T0320029

NBER Macroeconomics Annual 2018

NBER Macroeconomics Annual 2018

Edited by
Martin Eichenbaum and Jonathan A. Parker

The University of Chicago Press
Chicago and London

NBER Macroeconomics Annual 2018, Number 33

Published annually by The University of Chicago Press.

Standing orders
To place a standing order for this book series, please address your request to The University of Chicago Press, Chicago Distribution Center, Attn. Standing Orders/Customer Service, 11030 S. Langley Avenue, Chicago, IL 60628. Telephone toll free in the US and Canada: 1-800-621-2736; or 1-773-702-7000. Fax toll free in the US and Canada: 1-800-621-8476; or 1-773-702-7212.

Single-copy orders
In the UK and Europe: Order from your local bookseller or direct from The University of Chicago Press, c/o John Wiley Ltd. Distribution Center, 1 Oldlands Way, Bognor Regis, West Sussex PO22 9SA, UK. Telephone 01243 779777 or Fax 01243 820250. E-mail: cs-books@wiley.co.uk

In the US, Canada, and the rest of the world: Order from your local bookseller or direct from The University of Chicago Press, Chicago Distribution Center, 11030 S. Langley Avenue, Chicago, IL 60628. Telephone toll free in the US and Canada: 1-800-621-2736; or 1-773-702-7000. Fax toll free in the U.S. and Canada: 1-800-621-8476; or 1-773-702-7212.

Special orders
University of Chicago Press books may be purchased at quantity discounts for business or promotional use. For information, please write to Sales Department—Special Sales, The University of Chicago Press, 1427 E. 60th Street, Chicago, IL 60637 USA or telephone 1-773-702-7723.

ISSN: 0889-3365
ISBN-13: 978-0-226-64572-8 (hc.:alk.paper)
ISBN-13: 978-0-226-64555-1 (pb.:alk.paper)
ISBN-13: 978-0-226-64569-8 (e-book)

10 9 8 7 6 5 4 3 2 1

Relation of the Directors to the Work and Publications of the NBER

1. The object of the NBER is to ascertain and present to the economics profession, and to the public more generally, important economic facts and their interpretation in a scientific manner without policy recommendations. The Board of Directors is charged with the responsibility of ensuring that the work of the NBER is carried on in strict conformity with this object.

2. The President shall establish an internal review process to ensure that book manuscripts proposed for publication DO NOT contain policy recommendations. This shall apply both to the proceedings of conferences and to manuscripts by a single author or by one or more co-authors but shall not apply to authors of comments at NBER conferences who are not NBER affiliates.

3. No book manuscript reporting research shall be published by the NBER until the President has sent to each member of the Board a notice that a manuscript is recommended for publication and that in the President's opinion it is suitable for publication in accordance with the above principles of the NBER. Such notification will include a table of contents and an abstract or summary of the manuscript's content, a list of contributors if applicable, and a response form for use by Directors who desire a copy of the manuscript for review. Each manuscript shall contain a summary drawing attention to the nature and treatment of the problem studied and the main conclusions reached.

4. No volume shall be published until forty-five days have elapsed from the above notification of intention to publish it. During this period a copy shall be sent to any Director requesting it, and if any Director objects to publication on the grounds that the manuscript contains policy recommendations, the objection will be presented to the author(s) or editor(s). In case of dispute, all members of the Board shall be notified,

and the President shall appoint an ad hoc committee of the Board to decide the matter; thirty days additional shall be granted for this purpose.

5. The President shall present annually to the Board a report describing the internal manuscript review process, any objections made by Directors before publication or by anyone after publication, any disputes about such matters, and how they were handled.

6. Publications of the NBER issued for informational purposes concerning the work of the Bureau, or issued to inform the public of the activities at the Bureau, including but not limited to the NBER Digest and Reporter, shall be consistent with the object stated in paragraph 1. They shall contain a specific disclaimer noting that they have not passed through the review procedures required in this resolution. The Executive Committee of the Board is charged with the review of all such publications from time to time.

7. NBER working papers and manuscripts distributed on the Bureau's web site are not deemed to be publications for the purpose of this resolution, but they shall be consistent with the object stated in paragraph 1. Working papers shall contain a specific disclaimer noting that they have not passed through the review procedures required in this resolution. The NBER's web site shall contain a similar disclaimer. The President shall establish an internal review process to ensure that the working papers and the web site do not contain policy recommendations, and shall report annually to the Board on this process and any concerns raised in connection with it.

8. Unless otherwise determined by the Board or exempted by the terms of paragraphs 6 and 7, a copy of this resolution shall be printed in each NBER publication as described in paragraph 2 above.

Contents

Editorial

Martin Eichenbaum, *Northwestern University and NBER*
Jonathan A. Parker, *MIT and NBER*

NBER's 33rd Annual Conference on Macroeconomics brought together leading scholars to present, discuss, and debate six research papers on central issues in contemporary macroeconomics. In addition, Ragu Rajan, former governor of the Reserve Bank of India and former chief economist and director of research at the International Monetary Fund, delivered a thought-provoking after-dinner talk comparing the economic institutions in India and China and drawing out their implications for the economic growth potential of each country. Finally, we had a special panel session on the macroeconomic effects of the Tax Cuts and Jobs Act of 2017, moderated by NBER President James Poterba and featuring three leading experts in this area: Wendy Edelberg, associate director for economic analysis at the Congressional Budget Office; Kent Smetters, Boettner Chair Professor of Business Economics and Public Policy at the University of Pennsylvania's Wharton School; and Mark Zandi, chief economist of Moody's Analytics. Video recordings of the presentations of the papers, summaries of the papers by the authors, and the lunchtime panel discussion are all accessible on the web page of the NBER Annual Conference on Macroeconomics.[1] These videos make a useful complement to this volume and make the content of the conference more widely accessible.

This conference volume contains edited versions of the six papers presented at the conference, each followed by two written comments by leading scholars and a summary discussion of the debates that followed each paper.

The first paper in this year's volume takes an important step in understanding the implications of an assumption that is commonly used in mainstream macro models: people routinely solve extremely complicated, infinite-horizon planning problems. This assumption is clearly wrong. So a key question is, When does this assumption lead to misleading conclusions? Michael Woodford's paper, "Monetary Policy Analysis When Planning Horizons Are Finite," addresses this question with applications to monetary policy in the New Keynesian (NK) model. Woodford models the way people make decisions by analogy to the way artificial intelligence programs are designed to play complex games like chess or go. The idea is to transform agents' infinite-horizon problems into a sequence of simpler, finite-horizon problems. Specifically, Woodford supposes that people work via backward induction over a finite set of periods given some value function that they assign to the terminal nodes. They then choose the optimal actions for their current control variables. Woodford extends his analytical framework to also consider how people learn value functions from experience. This extension is important because it allows people to change their behavior in response to very persistent changes in policy or fundamentals.

Woodford uses his framework to assess the robustness of two key properties of the NK model. First, the standard NK model features a multiplicity of equilibria. Second, the simple NK model features the "forward guidance puzzle." That is, the effects on output of monetary policy commitments about future actions are very large and increasing in the temporal distance between when actions are announced and implemented.

Woodford shows that neither of these properties is robust in his alternative framework. Specifically, he shows that his variant of the NK model has a unique equilibrium. This equilibrium shares many of the properties emphasized in the NK literature. But Woodford's version of the NK model does not give rise to the forward guidance puzzle. As a final application, Woodford examines the implications of a central bank commitment to maintain a fixed nominal interest rate for a lengthy period of time.

The discussants focused on making clear the key mechanisms at work in Woodford's framework. They also emphasized the similarity between the implications of his analysis and a growing literature that is bringing insights from behavioral economics and bounded rationality into macroeconomics. Woodford's paper and that literature are helping us separate the wheat from the chaff of the NK model's predictions.

Our second paper is particularly ambitious and takes up one of the central questions in macrofinancial policy, which is whether the US financial sector is safer than it was prior to the 2007–8 financial crisis. At the time of the crisis, the US government provided significant support for banks and a wide range of financial institutions. Following the crisis, the government overhauled and reformed the regulation of the US financial system. Today, the banking sector is more profitable, more concentrated, and subject to more regulatory oversight than in the precrisis period. "Government Guarantees and the Valuation of American Banks," by Andrew G. Atkeson, Adrien d'Avernas, Andrea L. Eisfeldt, and Pierre-Olivier Weill, takes up the question: Have US banks become more resilient or not? This question arises because, post crisis, banks have lower levels of book leverage, but they also have higher levels of market leverage and higher market prices of credit risk.

To answer the central question, the paper studies the history of the ratio of the market values of banks to their book values, a ratio that the paper decomposes into the value of the franchise. Movements in this ratio capture changes in the profitability of the business arm of the banks and the value of the government guarantees of bank liabilities. So this ratio helps measure the extent to which regulatory reforms have or have not reduced the extent to which government support in crisis is an asset for the banking sector. The authors calculate that, relative to the precrisis period, there has been both a reduction in the franchise value of banks and a similar-sized reduction in the value of (uncertain) government guarantees. The authors conclude that, consistent with the observed market price of bank credit risk, banks have not become safer.

The paper draws on existing models and assumptions about the economics of banking. The discussants consider the importance of two key assumptions. First, the authors' analysis relies on a degree of noncompetitiveness. Subsidies to the cost of any business in a reasonably competitive industry should, through competition in the product market, ultimately lead to no change in the ratio of market value to book value. Second, banks may face substantial interest rate risk. This possibility does not change the conclusion that banks are not safer now than in the precrisis period, but it does lead one to question whether the value of government guarantees has or has not declined.

One of the biggest current debates in macroeconomics is why the labor share of output has been declining, a phenomenon that is related both to the recent anemic growth in real wages and to the increasingly unequal distribution of income. Our third paper, "Accounting for Factorless Income," by Loukas Karabarbounis and Brent Neiman, studies the three main possibilities for why the labor share of income has been declining while the measured capital share has not risen to offset it. The authors' careful analysis demonstrates the plausibility of different ways to allocate the share of output that is not measured either as capital income (from the rental rate on capital times the capital stock) or as labor income (from total payments to workers). One possibility is that this "factorless income" could be due to an increase in pure profits of firms, reflecting, for example, a rise in markups. The other possibilities are that one is mismeasuring the capital share by either mismeasuring the capital stock or the rental rate on capital. The paper shows that these two possibilities—increases in pure profits or underestimation of the capital stock—are each unlikely to account for the rise in factorless income. Assuming either is the cause implies movements in other quantities that appear to be implausible based on the observable evidence. For example, the assumption that factorless income is pure profits would imply that profit rates were even higher in the 1960s and 1970s than they have been in recent decades, and would require highly volatile evolutions of factor-specific technology. The authors conclude that the most likely source of factorless income is mismeasurement of the rate of return, although the paper also cautions against monocausal explanations in general.

Both the general discussion and discussants questioned whether the same theory need explain both the large fluctuations in the share of factorless income and its trend behavior. One discussant also thought that the rental rate of capital might be closely related to or influenced by the risk premium in the economy, which fluctuates substantially and without much correlation with the risk-free interest rate that lies at the heart of the measured capital rental rate.

The fourth paper in this year's volume explores the persistent decline in the risk-free interest rate after the 2008 financial crisis. "The Tail That Keeps the Riskless Rate Low" by Julian Kozlowski, Laura Veldkamp, and Venky Venkateswaran takes the view that the financial crisis was a very unusual event that caused people to reassess upward the probability of large adverse macro tail events. The rise in perceived tail risk led to a persistent increase in the demand for safe liquid assets.

Such a reassessment would not occur in a world where people had rational expectations and, improbably, knew the true probability of rare events. In the framework of this paper, people do not have strict rational expectations. Instead they use aggregate data and statistical tools to estimate the distribution of the shocks affecting the economy. The authors embed their learning mechanism in a standard general equilibrium where people are subject to liquidity constraints. Critically, in their model, the occurrence of a rare event leads to a persistent rise in the demand for safe and liquid assets. The authors argue that this mechanism is quantitatively important and can account for various other features of asset prices, including the behavior of the equity premium after the crisis.

The discussants focused on the quantitative implications of the authors' model, raising interesting questions about the relative importance of the safety and liquidity characteristics of risk-free assets and whether the authors' framework could in fact simultaneously explain the decline in the risk-free rate and the continued high returns to equity.

This paper is part of a larger literature that tries to depart from the more heroic aspects of traditional rational expectations. Instead of endowing people with comprehensive information about their environment, the authors focus on the process by which information is accumulated. That process leads to a novel and potentially important source of propagation of large, rare shocks. This paper is interesting both from a methodological and a substantive point of view.

The fifth paper in this volume, "The Transformation of Manufacturing and the Decline in US Employment," by Kerwin Kofi Charles, Erik Hurst, and Mariel Schwartz, documents the dramatic changes in the manufacturing sector and the large decline in employment rates and hours worked among prime-age Americans since 2000. It is hard to overstate the importance of these twin phenomena.

Charles et al. examine how much, and by what mechanisms, changes in manufacturing since 2000 affected the employment rates of prime-age men and women. The paper argues that the decline of the manufacturing sector played a major role in the declining participation rate of prime-age workers, particularly less educated prime-age men. The paper goes on to examine how the impact of Chinese import competition compares with the effects of other factors, like automation, on the decline in manufacturing employment. Significantly, the authors conclude that the China trade effect was small relative to other factors. This conclusion leads them to the view that policies aimed at mitigating the negative effects of trade on labor markets are unlikely to reverse the observed decline of employment in manufacturing.

The fact that wages fell along with employment supports the view that the decline in manufacturing employment reflects a decline in the demand for labor rather than a negative shift in the supply of labor to the manufacturing sector. More surprisingly, the authors show that the fall in employment caused a decline in health among the affected population of workers, as evident by a rise in failed drug tests and the increased use of opioids. The overall picture that emerges from the paper is of a technologically driven decline in employment with a large, persistent negative impact on the welfare of a key segment of the population.

Declining employment in the manufacturing sector is not a new phenomenon. But the post-2000 decline was associated with much larger and more persistent declines in overall employment than had been the case. The authors explore the importance of different forces that might explain this important change. Their analysis points to a large decline in the willingness of workers to move across regions in response to a local manufacturing shock. Why that should be so remains an unsolved and important mystery.

Both discussants provided historical perspective on the post-2000 era. For example, the post-2000 decline in manufacturing employment as a percentage of overall employment is consistent with the trend behavior of that variable. But the decline in the level of employment in the manufacturing sector is unprecedented. This fact poses an interesting challenge for how to interpret some of the authors' empirical findings. A broader question that remains unresolved is, What's so special about manufacturing? After all, there have been many other large sectoral reallocations in US history. But none of those episodes seem to have had such a profound negative impact on labor, especially less-educated workers. Valerie Ramey offers one explanation. But "What's so special about manufacturing?" remains an important and open question.

Our final paper is perhaps the most topical paper in the volume and takes up the question of how economies respond to tax reforms that involve "border adjustment taxes" (BATs) and similar policies. BATs are credits against domestic taxes for exported goods or services and are central features of value-added tax systems. Recent discussions of US tax reform considered BATs as part of a plan to move the US tax system toward a system that was closer to a consumption-based and territorial-based system. Existing academic work on BATs has focused on the fact that they are neutral in the long run because exchange rate movements undo the changes in import and export costs (from Lerner symmetry). In "The Macroeconomics of Border Taxes," Omar Barbiero, Emmanuel Farhi, Gita Gopinath, and Oleg Itskhoki show how changes in BATs can lead to business cycles in the short and medium term in an open-economy NK dynamic stochastic general equilibrium model in which nominal prices do not adjust immediately and fully to their long-run values.

In the authors' model, the introduction of a BAT is far from neutral. It reduces both exports and imports, yet has only a minor negative effect on output as the dollar appreciates by roughly the amount of the BAT. Neutrality fails because exporters fail to pass along the benefits of the BAT due to price stickiness so the BAT reduces overall trade. In the model, the BAT leads to an appreciation of the dollar, which would lead the United States to lose significant wealth due to its negative net asset position.

An alternative approach to adding a BAT to the current US tax system would be to move to a value-added tax. The paper shows that although this would avoid significant movement in the exchange rate, it would cause a significant recession. The paper elucidates nicely how the specific implementation of tax policies interacts with the currency in which trade is denominated. As such, the United States and other countries might experience quite different cyclical responses to identical policies. Among other issues, the discussants and the ensuing debate considered whether the level of price stickiness that one might observe or estimate in usual times would apply to a situation in which a BAT was implemented.

As in previous years, the editors posted and distributed a call for proposals in the spring and summer prior to the conference and some of the papers in this volume were selected from proposals submitted in response to this call. Other papers are commissioned on central and topical areas in macroeconomics. Both are done in consultation with the advisory board, which we thank for its input and support of both the conference and the published volume.

The authors and the editors would like to take this opportunity to thank Jim Poterba and the National Bureau of Economic Research for their continued support of the *NBER Macroeconomics Annual* and the associated conference. We would also like to thank the NBER conference staff, particularly Rob Shannon, for his continued excellent organization and support. We would also like to thank the NBER Public Information staff and Charlie Radin in particular for producing the high-quality multimedia content. Financial assistance from the National Science Foundation is gratefully acknowledged. Gideon Bornstein and Nathan Zorzi provided invaluable help in preparing the summaries of the discussions. And last but far from least, we are grateful to Helena Fitz-Patrick for her invaluable assistance in editing and publishing the volume.

Endnotes

For acknowledgments, sources of research support, and disclosure of the authors' material financial relationships, if any, please see http://www.nber.org/chapters/c14068.ack.

1. NBER Annual Conference on Macroeconomics, http://www.nber.org/macroannual conference2018/macroannual2018.html.

Abstracts

1 Monetary Policy Analysis When Planning Horizons Are Finite
Michael Woodford

It is common to analyze the effects of alternative possible monetary policy commitments under the assumption of optimization under rational (or fully model-consistent) expectations. This implicitly assumes unrealistic cognitive abilities on the part of economic decision makers. The relevant question, however, is not whether the assumption can be literally correct, but how much it would matter to model decision making in a more realistic way. A model is proposed, based on the architecture of artificial intelligence programs for problems such as chess or go, in which decision makers look ahead only a finite distance into the future and use a value function learned from experience to evaluate situations that may be reached after a finite sequence of actions by themselves and others. Conditions are discussed under which the predictions of a model with finite-horizon forward planning are similar to those of a rational expectations equilibrium, and under which they are instead quite different. The model is used to re-examine the consequences that should be expected from a central bank commitment to maintain a fixed nominal interest rate for a substantial period of time. "Neo-Fisherian" predictions are shown to depend on using rational expectations equilibrium analysis under circumstances in which it should be expected to be unreliable.

2 Government Guarantees and the Valuation of American Banks
Andrew G. Atkeson, Adrien d'Avernas, Andrea L. Eisfeldt,
and Pierre-Olivier Weill

Banks' ratio of the market value to book value of their equity was close to 1 until the 1990s, then more than doubled during the 1996–2007 period, and fell again to values close to 1 after the 2008 financial crisis. Some economists argue that the drop in banks' market-to-book ratio since the crisis is due to a loss in bank franchise value or profitability. In this paper we argue that banks' market-to-book ratio is the sum of two components: franchise value and the value of government guarantees. We empirically decompose the ratio between these two components and find that a large portion of the variation in this ratio over time is due to changes in the value of government guarantees.

3   Accounting for Factorless Income
Loukas Karabarbounis and Brent Neiman

Comparing US gross domestic product to the sum of measured payments to labor and imputed rental payments to capital results in a large and volatile residual or "factorless" income. We analyze three common strategies of allocating and interpreting factorless income, specifically that it arises from economic profits (case Π), unmeasured capital (case K), or deviations of the rental rate of capital from standard measures based on bond returns (case R). We are skeptical of case Π because it reveals a tight negative relationship between real interest rates and economic profits, leads to large fluctuations in inferred factor-augmenting technologies, and results in profits that have risen since the early 1980s but that remain lower today than in the 1960s and 1970s. Case K shows how unmeasured capital plausibly accounts for all factorless income in recent decades, but its value in the 1960s would have to be more than half of the capital stock, which we find less plausible. We view case R as most promising as it leads to more stable factor shares and technology growth than the other cases, though we acknowledge that it requires an explanation for the pattern of deviations from common measures of the rental rate. Using a model with multiple sectors and types of capital, we show that our assessment of the drivers of changes in output, factor shares, and functional inequality depends critically on the interpretation of factorless income.

4   The Tail That Keeps the Riskless Rate Low
Julian Kozlowski, Laura Veldkamp, and Venky Venkateswaran

Riskless interest rates fell in the wake of the financial crisis and have remained low. We explore a simple explanation: this recession was perceived as an extremely unlikely event before 2007. Observing such an episode led all agents to reassess macro risk, in particular the probability of tail events. Since changes in beliefs endure long after the event itself has passed, perceived "tail risk" remains high, generates a demand for riskless liquid assets, and continues to depress the riskless rate. We embed this mechanism into a simple production economy with liquidity constraints and use observable macro data, along with standard econometric tools, to discipline beliefs about the distribution of aggregate shocks. When agents observe an extreme adverse realization, they re-estimate the distribution and attach a higher probability to such an event recurring. As a result, even transitory shocks have persistent effects because once observed, the shocks stay forever in the agents' data set. We show that our belief revision mechanism can help explain the persistent nature of the fall in risk-free rates.

5   The Transformation of Manufacturing and the Decline in US Employment
Kerwin Kofi Charles, Erik Hurst, and Mariel Schwartz

Using data from a variety of sources, this paper comprehensively documents the dramatic changes in the manufacturing sector and the large decline in employment rates and hours worked among prime-age Americans since 2000. We use cross-region variation to explore the link between declining manufacturing employment and labor market outcomes. We find that manufacturing decline in a local area in the 2000s had large and persistent negative effects on local employment rates, hours worked, and wages. We also show that declining local manufacturing employment is related to rising local opioid use and deaths. These results suggest that some of the recent opioid epidemic is driven by demand factors in addition to increased opioid supply. We conclude the paper with a discussion of potential mediating factors associated with declining manufacturing labor demand, including public and private transfer receipt, sectoral switching, and interregion mobility. We conclude that the decline in manufacturing employment was a substantial cause of the decline in employment rates during the 2000s, particularly for less educated prime-age workers. Given the trends in both capital and skill deepening within this sector, we further conclude that many policies currently being discussed to promote the manufacturing sector will have only a modest labor market impact for less educated individuals.

6   The Macroeconomics of Border Taxes
Omar Barbiero, Emmanuel Farhi, Gita Gopinath, and Oleg Itskhoki

We analyze the dynamic macroeconomic effects of border adjustment taxes (BAT), both when they are a feature of corporate tax reform (C-BAT) and for the case of value-added tax (VAT). Our analysis arrives at the following main conclusions. First, C-BAT is unlikely to be neutral at the macroeconomic level, as the conditions required for neutrality are unrealistic. The basis for neutrality of VAT is even weaker. Second, in response to the introduction of an unanticipated permanent C-BAT of 20% in the United States, the dollar appreciates strongly, by almost the size of the tax adjustment, and US exports and imports decline significantly, while the overall effect on output is small. Third, an equivalent change in VAT, in contrast to the C-BAT effect, generates only a weak appreciation of the dollar and a small decline in imports and exports, but has a large negative effect on output. Last, border taxes increase government revenues in periods of trade deficit; however, given the net foreign asset position of the United States, they result in a long-run loss of government revenues and an immediate net transfer to the rest of the world.

1

Monetary Policy Analysis When Planning Horizons Are Finite

Michael Woodford, *Columbia University and NBER*

It has become commonplace—certainly in the scholarly literature but also increasingly in central banks and other policy institutions—to analyze the predicted effects of possible monetary policies using dynamic stochastic general equilibrium models, in which both households and firms are assumed to make optimal decisions under rational expectations. Since the methodological revolution in macroeconomics initiated by Kydland and Prescott (1982), this has come to mean assuming that economic agents formulate complete state-contingent intertemporal plans over an infinite future. Yet such a postulate is plainly heroic, as the implicit assumptions made about the knowability of all possible future situations, the capacity of people to formulate detailed plans before acting, and the ability of individuals to solve complex optimization problems in real time are well beyond the capabilities even of economists, let alone members of society in general.

Most if not all macroeconomists who use models of this kind probably do so on the assumption that such models represent a useful idealization—that while not literally correct, their predictions are approximately correct, while their logical simplicity makes them convenient to use in thinking through a variety of thought experiments of practical interest. Yet their use in this way requires that one have some basis for judgment about the degree to which, and the circumstances under which, one should expect the predictions of an admittedly idealized model to be approximately correct nonetheless. The issue of the conditions under which an idealized model can approximate a more complex reality deserves analysis rather than simply being a matter of faith (or badge of professional identity), as it too often is.

I propose an approach to macroeconomic analysis that makes less extreme cognitive demands than conventional rational expectations equilibrium analysis and thus allows us to pose the question of the degree to which the conclusions of the conventional analysis should be at least approximately valid even in a world in which people are only boundedly rational. It allows us to identify circumstances under which the predictions of the conventional analysis can be correct, or at least approximately correct, without people having to have such extraordinary cognitive capacities as the rational expectations analysis would seem, on its face, to require.

It can also address a conceptual problem with rational expectations analysis, which is providing a ground for selection of a particular solution as the relevant prediction of one's model, under circumstances where an infinite-horizon model admits a large number of potential rational expectations equilibria. The boundedly rational solution concept proposed here is necessarily unique, and so, in cases in which it coincides with a rational expectations equilibrium (or approaches one as the limit on computational complexity is relaxed), it provides a reason for using that particular rational expectations equilibrium as the predicted effect of the policy in question.

At the same time, the proposed approach will not always result in predictions similar to those of any rational expectations equilibria; in such cases, it provides a reason to doubt the practical relevance of conclusions from rational expectations analysis. In particular, I will argue that conclusions about the effects of central bank "forward guidance" based on rational expectations analysis are sometimes quite misleading, as they depend on assuming the validity of rational expectations analysis under circumstances in which a more realistic (though still highly sophisticated) model of human decision making would lead to quite different conclusions.

This proposed approach proceeds from the observation that in the case of complex intertemporal decision problems, people—even experts—are not able to "solve" such problems using the sort of backward induction or dynamic programming approaches that are taught in economics classes. It posits that, rather than beginning by considering all possible final situations, valuing them, and then working back from such judgments about the desirability of the end point to reach a conclusion about the best first action to take in one's current situation, people actually start from the specific situation that they are in and work forward from it to some finite extent, considering alternative situations that can be reached through some finite sequence of possible actions; however, they necessarily truncate this process of "forward planning" before all of the consequences of their earlier actions have been realized.[1]

And rather than supposing that people should be able to deductively compute a correct "value function" for possible interim situations that they might be able to reach—through some algorithm such as value-function iteration, which requires that a decision maker begin by specifying the set of possible states for which values must be computed—this model recognizes that while people have some ability to learn the values of particular situations by observing their average consequences over a body of actual or simulated experience, such a tactic necessarily requires a coarse classification of possible situations to make such averaging feasible. It is because of the coarseness of the state space for which a value function can be learned, relative to the more fine-grained information about one's current situation that can be made use of in a forward-planning exercise, that forward planning is useful, even when only feasible to some finite distance into the future. Our proposed approach makes use of both (finite-depth) forward planning and (coarse) value-function learning to take advantage of the strengths of each while mitigating the most important weaknesses of each.

The paper proceeds as follows. Section I introduces the basic approach to modeling boundedly rational intertemporal decision making that I propose. Section II then shows how this approach can be applied to monetary policy analysis, in the context of a simple but relatively standard microfounded New Keynesian model. In the analysis developed in this section, the coarse value function that decision makers use to value potential situations at the horizon at which their forward planning is truncated is taken as given, though motivated as one that would be optimal in a certain kind of relatively simple environment. Section III applies the framework developed in Section II to the specific problem of analyzing the effects of an announcement that a new approach to monetary policy will be followed for a period of time, as in recent experiments with forward guidance, and compares the conclusions from our boundedly rational analysis with conventional rational expectations analyses. Section IV then extends the analytical framework to also consider how value functions are learned from experience, allowing them to eventually change in response to a sufficiently persistent change in either policy or fundamentals. This allows us to consider the validity of the proposition that the Fisher equation should hold in the long run, regardless of how inflationary or deflationary monetary policy may be, and of the "neo-Fisherian" conclusions that are sometimes drawn from this proposition. Section V concludes.

I. How Are Complex Intertemporal Decisions Made?

In practice, even in highly structured environments such as the games of chess or go—where clear rules mean that the set of possible actions in any situation can be completely enumerated, and the set of situations that can ever possibly be encountered is also finite, so that in principle all possible strategies can be exhaustively studied—it is not possible even for the most expert players, whether human or artificial intelligence programs, to discern the optimal strategy and simply execute it. Indeed, tournament play would not be interesting, and the challenge of designing better programs would not continue to engage computer scientists, were this the case. This fact reveals something about the limitations of the kinds of computational strategies that economists use to compute optimal decision rules in classroom exercises.

But it is also worth considering how the best players approach these problems in practice—in particular, the approaches used by state-of-the-art artificial intelligence programs, since these are now the best players in the world and (more to the point) we know how they work. If we wish to assume in economic models that the people who make up the economy should be highly rational and do a good job of choosing strategies that serve their interests—but not that they have magical powers—then it would seem reasonable to assume that they make decisions using methods similar to those used by the most effective artificial intelligence programs.[2]

Programs such as Deep Mind for chess (Campbell, Hoane, and Hsu 2002) or AlphaGo for the game of go (Silver et al. 2016) have the following basic structure. Whenever it is the computer's turn to move, it begins by observing a precise description of the current state of the board. Starting from this state, it considers the states that it is possible to move to through a legal move, the possible situations that can arise as a result of any legal responses by the opponent in any such state, the possible states that can be moved to through a legal move from the situation created by the opponent's move, and so on; it creates a tree structure with the current state of the board as its root.

Once the tree is created, values are assigned to reaching the different possible terminal nodes (the nodes at which the process of "tree search" is truncated). Different hypothetical sequences of moves, extending forward until a terminal node is reached, can then be valued according to the value of the terminal node that they would allow one to reach. This allows the selection of a preferred sequence of moves: a finite-horizon plan (though not a plan for the entire rest of the game). The move that is taken is then the first move in the preferred sequence. However, the finite-horizon plan chosen at one stage in the game need not be continued; instead, the forward-planning exercise is repeated each time another move must be selected, looking further into the future as the game progresses and hence possibly choosing a new plan that does not begin by continuing the one selected at the time of the previous move.

Such a tree-search procedure would be fully rational if the complete game tree (terminating only at nodes at which the game has ended) were considered. But except in special circumstances, such as possibly near the end of a game, this is not feasible. Hence a tree of only a finite "depth" must be considered before choosing a current action. The best programs use sophisticated rules to decide when to search further down particular branches of the game tree and when to truncate the search earlier, in order to deploy finite computational resources more efficiently. In the model proposed, however, we simply assume a uniform depth of search k; that is, a decision maker is assumed to consider all of the possible states that can be reached through a feasible sequence of actions over the next k periods. Our focus here is on comparing a model with finite-horizon forward planning with one in which the complete (unbounded) future is considered, and on considering how the length of the finite horizon matters.

Another crucial aspect of such a program is the specification of the function that is used to evaluate the different terminal nodes. It is important to note that the answer cannot be that the value assigned to a terminal node should be determined by looking at the states further down the game tree that can be reached from it; the whole point of having a value function with which to evaluate terminal nodes is to allow the program to avoid having to look further into the future and thus have to consider an even larger number of possible outcomes. The value function must be learned in advance, before a particular game is played, on the basis of an extensive database of actual or simulated play, and represents essentially an empirical average of the values observed to follow from reaching particular states.

If sufficient prior experience were available to allow a correct value function (taking into account a precise description of the situation that has been reached) to be learned, then truncation of the forward planning at a finite depth would not result in suboptimal decisions. Indeed, there would be no need for multistage forward planning at all; one could simply consider the positions to which it is possible to move from one's current position, evaluate them, and choose the best move on this basis. The only reason that forward planning (to the depth that is feasible) is useful is that in practice, a completely accurate value function cannot be learned, even from a large database of experience; there are too many possible states that might in principle need to be evaluated for it to be possible to observe all of the outcomes that might result from each one of them and tabulate the average values of each. Thus, in practice, the value function used by such a program must evaluate a situation based on a certain set of "features," that provide a coarse description of the situation but do not uniquely identify it.

The degree to which forward planning should be used, before resorting to the use of a value function learned from prior experience to evaluate the situations that may be reached under alternative finite-horizon action plans, reflects a trade-off between the respective strengths and weaknesses of the two approaches. Evaluation of possible situations using the value function is quick and inexpensive once the value function has once been learned; however, it has the disadvantage that, for it to be feasible to ever learn the value function, the value function can take into account only a coarse description of each of the possible situations.

Forward planning via tree search can instead take into account very fine-grained information about the particular situation in which one currently finds oneself, because it is only implemented for a particular situation once one is in it, but it has the disadvantage that the process of considering all possible branches of the decision tree into the future rapidly becomes computationally burdensome as the depth of search increases. Finite-horizon forward planning to an appropriate depth makes use of fine-grained information when it is especially relevant and not overly costly (i.e., when thinking about the relatively near future) but switches to the use of a more coarse-grained empirical value function to evaluate possible situations when thinking about the further future.

A final feature of such algorithms deserves mention. If the intertemporal decision problem is not an individual decision problem but instead one in which outcomes for the decision maker depend on the actions of others as well—an opponent, in the case of chess or go, or the other households and firms whose actions determine market conditions, in a macroeconomic model—then the algorithm must include a model of others' behavior to deduce the consequences of choosing a particular sequence of actions. It makes sense to assume that those others will also behave rationally, but it will not be possible to compute their predicted behavior using an algorithm that is as complex as the forward-planning algorithm that one uses to make one's own decision.

In particular, if the algorithm used to choose one's own plan of action looks forward to possible situations after k successive moves, it cannot also model the opponent's choice after one's first move by assuming that the opponent will look forward to possible situations after k successive moves, considering what one should do after the first reply by simulating the result of looking forward to possible situations after k more moves, and so on. Continuation of such a chain of reasoning would amount to reasoning about possible situations that can be reached after many more than just k successive moves. For the complexity of the decision tree that must be considered to be bounded by looking out only to some finite depth, it becomes necessary to assume an even shorter horizon in the forward planning that one simulates on the part of other people whose behavior at a later stage of the tree must be predicted. This idea is made concrete in Section II.A (An Optimal Finite-Horizon Plan) in the context of a general equilibrium analysis.

The proposed approach has certain similarities to models of boundedly rational decision making discussed by Branch, Evans, and McGough (2012). Branch et al. assume that decision makers use econometric models to forecast the future evolution of variables, the future values of which matter to their intertemporal decision problem, and compare a variety of assumptions about how those forecasts may be used to make decisions; in particular, they discuss models in which decision makers solve only a finite-horizon problem, and hence only need to forecast over a finite horizon. A crucial difference between their models and the one proposed here is that in those models, the same econometric model is used both to forecast conditions during the (near-term) period for which a finite-horizon plan is chosen and to estimate the value of reaching different possible terminal nodes. Instead, I emphasize that the types of reasoning involved in finite-horizon forward planning, on the one hand, and in the evaluation of terminal nodes, on the other, are quite different and that the sources of information that are taken into account for the two purposes are accordingly quite different. This has important consequences for this analysis of the effects of central bank forward guidance, which we assume is taken into account in forward planning (based on the decision maker's complete information about the current situation) but not in the value function (which necessarily classifies situations using only a limited set of features, with which there must have been extensive prior experience).

II. A New Keynesian Dynamic Stochastic General Equilibrium Model with Finite-Horizon Planning

I now illustrate how the proposed approach can be applied to monetary policy analysis, by deriving the equations of a New Keynesian dynamic stochastic general equilibrium model similar to the basic model developed in Woodford (2003) but replacing the standard assumption of infinite-horizon optimal planning by a more realistic assumption of finite-horizon planning. I begin by deriving boundedly rational analogs of the two key structural equations of the textbook New Keynesian model—the "New Keynesian IS relation" and the "New Keynesian Phillips curve"—and then discuss the implications of the modified equations for an analysis of the effects of forward guidance regarding monetary policy.

A. Household Expenditure with a Finite Planning Horizon

We assume an economy made up of a large number of identical households, each of which represents a "dynasty" of individuals that share a single intertemporal budget constraint, and earn income and spend over an infinite horizon. At any point in time t, household i wishes to maximize its expected utility from then on,

$$\hat{E}_t^i \sum_{\tau=t}^{\infty} \beta^{\tau-t} [u(C_\tau^i; \xi_\tau) - w(H_\tau^i; \xi_\tau)],$$

where C_τ^i is the expenditure of i in period τ on a composite good, H_τ^i is hours worked in period τ, and ξ_τ is a vector of exogenous disturbances that can include disturbances to the urgency of current expenditure or the disutility of working. As usual, we suppose that for each value of the disturbance vector, $u(\cdot; \xi)$ is an increasing, strictly concave function; $w(\cdot; \xi)$ is an increasing, convex function; and the discount factor satisfies $0 < \beta < 1$. The composite good is a Dixit-Stiglitz aggregate

$$C_\tau^i \equiv \left[\int_0^1 (C_\tau^i(f))^{\frac{\theta-1}{\theta}} df \right]^{\frac{\theta}{\theta-1}} \tag{1}$$

of the household's expenditure $C_\tau^i(f)$ on each of a continuum of differentiated goods indexed by f, where $\theta > 1$. The operator $\hat{E}_t^i[\cdot]$ indicates the expected value under the subjective expectations of household i at time t, which we have yet to specify.

In the present subsection, we shall be concerned purely with the household's planning of its state-contingent expenditure C_τ^i on the composite good, given the expected evolution of the price P_τ of the composite good (a Dixit-Stiglitz index of the prices of the individual goods) and the household's income from working and from its share in the profits of firms. Both the question of how the household allocates its spending across the different individual goods and how its hours of work are determined are left for later. Here we note simply that we assume an organization of the labor market under which each household is required to supply its share of the aggregate labor H_τ demanded by firms; hence the expected evolution of $H_\tau^i = H_\tau$ is independent of household i's intentions with regard to spending and wealth accumulation. Moreover, each household's total income other than from its financial position (saving or borrowing) will simply equal its share of the total value Y_τ of production of the composite good. The evolution of this income variable is outside the control of an individual household i.

We further simplify the household's problem by supposing that there is a single kind of traded financial claim, a one-period riskless nominal debt contract promising a nominal interest rate i_τ (i.e., 1 dollar saved in period τ buys a claim to $1 + i_\tau$ dollars in period $\tau + 1$) that is controlled by the central bank. We denote the financial wealth carried into period t by household i by the variable B_t^i, defined as the nominal value of claims maturing in period t deflated by the price index P_{t-1}; this definition makes B_t^i a real variable that is purely predetermined (dependent only on decisions made at date $t - 1$). The household's financial position evolves in accordance with a flow budget constraint

$$B_{\tau+1}^i = (1 + i_\tau)[B_\tau^i / \Pi_\tau + Y_\tau - C_\tau] \qquad (2)$$

for each period $\tau \geq t$, where $\Pi_\tau \equiv P_\tau / P_{\tau-1}$ is the gross inflation rate between period $\tau - 1$ and period τ.

The problem considered in this subsection is the household's choice of an intended path of expenditure $\{C_\tau^i\}$, where spending in any period τ may depend on the aggregate state s_τ at that time, together with the associated path for its financial position $\{B_{\tau+1}^i\}$ implied by equation (2). (Here we use the notation s_τ for the complete state vector, including both the exogenous disturbances ξ_τ and any policy decisions that have been announced as of date τ.) These are chosen to maximize the expected discounted sum of utility from expenditure because the disutility of working can be taken as given for present purposes, given an existing financial position B_τ^i and the expected evolution of the variables $\{i_\tau, \Pi_\tau, Y_\tau\}$ in periods $\tau \geq t$.

An Optimal Finite-Horizon Plan

Rather than assuming that the household chooses a complete infinite-horizon state-contingent expenditure plan—and that it must accordingly consider the possible paths of the variables $\{i_\tau, \Pi_\tau, Y_\tau\}$ over an infinite future—we shall suppose that the household engages in explicit forward planning for only k periods into the future. This means that in period t (and given the state s_t at that time), the household chooses state-contingent values $\{C_\tau^i(s_\tau)\}$ only for the possible states s_τ that may be reached at dates $t \leq \tau \leq t + k$.

This plan is chosen to maximize the finite-horizon objective

$$E_t^k \left[\sum_{\tau=t}^{t+k} \beta^{\tau-t} u(C_\tau^i; \xi_\tau) + \beta^{k+1} v(B_{t+k+1}^i; s_{t+k}) \right], \tag{3}$$

where the evolution of $B_{\tau+1}^i$ for $t \leq \tau \leq t + k$ under the finite-horizon plan is given by equation (2), and $v(B_{t+k+1}^i; s_{t+k})$ is the value function that the household uses to estimate the continuation value of its problem at each of the possible states s_{t+k} at which it truncates the forward-planning exercise. Here the operator $E_t^k[\cdot]$ indicates the expectations at time t of a decision maker that plans k periods ahead regarding the probabilistic evolution of the variables outside her control. The information set of such a decision maker is assumed to include the current exogenous state s_t, and the equilibrium realizations of all endogenous variables at dates $t - 1$ or earlier; the conditional probabilities of future exogenous states are assumed to be correctly known, while the values of endogenous variables at date t or later (conditional on the exogenous state that is reached) are computed using the model's structural equations, as discussed further below. These expectations differ from model-consistent or "rational" expectations only because of the truncation of the household's planning horizon and so are the same for all households with planning horizon k.

The household's finite-horizon plan will satisfy a set of first-order conditions (FOCs),

$$u_c(C_\tau^i; \xi_\tau) = \beta E_t^k[((1 + i_\tau)/\Pi_{\tau+1}) u_c(C_{\tau+1}^i; \xi_{\tau+1})|s_\tau], \tag{4}$$

for each possible state s_τ (given the state s_t at the time of the planning) at each date $t \leq \tau \leq t + k - 1$, and

$$u_c(C_{t+k}^i; \xi_{t+k}) = \beta(1 + i_{t+k}) v_B(B_{t+k+1}^i; s_{t+k}) \tag{5}$$

for each possible state s_{t+k} at which the forward planning is truncated. (The expectation operator $E_t^k[\cdot|s_\tau]$ refers to the expectations that the decision maker at date t expects to have, conditional on reaching state s_τ.) Conditions (4)–(5) together with the budget constraints (2) determine a state-contingent plan $\{C_\tau^i, B_{\tau+1}^i\}$ for periods $t \leq \tau \leq t + k$.

If we were to assume that the household's expectations $E_t^k[\cdot]$ are fully model-consistent expectations and that the value function $v(B; s_{t+k})$ corresponds to the true (model-consistent) value of the household's continuation problem for any level of net saving B chosen in state s_{t+k}, then this system of equations would characterize the household's optimal infinite-horizon expenditure plan. We assume instead that the household's plan is only boundedly rational, in two respects.

First, we assume that although in period t, the household chooses planned expenditure for periods t through $t + k$, it does not subsequently implement this plan (beyond the level of spending C_t^i chosen for the current period). When it reoptimizes in the following period, it will not generally choose to continue with the plan chosen in period t (because in period $t + 1$, it looks forward to period $t + k + 1$ rather than truncating the planning at period $t + k$). This is however neglected by the household when it chooses a spending plan in period t. Indeed, we cannot assume that the household in period t has model-consistent expectations about its spending in the different states that may be reached in period $t + 1$, for this would require that the household use the model structural equations to calculate what should be expected to happen in period $t + k + 1$, rather than truncating the deductive forward planning in period $t + k$. Instead, we suppose that the household calculates as if in period $t + 1$ it will plan forward only $k - 1$ periods into the future, in period $t + 2$ it will plan forward only $k - 2$ periods into the future, and so on.

And while we assume that the household correctly understands the equations of the structural model (including the policy rule announced by the central bank) and uses them in the planning exercise to deduce the values of Π_τ, Y_τ, and i_τ that should be expected in each possible state s_τ for $t \leq \tau \leq t + k$, this does not suffice to imply model-consistent expectations of those variables. According to our model, aggregate expenditure in period $t + j$ (for some $1 \leq j \leq k$) is determined by the planning decisions of households in period $t + j$ that (if they have $k - period$ planning horizons) look forward to the anticipated model-based determination of variables as far in the future as period $t + j + k$. But for the household's planning not to require it to consider what the model equations imply about states further in the future than period $t + k$, we assume that the household assumes that in period $t + j$, spending and pricing decisions will be made by households and firms with only $(k - j)$-period planning horizons.

Thus, if we let Π_t^k, Y_t^k, and i_t^k be the model-consistent solutions for the endogenous variables in period t (given the state s_t reached at that time) in a model where all decision makers are assumed to have planning horizons of length k, then the expectations used in period t by a household with a k-period planning horizon are assumed to satisfy

$$E_t^k[Z_\tau] = E_t Z_\tau^{t+k-\tau}$$

for any endogenous variable Z_τ in period τ ($t \leq \tau \leq t + k$), where $E_t[\cdot]$ now refers to the model-consistent expectation conditional on being in state s_t. Similarly, we assume that the expectations about the following period that the household expects (in its period-t planning exercise) to hold in any future state $s_t (t + 1 \leq \tau \leq t + k)$ are given by

$$E_t^k[Z_{\tau+1}|s_\tau] = E_\tau Z_{\tau+1}^{t+k-\tau}.$$

Hence the household's Euler equation (4) can alternatively be written

$$u_c(C_\tau^j; \xi_\tau) = \beta E_\tau[((1 + i_\tau^j)/\Pi_{\tau+1}^{j-1}) u_c(C_{\tau+1}^{j-1}; \xi_{\tau+1})], \tag{6}$$

for any planning horizon $j \geq 1$. We can also use equation (5) to obtain a corresponding FOC for a household with a zero-period planning horizon:

$$u_c(C_\tau^0; \xi_\tau) = \beta(1 + i_\tau) v_B(B_{\tau+1}^0; s_\tau), \tag{7}$$

where $B_{\tau+1}^0$ is the wealth carried into period $\tau + 1$ by a household with a zero-period planning horizon in period τ. We now have a system of equations (consisting of eq. [6] for each of the periods $t \leq \tau \leq t + k$, and eq. [7] for the period $\tau = t + k$), now involving only model-consistent conditional expectations, to determine the state-contingent plan chosen in period t by a household with a k-period planning horizon.

The second respect in which we depart from fully model-consistent expectations is that we do not assume that the value function $v(B; s_{t+k})$, used to evaluate possible situations at the point where forward planning is truncated, necessarily corresponds to the model-implied continuation value of the household's discounted expected utility conditional on reaching state s_{t+k}. As discussed earlier, we suppose that the value function is learned by averaging past experience rather than by using the model structural equations to deduce what should happen further in the future and that it will not be practical to learn the value of wealth conditioning on all details of the complete state vector s_{t+k}.

To simplify the current presentation, we suppose that the value function is not state-contingent at all, though households are assumed to correctly learn the average continuation value $v(B)$ associated with a given level of real wealth B.[3] In particular, we assume in our treatment of forward guidance below that the value function $v(B)$ does not take any account of the consequences of any announcement by the central bank of a change in the monetary policy that will be implemented at dates beyond the planning horizon (though this would be part of the complete state vector s_{t+k}.). We do assume that the value function reflects one simple kind of state-dependence: households are assumed to recognize that it is their real financial position, rather than their nominal position, that should determine the value of their continuation problem so that the price level anticipated for period $t + k$ is taken into account.

I defer until Section IV a discussion of how the value function is assumed to be learned from experience. We first examine the equilibrium consequences of finite-horizon planning under the assumption of a given value function $v(B)$, setting aside the question of how the function should eventually shift over time in response to further experience.[4] For the sake of concreteness, we further suppose that the economy has for a long time been in a stationary equilibrium in which there have been no real disturbances and monetary policy has maintained a constant inflation rate $\overline{\Pi}$; that, as a result, output and the nominal interest rate have been constant as well, with values $\overline{Y}$ and $\overline{\iota}$ respectively; and that households and firms have eventually learned value functions that are correct for this stationary environment. (We assume that $\overline{\Pi} > \beta$, so that the implied stationary nominal interest rate $\overline{\iota} = \beta^{-1}\overline{\Pi} - 1$ is positive.)

In such an environment, a household's correct continuation value function is the function $v(B)$ that solves the Bellman equation,

$$v(B) = max_C\{u(C) + \beta v(B')\} \quad s.t.\, B' = \beta^{-1}[B + (\overline{Y} - C)\overline{\Pi}],$$

where $\overline{Y}$ is the stationary equilibrium level of output when households and firms optimize using model-consistent expectations (perfect foresight). The solution to this problem is easily seen to be

$$v(B) = (1 - \beta)^{-1} u(\overline{Y} + (1 - \beta)B/\overline{\Pi}). \tag{8}$$

This is the value function that we shall assume that households use, until our consideration of learning dynamics in Section IV.

Log-linear approximation of the optimal plan

Suppose now that there are no real disturbances and that the central bank uses its policy instrument to maintain the target inflation rate $\overline{\Pi}$ at all times. If households and firms act on the basis of finite-horizon plans, but use correct value functions, then actions are the same as if they chose their actions on the basis of infinite-horizon optimization, and hence all aspects of the equilibrium will be the same. If all households start with identical financial positions ($B_t^i = 0$, since financial claims are in zero net supply), then in this equilibrium $C_t^i = \overline{C} = \overline{Y}$ for each household at all times.[5]

If instead we allow for real disturbances and/or time variation in monetary policy, equilibrium dynamics with finite-horizon planning will not generally coincide with the predictions of rational expectations equilibrium analysis. However, in the case of small enough departures from the assumptions of the perfect-foresight steady state, we can approximately characterize these dynamics through a perturbation of the solution just computed in the case of zero disturbances and the constant policy. A first-order perturbation solution for the representative household's finite-horizon spending plan is obtained by linearizing the structural equations (2), (5), and (6) around the stationary solution.

We write the linearized equations in terms of percentage deviations from the stationary values of the variables, using the notation

$$c_t \equiv \log(C_t/\overline{C}), \quad y_t \equiv \log(Y_t/\overline{Y}), \quad b_t^i \equiv B_t^i/(\overline{\Pi}\,\overline{Y}),$$
$$\pi_t \equiv \log(\Pi_t/\overline{\Pi}), \quad \hat{\imath}_t \equiv \log(1 + i_t/1 + \overline{\imath}).$$

Then if we let $\sigma \equiv -u_c(\overline{C})/(u_{cc}(\overline{C})\overline{C}) > 0$ be the intertemporal elasticity of substitution of household expenditure and parameterize disturbances to the urgency of spending by the quantity g_t such that to first order,

$$\log(u_c(C_t^i; \xi_t)/u_c(\overline{C}; \bar{\xi})) = -\sigma^{-1}(c_t^i - g_t),$$

equation (6) can be linearized to yield

$$c_\tau^j - g_\tau = E_\tau[c_{\tau+1}^{j-1} - g_{\tau+1}] - \sigma[\hat{\imath}_\tau^j - E_\tau \pi_{\tau+1}^{j-1}]. \tag{9}$$

Here the value of c_τ^j for any horizon j and period τ is understood to depend not only on the aggregate state s_τ at that time but also on the financial position with which households with a planning horizon of j periods are assumed to start the period.

Similarly, equation (8) implies that to a log-linear approximation, the marginal value of wealth used in evaluating potential financial positions when forward planning is terminated is equal to

$$\log(v'(B^0_{\tau+1})/v'(\overline{B})) = -(1-\beta)\sigma^{-1}b^0_{\tau+1}.$$

Hence equation (7) can be linearized to yield

$$c^0_\tau - g_\tau = -\sigma\hat{\imath}^0_\tau + (1-\beta)b^0_{\tau+1}. \tag{10}$$

Here the solutions for c^0_τ, $\hat{\imath}^0_\tau$ and $b^0_{\tau+1}$ all depend on both the aggregate state s_τ and the financial position of the household at the beginning of period τ. Finally, the flow budget constraint (2) can be linearized to yield

$$b^j_{\tau+1} = \beta^{-1}[b^{j+1}_\tau + y^j_\tau - c^j_\tau] \tag{11}$$

for any horizon $j \geq 0$. Conditions (9) and (11), setting $\tau = t + k - j$ for each $0 \leq j \leq k$, and condition (10) for $\tau = t + k$, together with model-consistent solutions for the variables $\{i^j_{t+k-j}, y^j_{t+k-j}, \pi^{j-1}_{t+k-j+1}\}$ for $0 \leq j \leq k$, then provide a system of simultaneous linear equations to solve for a linear approximation to the optimal plan of a household with a k-period planning horizon in period t. The solution for optimal expenditure in period t (the period in which the planning is undertaken) is given by

$$c^k_t = g_t + (1-\beta)b_t + (1-\beta)\sum_{j=0}^{k}\beta^j\,\mathrm{E}_t[y^{k-j}_{t+j} - g_{t+j}]$$

$$\tag{12}$$

$$-\sigma\sum_{j=0}^{k-1}\beta^{j+1}\,\mathrm{E}_t[\hat{\imath}^{k-j}_{t+j} - \pi^{k-j-1}_{t+j+1}] - \sigma\beta^{k+1}\,\mathrm{E}_t\hat{\imath}^0_{t+k},$$

where b_t is the household's financial position at the beginning of period t. This is the aspect of the plan chosen in period t that is actually implemented.

To determine aggregate expenditure in period t, it is also necessary to determine the state-contingent values $\{i^j_{t+k-j}, y^j_{t+k-j}, \pi^{j-1}_{t+k-j+1}\}$ of aggregate state variables used in the planning exercise. Let us assume for now that all households have identical planning horizons, and also start with identical financial positions.[6] Then they make identical decisions at all times, and thus necessarily begin each period with a financial position $b_t = 0$. It is assumed that each household has the structural knowledge required to deduce this, and correctly assumes that $b^j_t = 0$ for each of the other households as well. Aggregate demand (and aggregate real income) is then given by $y^k_t = c^k_t$. It follows from equation (11) that $b^k_{t+1} = 0$

for each household, and each household is assumed to have the structural knowledge required to deduce that this will be true for all other households. Thus in predicting the spending decisions of other households in period $t+1$ (which are assumed then to have planning horizons of only $k-1$ periods), these households are each assumed to enter period $t+1$ with financial positions $b^i_{t+1} = 0$. The level of spending that each is expected to choose in period $t+1$ is then given by equation (12), except with t replaced by $t+1$ and k replaced by $k-1$, again assuming initial financial wealth of zero.

The same argument applies in each successive period of the household's planning exercise. It follows that the value y^{k-j}_{t+j} assumed in the planning exercise (for any $1 \le j \le k$ and any possible state s_{t+j}) is equal to the value c^{k-j}_{t+j} implied by equation (12) when t replaced by $t+j$, k is replaced by $k-j$, and b_{t+j} is set equal to zero. The value of π^{k-j}_{t+j} assumed is the one implied by the model of firm planning described in the next section, when firms assume this model of aggregate demand determination.

And finally, interest-rate expectations are assumed to be based on knowledge of the central bank's reaction function, which we assume also to be a log-linear relation of the form

$$\hat{\imath}_t = \hat{\imath}^*_t + \phi_{\pi,t}\pi_t + \phi_{y,t}y_t, \tag{13}$$

where the coefficients may be time-dependent (though independent of the realizations of the endogenous variables), to allow for forward guidance experiments, as discussed in Section III. The interest-rate expectations $\hat{\imath}^{k-j}_{t+j}$ used in a forward-planning exercise at time t are thus assumed to satisfy

$$\hat{\imath}^j_\tau = \hat{\imath}^*_\tau + \phi_{\pi,\tau}\pi^j_\tau + \phi_{y,\tau}y^j_\tau, \tag{14}$$

for any planning horizon $j \ge 0$ and any date $t \le \tau \le t+j$; in the latter expression, the time-dependent coefficients are assumed to be the ones implied by policy announcements as of period t.

It follows that for any $j \ge 1$, the aggregate expenditure of households with a planning horizon of j periods must satisfy the recursive relationship

$$y^j_t - g_t = E_t[y^{j-1}_{t+1} - g_{t+1}] - \sigma(\hat{\imath}^j_t - E_t\pi^{j-1}_{t+1}), \tag{15}$$

while the aggregate expenditure of households with a zero-period planning horizon must satisfy

$$y^0_t - g_t = -\sigma\hat{\imath}^0_t. \tag{16}$$

These equations can be solved recursively to determine predicted aggregate demand. Equation (16) can be solved for y_{t+k}^0, given a solution for π_{t+k}^0 and the central bank's reaction function (14). Using this solution for y_{t+k}^0, equation (15) can then be solved for y_{t+k-1}^1, given solutions for π_{t+k-1}^1 and π_{t+k}^0 and the central bank's reaction function. Using this solution for y_{t+k-1}^1, equation (15) can then be solved for y_{t+k-2}^2, and so on. The model's prediction for aggregate expenditure y_t^k in period t is then given by the solution for y_t^k.

B. Price Setting by Firms with a Finite Planning Horizon

We turn now to inflation determination through the price-setting decisions of firms. Each differentiated good f is assumed to be sold by a monopolistically competitive producer (also indexed by f) that sets the price P_τ^f of good f each period. The objective of each firm is assumed to be maximization of the average value to shareholders of the stream of earnings generated by the firm's pricing policy.

We assume for simplicity that shares in the firms are not traded and that each household i receives an equal share of the earnings of all firms. Firms are assumed to value incremental earnings in different aggregate states in proportion to the average marginal utility of additional real income to their shareholders in those different states, averaging the marginal utilities of the different households.[7] This is in proportion to the quantity

$$\lambda_t \equiv \int u_c(C_t^i; \xi_t)\, di. \tag{17}$$

Hence a firm's objective is assumed to be the maximization of

$$\hat{\mathrm{E}}_t^f \sum_{\tau=t}^{\infty} \beta^{\tau-t} \lambda_\tau H(P_\tau^f/P_\tau; Z_\tau), \tag{18}$$

where $H(r_\tau^f; Z_\tau)$ represents the real profits of firm f in period τ if its relative price is $r_\tau^f \equiv P_\tau^f/P_\tau$; Z_τ is a vector of real state variables at date τ (specified below) that are outside the control of the individual firm under the assumption of monopolistic competition but that matter for the firm's real profits; and the operator $\hat{\mathrm{E}}_t^f[\cdot]$ indicates the expectations used by firm f in a planning exercise at date t.

Staggered price adjustment. As in the models of Calvo (1983) and Yun (1996), we assume that only a fraction $1 - \alpha$ of all goods prices are recon-

sidered in any period and that the particular prices reconsidered are a
random selection from the set of goods. In a period t in which the price
of good f is not reconsidered, we assume that $P_t^f = P_{t-1}^f \cdot \overline{\Pi}$. In other
words, we assume (as in Yun 1996) that prices are automatically in-
creased at the target inflation rate when the optimality of this default
pricing rule is not considered. This assumption implies that in the absence of aggregate disturbances or changes in monetary policy, the equilibrium prices of all goods will be the same as in a perfect-foresight equilibrium with flexible prices, despite the fact that not all prices are
reconsidered each period. Staggered pricing matters for equilibrium dynamics only to the extent that there are disturbances and/or temporary
shifts in the central bank's reaction function.

In a period t in which the price of good f is reconsidered, we assume
that the firm chooses a new price P_t^f so as to maximize its subjective assessment of the objective (18). But as in the previous section, we assume
that the firm plans ahead for only k periods and evaluates possible situations in period $t + k$ using a value function to estimate the value of its
continuation problem. Furthermore, when choosing a new price in period t, the firm need only consider the consequences for future states
in which it has not yet reconsidered its price more recently than period
t. Hence P_t^f is chosen to maximize

$$\hat{E}_t^f \left[\sum_{\tau=t}^{t+k} (\alpha\beta)^{\tau-t} \lambda_\tau H(P_t^f \overline{\Pi}^{\tau-t}/P_\tau; Z_\tau) + (\alpha\beta)^{k+1} \tilde{v}(P_t^f \overline{\Pi}^k/P_{t+k}; s_{t+k}) \right], \quad (19)$$

where $\tilde{v}(r_{t+k}^f; s_{t+k})$ represents the firm's estimate of the value of discounted
real profits from period $t + k + 1$ onward, conditional on reaching state s_{t+k}
in period $t + k$, not reconsidering its price in any of the periods between
$t + 1$ and $t + k + 1$, and having a relative price of r_{t+k}^f in period $t + k$.

In a stationary perfect-foresight equilibrium in which the central bank
maintains a constant inflation rate $\overline{\Pi}$, the real variables Z_t have constant
values $\overline{Z}$ that satisfy

$$H_r(1; \overline{Z}) = 0, \quad (20)$$

and the price of each good satisfies $P_t^j = P_t$ at all times. (The allocation of
resources in this stationary equilibrium is the same as in a stationary
equilibrium with perfectly flexible prices.) As in the previous section,
we assume that the value function used by firms is optimal for this stationary equilibrium, which is assumed to have prevailed for some time
prior to the period in which we seek to analyze the effects of a change

in monetary policy. But again we simplify by assuming that the value function is not state-dependent; thus we assume that

$$\tilde{v}(r) = (1 - \alpha\beta)^{-1}\bar{\lambda}H(r; \overline{Z}), \qquad (21)$$

where $\bar{\lambda} \equiv u_C(\overline{C}; \bar{\xi})$ is the constant value of λ_t in the perfect-foresight steady state.

It follows that the FOC for maximization of equation (19) is given by

$$\hat{E}_t^f\left[\sum_{\tau=t}^{t+k}(\alpha\beta)^{\tau-t}\,\lambda_\tau H_r(P_t^f\overline{\Pi}^{\tau-t}/P_\tau; Z_\tau)\frac{P_t\overline{\Pi}^{\tau-t}}{P_\tau} + \frac{(\alpha\beta)^{k+1}}{1 - \alpha\beta}\,\bar{\lambda}H_r(P_t^f\overline{\Pi}^k/P_{t+k}; \overline{Z})\frac{P_t\overline{\Pi}^k}{P_{t+k}}\right] = 0.$$

Log-linearizing this condition around the values that hold in the perfect-foresight steady state yields

$$\hat{E}_t^f\left\{\sum_{\tau=t}^{t+k}(\alpha\beta)^{\tau-t}\,[p_t^f - \sum_{s=t}^{\tau}\pi_s - m_\tau] + \frac{(\alpha\beta)^{k+1}}{1 - \alpha\beta}\,[p_t^f - \sum_{s=t}^{t+k}\pi_s]\right\} = 0, \qquad (22)$$

using the notation

$$p_t^f \equiv \log\left(\frac{P_t^f}{P_{t-1}\overline{\Pi}}\right), \qquad m_t \equiv -H_{rr}(1; \overline{Z})^{-1}H_r(1; Z_t).$$

(Note that m_t is a function of real variables outside the control of firm f and is of only first order in the deviations of these variables from their steady-state values. To a linear approximation, it measures the percentage deviation of the average real marginal cost of supplying output from its steady-state level.)

As in the previous section, we assume that the firm's expectations $\hat{E}_t^f[\cdot]$ are deduced from the model structural equations but that endogenous variables determined in period τ are determined by the decisions of households and firms with planning horizons of $t + k - \tau$ periods, for any $t \le \tau \le t + k$. (The endogenous variables referred to here now include the variables Z_t, along with i_t, Π_t, and Y_t.) It then follows from equation (22) that any firm f that reconsiders its price in period t, and plans ahead for k periods, will choose a new relative price $p_t^f = p_t^{*k}$, where the optimized relative price is given by

$$p_t^{*k} = E_t\sum_{\tau=t}^{t+k}(\alpha\beta)^{\tau-t}\,[\pi_\tau^{t+k-\tau} + (1 - \alpha\beta)m_\tau^{t+k-\tau}]. \qquad (23)$$

As usual, the Dixit-Stiglitz price index is defined as

$$P_t \equiv \left[\int (P_t^f)^{1-\theta} df \right]^{\frac{1}{1-\theta}}.$$

This implies that when we log-linearize around the stationary equilibrium with constant inflation rate $\overline{\Pi}$, we obtain (to a first-order approximation)

$$\pi_t^k = (1 - \alpha) p_t^{*k}.$$

Equation (23) then implies that

$$\pi_t^k = (1 - \alpha) E_t \sum_{\tau=t}^{t+k} (\alpha\beta)^{\tau-t} [\pi_\tau^{t+k-\tau} + (1 - \alpha\beta)m_\tau^{t+k-\tau}].$$

A similar equation holds if we replace k by any horizon $j \geq 0$. We then see that the $\{\pi_t^j\}$ for different finite horizons satisfy a simple recursion of the form

$$\pi_t^j = \frac{(1 - \alpha)(1 - \alpha\beta)}{\alpha} m_t^j + \beta E_t \pi_{t+1}^{j-1} \tag{24}$$

for any $j \geq 1$, with the special form

$$\pi_t^0 = \frac{(1 - \alpha)(1 - \alpha\beta)}{\alpha} m_t^0 \tag{25}$$

when the planning horizon is of length 0. Equations (24)–(25) can be solved forward to yield

$$\pi_t^k = \frac{(1 - \alpha)(1 - \alpha\beta)}{\alpha} \sum_{\tau=t}^{t+k} \beta^{\tau-t} E_t m_\tau^{t+k-\tau}$$

as the solution for equilibrium inflation given expectations regarding the determination of m_τ. If all firms have a k-period planning horizon, then the actual inflation rate will be given by $\pi_t = \pi_t^k$.

Determinants of real marginal cost. It remains to discuss how the variable m_t is jointly determined along with the other variables in our model. This requires that we consider further the form of the firm's profit function. Real profits each period are equal to real sales revenues minus the firm's real wage bill. As usual, Dixit-Stiglitz preferences (1) imply that the demand for good f is equal to $Y_t(r_t^f)^{-\theta}$, where Y_t is aggregate demand for the composite good; hence the real revenues of firm f are equal to $Y_t(r_t^f)^{1-\theta}$.

We assume that each firm produces its differentiated good using labor as the only variable input, with a production function $Y_t(f) = A_t H_t(f)^{1/\phi}$, where $H_t(f)$ is the labor hired by firm f, A_t is an exogenous common productivity factor, and $\phi \geq 1$ indicates the degree of diminishing returns to scale. Real labor costs are therefore equal to $W_t(Y_t(f)/A_t)^\phi$, where W_t is the real wage in period t.

We assume that wages are determined in the following way. The household suppliers of labor are represented in wage negotiations by representatives that each bundle the labor of a representative sample of the different household types in the economy and offer to supply a certain number of total hours by members of their group at a given wage; when a given number of hours are agreed upon for a given wage, each household in the group must supply that number of hours, and receives the same wage. There are a large number of such representatives (each bargaining on behalf of an identical group of households), so none has any market power. The representative chooses a number of hours H_t that the group will offer to work so as the maximize the average utility of the households in the group; this results in an FOC for optimal labor supply of the form

$$v_H(H_t; \xi_t) = \lambda_t W_t,$$

where λ_t is again defined by equation (17). Note that this is the relationship between wages and hours that would hold in a representative-household model of the kind assumed in Woodford (2003); here, as in Woodford (2013), we assume a labor market organization that implies a similar relationship even when the subjective marginal utilities of income of households may differ because of their boundedly rational expectations.

Real profits are then given by

$$H(r_t^j; Z_t) \equiv Y_t(r_t^f)^{1-\theta} - \lambda_t^{-1} w((Y_t/A_t)^\phi (r_t^f)^{-\theta\phi}; \xi_t),$$

where

$$w(H_t; \xi_t) \equiv v_H(H_t; \xi_t) \cdot H_t.$$

(The vector Z_t is now seen to have as its elements the endogenous variables Y_t and λ_t, and the exogenous variables A_t and the elements of ξ_t that affect the disutility of labor.)

Differentiating this profit function to obtain H_r, we can use equation (20) together with the requirement that $\bar{\lambda} = u_C(\bar{Y}; \bar{\xi})$ to determine the steady-state values $\bar{Y}$ and $\bar{\lambda}$. We can also differentiate the function H_r, obtaining

$$m_t = [1 + (\phi - 1)\theta]^{-1} \cdot [(1 + v)\phi(y_t - a_t) - y_t - \hat{\lambda}_t + \xi_t^m],$$

where

$$v \equiv \bar{H}w_{HH}/w_H > 0, \quad a_t \equiv \log(A_t/\bar{A}), \quad \hat{\lambda}_t \equiv \log(\lambda_t/\bar{\lambda}),$$
$$\xi_t^m \equiv \log(w_H(\bar{H}; \xi_t)/w_H(\bar{H}; \bar{\xi})).$$

If all households have a planning horizon j, we have $\lambda_t^j = -\sigma^{-1}(y_t^j - g_t)$, from which it follows that

$$m_t^j = \xi(y_t^j - y_t^*),$$

where y_t^* is a linear combination of the exogenous terms g_t, a_t, and ξ_t^m identifying (to a linear approximation) the percentage change in the flexible-price equilibrium level of output,[8] and

$$\xi \equiv \frac{(\phi - 1) + v\phi}{1 + (\phi - 1)\theta} > 0.$$

It follows that the recursive system (24)–(25) can alternatively be written as

$$\pi_t^j = \kappa(y_t^j - y_t^*) + \beta E_t \pi_{t+1}^{j-1} \tag{26}$$

for any $j \geq 1$, and

$$\pi_t^0 = \kappa(y_t^0 - y_t^*), \tag{27}$$

where

$$\kappa \equiv \frac{(1 - \alpha)(1 - \alpha\beta)}{\alpha} \cdot \xi > 0.$$

The system of equations consisting of equations (14), (15)–(16), and (26)–(27) can then be solved recursively to obtain solutions for the evolution of the variables $\{i_t^j, \pi_t^j, y_t^j\}$ for any planning horizon $j \geq 0$. Finally, if the actual planning horizon of firms is always k periods, then the model's prediction for equilibrium inflation will be $\pi_t = \pi_t^k$.

C. *Heterogeneous Planning Horizons*

Thus far, we have assumed that the planning horizon of all households and firms is of some finite length, k periods. However, there is no reason to suppose that this must be uniform across decision makers or even that it must be the same each time that a decision is made for a given decision maker. We can easily extend the model to allow for heterogeneity in the length of planning horizons while still treating this as an exogenous parameter for the decision maker, rather than another decision.

We have discussed how to compute y_t^j, the overall spending that would be undertaken by households with a planning horizon of j periods, and π_t^j, the average rate of price increase in excess of the target inflation rate on the part of firms with a planning horizon of j periods, for arbitrary values of j. These calculations did not depend on whether any households or firms actually have planning horizons of length j. In the earlier discussion, we used the notation k for the length of actual planning horizons, but to determine the behavior of households and firms with planning horizons of length k, it has been necessary to consider the counterfactual behavior of households and firms with planning horizons $0 \le j \le k$. In the calculation of y_t^j or π_t^j, the fact that actual planning horizons are of length k was never used. Households with planning horizons of length j are assumed to expect that their current-period income will result from the spending decisions of other households that also have planning horizons of length j, that their income in the following period will result from the decisions of other households whose planning decisions are all of length $j-1$, and so on—even if actual planning horizons are all of length k. This was necessary to allow decisions to be made without having to think about what anyone should think about conditions more than k periods in the future.

Hence the equations stated earlier for the determination of $\{y_t^j, \pi_t^j, \hat{\imath}_t^j\}$ for different horizons j continue to apply, even if we assume that a variety of different lengths of planning horizons are actually used. Suppose that each period, a fraction ω_j of households have planning horizons of length j (for $j \ge 0$), and similarly that a fraction $\tilde{\omega}_j$ of firms have planning horizons of length j, where the sequences $\{\omega_j, \tilde{\omega}_j\}$ satisfy $\Sigma_j \omega_j = \Sigma_j \tilde{\omega}_j = 1$. The particular households with planning horizons of a given length may or may not remain the same from period to period; what matters is that we assume stable population fractions. Then aggregate real expenditure (and hence real income) in period t will be given by

$$y_t = \sum_j \omega_j y_t^j, \tag{28}$$

and the overall rate of inflation will be given by

$$\pi_t = \sum_j \tilde{\omega}_j \pi_t^j, \tag{29}$$

to a log-linear approximation in each case.

The assumption of heterogeneous planning horizons introduces a complication worth mentioning relative to the earlier discussion. Households with planning horizon k will assume that they will receive income in the current period equal to y_t^k because they assume the planning horizons of others to be the same as their own, but they will actually receive income y_t given by equation (28). Therefore if they start with a financial position $b_t^i = 0$ and choose a level of expenditure that they expect to imply $b_{t+1}^i = 0$ as well, this will generally not be the case, as their income will be different from what they had expected. However, it continues to be the case that the aggregate financial position of households will be zero, as planned. And because the approximate expenditure rules derived earlier are linear in b_t^i, the heterogeneous evolution of financial positions across the population of households is of no consequence for the evolution of aggregate demand, aggregate income, or wage setting, and thus the evolution of real marginal costs.

It should also be noted that the existence of equilibrium requires that the sums in equations (28)–(29) converge. If there exists a finite upper bound on the planning horizons of both households and firms, then this is not an issue, since each of the individual quantities y_t^j and π_t^j is necessarily well defined and finite. In the case that there is no upper bound on planning horizons, convergence of the sums depends on how y_t^j and π_t^j behave for large j. If these quantities converge as j is made large, there is again no problem; however, it is possible to define policies (e.g., the case of a permanent interest-rate peg, discussed below) under which y_t^j and π_t^j grow explosively as j is increased. In such a case, the existence of an equilibrium depends on ω_j and $\tilde{\omega}_j$ going to zero rapidly enough for large j. Because forward planning over extremely long horizons is unlikely to be within anyone's cognitive capacities, we regard this as a plausible assumption, even in the case of a policy commitment of such an extreme kind.

Allowing for potentially unbounded length of planning horizons is convenient for at least one reason: it allows us to analyze the consequences of finite planning horizons in a case in which the state space of our model is no more complex than under the rational expectations analysis. In the special case in which $\omega_j = \tilde{\omega}_j = (1 - \rho)\rho^j$ for some $0 < \rho < 1$, we can average equations (15)–(16) to obtain

$$y_t - g_t = \rho\, E_t[y_{t+1} - g_{t+1}] - \sigma\,(\hat{\imath}_t - \rho E_t \pi_{t+1}). \tag{30}$$

Similarly, we can average equations (26)–(27) to obtain

$$\pi_t = \kappa\,(y_t - y_t^*) + \beta\rho E_t \pi_{t+1}. \tag{31}$$

These two conditions, together with a specification of the central bank reaction function (13), provide a complete system of three equations per period to solve for the evolution of the three endogenous variables $\{y_t, \pi_t, \hat{\imath}_t\}$.

While conditions (30)–(31) are necessary for given paths to be consistent with finite-horizon optimization by households and firms, they are not sufficient conditions. It is still necessary to validate any candidate solution by computing the paths $\{y_t^j, \pi_t^j, \hat{\imath}_t^j\}$ for each planning horizon j and verifying that the sums (28)–(29) converge. This will often be the case but need not be, as discussed in the next section.

The conditions (30)–(31) are quite similar to the equilibrium conditions of the standard New Keynesian model with rational expectations (discussed further in Sec. III), differing only in the appearance here of the factor $\rho < 1$ that decreases the influence of the expectational terms in both equations. Exactly this kind of modification of the standard model is also proposed by Gabaix (2017), albeit on somewhat different grounds.[9] Our proposal is not equivalent to that of Gabaix, however, because of the requirement that the sums (28)–(29) must converge; this leads to importantly different conclusions about the consequences of an interest-rate peg, for example.[10]

III.   Comparison with Rational Expectations Equilibrium Analysis

Under the assumption of infinite-horizon optimization with rational (i.e., model-consistent) expectations, the variables $\{y_t, \pi_t, \hat{\imath}_t\}$ must instead evolve in accordance with the equations

$$y_t - g_t = E_t[y_{t+1} - g_{t+1}] - \sigma\,(\hat{\imath}_t - E_t \pi_{t+1}), \tag{32}$$

and

$$\pi_t = \kappa\,(y_t - y_t^*) + \beta E_t \pi_{t+1} \tag{33}$$

for all t, along with the central bank reaction function (13). Solutions to this system of equations under different assumptions about policy have been extensively discussed (see, e.g., Woodford 2003).

If the limiting values

$$y_t^\infty \equiv \lim_{k \to \infty} y_t^k, \qquad \pi_t^\infty \equiv \lim_{k \to \infty} \pi_t^k, \qquad \hat{\imath}_t^\infty \equiv \lim_{k \to \infty} \hat{\imath}_t^k \qquad (34)$$

are well defined, then it follows from equations (15) and (26) that these limiting processes must satisfy both of the equations (32)–(33) each period, that is, they must describe a rational-expectations equilibrium. It might seem from this that standard analyses of the rational-expectations equilibria consistent with a given policy commitment are therefore equivalent to the predictions of our model with finite-horizon planning, in the case that planning horizons are assumed to be long.

This is not quite true, however, for two reasons. First, in general, the equation system consisting of equation (13) together with equations (32)–(33) admits of a large multiplicity of solutions but not all of these solutions can correspond to the large-k limit of the predictions of the finite-horizon model. The predictions of the finite-horizon model are always uniquely determined for any horizon k, and if the sequence converges the limit must be unique as well. Thus in cases where the limiting values are well defined, these limiting values provide an interpretation of how the behavior described by a rational-expectations equilibrium can arise; however, they also provide a selection criterion that identifies a single solution among the large set of possible rational-expectations solutions as the one that should be expected. This clarifies an important issue for monetary policy analysis.

Second, it is not always the case that the sequence of finite-horizon decisions converges as k is made large. In such a case, none of the rational-expectations solutions are similar to the behavior predicted by our model, regardless of what one might think is a realistic range of values for k.

To see why, it is useful to write our equilibrium relations in vector form. If we use equation (13) to substitute for $\hat{\imath}_t$ in equation (32), we can write the equation system defining a rational-expectations equilibrium as a two-dimensional system,

$$x_t = M_t \cdot E_t x_{t+1} + N_t \cdot u_t, \qquad (35)$$

using the vector notation

$$x_t \equiv \begin{bmatrix} y_t - g_t \\ \pi_t \end{bmatrix}, \qquad u_t \equiv \begin{bmatrix} i_t^* + \phi_y g_t \\ g_t - y_t^* \end{bmatrix},$$

and where M_t and N_t are 2×2 matrices of coefficients that depend on the coefficients of the monetary policy reaction function (but are time-invariant if the reaction function is time-invariant).[11]

Using the same notation, the conditions that define an equilibrium with finite-horizon planning can be written in the form

$$x_t^j = M_t \cdot E_t x_{t+1}^{j-1} + N_t \cdot u_t, \qquad (36)$$

for any $j \geq 1$. For the case $j = 0$, we instead have simply

$$x_t^0 = N_t \cdot u_t. \qquad (37)$$

A.   Announcement of a Change in Monetary Policy

We can illustrate the use of this apparatus by considering our model's predictions about a "forward guidance" experiment of the following sort. Suppose that it is announced at date $t = 0$ that from period zero until some horizon $t = T$, monetary policy will follow a rule of the form (13) with some constant coefficients (i^*, ϕ_π, ϕ_y); we further suppose that $i^* \neq 0$, so that the "new" policy rule is not consistent with the steady state with inflation rate $\bar{\Pi}$ that we suppose has prevailed prior to the policy experiment. However, it is also understood that from $t = T$ onward, policy will revert to the central bank's "normal" rule, which involves $i_\tau^* = 0$ for all $\tau \geq T$. We wish to consider the effects of announcing a new policy that will be maintained for a specified period of time.[12] Note that we will have constant matrices $M_t = M$, $N_t = N$ for all $t < T$. We assume for simplicity that there are no real disturbances.

For any $\tau \geq T$, we observe that because $u_\tau = 0$, equation (37) implies that $x_\tau^0 = 0$. Then, proceeding recursively, we can use equation (36) to show that $x_\tau^j = 0$ for any $j \geq 0$. Hence regardless of the forecast horizon, for all periods $\tau \geq T$ the outcome will be the steady state with inflation equal to $\bar{\Pi}$; note that this is one of the possible rational-expectations equilibria for the period after time T.

In fact, there is a unique rational expectations equilibrium with $x_\tau = 0$ for $\tau \geq T$, namely the solution in which

$$x_t^{RE} = (I + M + M^2 + \dots + M^{T-t-1})Nu^* = (I - M^{T-t})(I - M)^{-1} Nu^* \qquad (38)$$

for all $t < T$. Here the final expression is valid only in the case that $I - M$ is nonsingular, which is true as long as

$$\phi_\pi + \frac{1-\beta}{\kappa} \phi_y \neq 1;$$

however, the first equality holds more generally. In these expressions, u^* is the constant value of u_t for all $t < T$, and M, N are the constant values of the matrices M_t, N_t for all $t < T$.

We can then solve the system (36)–(37) recursively for periods $t < T$, to show that $x_t^j = x_t^{RE}$ for any $j \geq T - t - 1$, while instead $x_t^j = x_{T-j-1}^{RE}$ for any $j < T - t - 1$. (The former result is also true in the case of exogenous disturbances, as long as they are sufficiently transitory; it requires only that $E_t u_\tau = 0$ for all $T \geq t$. The latter result is more special, as it relies on our assumption that $u_\tau = u^*$, a constant vector, for all $\tau < T$.) It follows that in the case of any temporary policy change (i.e., case in which T is finite), the limits (34) exist and are given by $x_t^\infty = x_t^{RE}$ for all t.

Thus in the case of a policy experiment of this kind, finite-horizon planning leads to the same predictions as a rational expectations analysis, if people's planning horizons are long enough ($j \geq T - t - 1$ for everyone), and one uses the right selection criterion to choose from among the large set of possible rational expectations solutions. If the policy change is relatively transitory, or people are given no reason to expect anything different from the "normal" reaction function except over a relatively near future, the length of people's planning horizons need not be very long. It is only necessary that most people's planning horizons be long enough for the predicted outcome to be approximately the same as the rational expectations prediction.

Matters are more complex in the case of a policy change that is expected to last for a long time. Consider the case in which (contrary to the assumption above) the change in policy is permanent. If the new policy satisfies the "Taylor principle," that is, the coefficients of the reaction function satisfy

$$\phi_\pi + \frac{1-\beta}{\kappa} \phi_y > 1; \tag{39}$$

then both eigenvalues of M are inside the unit circle.[13] In this case, equation (38) implies that

$$\lim_{T \to \infty} x_t^{RE} = x_{ss}^{RE} \equiv (I - M)^{-1} N u^*.$$

This identifies one of the possible rational expectations equilibria consistent with such a policy commitment: one in which the economy moves immediately to the new stationary equilibrium consistent with the new policy.

It then follows that

$$\lim_{k \to \infty} x_t^k = x_{ss}^{RE}$$

as well, for all $t \geq 0$ (all dates after the announcement of the permanent change in policy). Thus we again find that the limits (34) are well defined; hence we again justify selection of a particular rational expectations equilibrium as the one that approximates what will happen if people have only finite planning horizons, as both those horizons are sufficiently long. And it is again the case that as long as we are confident that most people's planning horizons are not too short, we should expect an outcome that is approximately the same as in a (suitably chosen) rational expectations equilibrium. How long horizons must be in order to be "not too short" depends on the largest eigenvalue of M, which depends on the strength of the policy feedback coefficients.

If instead the inequality in equation (39) is reversed, as will be the case if neither response coefficient is very large, the results are quite different. Because in this case M has an eigenvalue greater than 1, the rational expectations solution x_t^{RE} does not have a well-defined limit as T is made large (it grows explosively). This is a troubling feature of the rational expectations analysis, even when applied to the case of a policy change of long but finite duration; it implies that the predicted outcome is very different depending on the exact value of T, which means that changes in expected policy that change only what is expected about policy very far in the future can have a substantial effect on immediate outcomes—an intuitively unappealing conclusion. Moreover, the large eigenvalue also implies that x_t^k does not have a well-defined limit as k is made large. Hence the outcome with finite-horizon planning need not be similar to the predictions of (any) rational expectations equilibrium, even if one supposes that the planning horizons of most households are quite long.

B. The Case of an Interest-Rate Peg

As a case of particular interest in which equation (39) is not satisfied, suppose that $\phi_\pi = \phi_y = 0$. This is the case in which the central bank promises to fix the short-term nominal interest rate at some level i^* up until date T, as in the case of a central bank that announces that its policy rate will remain at its effective lower bound for a stated period of time. Suppose furthermore that $i^* < 0$, meaning not that the nominal interest rate is negative, but that it is lower than its level in the steady state with constant inflation at the target rate $\overline{\Pi}$.

In this case, $Nu^* \ll 0$ and $M \gg 0$, so that equation (38) implies that both elements of x_t^{RE} are positive and monotonically increasing as T is increased. Moreover, because M has an eigenvalue that is greater than 1, both elements of x_t^{RE} are predicted to grow without bound for large enough T. This implies that a commitment to keep the interest rate at a low level should be a stimulative policy, increasing both output and inflation. Moreover, even if a real disturbance would (in the absence of a countervailing change in monetary policy) significantly lower output and inflation, and even if the shock is so severe that a contemporaneous response of monetary policy alone cannot offset it because of the constraint imposed by the effective lower bound on nominal interest rates, it should be possible to fully offset the contractionary effects of the shock by committing to keep the nominal interest rate at the lower bound for a sufficiently long time. This is because, under the rational expectations analysis, the effects of a commitment to keep the nominal interest rate low can be unboundedly large as long as T is long enough.

This result, however—that forward guidance should not only be effective but should have effects that can be unboundedly large (and that grow explosively with the length of the commitment)—has met with some skepticism, so the results predicted by standard models under rational expectations have been termed a "forward guidance puzzle" (Del Negro, Giannoni, and Patterson 2015). An analysis under the assumption of finite-horizon planning also predicts that forward guidance should be effective, up to a point; as long as $T \leq t + k + 1$, the model predicts that $x_t^k = x_t^{RE}$, so that both elements of x_t^k will be increased by increasing T. But once $T = t + k + 1$, further increases in T are predicted to have no further effect on x_t^k, which will be given by

$$x_t^k = (I - M^{k+1})(I - M)^{-1} Nu^*, \tag{40}$$

for all $T \geq t + k + 1$. The predicted effects of forward guidance are bounded, no matter how long the commitment might be.[14] This is a more empirically plausible result; it also avoids the uncomfortable prediction of the rational expectations analysis, that changes in policy commitments far in the future (leaving expected policy over the next several decades unchanged) should have any material effect on macroeconomic outcomes now.

The conclusions from a rational expectations analysis are even more paradoxical in the case of a thought experiment in which the central bank commits to peg the nominal interest rate forever. Cochrane (2017) suggests that standard New Keynesian models imply that such a policy should have perfectly well-behaved effects, on the ground that there are well-behaved (nonexplosive, stationary) rational expectations equilibria consistent with an expectation that such a policy rule will be followed forever. However, all of these rational expectations equilibria have the property that at least eventually (for large enough t) the average inflation rate should be lower, the lower the nominal interest rate that the central bank commits to maintain. And many of them involve lower inflation immediately, and not merely in the long run. Indeed, if one uses a "minimum-state-variable criterion" to select the rational expectations equilibrium that is expected to occur, a permanent interest-rate peg with $i^* < 0$ (and no current or expected future real disturbances) should lead to an immediate jump to the new stationary equilibrium with a constant inflation rate and the interest rate i^*.[15] Because of the Fisher equation, this will be an inflation rate that is lower the lower the pegged interest rate is.

Such observations suggest that a commitment to a permanently low nominal interest rate should be expected to be a deflationary policy rather than an inflationary one; one might then wonder, on the principle that changes in expected policy far in the future should make little difference in the present, if a commitment to a low nominal interest rate for a long though finite time should not be deflationary as well. The conclusions from an analysis that assumes that planning horizons are finite are, however, quite different.

As indicated, if people's planning horizons are of some finite length k, then a commitment to peg the nominal interest rate at a lower level than the one consistent with the steady state with inflation rate $\bar{\Pi}$ necessarily results in higher output and inflation. These stimulative effects are predicted to be larger, the longer the length T of the commitment; however, once $T \geq t + k + 1$, there are no further effects in period t of lengthening the commitment. The predicted effects are also given by equation (40) in the case of a commitment to a permanent interest-rate peg. These effects are positive, though bounded; they are quite unlike the effects that should be observed under any of the rational expectations equilibria consistent with such a commitment, at least as regards the levels of output and inflation predicted as t increases.

Thus an analysis based on finite planning horizons provides no support for the neo-Fisherian proposal that the way an economy experiencing chronic low inflation can raise its inflation rate is by committing to peg the nominal interest rate at a higher level. However, the prediction just derived for the case of a commitment to a permanent interest-rate peg is not entirely satisfactory. It implies that the inflation rate and nominal interest rate should fail to conform to the Fisher equation, even in the long run, and even though (in the thought experiment just presented) both are forever constant at levels incompatible with the Fisher equation.

How can this be? In a situation where output and inflation are given by equation (40) each period (or by an average of this quantity for different values of k, in accordance with the distribution of planning horizons in the population), and the interest rate is pegged at i^*, households are modeled as choosing a constant level of expenditure each period despite facing a constant real rate of interest that differs from their rate of time preference. The reason that this is possible, despite their intertemporal planning, is that they are modeled as using a value function $v(B)$—to evaluate potential levels of financial wealth at times where they truncate their forward planning—that would be sensible in a stationary equilibrium with an inflation rate of $\overline{\Pi}$, but that does not represent a correct evaluation of the value to them of a given level of financial wealth, even on average, in the environment in which they find themselves after the change in policy.

And while we have justified our assumption of a particular value function by assuming that prior to the policy experiment, households have had considerable experience with a regime in which inflation was kept close to $\overline{\Pi}$ and the economy was stable enough for them to come to have correct expectations (including a correct estimate of the value of financial wealth) in that environment, it is not plausible to suppose that they would continue to use this value function if the new policy regime is maintained forever—especially if macroeconomic conditions under the new regime are simple and predictable, as implied by the earlier thought experiment. A more satisfactory analysis of the effects of long-lasting policy changes (or for that matter of long-lasting changes in other fundamentals, such as the effects of a permanent change in productivity) requires that we consider how the estimated value functions of households and firms should be shaped by further experience.

IV.   Learning the Value Functions

In the analysis thus far, we have treated the value functions $v(B)$ and $\tilde{v}(r)$ as fixed and equal to the correct continuation value functions in a stationary environment with no real disturbances and a constant inflation rate $\overline{\Pi}$. If we are interested in analyzing the effects of relatively transitory departures from such an environment—the effects of transitory real disturbances and/or transitory changes in monetary policy—then it may suffice to assume that these value functions continue to be used in the face of such disturbances. But if we wish to analyze the effects of more persistent changes—as in the discussion of the consequences of a permanent interest-rate peg—then the assumption that the value functions should remain forever equal to these ones is unappealing.

The value functions are intended to represent values that decision makers have learned by averaging their past experience with different states, and a sufficient amount of experience with an environment that persistently differs from the stationary equilibrium with inflation rate $\overline{\Pi}$ should eventually cause the value functions to change. In particular, if a new stationary equilibrium is eventually established, it makes sense to suppose that (at least in the long run) the value functions should be optimal for that new stationary equilibrium, and not for some previous stationary equilibrium far in the past.

A.   Updating Beliefs

I now illustrate how adaptive learning of the value functions can be incorporated into our analysis. Again we consider first the problem of a household. We cannot suppose that $v(B)$ is a simple average of the household's utility levels on previous occasions when real wealth was equal to B. First, there is the problem that many possible values of B that need to be considered in the planning exercise will never have been previously experienced. More important, there is the problem that the value function is intended to assess the value of the household's (infinite-horizon) continuation problem—the expected discounted utility flow over an unbounded sequence of subsequent periods—and the actual value of the household's discounted utility over an unbounded period of time is never observed. But both of these problems can be solved by assuming that what the household averages is not its actual discounted utility following a period in which it has a particular financial position, but rather an estimate of its discounted utility that it computes as part of the finite-horizon forward-planning exercise.

Suppose that household i enters period t with a financial position B_t^i, learns the current state s_t, and engages in forward planning using its current estimate $v_t(B)$ of its value function. (The time subscript indicates that we no longer assume that the same value function is used at all times.) Through this exercise (described in Sec. II.A), it chooses a state-contingent expenditure plan for periods t through $t + k$ to maximize the estimated value of the objective (3). As part of this calculation, it obtains an estimated value for its continuation utility from period t onward, the maximized value of equation (3). Furthermore, the household can perform this same calculation for any hypothetical value of B. In this way, the household obtains an estimated value function $v_t^{est}(B)$ for any value of B. Note that this calculation is performed only for the particular state s_t in which the household finds itself, and not for all of the possible states that it might ever be in—so that the calculation remains much less expensive than a computation of the true value function.

We may then suppose that the household revises its estimate of the value function for use in future periods' forward-planning exercises based on a comparison of its new estimate $v_t^{est}(B)$ with the assumption $v_t(B)$ used in its forward planning.[16] Specifically, let us suppose that

$$v_{t+1}(B) = \gamma v_t^{est}(B) + (1 - \gamma)v_t(B), \tag{41}$$

where the "gain parameter" $0 < \gamma < 1$ indicates the rate at which discrepancies between the assumed value function and the new estimate are corrected by adjusting the assumed value function.

Similarly, suppose that a firm f that reconsiders its price in period t engages in forward planning using its current estimate $\tilde{v}_t(r)$ of its value function. Through this exercise (described in Sec. II.B), it chooses a new price to maximize the estimated value of the objective (19). As part of this exercise, it must compute an estimate of what the value of equation (19) would be for any choice of P_{t}^f; let this estimate be denoted $\tilde{v}_t^{est}(P_t^f/(P_{t-1}\overline{\Pi}))$. This then implies an estimate for the continuation value function used in forward planning, for any value of r. We may then suppose that the firm revises its estimate of its value function using an error-correction rule of the form

$$\tilde{v}_{t+1}(r) = \tilde{\gamma}\tilde{v}_t^{est}(r) + (1 - \tilde{\gamma})\tilde{v}_t(r), \tag{42}$$

where the gain parameter $\tilde{\gamma}$ of firms need not be the same as that of households.

In the case that there are no real disturbances and monetary policy maintains a constant inflation rate $\overline{\Pi}$, assumption of a value function

$v^*(B)$ defined by equation (8) on the part of households, and of a value function $\tilde{v}^*(r)$ defined by equation (21) on the part of firms, will result in estimated value functions $v^{est}(B)$ and $\tilde{v}^{est}(r)$ that are also equal to $v^*(B)$ and $\tilde{v}^*(r)$ respectively. Hence the value functions $(v^*, \tilde{v}^*)$ constitute a fixed point of the dynamics defined by equations (41)–(42) in such a situation. We wish now to consider a local approximation to the dynamics implied by equations (41)–(42), through a perturbation of this solution.

B. Log-Linearization of the Learning Dynamics

We first consider a local approximation to equation (41). The structural equations defining the household's optimal finite-horizon plan involve the derivative $v'(B)$ of the value function; hence a log-linear approximation to those equations, of the kind used above to approximate the optimal plan, will involve a log-linear approximation to $v'(B)$. We parameterize this as

$$\log(v'_t(B)/v^{*'}(0)) = -\sigma^{-1}\left[\nu_\tau + \chi_t \cdot b\right].$$

Using this approximation, we can, as in Section II.A (Log-Linear Approximation of the Optimal Plan), compute a log-linear approximation to the household's optimal finite-horizon plan in period t, as a function of the assumed coefficients (ν_t, χ_t). This solution gives approximate values for variables such as c^i_t that are linear functions of b^i_t.

If we let $C^i_t(B)$ be the optimal expenditure plan of the household under the counterfactual assumption $B^i_t = B$, then the derivative of the estimated value function will equal

$$v^{est'}_t(B) = \hat{E}^i_t[u_C(C^i_t(B); \xi_t)/\Pi_t].$$

Hence to a log-linear approximation,

$$\log(v^{est'}_t(B)/v^{*'}(0)) = -\sigma^{-1}(c^k_t(b) - g_t) - \pi^k_t,$$

where k is the length of the planning horizon of the household (and the planning horizon assumed for the firms that revise their prices in period t). Our log-linear approximation to the optimal household plan, $c^k_t(b) = c^k_t(0) + (c^k_t)' \cdot b$, allows us to express the right-hand side of this equation as a linear function of b. Approximating the left-hand side as $-\sigma^{-1}\left[\nu^{est}_\tau + \chi^{est}_t \cdot b\right]$, and equating coefficients, we obtain

$$v_t^{est} = y_t^k - g_t + \sigma\pi_t^k, \tag{43}$$

$$\chi_t^{est} = (c_t^k)'. \tag{44}$$

A log-linear approximation to equation (41) can be written as

$$[v_{t+1} + \chi_{t+1}b] = \gamma \left[v_t^{est} + \chi_t^{est}b\right] + (1-\gamma)\left[v_t + \chi_t b\right]. \tag{45}$$

Equating coefficients on the two sides of equation (45), we obtain separate updating equations for v_t and χ_t.

The implied learning dynamics for χ_t turn out to be independent of the pricing behavior of firms. If the household's planning horizon is k periods, the right-hand side of equation (44) is equal to $gk(\chi_t)$, where

$$g_k(\chi) \equiv \frac{\chi}{\beta^{k+1} + \left(\frac{1-\beta^{k+1}}{1-\beta}\right)\chi},$$

and equation (45) then implies that

$$\chi_{t+1} = \gamma g_k(\chi_t) + (1-\gamma)\chi_t.$$

This is an autonomous nonlinear difference equation for the evolution of χ_t. One observes furthermore that for any $\chi > 0$, $g_k(\chi)$ is greater than, less than, or equal to χ if and only if χ is less than, greater than, or equal to $1 - \beta$. Hence the difference equation implies monotonic convergence of χ_t to the fixed point $1 - \beta$, from any initial condition $\chi_0 > 0$; this is true for any value of the gain parameter and is unaffected by exogenous shocks or shifts in monetary policy.

Because there is necessarily eventual convergence of this parameter, we assume in our analysis that convergence has already occurred and let $\chi_t = 1 - \beta$ at all times. With this simplification, our analysis of learning dynamics reduces to an analysis of the adjustment of the coefficient v_t. Equation (45) implies that

$$v_{t+1} = \gamma v_t^{est} + (1-\gamma)v_t, \tag{46}$$

where v_t^{est} is given by equation (43).

We can compute a similar local approximation to equation (42). The FOC characterizing the firm's optimal price adjustment depends on the derivative $\tilde{v}'(r)$ of the firm's value function, and log-linearization of this condition requires a log-linear approximation to $\tilde{v}'(r)$. Suppose that we parameterize this as

$$\tilde{v}'_t(r) = -\frac{\bar{\lambda}}{1 - \alpha\beta} H_{rr}(1; \overline{Z}) \cdot [\tilde{\nu}_t - \tilde{\chi}_t \cdot \log r].$$

The log-linearized FOC can then be solved for a linear approximation to the solution for p_t^f, as a function of the coefficients $\tilde{\nu}_t$ and $\tilde{\chi}_t$ used in the approximate value function.

The firm's estimated value function $\tilde{v}_t^{est}(P_t^f/(P_{t-1}\overline{\Pi}))$ is simply the estimated value of the objective (19). The derivative $\tilde{v}_t^{est'}(r)$ is obtained by differentiating this expression. Linearizing this, as in the derivation of equation (22), we obtain

$$\tilde{v}_t^{est'}(r) = -\bar{\lambda} H_{rr} \cdot \left(\frac{1 + (\alpha\beta)^{k+1}(\tilde{\chi}_t - 1)}{1 - \alpha\beta} \right) \cdot [p_t^{*k} - \log r],$$

where p_t^{*k} is the optimal log relative price (now dependent on $\tilde{\nu}_t$ and $\tilde{\chi}_t$), the value of $\log r$ that maximizes $\tilde{v}_t^{est}(r)$.

Then if we write $\tilde{v}_t^{est'}(r)$ in log-linear form,

$$\tilde{v}_t^{est'}(r) = -\frac{\bar{\lambda}}{1 - \alpha\beta} H_{rr}(1; \overline{Z}) \cdot [\tilde{\nu}_t^{est} - \tilde{\chi}_t^{est} \cdot \log r],$$

and equate coefficients, we obtain

$$\tilde{\chi}_t^{est} = \tilde{g}(\chi_t) \equiv [1 + (\alpha\beta)^{k+1}(\tilde{\chi}_t - 1)], \tag{47}$$

$$\tilde{\nu}_t^{est} = g(\chi_t) \cdot p_t^{*k}. \tag{48}$$

Equating coefficients in a log-linear approximation to equation (42), we obtain updating equations for the coefficients of the form

$$\tilde{\nu}_{t+1} = \tilde{\gamma}\tilde{\nu}_t^{est} + (1 - \tilde{\gamma})\tilde{\nu}_t, \tag{49}$$

$$\tilde{\chi}_{t+1} = \tilde{\gamma}\tilde{\chi}_t^{est} + (1 - \tilde{\gamma})\tilde{\chi}_t. \tag{50}$$

Substituting equation (47) into equation (50), we see that the evolution of $\tilde{\chi}_t$ is determined by an autonomous linear difference equation,

$$\tilde{\chi}_{t+1} = \tilde{\gamma}\tilde{g}(\tilde{\chi}_t) + (1 - \tilde{\gamma})\tilde{\chi}_t.$$

Moreover, we observe that $\tilde{g}(\tilde{\chi})$ is greater than, less than, or equal to $\tilde{\chi}$ if and only if $\tilde{\chi}$ is less than, greater than, or equal to 1. Hence the updating equation implies monotonic convergence of $\tilde{\chi}_t$ to the fixed point of 1, starting from any initial estimate $\tilde{\chi}_0$, and regardless of the paths of exogenous disturbances or of monetary policy.

We shall accordingly assume in our analysis that convergence has already occurred, and that $\tilde{\chi}_t = 1$ at all times. In this case, equation (48) reduces to

$$\tilde{v}_t^{est} = p_t^{*k} = (1 - \alpha)^{-1} \pi_t^k, \tag{51}$$

and the dynamic evolution of $\tilde{v}_t$ is then given by equation (49) with this substitution. The log-linearized learning dynamics are then described by the system of equations consisting of equations (46) and (49) for the evolution of v_t and $\tilde{v}_t$ respectively, where the right-hand sides of both equations can be expressed as linear functions of the current values of the coefficients $(v_t, \tilde{v}_t)$.

C. Equilibrium Dynamics with Learning

To describe the complete dynamics of both actions and beliefs, we must consider how the endogenous variables y_t^k and π_t^k (that appear in the expressions [43] and [51] for the coefficients of the estimated value functions) are affected by variations in the coefficients $(v_t, \tilde{v}_t)$. This requires us to review the derivations of our log-linear approximations to the optimal decision rules, now allowing a more general specification of the value functions.

Let the predicted equilibrium evolution of each of the endogenous variables $(y_t^j, \pi_t^j, \hat{\imath}_t^j)$ be expressed as a sum of two components,

$$y_t^j = \tilde{y}_t^j + \bar{y}_t^j, \quad \pi_t^j = \tilde{\pi}_t^j + \bar{\pi}_t^j, \quad \hat{\imath}_t^j = \tilde{\imath}_t^j + \bar{\imath}_t^j,$$

where in each case the tilde component means the predicted value for the variable under the assumption that $v_t = \tilde{v}_t = 0$ in all periods, but taking account of exogenous shocks and policy changes, while the bar component represents the discrepancy from this prediction as a result of variation in v_t and $\tilde{v}_t$. The evolution of the variables $\{\tilde{y}_t^j, \tilde{\pi}_t^j, \tilde{\imath}_t^j\}$ for all horizons $j \geq 0$ then continues to be described by the equations derived in Section II. It remains only to compute the values of the bar terms, that is, the effects on the endogenous variables of perturbation of the value functions.

The log-linear approximations to the FOCs for the household's problem remain as stated in Section II.A (Log-Linear Approximation of the Optimal Plan), except that log-linearization of equation (7) now yields

$$c_\tau^0 - g_\tau = -\sigma \hat{i}_\tau^0 + (1 - \beta)b_{\tau+1}^0 + \nu_t \tag{52}$$

as a generalization of equation (10). Here the variables all refer to state-contingent values at date τ that are contemplated by the household in its planning exercise at date t; in that exercise, the household assumes that all households will use the value function parameterized by ν_t in evaluating terminal states, even in decisions that it imagines them making in periods $\tau > t$.

Because the household's calculations incorporate the requirement that $y_\tau^j = c_\tau^j$, the log-linearized household Euler equations (9) imply that

$$\bar{y}_t^j = \bar{y}_t^{j-1} - \sigma[\bar{i}_t^j - \bar{\pi}_t^{j-1}] \tag{53}$$

for each $j \geq 1$. Note that the effects of ν_t and $\tilde{\nu}_t$ on the household's period-t calculation of y_τ^{j-1} or π_τ^{j-1} for dates $\tau > t$ are identical to the effects of those belief shifts on the value of y_t^{j-1} and π_t^{j-1}; this allows us to make reference purely to period-t variables in equation (53).

The household's log-linearized flow budget constraint also continues to be given by equation (11). Because the household understands that $y_\tau^j = c_\tau^j$, the flow budget constraint implies that in the household's optimal plan, $b_{\tau+1}^j = 0$ each period. Hence (52) requires that

$$\bar{y}_t^0 = -\sigma \bar{i}_t^0 + \nu_t. \tag{54}$$

The system consisting of equations (53)–(54) can be solved recursively to obtain $\bar{y}_t^j$ for any $j \geq 0$.

We turn next to optimal price setting by firms. The FOC for the pricing decision of a firm that reconsiders its price in period t, and has a planning horizon of k periods, can be log-linearized as above to yield the solution

$$p_t^{*k} = E_t^k \sum_{\tau=t}^{t+k} (\alpha\beta)^{\tau-t} \left[\pi_\tau + (1 - \alpha\beta)m_\tau\right] + (\alpha\beta)^{k+1}\tilde{\nu}_t, \tag{55}$$

generalizing equation (23). Note that we now use the operator $E_t^k[\cdot]$ rather than $E_t[\cdot]$ because the predictions about decisions made in periods $\tau > t$ used in the firm's forward planning in period t are no longer model-consistent; this is because the firm assumes in period t that value functions parameterized by ν_t and $\tilde{\nu}_t$ will also be used in periods $\tau > t$, while genuinely model-consistent expectations would take account of the predictable evolution of beliefs.

The solution (55) implies as before that for any $j \geq 1$,

$$p_t^{*j} = \mathrm{E}_t^k \left[\pi_t + (1 - \alpha\beta)m_t + \alpha\beta \, p_{t+1}^{*j-1} \right].$$

From this it follows that

$$\overline{\pi}_t^j = \kappa\overline{y}_t^j + \beta\overline{\pi}_t^{j-1} \tag{56}$$

for all $j \geq 1$. Again we use the fact that the effects of v_t and $\tilde{v}_t$ on the household's period-t calculation of y_τ^{j-1} or π_τ^{j-1} for dates $\tau > t$ are identical to the effects of those belief shifts on the value of y_t^{j-1} and π_t^{j-1}. The solution (55) also implies that

$$\overline{\pi}_t^0 = \kappa\overline{y}_t^0 + (1 - \alpha)\beta\tilde{v}_t. \tag{57}$$

The system consisting of equations (56)–(57) can be solved recursively to obtain $\overline{\pi}_t^j$ for any $j \geq 0$.

Finally, the central bank reaction function (13) implies that

$$\overline{i}_t^j = \phi_{\pi,t}\overline{\pi}_t^j + \phi_{y,t}\overline{y}_t^j \tag{58}$$

for any $j \geq 0$. Equations (53)–(54), (56)–(57), and (58) form a complete system that can be solved for the values of $\{\overline{y}_t^j, \overline{\pi}_t^j, \overline{i}_t^j\}$ for all $j \geq 0$, as linear functions of v_t and $\tilde{v}_t$. Note that these are all static relationships, as they relate purely to the way that given perturbations of the value functions influence the calculations of households and firms in the forward planning that takes place in a single period t.

Once we have solved for both the tilde variables and the bar variables, we have obtained complete solutions for the variables $\{y_t^j, \pi_t^j, i_t^j\}$ at any point in time t, as linear functions of the belief coefficients v_t and $\tilde{v}_t$. Updating of the belief coefficients then requires that we calculate the implied values of the estimates v_t^{est} and $\tilde{v}_t^{est}$.

We recall that v_t^{est} is given by equation (43) if all households have planning horizons of length k. We can, however, allow for heterogeneity in the length of planning horizons; in this case, there will also be heterogeneity in the updating of value functions. However, in the linear equations (54) and (57), it is only the population averages of the belief coefficients v_t and $\tilde{v}_t$ that matter for the determination of aggregate variables such as y_t and π_t, and we shall assume from here on that the variables v_t and $\tilde{v}_t$ refer to these averages. The linear updating equations (46) and (49) continue to hold when we interpret v_t and $\tilde{v}_t$ as population averages, as long as v_t^{est} and $\tilde{v}_t^{est}$ are also now understood to refer to population averages.

In this case, equation (43) must be replaced by the more general form

$$v_t^{est} = \sum_j \omega_j \left[y_t^j - g_t + \sigma \pi_t^j \right], \tag{59}$$

where ω_j is the fraction of households each period with planning horizons of length j. Similarly, equation (51) must be replaced by the more general form

$$\tilde{v}_t^{est} = (1 - \alpha)^{-1} \sum_j \tilde{\omega}_j \pi_t^j, \tag{60}$$

where $\tilde{\omega}_j$ is the fraction of firms each period with planning horizons of length j.

The complete system of equations to describe the evolution of output, inflation, and interest rates, taking into account learning dynamics, then consists of the following sets of equations: (i) equations (14), (15)–(16), and (26)–(27) compose a forward-looking system of equations that can, however, be solved recursively to obtain solutions for the evolution of the variables $\{\tilde{y}_t^j, \tilde{\pi}_t^j, \tilde{\imath}_t^j\}$ as functions of the exogenous disturbances and changes in monetary policy; (ii) equations (53)–(54), (56)–(57), and (58) compose a static system of linear equations to solve for the values $\{\overline{y}_t^j, \overline{\pi}_t^j, \overline{\imath}_t^j\}$ as linear functions of v_t and $\tilde{v}_t$; (iii) equations (59)–(60) allow the estimates v_t^{est} and $\tilde{v}_t^{est}$ to be computed from the solution for the evolution of the variables $\{y_t^j, \pi_t^j\}$ along with the exogenous disturbances; and (iv) equations (46) and (49) describe the evolution of the belief variables v_t and $\tilde{v}_t$ given these estimates.

D. A Useful Special Case

This system of linear equations is, in general, relatively complex and high dimensional, although the causal structure is relatively simple, and (at least if there is a finite upper bound on the planning horizons of both households and firms) a unique solution necessarily can be computed without inverting any large matrices. Further insight into the kind of dynamics implied by this system can be obtained by considering again the special case in which $\omega_j = \tilde{\omega}_j = (1 - \rho)\rho^j$ for some $0 < \rho < 1$. In this case, we can decompose each of our aggregate variables into two components,

$$y_t = \tilde{y}_t + \overline{y}_t, \qquad \pi_t = \tilde{\pi}_t + \overline{\pi}_t, \qquad \hat{\imath}_t = \tilde{\imath}_t + \overline{\imath}_t,$$

where we define $\tilde{y}_t \equiv (1 - \rho)\Sigma_j \rho^j \tilde{y}_t^j$, and similarly for the other variables.

The paths of the variables $\{\tilde{y}_t, \tilde{\pi}_t, \tilde{\iota}_t\}$ then must satisfy equations (13) and (30)–(31). This means that the actual dynamics $\{y_t, \pi_t, \iota_t\}$ must satisfy

$$y_t - g_t - \overline{y}_t = \rho \, E_t[y_{t+1} - g_{t+1} - \overline{y}_{t+1}] - \sigma[(\hat{\iota}_t - \overline{\iota}_t) - \rho E_t(\pi_{t+1} - \overline{\pi}_{t+1})], \quad (61)$$

$$\pi_t - \overline{\pi}_t = \kappa(y_t - y_t^* - \overline{y}_t) + \beta \rho E_t[\pi_{t+1} - \overline{\pi}_{t+1}], \quad (62)$$

and

$$\hat{\iota}_t - \overline{\iota}_t = \hat{\iota}_t^* + \phi_{\pi,t}(\pi_t - \overline{\pi}_t) + \phi_{y,t}(y_t - \overline{y}_t). \quad (63)$$

This provides a purely forward-looking system of equations to solve for the deviations of the variables $(y_t, \pi_t, \hat{\iota}_t)$ from their "trend" components $(\overline{y}_t, \overline{\pi}_t, \overline{\iota}_t)$. In the case that the coefficients (ϕ_π, ϕ_y) do not vary over time, it is furthermore a linear system with constant coefficients. Using equation (63) to substitute for $\hat{\iota}_t - \overline{\iota}_t$ in equation (61), we can write this as a two-dimensional system,

$$[x_t - \overline{x}_t] = \rho M \cdot E_t[x_{t+1} - \overline{x}_{t+1}] + N \cdot u_t, \quad (64)$$

using the same matrix-vector notation as in equation (35) but now also defining the vector

$$\overline{x}_t \equiv \begin{bmatrix} \overline{y}_t \\ \overline{\pi}_t \end{bmatrix}.$$

Similarly, we can average equations (53)–(54) over the different horizons j to obtain

$$\overline{y}_t = \rho \overline{y}_t - \sigma[\overline{\iota}_t - \rho \overline{\pi}_t] + (1 - \rho)v_t,$$

which can be written more simply as

$$\overline{y}_t = -\frac{\sigma}{1 - \rho}[\overline{\iota}_t - \rho \overline{\pi}_t] + v_t. \quad (65)$$

And we can average equations (56)–(57) over the different horizons j to obtain

$$\overline{\pi}_t = \kappa \overline{y}_t + \beta \rho \overline{\pi}_t + (1 - \rho)(1 - \alpha)\beta \tilde{v}_t,$$

which can be written more simply as

$$\overline{\pi}_t = \frac{\kappa}{1 - \beta \rho} \overline{y}_t + \frac{(1 - \rho)(1 - \alpha)\beta}{1 - \beta \rho} \tilde{v}_t. \quad (66)$$

And finally, (58) can be averaged to obtain

$$\bar{\imath}_t = \phi_{\pi,t}\bar{\pi}_t + \phi_{y,t}\bar{y}_t. \tag{67}$$

This is a system of three simultaneous equations that can be solved for $(\bar{y}_t, \bar{\pi}_t, \bar{\imath}_t)$ as linear functions of v_t and $\tilde{v}_t$.

In particular, we obtain a solution of the form

$$\bar{x}_t = \Xi \begin{bmatrix} v_t \\ \tilde{v}_t \end{bmatrix} \tag{68}$$

for the elements of $\bar{x}_t$, where (as long as $\phi_\pi, \phi_y > 0$) Ξ is an invertible 2×2 matrix. We can then write an evolution equation for the trend components $\bar{x}_t$ through a linear transformation of the laws of motion (46) and (49) for v_t and $\tilde{v}_t$.

We note that the system (59)–(60) can be written in the form

$$\begin{bmatrix} v_t^{est} \\ \tilde{v}_t^{est} \end{bmatrix} = \Phi x_t, \tag{69}$$

where Φ is a 2×2 matrix of coefficients. Then the evolution equation for the trend components can be written as

$$\bar{x}_{t+1} = \Lambda \bar{x}_t + Q x_t, \tag{70}$$

where

$$\Lambda \equiv \Xi[I - \Gamma]\Xi^{-1}, \qquad Q \equiv \Xi\Gamma\Phi,$$

and Γ is the 2×2 diagonal matrix with diagonal elements $(\gamma, \tilde{\gamma})$. Note that the eigenvalues of Λ are $1 - \gamma$ and $1 - \tilde{\gamma}$; thus both eigenvalues are inside the unit circle, and if the variables x_t remain constant over time, the trend variables $\bar{x}_t$ necessarily converge to constant values as well, though this convergence may be slow if γ and $\tilde{\gamma}$ are small. The dynamics of x_t and $\bar{x}_t$ are then completely determined by equations (64) and (70), given a specification of the exogenous disturbance processes, monetary policy, and an initial condition for $\bar{x}_0$.

We thus obtain a "hybrid" New Keynesian model, in which deviations of output and inflation from their trend values are determined in a purely forward-looking way (though the system [64] is somewhat less forward-looking than in the standard model, if ρ is significantly less than 1), but in which there are persistent fluctuations in the trend values (quite persistent, if the revision of estimated value functions is slow), determined in a purely backward-looking way. The model thus produces persistent dynamics of both output and inflation, without any need for hypotheses of habit-persistence in preferences, costs of adjusting the rate of investment spending, or automatic indexation of prices to past inflation, of the kind often assumed in econometric New Keynesian models. Like the models of Milani (2007) and Slobodyan and Wouters (2012), the model proposed here generates persistence as a result of learning from past experience. However, unlike those models, the model proposed here does not make expectations purely backward-looking, so that forward guidance (and other special, circumstantial sources of information) is not implied to be irrelevant.

E. Long-Run Equilibrium, the Fisher Equation, and the Neo-Fisherian Fallacy

We return now to consideration of the validity of the proposition that the Fisher equation should hold in a long-run equilibrium. In our model that has been augmented to allow adaptive learning of the value functions, this proposition is correct. Consider a situation in which the central bank's reaction function is constant over time but not necessarily consistent with the inflation rate $\overline{\Pi}$ assumed in the stationary equilibrium around which we have log-linearized our model equations; in addition, suppose that all exogenous states are also constant over time ($\xi_t = \bar{\xi}$ for all t). Given this, let us consider whether it is possible to have a stationary equilibrium in which the endogenous variables ($y_t, \pi_t, \hat{\imath}_t$) are all constant over time.

If so, the values of v_t^{est} and $\tilde{v}_t^{est}$ will also be constant over time, from which it follows that v_t and $\tilde{v}_t$ will necessarily converge and eventually be constant as well. This in turn means that the trend components ($\overline{y}_t, \overline{\pi}_t, \overline{\imath}_t$) must eventually take constant values as well. Hence we consider the possibility of stationary solutions in which each of these variables takes a value that is independent of time. For simplicity, we treat here only the case of exponentially distributed planning horizons just discussed, though a version of the Fisher equation holds in more general cases as well.

In such a solution, equation (61) requires that

$$(1 - \rho)(y - \overline{y}) = -\sigma[(\hat{\imath} - \overline{\imath}) - \rho(\pi - \overline{\pi})]. \tag{71}$$

In addition, equation (65) requires that

$$\overline{y} = -\frac{\sigma}{1 - \rho}[\overline{\imath} - \rho\overline{\pi}] + \nu.$$

Moreover, equation (46) requires that $\nu = \nu^{est}$, which using equation (59) can be seen to imply that

$$\nu = y + \sigma\pi.$$

Using these latter two equations to substitute for $\bar{y}$ and ν, we find that equation (71) requires that

$$\hat{\imath} = \pi.$$

That is, deviations of the constant inflation rate from the value $\overline{\Pi}$ of the steady state around which we have log-linearized must be associated with deviations of the nominal interest rate of exactly the same size. The Fisher equation must hold in any long-run stationary equilibrium, once we take account of the endogenous adjustment of the beliefs that are reflected in the value function of households.

Does this mean, then, that a commitment to maintain a constant nominal interest rate forever must eventually bring about a level of inflation consistent with the Fisher equation, so that commitment to maintaining a low nominal interest rate must eventually be disinflationary or even deflationary, while commitment to keep the nominal interest rate must eventually result in correspondingly high inflation in accordance with neo-Fisherian reasoning? No. We have shown that if such a policy were to lead, at least in the long run, to a stationary equilibrium, it would have to be one consistent with the Fisher equation; however, there is no reason to expect that such a policy—however credible it may be that it will be maintained in perpetuity—should lead to a stationary equilibrium, even in the long run.

Let us return to the thought experiment considered in Section III.B, in which the central bank pegs the nominal interest permanently at a level lower than the constant level associated with the stationary equilibrium with inflation rate $\overline{\Pi}$, but let us now consider the consequences of adaptation of the estimated value functions. The outcome calculated in Section III.B assumes that $\nu_t = \tilde{\nu}_t = 0$. If this were to remain true forever, then one would have constant values for output and inflation given by equation (40), which implies that both inflation and output are higher than their values in the stationary equilibrium with the target inflation rate. (In fact, π_t^k and y_t^k are higher for arbitrary k; so this conclusion is true regardless of the assumed distribution of forecast horizons.) If this were to remain true permanently, the inflation rate and nominal interest rate would fail to conform to the Fisher equation, even in the long run.

But in such a situation, the estimated value functions should not remain the ones that were appropriate to the previous steady state. As discussed in Section III.B, in this thought experiment $Nu^* \ll 0$. Moreover, in the case in which ρ is small enough for the infinite sums $\Sigma_j \omega_j \tilde{x}_t^j$ to converge, we have $(I - \rho M)^{-1} \gg 0$, and we can solve equation (64) forward to obtain

$$[x_t - \bar{x}_t] = \tilde{x} \equiv [I - \rho M]^{-1} Nu^* \gg 0$$

at each date t. Substitution of this system of equations together with equation (68) into equation (69) yields

$$\begin{bmatrix} v_t^{est} \\ \tilde{v}_t^{est} \end{bmatrix} = \Phi \tilde{x} + \Phi \Xi \cdot \begin{bmatrix} v_t \\ \tilde{v}_t \end{bmatrix} \tag{72}$$

for each date.

We further observe that in the case of an interest-rate peg, $\Xi \gg 0$ and hence $\Phi \Xi \gg 0$. It then follows from equation (72) that in the case of any beliefs satisfying $v_t, \tilde{v}_t \geq 0$, we must have $v_t^{est}, \tilde{v}_t^{est} > 0$. Then, because v_{t+1} is specified to be a weighted average of v_t and v_t^{est}, we must have $v_{t+1} > 0$, and similarly for $\tilde{v}_{t+1}$. We can then show recursively that starting from initial values $v_0 = \tilde{v}_0 = 0$ (beliefs consistent with the previous steady state), we must have $v_t, \tilde{v}_t > 0$ for all $t > 0$. It then follows from equation (68) that $\bar{x}_t \gg 0$ for all $t > 0$, and hence that

$$x_t = \tilde{x} + \bar{x}_t \gg 0$$

for all dates t after the policy change. But this means that the levels of output and inflation can never converge to the long-run steady state consistent with the Fisher equation, since in this steady state both elements of x_t must be negative.

Because the dynamics implied by our system of equations are linear, the fact that there is no convergence to the unique steady state means that the dynamics must diverge explosively. Thus once learning dynamics are taken into account, the model predicts an explosive inflationary spiral that should continue until the interest-rate peg is abandoned, as in the famous analysis of an interest-rate peg by Friedman (1968). Similarly, the model implies that commitment to maintaining a fixed high interest rate should never succeed in bringing about a correspondingly high rate of inflation.

Similar conclusions about the instability of learning dynamics under an interest-rate peg have been obtained in the context of New Keynesian models based on intertemporal optimization by authors including Bullard and Mitra (2002), Preston (2005), and Evans and McGough (2017).[17] The present model illustrates, however, that such conclusions can be obtained without modeling expectations as purely backward looking, as these authors do. The present analysis does allow central bank announcements about intended future policy to influence behavior immediately, even before any change in actual central bank behavior occurs, because it is assumed that households and firms should both take into account such information in their forward-planning exercises. But this does not imply dynamics that converge to a stationary equilibrium consistent with the Fisher equation.

V. Conclusions

The analysis shows that care must be used in drawing conclusions about contemplated monetary policies using rational expectations equilibrium analysis. I do not mean to suggest that such analysis is never useful. In some cases, the rational expectations equilibrium outcome (with a suitable equilibrium selection) should provide a reasonable approximation to what a more realistic model with finite-horizon forward planning would imply, at least if many people are somewhat forward-looking.

For example, this should be the case if one is interested in computing predicted responses to economic disturbances that are (i) relatively transitory and (ii) recurrent enough for people to have learned their serial correlation from experience, when (iii) the central bank's reaction function satisfies the Taylor principle, equation (39). In such a case, the decisions that result from forward planning are not very sensitive to the length of the horizon over which people plan; and as a consequence, the limit as the horizon length k is made unboundedly large is well defined and corresponds to a particular selection from among the rational expectations equilibrium solutions.

But for some questions, there is no selection criterion under which rational expectations equilibrium analysis provides reliable predictions. The question of predicting the effects of a central bank commitment to maintain its nominal interest-rate target at a low level for a considerable period of time is such a case. We have seen that in this case, finite-horizon forward planning does not result in outcomes similar to any of the rational expectations equilibria consistent with such a policy, no matter how long people's planning horizons may be or how rapidly they may adjust their estimated value functions to reflect more recent experience.[18]

Avoiding misleading conclusions is only possible by considering the implications of explicit models of boundedly rational cognition and by examining the extent to which they lead to results similar to those of the more familiar rational expectations analyses. The example provided is intended to show how such analyses can be tractable, in a setting that is no less general than those often used in rational expectations analyses of alternative policies. It is offered in the hope that analyses in this style will become more common in the monetary policy literature and that more robust conclusions about policy can be reached as a result.

Endnotes

Prepared for the NBER Macroeconomics Annual conference, April 12–13, 2018. I would like to thank Roger Farmer, Xavier Gabaix, Mariana García-Schmidt, Marc Giannoni, Jennifer La'O, Guido Lorenzoni, Bentley MacLeod, Benoit Mojon, and Argia Sbordone for helpful discussions. For acknowledgments, sources of research support, and disclosure of the author's material financial relationships, if any, please see http://www .nber.org/chapters/c14077.ack.

1. Earlier proposed models of boundedly rational economic decision making in this spirit include Jéhiel (1995), MacLeod (2002), and Gabaix et al. (2006).

2. The kind of decision-making algorithm proposed here—called "planning-to-habit" by Keramati et al. (2016)—has also been used to describe the behavior of nonexpert human decision makers in settings where less extensive training has been possible.

3. It is not an essential feature of our method that the value function be so simple. The key assumption for our analysis of forward guidance is that we suppose that an announcement of a new monetary policy does not change the value functions that households or firms use in their finite-horizon planning. It is particularly plausible to suppose that the value functions should ignore this aspect of the state, as in the case of a policy that has never been used previously so that there will have been no opportunity to learn the consequences of this kind of policy change from experience.

4. The issue of the endogeneity of the value function can be abstracted from when we are concerned only with the effects of relatively transitory disturbances, including short-lived changes in monetary policy.

5. In the present analysis, we abstract from both government spending and government debt issuance; extension of the model to consider the effects of fiscal policy as well is left for a future study.

6. The analysis is generalized to allow for heterogeneous planning horizons in Sec. II.C.

7. In the exposition in the previous section, we have assumed that all households solve an identical problem, with a k-period planning horizon. If so, in equilibrium all households value additional income in the same way, and we can simply refer to the marginal utility of income of the representative household. However, the exposition in this section allows for possible heterogeneity in households' planning horizons, in preparation for the discussion in Sec. II.C.

8. Note that in a flexible-price equilibrium, one would have $H_r(1; Z_t) = 0$ at all times, meaning that (in a linear approximation) $m_t = 0$ at all times, which requires that $y_t = y_t^*$ to first order.

9. The interpretation proposed by Gabaix is one in which people solve infinite-horizon decision problems, but under distorted beliefs about the laws of motion of variables that need to be forecasted, which are biased so as not to differ too much from a simpler "default" model.

10. The discussion by Gabaix of how the "default" model should endogenously respond to experience is also different from the model of learning proposed in Sec. IV, and this also matters for our conclusions about the long-run effects of a permanent policy change.

11. We define the first element of x_t to be $y_t - g_t$, rather than simply y_t or the "output gap" $y_t - y_t^*$, for convenience in writing eq. (70). Note that if we can solve the system of equilibrium conditions for the path of $y_t - g_t$, then we also have the solution for the path of y_t or $y_t - y_t^*$, simply by adding the appropriate exogenous variable.

12. See García-Schmidt and Woodford (2015) for discussion of the connection between such a thought experiment and recent debates about the effects of forward guidance.

13. See Woodford (2003) or García-Schmidt and Woodford (2015) for demonstrations of this, and further discussion.

14. The discussion here assumes a finite planning horizon k for all decision makers, but it suffices that there be some finite upper bound on the length of planning horizons. If instead there is no finite upper bound, but the distribution of planning horizons $\{\omega_j\}$ is the same for both households and firms, then the predicted effects of forward guidance will still be bounded as long as $\sum_j \omega_j M^j$ is still a convergent sum, that is, as long as ω_j approaches zero sufficiently rapidly for large j.

15. See García-Schmidt and Woodford (2015) for further discussion of this argument.

16. This model of learning is related to the model of "value function learning" proposed by Evans and McGough (2015). Like us, they assume that an estimated value function v_t^{est} is computed each period as part of a finite-horizon forward-planning calculation using the currently assumed value function. The value function v_t used in the forward planning is then estimated econometrically, using the sequence of past calculated values $\{v_{t-1}^{est}, v_{t-2}^{est}, ...\}$ as data. Our specification (41) can be viewed as a constant-gain recursive estimation procedure for such a problem.

17. Gabaix (2017) obtains a different conclusion about the long-run effects of an announced permanent peg of the nominal interest rate at a different level than has prevailed in the past. However, this is because he assumes that the interest-rate peg is accompanied by central bank guidance that directly affects people's expectations (because their "default model" is influenced by central bank guidance), and that the way that this guidance, to the extent that it is accepted, implies that one should expect the inflation rate that makes the new interest-rate peg consistent with the Fisher equation. That is, Gabaix assumes that people's beliefs should be at least partially neo-Fisherian, even when their experience points in the opposite direction.

18. The fragility of rational expectations equilibrium results in this case is also shown by the related work of García-Schmidt and Woodford (2015), who relax the assumption of optimization under rational expectations in a different way.

References

Branch, William, George W. Evans, and Bruce McGough. 2012. "Finite Horizon Learning." In *Macroeconomics at the Service of Public Policy*, ed. T. J. Sargent and J. Vilmunen. Oxford: Oxford University Press.

Bullard, James, and Kaushik Mitra. 2002. "Learning about Monetary Policy Rules." *Journal of Monetary Economics* 49:1105–29.

Calvo, Guillermo A. 1983. "Staggered Prices in a Utility-Maximizing Framework." *Journal of Monetary Economics* 12:383–98.

Campbell, Murray, A. Joseph Hoane Jr., and Feng-Hsiung Hsu. 2002. "Deep Blue." *Artificial Intelligence* 134:57–83.

Cochrane, John H. 2017. "Michelson-Morley, Fisher, and Occam: The Radical Implications of Stable, Quiet Inflation at the Zero Bound." Working paper, Stanford University.

Del Negro, Marco, Marc P. Giannoni, and Christina Patterson. 2015. "The Forward Guidance Puzzle." Staff Report no. 574, Federal Reserve Bank of New York.

Evans, George W., and Bruce McGough. 2015. "Learning to Optimize." Working paper, University of Oregon.

———. 2017. "Interest Rate Pegs in New Keynesian Models." Working paper, University of Oregon.

Friedman, Milton. 1968. "The Role of Monetary Policy." *American Economic Review* 58:1–17.

Gabaix, Xavier. 2017. "A Behavioral New Keynesian Model." Working paper, Harvard University.

Gabaix, Xavier, David Laibson, Guillermo Moloche, and Steven Weinberg. 2006. "Costly Information Acquisition: Experimental Analysis of a Boundedly Rational Model." *American Economic Review* 96:1043–68.

García-Schmidt, Mariana, and Michael Woodford. 2015. "Are Low Interest Rates Deflationary? A Paradox of Perfect-Foresight Analysis." Working Paper no. 21614, NBER, Cambridge, MA.

Jéhiel, Philippe. 1995. "Limited Horizon Forecast in Repeated Alternate Games." *Journal of Economic Theory* 67:497–519.

Keramati, Mehdi, Peter Smitenaar, Raymond J. Dolan, and Peter Dayan. 2016. "Adaptive Integration of Habits into Depth-Limited Planning Defines a Habitual-Goal-Directed Spectrum." *Proceedings of the National Academy of Sciences USA* 113:12868–73.

Kydland, Finn E., and Edward C. Prescott. 1982. "Time to Build and Aggregate Fluctuations." *Econometrica* 50:1345–70.

MacLeod, W. Bentley. 2002. "Complexity, Bounded Rationality, and Heuristic Search." *Contributions to Economic Analysis and Policy* 1 (1): article 8.

Milani, Fabio. 2007. "Expectations, Learning and Macroeconomic Persistence." *Journal of Monetary Economics* 54:2065–82.

Preston, Bruce. 2005. "Learning about Monetary Policy Rules When Long-Horizon Expectations Matter." *International Journal of Central Banking* 1:81–126.

Silver, David, Aja Huang, Chris J. Maddison, Arthur Guez, Laurent Sifre, George van den Driessche, Julian Schrittwieser, et al. 2016. "Mastering the Game of Go with Deep Neural Networks and Tree Search." *Nature* 529:484–89.

Slobodyan, Sergey, and Raf Wouters. 2012. "Learning in a Medium-Scale DSGE Model with Expectations Based on Small Forecasting Models." *American Economic Journal: Macroeconomics* 4:65–101.

Woodford, Michael. 2003. *Interest and Prices: Foundations of a Theory of Monetary Policy.* Princeton, NJ: Princeton University Press.

———. 2013. "Macroeconomic Analysis without the Rational Expectations Hypothesis." *Annual Review of Economics* 5:303–46.

Yun, Tack. 1996. "Nominal Price Rigidity, Money Supply Endogeneity, and Business Cycles." *Journal of Monetary Economics* 37:345–70.

Comment

Jennifer La'O, *Columbia University and NBER*

I. Introduction

In most macroeconomic models, time is infinite. Agents are endowed with rational expectations including the cognitive ability to solve complex infinite-horizon planning problems. This is a heroic assumption; but when does it matter? In "Monetary Policy Analysis When Planning Horizons Are Finite," Michael Woodford reconsiders this unrealistic feature, introduces a novel bounded-rationality framework to address it, and explores under what circumstances this affects the policy conclusions of the standard New Keynesian paradigm.

Woodford develops a new cognitive framework in which agents transform their infinite-horizon problem into a sequence of simpler, finite-horizon ones. The solution method used by the agent is to backward induct over a finite set of periods given some perceived value function he has assigned to his perceived terminal nodes. This solution method seems quite natural; in fact, Woodford is motivated by a beautiful analogy to how state-of-the-art artificial intelligence (AI) programs play the games of chess or go.

Take chess—a game with a finite strategy space and thereby in theory solvable via backward induction. In practice, however, the space of strategies is so large that solving the game in this fashion would require unfathomable processing power. Consider then the most effective AI programs. A typical decision-making process may be described as follows: at each turn, the machine looks forward at all possible moves for both itself and its opponent a finite number of turns, thereby creating a decision tree with finite nodes. It assigns a value to each of the different possible terminal nodes; these values may be based on past experience or data. Finally, given these terminal node values, the machine backward inducts along its decision tree to choose its optimal move for the current turn.[1]

Inspired by this method, Woodford develops a similar cognitive behavioral approach for economic agents and applies it to the standard New Keynesian model. He shows that this feature helps resolve two well-known and controversial problems within the New Keynesian literature. The first is the problem of equilibria indeterminacy: Woodford's model with finite-planning horizons reduces the set to a unique equilibrium.[2] The second is the well-known problem of the unbounded and unrealistic effectiveness of monetary policy announcements at the zero lower bound—what is known as the "forward guidance puzzle."

In this discussion I begin in Section II with a simple example of a single-household finite-horizon planning problem to illustrate the basic cognitive framework. I then review how Woodford applies this approach to the standard New Keynesian model in Section III. In Section IV I compare Woodford's model with a few recent papers in the monetary literature that consider similar yet distinct departures from rational expectations. Finally, in Section V I briefly discuss how these contributions help resolve certain puzzles in the New Keynesian literature, after which I conclude.

II. A Simple Example

To illustrate the basic idea behind the bounded rationality framework proposed by Woodford in this paper, I begin with a simple example of a single household consumption-savings problem. Suppose time is discrete and infinite: $t = 0, \ldots , \infty$. The objective of the household is to choose a consumption and asset holdings sequence $\{c_t, a_{t+1}\}_{t=0}^{\infty}$ to maximize lifetime utility given by

$$\max_{c,a} \sum_{t=0}^{\infty} \beta^t u(c_t) \tag{1}$$

subject to its per-period budget constraint,

$$c_t + a_{t+1} = y_t + (1 + r)a_t, \tag{2}$$

where y_t is income in period t, r is the real interest rate, and the initial asset level a_o is given. Let the real interest rate be exogenous and equal to the discount rate: $\beta(1 + r) = 1$. We may assume the usual regularity conditions on utility: $u' > 0$, $u'' < 0$, the Inada conditions, along with the no-Ponzi-game condition.

Furthermore, let's make the simplifying assumption of no uncertainty. Suppose income in each period is a known constant: $y_t = y$, for all t.

A. Infinite-Horizon Rational Expectations

Let us first consider the standard method of solving this problem: consider a rational agent who takes into account the entire infinite horizon. Under this framework, the rational household's problem may be solved using dynamic programming as in Stokey and Lucas (1989). In particular, we can reformulate the sequence problem in (1) into the familiar Bellman equation seen here:

$$V(a) = \max_{a'} u(y + (1 + r)a - a') + \beta V(a'). \qquad (3)$$

This is a stationary Bellman equation: the problem of the household is the same in any given period. The household enters a period with asset state a, then chooses its control a' to maximize the functional equation in (3) where $V(a')$ is the household's continuation value of carrying a' assets into the following period.

The first thing to note about the recursive formulation of the infinite-horizon sequence problem is that the Bellman equation is a finite-horizon problem! That is, given some continuation value function $V(a')$, the problem of the household becomes a simple, finite, one-period-ahead backward induction problem of choosing how much to consume and how much to save today.

Thus, the beauty of the recursive formulation used in dynamic programming is that under certain conditions, one may transform an infinite-horizon problem into a finite-horizon one that may be solved using backward induction. The only conceptual difference is that the stationary value function $V(a)$ is the fixed point that satisfies the Bellman equation in all periods.

It is straightforward to show that the fixed-point solution to the Bellman equation in (3) is characterized by the following stationary consumption and savings policy functions,

$$c = C^*(a) \equiv y + ra \text{ and } a' = A^*(a) \equiv a, \forall t, \qquad (4)$$

and a corresponding value function given by

$$V^*(a) = \frac{1}{1 - \beta} u(y + ra), \forall t. \qquad (5)$$

That is, the rational expectations infinite-horizon agent consumes her full income each period along with the annuity value of her wealth; as a result, her asset position remains constant. Her value function is simply the discounted value in utils of her constant consumption stream.

B.   Finite-Horizon Boundedly Rational Agent

Consider now the boundedly rational agent proposed by Woodford. Consider an agent who, despite facing the infinite-horizon sequence problem in (1), only has the ability to contemplate and process a finite horizon; suppose the agent's horizon is $T < \infty$. The boundedly rational agent thereby solves a sequence of finite-horizon problems. In any period t the agent's problem is to maximize the following objective

$$\sum_{t=0}^{T} \beta^t u(c_t) + \beta^{T+1} V_{T+1}(a_{T+1}) \tag{6}$$

subject to the same per-period budget constraint given in (2). One may reformulate this finite horizon problem with a nonstationary Bellman equation as follows:

$$V_t(a) = \max_{a'} u(y + (1 + r)a - a') + \beta V_{t+1}(a'). \tag{7}$$

Given a terminal continuation value function $V_{T+1}(a)$, the agent solves for his optimal path of consumption and assets via backward induction according to equation (7).

   The question then becomes: where does this terminal continuation value come from? First, suppose the continuation value function is "correct," that is, it coincides with the stationary rational expectations infinite-horizon value function given in (5). Specifically, suppose the terminal value function were given by

$$V_{T+1}(a) = V^*(a) = \frac{1}{1 - \beta} u(y + ra).$$

If this were the case, then it is clear that the backward induction problem in (7) would coincide with the stationary Bellman equation in (3) in all periods. As a result, the finite-horizon solution would be identical to the infinite-horizon solution, and the boundedly rational agent would behave exactly as if he were rational. Put more simply, this is a restatement of the fact that the standard Bellman equation is a backward induction problem with a particular value function—that which is the unique fixed point of the infinite-horizon's recursive formulation.

But now suppose that the boundedly rational agent's terminal continuation value does not coincide with the infinite-horizon one. For pedagogical purposes, suppose that the agent truly believes that period T is his terminal node and he dies the following period. Accordingly, let the perceived value of carrying assets into the following period after death be set equal to zero: $V_{T+1}(a) = 0$. With this terminal continuation value, the agent solves for his optimal path of consumption and assets over his finite lifespan via backward induction. The solution to this problem is given by consumption and savings policy functions:

$$C_t(a) = y + \frac{1-\beta}{1-\beta^{T-t+1}}(1+r)a \text{ and } A_{t+1}(a) = \frac{1-\beta^{T-t}}{1-\beta^{T-t+1}}a. \qquad (8)$$

Note that $C_t(a) > C^*(a)$ and $A_{t+1}(a) < A^*(a)$ for all t, and that $A_{T+1}(a) = 0$. That is, if the boundedly rational agent believes that he dies in exactly T periods, then it is optimal for him to consume a constant amount every period—but an amount that is greater than that of the rational infinite-horizon agent. As a result, the boundedly rational agent plans to eat into his life savings until he has none left following the last period of his finite life. From the perspective of the agent in period t, his optimal asset path should appear as in figure 1a: monotonically decreasing over time so that it is exactly equal to zero at terminal date T.

But now consider what happens in the following period, at date $t + 1$. When the boundedly rational agent enters this period, he now realizes that in fact the world doesn't end for him at time T, it instead ends at date $T + 1$! With his newfound extra period of life, he must plan for his bright future: he performs the same backward induction argument as before, but now with a lower incoming value of assets. He again chooses to consume a constant amount each period and his revised plan for asset holdings is represented in figure 1b as a new, monotonically decreasing curve that it is exactly equal to zero at terminal date of $T + 1$.

This means that in every consecutive period, the agent wakes up and realizes that he has one more period of life. Every day he thus chooses a new declining asset path that is slightly at odds with the one he chose the day before. As a result, the boundedly rational agent's actual asset path becomes the upper envelope of his sequence of perceived asset paths (see figure 1c).

This simple example thereby illustrates that there are in fact two key deviations from rationality for the boundedly rational agent. The first is that in order for his actions to deviate from those of the rational agent, it must be that his continuation values at his perceived terminal nodes

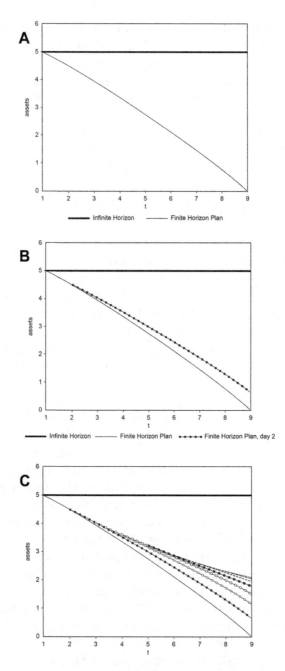

Fig. 1. Finite-horizon asset plans in the simple example: (*a*) optimal asset path; (*b*) revised plan for asset holdings; (*c*) actual asset path.

differ from those of the rational infinite-horizon agent. The second deviation is that the boundedly rational agent acts as if he is truly solving a finite-horizon problem. But this is another fiction: the agent doesn't realize that tomorrow he will wake up to face a new finite-horizon problem and will devise a new optimal course of action that may not correspond to his last.[3]

III. Application to the New Keynesian Framework

Woodford's novel bounded-rationality framework of finite-horizon planning can be applied to any model of economic actors. In this paper he applies this approach to the standard New Keynesian dynamic stochastic general equilibrium model. Consider the standard infinite-horizon New Keynesian model with infinitely lived, utility-maximizing households and monopolistically competitive price-setting firms.[4] Rationality is typically assumed on both the side of households and firms. By log-linearization around the steady state, the standard model reduces to the following familiar set of three equations: (i) the Euler equation (or, the modern IS curve),

$$\tilde{y}_t = E_t \tilde{y}_{t+1} - \sigma(i_t - E_t \pi_{t+1}), \tag{9}$$

where $\tilde{y}_t$ is the output gap at time t, i_t is the nominal interest rate, and $E_t \pi_{t+1}$ is expected next-period inflation; (ii) the New Keynesian Phillips curve,

$$\pi_t = \beta E_t \pi_{t+1} + \kappa \tilde{y}_t; \tag{10}$$

and (iii) a central bank reaction function, namely, monetary policy. The first equation is the household's standard log-linearized Euler equation. The second is the result of staggered nominal price-setting by the forward-looking firms. The third equation closes the model with some specification for monetary policy. This is typically stated in the form of a Taylor rule, but for the purposes of this discussion I abstract from the details of this equation.

Woodford applies his bounded-rationality framework of finite planning horizons to the agents in a typical New Keynesian model: both households and firms. As in the standard model, households earn income and choose their optimal plans for consumption and savings to maximize lifetime expected utility. But unlike the standard model, here households have finite planning horizons: they choose a plan for consumption and savings for only k periods in the future. In Woodford's general formulation, households are endowed with a value function defined over their control variables and all possible exogenous states at their perceived terminal planning node, $t + k$. In order to solve for their optimal plan, they backward induct using these k-period ahead continuation values.

A similar procedure is applied to the firms. As in the standard model, monopolistically competitive firms choose nominal prices in a staggered fashion à la Calvo. Applying his framework, Woodford assumes that firms plan ahead for only k periods in the future and backward induct using a value function defined over their controls and all possible exogenous states at date $t + k$.

Households and firms each period are assumed to make optimal plans conditional on their k-period ahead continuation values. Aside from the two deviations from rationality alluded to above in my simple example, households and firms are "rational" or "knowledgeable" in all other senses: they know all current and past states as well as past realizations of all endogenous variables, they have the correct perception of the conditional probabilities of future exogenous states and the law of motion of endogenous outcomes conditional on these states, and they can perform their backward induction operations given perceived value functions without error.

What then matters is the determination of the terminal node continuation value. Again, if the continuation value function were the same as that of the fully rational infinite-horizon agent, then despite their constrained planning abilities, the boundedly rational agents would still behave rationally; in this case the model would simply reduce to the standard one.

Woodford begins by endowing agents with a specific value function for their terminal node, one that is non-state-dependent. In particular he assumes the value function that would arise in the perfect-foresight steady-state equilibrium. This seems like a fairly natural assumption: it is as if the economy had been resting for a prolonged period of time at its steady state with a constant inflation rate and zero real disturbances. Households and firms have had enough time to learn their proper values as functions over their controls in steady state, but not how these values should behave in response to shocks. As a result, when choosing their optimal plan they use a terminal node continuation value that is perfectly flat across exogenous states.[5]

Woodford furthermore considers a beautiful extension in which he allows for heterogeneity in the length of planning horizons. Rather than imposing that all households and firms have the same finite planning horizon, he supposes that a fraction $(1 - \rho)\rho^k$ of the population have planning horizon of length $k = 0, 1, \ldots, \infty$ for some parameter $\rho \in (0, 1)$. This extension with heterogeneity and unbounded support of finite planning horizons is quite useful as it reduces the state space of the model back to that of the original rational expectations framework. In particular, the equilibrium characterization elegantly results in a modified Euler equation (or modern IS curve) given by

$$\tilde{y}_t = \rho E_t \tilde{y}_{t+1} - \sigma(i_t - \rho E_t \tilde{\pi}_{t+1}), \tag{11}$$

and a modified New Keynesian Phillips curve given by

$$\pi_t = \rho \beta E_t \pi_{t+1} + \kappa \tilde{y}_t. \tag{12}$$

Comparing equations (11)–(12) with their counterparts in the standard rational expectations framework (9)–(10), one observes that the only real difference between the two models is that the boundedly rational one features aggregate attenuation of expectations of future variables: future expectations of inflation and the output gap are dampened by the parameter $\rho \in (0, 1)$. The economy on the whole acts as if it were myopic.

The forces behind this attenuation are fairly intuitive. Consider first the agents with the longest planning horizons, those with $k \to \infty$. These are the rational types: conditional on the equilibrium law of motion for endogenous variables, these agents behave with near rationality. Thus, if the entire population were to consist of these agents, as it does in the limit as ρ approaches 1, then the model indeed converges to the standard rational expectations equilibrium.

Consider now the most boundedly rational types, the agents with the shortest planning horizons: those with $k = 0$ or $k = 1$. These agents are effectively making static decisions. Because their continuation values are completely independent of shocks, these values do not fully and accurately reflect the future. As a result, these agents need not form expectations of future variables and they behave as if the economy were perpetually in steady state. If one were to increase the population size of these most boundedly rational types, that is, decrease ρ toward zero, then the economy would behave on the whole with greater myopia. This would be not only due to the greater presence of the behavioral types, but also due to the general equilibrium expectations formed by the more rational types.

In summary, equations (11) and (12) replace equations (9) and (10) of the standard rational expectations model, respectively. These two equations along with a suitable central bank reaction function provide a complete system of three equations per period in three unknowns, $(\tilde{y}_t, \pi_t, i_t)$, and thereby fully characterize the equilibrium of this model.

IV.   Bounded Rationality in Monetary Models: A Brief User's Guide

Consider again Woodford's original question: do boundedly rational agents' finite-planning capacities matter within the context of the standard New Keynesian model? The answer he provides is undoubtedly yes, it does matter. To the extent to which the population of households and firms have short, finite planning horizons and continuation values do not fully reflect the future, the current impact of movements in future expectations within the standard Euler equation and New Keynesian Phillips curve are attenuated. Rather than focus on the implications of this feature, allow me to make a slight detour and compare Woodford's work with certain recent models that also depart from the standard model.

Consider first the sparsity model of Gabaix (2014). In his bounded rationality framework, Gabaix introduces agents with limited capacity to pay attention to all variables in the world. Agents choose optimally which variables to pay attention to, subject to a linear cost of attention. The linearity results in agents optimally choosing to pay attention to some variables but to pay zero attention to others. Hence agents' simplified versions of the world are "sparse." Gabaix (2016) applies his sparsity framework to the typical New Keynesian paradigm. His application results in the following modified Euler equation and New Keynesian Phillips curve:

$$\tilde{y}_t = m^h E_t \tilde{y}_{t+1} - \sigma(\bar{\iota}_t - E_t \pi_{t+1})$$

$$\pi_t = \beta m^f E_t \pi_{t+1} + \kappa \tilde{y}_t$$

where $m^h, m^f \in [0, 1]$. Similar to Woodford, the Gabaix (2016) sparsity version of the standard New Keynesian model also features a dampening of future expectations in the Euler equation and the Phillips curve. This macro attenuation is the result of cognitive discounting in the agents' perceived law of motion of exogenous states.

One need not even stray away from rational expectations to generate such features—consider the recent work of Angeletos and Lian (2016).

Standard macroeconomic models not only endow agents with rational expectations but also impose common knowledge. This means that agents not only share the same information about present and future shocks, but that they also face zero uncertainty about the general equilibrium reaction to these shocks—equivalently, they face zero uncertainty about the actions of others. Beginning with the seminal work of Morris and Shin (2002) and Woodford (2003a), a large literature has explored the aggregate implications of relaxing common knowledge in macro environments with strategic interactions.[6] One of the main lessons from this literature is that strategic complementarity in actions leads agents to put greater weight on higher-order beliefs; higher-order beliefs in turn are more anchored to agents' priors, and thereby dampen the equilibrium impact of aggregate shocks.

Angeletos and Lian (2016) show that a certain type of dynamic strategic interaction emerges quite naturally in the standard New Keynesian model. In both the consumption-savings decisions of individual households and the forward-looking behavior of price-setting firms, optimal decisions today depend positively on expectations of future decisions of others. The further an event is in the future, the more iterations of forward-looking general equilibrium behavior are needed, the more agents must form beliefs over what other agents will do, and hence the greater the anchoring of their actions to the prior. As a result, the Angeletos and Lian model aggregates to the following modified Euler equation and New Keynesian Phillips curve:

$$\tilde{y}_t = \Lambda E_t \tilde{y}_{t+1} - \sigma(\tilde{\imath}_t - \lambda E_t \pi_{t+1})$$

$$\pi_t = \beta \Gamma E_t \pi_{t+1} + \kappa \gamma \tilde{y}_t$$

where $\Lambda, \lambda, \Gamma, \gamma \in [0,1]$. Thus, while the Angeletos and Lian model features no departure from rationality, it still generates a similar aggregate weakening of future expectations.

Third, consider the recent paper by Farhi and Werning (2017). These authors depart from the standard New Keynesian framework in two ways. First, they allow for incomplete markets: households face idiosyncratic income risk and occasionally binding borrowing constraints as in a Bewley-Aiyagari-Huggett economy. Second, agents are boundedly rational in the form of k-level thinking.[7] Similar to Angeletos and Lian (2016), this latter feature implies a lack of common knowledge: agents must not only form beliefs about future shocks, but must also forecast their general equilibrium effects. This amounts to forming beliefs of the beliefs of other agents. As with informational frictions, k-level thinking attenuates these higher-order beliefs. Thus, a similar aggregate dampening of future expectations must also arise in Farhi and Werning.

V. Implications for Forward Guidance and Conclusion

Woodford's model of boundedly rational agents with finite-planning horizons is a novel departure from the standard rational expectations New Keynesian paradigm. While this departure may differ from those featured in Gabaix (2016), Angeletos and Lian (2016), and Farhi and Werning (2017), it is clear that all four of these papers generate similar (albeit nonidentical) aggregate implications. In particular they all work toward mitigating the current impact of future expectations.

Attenuation of future beliefs is useful for a number of reasons. First, Woodford illustrates how this feature helps resolve the indeterminacy of equilibria in the standard model. He furthermore demonstrates how this feature may also resolve the well-known forward guidance puzzle, namely, the excessive and unreasonable power of monetary policy announcements regarding interest rate changes in the far future. In fact, all four of the models considered tackle this issue essentially by killing the extreme forward-looking nature of the standard rational expectations paradigm. Instead, with aggregate dampening of future expectations, announcements of interest rate changes in the far future have negligible effects today.

There appears to be an urgency in the monetary literature to liberate models from the inordinate amount of forward-looking behavior embedded in the Euler equation and the New Keynesian Phillips curve. Woodford's work as well as the three other papers mentioned above compose a movement toward replacing the "old" New Keynesian model with a "new" New Keynesian model: the same, familiar set of three equations but with mitigated effects of future beliefs. Moving forward, it would appear to me that empirically distinguishing between these models may be nearly impossible given that they offer such similar time-series predictions. Rather, it would perhaps be more fruitful to tease out reduced-form estimates of these aggregate attenuation parameters from the macro data; for example, along the lines of previous empirical work by Gali and Gertler (1999) and Gali, Gertler, and Lopez-Salido (2005). One hopes that these exciting recent developments in theory will spur new empirics.

Appendix

Proofs for the Simple Example

The Infinite-Horizon Problem

Consider the infinite-horizon version of the Bellman equation in (3). We may guess and verify that the value function takes the form in (5). Given this guess, the Bellman equation may thereby be written as

$$V(a) = \max_{a'} u(y + (1+r)a - a') + \beta \frac{1}{1-\beta} u(y + ra').$$

Taking the first-order condition of this expression with respect to a' we get

$$-u'(y + (1+r)a - a') + \beta \frac{1}{1-\beta} ru'(y + ra') = 0.$$

Using the assumption that $\beta (1 + r) = 1$, this reduces to

$$u'(y + (1+r)a - a') = u'(y + ra').$$

Solving this expression for a' we obtain the following policy function for assets:

$$a' = A^*(a) = a.$$

Similarly, for consumption we have $c = y + (1+r)a - A^*(a) = y + ra$, thereby verifying the policy functions found in (4) as well as the value function in (5). QED.

The Finite-Horizon Problem

Consider the finite-horizon version of the Bellman equation in (7). We may guess and verify that the value function takes the following form.

$$V_t(a) = \frac{1 - \beta^{T-t+1}}{1-\beta} u \left(y + \frac{1-\beta}{1-\beta^{T-t+1}} (1+r)a \right). \tag{13}$$

We next prove by induction that the value function and the policy functions above are correct for all $t \le T$; that is, we assume this is correct for $t + 1$ and show that it is correct for t.

First consider terminal period $t = T$ and suppose the household enters the period with assets a_T. Given that the value for this household in period T is zero: $V_{T+1}(a_{T+1}) = 0$, the Bellman equation in (7) implies that

$$V_T(a_T) = u(y + (1 + r)a_T).$$

This verifies the value function in (13) holds for period $t = T$.

Next consider any date $t < T$. Assuming (13) is true for time $t + 1$, the Bellman equation in (7) written for time t is given by

$$V_t(a) = \max_{a'} u(y + (1 + r)a - a') + \beta \frac{1 - \beta^{T-t}}{1 - \beta} u\left(y + \frac{1 - \beta}{1 - \beta^{T-t}}(1 + r)a'\right).$$

Taking the first order condition of this expression with respect to a' we get

$$-u'(y + (1+r)a - a') + \beta \frac{1 - \beta^{T-t}}{1 - \beta} u'\left(y + \frac{1 - \beta}{1 - \beta^{T-t}}(1 + r)a'\right) \frac{1 - \beta}{1 - \beta^{T-t}}(1 + r) = 0.$$

Using the assumption that $\beta(1 + r) = 1$, this reduces to

$$u'(y + (1 + r)a - a') = u'\left(y + \frac{1 - \beta}{1 - \beta^{T-t}}(1 + r)a'\right).$$

Solving this expression for a' we obtain the following policy function for assets:

$$a' = A_{t+1}(a) = \frac{1 - \beta^{T-t}}{1 - \beta^{T-t+1}} a,$$

Similarly, for consumption we have

$$c = C_t(a) = y + (1 + r)a - A_{t+1}(a) = y + \left(\frac{1 - \beta}{1 - \beta^{T-t+1}}\right)(1 + r)a.$$

Finally, plugging these policy functions into the Bellman equation in (7), we verify that the value function at time t indeed satisfies (13). QED.

Alternative Way to Obtain the Infinite-Horizon Solution

Finally, consider the limit of the finite-horizon solution as $T \to \infty$. In this limit, the finite-horizon value function in (13) converges to $V_t(a) \to V^*(a)$ and the finite-horizon consumption and asset policy functions in (8) converge to

$$C_t(a) \to C^*(a) = y + ra,$$
$$A_t(a) \to A^*(a) = a.$$

Therefore, the consumption and asset policy functions converge to the stationary infinite-horizon functions found in (4). QED.

Endnotes

Email: jenlao@columbia.edu. I thank Guido Lorenzoni, Marios Angeletos, and Xavier Gabaix for their valuable comments and suggestions. For acknowledgments, sources of research support, and disclosure of the author's material financial relationships, if any, please see http://www.nber.org/chapters/c14078.ack.
 1. See, e.g., the pioneering work at IBM on chess machine Deep Blue (Campbell, Hoane, and Hsu 2002).
 2. While the problem of the New Keynesian model's admitting a large multiplicity of equilibria—some with explosive paths—is well known, this issue has recently been revived by John Cochrane in a number of papers (see, e.g., Cochrane 2011, 2018). One contribution of Woodford's finite-horizon model may be to view it as a selection criterion over the set of infinite-horizon rational expectations equilibria: it selects the equilibrium that corresponds to the uniquely determined equilibrium of the finite-horizon planning economy as the horizon approaches infinity.
 3. This feature is also true for the chess-playing AI programs: at each turn they may choose a new course of action that may be at odds with their previous plan.
 4. See, e.g., the standard model developed in Woodford (2003b).
 5. Woodford also considers a version of his model where agents learn over time about their continuation values. This is a very interesting extension which could in itself be the basis of an entirely separate paper.
 6. For example, Angeletos and La'O (2009, 2013) demonstrate how in a real business cycle model devoid of nominal frictions, demand externalities lead to strategic complementarity among firms. If one then relaxes common knowledge and allows firms to have heterogeneous information, strategic complementarity leads them to place more weight on common sources of information, thereby opening the door for sentiment-driven business cycles while dampening the aggregate effects of total factor productivity shocks.
 7. Similar deviations from rational expectations in macroeconomic settings can be found in Evans and Ramey (1992, 1995, 1998) and García-Schmidt and Woodford (2015).

References

Angeletos, G.-M., and J. La'O. 2009. "Noisy Business Cycles." *NBER Macroeconomics Annual* 24:319–78.
———. 2013. "Sentiments." *Econometrica* 81:739–79.
Angeletos, G.-M., and C. Lian. 2016. "Forward Guidance without Common Knowledge." Working Paper no. 22785, NBER, Cambridge, MA.
Campbell, M., A. J. Hoane, and F. Hsiung Hsu. 2002. "Deep Blue." *Artificial Intelligence* 134:57–83.
Cochrane, J. H. 2011. "Determinacy and Identification with Taylor Rules." *Journal of Political Economy* 119:565–615.
———. 2018. "Michelson-Morley, Fisher, and Occam: The Radical Implications of Stable Quiet Inflation at the Zero Bound." *NBER Macroeconomics Annual* 32:113–226.

Evans, G. W., and G. Ramey. 1992. "Expectation Calculation and Macroeconomic Dynamics." *American Economic Review* 82:207–24.

———. 1995. "Expectation Calculation, Hyperinflation and Currency Collapse." In *The New Macroeconomics: Imperfect Markets and Policy Effectiveness*, ed. H. D. Dixon and N. Rankin. Cambridge: Cambridge University Press.

———. 1998. "Calculation, Adaptation, and Rational Expectations." *Macroeconomic Dynamics* 2:156–82.

Farhi, E., and I. Werning. 2017. "Monetary Policy, Bounded Rationality, and Incomplete Markets." Working Paper no. 23281, NBER, Cambridge, MA.

Gabaix, X. 2014. "A Sparsity-Based Model of Bounded Rationality." *Quarterly Journal of Economics* 129:1661–710.

———. 2016. "A Behavioral New Keynesian Model." Working Paper no. 22954, NBER, Cambridge, MA.

Gali, J., and M. Gertler. 1999. "Inflation Dynamics: A Structural Econometric Analysis." *Journal of Monetary Economics* 44:195–222.

Gali, J., M. Gertler, and J. David Lopez-Salido. 2005. "Robustness of the Estimates of the Hybrid New Keynesian Phillips Curve." *Journal of Monetary Economics* 52:1107–18.

García-Schmidt, M., and M. Woodford. 2015. "Are Low Interest Rates Deflationary? A Paradox of Perfect-Foresight Analysis." Working Paper no. 21614, NBER, Cambridge, MA.

Morris, S., and H. S. Shin. 2002. "Social Value of Public Information." *American Economic Review* 92:1521–34.

Stokey, N. L., and R. E. Lucas Jr. 1989. *Recursive Methods in Economic Dynamics*, with E. C. Prescott. Cambridge, MA: Harvard University Press.

Woodford, M. 2003a. "Imperfect Common Knowledge and the Effects of Monetary Policy." In *Knowledge, Information, and Expectations in Modern Macroeconomics: In Honor of Edmund S. Phelps*, ed. Philippe Aghion, Roman Frydman, Joseph Stiglitz, and Michael Woodford. Princeton, NJ: Princeton University Press.

———. 2003b. *Interest and Prices: Foundations of a Theory of Monetary Policy*. Princeton, NJ: Princeton University Press.

Comment

Guido Lorenzoni, Northwestern University and NBER

"Monetary Policy Analysis When Planning Horizons Are Finite" by Michael Woodford fits in a fast-growing literature that attempts to introduce forms of bounded rationality in macroeconomic models. Bounded rationality can be introduced in a variety of ways, depending on how we describe the agents' limited ability to process information, to form forecasts, and to compute optimal plans. The paper I am discussing captures bounded rationality by giving agents a finite planning horizon and exploring in depth a variety of consequences of this modeling assumption. The paper provides a nice motivation for the exercise by connecting the macro literature to existing work in artificial intelligence.

In this discussion I want to make two points, one on the role of general equilibrium effects and one on difference between finite lives and finite planning horizons.

There is one dimension of bounded rationality that appears in different forms in a variety of models: the limited capacity of agents to think through general equilibrium effects in their environment. My first point is that this limited capacity for general equilibrium thinking also plays an important role in this paper. To make this point, let me use a simple example of the "forward guidance puzzle" (Del Negro, Giannoni, and Patterson 2012), inspired by Farhi and Werning (2017).

Take an infinitely lived consumer, with standard time-separable preferences, who receives a deterministic stream of labor income $\{Y_t\}$ and has access to a single bond that pays the real interest rate r_t. The optimal behavior of this consumer can be derived from the Euler equation

$$U'(C_t) = \beta(1 + r_t)U'(C_{t+1})$$

and the intertemporal budget constraint

$$C_t - Y_t + \frac{1}{1+r_t}(C_{t+1} - Y_{t+1}) + \frac{1}{1+r_t}\frac{1}{1+r_{t+1}}(C_{t+2} - Y_{t+2}) + \dots = 0.$$

Assume that the consumer starts with zero wealth. Suppose the real interest rate has been stable at $r_t = r^* = 1/\beta - 1$ and, unexpectedly, at time t, the consumer learns that the central bank, at some future date $t + J$, will temporarily raise the interest rate to $r_{t+J} > r^*$. What is the effect of this shock?

The Euler equation implies that consumption will be constant between periods t and $t + J - 1$ and then will be constant again from $t + J$ onward. So the present value of consumption in the intertemporal budget constraint will take the form

$$(1 + \beta + \beta^2 + \dots + \beta^{J-1})C_t + \beta^{J-1}\left(1 + \frac{1}{1-\beta}\frac{1}{1+r_T}\right)C_{t+T}.$$

Inspecting this expression suggests, correctly, that as $J \to \infty$ we will get

$$C_t = \sum_{j=0}^{\infty} \beta^j Y_{t+j}.$$

From this simple derivation it seems that, as the time of the intervention is moved further into the future, the intervention will have no effect on consumer spending today. So it would appear that there is no forward guidance puzzle after all! What is missing from the argument here is that this was purely a partial equilibrium exercise, taking as given the path of income $\{Y_t\}$.

Suppose now that we build a simple representative agent economy around the consumer above. Suppose output is produced linearly using only labor. To introduce an extreme form of nominal rigidity, suppose wages and prices are fixed so output and labor income is simply determined by demand in the goods market

$$Y_{t+j} = C_{t+j}.$$

Assume now that the representative consumer realizes that all other consumers are behaving identically and is aware of the goods market clearing condition above. To solve for the equilibrium of this economy, we can now ignore the intertemporal budget constraint—which is trivially satisfied since $C_t = Y_t$ for all t—and only use the Euler equation. As a terminal condition, we use the assumption that after $t + J$ the central bank leads the economy to the natural level of output Y^*.[1] Now repeated use of the Euler equation gives

$$U'(C_t) = U'(C_{t+1}) = \ldots = U'(C_{t+J}) = \beta(1 + r_{t+J})U'(Y^*).$$

This gives us a simple version of the forward guidance puzzle: the effect of increasing r_{t+J} on consumption C_t is the same, irrespective of how far in the future the shock is expected to occur. One can get even stronger forms of the puzzle by adding details of the New Keynesian model, like a Phillips curve and a central-bank policy formulated in terms of nominal rates, so effects on future inflation will affect the real interest rate. Going in that direction one can find examples in which the effect on C_t increases without bounds as J increases. But for my point here, this simple version is enough. Comparing the partial equilibrium response and the general equilibrium response highlights that it is crucial that consumers form expectations about future income levels by being fully aware that other agents are responding like themselves and that their responses are affecting equilibrium incomes.

One of the most direct ways of capturing the idea that agents have limited grasp of the general equilibrium forces that an external shock sets in motion is the idea of k-level rationality (see Crawford, Costa-Gomes, and Iriberri 2013). García-Schmidt and Woodford (2015) first proposed to use a version of k-level rationality in monetary models. The present paper offers a different approach to bounded rationality, but what I want to point out here is that limits to general equilibrium thinking are still very much central to its argument. To see that, let me begin with the value function used in the finite-horizon plans of the model presented in this paper. Still using my simple deterministic example, the value function for an individual saver with labor income $\{Y_{t+j}\}$ and access to a single bond can be defined as follows:[2]

$$V_t(B_t) = \max \sum_{j=0}^{\infty} \beta^j U(C_{t+j}) \quad \text{s. t.} \sum_{j=0}^{\infty} Q_{t+j|t}(C_{t+j} - Y_{t+j}) = B_t.$$

Assume now that the interest rate and income are fluctuating around the values r^* and Y^*. Then the approximate value function that the agents in this model will use is not the one defined above, but one that abstracts from the fluctuations in interest rates and income; that is, one that uses the intertemporal budget constraint

$$\sum_{j=0}^{\infty} \beta^j(C_{t+j} - Y^*) = B_t.$$

This approximate value function is

$$V(B_t) = \frac{1}{1-\beta} U((1-\beta)B_t + Y^*). \tag{1}$$

To compute the response at date t of an agent with planning horizon j we need to proceed recursively. Start from an agent at date $t + j - 1$ and an horizon of 1 and look at his response. Then use this response to compute the general equilibrium expectations of an agent at $t + j - 2$ with a planning horizon of two periods, and so on and so forth until we reach t. Proceeding in this way, it is easy to show that the agents in the model Woodford presents will not respond at all to an anticipated shock at $t+J$ if their planning horizon is smaller than J. What I want to remark is that this result relies on the fact that even though the agents are allowed to use full general equilibrium reasoning within their planning horizon, the use of the value function (1), by replacing the present value of future labor income with the fixed value Y^*, is essentially stopping general equilibrium reasoning beyond the planning horizon, and that plays an important role. It is useful to add that limits to general equilibrium thinking feature in a variety of approaches that have been used to address the forward guidance puzzle in the recent literature: in Gabaix (2016) by introducing a myopia parameter in agents' forecasting equations, in Angeletos and Lian (2018) and Wiederholt (2014) by keeping rational expectations but ruling out common knowledge, and in Farhi and Werning (2017) by using a combination of heterogeneity and k-level rationality.

The second point I want to make is to answer a naive question: If the idea is to give agents a limited future horizon, isn't it enough to give agents finite lives? The answer is no, and again the crucial issue is not how long agents live but how far in the future they think about general equilibrium effects. To see why, consider a simple overlapping generations economy, with two-period lived agents who receive labor income only when young. Agents save by holding a Lucas tree, in unit supply, with price P_t and dividend D_t. The preferences of agents born at time t are represented by the utility function

$$\ln(C_{1t}) + \beta \ln(C_{2t+1}).$$

Their budget constraints are

$$C_{1t} = W_t N_t - P_t S_t,$$

$$C_{2t+1} = (P_{t+1} + D_{t+1})S_t,$$

where S_t are holdings of the tree. Again, I assume a linear production function that uses only labor and make the extreme assumption of fixed wages and prices (with prices normalized to 1). Let me assume that dividends are proportional to total output produced by labor, which I denote by Y_t. Namely, set $D_t = \delta Y_t$. Optimal behavior of young agents imply that they consume

$$C_{1t} = \frac{1}{1+\beta} W_t N_t.$$

Old agents consume the value of the tree they sell

$$C_{2t} = P_t + D_t.$$

Good market clearing takes the form

$$C_{1t} + C_{2t} = Y_t + D_t = (1+\delta)Y_t.$$

Suppose labor productivity is 1 and labor supply is 1. A stationary equilibrium with full employment has $W_t = 1$ and $Y_t = N_t = 1$. The goods market clearing condition at full employment then requires the asset price to satisfy

$$P_t = P^* \equiv \frac{\beta}{1+\beta},$$

and no arbitrage between bonds and trees require the interest rate to be $r = r^*$, where

$$P^* = \frac{P^* + \delta}{1+r^*}.$$

Consider an economy where the central bank is keeping the real rate at $r = r^*$ and consider the effect of a one-time, anticipated increase in the interest rate at $t + J$. Repeatedly using the no-arbitrage condition between bonds and trees implies that

$$P_t = \frac{1+r^*}{1+r_{t+J}} P^*.$$

Assuming complete nominal price and wage rigidity as in the example above, good market clearing now gives

$$\frac{1}{1+\beta} Y_t + P_t = Y_t,$$

which then implies

$$Y_t = \frac{1 + r^*}{1 + r_{t+J}}.$$

Once again we have a basic form of the forward guidance puzzle: the effect of an intervention is the same even if the intervention happens very far in the future. Even though agents live only two periods, they correctly forecast the effect of future policy on asset prices in the future, and these determine asset prices today, thus affecting real activity.

If some agents, at some future date, use the approximate value function

$$V(S_{t+j}) = \beta \ln \left((Q^* + D^*) S_{t+j} \right),$$

or if agents at t form expectations on the behavior of these agents by attributing them this value function, then the chain of general equilibrium reasoning is broken and we move in the direction of Woodford. So finite lives are different from finite planning horizons. Agents with finite lives can still look beyond their lifetime to make forecast about future economic variables. Only when they start making simplifications in thinking about these future outcomes do we start to see the type of effects that this and other papers are after.

This simple overlapping generations example allows me to make one more point. This example has two predictions: one is that the asset price Q_t will be very sensitive to forecasts about future central bank actions; the second is that consumption and real activity will also be very sensitive. In the model, these two predictions are strictly intertwined. However, the first prediction sounds much more palatable than the second. In other words, it seems like it could make sense to build models where financial market prices are determined by agents that look relatively far into the general equilibrium consequences of some shock, while other, real variables are determined by decision makers that use less general equilibrium thinking. Some combination along these lines seems a promising avenue for future research in this area.

Before concluding, I want to add a comment on Section IV of the paper, in which Woodford combines finite-horizon planning and some form of learning. Finite-horizon planning seems a good way of capturing what happens when agents are used to a given environment and are forced to think about the effects of an "unusual" shock, so they have to form conjectures about other agents' behavior by thinking through the optimization problems these other agents are solving. If this reasoning is boundedly rational, these agents will make systematic mistakes. Eventually one imagines that agents will learn from these mistakes and adapt. Section IV of the paper captures this adaptation by introducing a form of learning and applying it to the following problem.

Consider a central bank that, instead of following a Taylor rule or some other responsive rule, just keeps the nominal interest rate fixed at some level below the natural interest rate of the economy. A model with finite planning horizons—or a model with other forms of bounded rationality like those listed above—will still be able to derive unique predictions about the behavior of this economy. The reason is that these models can basically be solved going backward starting at some future date and expectations are always uniquely derived. And the model predictions will be that inflation is stable at some level above the reference steady state used to conduct the exercise.

The question is, is this a desirable property of this class of models? In this paper, Woodford argues that it is not. If the central bank follows a nominal interest rate peg below the natural rate, we expect inflation to be systematically higher than what people expect, and we expect agents to start adjusting their inflation expectations upward. The logic of the accelerationist hypothesis suggests that, absent any reaction of the central bank, we will see inflation increasing without bounds. Adding learning to the model, Woodford shows that an interest rate peg does indeed lead to explosive inflation dynamics.

I see that part of the paper as providing a very useful general warning. Introducing bounded rationality in macro models is a desirable development, but we want to avoid making so many assumptions about the way in which agents simplify their optimization problems that we end up ruling out pathological outcomes under any possible policy regime. Identifying policy regimes that lead to various forms of instability is an important task of macro modeling. Combining bounded rationality and learning seems a good way to make progress in that direction.

Endnotes

For acknowledgments, sources of research support, and disclosure of the author's material financial relationships, if any, please see http://www.nber.org/chapters/c14079.ack.

1. Here, I am implicitly assuming labor supply is inelastic at some level $\bar{N}$, so $Y^* = \bar{N}$. This would cause some problems if I wanted to experiment with a reduction in r_{t+j} and insisted that wages be rigid both downward and upward. Of course there are many ways around this issue, e.g., having only downward wage rigidity, introducing an initial shock that makes the economy start below full employment, or introducing full-blown sticky prices and wages.

2. I use the notation $Q_{t+j|t} = [1/(1 + r_t)][1/(1 + r_{t+1})]...[1/(1 + r_{t+j})]$.

References

Angeletos, G.-M., and C. Lian. 2018. "Forward Guidance without Common Knowledge." *American Economic Review* 108 (9): 2477–512.

Crawford, V. P., M. A. Costa-Gomes, and N. Iriberri. 2013. "Structural Models of Nonequilibrium Strategic Thinking: Theory, Evidence, and Applications." *Journal of Economic Literature* 51 (1): 5–62.

Del Negro, M., M. Giannoni, and C. Patterson. 2012. "The Forward Guidance Puzzle." Staff report, Federal Reserve Bank of New York.

Farhi, E., and I. Werning. 2017. "Monetary Policy, Bounded Rationality, and Incomplete Markets." Working Paper no. 23281, NBER, Cambridge, MA.

Gabaix, X. 2016. "A Behavioral New Keynesian Model." Working Paper no. 22954, NBER, Cambridge, MA.

García-Schmidt, M., and M. Woodford. 2015. "Are Low Interest Rates Deflationary? A Paradox of Perfect-Foresight Analysis." Working Paper no. 21614, NBER, Cambridge, MA.

Wiederholt, M. 2014. "Empirical Properties of Inflation Expectations and the Zero Lower Bound." Working paper, Goethe University Frankfurt.

Discussion

Xavier Gabaix welcomed the broader agenda to which the paper contributes and that recognizes a larger role for behavioral features in macroeconomic models. Gabaix was curious about the ability of Woodford's model to obtain Fisher neutrality in the long run while resolving the "forward guidance puzzle." He followed up on a point raised by Jennifer La'O during her discussion and noted that several recent papers pursue an exercise similar to Woodford's but consider different behavioral frictions. Gabaix asked how the predictions of the model at the aggregate level differed from the ones in these papers and suggested that these alternative models should be judged in light of these predictions. Finally, he offered a broader comment about the role of bounded rationality for decisions at the micro and macro levels. According to estimates of his, the discount factor is roughly 0.85 per quarter in a macro context, suggesting a planning horizon of 2 years. Gabaix concluded that agents can be very patient at the micro level, when making professional and familial decisions, but may have a more limited attention to macro disturbances.

The author pointed out that there is indeed a formal similarity between the reduced-form equations he obtained and those associated with other behavioral frictions, including sparsity in the case of Gabaix ("A Behavioral New Keynesian Model" [Working Paper, Harvard University, 2018]). He emphasized that his model differs from other contributions, not only in terms of the foundations but also in terms of predictions at the aggregate level. An important difference, he argued, is that his model resolves the issue of multiplicity of equilibria. Another difference he mentioned is that his model allows for learning dynamics. The learning component has crucial implications for long-lasting policy experiments, such as a permanent interest rate peg. On this point, the author clarified that adaptive learning of the value functions is the very mechanism that allows one to obtain Fisher neutrality in the long run, while the truncation of the forward planning horizon allows resolution of the forward guidance puzzle.

Andrew Atkeson spoke next and noted some similarity between the adaptive learning of the value function in the paper and the characterization of equilibrium payoffs in various infinitely repeated games, including those of Dilip Abreu, David Pearce, and Ennio Stacchetti ("Optimal Cartel Equilibria with Imperfect Monitoring," *Journal of Economic Theory* 39, no. 1 [1986]: 251–69). He pointed out that the author's model admits a unique equilibrium, whereas such infinitely repeated games typically admit multiple ones, and inquired about the reason for this difference. The author clarified that the source of uniqueness in his model lies in the fact that the value function is initially anchored by past experience and then learned empirically. He added that uniqueness of the equilibrium in his model holds for any initial condition (in the form of past experience), but he noted that there may still be multiple stationary equilibria to which the economy could converge.

Three topics dominated the rest of the discussion: heterogeneity in the degree of rationality and information, the role of expectations in general equilibrium, and the endogeneity of the planning horizon.

Emmanuel Farhi's comments were related to the first topic. Farhi started by contrasting two empirical regularities: the yield curve is very reactive to announcements about future monetary policy, whereas the response of real variables is muted. These regularities, he argued, suggest the presence of heterogeneity in bounded rationality. He inquired about the possibility that this heterogeneity could create arbitrage opportunities across assets in the model. Farhi finally noted that this heterogeneity, together with the particular form of bounded rationality considered in the paper, should have clear, testable implications regarding patterns of trading in assets between agents with various degrees of rationality. He invited the author to investigate whether these patterns hold empirically to verify his theory. The author responded that the paper allows for such heterogeneity as part of an extension. The model features a single asset, he clarified, ruling out arbitrage across assets. He agreed that the testable implications about the patterns of trading in assets deserve to be investigated empirically. Laura Veldkamp also highlighted that heterogeneity in finite planning horizon could lead to contractual relations between agents, with less sophisticated agents delegating certain decisions to more sophisticated ones.

Alp Simsek was the first to comment on the role of expectations in general equilibrium. He insisted on the importance of asset prices in models that depart from the assumptions of perfect rationality and common knowledge. Asset prices can help modulate the effects of these departures, he argued, by revealing information and allowing agents to react to it. This, in turn, could potentially reestablish the forward guidance puzzle. Simsek suggested that some restrictions on the ability of agents to pay attention to or process this information would be required. Simsek noted that such restrictions would then raise another set of issues related to speculation, which have little to do with the truncation of the planning horizon.

The author replied that asset prices in his model play a role similar to the one advocated by Simsek. Referring to Guido Lorenzoni's discussion, he pointed out that asset prices reflect information about variables beyond the truncated planning horizon. Furthermore, asset prices affect agents' behaviors by conveying information about the underlying shocks, through the adaptive learning of the value functions. Referring again to Lorenzoni's discussion, the author confirmed that the truncation of the planning horizon is similar to reducing the number of rounds of general equilibrium reasoning, but he emphasized that both concepts are not equivalent. He reminded the audience that the adaptive learning of the value functions is conditioned on a coarse state space. As a consequence, the effective limit on the ability of general equilibrium reasoning depends on which variables are used as part of this learning process. Some variables may allow one to learn the general equilibrium effects of some shocks, whereas others will not.

On the same subject, George-Marios Angeletos offered comments about the nature of belief formation in the model. Considering finite planning horizon, he argued, introduces two frictions. The first friction, which he didn't consider particularly important per se, affects the decision-theoretic part (given beliefs) by truncating the planning horizon. He noted that this friction would map into the discount factor for a representative agent, which does not appear in the Euler equation after log-linearization. The second friction, which he viewed as the substantial contribution of the paper, affects beliefs about equilibrium objects. Angeletos emphasized that expectations about endogenous variables in the long run are crucial for the predictions of Keynesian models and are at the heart of the forward guidance puzzle. He emphasized that relaxing the assumption of rationality is one particular approach to affect these expectations. An alternative approach consists of relaxing the assumption of common knowledge, he said, referring to his own work on the subject and including Angeletos and Chen Lian ("Forward Guidance without Common Knowledge," *Amer-*

ican Economic Review 108, no. 9 [2018]: 2477–512). He argued that more evidence is required to determine what particular approach is more realistic.

The author highlighted that the importance of expectations about endogenous variables in this class of models depends crucially on the exact policy regime. Such expectations matter less when monetary policy commits to a Taylor rule, compared with the case of an interest rate peg. The author shared Angeletos's opinion that relaxing the assumption of common knowledge is an interesting avenue, and mentioned his own work on the subject, including Mariana García-Schmidt and Michael Woodford ("Are Low Interest Rates Deflationary? A Paradox of Perfect-foresight Analysis" [Working Paper no. 21614, NBER, Cambridge, MA, 2015]). Finally, he argued that finite horizon planning captures some of the effects of relaxing the assumption of common knowledge.

On the topic of endogeneity of the planning horizon, Veldkamp suggested modeling finite planning horizon as a rational choice subject to computational costs, instead of a cognitive limitation. She suggested investigating whether this choice is associated to strategic complementarity or substitutability. The author was sympathetic to the view that finite horizon planning is the result of a cost-benefit trade-off. He cautioned against a naive approach by which the agent would first compare her outcomes with various planning horizons before choosing the optimal one, which he viewed as unrealistic. The author advocated for a more boundedly rational approach by which the agent decides whether to incur a cost to reason one step forward. He referred to Gabaix and David Laibson ("Shrouded Attributes, Consumer Myopia, and Information Suppression in Competitive Markets," *Quarterly Journal of Economics* 121, no. 2 [2006]: 505–40), and drew an analogy with how artificial intelligence explores its options in a game of chess.

Jonathan Parker followed up on this analogy and noted that recent developments in computations methods for heterogeneous agent models allow for large state spaces, in contrast to the coarser one considered in the author's paper. He referred to a paper by SeHyoun Ahn and colleagues ("When Inequality Matters for Macro and Macro Matters for Inequality," in *NBER Macroeconomics Annual 2017*, vol. 32, ed. Martin Eichenbaum and Jonathan A. Parker [Chicago: University of Chicago Press, 2018]) and recent contributions using machine learning to approximate value functions. Parker also pointed out that a relevant welfare criterion for policy should account for heterogeneity in planning horizon. The author responded that recent computational methods are powerful to deal with rich state spaces, but struggle with high dimensionality. He noted that the relevant state space in his model can be of high dimensionality, depending on the number of variables that the agent pays attention to as part of the adaptive learning process.

Gregory Mankiw inquired about imperfect credibility of policy makers, and its importance relative to bounded rationality, to explain the forward guidance puzzle. The author acknowledged that the commitment of the Federal Reserve regarding forward guidance was hedged and might have played a role in dampening the effect of accommodative monetary policy.

2

Government Guarantees and the Valuation of American Banks

Andrew G. Atkeson, *University of California, Los Angeles, and NBER*
Adrien d'Avernas, *Stockholm School of Economics*
Andrea L. Eisfeldt, *University of California, Los Angeles, and NBER*
Pierre-Olivier Weill, *University of California, Los Angeles, and NBER*

I. Introduction

Are banks safer today than they were in 2007? Book measures of leverage indicate that regulations postcrisis have shored up the US banking system (see Yellen 2017); however, market measures of leverage and bank credit risk are actually higher than precrisis levels (Sarin and Summers 2016). Do book or market measures more accurately depict the safety of the US banking system? The answer depends on the quantitative drivers of the difference between the market and book values of bank assets. In this paper, we provide a decomposition of banks' market-to-book values into a component driven by bank profitability, or "franchise value," and a component driven by the value of explicit and implicit government guarantees. We find that, quantitatively, about half of the elevated market values of banks from the mid-1990s to 2007 arose from the ability of bank equity holders to capitalize the value of the government safety net. Under current regulatory limitations on leverage, the ability of banks to capture the value of government guarantees is constrained, and, as a result, market-to-book ratios are lower.

The key to understanding the difference between book and market measures of bank leverage is a decomposition of the drivers of banks' market value of equity versus book value of equity into two components, franchise value and the value of government guarantees. Building on this idea, we provide and apply a measurement framework to quantitatively assess the drivers of bank valuation and bank safety using market and accounting data. Our decomposition can be written simply as

$$\frac{\text{MVE}}{\text{BVE}} = 1 + \underbrace{\frac{\text{FVE} - \text{BVE}}{\text{BVE}}}_{\substack{\text{franchise} \\ \text{value}}} + \underbrace{\frac{\text{MVE} - \text{FVE}}{\text{BVE}}}_{\substack{\text{government} \\ \text{guarantees}}}.$$

where MVE indicates market value of bank equity, BVE indicates book value of bank equity, and FVE indicates fair value of bank equity. The first component of banks' market-to-book equity ratios is the ratio of the gap between the fair value of bank equity and the book value of bank equity divided by the book value of bank equity. We define the fair value of bank equity as the difference between the fair value of all of the bank's assets and the fair value of all of the bank's liabilities. Fair values are measured as the discounted present value of all of the cash flows associated with bank assets and liabilities, not considering the contribution to bank value from government guarantees. The difference between the fair value and book value of bank equity, then, is the gap between the market value and book value of the bank's business arms, which we refer to as the franchise value of the bank.

The second component is the ratio of the gap between the market value of bank equity and the fair value of bank equity to the book value of bank equity. The market value of bank equity includes the discounted present value of cash flows associated with taxpayer bailouts of banks' liability holders in times of distress. By definition, this second component reflects the contribution to bank equity valuation from bank risk taking with the support of government guarantees for bank liabilities.

The implications of observations on the market-to-book values of equity for bank financial soundness depend critically on which of these two components, franchise value or government guarantees, accounts for most of the movement in bank equity valuation. As emphasized by Keeley (1990), Sarin and Summers (2016), and Chousakos and Gorton (2017), to the extent that the market-to-book value of equity is high because banks have high franchise value, a high market-to-book value of equity is a manifestation of economic capital not recorded on banks' balance sheets, and indicates that banks have less risk of default in a crisis.

In contrast, to the extent that high market-to-book values of equity are due to the value of government guarantees, then high valuations of bank equity are a signal of risk in banks and of a large taxpayer contingent liability for bank bailouts in a crisis. As we show in our model below, in this case, increases in book or regulatory capital should be expected to reduce bank market-to-book ratios and accounting profitability. The reduction in bank's market-to-book ratios has an upside, namely, a lower liability forcing taxpayers to bail out bank debt and deposits in a crisis.[1]

Our paper is closely related in its objective to that of Haldane, Brennan, and Madouros (2010). These authors ask whether the evolution of bank profitability and valuation prior to the financial crisis reflected an increase in the economic profitability of bank loan making and deposit taking (what we term "franchise value") or, instead, a return by bank owners to risk taking backed by government guarantees. They examine how increases in bank leverage and risk taking might account for the rise in bank accounting profitability from the mid-1990s until the financial crisis. We extend their analysis to provide a quantitative accounting of the evolution of US bank valuations and the relative contributions from franchise values and value from risk taking backed by government guarantees. Our accounting indicates that there has been a reduction in bank franchise values from before the 2008 crisis to now, mostly stemming from a lower fair value of core deposits. However, our main finding is that there has been an equally large decline in banks' capitalized values from government guarantees.

Our framework allows us to assess which channel for capturing the value of government guarantees, namely, risk taking, leverage, or prospects for growth of banks' balance sheets, has declined in importance since the crisis.

It does not appear that regulation has succeeded in reducing risk taking by banks. In particular, our accounting indicates that bank equity would still be wiped out in a crisis of the magnitude observed in 2008. This finding is driven by two observations. First, bank accounting profitability is still quite high relative to available riskless rates of return even after adjustment for the fair value of bank assets and liabilities. This observation implies that banks' assets are still quite exposed to aggregate risk.[2] Second, the market signals from bank equity and debt reviewed by Sarin and Summers (2016) still signal considerable risk to subordinated claims on US banks, suggesting that the market perceives that bank equity and subordinated debt would still be wiped out in a crisis.

Instead, we find that the reduction of the value of government guarantees to bank equity is due primarily to the increase in bank regulatory capital and a reduction in the growth rate of banks' balance sheets. With greater regulatory or book capital, equity suffers more of the loss to bank assets in a crisis. Holding fixed the drop in bank asset values in a crisis, the taxpayer contribution required to honor deposit guarantees is smaller. Moreover, with lower expected growth, equity is not able to grow implicit guarantees in advance of the next crisis.

Our accounting model suggests that moves to lighten the regulatory burden on banks going forward may lead to substantially greater bank risk exposure. The value of government guarantees to bank equity is highly sensitive to small changes in the risk exposure of bank assets. If regulators allow even a moderate increase in risk taking by banks, we should see a significant jump in bank valuations and accounting profitability. The temptation will be to interpret this increase in bank valuations and accounting profitability as a restoration of bank franchise value previously damaged by regulation. Instead, we argue that it would properly be interpreted as a return to the days in which taxpayers had a large contingent liability to bail out banks in a crisis.

The remainder of our paper is organized as follows. In Section II, we document the facts on bank valuation and profitability that we focus on in our accounting exercise. In Section III we present the model we use for measurement. We define the book and fair values of items on banks' balance sheets. We show that to construct a fair value balance sheet for banks, one must measure the fair values of bank loans and deposits, as well as banks' growth opportunities to earn future profits from originating new loans and acquiring new deposits. We establish the result that in the absence of government guarantees, the market value of bank equity is equal to the fair value of bank equity, regardless of the risk in the banks' assets and regardless of bank equity's decisions to default on bank subordinated liabilities in a crisis. In the presence of government guarantees, we show that equity holders obtain a market value in excess of fair value by taking on risk, boosting dividends in normal times and defaulting during crises.

The concept of the fair value of bank equity for banks is very similar to the concept of the value of equity absent violations of the Miller and Modigliani (1958) theorem from the familiar adjusted present value formula in corporate finance. The difference between the fair value of bank equity and the market value of equity stems from a nonzero net present value of banks' financing decisions. In particular, implicit and explicit guarantees lead to a positive net present value of debt financing for US banks because of the injection of taxpayer funds into the bank in the event of a crisis. We use the terminology "fair value of bank equity" for two reasons. First, our concept of fair value is related to that used in financial institution accounting. Second, we include the franchise value of a bank's deposit business in the fair value of equity, despite the fact that the value of the deposit business depends on the bank's capital structure.[3]

The quantitative value of government guarantees depends critically on the risk-neutral probability of a crisis state. In Section IV, we use data on the realized returns on broad portfolios of corporate bonds from Asvanunt and Richardson (2016) as well as estimates of the credit risk premium from Berndt et al. (2017) to measure exposure to aggregate credit risk and to calibrate the risk-neutral probability of a crisis. Based on these data, we calibrate the risk-neutral probability of the crisis state to 5% on an annual basis. Under the assumption that marginal utility is high in the crisis state, 5% is an upper bound on the objective probability of a crisis, and thus crises are rare events.

In Section V we use a stylized, two-state model of a bank to demonstrate that, under reasonable parameters describing bank leverage and aggregate credit risk, the observed drop in bank valuations since 2007 can easily be generated by a decline in the value of government guarantees to bank equity. The stylized bank issues liabilities insured with a government guarantee and holds only marketable securities exposed to aggregate credit risk. By definition, this bank has no franchise value. However, with guaranteed liabilities and assets with the same distribution of excess returns as those on BBB-rated corporate bonds, the bank trades at a market-to-book ratio of equity of 2 given book leverage of 90%. Leverage is key to this valuation. If book leverage is constrained to 85%, the market-to-book ratio of this bank falls from 2 to close to 1. The entire decline is due to the reduction in the size of taxpayers' exposure to bailouts in the crisis state.

With confirmation of the quantitative plausibility of guarantees as main drivers of bank equity values in hand, we turn in Section VI to a complete accounting exercise. We construct estimates of the book value, the fair value, and the market value of banks in the 1970–85, 1996–2007, and 2011–17 time periods. We model each time period as one in which only the "normal" state is realized. We collect data on the book value of items on banks' balance sheets from bank regulatory reports. To construct a fair value version of banks' balance sheets, we use banks' reports of the fair value of their loans found in the footnotes of banks' annual reports since the mid-1990s as well as two measures of the fair value of bank deposits. The first is a measure of the fair value of bank deposits from the Portfolio Value Model developed by the Office of Thrift Supervision (OTS). The second is a measure of the fair value of deposits derived from the measure of core deposit intangibles recorded on bank books when one bank acquires another.[4] We then use a Gordon (1962) dividend growth model to value bank equity using observed accounting returns for banks, our calibration of the risk-neutral probabilities of the normal and crisis states, and measures of the riskless interest rate and the growth rate of bank balance sheets in normal times from each of these three time periods.

Using our model for measurement, we find the following results for banks' market-to-book equity values, and the contribution from franchise values and government guarantees.

In the early period from 1970 to 1985, according to our model, banks did not have large franchise values and did not derive value from risk taking with government guarantees. Our model yields a market-to-book equity value of 1, which matches the observed ratio for financial firms for that time period.

In contrast to this early period, in the precrisis, postderegulation period from 1996 to 2007, our model predicts that banks' market-to-book equity ratio was 2.24, which closely matches the observed average ratio of 2.12 over this time period. We find that the excess in market over book values was driven mainly by the value of government guarantees. In particular, we find that banks' franchise values contributed (FVE – BVE) / BVE = 0.34 and the value of government guarantees contributed (MVE – FVE) / BVE = 0.91 to the total gap between market and book values of (MVE – BVE) / BVE = 1.24 implied by our model. Hence, we find that government guarantees contribute roughly three times more than franchise value to the market-to-book ratio of equity over this precrisis window. Our model suggests that the value of government guarantees was so high in this time period because, starting in the late 1990s, banks took on significantly more risk, as evidenced by significantly higher realized accounting returns in banking relative to riskless benchmarks.

This accounting evidence of risk taking by banks continues past the 2008 crisis. However, due to changes in book leverage and the growth rate of bank assets over time, this risk taking by banks has had a smaller effect on the market value of bank equity since the crisis. For the 2011 to 2017 time period, our model implies that banks' market-to-book equity ratios should have averaged a much lower value of 1.19. In the data, the market-to-book ratio in banking averaged 0.98 over this time period. In the postcrisis data, about half of the excess of market over book values of equity stem from franchise value and half from government guarantees.

Finally, in Section VII, we conclude. Our valuation estimates indicate that regulation-induced reductions in book leverage have succeeded in reducing the market value of the funds that taxpayers will need to contribute in a bailout, consistent with the views of Yellen (2017) and the important contribution by Admati and Hellwig (2013), which provides strong arguments for lower bank leverage. In contrast, we also show that the risk of equity and subordinated debt being wiped out has not gone down substantially, which explains the observations of high market leverage as well as market measures of bank credit riskiness in Sarin and Summers (2016).

In appendix A, we present proofs of several propositions regarding the impact of changes in leverage, risk taking, and economic profitability on banks' accounting profitability and market-to-book ratios. In appendix B, we discuss in greater detail several of our modeling assumptions and compare our results on the value of government guarantees to other measures of the value of government guarantees in the literature.

II.   Historical Data on the Valuation

In this section we develop the main stylized facts describing changes in bank valuation, leverage, profitability, and market credit risk measures. These facts motivate our study and support the calibration of our model.[5]

A.   Bank Valuation

We measure the valuation of the banking sector in each time period as the ratio of market-to-book value of equity for the entire sector in each quarter from 1991 to 2017.[6] We display this market-to-book value of equity for the US banks over the time period 1991–2017 in figure 1.

This figure shows a substantial increase in the ratio of the market-to-book value of equity for US banks in the mid-1990s and a sharp reduction in this ratio after the financial crisis. In particular, we find that the market-to-book ratio in banking averaged 2.12 over the 1996–2007 time period and 0.97 over the 2011–17 time period. This pattern of bank valuations over time is consistent with the findings in Chousakos and Gorton (2017) and Minton, Stulz, and Taboada (2017) regarding the valuation of bank equity relative to balance sheet benchmarks.

Keeley (1990) provides evidence on the valuation of banks in the 1970s. He finds that market-to-book values of bank equity were closer to 1 during that time period. To confirm that finding, in figure 2, we examine the ratio of the market-to-book value of equity for the US financial sector from 1975 to the present together with our series for bank holding companies over the 1986–2017 time period.[7] Note that the market-

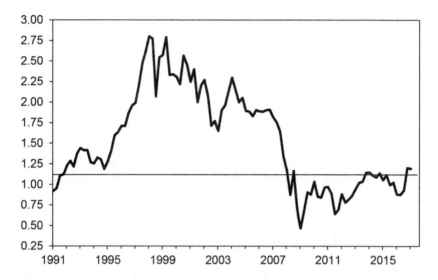

Fig. 1. Market-to-book value of equity for bank holding companies. The ratio is computed as the sum of the market value of equity across bank holding companies divided by the sum of the book value of equity across bank holding companies. The book value of equity comes from the Holding Company Data of the Federal Reserve Bank of Chicago (2019) and corresponds to item 28 of Schedule HC from FR Y-9C reports. The market value of equity comes from the Center for Research in Security Prices database.

to-book value of equity for the US financial sector corresponds closely to that for bank holding companies over the time period for which we have data for both series. Figure 2 shows that the ratio of the market-to-book value of equity for the financial sector from 1975 into the early 1990s was close to 1.

Consistent with the findings of Minton et al. (2017), we find similar patterns of bank valuations over time for large and small bank holding companies. In figure 3, we show the ratios of the market-to-book value of equity for bank holding companies with assets of more than $250 billion and those with assets from $10 to $250 billion.[8] These data on the valuation of large and smaller banks suggest that fluctuations in bank market valuations are not driven by valuations of the investment banking activities of the largest bank holding companies.

B. Bank Financial Soundness

In what follows, we consider the implications of the data on bank valuations presented above as an indicator of bank financial soundness. The

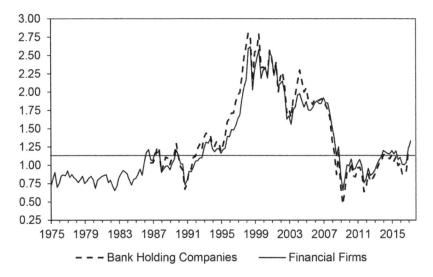

Fig. 2. Market-to-book value of equity for bank holding companies and financial firms. The ratio is computed as the sum of the market value of equity across bank holding companies divided by the sum of the book value of equity across bank holding companies. The book value of equity comes from the holding company data of the Federal Reserve Bank of Chicago (2019) and corresponds to item 28 of Schedule HC from FR Y-9C reports. The market value of equity comes from the Center for Research in Security Prices database. We use financial firms with a standard industry classification code between 6000 and 6199 to go back to 1975.

connection to bank financial soundness is through bank leverage. It is common to evaluate bank leverage on both a book and a market basis.

Bank capital regulation is applied to banks' book leverage, that is, the ratio of the book value of debt to the book value of assets (we abstract here from risk weighting of assets). Figure 4 shows book leverage for bank holding companies over the period 1991–2017. Book leverage has declined steadily over this time period.

We plot market leverage for bank holding companies, defined as the ratio of the book value of debt to the market value of assets, over this time period in figure 5.[9] Bank market leverage shows a pattern over time that is different from that of book leverage. Specifically, bank market leverage was relatively low in the period before the 2008 crisis and it is high in the period since that crisis.

C. Bank Profitability

Accounting measures of bank profitability are a key input into our accounting for the market valuation of banks. As we will show in our

Fig. 3. Market-to-book value of equity for bank holding companies. We use the gross domestic product implicit price deflator with base year 2009 as the deflator of the $205 billion threshold. We then take the average of the ratios of market-to-book value of equity within each group. We use the same data as in figure 1.

model, bank profits in normal times are driven both by banks' exposure to crisis risk (consistent with the findings of Meiselman, Nagel, and Purnanandam [2018]) and by sources of franchise value. Here we document the accounting data that we target.

Figure 6 displays the accounting return on equity (ROE) for US bank holding companies over the period 1991–2017. ROE is measured as the ratio of bank net income to the book value of bank equity. Figure 6 shows that the ROE for bank holding companies was high at just under 15% from the mid-1990s into 2007, and it has been substantially lower since the 2008 crisis.

Figure 7 shows the corresponding accounting profitability of bank holding companies over this time period measured in terms of bank return on assets (ROA; the ratio of net income to total book assets). Here we find that the ROA for bank holding companies was consistently above 1% from the mid-1990s into 2007 and has been below 1% since the 2008 crisis.

The high accounting profitability of banks in the period from the mid-1990s into 2007 was unusual in a longer historical perspective. In figure 8,

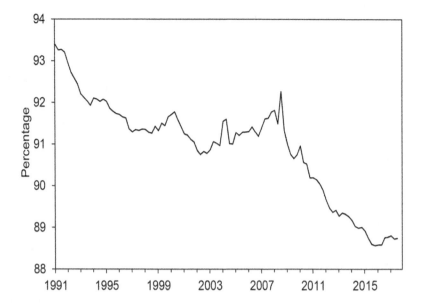

Fig. 4. Book leverage for bank holding companies. This figure reports book leverage from the Federal Reserve Bank of New York (2017). The ratio is computed as the sum of liabilities across bank holding companies divided by the sum of total assets across bank holding companies.

we show the ROA for commercial bank subsidiaries reported in the Federal Deposit Insurance Corporation (FDIC) historical statistics on banking from 1934 to 2017 (FDIC 2019b). This figure shows that the ROA for banks was consistently under 1% until the mid-1990s. Then, as in the bank holding company data in figure 7, banks had an ROA consistently above 1% from the mid-1990s into 2007, and then a lower ROA since the 2008 crisis.

D. Spreads on Subordinated Debt

As we apply our accounting model, we need to confirm that it is consistent with the evolution of market signals of the risk exposure of bank equity and subordinated debt to a crisis. Sarin and Summers (2016) provide a convincing review of those equity and debt market signals and conclude that these signals have not improved from levels observed before the 2008 crisis. In our accounting model, we focus on matching data on spreads on banks' subordinated debt. In figure 9 we present data on these corporate bond spreads from 1991 to 2017. For a sample of firms covered by Standard & Poor's Compustat database and the Center for

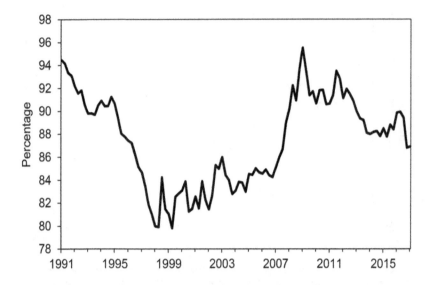

Fig. 5. Market leverage for bank holding companies. The ratio is computed as the sum of the book value of liabilities across bank holding companies divided by the sum of the market value of total assets across bank holding companies. The book value of liabilities comes from the Holding Company Data of the Federal Reserve Bank of Chicago and corresponds to item 21 of Schedule HC from FR Y-9C reports. The market value of assets is calculated as the sum of the book value of liabilities and the market value of equity coming from the Center for Research in Security Prices database.

Research in Security Prices, we matched month-end secondary market option-adjusted credit spreads of their outstanding senior unsecured bonds from the Lehman/Warga and Bank of America Merrill Lynch (BAML) databases.[10]

In figure 9, the thick solid line corresponds to averages of the natural log of option-adjusted spreads on bank holding company bonds calculated by BAML.[11] The other lines correspond to averages of option-adjusted spreads on bonds of nonfinancial firms within a certain credit rating.[12] Starting from the bottom and going up, these lines correspond to AAA- and AA-rated bonds together in one line, A-rated bonds, BBB-rated bonds, BB-rated bonds, and B-rated bonds. Thus, in this figure, we see how the level of bank bond spreads has evolved over time and how these spreads have moved relative to those of nonfinancial firms. We see that the level of bank bond spreads has risen both in absolute terms since before 2008 and in relative terms compared with nonbank bonds. Before the crisis, bank bond spreads were in line with those of A-rated firms. After the crisis, bank bond spreads are in line with those of BBB-rated

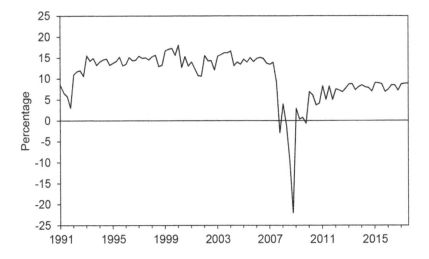

Fig. 6. Return on equity for bank holding companies. This figure reports the quarterly annualized return on equity from the Federal Reserve Bank of New York (2017). The ratio is computed as the sum of net income across bank holding companies divided by the sum of total equity across bank holding companies. Net income corresponds to item 14 of Schedule HI from FR Y9-C reports. The book value of equity corresponds to item 28 of Schedule HC from FR Y-9C reports.

firms. The average level of bank holding companies' corporate bond option-adjusted spreads was 93 basis points (bp) over the period 1996–2007 and 151 bp over the period 2011–17.

III.   An Accounting Model

We now present the model we use to define the concepts of book, fair, and market values of equity and to establish the results that FVE – BVE is a measure of the franchise value of the bank and MVE – FVE is a measure of the market value of the taxpayer injections of resources needed to honor government guarantees of bank liabilities.

A representative bank operates a loan-making arm and a government-guaranteed deposit-taking arm.[13] Deposits are fully guaranteed by the government. Every period, the loan-making arm makes new loans and the deposit arm takes in new government-guaranteed deposits. The bank also issues subordinated debt. Both the loan-making and the deposit-taking arms are subject to shocks: shocks to the prepayment rate and default rate of loans, to the withdrawal rate of deposits, and to the growth rate of the balance sheet achieved through origination of new loans and

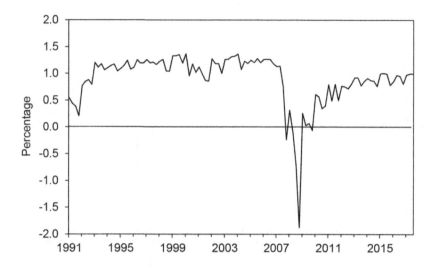

Fig. 7. Return on assets for bank holding companies. This figure reports the quarterly annualized return on assets from the Federal Reserve Bank of New York (2017). The ratio is computed as the sum of net income across bank holding companies divided by the sum of total assets across bank holding companies. Net income corresponds to item 14 of Schedule HI from FR Y9-C reports. The book value of assets corresponds to item 12 of Schedule HC from FR Y-9C reports.

deposits. We assume that the vector of shocks is independently and identically distributed over time under the risk-neutral probability measure but that the shocks can be contemporaneously correlated. After observing the realized shocks, equity holders have the option to default. In that case, the subordinated debt holders take over the bank and auction it off immediately to new owners. The government makes a contribution of taxpayer funds to the sale sufficient to ensure that the new owners of the bank are willing to assume the bank's deposit liabilities and pay a nonnegative price for the bank to the holders of the subordinated debt.

A.   The Loan-Making Arm

Let L denote the total face value, or book value, of the loans on the bank's balance sheet. Every period, every dollar of loan pays a coupon c_L, net of servicing cost. Then the face value of the loan is prepaid with probability μ'_L, and default on the face value of the loan occurs with probability δ'_L. We use the prime notation, μ'_L and δ'_L, to indicate that the probability of prepayment and default are themselves random var-

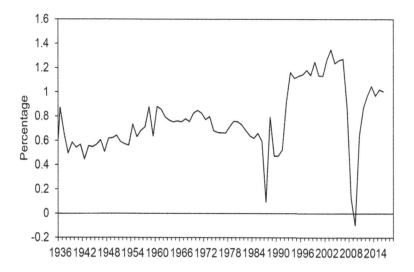

Fig. 8.   Return on assets for FDIC-insured banks. This figure reports the return on assets from the consolidated annual financial statements of FDIC-insured institutions. The ratio is computed as the sum of net income across FDIC-insured institutions divided by the sum of total assets across FDIC-insured institutions.

iables, representing aggregate risk of prepayment and default. The fair value of the loans on the bank's balance sheet is $v_L \times L$, where the ratio of fair-to-book value for the stock of loans on the balance sheet solves the asset pricing equation

$$v_L = \frac{1}{1+i} \hat{\mathbb{E}}[c_L + \mu'_L + (1 - \mu'_L - \delta'_L)v_L], \tag{1}$$

where i is the risk-free rate and $\hat{\mathbb{E}}[\cdot]$ denotes expectations under the risk-neutral probability measure. Solving for v_L we obtain:

$$v_L = \frac{c_L + \bar{\mu}_L}{i + \bar{\mu}_L + \bar{\delta}_L},$$

where the "bar" notation denotes the expectation given risk-neutral probabilities, for example $\bar{\mu}_L = \hat{\mathbb{E}}[\mu'_L]$. That is, v_L is the present value of receiving the coupon c_L and the average prepayment $\bar{\mu}_L$, until the loan is either prepaid or defaulted on.

Next, let us calculate the fair value of the loan-making arm of the bank. We assume that the bank grows at rate g' and impose the standard growth condition $\bar{g} < i$. To achieve that growth, the bank must make new

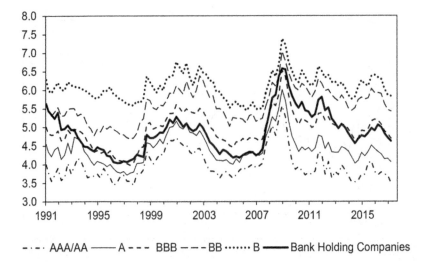

Fig. 9. Corporate bond log option-adjusted spreads. The thick line is the average corporate bond log option-adjusted spread of publicly traded bank holding companies from the Lehman/Warga and Merrill Lynch databases from 1986 to 2016. The other lines show the average for publicly traded nonfinancial firms within rating groups AAA or AA, A, BBB, BB, and B.

loans at a rate $\mu'_L + \delta'_L + g'$ so as to replace the principal prepaid, μ'_L, and written down, δ'_L, and achieve net growth rate g' in the book value of its loans. We assume that the bank incurs origination costs at rate $\phi_L > 0$ per dollar of new loans. Therefore, the contribution to the bank dividend, or free cash flow, generated by the loan-making arm is $\mathrm{DIV}'_L \times L$, where the dividend rate is

$$\mathrm{DIV}'_L = c_L + \mu'_L - (1 + \phi_L)(\mu'_L + \delta'_L + g').$$

The first term is the coupon, the second term is the prepayment rate, and the third term is the sum of the principal and origination cost for new loans. The fair value of the loan-making arm is the risk-neutral expected present value of these free cash flows. Therefore, the fair value of the loan-making arm is $\mathrm{FVL} \times L$, where the fair value ratio solves

$$\mathrm{FVL} = \frac{1}{1+i} \hat{\mathbb{E}}[\mathrm{DIV}'_L + (1+g')\mathrm{FVL}]. \tag{2}$$

Taking the difference between the pricing equation for FVL, (2), and v_L, (1), we obtain

$$\mathrm{FVL} - v_L = \frac{1}{1+i} \hat{\mathbb{E}}[(\mu'_L + \delta'_L + g')(v_L - (1 + \phi_L)) + (1+g')(\mathrm{FVL} - v_L)].$$

Solving for FVL, we obtain

$$\text{FVL} = v_L + \frac{\bar{\mu}_L + \bar{\delta}_L + \bar{g}}{i - \bar{g}} (v_L - (1 + \phi_L)). \tag{3}$$

Assuming that banks only make investments with positive net present value, we have that $v_L \geq 1 + \phi_L$. Thus, the fair value of the loan-making arm exceeds the book value for two reasons: value from assets in place and value from growth opportunities. First, the present value of all the payments to be received from each outstanding loan, v_L, exceeds its book value of 1. Second, each time the bank will issue a new loan, it will make a profit equal to the net present value, $v_L - (1 + \phi_L)$.

B. The Deposit-Taking Arm

Let D denote the total face value, or book value, of the deposits on the bank's balance sheet. Every period, every dollar of deposits costs the bank c_D, equal to the sum of the interest rate paid on deposits and the servicing cost. The deposit is withdrawn with probability of repayment, μ_D. As before, we use the prime notation, μ'_D, to indicate that the probability is random, representing aggregate run or funding risk. Hence, the fair value of the deposits on the bank's balance sheet is $-v_D \times D$, where the ratio of the fair-to-book value of deposits solves

$$v_D = \frac{1}{1 + i} \hat{\mathbb{E}}[c_D + \mu'_D + (1 - \mu'_D)v_D] \Rightarrow v_D = \frac{c_D + \bar{\mu}_D}{i + \bar{\mu}_D}.$$

Next, let us calculate the fair value of the deposit-taking arm of the bank. We again assume that the bank grows at rate g'. Hence, to achieve that growth, the bank must take new deposits at a rate $\mu'_D + g'$ so as to replace the deposits withdrawn, μ'_D, and achieve net growth of the book value of deposits of g'. We assume that, when it originates new deposits, the bank incurs costs at rate ϕ_D. Therefore, the contribution to bank dividends, or free cash flow, generated by the deposit-taking arm is $-\text{DIV}'_D \times D$, where the dividend rate solves

$$\text{DIV}'_D = c_D + \mu'_D - (1 - \phi_D)(\mu'_D + g').$$

The fair value of the deposit-taking arm is $-\text{FVD} \times D$, where

$$\text{FVD} = \frac{1}{1 + i} \hat{\mathbb{E}}[\text{DIV}'_D + (1 + g')\text{FVD}]. \tag{4}$$

Taking the difference between the equations for FVD and v_D, we obtain that

$$\text{FVD} - v_D = \frac{1}{1+i}\hat{\mathbb{E}}[(\mu_D' + g')(v_D - (1 - \phi_D)) + (1 + g')(\text{FVD} - v_D)].$$

Solving for FVD $- v_D$, we obtain:

$$\text{FVD} = v_D - \frac{\bar{\mu}_D + \bar{g}}{i - \bar{g}}(1 - \phi_D - v_D).$$

Assuming as before that the bank invests only in projects with positive net present value, we have that $v_D + \phi_D \leq 1$. This implies that the fair value of the deposit-taking arm exceeds the book value for two reasons. First, the present value of the payment to be made on outstanding deposits is less than the face value of 1. Second, each time the bank takes a new deposit, it makes a profit equal to the net present value, $1 - v_D - \phi_D$.

C. Subordinated Debt

In addition to deposits, we assume that the bank also issues subordinated debt.[14] We assume that subordinated debt takes the form of one-period defaultable debt with face value $1 + i$. We denote the price of a unit of subordinated debt by v_B. To determine v_B, we need to study the default decision of equity.

The Default Decision of Equity

Suppose that equity enters the period with L loans, D deposits, and B subordinated debt. If equity does not default, subordinated debt is paid principal and interest $(1 + i)B$ out of the bank's free cash flows $\text{DIV}_L'L - \text{DIV}_D'D$. In these states, equity issues new subordinated debt in quantity $(1 + g')B$ at price v_B. Thus, the dividend to equity in the event that equity does not default is $DIV_E' \times L$, where

$$DIV_E' = DIV_L' - DIV_D'\Theta_D - (1 + i)\Theta_B + v_B(1 + g')\Theta_B, \tag{5}$$

with $\Theta_D \equiv D / L$ and $\Theta_B \equiv B / L$. If, on the other hand, equity chooses to default, then it receives zero dividend and gives up all future claims on the bank. Hence, the default decision is obtained as the solution of the following Bellman equation:

$$\text{MVE} = \max \frac{1}{1+i} \hat{\mathbb{E}}[I'\{\text{DIV}'_E + (1+g')\text{MVE}\}] \qquad (6)$$

with respect to repayment decisions $I' \in \{0, 1\}$, where the prime notation indicates that the repayment decision will depend on the vector of shocks realizations, $(\mu'_L, \delta'_L, \mu'_D, g')$. Clearly, this implies that equity defaults if

$$\text{DIV}'_E + (1+g')\text{MVE} < 0. \qquad (7)$$

The Valuation of Subordinated Debt

Now let us turn to the valuation of subordinated debt. If there is default, $I' = 0$, then subordinated debt is not paid its principal and interest $1 + i$. Instead, subordinated debt holders immediately resell the bank to new owners at price R'. The bank is sold inclusive of some government support $T' \geq 0$ per unit of assets. After purchasing the bank, new owners receive the current free cash flow from loans and deposits, and issue new subordinated debt at price $(1 + g')v_B$. New owners do not have to repay current subordinated debt owners. All in all, this implies that the price at which new owners purchase the bank from subordinated debt holders is, per unit of asset,

$$R'\Theta_B = T' + \text{DIV}'_E + (1+i)\Theta_B + (1+g')\text{MVE}. \qquad (8)$$

The first term, T', is the government support received by subordinated debt holders and immediately resold, bundled with the rest of the bank, to new owners. The second term, DIV'_E, is the dividend received by the new owners. The third term adjusts the payout to the new owners for the fact that new owners do not have to repay principal and interest, $(1 + i)\Theta_B$, to current subordinated debt owners. The last term is the continuation value of new owners. We assume that the government support, T', is chosen so that

$$0 \leq R' \leq 1+i. \qquad (9)$$

The left-hand inequality reflects limited liability for subordinated debt holders. The right-hand inequality imposes that the government does not pay more than principal and interest on outstanding subordinated debt.

Given that, in case of default, subordinated debt holders resell the bank at price $R'\Theta_B$, the selling price of subordinated debt is

$$v_B = \frac{1}{1+i}\hat{\mathbb{E}}[(1+i)I' + (1-I')R'].\tag{10}$$

Finally, we can compute the fair value of the subordinated debt arm of the bank as before:

$$\text{FVB} = \frac{1}{1+i}\hat{\mathbb{E}}[(1+i)I' + (1-I')R' - (1+g')v_B + (1+g')\text{FVB}],$$

and one sees by direct comparison that $\text{FVB} = v_B$.

D. Book, Fair, and Market Value of Equity

Book Value

Banks hold loans and deposits on their books at face values. Banks hold subordinated debt on their books at market value. The book value of bank equity is the difference between the book value of bank assets and the book value of bank liabilities. Hence, the ratio of the book value of bank equity to the book value of bank assets is given by

$$\text{BVE} = 1 - \Theta_D - \Theta_B v_B.$$

Define $\Theta = \Theta_D + \Theta_B v_B$. Then Θ is the book leverage of the bank. We thus have $\text{BVE} = 1 - \Theta$.

Fair Value

The fair value of bank equity, on the other hand, is the difference between the fair value of bank assets and the fair value of bank liabilities not including the value of government guarantees. The ratio of the fair value of bank equity to the book value of bank assets is given by

$$\text{FVE} = \text{FVL} - \Theta_D\text{FVD} - \Theta_B v_B.\tag{11}$$

Because $\text{FVL} \geq 1$ and $\text{FVD} \leq 1$, it follows that the fair value of bank equity exceeds the book value.

Note that the difference between the fair value and book value of bank equity is given by

$$\text{FVE} - \text{BVE} = (\text{FVL} - 1) - \Theta_D(1 - \text{FVD}),$$

which is the gap between the fair value and book value of the bank's loans and deposits. Accordingly, we define the franchise value of the bank (relative to total book assets) to be the difference between the fair value and book value of bank equity because this gap corresponds to the gap between the fair value and book value of the bank's business arms.

Market versus Fair Value

To compare the fair value of equity to the market value of equity, we use a budget identity in the tradition of Miller and Modigliani (1958). We start from the observation that shareholders and subordinated debt holders do not make all payments on deposits: in a severe default, some of the payments are made by the government. Hence, we have the standard result that the sum of the market values of equity and subordinated debt are equal to the fair value of the bank's two business arms, plus the market value of all the payments made by the government (shown as MVG)

$$\text{MVE} + \Theta_B v_B = \text{FVL} - \Theta_D \text{FVD} + \text{MVG},$$

where MVG is defined recursively from

$$\text{MVG} = \frac{1}{1+i} \hat{\mathbb{E}}[(1 - I')T' + (1 + g')\text{MVG}]. \tag{12}$$

Subtracting the value of the bank's subordinated debt from both sides gives us

$$\text{MVE} = \text{FVE} + \text{MVG}. \tag{13}$$

This identity is straightforward to formally verify using equations (2)–(6), (8), and (10)–(12).

Equation (13) implies that, in the absence of government guarantees, the market value of bank equity is equal to the fair value of bank equity regardless of the risk in bank assets and bank equity's strategy for default.[15] It follows from this decomposition that, as long as the bank defaults with positive probability and the government contributes resources to bail out bank liabilities, then the market value of bank equity exceeds the fair value of bank equity.

Notice as well that, in our model, equity does not directly receive payments due to government guarantees upon default. Only debt receives these payments. Yet, equity indirectly profits from these payments. This is because equity reaps the benefit of issuing risk-free liabilities without bearing the full cost of making these liabilities risk free: equity only repays liabilities in good times, and the government repays in bad times. Equation (13) shows that the market value of equity capitalizes the present value of all future government contributions.

Finally, using our definition of the market value of government guarantees, we obtain the following decomposition of the market-to-book ratio of equity:

$$\frac{MVE}{BVE} = 1 + \frac{FVE - BVE}{BVE} + \frac{MVE - FVE}{BVE} = 1 + \frac{FVE - BVE}{BVE} + \frac{MVG}{BVE}.$$

Both the second and the third terms are positive. The second term reflects the franchise value of the bank relative to the book value of bank equity. The third term reflects the market value of government guarantees relative to the fair value of bank equity.

E. Comparative Statics for the Market-to-Book Ratio

As we argued earlier, the market-to-book equity ratio dropped dramatically after the financial crisis of 2008. This drop has been interpreted by Sarin and Summers (2016) as a signal that banks have become riskier. In what follows, we provide comparative statics to demonstrate that, in fact, whether a drop in the market-to-book ratio signals an improvement or a deterioration in bank safety depends on the forces driving the decline. For instance, if the drop is the consequence of a decrease in bank franchise value, it indicates that banks are riskier. But if the drop is the consequence of a decrease in risk taking (perhaps due to more stringent regulation), it indicates that banks are safer, not riskier.

We focus on the case in which the bank does not issue subordinated debt ($B = 0$). This case is appropriate because, in the data, banks issue very little subordinated debt. In this case, the cash injections from the government in the case of default by bank equity are whatever is needed to pay off depositors. In terms of the equations above, the cash transfer from the government in the event of default is

$$T' = -[DIV'_L - DIV'_D \Theta_D + (1 + g')MVE]$$

per unit of asset.

Franchise Value

The first comparative static is with respect to a decrease in bank franchise value. Formally, consider any change in parameter, besides growth and leverage, that decreases the equity dividend rate in all states. This includes, for example, a decrease in loan coupon, c_L, an increase in average prepayment, $\bar{\mu}_L$, an increase in average default, $\bar{\delta}_L$, or an increase in deposits coupon, c_D.

Lemma 1 (rents and quasi-rents).   Consider a decrease in rents or quasi-rents. Then:

- The franchise value, (FVE − BVE) / BVE, decreases.
- The market-to-book ratio, MVE / BVE, decreases.
- The value of the government guarantee, MVG / BVE, increases. QED.

It is intuitive that a decrease in the bank's economic profitability reduces both the market value and the fair value of bank equity. The key point is that it reduces the franchise value by more. Indeed, for the franchise value, the decrease in profitability matters in all states, both those in which the bank defaults ($I' = 0$) and those in which it does not ($I' = 1$). For the market value, it only matters in nondefault states, $I' = 1$. On net, this implies that MVE − FVE = MVG must increase.

This comparative statics exercise illustrates that a decrease in the market-to-book equity ratio, if driven by a decrease in bank franchise value, can be interpreted, following Sarin and Summers (2016), as a decrease in bank safety.

Risk Taking

Second, we consider the impact of an increase in risk taking, defined as follows. Assume that the shocks $x' \equiv (\delta'_L, \mu'_L, \mu'_D, g')$ have a factor structure, that is $x' = \bar{x} + A\Sigma\varepsilon'$ for some vector of mean zero, unit variance, and contemporaneously independent shocks, $\varepsilon' = (\varepsilon'_1, \varepsilon'_2, ..., \varepsilon'_N)$, some $4 \times N$ matrix A, and some $N \times N$ positive diagonal matrix $\Sigma = \text{diag}(\sigma_1, ..., \sigma_N)$. We define a decrease in risk taking as a decrease in σ_n, for some $n \in \{1, ..., N\}$.

Lemma 2 (risk taking).   Consider a decrease in risk taking. Then:

- The market-to-book ratio, MVE / BVE, decreases.
- The franchise value, (FVE − BVE) / BVE, stays the same.
- The government guarantee, MVG / BVE, decreases.

The decrease in risk leaves the franchise value constant because bank franchise value only depends on the mean of shocks under the risk-neutral probabilities. The decrease in risk decreases the market-to-book ratio value because of a usual option valuation effect: the payoff of equity is convex, so a decrease in risk reduces the upside by more than the downside.

This comparative statics exercise illustrates that a decrease in the market-to-book equity ratio for a bank, if driven by a decrease in risk of the bank, can be interpreted as signal of an increase in bank safety.

Leverage

The last comparative statics exercise is with respect to leverage, Θ.

Lemma 3 (leverage).   Consider a decrease in leverage. Then:

- The market-to-book ratio, MVE / BVE, decreases.
- The franchise-value, (FVE – BVE) / BVE, decreases.
- The government guarantee, MVG / BVE, decreases.

To understand this comparative statics result, notice that a decrease in leverage has two effects on bank safety going in opposite directions. On the one hand, it makes it less profitable to operate a bank, so it increases incentives to default. Correspondingly, we find that the franchise value decreases. On the other hand, it also increases the bank's equity cushion, so it reduces incentives to default. Correspondingly, we find that the government guarantee decreases.[16]

This comparative statics exercise illustrates that a decrease in the market-to-book equity ratio for a bank, if driven by a decrease in book leverage, can be interpreted, following Yellen (2017), as a signal of an increase in bank safety.

F.   *What Triggers Default*

The Default Region

In this paragraph, we investigate the multiple dimensions of banks' default risk: we ask which types of shocks bring the bank closer to default, in the sense of decreasing the sum of current dividends and continuation payoffs, $DIV'_E + (1 + g')MVE$.

Lemma 4.   Holding every other shock realization the same, the bank is strictly closer to default if:

- Loan delinquency, δ'_L, increases.
- Loan prepayment, μ'_L, increases and $\phi_L > 0$.

- Deposit withdrawal, μ'_D, increases and $\phi_D > 0$.
- Balance sheet growth, g', decreases and either $\text{MVG} > 0$, $v_L > 1 + \phi_L$, or $v_D < 1 - \phi_D$.

Loan delinquencies create losses and so bring the bank closer to default. Loan prepayment also brings the bank closer to default because the cost of replacing a loan on the balance sheet exceeds its face value, $1 + \phi_L > 1$. When loan making has zero net present value, $v_L = 1 + \phi_L$, this observation becomes equivalent to the standard intuition that prepayment must create a loss for the bank, which is long premium bonds (loans). Conversely, deposit withdrawal also brings the bank closer to default. Indeed, the cost of honoring a withdrawal is greater than the benefit of replacing the deposit on the balance sheet $1 > 1 - \phi_L$. When deposit taking has zero net present value, $v_D = 1 - \phi_D$, this is equivalent to the standard intuition that prepayment creates a loss for the bank, which is short discount bonds (deposits). Finally, negative shocks to the growth rate of the bank's balance sheet also bring the bank closer to default as long as growth opportunities have strictly positive value. Growth opportunities can arise in our model if the value of government guarantees is positive, loan making has positive net present value, or deposit taking has positive net present value. Lemma 4 illustrates the commonly held view that a bank's default risk has multiple dimensions, such as credit risk (δ'_L), prepayment risk (μ'_L), run risk (μ'_D), or growth opportunity risk (g').

Default and Accounting Profitability

Although risk has multiple dimensions, the bank's default decision ultimately depends on the overall performance of its portfolio, as measured by the sum of current dividends and continuation payoff, $\text{DIV}'_E + (1 + g')\text{MVE}$. In this paragraph, we relate the bank's overall performance to standard measures of accounting profitability. First, we note that

$$\text{DIV}'_E = \text{ROA}' - g'\text{BVE} - (1 - v_B)\Theta_B,$$

where ROA' is the bank's return on assets. That is, the dividend of equity, per unit of assets, is equal to the ROA' adjusted for the cost of growing assets in excess of liabilities, $g'\text{BVE}$, and the cost of issuing subordinated debt at a discount. Dividing both sides by BVE, and keeping in mind that $\text{ROE}' \equiv \text{ROA}' / \text{BVE}$, we obtain that

$$\frac{\text{DIV}'_E}{\text{BVE}} = \text{ROE}' - g' - (1 - v_B)\frac{\Theta_B}{\text{BVE}}.$$ (14)

Hence, the bank defaults whenever

$$\text{ROE}' + g'\left(\frac{\text{MVE}}{\text{BVE}} - 1\right) - (1 - v_B)\frac{\Theta_B}{\text{BVE}} < -\frac{\text{MVE}}{\text{BVE}}.$$ (15)

That is, the bank defaults whenever the ROE, properly adjusted for the benefit of current growth opportunities, falls below the negative of the market-to-book ratio.[17]

G. Two-State Valuation

In this subsection, we develop the valuation formulas that we implement in the remainder of the paper. Because default is a binary decision, a bank's valuation ultimately depends on probabilities and payoffs for two events: repayment ($I' = 1$) and default ($I' = 0$). Hence, we can value the bank as if there were only two states. Of course, these two events are determined by the optimal default decision for equity, but given that decision, we can use the following valuation formulas.

Formally, let $q(n) \equiv \hat{\mathbb{E}}[I']$ denote the risk-neutral probability for the event of repayment, which we will refer to as "normal times." Vice versa, let $q(c) = 1 - q(n)$ denote the total risk-neutral probability for the event of default, or "crisis time." For any random variable x', we let $x(n) \equiv \hat{\mathbb{E}}[x'|I' = 1]$ denote the risk-neutral expectation conditional on a normal time and $x(c) = \mathbb{E}[x' \mid I' = 0]$ denote the expectation conditional on a crisis. Again, let $\bar{x} \equiv \hat{\mathbb{E}}[x']$ denote the unconditional expectation of that variable under the risk-neutral probabilities.

With this notation, we obtain using equations (6) and (14)

$$\frac{\text{MVE}}{\text{BVE}} = \frac{q(n)}{1 + i - q(n)(1 + g(n))}\left[\text{ROE}(n) - g(n) - (1 - v_B)\frac{\Theta_B}{\text{BVE}}\right],$$ (16)

a formula that will prove to be convenient for our quantitative exercises.

Likewise we can obtain a formula for the market value of government guarantees, assuming for simplicity either that there is no subordinated debt ($\Theta_B = 0$) or that this debt is fully bailed out in default (so that $v_B = 1$):

$$\frac{\text{MVG}}{\text{BVE}} = -\frac{q(c)T(c)}{i - \bar{g}},$$ (17)

where $T(c)$ is the expectation of the cash injection from the government required to sell the failed bank, conditional on bank failure. That is,

$$T(c) = -\left[\text{ROE}(c) + (1 + g(c))\frac{\text{MVE}}{\text{BVE}}\right].$$

In what follows, it is useful for us to compute the value of government guarantees in terms of banks' realized accounting returns and balance sheet growth rates conditional on not defaulting relative to the unconditional expectation of these accounting returns. Now take unconditional expectations in (14) and recall that $\text{FVE} = \overline{\text{DIV}}_E / (i - \bar{g})$. Under the assumption that either $\Theta_B = 0$ or $v_B = 1$, we obtain after rearranging that the unconditional expectation of the accounting ROE for a bank is given by

$$\overline{\text{ROE}} = i\left(\frac{\text{FVE}}{\text{BVE}}\right) - \bar{g}\left(\frac{\text{FVE} - \text{BVE}}{\text{BVE}}\right). \tag{18}$$

We can then write the market value of government guarantees by taking the difference between the market value and fair value of bank equity as

$$\frac{\text{MVG}}{\text{BVE}} = \frac{q(n)}{1 + i - q(n)(1 + g(n))}\left[(\text{ROE}(n) - g(n)) - (\overline{\text{ROE}} - \bar{g})\right]$$
$$- \left[1 - \frac{q(n)(i - \bar{g})}{1 + i - q(n)(1 + g(n))}\right]\frac{\text{FVE}}{\text{BVE}}. \tag{19}$$

This formula for the value of government guarantees is useful for understanding the source of the value of these guarantees. The value of these guarantees is broken into two components. The first component is represented by the term

$$\frac{q(n)}{1 + i - q(n)(1 + g(n))}\left[(\text{ROE}(n) - g(n)) - (\overline{\text{ROE}} - \bar{g})\right].$$

This term represents the expected discounted present value of the realized excess return (dividend) that the owners of the bank earn from risk taking until the first time that a crisis occurs. The second component is represented by the term

$$- \left[1 - \frac{q(n)(i - \bar{g})}{1 + i - q(n)(1 + g(n))}\right]\frac{\text{FVE}}{\text{BVE}}.$$

This term represents the expected discounted value of the loss that the owners of the bank will suffer when they default because they must give up their equity in the bank.

IV.   Calibrating Aggregate Credit Risk

Our findings regarding the value of government guarantees to bank equity require that banks be exposed to a risk that involves a small probability of a very negative outcome. We document that aggregate credit risk has this feature. Broad portfolios of corporate bonds experienced large negative realized excess returns in 2008. These portfolios earn relatively small realized excess returns from their exposure to this risk in normal times.[18]

We build on existing studies of bank risk exposure. Begenau, Piazzesi, and Schneider (2015) is an important study of banks' exposure to interest rate risk and credit risk. They estimate the size of banks' exposure to these risks in terms of factor portfolios. They find that banks increased their exposure to both interest rate risk and credit risk in advance of the financial crisis. Building on their study, we model bank exposure to credit risk directly in terms of the excess returns on portfolios of corporate bonds with different credit ratings financed with risk-free debt.[19] In our model, we abstract from the impact of interest rate risk on banks' profitability and valuation.[20] We discuss this assumption further in appendix B.

In this section, we rely on the insight from Subsection III.G that a bank's valuation ultimately depends on the bank's expected risk-neutral performance in two states: a crisis state in which the bank finds it optimal to default and a normal state in which the bank finds it optimal to repay. We use data on the total returns on portfolios of corporate bonds in excess of returns on similar maturity bonds without credit risk to calibrate the risk-neutral probabilities $q(c)$ of a crisis. Our calibration of the risk-neutral probability of the normal state $q(n)$ determines the trade-off investors face between exposure to negative realized excess returns in the crisis state c and reward in terms of positive realized excess returns in the normal state n.

Our calibration of the risk-neutral probabilities $q(s)$ is based on the asset pricing equation for excess returns on any two fairly priced assets:

$$q(n)(R(n) - R^f(n)) + (1 - q(n))(R(c) - R^f(c)) = 0. \qquad (20)$$

To focus on credit risk, we let $R(s)$ denote the realized returns on a portfolio of corporate bonds with a given credit rating below AAA, and we let $R^f(n)$ denote the realized returns on a portfolio of AAA-rated bonds.

We also use information from recent studies of the expected credit risk premium on investment-grade corporate bonds relative to similar duration Treasury bonds by Asvanunt and Richardson (2016) and Berndt et al. (2017). The expected risk premium on any asset relative to another asset is the expected value of the excess return under the physical probabilities $p(s)$. As long as realized excess returns on corporate bonds in the normal state are positive, estimates of expected risk premia on corporate bonds are a lower bound on the realized excess return on these bonds in the normal state. That is, under these assumptions we have the inequality

$$R(n) - R^f(n) \geq p(n)(R(n) - R^f(n)) + (1 - p(n))(R(c) - R^f(c)). \quad (21)$$

Corporate bonds are useful for studying the nature of aggregate credit risk as these bonds are traded, and hence their returns can easily be measured for different credit ratings. We measure the credit risk in corporate bonds using BAML Total Return Indices for portfolios of bonds of different credit ratings.[21] To measure credit risk, we examine the total returns on bonds rated AA, A, BBB, BB, B, and the BAML High Yield Total Return Index in excess of the total returns on bonds with a rating of AAA.[22] See table 1 for a presentation of these data.

The realized excess returns on the BAML portfolios for 2008 were increasingly negative as the rating of the bond portfolio declines, consistent with the hypothesis that bonds with a lower credit rating are more exposed to aggregate credit risk. For the most part, the realized excess returns on these bond portfolios in the noncrisis years of 1997–2007 and 2011–17 are increasing as the credit rating of the bond portfolio declines, consistent with the hypothesis that investors were compensated in normal times for exposure to this risk.

Table 1
Realized Annualized Excess Returns and Credit Risk Premium on Corporate Bonds

	AA	A	BBB	BB	B	HY
Returns BAML 2008, %	−5.00	−12.30	−15.76	−23.90	−32.73	−31.09
Returns BAML 1997–2007/2011–17, bp	−21	9	33	111	31	77
Premium BDDF 2002–15, bp	13	26	57	143	242	. . .
Premium AV 1988–2014, bp	. . .	50[a]	. . .	. . .	. . .	248
$R(n) - R^f(n)$ if $q(n) = .95$, bp	26	65	84	126	172	164

Note: BAML = Bank of America Merrill Lynch; bp = basis points; HY = high yield; AV = Asvanunt and Richardson (2016); BDDF = Berndt et al. (2017). The last line is calculated as $R(n) - R^f(n) = -(1 - q(n))/q(n) [R(c) - R^f(c)]$, where $R(c) - R^f(c)$ is the realized BAML excess return in 2008.
[a]bp for investment grade.

Next, consider the evidence on the expected credit risk premium, which, through equation (21), puts a lower bound on the realized excess returns on corporate bonds in normal times. In table 1, we present the expected credit risk premia estimated by Asvanunt and Richardson (2016) over the 1988–2014 time period and by Berndt et al. (2017) over the 2002–15 time period.[23]

To map these data to our model, we use the realized excess returns on these various portfolios as a measure of the realized excess return on a portfolio of assets with the credit risk in corporate bonds in the crisis state c, which we denote by $R(c) - i$.[24] Thus, given a choice of $q(n)$, our model implies a predicted realized excess return for each of these bond portfolios in normal times $R(n) - i$. In the last line of table 1, we present the model's predictions for these realized excess returns in the normal state under the hypothesis that the risk-neutral probability of the normal state is $q(n) = 0.95$.

Based on these observations, in what follows, we use a calibration of the risk-neutral probability of the normal state of $q(n) = 0.95$.

V.   Applying the Model to a Stylized Bank

We now use our model to study the implications of government guarantees for the market valuation of a stylized bank that has no franchise value because all of its assets and liabilities are simply marketable securities. We do so to make a simple quantitative illustration of the two comparative statics results that we considered in lemmas 2 and 3.

In particular, we first show that, in the presence of government guarantees, it is quantitatively plausible that observed variations in bank accounting profitability and market valuations in normal times can be accounted for by small changes in bank exposure to the aggregate credit risk in investment-grade corporate bonds. We demonstrate that a bank with government guarantees, plausible amounts of book equity, and assets with exposure to aggregate credit risk of BBB-rated corporate bonds can capture enough value from government guarantees to boost the ratio of the market-to-book value of its equity to 2.

We then use this stylized model to demonstrate the result in lemma 3: a reduction in book leverage can result in a substantial decline in the accounting profitability and market valuation of the bank, even if it implies that the bank is becoming safer in the sense that the market value of the government guarantees is getting smaller. Specifically, this exercise demonstrates that higher regulatory capital standards should be expected to significantly reduce the accounting profitability and valuation of a risk-taking bank.

Our stylized bank holds on its asset side a portfolio of marketable securities with exposure to the credit risk observed in corporate bonds with different credit ratings and finances its portfolio with wholesale deposits backed by a full government guarantee. Accordingly, because all of the bank's assets and liabilities are obtained through transactions in capital markets, we assume that the fair value of this bank's assets and liabilities is equal to the book value. That is, we assume that $v_L = v_D = 1$ and that there are no costs of originating new loans or deposits $\phi_L = \phi_D = 0$. The book leverage of the bank is Θ. Thus, the book value and the fair value of the bank's equity are given by $1 - \Theta$.

The assets of this stylized bank earn gross returns $1 + R(s)$ realized in state s. We assume that the bank reinvests to have its portfolio of assets and liabilities grow at rates $g(s)$. With these assumptions, the free cash flow of the bank is given by

$$\mathrm{DIV}_E(s) = (R(s) - i) + (1 - \Theta)(1 + i) - (1 + g(s))(1 - \Theta).$$

The accounting ROE for this stylized bank is given by

$$\mathrm{ROE}(s) = \frac{R(s) - \Theta i}{1 - \Theta}.$$

The market value of this bank is given by equation (6). The decision of bank equity to default $I(s)$ is governed by equation (7). With only two states, the ratio of the market value of equity to its book value is given by the maximum of the value given from equation (16) and the ratio of the fair-to-book value of equity (corresponding to no default). Hence, it is optimal for the bank to default in the crisis state if

$$\frac{q(n)}{1 + i - q(n)(1 + g(n))}[\mathrm{ROE}(n) - g(n)] > \frac{\mathrm{FVE}}{\mathrm{BVE}}. \tag{22}$$

For our stylized bank, the ratio FVE / BVE = 1.

A. Risk and Bank Valuation

We now examine the implications of our stylized model for the market valuation and accounting profitability of stylized banks that have different exposures to aggregate credit risk as indexed by their realized excess returns in the crisis state $R(c) - i$ and different levels of leverage Θ. We calibrate our stylized model to a risk-neutral probability of the normal state of $q(n) = 0.95$ and hence a risk-neutral probability of a crisis of $q(c) = 0.05$. We set the risk-free interest rate to $i = 5\%$ and the growth rate of the book balance sheet in normal times of $g(n) = 7.5\%$.[25]

To model banks with different exposures to aggregate credit risk, we consider four banks that differ in their realized excess returns in the crisis state. We calibrate these crisis excess returns to those observed for the different BAML bond portfolios in 2008 discussed above in table 1. We refer to these four banks with different risk profiles as the AA, A, BBB, and BB banks.

We now examine how the market valuation and accounting profitability of our four stylized banks vary with these banks' exposure to credit risk. We consider first a value for leverage in these banks of $\Theta = 0.90$.

With the parameters we have set, we show that the realized accounting ROEs for these banks in the normal state (ROE(n)) are rising sharply in bank exposure to credit risk (see the first row of table 2). Thus, we see that it is quite plausible that large differences in banks' observed accounting ROEs in normal times can be accounted for by differences in their exposure to the aggregate credit risk in investment-grade corporate bonds.

Which of these banks chooses to default in the crisis state? From equation (22), we have that the banks with A-, BBB-, and BB-rated assets would all choose to default in the crisis state. Only the safest bank, the bank with AA-rated assets, would choose not to default.

Now consider the implications of our model for the market valuation of these banks. The safest bank, the bank with AA-rated assets, does not default in the crisis state. Hence, the market value of its equity is equal to the fair value of its equity, which, in turn, is equal to the book value of its equity. Hence, it trades at a market-to-book value of 1.

To value the three riskier banks that choose to default in the crisis state, we use equation (16). From this equation, we have that the bank

Table 2
Profitability and Valuation of Stylized Banks by Rating of Bank Assets

	AA	A	BBB	BB
$\Theta = .90$:				
ROE(n), %	7.63	11.47	13.40	17.58
MVE / BVE	1	1.31	1.95	3.33
$\Theta = .85$:				
ROE(n), %	6.75	9.32	10.60	13.39
MVE / BVE	1	1	1.02	1.95

with A-rated assets trades at a market-to-book ratio of 1.31, the bank with BBB-rated assets at a ratio of 1.95, and the bank with BB-rated assets at a ratio of 3.33 (see the second row of table 2.) Thus, we see that the market valuation of these banks rises sharply with their exposure to aggregate credit risk. Moreover, our stylized bank can attain a market-to-book ratio close to 2 simply from exposure to the aggregate credit risk in BBB bonds.

The results in table 2 from this simple numerical exercise make clear the quantitative implications of lemma 2. Specifically, we see that, in the presence of government guarantees, it is entirely plausible that large changes in banks' accounting profitability and market valuations can be accounted for by small changes in banks' exposure to the aggregate credit risk in investment-grade corporate bonds.

B.   Equity Capital, Bank Accounting Profits, and Valuation

We now illustrate the comparative statics exercise in lemma 3. Specifically, we now consider the accounting profitability and valuation of our stylized banks with a value for leverage in these banks of $\Theta = 0.85$. Results are reported in the lower half of table 2.

The realized accounting ROEs for these banks in the normal state ($\text{ROE}(n)$) are substantially reduced relative to the example above with lower equity capital (cf. first and third rows of table 2.)

Which of these banks chooses to default in the crisis state? From equation (22), we have that now only the two riskiest banks, the banks with BBB and BB assets, would choose to default in the crisis state. The banks with AA and A assets would not choose to default in the crisis state.

This reduction in banks' book leverage has a striking impact on their market valuations (cf. second and fourth rows of table 2.) Now, the banks with AA- and A-rated assets both trade at a market-to-book ratio of 1. The BBB bank now trades at a market-to-book ratio of only 1.02 instead of 1.95. Although this bank continues to default in the crisis state (and hence with the same probability), with lower leverage, the equity of this bank derives much less value from the government guarantees.

The results in table 2 from this second simple numerical exercise highlight the quantitative implications of lemma 3, that is, the prediction of our model that an increase in bank capital following a crisis should be expected to substantially reduce bank market valuations and accounting profitability relative to what was observed prior to that crisis.

C. Risk Taking and Accounting Profitability

As shown in table 2, the accounting profitability of our stylized bank rises in the risk exposure of its assets.[26] We can use the benchmark for accounting profitability in equation (18) to decompose the accounting profitability of banks observed in normal times into a component that is due to exposure to aggregate risk $\text{ROE}(n) - \overline{\text{ROE}}$ and a component that is due to the fair value of bank equity $\overline{\text{ROE}}$.

For our stylized banks in which FVE = BVE, we have $\overline{\text{ROE}} = i$, which we calibrate to $i = 5\%$. For each of our stylized banks, we see that they show accounting profitability in normal times in excess of this benchmark, with this gap increasing as the credit quality of the bank's assets is reduced. Note that this excess accounting profitability for the BBB bank with book leverage of $\Theta = 0.9$ is 840 bp. When book leverage is reduced to $\Theta = 0.85$, this excess profitability is reduced to 560 bp. The risk-neutral expectation of the bank's accounting profitability, however, is unchanged at $\overline{\text{ROE}}$ regardless of risk taking. A bank that takes risks succeeds at raising its accounting profitability in normal times at the expense of reducing its profitability in the crisis state. From equation (19) and our quantitative results, we see how this impact of risk taking on accounting profitability translates into higher valuations of government guarantees.

VI. Accounting for the Valuation of US Banks

In this section, we use our model to provide a full accounting of the evolution of the market valuation of banks for three time periods: 1970–85, 1996–2007, and 2011–17. We choose these time periods to correspond to "normal" states as opposed to crisis states. We omit the time period between 1986 and 1995 because this was a period of rapid change in the regulatory environment and business models for banking and of substantial volatility in bank earnings and valuations. We omit the years 2008–10 as these correspond to a crisis period in banking. Table 3 summarizes all the parameters and results of this section. Our accounting proceeds in two steps.

In the first step, we construct a measure of the fair value of bank equity, using data on the book value of items on banks' balance sheets together with data reported in the footnotes of banks' annual reports and results from the Portfolio Value Model created by the OTS. We do so using equations (3), (4), and (11). The inputs required here are the values of

Table 3
Calibration and Results

	1970:1–1985:12	1996:1–2007:12	2011:1–2017:12	Name	Source
Calibration:					
Θ, %	93.86	91.80	88.87	Leverage	FR Y-9C Reports 1-RC28/RC12
$\Theta_B v_B$, %	.41	1.33	.74	Subordinated debt	FR Y-9C Reports RC19/RC12
i, %	10.79	4.81	1.34	Risk-free rate	5-year Treasury yield
$g(n)$, %	10.0	7.5	2.4	Expected growth of balance sheet	
v_L	1	1.009	1.002	Fair-to-book value of loans	Annual reports
v_D	1	.978	.99	Fair-to-book value of deposits	OTS estimates
$ROA(n)$, %	.717	1.22	.825	Return of assets in s^n	FRY-9C Reports RI14/A
Results:					
MVE / BVE	1	2.24	1.19	Market-to-book value of equity	Accounting model
[FVE – BVE] / BVE	0	.33	.10	Franchise value/book equity	Accounting model
[MVE – FVE] / BVE	0	.91	.09	Value of government guarantees/book equity	Accounting model
$\overline{ROE}$, %	10.79	5.80	1.64	Return on equity with no asset risk	Accounting model
$ROE(n) - \overline{ROE}$, bp	89	908	577	Excess returns in normal times	Accounting model

the ratio of the fair-to-book value of loans v_L, the ratio of the fair-to-book value of deposits v_D, and an assumption regarding the value of growth opportunities in loan making, $FVL - v_L$, and deposit taking, $FVD - v_D$. This first step gives us a measure of the ratio of the franchise value of banks relative to the book value of bank equity implied by (FVE – BVE) / BVE.

In the second step, we construct a measure of the model's implications for the market value of bank equity. This measure is the maximum of the fair value of bank equity and the market value of bank equity conditional on equity defaulting in the crisis state from equation (16).[27] The inputs required here are measures of the risk-free interest rate i, a measure of the growth rate of the bank balance sheet in normal times $g(n)$, a measure of the bank's free cash flow to equity in the normal state $DIV_E(n)$ given observed accounting profitability, and our calibration of the risk-neutral probability of the normal state $q(n) = 0.95$. Hence, this second step gives us a measure of the ratio of the market value of government guarantees to the fair value of bank equity implied by (MVE − FVE) / BVE.

A. First Step: Fair Value of Equity

Measurement of Franchise Value in Banking

From equation (11), the fair value of bank equity, and hence the franchise value of the bank, is determined by the fair value of the current stock of bank loans relative to its book value v_L, the fair value of the current stock of deposits relative to its book value v_D, the leverage of the bank Θ_D, and the value of the bank's opportunities to originate new loans and deposits. Note that the subordinated debt of the bank is recorded on the balance sheet at its market price, so we are able to read $\Theta_B v_B$ off bank balance sheets.

To measure v_L, our paper relies on banks' estimates of the fair value of their loans presented in the footnotes to the financial statements in their annual reports.[28] To measure v_D, we rely on estimates of the fair value of bank deposits from a model developed by the OTS. We assume that banking is competitive in the sense that loan and deposit origination is a zero net present value activity, that is, $\phi_L = (v_L - 1)$ and $\phi_D = (1 - v_D)$. This implies that the gap between the fair value and the book value of bank equity relative to the book value of bank assets is given by $(v_L - 1) - \Theta_D(1 - v_D)$.

The methods that banks and the OTS use to estimate the fair value of loans and deposits are related to the internal cost-accounting models banks develop to evaluate the risk versus the profitability of their lending and deposit-taking units. This methodology is commonly referred to as "funds transfer pricing."[29] This methodology is also related to the methodology that the Bureau of Economic Analysis uses when it measures value added in banking. In particular, the Bureau of Economic Analysis methodology attributes a portion of banks' net interest income to implicit charges for service provision, which they refer to as "financial intermediation services implicitly measured."[30]

Loan Fair Values

First consider our data on the fair value of bank loans. Banks have been required since the mid-1990s to report an estimate of the fair value of their loans in the footnotes to their annual reports. We collected data from the footnotes in bank annual reports on the fair and book values of bank loan portfolios for the period 1995–2016 for 19 large bank holding companies.[31] We compute a ratio of the fair-to-book value of loans for the banking sector by taking the sum of loan fair values across these banks divided by the sum of loan book values. The resulting ratios from these data are shown in figure 10. In normal times, these ratios range between 1.00 and 1.02. Thus, consistent with the finding of Begenau and Stafford (2018) that bank assets have not substantially outperformed passive portfolios of securities, we find that according to bank models of loan fair values, the gap between loan fair values and book values is small.

The coefficient v_L in our model refers to the ratio of the fair value to book value of all bank assets. To obtain an estimate of v_L to be used in our model, we must convert the figure for the ratio of the fair-to-book value of bank loans to a fair-to-book value of all bank assets. We do

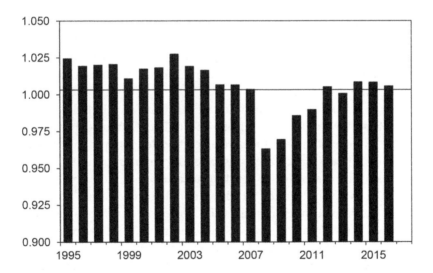

Fig. 10. Fair-to-book value of loans. The ratio is computed as the sum of the fair value of loans across bank holding companies divided by the sum of the book value of loans across bank holding companies. Observations of fair value of loans come from notes in the annual reports of bank holding companies. See, for example, note 22, "Fair Value of Financial Instruments," on page 208 of the Bank of America (2017) 2016 annual report. We collected observations for Bank of America, Citigroup, JPMorgan Chase, Wells Fargo, American International Group, MetLife, American Express, Huntington Bancshares, Fifth Third Bank, Washington Mutual, SunTrust Banks, Regions Financial Corporation, PNC Financial Services, National City Corporation, Zions Bancorporation, Countrywide Financial, Comerica, KeyCorp, and US Bancorp.

so as follows. We treat all earning bank assets that are not loans as having fair values equal to book values.[32] We also treat all nonearning bank assets as having fair values equal to book values.[33] If we denote the ratio of fair-to-book value of bank loans taken from bank annual reports by $\tilde{v}_L$ and the ratio of bank loans in the data to total assets in the data by $\tilde{L}$, these assumptions give us that v_L in our model is given by

$$v_L = 1 + (\tilde{v}_L - 1)\tilde{L}.$$

We report the implied values of v_L in table 3. We do not have data for the 1970–85 time period. We set $v_L = 1$ for this time period.

Deposit Fair Values

Now consider our data for the fair value of bank deposits. Banks do not report on the fair value of their deposits. Instead, we rely on estimates of the fair value of deposits constructed by the OTS in its Portfolio Value Model.[34] Their estimate of the ratio of the fair-to-book value of deposits (which they refer to as the intangible value of deposits) is an estimate of the interest savings to the bank that arise if current depositors leave their funds in their demand accounts or roll over their funds in time deposits at rates below prevailing wholesale interest rates (or a combination of both).

The OTS published estimates of the fair value of selected assets and liabilities on a quarterly basis from 1997 to 2011.[35] We use the OTS estimates of the intangible value of retail certificates of deposit, transaction accounts, money market accounts, passbook savings accounts, and non-interest-bearing accounts to construct an estimate of the fair value of deposits in banks in the data, which we denote by $\tilde{v}_D$.[36]

We check the results from the OTS Portfolio Value Model for the intangible value of deposits against accounting data on the core deposit intangibles that banks record when one bank purchases another bank. Davis (2017) charts three reports on average core deposit intangibles recorded from whole bank transactions from 2000 to 2017. Core deposit intangibles range from 2.5% to 3% in the early 2000s and have fallen to roughly 1% since the crisis. These estimates imply a large drop in the gap between the book value and fair value of deposit liabilities across these two time periods. This finding is consistent with the discussion in Fine and Rohde (2013).

As with loans, the concept of v_D in our model corresponds to the ratio of the fair value to book value of all bank liabilities. In addition to depos-

its, bank liabilities include fed funds purchased, repo, and trading liabilities.[37] We assume that these liabilities are all carried on the books at fair
value. Hence, if $\tilde{D}$ denotes the ratio of deposits to total assets in the data,
our model concept of v_D is given by

$$v_D = 1 - (1 - \tilde{v}_D)\frac{\tilde{D}}{\Theta},$$

where $\tilde{D}/\Theta$ is the ratio of deposits to total liabilities in the data.

We report the implied values of v_D in table 3. Again, we do not have
data for the 1970–85 time period. We set $v_D = 1$ for this time period. We
find significant gaps between the fair and book values of bank deposits,
particularly during the 1996–2007 time period.[38]

Bank Leverage

The sources we use to measure bank leverage Θ (and accounting profitability and growth of assets) are as follows. For the 1970–85 time period, we use data from the FDIC's (2019b) historical statistics on banking. This source provides data on bank income statements and balance
sheets on an annual basis from 1934 through 2017. For the 1996–2007 and
2011–17 time periods, we use data on bank holding companies from the
Federal Reserve Bank of New York's (2019) report "Quarterly Trends for
Consolidated US Banking Organizations." This source provides quarterly data on bank holding company income statements and balance
sheets on a quarterly basis from 1991 through 2017Q3. The values of the
ratio of the fair value of bank subordinated debt to total assets ($\Theta_B v_B$) for
these three time periods are from line 19 from Schedule HC on the bank
holding company FR Y-9C reports. These data are presented in the top
panel of table 3.

Results on Bank Franchise Values

Bank franchise parameters give us the following results for the ratio of
the fair value of bank equity to the book value of bank equity presented
in the bottom panel of table 3. We estimate that the ratio of the fair value
of bank equity relative to the book value of bank equity was 1.33 for
bank holding companies in the 1996–2007 time period and 1.10 for bank
holding companies in the 2011–17 time period. Thus, our estimates imply that bank franchise values have fallen considerably relative to bank
book equity—from 33% in 1996–2007 to 10% in 2011–17.

B.   Second Step: Market Value of Equity

We now turn to the second step of our accounting, that of measuring the model's implications for the market value of bank equity. For this step, from equation (16) we require measures of the following parameters: $q(n), i, g(n)$, and ROE(n). These parameters are presented in the top panel of table 3, where we compute $\text{ROE}(n) = \text{ROA}(n) / (1 - \Theta)$.

We use our calibration of the risk-neutral probability of the normal state of $q(n) = 0.95$ for all time periods that we consider.

To calibrate the level of the riskless interest rate i for each of our three normal time periods, we consider the constant maturity yield on 5-year Treasury securities as reported in the top panel of table 3. To calibrate the growth rate of assets in the normal state $g(n)$, we examine the average of the growth rate of bank total assets in the time periods under consideration. We use values of the growth rate of banks in normal times g (n) of 10.0% for 1970–85, 7.5% for 1996–2007, and 2.4% for 2011–17.

To compute equity dividends in normal times $\text{DIV}_E(n)$, we use

$$\text{DIV}_E(n) = \text{ROA}(n) - (1 - v_B)\Theta_B - g(n)\text{BVE}.$$

To estimate the market price of subordinated debt v_B, we use data on banks' bond spreads as described in Section II. We have that $v_B = (1 + i)/(1 + y)$ where y is the yield on subordinated debt. We calibrate the spreads on bank-subordinated debt $y_B - i$ to 93 bp for 1996–2007 and 147 bp for 2011–17. We do not have data for the 1970–85 time period. We use a spread of 100 bp for this time period. This calibration implies values of v_B equal to 0.991 for 1970–85 and 1996–2007 and 0.986 for 2011–17. Using these data, we have implied values of Θ_B.

C.   Results

Our results are presented in the bottom panel of table 3.

Our model predicts that during the 1970–85 time period, banks would not choose to default in the crisis state, and hence they derived no value from government guarantees. This implies that the market-to-book ratio of banks during this time period should equal the ratio of the fair value to book value of equity and that government guarantees did not add to the market value of bank equity.

Our model predicts that during the 1996–2007 time period, banks would choose to default in the crisis state and that the model-implied ratio of market-to-book value of equity was 2.24. This value is quite close to the observed average value in the data of 2.12. As a result, we argue that our model can account for observed bank valuations during the 1996–2007 time period. Because the predicted ratio of the fair-to-book value of equity during this time period was only 1.33, our model implies that banks derived a substantial portion of their market value of equity from government guarantees (roughly 91% of their book value of equity).

Our model predicts that during the 2011–17 time period, banks would choose to default in the crisis state and that the model-implied ratio of market-to-book value of equity was 1.19. This figure is close to the model's predictions for the ratios of the fair-to-book value of bank equity of 1.10 discussed above. Hence, our model predicts that banks currently do not derive much of their market value from government guarantees. Our model actually overpredicts the ratio of the market-to-book value of bank equity relative to the data. In the data, this figure averages 0.98 over this time period.

What forces drive our finding that the market value of government guarantees was large relative to the book value of bank equity in the period 1996–2007 but not in the other two time periods? The forces that we focus on here are changes in the book value of bank leverage and the risk in bank assets.

We have seen that the book value of bank leverage has declined steadily across the three time periods that we study. This finding raises the question of why the market value of government guarantees was not high in the 1970–85 time period.

The answer lies in the amount of aggregate risk in bank assets. To derive this answer, we use equation (18) to measure the excess accounting ROE of banks in normal times for these three time periods.[39] We find a value of $ROE(n) - \overline{ROE}$ of only 89 bp in the 1970–85 time period. This excess accounting return to equity contrasts sharply with the value of 908 bp in the 1996–2007 time period and the value of 577 bp for the 2011–17 time period. Based on this evidence, we argue that risk taking by banks in terms of the exposure in bank assets rose sharply from the 1970–85 time period to the 1990s and beyond. This evidence suggests that the risk in bank assets has declined only modestly since the crisis of 2008.[40]

VII. Conclusion

In this paper, we have shown that a large part of the evolution of bank valuations from 1970 to the present can be explained by changes in the value of government guarantees. By increasing leverage and exposure to losses in credit crisis states, bankers increase the capitalized value of government guarantees. We show that changes in the capitalized value of these guarantees, driven mainly by changes in bank leverage, risk taking, and the growth rate of banks' balance sheets, have been at least as important as banks' true franchise values in determining the value of US banks over time.

Our paper has important implications for bank regulation. Indeed, we show that very small changes in banks' exposure to aggregate credit risk, as well as small changes in bank leverage, have very large effects on taxpayers' liability to bail out banks in a crisis. Currently, bank book leverage is lower than precrisis levels. The larger bank equity cushion has reduced the value of taxpayers' liability to bail out banks in a crisis. However, data on bank profitability and market measures of bank credit risk indicate that banks have not substantially reduced their exposure to aggregate risk. As a result, current data suggest that bank equity and subordinated debt would again be wiped out in a credit crisis of the magnitude of 2008.

To conclude, our accounting model suggests that moves to lighten the regulatory burden on banks going forward may lead to substantially greater bank risk exposure. The value of government guarantees to bank equity is highly sensitive to small changes in the risk exposure of bank assets. If regulators allow even a moderate increase in risk taking by banks, we should see a significant jump in bank valuations and accounting profitability. The temptation will be to interpret this increase in bank valuations and accounting profitability as a restoration of bank franchise value previously damaged by regulation. Instead, we argue that it would properly be interpreted as a return to the days in which taxpayers had a large contingent liability to bail out banks in a crisis.

Appendix A

Omitted Proofs

A.1. Proof of Lemma 1

It is clear from the Bellman equations that a decrease in profitability decreases both market and fair value of bank equity. Because $BVE = 1 - \Theta$ is not affected by profitability, it follows that both MVE / BVE and FVE / BVE decrease. To sign the net impact on market value of all the payments made by the government, recall the Bellman equation for fair value of bank equity:

$$FVE = \frac{1}{1+i} \hat{\mathbb{E}}[DIV'_E + (1+g')FVE].$$

Subtract this Bellman equation for fair value of bank equity from the Bellman equation for market value of bank equity, (24).

MVE − FVE

$$= \frac{1}{1+i} \hat{\mathbb{E}}[\max\{-DIV'_E - (1+g')FVE, (1+g')(MVE - FVE)\}]$$

$$= \frac{1+\bar{g}}{1+i} (MVE - FVE)$$

$$+ \frac{1}{1+i} \hat{\mathbb{E}}[\max\{-DIV'_E - (1+g')FVE - (1+g')(MVE - FVE), 0\}].$$

Let $\rho \equiv (MVE - FVE) / BVE$ and recall that $BVE = 1 - \Theta$ and that $FVE = \overline{DIV}_E/(i - \bar{g})$. Dividing through both sides by $1 - \Theta$ and rearranging, we obtain

$$\rho(i - \bar{g}) = \hat{\mathbb{E}}\left[\max\left\{-\frac{DIV'_E + (1+g')\frac{\overline{DIV}_E}{i-\bar{g}}}{1-\Theta} - (1+g')\rho, 0\right\}\right]. \quad (23)$$

The left-hand side is strictly increasing in ρ and the right-hand side is weakly decreasing. It is clear that any parameter that decreases dividends in all states, besides growth and leverage, increases the right-hand side. This implies that following any change in parameter that decreases dividends in all states, besides growth and leverage, ρ must increase.

A.2. Proof of Lemma 2

Recall the equation for MVE:

$$MVE = \frac{1}{1+i} \hat{\mathbb{E}}[\max\{0, DIV'_E + (1+g')MVE\}]. \quad (24)$$

Subtract $(1 + \bar{g})/(1 + i)MVE/BVE$ from both sides to obtain

$$(i - \bar{g})MVE = \hat{\mathbb{E}}[\max\{-(1+g')MVE, DIV'_E\}].$$

The left-hand side is strictly increasing in MVE, is equal to zero when MVE = 0, and goes to infinity as MVE → ∞. The right-hand side is decreasing and positive. Hence, there exists a unique solution.

By definition, an increase in risk taking keeps $\bar{g}$ the same, so it leaves the left-hand side the same. It is easy to see that it increases the right-hand side. Indeed, rewrite the right-hand side as

$$-(1 + \bar{g})\text{MVE} + \hat{\mathbb{E}}[\max\{0, \text{DIV}'_E + (1 + g')\text{MVE}\}]$$

$$= -(1 + \bar{g})\text{MVE} + \hat{\mathbb{E}}\left[\max\left\{0, a + \sum_{n=1}^{N} k_n \sigma_n \varepsilon'_n\right\}\right]$$

for some coefficients a and k_n because the dividend is an affine function of shocks and the shocks are affine functions of the εs. Now it is easy to see that, for any mean 0 random variable, the function $\sigma \mapsto \mathbb{E}[\max\{0, a + b\sigma\varepsilon\}]$ is increasing in σ, so the result follows.

A.3. Proof of Lemma 3

Start from the right-hand side of (23). Let

$$N(\Theta) \equiv \text{DIV}'_E + (1 + g')\frac{\overline{\text{DIV}_E}}{i - \bar{g}}.$$

It is clear from the expression of DIV'_E that $N(\Theta)$ is decreasing in Θ and that $N(\Theta) < 0$ whenever the right-hand side of the Bellman equation (23) is positive. Therefore:

$$-\frac{\partial}{\partial \Theta}\left(\frac{N(\Theta)}{1 - \Theta}\right) = -\frac{\partial N(\Theta)/\partial \Theta}{1 - \Theta} - \frac{N(\Theta)}{(1 - \Theta)^2} > 0$$

whenever the right-hand side of the Bellman equation (23) is positive. This implies that a decrease in Θ decreases ρ.

A.4. Proof of Lemma 4

We have

$$\text{DIV}'_E + (1 + g')\text{MVE} = \text{DIV}'_L - \Theta_D\text{DIV}'_D - (1 + i)\Theta_B + v_B(1 + g')\Theta_B$$

$$= c_L + \mu'_L - (1 + \phi_L)(\mu'_L + \delta'_L + g')$$

$$- \delta_D[c_D + \mu'_D - (1 - \phi_D)(\mu'_D + g')]$$

$$- (1 + i)\Theta_B + v_B(1 + g')\Theta_B + (1 + g')\text{MVE}.$$

Clearly, the partial derivative with respect to δ_L' is strictly negative, the partial derivative with respect to μ_L' is strictly negative if $\phi_L > 0$, and the partial derivative with respect to μ_D is strictly negative if $\phi_D > 0$.

The partial derivative with respect to g' is equal to

$$-(1 + \phi_L) + \Theta_D(1 - \phi_D) + v_B\Theta_B + \text{MVE}.$$

Now use that $\text{MVE} \geq \text{FVE} = \text{FVL} - \Theta_D\text{FVD} - \Theta_B v_B$ to obtain that the partial derivative with respect to g' is greater than

$$\text{FVL} - (1 + \phi_L) + \Theta_D(1 - \phi_D - \text{FVD}) \geq 0,$$

because $\text{FVL} \geq v_L \geq 1 + \phi_L$, and $\text{FVD} \leq v_D \leq 1 - \phi_D$. Hence, the partial derivative is positive. Clearly, the partial derivative is strictly positive if $\text{MVE} > \text{FVE}$, $v_L > 1 + \phi_L$, or $v_D < 1 - \phi_D$.

Appendix B

Frequently Asked Questions

Here we address several questions that have been asked about our modeling and measurement of the fair value of banks and of the value of government guarantees for banks. These questions are as follows.

1. In our measurement of the franchise value of banks, we have focused on measuring the gap between the fair value and book value of banks' loans and deposits. Would consideration of the gap between the fair value and book value of the other assets and liabilities on banks' balance sheets have a substantial impact on our measurement of banks' franchise value?

2. In our measurement of the franchise value of banks, we have assumed that bank equity does not derive value from banks' noninterest income other than service charges on deposits. Noninterest income has grown considerably as a portion of banks' operating income over the past several decades. Would consideration of the contribution of noninterest income to dividends to bank equity substantially affect our measurement of bank franchise value?

3. In our model of the value of government guarantees for stylized banks, we have focused on aggregate credit risk and abstracted from the role of interest rate risk. How would consideration of interest rate risk affect our measurement of the value of government guarantees?

4. In our model of the value of government guarantees for banks, we have assumed that banks' opportunity to grow their balance sheets con-

tributes to the value of these guarantees. What justification do we have for this assumption? Why is it that competition between banks does not eliminate the value of this growth opportunity?

5. In our valuation model for banks, we use a discrete time model and consider each time period to be 1 year. Hence, we have implicitly assumed that banks are required to meet capital standards only once per year (at the beginning of each time period) and that the risks to bank assets and liabilities over a 1-year horizon is the relevant horizon for measuring bank risks. How should one interpret this assumption? And what impact would it have to use a longer or shorter time period in our analysis?

6. How do results from our model of the value of government guarantees compare to other estimates in the literature?

We address each of these questions in the subsections below.

Question 1: A Full Accounting for Fair Value of the Balance Sheet

In our measurement of the franchise value of banks, we have focused on measuring the gap between the fair value and book value of banks' loans and deposits. Would consideration of the gap between the fair value and book value of the other assets and liabilities on banks' balance sheets have a substantial impact on our measurement of banks' franchise value?

Based on work by Nissim and Penman (2007) and Calomiris and Nissim (2014), we argue that the answer to this question is no.

As described by Calomiris and Nissim (2014), banks have been required to report their own estimates of the fair value of their financial assets and liabilities in the footnotes to their annual reports for several decades now. Specifically, these authors report that "the measurement of the disclosed fair value of equity is made possible by an accounting change in 1992. Since 1992 on an annual basis, and since Q2:2009 on a quarterly basis, companies are required to disclose the estimated fair value of their financial assets and liabilities as of the balance sheet date. These disclosures are quite comprehensive. They include essentially all loans, securities, debts payable, time deposits, derivatives, and most other financial instruments" (406). In figure 2 of their paper, they plot the mean and median of the ratio of the disclosed fair value to disclosed book value of equity for the bank holding companies in their sample from the end of 2000 through mid-2013. As is evident in this figure, the ratio of disclosed fair value to disclosed book value of equity is very stable over time and very close to 1. These results indicate that banks' estimates of the fair value of items on their balance sheets are very close to the book value of these items.

Note that these disclosed estimates of the fair value of bank assets and liabilities do not include estimates of the fair value of deposits with no defined maturity (demand deposits). This is why we have focused on estimating the ratio of the fair value to book value of these deposits using alternative data from the Office of Thrift Supervision Portfolio Value Model and from estimates of core deposit intangibles from bank transactions.

Nissim and Penman (2007) provide a comprehensive discussion of the gap between the fair and book values of all of the items on banks' balance sheets. Using data from before the crisis, they report,

On average, 36% of banks' reported assets (cash and balances due, federal funds sold, securities purchased under resell agreements, available-for-sale securities, and trading assets) and 16% of their liabilities (federal funds purchased, securities sold under repurchase agreements, and trading liabilities) were reported on the balance sheet at or close to fair value. Another 52% of assets (loans, held-to-maturity securities, and other financial assets) and 34% of liabilities (time deposits and debt) were subject to Statement of Financial Accounting Standard (SFAS) 107 and SFAS 115 fair value disclosure requirements. Thus, for approximately 88% of BHCs' [bank holding companies'] reported assets and 50% of their liabilities, fair value estimates were generally available during the sample period. (6)

They further conclude that the difference between the fair and book values of existing assets is likely of "secondary importance."

Question 2: Noninterest Income and Bank Value

In our measurement of the franchise value of banks, we have assumed that bank equity does not derive significant value from banks' noninterest income other than service charges on deposits.[41] Noninterest income has grown considerably as a portion of banks' operating income over the past several decades. This has been especially true for the largest banks. Here we consider the question of whether the contribution of noninterest income to dividends to bank equity substantially affect our measurement of bank franchise value.

On the basis of cross-sectional data on overall bank accounting profitability and bank equity valuations, we argue that it is unlikely that bank equity derives significant value from activities that generate noninterest income other than service charges on deposits. This is because, although noninterest income has become relatively more important for larger banks, there does not appear to be significant systematic variation across banks of different size in accounting profitability and equity valuation.

The main categories of bank holding company noninterest income are as follows: service charges on deposits; income from fiduciary activities; fees and commissions from securities brokerage; investment banking, advisory, and underwriting fees and commissions; fees and commissions from annuity sales; underwriting income from insurance and reinsurance activities; income from other insurance activities; venture capital revenue; net servicing fees; net securitization income; and trading revenue. The main sources of noninterest expense are expenses for salaries and employee benefits, premises, and intermediate inputs.

Copeland (2012) analyzes the evolution of noninterest income for bank holding companies of different sizes over the period 1994–2010. He finds that the most dramatic growth of nontraditional sources of noninterest income has occurred for the largest bank holding companies, whereas smaller bank holding companies have not seen much of a change in the size and sources of their noninterest income. In figure B1 we show the change in importance of noninterest income in bank net operating revenue by bank size over the period 1991 to the present as reported in the Federal Reserve Bank of New York's (2019) "Quarterly Trends for Consolidated US Banking Organizations." These data clearly

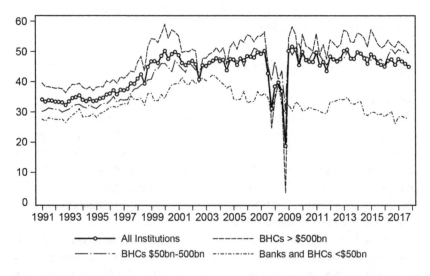

Fig. B1. Noninterest income share by bank size. Noninterest income as a percentage of net operating revenue. Net operating revenue is defined as the sum of net interest income and noninterest income (Federal Reserve Bank of New York 2017).

show that noninterest income is more important for larger bank holding companies and that this has been increasingly true over time.

We argue that bank equity does not derive significant value from
banks' noninterest income other than service charges on deposits based
on two cross-sectional observations regarding bank accounting overall
profitability and equity valuations. Each of these observations in cross-
sectional data indicates that larger banks are neither more profitable nor
more highly valued than medium-sized banks. Thus, it appears that the
advantage large banks have in generating noninterest income does not
translate into an advantage in terms of overall profitability or valuation.

First, we consider data from the Federal Reserve Bank of New York's
(2019) "Quarterly Trends for Consolidated US Banking Organizations"
report on bank holding companies' accounting ROE by bank size over
the time period 1991 to the present. As shown in figure B2, over the time
period 1991 to the present, banks' accounting ROE does not show significant variation across bank size categories. In particular, the time series
variation in this measure of accounting profitability is substantially larger
than the cross-sectional variation at a point in time.[42]

Next we consider data on the valuation of banks by bank size. Figure 3
shows measures of the ratio of the market-to-book value of equity by
bank size for the period 1991 to the present. Here again, we see that
the variation in the ratio of the market-to-book value of equity over time
is substantially larger than the variation of this ratio in the cross-section

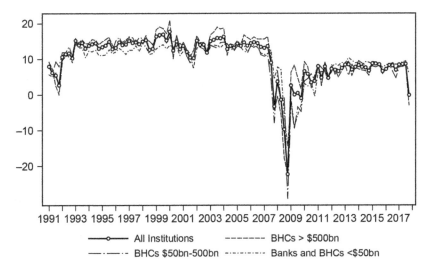

Fig. B2. Return on equity by BHC size (Federal Reserve Bank of New York 2017)

at a point in time. Minton et al. (2017) conduct a more thorough study of the relationship between bank size and bank valuation and arrive at the conclusion that there is strong cross-sectional evidence that the valuation of large banks falls with size (as is evident in our fig. 3). Moreover, they find that banks with more trading assets are worth less than banks with fewer trading assets.

Question 3: Interest Rate Risk

In our model of the value of government guarantees, we have assumed that the risks that banks face are independent and identically distributed (i.i.d.) over time. With this stark modeling assumption, we can derive very simple formulas for the value of government guarantees based on a few parameters. We see this simplicity as the main advantage of our modeling framework.

One cost of this assumption is that we are unable to account explicitly for interest rate risk. This is because our assumption forces us to keep the risk-free interest rate i constant over time. Hence, the term structure of interest rates in our model is always constant at all maturities. Clearly, the interest rate risk associated with banks' maturity transformation and interest rate derivatives is an important risk to bank asset values. What is the impact of this omission of interest rate risk on our valuation exercise?

We conjecture that one could capture the impact of interest rate risk and other risks on the value of government guarantees in our model in a reduced-form manner as follows. As shown in equation (16), in our model, the market value of bank equity is determined by a handful of parameters. These are the risk free rate i, the expected growth rate of the bank conditional on not defaulting $g(n)$, the risk-neutral probability of bank failure $1 - q(n)$, and the bank's ROE conditional on not defaulting $ROE(n)$. To derive these parameters from an underlying model, one must choose a state space S and associated risk-neutral probabilities $q(s)$ and then directly specify the excess returns on the bank's portfolio of assets $R(s) - i$ together with the growth rates of the bank's portfolio $g(s)$. These choices imply bank dividends to equity $DIV_E(s)$ as a function of the state. One would then solve equation (6) for the default decision. As shown in equations (16) and (17), the valuation of bank equity and government guarantees then reduces to the same two-state version of our model studied in Sections V and VI.

To summarize, the reduced-form risks that determine bank default and valuation in our model are the risks to bank dividends $DIV_E(s)$ and to the growth of the bank $g(s)$. As discussed in lemma 2, the model can accommodate a wide array of underlying fundamental risks. As discussed in Section V, we can also model these fundamental risks directly in terms of realized excess returns on the banks' portfolio of assets.

Begenau et al. (2015) is an important study of the joint distribution of interest rate and credit risk faced by banks. Future work should incorporate results from their model of the returns banks obtain from exposure to these risks to improve the computation of the implied value of government guarantees.

Question 4: Government Guarantees and the Value of Growing a Bank

In our model of the value of government guarantees for banks, we have assumed that banks' opportunity to grow their balance sheets contributes to the value of these guarantees. That is, we assume that (i) the government guarantee is a regulatory rent, (ii) the value of which accrues to the owners of bank liabilities (insured debt and equity), and that (iii) bankers can expand the value of this rent by growing their bank.[43] What justification can we provide for these assumptions?

It is widely observed that the federal safety net for banking is a regulatory rent for this sector. The Federal Reserve System, in its role as primary regulator of bank holding companies, recognizes the nature of the apparent profit opportunity of setting up or expanding a bank holding company to take advantage of government guarantees and imposes restrictions on bank holding companies as a result (see also Kane 2014).[44]

Our second assumption is perhaps more controversial. Why do the owners of incumbent banks capture the value of these rents? Why doesn't competition for these rents dissipate these rents?[45]

We conjecture that the answer to this question is based on the observation that entry into banking and growth of incumbent banks are constricted through a somewhat opaque exercise of regulatory discretion by bank supervisors. This discretion is based on both the Bank Holding Company Act and its subsequent modifications and through the direct supervision of bank subsidiaries.[46] Thus, it is reasonable to expect that the owners of an incumbent bank with permission to issue government-backed liabilities would enjoy a quasi-rent from government guarantees earned as compensation for past expenditures on rent seeking to gain permission to establish an incumbent bank under the federal safety net. This is one classic definition of the *charter value* of a bank.

Our third assumption is the most controversial. Why would owners of incumbent banks in the early 1990s capture value from the opportunity to grow their bank rapidly over the next two decades under a vastly expanded federal safety net? Why did increased competition following deregulation fail to dissipate the rents associated with this growth opportunity? We conjecture that a full answer to this question would be based on the observation that most of these rents from this growth opportunity were offered to and captured by incumbents who grew dramatically larger to take advantage of the specific benefits offered to banks that could achieve the scale needed to be labeled "too big to fail."[47] Thus, we conjecture that the resolution of the Tullock paradox in this case would be based on the argument that in the transition from a fragmented, highly constrained banking sector in the 1970s to the large sector now dominated by a few very large banks, owners of larger incumbent banks did indeed capture most of the value of the growth opportunity to expand the scope of the federal safety net for finance due to increasing returns to scale in rent seeking in finance.[48]

Based on these observations, we interpret the assumption that the growth of banking $g(s)$ is an exogenous parameter in our model as a constraint imposed by regulation. Our assumption that owners of incumbent banks do not need to incur noninterest lobbying expenses to gain permission to expand their bank is based on a conjecture that these rent-seeking expenses were quite small relative to the value of the expanded government guarantee obtained.[49] This is a conjecture that should be evaluated more closely in future work.

Question 5: The Impact of the Length of the Time Period on Valuation

In our valuation model for banks, we use a discrete time model and consider each time period to be 1 year. Hence, we have implicitly assumed that banks are required to meet capital standards only once per year (at the beginning of each time period) and that the risks to bank assets and liabilities over a 1-year horizon is the relevant horizon for measuring bank risks. We choose this time period based on the observation that larger banks are required to undergo a full examination annually. This convention of an annual review of bank balance sheets has continued post crisis with the implementation of annual stress tests and approval of capital plans for larger banks.

What is the impact of this choice of time period on our valuation exercise? The answer to this question depends on the nature of the risks that banks face.

For example, if one assumes that the value of bank assets follows a diffusion, as is typically assumed in a Merton- or Leland-style structural credit risk model, then it is essentially impossible for a bank with a positive equity position to fail over a short time horizon.[50] This implies that, in this case, if regulators were to examine banks frequently enough and force them to meet capital standards based on a mark-to-market accounting of their balance sheet often enough, then the failure of a bank would occur with vanishing probability.[51]

In contrast, if one assumes that the value of bank assets is subject to the risk of a discrete jump downward large enough to trigger default that occurs with some Poisson rate over time (often called "jump to default" risk), then more frequent examination of the bank, in and of itself, does not significantly reduce the probability of bank failure over a given time horizon. The only option for reducing the risk of bank failure in this case is to raise the capital standard for the bank so that a downward jump in its asset value, should it occur, no longer triggers failure of the bank. In interpreting our model, we opt for this second approach to modeling the risk within banks.

There is a large literature in finance, both in option pricing and structural credit risk modeling, that indicates that the risk of discrete jumps in asset values is significant and important in understanding the pricing of options and credit risk (see, e.g., Broadie, Chernov, and Johannes 2007). Certainly, during the crisis of 2007–9, the transition of the financial system from a mildly distressed state in the late summer of 2008 to a severely distressed state by late September of 2008 was extremely rapid. Likewise, the large negative realized excess return on corporate credit portfolios in 2008 that we use in our measurement exercise was concentrated in the last few months of 2008.

Based on these observations that the risk of jump to default is likely to be an important driver of the risk of bank failure, we conjecture that the choice of the length of a time period in our model does not have a substantial impact on our results.

Question 6: Comparison to Other Estimates in the Literature

Our finding of large capitalized values of government guarantees in the period before 2008 follows a large literature on the impact of government guarantees on the value of bank debt and equity. Li, Qu, and Zhang (2011); the Government Accountability Office (2014); and Acharya, Anginer, and Warburton (2016) have published recent studies of the impact of government guarantees on the pricing of bank bonds. Schweikhard and Tsesmelidakis (2012) study the impact of government guarantees on bank credit default swap spreads relative to equity-based estimates of banks' probability of default. Gandhi and Lustig (2015) and Gandhi, Lustig, and Plazzi (2017) study the impact of government guarantees on the pricing of bank equity. Kelly, Lustig, and Van Nieuwerburgh (2016) study the impact of government guarantees on the pricing of options on bank equity. This paper highlights the impact of guarantees on option pricing due to guarantees against an aggregate or systemic shock to the financial sector as opposed to an idiosyncratic shock to an individual bank. All of this literature finds a significant impact of government guarantees on the pricing of bank debt and equity, particularly for larger banks.

Several studies have focused on quantifying the value of these government guarantees to owners of bank debt and equity. Here we focus on comparing our results to two of these studies in particular. The first of these is presented in Ruud (2007). This paper presents an estimate of the fair value of government guarantees to banks based on methodology used by Lucas and McDonald (2006) to measure the value of government support for Fannie Mae and Freddie Mac. The second of these is presented in Tsesmelidakis and Merton (2013). This paper uses results from Schweikhard and Tsesmelidakis (2012) to derive an estimate of the ex ante and ex post values of government support during the recent financial crisis.

Ruud (2007) applies a Merton-style structural credit risk model to assess the value of deposit insurance for 231 publicly traded banks, using data from 2004 to estimate the inputs of equity volatility and leverage needed for the model. She extrapolates results from these calculations to find a fair value of expected payouts from the FDIC (net of the recovery value from selling what remains of the failed bank) over a 5-year horizon of only $4 billion.

Tsesmelidakis and Merton (2013) is a detailed study of the pricing of bank bonds for 74 large financial firms. They use the Merton-type model of bond spreads in Schweikhard and Tsesmelidakis (2012) calibrated to match the pricing of bonds of nonfinancial firms to measure the impact of government guarantees on the pricing of bank bonds over the period 2007–10. They calculate that these guarantees amounted to a wealth transfer of $365 billion over this time period. They refer to this number as a valuation of implicit guarantees as it does not include the value of explicit deposit insurance. They divide this number into two components. The first is the benefit obtained by shareholders from being able to issue bonds at a higher price. They value this component at $129 billion. The remainder is the amount gained by incumbent bondholders ex post when the negative shock of the financial crisis occurs. The ex ante figure of $129 billion is conceptually closer to the value of government guarantees that we compute.

We find a larger value of government guarantees for the period 1996–2008 than is found in these other two papers. There are two significant methodological differences between our model for estimating the value of government guarantees and the models presented in these other papers that account for the differences in the estimates obtained in our paper and in these other papers.

First, from equation (12), we value government guarantees as a growing perpetuity. That is, we take into account that when a regulator sells what remains of a failed bank to new owners, the prospect that these new owners will also benefit from continued government guarantees affects the sale price and thus the recovery value of a failed bank (as noted in equation [8] in our model). In contrast, the papers by Ruud (2007) and Tsesmelidakis and Merton (2013) measure the value of guarantees over a fixed time horizon and consider the recovery value of a failed bank to be a fixed parameter that is not included in the measure of government guarantees. To facilitate a comparison of our measure of the value of government guarantees as a growing perpetuity to measures of the value of these guarantees over a fixed horizon, one can use equation (12) to convert our estimates of the value of government guarantees to any finite time horizon of T years using a standard annuity formula

$$\text{MVG}^T = \left[1 - \left(\frac{1+\bar{g}}{1+i}\right)^T\right]\text{MVG}.$$

For example, to convert the ex ante value of government guarantees obtained from our model to a value over a horizon of 5 years as in Ruud (2007) with a risk-free interest rate of $i = 0.05$ and expected growth of the bank balance sheet of $\bar{g} = 0.025$, we have that the value of government guarantees over a 5-year horizon is 11.4% of the estimate obtained in our paper for the value of these guarantees over an infinite horizon.

Note that this adjustment for the time horizon is sufficient to reconcile our estimate of the value of government guarantees with that obtained in Tsesmelidakis and Merton (2013). Specifically, if one converts their estimate of the benefit to bank shareholders of $129 billion from issuing bonds at a premium over a 4-year period to an infinite horizon, one would obtain an estimate of the value of government guarantees in the neighborhood of $1 trillion.

The second methodological difference between our study and these other studies is the approach we take to calibrating the parameters of the measurement model. As shown in equation (19), in applying our model in Section V, we measure the value of government guarantees using a measure of the fair value of bank assets and observed bank accounting profitability. Our measure of the risk that banks face is consistent with a small probability of a large negative shock to the bank's balance sheet.[52] In contrast, the approach followed by Ruud (2007) and Tsesmelidakis and Merton (2013) is based on the structural model of Merton as applied to banks in Merton (1977). In these models, the risk in bank assets is measured using observations on the volatility of bank equity and measures of bank market leverage.

Note that if one assumes a model in which risk to bank dividends and growth is i.i.d. and in which banks reset balance sheets to conform with regulatory limits on leverage once a year, as we have done, then the valuation formulas for bank equity and the value of government guarantees are given as in equations (17) and (19) conditional on a solution for the default decision from equation (15) regardless of the approach used for measuring the risks to the bank's ROE and to the growth of the bank's balance sheet.[53] Thus, the other principal difference in methodology that accounts for the difference between our estimate of the value of government guarantees and the estimates presented in Ruud (2007) and Tsesmelidakis and Merton (2013) is that our model assumes a large downside tail risk for banks.

Endnotes

All errors are ours. Author email addresses: Atkeson (andy@atkeson.net), d'Avernas (adrien.davernas@hhs.se), Eisfeldt (andrea.eisfeldt@anderson.ucla.edu), Weill (poweill@econ.ucla.edu). For acknowledgments, sources of research support, and disclosure of the authors' material financial relationships, if any, please see http://www.nber.org/chapters/c14085.ack.

1. A closely related point is made by Admati and Hellwig (2013) and Admati et al. (2013), who argue that, to the extent that leverage reduces banks' cost of capital, it is due to distortions from government subsidies to bank debt.

2. Meiselman, Nagel, and Purnanandam (2018) show that high rates of accounting profitability for banks in good times is a signal of bank exposure to tail risk in bad times, and apply this idea successfully to the cross-section of US bank values during the crisis.

3. We note that there are no deadweight costs from bank failure in our model but instead a bankruptcy benefit, which is a transfer from taxpayers to banks.

4. We impose the assumption that banks do not derive value from the opportunity to originate new loans or deposits.

5. We collect financial information on bank holding companies from the "Quarterly Trends for Consolidated US Banking Organizations" report from the Federal Reserve Bank of New York (2019) and from the holding company data of the Federal Reserve Bank of Chicago (2019). To construct market prices, we merge this data set with Standard & Poor's Compustat and the Center for Research in Security Prices (CRSP) databases using the CRSP-FRB links from the Federal Reserve Bank of New York. Our sample of public bank holding companies consists of 1,128 banks and 40,468 bank-quarter observations from 1986 to 2016 and covers 93% of total assets of all FDIC-insured institutions in the fourth quarter of 2016. To have a longer historical perspective, we also use the consolidated annual financial statements of FDIC-insured institutions from 1935 to 2016 available in the FDIC (2019b) historical statistics on banking. We obtain corporate bond credit spreads from the Lehman/Warga and Bank of America Merrill Lynch (BAML) databases.

6. We construct the market-to-book value of equity for the sector as the sum of the market value of equity across bank holding companies in our sample divided by the sum of the book value of equity across the same bank holding companies. This ratio corresponds to a value-weighted average of the market-to-book value of equity across bank holding companies.

7. The CRSP-FRB linked database starts in 1986. Therefore, we use financial firms with a standard industry classification code in between 6000 and 6999 to go back to 1975.

8. We use the gross domestic product implicit price deflator with base year 2009 as the deflator.

9. The market value of assets is defined as the book value of debt plus the market value of equity.

10. We eliminate all observations with credit spreads below 5 basis points (bp) and greater than 3,000 bp. In addition, we drop very small corporate issues (equity market value of less than $1 million) and all observations with a remaining term to maturity of less than 6 months or more than 20 years. Some firms tend to have many different corporate bond securities outstanding. To avoid overweighting firms that issue a lot of different securities, when different prices were available for the same firm, we keep only the security with time to maturity closest to 8 years (sample average). Financial, utility, and public administration firms are also excluded from the sample. Restricting to unique credit spreads' monthly observations for each firm eliminates 45% of the data set; other restrictions affect less than 5% of the rest.

11. Option-adjusted spreads roughly follow a log-normal distribution with time-varying mean and standard deviation.

12. We define "nonfinancial firms" as firms with a standard industry classification code not between 6000 and 6999.

13. In the data, banks also manage a portfolio of marketable securities on both the asset and liability side of their balance sheet including federal funds and repo (a securities arm) and conduct a wide range of fee-for-service business (a fee-for-service arm). Here we assume that the securities arm of the bank has no franchise value, but that it can contribute to the risk exposure of the bank and hence to the value of government guarantees. This assumption is in line with the assumptions used by the Bureau of Economic Analysis to construct its measure of value added in banking (see Hood 2013). We assume that the fee-for-service arm of the bank does not generate franchise value for the bank because the costs of labor and physical premises required to conduct these activities soak up all of the revenue associated with these activities (in discounted present value). We discuss this assumption in greater detail in app. B. We discuss how we map the accounting items in bank holding company regulatory reports on their income statements and balance sheets (form FR Y-9C) into our accounting model when we do our full accounting in Section VI.

14. In our model, we assume that the bank issues deposits that are default free, as they are guaranteed by the government. We include subordinated debt in the model to allow some of the liabilities of the bank to suffer losses in default. Subordinated debt is distinct from repo and derivatives exposures that are collateralized and hence protected in the event of bank failure by specific assets within the bank. A normal firm without government guarantees would have no deposits, and all of its liabilities would be subordinated

debt. In the data, banks issue very little subordinated debt; however, the credit spreads on these bonds are informative about banks' default risk.

15. For a bank with positive deposits (with no risk of default) to operate without government guarantees, we must allow for unlimited liability for subordinated debt in the event of default. Before deposit insurance, it was standard for bank investors to be liable to inject resources in the event of failure of the bank, either as partners or through double liability of bank shares (see, e.g., Macey and Miller 1992).

16. See Elenev, Landvoigt, and Nieuwerburgh (2018) for related results in a large-scale macroeconomic model.

17. Note that the presence of government guarantees affects the default decision in our model through the effect on MVE. Lucas and McDonald (2010) emphasize the importance of this effect in explaining the difference in implied values of government guarantees recovered from credit spread versus option data.

18. Giesecke et al. (2011) present data on default rates for corporate bonds over the period from 1866 to 2008. They find evidence of repeated events of clustered defaults much worse than those experienced during the Great Depression. Moody's (2018) provides an update of these data. These data suggest that, for bonds, 2008 was not a unique event in history.

19. See also Begenau, Bigio, and Majerovitz (2018), which documents the magnitude of losses on the market value of bank equity in the 2008 crisis.

20. A rapidly growing new literature on the interest rate risk inherent in banks' portfolios argues that maturity transformation does not expose banks to significant interest rate risk. See, e.g., English, Van den Heuvel, and Zakrajsek (2012); Landier, Sraer, and Thesmar (2013); Drechsler, Savov, and Schnabl (2017a, 2017b); see also Di Tella and Kurlat (2017).

21. These indices are available on the website for the FRED database at the Federal Reserve Bank of St. Louis (https://fred.stlouisfed.org).

22. Bonds with ratings of AAA, AA, A, and BBB are considered investment grade. Bonds with ratings of BB and below are considered high yield.

23. See table 3 of Berndt et al. (2017) for the median credit risk premia by credit rating.

24. In our model, we abstract from interest rate risk. Clearly, the BAML portfolio of AAA bonds is not completely riskless because it is subject to interest rate risk, so its return does not correspond to the riskless rate i. Thus, we take the gap between the returns of these bond portfolios and the portfolio of AAA bonds to control for interest rate risk and use this measure of realized aggregate credit risk in the crisis state to calibrate $R(c) - i$ in our model.

25. These values are representative of those observed in the data for the 1996–2007 time period. With this calibration, if our stylized bank chooses to default in the crisis state, then its price-dividend ratio in the normal state as given in eq. (16) is equal to 33 regardless of the riskiness of the bank.

26. Meiselman et al. (2018) use a closely related model to study the accounting profitability of a bank as a measure of the risk to which its assets are exposed using cross-sectional data.

27. The default decision is given in eq. (22).

28. For background information on these reports on loan fair values, see Calomiris and Nissim (2014); Knott et al. (2014); Nissim (2003); Nissim and Penman (2007); Tschirhart et al. (2007).

29. Hutchison and Pennacchi (1996); Janosi, Jarrow, and Zullo (1999); Jarrow and van Deventer (1998); O'Brien (2000); and Sheehan (2013) develop fair value models for loans and deposits. For a discussion of banks' models for funds transfer pricing, see Dermine (2012); Grant (2011); Wyle and Tsaig (2011).

30. Wang, Basu, and Fernald (2008) and Basu, Inklaar, and Wang (2011) study the measurement of financial intermediation services implicitly measured (FISIM), and Hood (2013) and Akritidis (2017) discuss the methods used in the United States and elsewhere to conduct this measurement. Haldane, Brennan, and Madouros (2010) focus on the impact of risk taking on measurement of FISIM in banking.

31. Bank of America, Citigroup, JPMorgan Chase, Wells Fargo, AIG, MetLife, American Express, Huntington Bancshares, Fifth Third Bank, Washington Mutual, SunTrust

Banks, Regions Financial, PNC Financial Services, National City Bank, Zions Bank, Countrywide, Comerica, KeyCorp, and US Bancorp.

32. These assets include cash and deposits due, securities, trading assets, fed funds sold, and reverse repo. We discuss banks' estimates of the fair values of these assets in app. B.

33. Bank nonearning assets such as premises, other real estate owned, intangible assets such as goodwill, and tax-related assets are all recorded at book values. We treat the fair value of these assets as equal to their book value. This is likely an overstatement of the fair value of these assets.

34. See OTS (2000) for a description of that model. See also Sheehan (2013).

35. These estimates are available on the website of the Office of the Comptroller of the Currency (US Treasury 2019).

36. The aggregation of these OTS fair value estimates requires considerable judgment on our part. With more time, perhaps a more precise estimate could be constructed.

37. Recall that we handle subordinated debt separately. We discuss banks' estimates of the fair value of these other bank liabilities in app. B.

38. This finding is consistent with the findings of Egan, Lewellen, and Sunderam (2017) regarding the importance of variation in the productivity of deposits in explaining the cross section of bank valuation. Similarly, Furlong and Kwan (2006) study the determinants of bank valuation in the cross section.

39. To implement this formula, we set $\bar{g} = i - 0.025$.

40. We do not directly address changes in the regulatory and economic environment that would account for the changes in bank risk taking and value derived from government guarantees that we document here. There is a large literature on the changes in the regulatory environment that increased the incentives for banks to take risks and become too big to fail. See, e.g., Boyd and Gertler (1994); Rolnick and Feldman (1998); Wilmarth (2002); Stern and Feldman (2004); Mishkin (2006). There is also a literature that examines the impact of equity-based incentives for CEOs on bank risk taking. See, e.g., Chesney, Stromberg, and Wagner (2012); Larcker et al. (2014); Boyallian and Ruiz-Verdú (2018).

41. Egan et al. (2017) is a recent study of the determinants of bank value that focuses on valuing the loan-making and deposit-taking arms of the bank.

42. The large decline in bank ROE in the final quarter of 2017 is largely due to the impact of the recent corporate tax cut on the valuation of banks' tax assets.

43. Note that our assumption that growth of the bank contributes to the value of government guarantees only applies to growth achieved through organic growth via new injections of bank equity. The opportunity to grow an individual bank through a strategy of acquisitions would not contribute to the value of the acquiring bank in our model because the acquiring bank would have to pay the shareholders of the acquired bank for the value of expanded government guarantees.

44. In a policy statement regarding the obligations of bank holding companies to insured bank subsidiaries, the Federal Reserve states that "the important public policy interest in the support provided by a bank holding company to its subsidiary banks is based upon the fact that, in acquiring a commercial bank, a bank holding company derives certain benefits at the corporate level that result, in part, from the ownership of an institution that can issue federally insured deposits and has access to Federal Reserve credit. The existence of the federal safety net reflects important governmental concerns regarding the critical fiduciary responsibilities of depository institutions as custodians of depositors' funds and their strategic role within our economy as operators of the payments system and impartial providers of credit. Thus, in seeking the advantages flowing from the ownership of a commercial bank, bank holding companies have an obligation to serve as sources of strength and support to their subsidiary banks." See FDIC (2019a).

45. This is the classic question raised in Tullock (1980) regarding the value of regulatory rents.

46. See Wilmarth (2002) and Omarova and Tahyar (2012) for a discussion of the evolution of this act and its impact on the growth of banking. A bank that is given a low CAMEL rating (supervisory rating system to classify a bank's overall condition) in an examination

by the FDIC or other bank regulator will face direct restrictions on its further growth under the regulatory framework of the FDICIA's policies for prompt corrective action.

47. There is a large literature on the changes in the regulatory environment that increased the incentives for banks to take risks and to grow to become too big to fail. See, e.g., Boyd and Gertler (1994); Berger, Kashyap, and Scalise (1995); Rolnick and Feldman (1998); Wilmarth (2002); Stern and Feldman (2004); Mishkin (2006); Avraham, Selvaggi, and Vickery (2012).

48. This is the apparent paradox pointed to in Tullock (1980) of the low costs of rent seeking relative to the gains from rent seeking.

49. Such expenses could be modeled in a manner parallel to the noninterest expenses ϕ_L and ϕ_D we assumed that banks incur to grow deposits and loans.

50. This is because asset value follows a diffusion. Thus, the probability of the event that bank asset values fall below a default threshold in a short period of time converges to zero as the time horizon shrinks to zero.

51. See the calculations illustrating this point in Hanson, Kashyap, and Stein (2011) and Flannery and Giacomini (2015).

52. Lucas et al. (2001) and Nagel and Purnanandam (2017) provide theoretical arguments that returns on bank portfolios should be expected to have a thick tail of extreme negative returns. Recall that our measure of the value of government guarantees for stylized banks in Section V is a proof of concept based on direct observation of the downside risk in portfolios of corporate bonds.

53. As discussed in Atkeson, Eisfeldt, and Weill (2017), the distribution of equity volatility across firms appears to experience regime shifts that have a dramatic impact on estimates of the risk in firm or bank assets derived from a Merton-type structural credit risk model. See, for example, estimates of the probabilities of default of European banks based on this method in Flannery and Giacomini (2015). These regime shifts suggest that it may be fruitful to move beyond an i.i.d. model of the risks facing banks to include shifts in regimes. See d'Avernas (2018) for a regime-switching model of equity volatility and bond spreads for nonfinancial firms in the United States.

References

Acharya, Viral V., Deniz Anginer, and A. Joseph Warburton. 2016. "The End of Market Discipline? Investor Expectations of Implicit Government Guarantees." https://papers.ssrn.com/sol3/papers.cfm?abstract_id=1961656.

Admati, Anat, and Martin Hellwig. 2013. *The Banker's New Clothes: What's Wrong with Banking and What to Do about It*. Princeton, NJ: Princeton University Press.

Admati, Anat R., Peter M. DeMarzo, Martin Hellwig, and Paul Pfleiderer. 2013. "Fallacies, Irrelevant Facts, and Myths in the Discussion of Capital Regulation: Why Bank Equity Is Not Expensive." Working Paper no. 2065 (October), Stanford Graduate School of Business. https://papers.ssrn.com/sol3/papers.cfm?abstract_id=2349739.

Akritidis, Leonidas. 2017. "Financial Intermediation Services Indirectly Measured (FISIM) in the UK Revisited." Technical report (April 24), UK Office for National Statistics, London.

Asvanunt, Attakrit, and Scott Richardson. 2016. "The Credit Risk Premium." https://papers.ssrn.com/sol3/papers.cfm?abstract_id=2563482.

Atkeson, Andrew G., Andrea L. Eisfeldt, and Pierre-Olivier Weill. 2017. "Measuring the Financial Soundness of US Firms, 1926–2012." *Research in Economics* 71 (3): 613–35.

Avraham, Dafna, Patricia Selvaggi, and James Vickery. 2012. "A Structural View of US Bank Holding Companies." *FRBNY Economic Policy Review* 18 (2): 65–81.

Bank of America. 2017. "2016 Annual Report." http://media.corporate-ir.net /media_files/IROL/71/71595/BOAML_AR2016.pdf.

Basu, Susanto, Robert Inklaar, and J. Christina Wang. 2011. "The Value of Risk: Measuring the Service Output of US Commercial Banks." *Economic Inquiry* 49 (1): 226–45.

Begenau, Juliane, Saki Bigio, and Jeremy Majerovitz. 2018. "Data Lessons on Bank Behavior." Working paper. https://economicdynamics.org/meetpapers /2018/paper_161.pdf.

Begenau, Juliane, Monika Piazzesi, and Martin Schneider. 2015. "Banks' Risk Exposures." Working Paper no. 21334 (July), NBER, Cambridge, MA. https:// www.nber.org/papers/w21334.

Begenau, Juliane, and Erik Stafford. 2018. "Do Banks Have an Edge?" Working Paper no. 18-060 (January), Harvard Business School. https://www.hbs .edu/faculty/Pages/item.aspx?num=53722.

Berger, Allen N., Anil K. Kashyap, and Joseph M. Scalise. 1995. "The Transformation of the US Banking Industry: What a Long Strange Trip It's Been." *Brookings Papers on Economic Activity* 1995 (2): 55–201.

Berndt, Antje, Rohan Douglas, Darrell Duffie, and Mark Ferguson. 2017. "Corporate Credit Risk Premia." https://papers.ssrn.com/sol3/papers .cfm?abstract_id=3077352.

Boyallian, Patricia, and Pablo Ruiz-Verdú. 2018. "Leverage, CEO Risk-Taking Incentives, and Bank Failure during the 2007–10 Financial Crisis." *Review of Finance* 22 (5): 1763–805.

Boyd, John H., and Mark Gertler. 1994. "The Role of Large Banks in the Recent US Banking Crisis." *Federal Reserve Bank of Minneapolis Quarterly Review* 18 (1): 2–21.

Broadie, Mark, Mikhail Chernov, and Michael Johannes. 2007. "Model Specification and Risk Premia: Evidence from Futures Options." *Journal of Finance* 62 (3): 1453–90.

Calomiris, Charles W., and Doron Nissim. 2014. "Crisis-Related Shifts in the Market Valuation of Banking Activities." *Journal of Financial Intermediation* 23 (3): 400–35.

Chesney, Marc, Jacob Stromberg, and Alexander F. Wagner. 2012. "Risk-Taking Incentives and Losses in the Financial Crisis." Working paper. https://www .tilburguniversity.edu/upload/28149ef9-b87a-4de8-a78e-145dea7408e1 _lhstromberg.pdf.

Chousakos, Kyriakos T., and Gary B. Gorton. 2017. "Bank Health Post-Crisis." Working Paper No. 23167 (February), NBER, Cambridge, MA. https://www .nber.org/papers/w23167.

Copeland, Adam. 2012. "Evolution and Heterogeneity among Larger Bank Holding Companies: 1994 to 2010." *FRBNY Economic Policy Review* 18 (2): 83–93.

d'Avernas, Adrien. 2018. "Disentangling Credit Spreads and Equity Volatility." Research Paper 18–9 (January), Swedish House of Finance, Stockholm. https:// papers.ssrn.com/sol3/papers.cfm?abstract_id=3108442.

Davis, Madeline G. 2017. "Core Deposit Intangible Asset Values and Deposit Premiums Update." Mercer Capital's Financial Reporting Blog. November 2017. https://mercercapital.com/financialreportingblog/core-deposit -intangible-asset-values-deposit-premiums-update/.

Dermine, Jean. 2012. "Fund Transfer Pricing for Deposits and Loans, Foundation and Advanced." Working paper 2012-55-FIN (May 24), INSEAD.

Di Tella, Sebastian, and Pablo Kurlat. 2017. "Why Are Banks Exposed to Monetary Policy?" Working Paper no. 24076, NBER, Cambridge, MA. https://www.nber.org/papers/w24076.pdf.

Drechsler, Itamar, Alexi Savov, and Philipp Schnabl. 2017a. "Banking on Deposits: Maturity Transformation without Interest Rate Risk." https://papers.ssrn.com/sol3/papers.cfm?abstract_id=2938236.

———. 2017b. "The Deposits Channel of Monetary Policy." *Quarterly Journal of Economics* 132 (4): 1819–76.

Egan, Mark, Stefan Lewellen, and Adi Sunderam. 2017. "The Cross Section of Bank Value." Working Paper no. 23291 (March), NBER, Cambridge, MA. https://www.nber.org/papers/w23291.

Elenev, Vadim, Tim Landvoigt, and Stijn Van Nieuwerburgh. 2018. "A Macroeconomic Model with Financially Constrained Producers and Intermediaries." Working Paper no. 24757 (June), NBER, Cambridge, MA. https://www.nber.org/papers/w24757.

English, William B., Skander J. Van den Heuvel, and Egon Zakrajsek. 2012. "Interest Rate Risk and Bank Equity Valuations." Finance and Economics Discussion Series 2012–26, Federal Reserve Board, Washington, DC. https://www.federalreserve.gov/pubs/feds/2012/201226/201226abs.html.

FDIC (Federal Deposit Insurance Corporation). 2019a. "FDIC Law, Regulations, Related Acts: 7500–FRB Regulations." https://www.fdic.gov/regulations/laws/rules/7500-5000.html.

FDIC (Federal Deposit Insurance Corporation). 2019b. "Historical Bank Data." https://banks.data.fdic.gov/explore/historical.

Federal Reserve Bank of Chicago. 2019. "Holding Company Data." https://www.chicagofed.org/banking/financial-institution-reports/bhc-data.

Federal Reserve Bank of New York. 2017. "Quarterly Trends for Consolidated US Banking Organizations, Fourth Quarter 2017." https://www.newyorkfed.org/medialibrary/media/research/banking_research/quarterlytrends2017q4.pdf?la=en.

Federal Reserve Bank of New York. 2019. "Quarterly Trends for Consolidated US Banking Organizations." https://www.newyorkfed.org/research/banking_research/quarterly_trends.html.

Fine, Aaron, and Frank Rohde. 2013. "Deposits: A Return to Value?" Executive brief, Oliver Wyman, New York. https://www.oliverwyman.com/content/dam/oliver-wyman/global/en/files/insights/financial-services/2013/Dec/Deposits%20-%20A%20Return%20to%20Value.pdf.

Flannery, Mark J., and Emanuela Giacomini. 2015. "Maintaining Adequate Bank Capital: An Empirical Analysis of the Supervision of European Banks." *Journal of Banking and Finance* 59:236–49.

Furlong, Frederick T., and Simon H. Kwan. 2006. "Sources of Bank Charter Value." Technical report (September), Federal Reserve Bank of San Francisco.

Gandhi, Priyank, and Hanno Lustig. 2015. "Size Anomalies in US Bank Stock Returns." *Journal of Finance* 70 (2): 733–68.

Gandhi, Priyank, Hanno Lustig, and Alberto Plazzi. 2017. "Equity Is Cheap for Large Financial Institutions." Working Paper no. 22355, NBER, Cambridge, MA. https://www.nber.org/papers/w22355.

Giesecke, Kay, Francis A. Longstaff, Stephen Schaefer, and Ilya Strebulaev. 2011. "Corporate Bond Default Risk: A 150-Year Perspective." *Journal of Financial Economics* 102 (2): 233–50.

Gordon, Myron J. 1962. *The Investment, Financing, and Valuation of the Corporation*. Homewood, IL: Irwin.

Government Accountability Office. 2014. "Large Bank Holding Companies: Expectations of Government Support." Technical Report 14–621 (July), Government Accountability Office, Washington, DC. https://www.gao.gov/products/GAO-14-621.

Grant, Joel. 2011. "Liquidity Transfer Pricing: A Guide to Better Practice." Financial Stability Institute Occasional Paper 10 (December), Bank for International Settlements, Basel. https://www.bis.org/fsi/fsipapers10.htm.

Haldane, Andrew, Simon Brennan, and Vasileios Madouros. 2010. "What Is the Contribution of the Financial Sector: Miracle or Mirage?" In *The Future of Finance: The LSE Report*, 87–120. London: London School of Economics and Political Science.

Hanson, Samuel G., Anil K. Kashyap, and Jeremy C. Stein. 2011. "A Macroprudential Approach to Financial Regulation." *Journal of Economic Perspectives* 25 (1): 3–28.

Hood, Kyle K. 2013. "Measuring the Services of Commercial Banks in the National Income and Product Accounts: Changes in Concepts and Methods in the 2013 Comprehensive Revision." *Survey of Current Business* 93:8–19.

Hutchison, David E., and George G. Pennacchi. 1996. "Measuring Rents and Interest Rate Risk in Imperfect Financial Markets: The Case of Retail Bank Deposits." *Journal of Financial and Quantitative Analysis* 31 (3): 399–417.

Janosi, Tibor, Robert A. Jarrow, and Ferdinando Zullo. 1999. "An Empirical Analysis of the Jarrow-van-Deventer Model for Valuing Non-Maturity Demand Deposits." *Journal of Derivatives* 7 (1): 8–31.

Jarrow, Robert, and Donald van Deventer. 1998. "The Arbitrage-Free Valuation and Hedging of Demand Deposits and Credit Card Loans." *Journal of Banking and Finance* 22:249–72.

Kane, Edward J. 2014. "Shadowy Banking: Theft by Safety Net." *Yale Journal on Regulation* 31 (3): 773–807.

Keeley, Michael C. 1990. "Deposit Insurance, Risk, and Market Power in Banking." *American Economic Review* 80 (5): 1183–200.

Kelly, Bryan, Hanno Lustig, and Stijn Van Nieuwerburgh. 2016. "Too-Systemic-to-Fail: What Options Markets Imply about Sector-Wide Government Guarantees." *American Economic Review* 106 (6): 1278–319.

Knott, Samuel, Peter Richardson, Katie Rismanchi, and Kallol Sen. 2014. "Understanding the Fair Value of Banks' Loans." Financial Stability Paper 31 (November), Bank of England, London. https://papers.ssrn.com/sol3/papers.cfm?abstract_id=2545783.

Landier, Augustin, David Alexandre Sraer, and David Thesmar. 2013. "Banks' Exposure to Interest Rate Risk and the Transmission of Monetary Policy." Working Paper no. 18857, NBER, Cambridge, MA. https://www.nber.org/papers/w18857.

Larcker, David F., Gaizka Ormazabal, Brian Tayan, and Daniel J. Taylor. 2014. "Follow the Money: Compensation, Risk, and the Financial Crisis." Research paper (September 8), Stanford Graduate School of Business. https://www.gsb.stanford.edu/faculty-research/publications/follow-money-compensation-risk-financial-crisis.

Li, Zan, Shisheng Qu, and Jing Zhang. 2011. "Quantifying the Value of Implicit Government Guarantees for Large Financial Institutions." Technical report (January), Moody's Analytics, New York.

Lucas, André, Pieter Klaassen, Peter Spreij, and Stefan Straetmans. 2001. "An Analytic Approach to the Credit Risk of Large Corporate Bond and Loan Portfolios." *Journal of Banking and Finance* 25 (9): 1635–64.

Lucas, Deborah, and Robert McDonald. 2006. "An Options-Based Approach to Evaluating the Risk of Fannie Mae and Freddie Mac." *Journal of Monetary Economics* 53 (1): 155–76.

———. 2010. "Valuing Government Guarantees: Fannie and Freddie Revisited." In *Measuring and Managing Financial Risk*, ed. Deborah Lucas, 131–54. Chicago: University of Chicago Press.

Macey, Jonathan R., and Geoffrey P. Miller. 1992. "Double Liability of Bank Shareholders: History and Implications." Faculty Scholarship Series 1642, Yale Law School. https://digitalcommons.law.yale.edu/cgi/viewcontent.cgi ?referer=https://www.google.com/&httpsredir=1&article=2677&context=fss _papers.

Meiselman, Ben, Stefan Nagel, and Amiyatosh Purnanandam. 2018. "Judging Banks' Risk by the Profits They Report." https://papers.ssrn.com/sol3/papers .cfm?abstract_id=3169730.

Merton, Robert C. 1977. "An Analytic Derivation of the Cost of Deposit Insurance and Loan Guarantees: An Application of Modern Option Pricing Theory." *Journal of Banking and Finance* 1 (1): 3–11.

Miller, Merton H., and Franco Modigliani. 1958. "The Cost of Capital, Corporation Finance, and the Theory of Investment." *American Economic Review* 48 (3): 261–97.

Minton, Bernadette A., René M. Stulz, and Alvaro G. Taboada. 2017. "Are Larger Banks Valued More Highly?" Working Paper no. 23212, NBER, Cambridge, MA. https://www.nber.org/papers/w23212.

Mishkin, Frederic S. 2006. "How Big a Problem Is Too Big to Fail? A Review of Gary Stern and Ron Feldman's 'Too Big to Fail: The Hazards of Bank Bailouts.'" *Journal of Economic Literature* 44 (4): 988–1004.

Moody's. 2018. "Annual Default Study: Corporate Default and Recovery Rates, 1920–2017." Technical report (February), Moody's Investors Service, New York. https://www.researchpool.com/download/?report_id=1751185&show_pdf _data=true.

Nagel, Stefan, and Amiyatosh Purnanandam. 2017. "Bank Risk Dynamics and Distance to Default." Unpublished paper. http://webuser.bus.umich.edu /amiyatos/BankCreditRisk_v5.pdf.

Nissim, Doron. 2003. "Reliability of Banks' Fair Value Disclosure for Loans." *Review of Quantitative Finance and Accounting* 20 (4): 355–84.

Nissim, Doron, and Stephen Penman. 2007. "Fair Value Accounting in the Banking Industry." Occasional paper series (May), CE-ASA, Columbia Business School. http://www.columbia.edu/~dn75/fair%20value%20accounting %20in%20the%20banking%20industry.pdf.

O'Brien, James M. 2000. "Estimating the Value and Interest Rate Risk of Interest-Bearing Transactions Deposits." Working Paper no. 00–53 (November), Finance and Economics Discussion Series (FEDS), Washington, DC. https:// papers.ssrn.com/sol3/papers.cfm?abstract_id=256712.

Office of Thrift Supervision. 2000. "Net Portfolio Value Model." Technical report (March), Office of Thrift Supervision, Washington, DC.

Omarova, Saule T., and Margaret E. Tahyar. 2012. "That Which We Call a Bank: Revisiting the History of Bank Holding Company Regulations in the United States." *Cornell Law Faculty Publications*, paper 1012. https://scholarship .law.cornell.edu/facpub/1012/.

Rolnick, Arthur J., and Ron J. Feldman. 1998. "Fixing FDICIA: A Plan to Address the Too Big to Fail Problem." Annual report essay (January), Federal Reserve Bank of Minneapolis.

Ruud, Judy. 2007. "The Fair Value of the Federal Deposit Insurance Guarantee." Working Paper 2007-13 (November), Congressional Budget Office, Washington, DC. https://www.cbo.gov/publication/19355.

Sarin, Natasha, and Lawrence H. Summers. 2016. "Have Big Banks Gotten Safer?" *Brookings Papers on Economic Activity.* https://www.brookings.edu/bpea-articles /have-big-banks-gotten-safer/.

Schweikhard, Frederic A., and Zoe Tsesmelidakis. 2012. "The Impact of Government Interventions on CDS and Equity Markets." Working paper. https://papers .ssrn.com/sol3/papers.cfm?abstract_id=1943546.

Sheehan, Richard G. 2013. "Valuing Core Deposits." *Journal of Financial Services Research* 43 (2): 197–220.

Stern, Gary H., and Ron J. Feldman. 2004. *Too Big to Fail: The Hazards of Bank Bailouts.* Washington, DC: Brookings.

Tschirhart, John, James M. O'Brien, Michael Moise, and Emily Yang. 2007. "Bank Commercial Loan Fair Value Practices." Working Paper no. 2007-29, Finance and Economics Discussion Series (FEDS), Washington, DC. https:// papers.ssrn.com/sol3/papers.cfm?abstract_id=1017604.

Tsesmelidakis, Zoe, and Robert C. Merton. 2013. "The Value of Implicit Guarantees." Working paper. https://papers.ssrn.com/sol3/papers.cfm?abstract _id=2231317.

Tullock, Gordon. 1980. "Efficient Rent-Seeking." In *Toward a Theory of the Rent-Seeking Society*, ed. James M. Buchanan, Robert D. Tollison, and Gordon Tullock, 97–112. College Station: Texas A&M University.

US Treasury. 2019. "Office of Thrift Supervision Asset and Liability Price Tables." Office of the Comptroller of the Currency. https://www.occ.gov/publications /publications-by-type/other-publications-reports/ots/ots-asset-liability-price -tables.html.

Wang, J. Christina, Susanto Basu, and John G. Fernald. 2008. "A General-Equilibrium Asset-Pricing Approach to the Measurement of Nominal and Real Bank Output." Working Paper no. 14616, NBER, Cambridge, MA. https:// www.nber.org/papers/w14616.

Wilmarth, Arthur E., Jr. 2002. "The Transformation of the US Financial Services Industry, 1975–2000: Competition, Consolidation, and Increased Risks." *University of Illinois Law Review* 2002 (2): 215–476.

Wyle, Robert J., and Yaakov Tsaig. 2011. "Implementing High Value Funds Transfer Pricing Systems." Technical report (September), Moody's Analytics. https://www.moodysanalytics.com/-/media/whitepaper/2011/11-01-09 -implementing-high-value-fund-transfer-pricing-systems.pdf.

Yellen, Janet L. 2017. "Financial Stability a Decade after the Onset of the Crisis" (speech). https://www.federalreserve.gov/newsevents/speech/yellen 20170825a.htm.

Comment

Juliane Begenau, Stanford University and NBER

Why are market-to-book ratios of banks so low since the financial crisis? Are banks safer since tighter financial regulations have forced banks to increase their capital ratios and thus lowered the value of the implicit government guarantee?[1] The paper attempts to answer these questions using a decomposition of the market-to-book ratio of banks into

$$\frac{\text{Market Value of Equity}}{\text{Book Value of Equity}} = 1 + \text{Franchise Value} + \text{Gov. Guarantee,}$$

where the franchise value is the difference between the fair and book value of bank equity. The franchise value is positive when banks can increase the value of their assets above their costs, as captured by the book value, or when banks have a funding advantage. A clever application of a standard valuation technique in finance, the Gordon growth model, allows the authors to calculate the model-implied market-to-book ratio and the franchise value of the aggregate US banking sector. The inputs to the model are simply a discount rate, the cash flow to bank equity, and a cash flow growth rate. This method is accurate as long as its inputs accurately capture the cash flow process, the risk, and the opportunity cost of capital for bank equity investors.[2] Using bank accounting data and corporate excess return data, the authors calculate banks' model implied franchise value and market-to-book ratio, that is, two of the three terms in the above equation. They conclude that the reduction in bank market valuation is primarily due to a reduction in the value of government guarantees.

In my comments, I first present a simplified version of the valuation method to highlight the authors' key assumptions. Second, I present evidence that banks are exposed to interest rate risk, leading me to argue that interest rate risk should be taken into account for a more compelling analysis. Last, I offer a different perspective on the reduction in market valuations.

To apply the Gordon growth model to banks, one needs first to identify banks' cash flow sources. For this exercise, it is useful to inspect the aggregate US bank balance sheet in figure 1. Banks hold approximately 30% of their assets in securities, broadly defined as cash, repurchase agreements, federal funds sold, mortgage-backed securities, and US Treasuries (USTs). Loans make up 55% of assets. More than 10% of assets are trading assets, such as interest rate derivatives. The remainder are fixed and intangible assets. Banks fund these assets with deposits and debt raised from the capital market. Thus, overall the balance sheet looks like a fixed-income portfolio.

Each balance sheet position derives its value from the cash flow it generates. Hence, the fair value at time zero of a balance sheet position i is

$$FV_0^i = E_t \sum_{t=1}^{\infty} \frac{CF_t^i}{1 + r_t^i},$$

(1)

where CF_t^i denotes the cash flow from position i at time t and r_t^i denotes the opportunity cost of capital for an investment with the same project

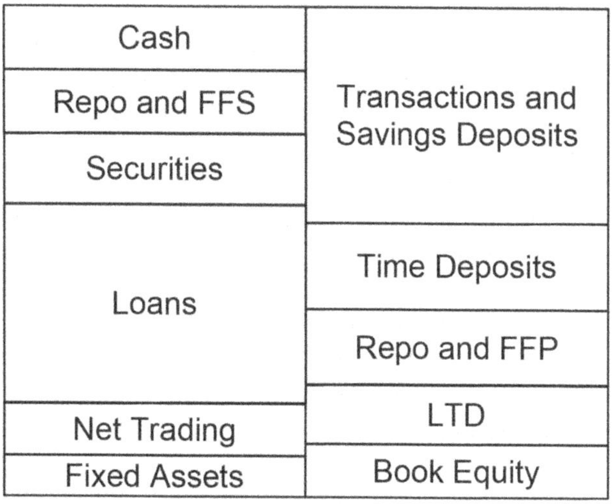

Cash	Transactions and Savings Deposits
Repo and FFS	
Securities	
Loans	Time Deposits
	Repo and FFP
Net Trading	LTD
Fixed Assets	Book Equity

Fig. 1. Aggregate balance sheet of US bank holding companies. This graphic approximates the relative share of assets and liabilities of the US aggregate banking sector from 2000–10. Repo denotes repurchase agreements. FFS = federal funds sold; FFP = federal funds purchased; LTD = long-term debt. "Net trading" is the difference between trading assets and trading liabilities.

length and risk as position i. To bring this discounted cash flow model to the data, we need accurate cash flow projections and the appropriate discount rate r_t^i for each balance sheet (and off-balance sheet) position. Note that the Gordon growth model used by the authors is a special case of equation (1) when CF_t^i is growing at a constant rate g, and the opportunity cost of capital r_t^i is constant over time. Equation (1) requires us to be thoughtful about the opportunity cost of each position. Banks' franchise value can only be positive if on net banks' positions have a higher return than their opportunity cost of capital. The authors sidestep this difficulty in their franchise value calculation by simply relying on fair value estimates on select balance sheet positions provided by banks and regulators. These positions are loans and deposits. The implicit assumption is that banks (regulators) have accurately estimated the cash flow process of loans (deposits) and the opportunity cost of capital. Moreover, the authors assume that any positive franchise value can only come from loans or deposits, implying that all nonloan assets have a fair-to-book value ratio of one.[3] This means that banks have either a funding advantage, that is, can issue deposits at below competitive rates, or earn more on loans than what it costs them to make loans. Yet the authors also assume that loans and deposits are issued competitively, which further obfuscates the origin of the franchise value for loans and deposits in the model. Without a clear articulation of how banks generate value with their balance sheet, it is a bit difficult to see how outside estimates from banks and regulators map into the authors' valuation model. Moreover, they rely heavily on the accuracy of these estimates, in particular regarding the risk and investors' opportunity cost calculation.

The value of the government guarantee is simply the difference between the model-implied market value of equity as described in Section VI.B of the paper and the model-implied franchise value. The model-implied market value of bank equity is also based on a Gordon growth model, with the key step being the valuation of cash flows in two states: nondefault and default. The authors assume that only credit risk matters for the default decisions of banks.

Interest Rate Risk

Given the fixed-income nature of bank balance sheet positions, the absence of interest rate risk in the valuation model of the paper is notable. Banks' balance sheet and off-balance sheet positions embed significant interest rate risk exposure that gets expressed in bank equity valuations (see, e.g., English, Van den Heuvel, and Zakrajšek 2018) and actual bank default rates.

In Begenau, Piazzesi, and Schneider (2015), we propose a method to estimate and measure this exposure in two steps. The first step is to decompose all book value positions of banks into their expected cash flows and compute the fair value of each position by applying equation (1). Riskier cash flows are discounted at the discount rate that reflects their underlying interest rate and credit risk.[4] For our second step, we use a replication argument that says that any fixed-income position can be replicated with a small number of bonds. This final step allows us to represent each balance sheet as an interest rate and credit risk factor portfolio. This factor portfolio mimics banks' exposures and allows me to also comment on the question of whether banks have gotten safer since the crisis.

To illustrate the first step of our method, take the loan portfolio of a bank. Its loan book is predominately reported at book value. Book values only coincide with fair values in the unlikely case that (1) the yield curve has not moved since the loan was originated and (2) the loan contains no credit risk. From the data, we observe the maturity and credit risk distribution, as well as the total dollar value of the position. Then, for each position of credit rating j and remaining maturity m, we calculate the implied coupon payments until the loan matures using the standard annuity formula. Because each coupon payment can be viewed as the face value of a zero-coupon bond, a loan book can be recast as a portfolio of zero-coupon bonds. The fair value of a zero-coupon bond equals just its appropriately discounted face value, where the discount rate reflects the duration and the risk of the bond.

Trading assets pose another challenge for our method. Trading assets are mainly derivatives of which interest rate swaps are the largest component. Even though banks report those positions at fair value, they do not report the trading direction of their derivatives. This means that we would not know whether a bank stands to win or to lose when interest rates rise. To fill this gap in the data, we estimate the trading direction of banks' interest rate derivative positions from profit and losses, notionals, and the history of interest rates. This allows us to conveniently represent the swap positions as a portfolio of bonds.

The end result of our estimation is a factor portfolio that has exposures to an interest rate factor as well as a credit risk factor, and is short in cash (see fig. 2). This portfolio intuitively resembles the maturity transforma-

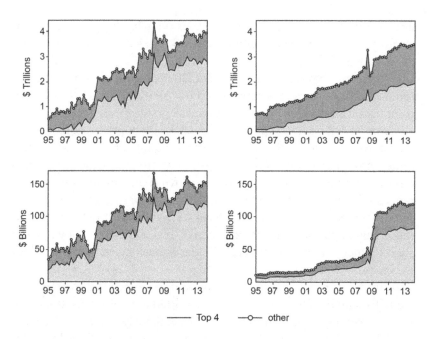

Fig. 2. Total factor exposures. This figure is reproduced from Begenau et al. (2015). Top row: exposures to interest rate risk (left panel) and credit risk (right panel). Black lines are total factor exposures of US banking sector; shading indicates contribution of top four bank holding companies (light) and all other banks (dark). Bottom row: gains or losses from one standard deviation realization of interest rate factor (left panel) and credit risk factor (right panel). Black lines are total gains/losses of US banking sector; shading indicates share of top four (light) and all others (dark).

tion and credit provision business of banks. Banks take on credit and interest rate risk when they make loans that are funded with shorter-term deposits or capital market debt.

Figure 2 shows the resulting interest rate and credit risk exposures of the aggregate banking sector. There are three notable points to make. First, for most of the sample, the interest rate risk exposure of banks (top left) dominates the credit risk exposure (top right). Second, the typical gains and losses due to interest rate risk (bottom left) exceed that of credit risk (bottom right). Third, consistent with the authors' conclusion that postcrisis regulations have not succeeded in reducing credit risk in banks' portfolios, the figure shows a doubling of the typical gains and losses on banks' credit exposure since the crisis. The reason is a rise in the conditional volatility of the credit factor post crisis, leading to higher expected gains and losses. Overall, though, interest rate risk still dominates.

For evidence on how interest rate risk matters for the default risk of banks, I plot the default rate of banks in figure 3 since the early 1970s together with the loan loss provision rate, which measures loan losses in a more timely manner. The top panel of figure 3 shows that bank default rates were much higher and persistently so during the savings and loan (S&L) crisis of the 1980s. The root causes for the S&L crisis (see, e.g., Hubbard 1991; White 1991; NCFIRRE 1993; FDIC 1997) were high interest rates. These hurt banks in three ways. First, faced with uncompetitively low deposit rates, depositors withdrew their funds to invest them in higher-yielding securities. Second, banks predominately held long-term and fixed-rate loans that were funded with short-term liabilities. The rise in funding rates meant banks incurred large losses. Third, high interest rates lowered the market value of assets and thus impaired banks' net worth. Attempts to salvage an impaired net worth position often involved investing in higher-yielding and therefore riskier assets, leading to credit losses later in the decade (see bottom panel of fig. 3).

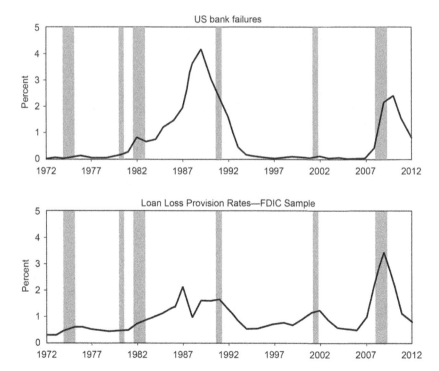

Fig. 3.   Bank default rates and credit risk (FDIC 2019). The gray bars denote recession periods as defined by NBER.

Taken together, this evidence suggests that interest rate risk should factor in both the risk-neutral probability calculation, as it may cause banks to default, as well as in the measurement of the franchise value.

Why Are Banks' Market Valuations Low?

Another interpretation of why bank valuation decreased over time comes from Begenau and Stafford (2018). In this paper, we directly measure the franchise value of banks from the perspective of shareholders by comparing banks against their closest capital market alternative. If banks are indeed the most efficient providers of products such as loans and deposits, we expect their competitive edge and therefore their franchise value to be large. The evidence that we bring to bear, however, challenges that very idea. Bank assets underperform a simple maturity-matched UST portfolio, and bank deposits are costlier than banks' non-deposit funding sources thanks to an expensive branch network.

As argued earlier, a significant source of risk for the aggregate banking sector comes from interest rates, consistent with the maturity transformation role of banks. In line with Begenau et al. (2015) and Atkeson et al., we assume that the portfolio of banks can be replicated with a bond portfolio. Similar exposures should be priced similarly.[5] Focusing on interest rate risk first, this implies that any asset should earn at least as much as required by its duration.

Based on a long-dated sample of commercial banks using data from the Federal Deposit Insurance Corporation, Table 1 compares the unlevered bank asset returns with the return of a maturity matched UST portfolio. To pick the appropriate maturity match for the UST portfolio, we take the average maturity of bank assets of 3 years from the data.[6] We compute the unlevered return on bank assets (ROA) as

$$\text{ROA}_t = \frac{\text{Net Income}_t - (1 - \tau)(\text{Deposit Income} - \text{Interest}_t - (1 - s)\text{OpEx}_t)}{\text{Assets}_{t-1}}$$

where τ denotes the tax rate and s the assumption for the share of operating expenses that are attributed to assets as opposed to deposits.[7] The net income variable is the correct numerator for the return on equity but not for the ROA. To calculate the ROA, we need to add back all interest expenses, deduct any deposit service fees from noninterest income, and add back the deposit share of operating expenses. To compare banks' smoothed book returns with capital market returns, we apply the same accounting method to the latter. Using the book value measure of the

Table 1
Unlevered Return on Bank Assets Compared with 3-Year US Treasury

Annual Percentage	Return on Assets			3-Year UST	
	s = 30%	s = 50%	s = 70%	MV	BV
Full sample 1960–2015:					
Mean	4.49	4.06	3.64	5.88	5.74
SD	1.73	1.69	1.65	4.41	2.60
Tstat t test $\mu^{Rep} - \mu^{B} = 0$				3.47	5.49
Correlations:					
UST 3-year MV	.70	.71	.72	. . .	. . .
UST 3-year BV	.90	.92	.93	. . .	. . .
1960–80:					
Mean	4.18	3.83	3.48	5.24	5.57
SD	1.82	1.78	1.73	3.00	2.36

Source: This table is an excerpt from table 2 in Begenau and Stafford (2018). The data are from FDIC (2019).
Note: UST = US Treasury; MV = market value; BV = book value; SD = standard deviation. We calculate the book value of the 3-year UST portfolio as BV(t+1) = BV(t) + interest income – purchases + proceeds. A share 1 – s of the operating expense is attributed to assets.

3-year UST portfolio significantly increases its correlation with bank ROA (see table 1).

The results (tabulated in table 1) suggest that bank assets underperform a maturity-matched portfolio by 1.68% per year on average. In short, bank assets do not earn the required return implied by their embedded interest rate exposure. The difference is large and not merely an artifact of our operating expense assumption. With roughly 3% of assets and 40% of equity, banks' operating expenses exceed even the cost of expensive investment vehicles such as hedge funds that have costs amounting to 4%–6% of invested capital.

Recent academic papers assert that deposits are an important source of bank value (see, e.g., Egan, Lewellen, and Sunderam 2017; Drechsler, Savov, and Schnabl 2018). One often cited reason is that deposits look cheaper compared with nondeposit funding options, as deposit rates are typically below other funding rates.[8] However, they are also associated with a costly branch network, as figure 4 shows. Operating expenses increase exponentially in the number of branches, and so do deposits. Based on cross-sectional regressions of log expenses on log deposits and log loans, a 1% change in deposits is associated with a 0.47% change in log expenses. Taking into account the operating expenses on deposits increases the average annual deposit cost rate from 2.91% to 4.89% over the

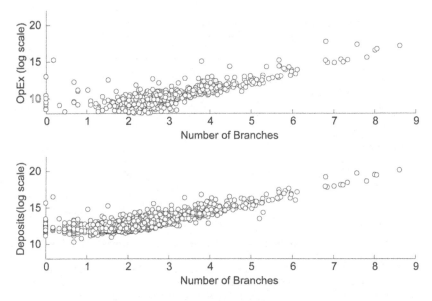

Fig. 4. Branches and expenses

period from 1960 to 2015, whereas nondeposit debt costs banks only 4.29%.[9] The scope for a funding advantage of banks is therefore small.

What can be taken away from this evidence? A positive franchise value means a firm has created value beyond the value of its inputs. It is a time-varying notion that depends on market conditions affecting the opportunity cost of capital. Valuation models take this into account by choosing a discount rate that represents the best alternative for the capital provider. By relying on banks' (regulators') static estimates of loan (deposit) fair values, the authors lean heavily on banks' (regulators') proper application of equation (1) instead of taking their valuation model more seriously and apply it directly to the data as in Begenau et al. (2015) and Begenau and Stafford (2018). Although the authors find a positive franchise value based on bank-supplied fair value estimates, the results in Begenau and Stafford (2018) suggest that banks have a negative franchise value. This discussion also affects the calculation of the model-implied market value of bank equity, as both the opportunity costs of capital and the default state calculation are sensitive to it. Certainly, it is plausible that higher capital cushions have reduced the value of government guarantees. But how much of the reduction in banks' market valuation is due to government guarantees, franchise value, or some unmodeled factor still remains to be ascertained.

Conclusion

Atkeson et al. present a useful and clever way to decompose aggregate bank valuation ratios into a government guarantee part and a franchise value part. The accounting model is very transparent and insightful to think through, as it requires an examination of the assumed sources of bank value. Using this decomposition, they claim that (1) bank valuations decreased since the crisis because of a sharp reduction in the value of government guarantees, and (2) despite that, banks have not become safer.

This discussion provides evidence that is consistent with the second conclusion, namely that banks have not decreased their overall risk exposure since the crisis. In fact, the evidence I bring to bear shows that banks' credit risk exposure has since doubled. I have also presented evidence that calls for a more skeptical stance toward the paper's first conclusion. The business model of banking is at its core an interest rate spread and volume business, both of which are sensitive to market interest rates. Without taking into account interest rate risk and investors' opportunity costs, the proposed valuation model is going to mismeasure the market and franchise value of banks. Notwithstanding some important details of the accounting exercise, Atkeson et al. shine a light on how to make productive use of banks' market and accounting data to speak to a first-order question.

Endnotes

Author's email address: begenau@stanford.edu. For acknowledgments, sources of research support, and disclosure of the author's material financial relationships, if any, please see http://www.nber.org/chapters/c14086.ack.
1. The evidence suggests that government guarantees are particularly important for large banks (Gandhi and Lustig 2015) and the aggregate banking sector (Kelly, Lustig, and Van Nieuwerburgh 2016).
2. Different states, such as default and nondefault, can be captured by computing the expected value of the discounted cash flows for each state.
3. In fact, banks' accounting rules require trading assets and most securities to be recorded at fair value, suggesting one avenue for a potential mismeasurement of banks' franchise value.
4. Begenau, Bigio, and Majerovitz (2018) show the problem with relying on the accounting measures provided by banks. Banks' book equity includes banks' own fair value estimates for most securities and trading assets but yet does not capture losses as well as market values do. Thus, caution should be exercised when taking fair value estimates from banks at face value as the authors do to calculate the franchise value.
5. We rely on this fundamental insight (see, e.g., Merton 1995; Merton and Bodie 1995) when we compare the return of banks against the return of a maturity-matched UST portfolio.
6. The data come from the quarterly regulatory filings of commercial banks. This calculation uses the remaining maturity for fixed-rate securities and the next repricing date for floating-rate securities.

7. Bank branches are a key driver of banks' operating expenses. Banks rely on bank branches to sustain their deposit franchise and to make loans.

8. Since the financial crisis and the ensuing low interest rate policy, even the funding advantage based on interest rates alone has dissipated. Drechsler et al. (2018) suggest that deposits are valuable because they insulate banks against interest rate risk. The evidence in English et al. (2018) is inconsistent with this interpretation, as the stock return of banks most reliant on core deposit funding reacts more negatively to interest rate shocks. Although net interest margins of these core-deposit-heavy banks remain constant, they lose deposits at higher rates, forcing them to either replace deposits with nondeposit funds or to shrink assets. The study shows that banks do both.

9. This calculation assumes an asset expense share of 50%. When 30% (70%) of expenses are allocated to assets, deposits cost 5.59% (4.10%).

References

Begenau, J., S. Bigio, and J. Majerovitz. 2018. "Banks Adjust Slowly—Evidence and Lessons for Modeling." Technical report, Stanford University.

Begenau, J., M. Piazzesi, and M. Schneider. 2015. "Banks' Risk Exposure." Technical report, Stanford University.

Begenau, J., and E. Stafford. 2018. "Do Banks Have an Edge?" Technical report, Stanford University.

Drechsler, I., A. Savov, and P. Schnabl. 2018. "Banking on Deposits: Maturity Transformation without Interest Rate Risk." Working Paper no. 24582 (May), NBER, Cambridge, MA.

Egan, M., S. Lewellen, and A. Sunderam. 2017. "The Cross Section of Bank Value." Working Paper no. 23291 (March), NBER, Cambridge, MA.

English, W. B., S. J. Van den Heuvel, and E. Zakrajšek. 2018. "Interest Rate Risk and Bank Equity Valuations." *Journal of Monetary Economics* 98:80–97.

FDIC (Federal Deposit Insurance Corporation). 1997. *History of the Eighties: Lessons for the Future.* https://www.fdic.gov/bank/historical/history/.

FDIC (Federal Deposit Insurance Corporation). 2019. "Commercial Banks—Historical Statistics on Banking." https://www5.fdic.gov/hsob/SelectRpt.asp?EntryTyp=10&Header=1.

Gandhi, P., and H. Lustig. 2015. "Size Anomalies in US Bank Stock Returns." *Journal of Finance* 70:733–68.

Hubbard, R. 1991. *Financial Markets and Financial Crises.* Chicago: University of Chicago Press.

Kelly, B., H. Lustig, and S. Van Nieuwerburgh. 2016. "Too-Systemic-to-Fail: What Option Markets Imply about Sector-Wide Government Guarantees." *American Economic Review* 106:1278–1319.

Merton, R. C. 1995. "A Functional Perspective of Financial Intermediation." *Financial Management* 24 (2): 23–41.

Merton, R. C., and Z. Bodie. 1995. "A Conceptual Framework for Analyzing the Financial System." In *The Global Financial System: A Functional Perspective,* ed. Dwight B. Crane et al., 3–31. Boston: Harvard Business School Press.

NCFIRRE (National Commission on Financial Institution Reform, Recovery, and Enforcement). 1993. *Origins and Causes of the S&L Debacle: A Blueprint for Reform: A Report to the President and Congress of the United States.* Washington, DC: National Commission on Financial Institution Reform, Recovery, and Enforcement.

White, L. J. 1991. *The S&L Debacle: Public Policy Lessons for Bank and Thrift Regulation.* New York: Oxford University Press.

Comment

Lawrence H. Summers, *Harvard University and NBER*

I salute the authors' endeavor to use market price to examine the riskiness of the financial system and to evaluate the change in the subsidy represented by government guarantees. As illustrated by my work with Natasha Sarin (Sarin and Summers 2016), which the authors reference, I believe that market information is at a minimum a valuable complement to accounting information in evaluating the health of banks. I would guess that their broad conclusion—that if a crisis like 2008 were to happen again, we would have insolvent banks—is correct. And I find it plausible that, as the authors believe, a combination of more regulatory capital, establishment of resolution procedures, and official commitments to move beyond too-big-to-fail have reduced the market's perception of implicit guarantees.

That said, I have to report that I'm almost entirely unconvinced by any of the authors' estimates and believe that all reflect arbitrary and in some cases implausible modeling assumptions. I do not believe they have any real basis for their claims about the extent to which declining franchise value, as opposed to capitalized government subsidies, is responsible for banks' low market-to-book equity ratios. It's not that I have clearly different views than the authors, just that I do not believe their measurements are convincing.

First, there are some real questions about the theory of subsidies that are raised by the kind of analysis that is done here. Let's imagine that the government decided to subsidize ice cream cones for all companies that sold ice cream cones. What would we expect? I think we would expect that there would be lower-priced ice cream cones. I think we would expect that the quantity of ice cream cones sold would go up. I think we would expect no change in the Q ratio of ice cream cone companies, if this was a competitive industry. If ice cream cones, and the production of ice cream cones, involved investment that took place with adjustment costs, we would expect some brief interval of higher profits before the industry expanded, but to the first approximation, the change in the Q ratio would be very small compared with the magnitude of the change in government subsidies.

Of course, matters would be different if ice cream cones were produced by a monopolist or if there were barriers to entry into ice cream cone production or limits on the expansion of ice cream cone producers. Then one would expect more capitalization of the subsidy into the market value of ice cream cone companies. Suppose an economist who for some reason didn't know the size of the subsidy sought to infer it from ice cream cone company stock prices. I do not think she would be taken seriously. There would be little basis for knowing how much of the subsidy was capitalized and how much in the market's view would be competed away. And there would be many other things happening economy-wide that would affect ice cream cone company stock prices.

Now, let's suppose that the key input into the production of bank loans is bank liabilities, and let's suppose that the government subsidizes bank liabilities. Then, if one assumes that the banking industry is competitive, it seems to me, one would reach an essentially parallel conclusion, that expanded subsidies from the government would lead to competition between all the banks, which would lead to expansion by the banks, but it would not lead to an increase in the long-term profitability on assets of banks.

Now, if banks were small compared with the loan industry, and so the pricing of loans didn't change, things would be different. Similarly, things would be different if the price of ice cream cones was fixed and only one small sector of ice cream cone manufacturers were subsidized. But that would surprise me as the right assumption with respect to bank loans. If the whole banking industry were a monopoly, one would expect that my analysis was wrong, as with ice cream cone monopolists.

I would guess that banks are closer to competitive than to being long-term monopolies, but the key point is that, as with ice cream cones, inferring the value of the subsidy from stock prices is implausible. In appendix B, "Question 4," the authors attempt to respond to this issue, but I have trouble following their argument.

Second, assume away this set of problems. It seems to me, there are a variety of more specific reasons to doubt the estimates the authors provide.

One point: When Sarin and I were doing our work, we thought a lot about changes in the "too-big-to-fail" subsidy and using option theory to deal with this aspect. I decided that if the government operated the way it would in the model—which is the government properly watched bank assets and liabilities, was in a position to liquidate those assets and liabilities, and liquidated banks as soon as assets equaled those liabilities—then, except for jumps, the government guarantee would be costless. So, the "too big to fail" subsidy would be all about jumps, and there really weren't that many jumps, in practice. After all, stock prices rarely move 5% in a day.

An actual valuation of the liability guarantee has to recognize that the government is not that smart; that the government isn't that good at measuring these things precisely; that the government is heavily influenced by politics; and, therefore, that the government would tend to be late to the party in recognizing asset value declines, particularly on illiquid assets like bank loans. There is also the point that the government will not be able to realize the same value from the assets that the banks could have as an ongoing concern. Why should you repay an institution that's about to close and will never be in a position to lend you money or do anything to you again?

So, the value of the put option represented by a government liability guarantee depends crucially on its horizon, which in turn depends upon these heavily institutional questions: How slow is the government, and what are the problems with the liquid markets assumption? It is right to apply option theory in principle. But I can't imagine why one would suppose that a two-state model that assumed that one was in a crisis or one was not in a crisis, that capital was checked annually, and that at some moment—like the trough of the 2008 crisis—liquidation was possible were reasonable approximations. Option theory when you do not know the strike price of the option or its horizon is not actually very helpful.

In addition, I will confidently predict that if you just looked at the stock market, in real terms, it would track fairly accurately Tobin's Q for the whole economy and the ratio of the market value to the book value of banks. This suggests that much of what is driving fluctuations in bank market-to-book ratios is broad economic factors. The authors suggest otherwise. This is because they do not reckon with the differences between marking to market and book value accounting. I would be very surprised if the fair value calculation that's used in the authors' calculations corresponds to an actual market value of loans when loan sales were attempted in 2008. The authors' procedure, in effect, smoothes franchise value very substantially and attributes the rest of the fluctuation in market value to fluctuating values in the government guarantee, and then, not very surprisingly, concludes that the fluctuating values of the government guarantee are a large part of what is going on.

Also, I was struck that a substantial part of the risk in the banking system must have to do with duration mismatches. Certainly, if one looks at specific institutions, there must be a number that, at any given moment, are substantially mismatched. This further reduced my confidence in the calibration.

Finally, I would simply suggest that it is almost impossible for me to believe that there was not a substantial behavioral element in the valuation of bank stocks in the run-up to the 2007 period. So, to somehow suggest that all of the valuation is best thought of as either a rational calculation of franchise value or as a value of a government guarantee seems to me pretty substantially unlikely.

Sarin and I recognized that it was a basically uninteresting comparison to look at various measures of bank volatility or various measures of required returns on preferred stock in the current period and compare those with the 2005 to 2007 period, which we took to obviously be distorted by investor misperceptions. We thought the interesting comparisons were with the pre-2005 period, which were plausibly without those misperceptions or at least had fewer of them.

For all these reasons, the authors' effort to calibrate the importance of franchise value versus government subsidy value is unconvincing, even if I wave aside the fact that I would expect the principal effect of the subsidies to flow into lending rates rather than bank stock prices.[1]

In addition, there are some subtle issues that I do not feel I fully understand having to do with the relationship between franchise value and bank capital. The authors write—and at times Sarin and I wrote—as if franchise value was a perfect substitute for bank capital. If the bank has more capital, it's a sounder bank. If the bank has more franchise value, it's got more capital, so it's a sounder bank. However, if a bank goes out of business it likely loses its franchise value. And so if I am thinking about my risk in lending to a bank, then if the bank is sitting with assets that it can sell, that is reassuring to me about the health of the bank. If the bank is sitting with franchise value, whose existence depends on people like me all not staging a run, that is at least a more problematic scenario. And so, the question of what the relationship is between franchise value and economic capital—and its relationship to stability—is delicate. Franchise value is an illiquid asset.

I don't think the treatment in this paper is quite right. It's clear to me that it's better to have franchise value than it is to not have franchise value, but it sure feels to me like it's better to have a dollar of book value of equity than to have a dollar of franchise value. Just how one compares these, I'm not sure. There's probably a big distinction here between big banks and small banks. If you're a little community bank and your franchise value takes the form of a bunch of sticky deposits, if you fail you're going to get sold to a somewhat bigger bank that's going to continue to have those deposits, so your franchise value is fine. If you're a large institution that cannot be sold, whatever your franchise value is exactly, it seems to me that it is a much more problematic thing from the point of view of your stability.

A final broad point: the large question that I don't think this paper resolves, and that I certainly don't think that Sarin and I resolve, is how best to integrate market value information and book information in assuring bank stability. I am reasonably sure that relying only on the market is foolish. You would conclude on the basis of a variety of measures—pricing of subordinated debt, option value calculations based on the volatility of equity, for example—that the banking system was extremely safe in 2007. So, I'm fairly sure that that is a serious mistake.

I am almost equally confident that ignoring market value information and relying on book accounting value is an egregious error. I would note that the chairman of the SEC proudly proclaimed that Bear Stearns's capital ratio was around 14% the week it failed. I would note that the relevant authorities professed Wachovia, Washington Mutual, and Citigroup all to be well capitalized and without problem as measured by capital ratios on the brink of their failure. I would note that surely the most egregious failure associated with the financial crisis, and one of the least remarked, is the failure of the authorities to do anything to stop dividends or force capital raising in the period from summer 2007 to summer 2008, when much could have been done and when markets were sending fairly clear signals that all was not well.

So it seems to me it is clear that some kind of two-key system is necessary, where regulators become alarmed either if accounting information provides grounds for alarm or if markets provide grounds for alarm, but as to how that best can be implemented, I have not seen what I would regard as substantially practical proposals.

And I would note, finally, that anyone who believes that this problem is in hand should ponder the fact that our regulatory authorities, as a group, proclaim each year some form of the proposition that I would regard as being at the edge of absurd.[2] That if the Dow were to fall to 10,000, if house prices were to fall 50% more than they fell during the 2008 crisis, if the unemployment rate were to reach double digits, that no major financial institution would suffer a loss of more than 5% of its capital or be in any need of raising capital.[3]

Whether we need to have a financial system that is fully insured against that contingency or whether we can rely on some broader public insurance for that fairly rare contingency is, I think, a legitimate question for debate. But to suppose as the Federal Reserve stress tests do that all major institutions could weather a storm much worse than 2008 without needing to raise capital seems to me highly dubious. Certainly extrapolations from market information on banks' health suggest cause for grave concern. All is not in hand.

Endnotes

For acknowledgments, sources of research support, and disclosure of the author's material financial relationships, if any, please see http://www.nber.org/chapters/c14087.ack.

1. The authors attempt to respond to some of these points in app. B. But I do not think they provide convincing defenses of their option horizon assumption, their use of fair value accounting, or their ignoring behavioral aspects of bank stock pricing.

2. In fact, Sarin and I are working on a follow-on paper that makes exactly this point (Sarin and Summers, forthcoming). A naive "market-based" stress test produces outcomes much less sanguine than the Federal Reserve's annual exercise.

3. For a description of the most recent severely adverse stress scenario, see Board of Governors of the Federal Reserve System (2018).

References

Board of Governors of the Federal Reserve System. 2018. *Dodd-Frank Act Stress Test 2018: Supervisory Stress Test Methodology and Results*. https://www.federalreserve.gov/publications/files/2018-dfast-methodology-results-20180621.pdf.

Sarin, Natasha, and Lawrence H. Summers. 2016. "Understanding Bank Risk through Market Measures." *Brookings Papers on Economic Activity* 2016 (2): 57–127.

Sarin, Natasha, and Lawrence H. Summers. Forthcoming. "On Market-Based Approaches to the Valuation of Capital." In *The Handbook of Financial Stress-Testing*. Cambridge: Cambridge University Press.

Discussion

The authors opened the discussion by addressing three concerns raised by the discussants. First, they pointed out their model assumes that asset holdings and liabilities grow at an exogenous rate. As a consequence, the balance sheet of banks is inelastic with respect to government guarantees, and the value of deposit insurance is not competed away, as noted by Lawrence Summers during his discussion. The authors agreed that changes in regulation or government guarantees could affect the size of the banking sector and that this issue is important for policy making. They argued that this response is slow due to adjustment costs in the banking sector, and the market-to-book ratio is expected to increase during the transition.

Second, the authors acknowledged that both the reaction time before bailout and the presence of jump risk are key determinants of the value of government guarantees, as emphasized by Summers. Their calibration assumes a market-to-book ratio of 2, corresponding to that observed during the period of interest, and a risk-neutral probability of a crisis of 5%. With a reaction time of a year, their model predicts a government bailout worth half of book equity. They noted that with a precrisis book equity value of banks around $1.1 trillion, this amounts to a subsidy of $550 billion. In the authors' view, this figure is comparable to the actual government support during crisis, which speaks in favor of a 1-year delay before bailout.

Third, the authors confirmed that their model abstracts from interest rate risk, as highlighted by Juliane Begenau as part of her discussion. They argued that such risk does not generate large enough losses over the course of a year to rationalize the value of government guarantees. Credit risk is more attractive in this respect, they mentioned, due to larger jumps and tail risk. In the authors' opinion, the role of interest rate risk during earlier episodes, including the savings and loans crisis, was associated with longer reaction times by regulators.

The next two comments were related to the timing and the nature of government interventions, and their importance for the value of government guarantees.

Robert Hall pointed out that the Dodd-Frank legislation requires orderly and timely resolution of impending failures. He noted that timely resolution should ensure that the government doesn't have to pay deposit insurance, absent unanticipated jumps. Similarly, he reminded the audience that orderly resolution takes the form of haircuts on subordinated creditors and does not involve liquidation. Hall suggested that the authors' assumptions are at odds with important features of the existing regulatory framework. The authors responded that subordinated debt was small precrisis (around 1%) and that the total loss-absorbing capacity postcrisis under the proposed regulation remained below 6%. They argued that the losses associated with a decline in asset values of 16% to 25% would exceed the loss-absorbing capacity and would require a bailout. In addition, the authors emphasized the importance of jumps in price options, and argued that such jumps are large in practice.

Benjamin Friedman agreed with the authors that delays in government interventions are important in practice. In his view, such delays cannot be explained by a slow response of regulators per se. They are instead due to the time required for banks and regulators to value the nonmarketed assets on banks' balance sheets, determine which loans should be classified, and decide what share of these loans to write down. Summers shared Friedman's view and noted that banks hold illiquid assets that are complicated to value. Summers also pointed out that current regulations allow for valuations of loans that are more sluggish than those produced by market-to-market accounting. He considered such valuation methods as a substantial contributor to the bad management during the financial crisis.

The authors agreed that such valuation issues might be important for traditional banks. They referred to recent work by Charles W. Calomiris and Doron Nissim ("Crisis-Related Shifts in the Market Valuation of Banking Activities," *Journal of Financial Intermediation* 23, no. 3 [2014]: 400–35) and Bernadette A. Minton, René M. Stulz, and Alvaro G. Taboada ("Are Larger Banks Valued More Highly?" [Working Paper no. 23212, NBER, Cambridge, MA, 2017]). This work documents that the market-to-book ratio declines with bank size as well as the size of the trading arm relative to the commercial activity arm. The authors also noted that banks' total exposure to aggregate risk is roughly similar across the size distribution of banks but that small banks are more exposed through their loan book and less through their trading book. Finally, the authors pointed out that their paper explains the large decline in market-to-book ratio during the crisis and its persistence since then, but does not explain its increase in the 1980s.

Summers also questioned the authors' estimates of the market value of banks. He noted that market equity corresponds to the value of an option on the underlying assets and liabilities of banks, rather than an estimate of the corresponding value of assets net of liabilities. In addition, he argued that the Gordon dividend growth model, which the authors use in their paper, typically fails to track the volatility of market value. The authors responded that they focus on long time periods and do not attempt to match short-term movements in market value. The authors also offered a more general comment about the relative importance of franchise value and government guarantees to explain the decline in market-to-book ratio during the financial crisis. They argued that the franchise value captures in part the difference between the risk-neutral probability assigned to a crisis by banks and that assigned by outside investors. A decline in the franchise value during the financial crisis suggests that banks were more pessimistic when reporting asset values than outside investors, which the authors viewed as unlikely.

Summers expressed skepticism about the paper's view that an erosion of too-big-too-fail guarantees could explain the recent decline in market-to-book ratio. Two alternative explanations seemed more plausible to him. Referring to Begenau's discussion, Summers suggested that the value added by banks might be intrinsically low and that increased competition by nonbanks and limits on overdraft fees dissipated rents. Alternatively, he suggested that the franchise value of banks reflects the degree of optimism of outside investors regarding the performance of the banking sector. Summers reiterated his view that pessimism about financial institutions is key to understanding the decline in market-to-book ratio since 2007. Jonathan Parker noted that the Dodd-Frank legislation might in fact have created more rents, especially for bigger banks, despite contrary claims from the banking sector. Martin Eichenbaum emphasized the intrinsic link between regulation and competition and cited Canada as an example of a country with high returns on investments, high regulation, and low competition. Finally, the authors clarified that they attribute the decline in the market-to-book ratio to a decrease in the option value of default. Such a decrease, they continued, is due to a higher loss-absorbing capacity rather than to more restrictive or more uncertain bailouts under the new regulations.

3

Accounting for Factorless Income

Loukas Karabarbounis, *University of Minnesota and NBER*
Brent Neiman, *University of Chicago and NBER*

I. Introduction

The value added produced in an economy equals payments accruing to labor and capital plus economic profits earned by producers selling at prices that exceed the average cost of production. Equivalently, the labor share of income, the capital share of income, and the profit share of income sum up to one. Separating these components of income is crucial in order to understand the economy's production technology, the evolution of competition across firms, and the responsiveness to various tax and regulatory policies.

Measurement of each of the three shares has proven a challenging task. Payments accruing to labor are most directly observable because they are commonly included in standard reporting for corporate financial and tax purposes. Direct measurements of the capital share and profit share are more difficult to obtain. This is because most producers own, rather than rent, their capital stocks, and capital accumulation is subject to factors that are difficult to observe, such as investment risk, adjustment costs, depreciation and obsolescence, and financial constraints. Additionally, various forms of capital such as brand equity and organizational capital are difficult to measure in practice. Given the relative ease of observing payments to labor, the labor share has historically been a more common focus of empirical work on factor shares than the capital share or the profit share.[1]

A large wave of recent work has documented a decline in the labor share starting around 1980. Karabarbounis and Neiman (2014) found this decline to be a global phenomenon, present within the majority of countries and industries around the world.[2] Most analyses of the US data that we are aware of, including our baseline analysis below, show that imputed payments to capital do not rise sufficiently during this period to fully offset the measured decline in payments to labor. As a result, there is a significant amount of residual payments—or what we label "factorless income"—that, at least since the early 1980s, has been growing as a share of value added. Formally, we define factorless income as the difference between measured value added Y and the sum of measured payments to labor WL and imputed rental payments to capital RK:

$$\text{Factorless Income} = Y - WL - RK, \tag{1}$$

where we obtain value added Y, payments to labor WL, and capital K from the national accounts and calculate the rental rate R using a standard formula as in Hall and Jorgenson (1967).

How should one interpret factorless income? A first method, case Π, embraces the possibility that firms have pricing power that varies over time and interprets factorless income as economic profits Π.[3] A second method, case K, emphasizes that capital stock estimates can be sensitive to initial conditions, assumptions about depreciation and obsolescence, and unmeasured investment flows in intangibles or organizational capital, and attributes factorless income to understatement of K.[4] A third method, case R, attributes factorless income to elements such as time-varying risk premia or financial frictions that generate a wedge between the imputed rental rate R using a Hall-Jorgenson formula and the rental rate that firms perceive when making their investment decisions.[5] When thinking about strategies that allocate factorless income, in short, we need to decide: "Is it Π, is it K, or is it R?"

The contribution of this paper is to assess the plausibility of each of these three methodologies to allocate factorless income and to highlight their consequences for our understanding of the effects of various macroeconomic trends. We begin our analyses in Section II in a largely model-free environment. Aside from a standard model-based formula for the rental rate of capital, we rely only on accounting identities and external measurements to ensure an internally consistent allocation of the residual income. Section III introduces a variant of the neoclassical growth model with monopolistic competition, multiple sectors and types of capital, and representative hand-to-mouth workers and forward-looking capitalists. In Section IV, we back out the exogenous driving processes such that the model perfectly reproduces the time series of all endogenous variables in the data as interpreted by each of the three cases. We then solve for counterfactuals in which we shut down various exogenous processes driving the economy's dynamics and assess how their effects on output, factor shares, and consumption inequality between capitalists and workers depend on the strategy employed for allocating factorless income.

Case II, where the residual is allocated to economic profits, is characterized by a tight negative comovement between the real interest rate, measured by the difference between the nominal rate on 10-year US Treasuries and expected inflation, and the profit share. Mechanically, the decline in the real interest rate since the early 1980s has driven the surge in the profit share since then, a pattern emphasized in Barkai (2016) and Eggertsson, Robbins, and Wold (2018). A focus on recent decades, however, masks a significant decline in the profit share between the 1970s and the 1980s. We find that the profit share, as interpreted under case II, is in fact lower today than it was in the 1960s and the 1970s when real rates were also low.

Further, case II requires both labor-augmenting and capital-augmenting technology to fluctuate wildly between the late 1970s and the early 1980s along with the rise and fall of the real interest rate. This extreme variability of technology is found regardless of whether the elasticity of substitution between capital and labor is above or below one. Our counterfactuals for case II imply that the significant decline in markups between the 1970s and the 1980s contributed to a decline in the relative consumption of capitalists and to an increase in the labor share. The subsequent rise in profits reverses these trends after the mid-1980s. Beginning from 1960, however, the effects of markups on output, factor shares, and inequality are muted because markups did not exhibit a significant trend over the past 55 years.[6]

We conclude that the large swings in the profit share and the volatility in inferred factor-augmenting technologies cast doubts on the plausibility of case II as a methodology to account for factorless income. De Loecker and Eeckhout (2017), however, use a different approach that also reveals a recent surge in profits. They demonstrate in Compustat data a significant rise in sales relative to the cost of goods sold (COGS) since the 1980s, a shift that underlies their estimate of an increase in markups. We demonstrate in these same data, however, that the increase in sales relative to COGS almost entirely reflects a shift in the share of operating costs that are reported as being selling, general, and administrative (SG&A) expenses instead of COGS. Using the sum of COGS and SG&A instead of COGS only, we find that the inferred markup is essentially flat over time.[7] The shift from COGS to SG&A—which we document also occurred in a number of other countries—is consistent with many possibilities, including changing classifications of what constitutes production, outsourcing, and greater intensity in the use of intangibles in production. It is also consistent with a rise in fixed costs, which opens the possibility of increasing markups without a rise in economic profits. Given this sensitivity, we remain skeptical of case II.

Case K attributes factorless income to unmeasured forms of capital. We calculate time series for the price, depreciation rate, and investment spending on unmeasured capital that fully account for factorless income. Many such series can be constructed, but we offer one where these variables do not behave implausibly after the 1980s. While the size of missing capital is broadly consistent with the inferred "e-capital" in Hall (2001) and the measured organizational capital in Eisfeldt and Papanikolaou (2013) after the 1980s, accounting for factorless income requires that in the years before 1970 the stock of missing capital be worth nearly 60% of the entire capital stock. Case K additionally implies that output growth deviates from the growth of measured gross domestic product (GDP) in the national accounts. We demonstrate that this deviation need not be significant in most years, with growth being within 0.5 percentage point of measured growth in all but 4 years since 1960. There are some years, however, when the growth rates deviate significantly.

Case K leads to far more reasonable inferences of labor-augmenting and capital-augmenting technology. While quantitative differences exist for the role of exogenous processes in driving the US dynamics, the key patterns generated under case K resemble those under case II. For example, similar to case II, we find that this case also assigns the most important role in accounting for the long-term increase in consumption inequality between capitalists and workers to the slowdown of labor-augmenting technology growth.

Our last case, case R, adjusts the opportunity cost of capital until it implies a rental rate such that equation (1) results in zero factorless income. We demonstrate that this adjusted opportunity cost component in firms' rental rate has been relatively stable, ranging during the last half century from levels slightly above 10% to levels slightly above 5%. We also find that this adjusted cost increased between the 1980s and the 2000s. This contrasts with the real interest rate based on US Treasury prices, which jumped by nearly 10 percentage points from the late 1970s to the early 1980s, before slowly returning to the near zero levels by the 2010s. Our case R results relate closely to the conclusion in Caballero, Farhi, and Gourinchas (2017) that rising risk premia have generated a growing wedge between Treasury rates and corporate borrowing costs in recent decades.[8] Among the three cases, we show that the fluctuations in both labor-augmenting and capital-augmenting technology are the smallest in case R.[9] Finally, case R attributes to the opportunity cost of capital the most important role for consumption inequality between capitalists and workers simply because this cost, and therefore capitalists' consumption growth, is higher than in the other cases.

Collectively, we view our results as tempering enthusiasm for any one of these ways to alone account for factorless income, especially so for case II and case K. The observation in case II of a post-1980 increase in profits has called for heightened enforcement of antitrust laws and calls to eliminate licensing restrictions and other barriers to entry. But our work leads to the conclusion that profits are only now returning to the historical levels of the 1960s and 1970s after having been unusually low in the 1980s and 1990s. Further, case II requires a narrative tightly linking lower interest rates to rising market power at high frequencies, such as through the greater ease of financing mergers, or tightly linking greater market power to lower interest rates, such as through reduced investment demand by monopolists. Case K plausibly accounts for recent movements of factorless income and, given the changing nature of production, we do not think it should be dismissed in terms of its implications for growth, factor shares, and investment. The case we explore requires an implausibly large unmeasured capital stock early in the sample in order to entirely account for factorless income. We acknowledge, however, the possibility that additional flexibility in the specification of missing capital accumulation may allow researchers to account for factorless income with less extreme values of initial missing capital. Case R in many ways produces the most stable outcomes. While we find it plausible that the cost of capital perceived by firms in making their investment decisions deviates from the cost of capital one would impute based on US Treasuries, we acknowledge that embracing this case more fully requires a thorough understanding of what causes time variations in this deviation; we currently do not offer such an explanation. Finally, we note that the interpretation of some key macroeconomic trends during the past 50 years proves largely invariant to the treatment of factorless income. For example, the rapid decline in the relative price of information technology (IT) investment goods and the slowdown in labor-augmenting technology growth play important roles for macroeconomic dynamics in all cases.

II. Three Strategies for Allocating Factorless Income

In this section we analyze the three strategies for allocating factorless income. We begin by populating the terms in equation (1) used to define factorless income. Our data cover the US economy and come from the Bureau of Economic Analysis (BEA), including the National Income and Product Accounts (NIPA) and Fixed Asset Tables (FAT). All our analyses begin in 1960, since the BEA began its measurement of a number of categories of intellectual property products in 1959 and refined its measure of research and development (R&D) in 1960.

We study the private sector and therefore remove the contribution of the government sector to nominal output Y and labor compensation WL in equation (1).[10] Some of our analyses distinguish between the business sector's value added ($P^Q Q$) and profits (Π^Q) and the housing sector's value added ($P^H H$) and profits (Π^H), where total output is $Y = p^Q Q + p^H H$ and total profits are $\Pi = \Pi^Q + \Pi^H$.

We impute rental payments to capital RK in equation (1) as the sum of those accruing to each of several types of capital j, so that $RK = \sum_j R^j K^j$. Similar to our treatment of output and compensation, we remove government capital and bundle the other capital types into three mutually exclusive groups: IT capital ($j = I$), non-IT capital ($j = N$), and residential or housing capital ($j = H$).[11] Profits in the housing sector are defined as $\Pi^H = P^H H - R^H K^H$.

Each rental rate R^j is constructed using data on capital prices ξ^j, depreciation rates δ^j, the real interest rate r, the tax rate on investment τ^x, and the tax rate on capital τ^k using the following formula:[12]

$$R_t^j = \frac{(1 + \tau_t^x)\xi_t^j}{1 - \tau_t^k} \left[\left(\frac{(1 + \tau_{t-1}^x)\xi_{t-1}^j}{(1 + \tau_t^x)\xi_t^j} \right) (1 + (1 - \tau_t^k)r_t) - (1 - \delta_t^j) - \frac{\tau_t^k \delta_t^j}{1 + \tau_t^x} \right]. \quad (2)$$

We derive equation (2) in Section III.D from the optimality conditions of a representative capitalist. Our baseline measure of the real interest rate equals the nominal rate on 10-year US Treasuries minus a 5-year moving average of realized inflation that proxies expected inflation.[13] Additional details on our data construction are found in the online replication file.[14]

Figure 1 plots the share of private sector value added paid to labor, or the labor share $s_L = WN/Y$, and the implied shares of each type of capital, $s_K^j = R^j K^j / Y$. We smooth all time series (throughout the paper) by reporting 5-year moving averages.[15] The labor share measure declines secularly, from levels near 60% before 1980 to 56% by 2016. The capital share calculations, done separately for each of the three types of capital, reveal a unique pattern for IT capital, which increased from zero to about 5% of value added around 2000. Non-IT capital and housing capital follow es-

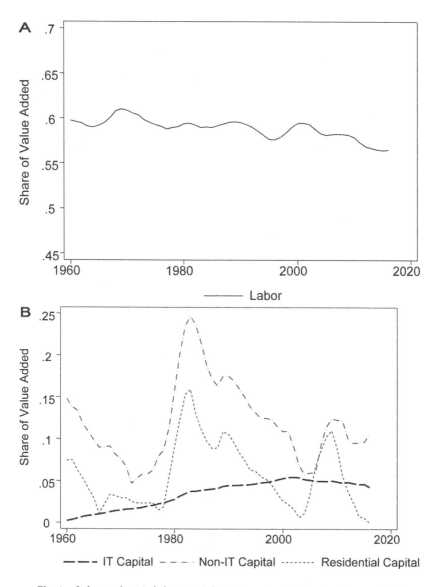

Fig. 1. Labor and capital shares in US private sector before allocating residual

sentially the same time-series patterns, which highlights that they are
driven by a common factor. Even in this 5-year smoothed form, the imputed capital income shares vary significantly. The sum of the labor
share and the four capital shares does not necessarily equal one—the residual is factorless income's share in value added.

A. Case II

The first approach attributes factorless income in equation (1) entirely to economic profits Π. Figure $2a$ plots the business sector's profit share, $s_{\Pi}^{Q} = \Pi^{Q}/(P^{Q}Q)$, implied by this approach. The solid black line plots s_{Π}^{Q}'s 5-year moving average against the left y-axis and shows that between 1960 and 1980 profits averaged just below 20% of business value added. The profit share collapses to essentially zero in the early 1980s before reverting by the 2000s to levels averaging about 15%.[16]

This rise in the profit share after the 1980s has been noted by recent analyses such as Karabarbounis and Neiman (2014), Rognlie (2015), and Barkai (2016) in relation to the decline in the labor share. We think it is important to emphasize, however, the critical role played by the real interest rate in reaching this conclusion. The dashed line in figure $2a$ is plotted against the y-axis on the right and shows the moving average of the real interest rate series used in these calculations. After hovering near low levels in the 1960s, the real interest rate jumps toward 10% in the early 1980s before slowly returning to the earlier low levels.[17] Comparing the real interest rate with the profit share, one notes that the real interest rate and the profit share are very tightly (negatively) correlated at both high and low frequencies. The series in figure $2a$, for example, have a correlation of $-.91$.[18]

A conclusion from figure $2a$ is that taking seriously case II and the implied behavior of profits requires a narrative that links the real interest rate to the profit share. There are such possibilities. For example, cheaper credit might be crucial for facilitating corporate mergers and acquisitions in a way that increases concentration and market power. Alternatively, a growing share of firms with higher market power might desire lower investment and result in a lower real interest rate. But the linkages between these variables must be tight and operate at relatively high frequency to account for these data.

Further, while the timing of the rise in profits from the early 1980s accords relatively well with the decline in the labor share, the even higher profit share early in the sample is difficult to reconcile with the conventional US macroeconomic narrative. Taken literally, these calculations imply that labor's share of business costs, $WL/(WL + R^{I}K^{I} + R^{N}K^{N})$, averaged roughly 85% in the 1960s and 1970s and dropped to roughly 70% in the 1980s before slowly climbing back up above 80% after 2000.

What are the implications of case II for the housing sector? Inspired by what is essentially the same exercise in Vollrath (2017), figure $2b$ plots the housing profit share $s_{\Pi}^{H} = 1 - R^{H}K^{H}/(P^{H}H)$.[19] Just as in the analyses of

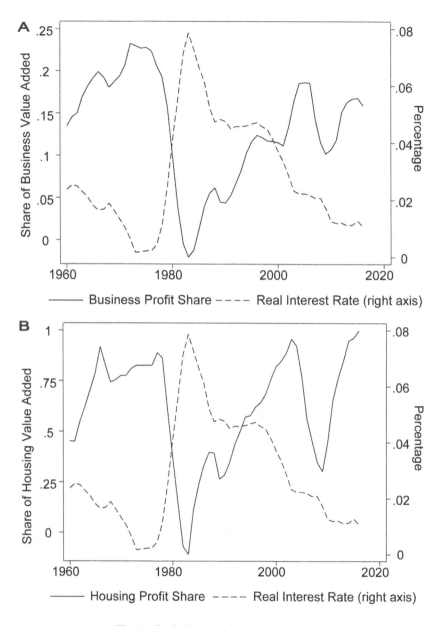

Fig. 2. Profit shares and interest rate, case II

capital rental costs for the business sector, we combine data on the real interest rate, housing depreciation rate, price of residential capital, and the stock of housing capital to measure housing capital rental costs. We find that s_{II}^{H} exhibits the same basic time-series patterns as s_{II}^{Q} but is dramatically more volatile.[20] The correlation of the business profit share s_Π^Q and the housing profit share s_Π^H is .78.

The surging profit share in housing may indeed reflect greater market power in housing rental markets. Over the past 10 years, for example, the Blackstone group has become a landlord of enormous scale, acquiring and renting out nearly 50,000 homes. Perhaps this is representative of increasing concentration in housing markets. Further, this measure of the profit share is less suited to the housing sector than to the business sector as it disregards risk and may miss labor costs. Still, the extremely volatile path of s_Π^H and its tight link to r contribute to our doubts that case II is the appropriate treatment of factorless income.

Another way to emphasize the critical role played by variations in the real interest rate for case II is to calculate the profit share under this methodology but using a constant real interest rate instead of time-varying Treasury rates. Using $r = .05$ yields the series for business and housing profit shares in figures 3a and 3b. Under this methodology the business profit share rises by only a few percentage points since the early 1980s instead of the nearly 20 percentage points seen in figure 2a. Further, the calculated profit shares during the Great Recession return to their low levels during the 1980s. We conclude that absent the variation in the real interest rate, case II would not point to surging profits.

Our basic conclusions remain largely undisturbed if we consider alternative measures of the labor share and additional alternative series for the real interest rate. First, we continue to use compensation to measure the labor share but use the Moody's AAA bond yield index instead of the 10-year Treasury yield as an input when calculating our rental rates R^j. Next, we construct an "Adjusted" labor share measure by adding to our baseline measure of compensation a fraction of proprietors' income and net taxes on production, where this fraction equals the share of labor compensation in the part of business value added other than proprietors' income and net taxes on production. As a third case, we assume the entire business sector has a labor share equal to that measured in the corporate sector.

Figure 4a shows our baseline labor share series, which is not impacted by changing the real interest rate series to "AAA." The series slowly declines in recent decades but is flatter than the private sector series shown in figure 1a due to the exclusion of housing, a difference uncovered and emphasized in Rognlie (2015). The "Adjusted" and "Corporate" lines exhibit somewhat different patterns, with the former dropping by most in the late 1970s and the latter dropping most since 2000.

Figure 4b shows the corresponding profit-share calculations. Unsurprisingly, the higher real interest rate (AAA) and higher labor share mea-

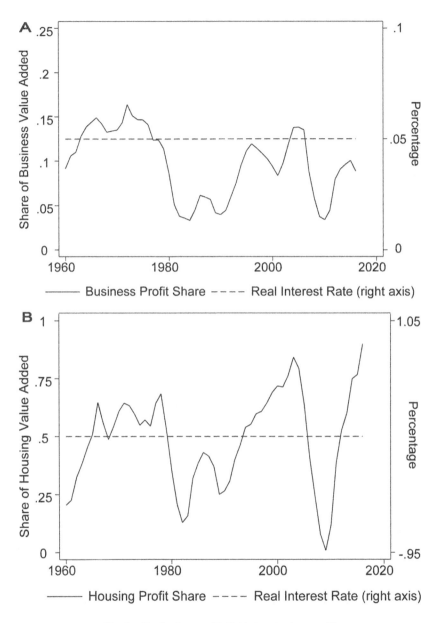

Fig. 3. Profit shares with flat interest rate, case II

sures (Adjusted and Corporate) result in a downward shift in the level of
the associated profit shares, including more periods with negative measured profit shares. However, consistent with our conclusion that the
time-series patterns in the real interest rate mechanically drive the evolu-

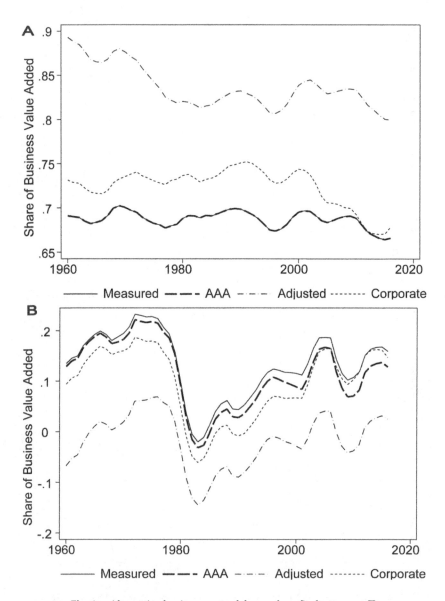

Fig. 4. Alternative business sector labor and profit shares, case II

tion of the calculated profit shares, all four lines in figure 4*b* move very
closely together.

Figure 5 shows that our conclusions remain unchanged when we use
alternative measures of inflation expectations to construct the real interest rate and the business profit share. The solid black line in figure 5*a*

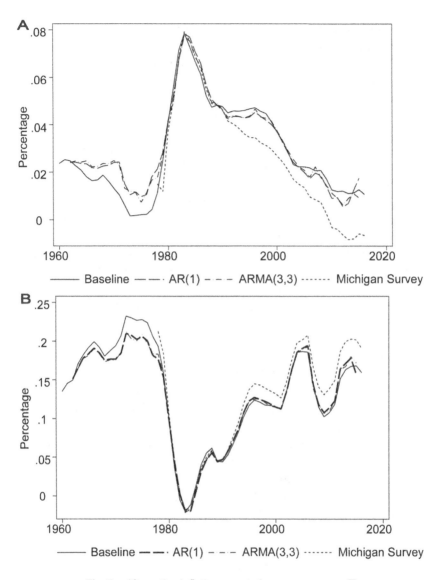

Fig. 5. Alternative inflation expectation measures, case II

shows the moving average of our baseline real interest rate, which uses a 5-year moving average of realized inflation rates to proxy for expected inflation. The corresponding profit share is shown by the solid black line in figure 5*b*. The other lines in figure 5*a* show the moving average of real interest rates constructed using an AR(1) process, an ARMA(3, 3) process, and the University of Michigan Survey of Consumers to measure expected inflation.[21] The corresponding profit shares are plotted in figure 5 and show essentially identical profit-share dynamics.

Calculations using aggregate data to show that the sum of s_L and s_K is declining are not the only evidence suggesting economic profits have increased since the 1980s. De Loecker and Eeckhout (2017) apply the methodology of De Loecker and Warzynski (2012) to Compustat data and uncover a striking rise in markups from 1.18 in 1980 to 1.67 by the end of their data, reproduced as the solid black line in figure 6a. With constant returns and absent fixed costs, this trajectory corresponds to an increase in s_Π^Q from about 15% to 40%. The inflection point of 1980 closely corresponds to the timing of the global labor share decline as documented in Karabarbounis and Neiman (2014).

De Loecker and Eeckhout (2017) use COGS as their proxy for variable costs. Their methodology is more involved, but the fall of COGS relative to sales in their sample appears to be the core empirical driver of their result. The long-dashed line in figure 6a simply plots the average across firms of the sales to COGS ratio in these same data and tracks the estimated markup trajectory quite well.[22]

This pattern plausibly reflects forces other than growing economic profits.[23] In particular, COGS suffers from some important shortcomings as a proxy for the behavior of spending on variable inputs. Compustat's data definitions describe it as including "all expenses directly allocated by the company to production, such as material, labor, and overhead." While materials align well with the notion of variable costs, it is unclear that only variable labor costs are included and overhead is unlikely to capture variable costs in the way desired. Further, as was first noted in this context by Traina (2018), the Compustat variable SG&A also includes some variable costs. SG&A is described in Compustat's data definitions as including "all commercial expenses of operation (e.g., expenses not directly related to product production) incurred in the regular course of business pertaining to the securing of operating income." Such expenses explicitly include categories such as marketing or R&D, where it is unclear if they should be variable costs in the sense desired for markup estimation, but also include bad-debt expenses, commissions, delivery expenses, lease rentals, retailer rent expenses, as well as other items that more clearly should be included as variable costs. Most importantly, Compustat itself explicitly corroborates the blurred line between COGS and SG&A when it states that items will only be included in COGS if the reporting company does not themselves allocate them to SG&A. Simi-

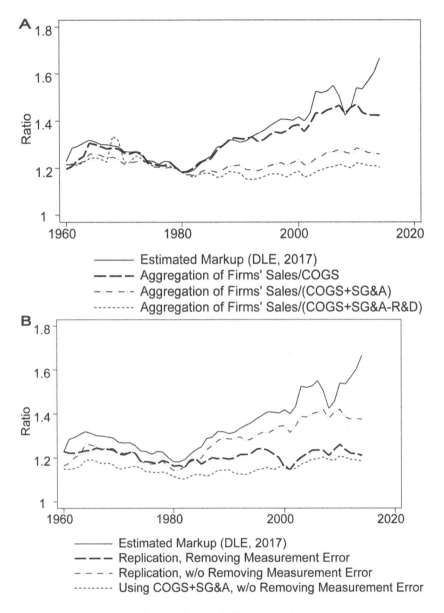

Fig. 6. Markups in Compustat data

larly, Compustat does not include items in SG&A if the reporting company already allocates them to COGS.

The dot-dashed line in figure 6a shows the average across firms of the ratio of sales to the sum of COGS and SG&A. There is a very mild increase in sales relative to this measure of operating costs. Put differently, the empirical driver of the rising markup result in Compustat data appears to be the shift in operating costs away from COGS and toward SG&A, not a shift in operating costs relative to sales.[24] This may be consistent with a rise in markups, but also might be consistent with other trends such as a rise in outsourcing (which could cause a reclassification of otherwise economically similar expenses), changing interpretations of what is meant by "production," or substitution of production activities performed by labor toward production activities performed by capital, the expenses of which may then be recorded by companies under a different category.[25]

Finally, we wish to emphasize that it is important to keep in mind the difference between markups of price over marginal cost and economic profits, which can be thought of as markups of price over average cost. For example, imagine that COGS perfectly captured variable costs and SG&A perfectly captured fixed costs of production. If this were the case, the fact that COGS declines relative to Sales would suggest an increase in markups on the margin. However, the rise in SG&A relative to Sales would, all else equal, reduce profits. Without adding more structure to quantify these relative forces, their overall effect on the average profit share is ambiguous. While markups on the margin are important for various questions of interest in economics, the average profit share is more salient for issues such as the decline in the labor share or the degree of monopoly power.

While we believe the evolution of the raw sales to COGS ratio is the proximate driver of the markup estimate in De Loecker and Eeckhout (2017), their methodology is more nuanced and sophisticated than a simple aggregation of raw operating ratios. To evaluate the sensitivity of their result to the choice of variable cost proxy, therefore, we would like to exactly implement their full methodology but substitute COGS+SG&A for COGS as the proxy of variable costs. The solid black line in figure 6b plots the headline result from De Loecker and Eeckhout (2017) and the long-dashed line shows our best effort to exactly replicate their calculations, leveraging the publicly available replication code for De Loecker and Warzynski (2012).[26] Our calculated series clearly fails to track theirs; we suspect the gap in our estimate reflects a different treatment of the variable used for the capital stock, which plays the largest role when running the first-stage nonparametric regression to purge out measurement errors.[27] Indeed, when we skip that step entirely, our estimated markup series comes much closer to theirs, and is plotted as the dot-dashed line. We use that same methodology but use COGS+SG&A as our proxy for variable cost and plot the implied markup as the short-dashed line, which confirms that substituting operating expenses for COGS reduces or eliminates the inferred rise of markups in Compustat data, consistent with the findings in Traina (2018).[28] The estimated markup rises only mildly since 1980.

The labor share decline since 1980 is a global phenomenon that was accompanied by flat or mildly declining investment rates in most countries.[29] This observation suggests that factorless income has risen in recent decades around the world. We evaluate the extent to which the ratio of sales to COGS or sales to COGS+SG&A has trended up in other countries using data from Compustat Global. Table 1 lists, for each country with at least 100 firms in the data, the linear trend (per 10 years) in Sales/COGS and Sales/(COGS+SG&A). There are a number of cases where the Sales/COGS ratio has significantly increased, including large economies such as India, Japan, Spain, the United Kingdom, and the United States. The remaining eight countries either experienced significant declines or insignificant trends. As with the US case, however, the scale and significance of the trends generally change if one instead considers Sales/(COGS+SG&A). In that case, the positive trends in the United Kingdom and United States, for example, remain statistically significant but drop in magnitude by roughly three-quarters. Statistically significant declines emerge in China, Italy, and Korea. Whereas a simple average of the trend coefficients on Sales/COGS is .041, the average trend coefficient for Sales/(COGS+SG&A) is .002. While Compustat's coverage in terms of time and scope varies significantly across countries, the results in table 1 cast further doubt that increasing markups can explain the bulk of rising factorless income in recent decades.

To recap case II, the large residual share of value added that is neither recorded as labor compensation nor imputed as payments to capital rises rapidly from the early 1980s. Fully embracing the interpretation of this residual as rising economic profits may offer a plausible story for labor share's decline since 1980 and carries important implications for a range of topics from asset pricing to competition policy. Our analysis, however, casts doubt on this strict interpretation of factorless income as profits. First, one must acknowledge that the same methodology driving inference about rising profit shares since 1980 reveals that profit-share levels in the 1960s and 1970s generally exceeded the levels reached today and this overall pattern is evident not only in the business sector but also in the housing sector. Second, one must directly link any story of economic profits to the real interest rate, as their tight negative comovement reveals the real interest rate as the mechanical driver of calculated profit shares.

Table 1
Trends in Markups in Compustat Global Data

Country	Trend (per 10 Years)		Years Covered		Firms Included	
	Sales/COGS	Sales/(COGS+SG&A)	Start	End	Min	Max
Brazil	−.038	−.002	1996	2016	128	284
	(.035)	(.029)				
China	−.008	−.021	1993	2016	314	3,683
	(.014)	(.007)***				
France	−.068	−.012	1999	2016	111	631
	(.039)*	(.011)				
Germany	.002	.034	1998	2016	119	668
	(.017)	(.008)***				
India	.118	.058	1995	2016	630	2,890
	(.041)***	(.024)**				
Italy	.004	−.057	2005	2016	202	264
	(.031)	(.018)***				
Japan	.059	.028	1987	2016	2,128	3,894
	(.008)***	(.004)***				
Korea	.000	−.032	1987	2016	419	1,682
	(.009)	(.005)***				
Russia	−.133	−.012	2004	2016	127	245
	(.097)	(.089)				
Spain	.274	−.026	2005	2016	102	128
	(.117)**	(.044)				
Taiwan	−.051	−.021	1997	2016	160	1,789
	(.026)**	(.018)				
United Kingdom	.280	.072	1988	2016	183	1,489
	(.015)***	(.007)***				
United States	.088	.021	1981	2016	3,136	8,403
	(.004)***	(.002)***				

Note: The table summarizes estimates of the linear trend in the Sales/COGS and the Sales/ (COGS+SG&A) ratios. Standard errors are displayed in parentheses.
*$p < .1$
**$p < .05$
***$p < .001$

B. Case K

We now consider a second approach, which attributes factorless business income entirely to a gap between the measure of capital in the national accounts and the quantity of capital used in production. The basis for this possibility is the idea that capital stocks are imputed and potentially suffer significant measurement difficulties. The mismeasurement may reflect faulty parametric assumptions in the perpetual inventory method used to impute capital stocks but may also reflect missing investment spending, as detailed in the influential work of Corrado, Hulten, and Sichel (2009).

Certain intangible investments are particularly good candidates for missing investment spending. For example, when a chain restaurant pays advertising firms or their own marketing executives to increase awareness and positive sentiment for their brand, conventional accounts treat this spending as intermediate expenses and not as investment, much like the treatment of their spending on food. When a management consultancy pays staff to develop internal knowledge centers to organize their industry expertise, this is treated as an input to their existing production and not as an investment in the firm's capital stock. The US BEA explicitly recognized the importance of various misclassified investment expenditures when it changed its treatment of software in 1999 and of R&D and artistic originals in 2013 and, accordingly, revised upward its historical series for investment and capital stocks.[30]

Let X^U equal the real value and ξ^U equal the price of unmeasured investment, which accumulates into an unmeasured capital stock K^U with an associated rental rate R^U. These magnitudes are related to measured income according to

$$\tilde{Y} = Y + \xi^U X^U = WL + R^I K^I + R^N K^N + R^H K^H + \Pi + R^U K^U, \qquad (3)$$

where $\tilde{Y}$ is unmeasured (or "revised") output which may differ from measured GDP Y.

To see how unmeasured investment matters for factorless income and output, consider two extreme cases. First, consider the case where there is unmeasured capital in the economy accumulated from past investment flows, so $R^U K^U > 0$, but current investment spending of this type equals zero: $\xi^U X^U = 0$. In this case, output is correctly measured and $\tilde{Y} = Y$. Capital income, however, is underestimated by $R^U K^U$. Alternatively, imagine that $R^U K^U = 0$ in some years, but there is unmeasured investment and $\xi^U X^U > 0$. This means that output is larger than measured GDP, but standard measures of RK correctly capture capital income. In cases in between these extremes both capital income and output will be mismeasured.

We can rearrange equation (3) so the left-hand side equals the gap between unmeasured capital income and unmeasured investment spending and the right-hand side contains only measured income terms and economic profits:

$$R^U K^U - \xi^U X^U = Y - WL - R^I K^I - R^N K^N - R^H K^H - \Pi^Q - \Pi^H. \qquad (4)$$

For any given paths of business sector profits Π^Q and housing sector profits Π^H, there will generally be many possible paths of R^U, K^U, ξ^U, and X^U that satisfy equation (4) for the years covered in our data. Most such paths, however, may not be economically sensible. To put more discipline on our exercise, we additionally require that R^U is generated like the other rental rates R^j in equation (2) and that capital and investment are linked through a linear capital accumulation equation $K_{t+1}^U = (1 - \delta^U)K_t^U + X_t^U$.

We solve for one set of paths $\{R^U, K^U, \xi^U, X^U\}$ as follows. First, we create a grid with different combinations of business profit-share levels s_Π^Q, depreciation rates δ^U, and values of the capital stock relative to measured GDP in 2010 (chosen because prices are normalized to one in 2009). For each combination of $\{s_\Pi^Q, \delta^U, (K^U / Y)_{2010}\}$, we consider a number of values for ξ_{2010}^U, the price of investment in 2010. Each resulting value of ξ^U in 2010 can be used to calculate a value for R^U in 2010 using equation (2) since $\xi_{2009}^U = 1$. Because the right-hand side variables of equation (4) are then all known for 2010 (we keep Π^H at its values from case II), and we have assumed values for $R^U K^U$ and ξ^U on the left-hand side, we can then back out the value for the remaining left-hand side term X_{2010}^U, real investment in unmeasured capital in 2010. Using the capital accumulation equation, we then calculate K^U in 2011 and start the sequence again.

We iterate forward in this way through 2015 and do the same in reverse to iterate backward from 2010 to 1960. This results in a series of thousands of possible paths for each node of the grid $\{s_\pi^Q, \delta^U, (K^U / Y)_{2009}\}$. From all those possibilities, we select the paths such that investment is nonnegative and where the variance and magnitude of the price and stock of unmeasured capital is minimized. Additional details on our exact algorithm and selection criteria are found in the online replication file.[31]

Figure 7 plots the 5-year moving average of key magnitudes describing the unmeasured investment where $s_\Pi^Q = 0.06$ and $\delta^U = 0.05$. Figure 7a shows a path for the price of unmeasured investment in terms of the price of nonhousing consumption. After having essentially flat or slightly declining investment prices from 1960 to 1980, the price grows rapidly at almost 13% per year until 2000. Prices are then fairly flat through 2010 and have declined at about 6% per year since then.

This price path may seem unusual, but as shown in figure 7a, the rate of price change is orders of magnitude smaller than that of IT capital. Further, though both IT and non-IT depreciation rates evolve over time in the data, we reduce our degrees of freedom and assume a constant value for δ^U. Allowing more flexibility in our choice of δ^U (or, similarly, allowing s_Π^Q to fluctuate around a constant level) would likely allow us to find paths of ξ^U with a bit less unusual behavior. Combined with the underlying real interest rate and depreciation rate, this price path translates into a path for the rental rate of unmeasured capital R^U, plotted in figure 7b, which comoves negatively with the non-IT rental rate. It has generally risen from near zero in the 1960s to nearly 15% in recent years.

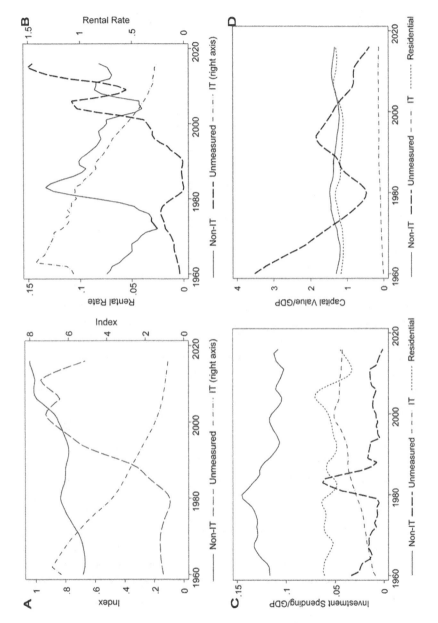

Fig. 7. Hypothetical paths governing missing investment and capital, case K

Figure 7c shows investment spending in each type of capital relative to revised output $\tilde{Y}$. It shows that investment spending on unmeasured capital need not be particularly large to account for factorless income. As shown in the figure, there is a surge in early 1980s investment in unmeasured capital. Recall that factorless income, or what case Π calls profits, is high prior to the early 1980s at nearly 25% of GDP and then plunges to less than zero before growing back to levels seen earlier. This investment surge in the early 1980s, combined with the rising rental rates from the 1990s onward as seen in figure 7b, helps match that pattern.

Finally, figure 7d plots the value of each capital stock relative to output, $\xi^j K^j / \tilde{Y}$. The figure shows that the value of this missing capital stock is at times quite large. Early in the sample, the capital stock is worth roughly three times output and accounts for more than half of the value of the capital stock. From 1970 onward, however, this capital would only need to be worth between one-half and twice of output. Over that period, unmeasured capital accounts for roughly 30% of the value of all capital in the economy and roughly 40% of all business capital.[32]

Under case K, the deviation of revised output from measured GDP equals unmeasured investment spending, which figure 7c shows to be quite low. Figure 8a compares moving averages of log changes in the two (real) output series, which are visually quite similar except for the key periods in the late 1970s and early 1980s. The 25th to 75th percentile range in the distribution of deviations of the two growth rates is −0.5 percentage point to 0.6 percentage point, with a median deviation equal to zero. There are some years, most notably 1982, in which the gap is large. Such gaps often represent shifts in the timing of growth periods, and indeed, measured growth during the subsequent 2 years exceeds revised growth by a total of 8.4%, undoing some of the 1982 gap.

An implication of case K is that the path of the revised labor share differs from that of the measured labor share. Figure 8b compares moving averages of these series. Though they largely move together, the revised labor share declines significantly in the early 1980s due to the surge in output from investment in unmeasured capital at that time. As a result, the revised labor share in the business sector does not end at a historic low as does the measured business labor share. Both series, however, exhibit almost parallel trends starting from the mid-1980s.

The magnitude of our estimates of unmeasured investment and capital for the post-1980 period is only moderately larger than other estimates in the literature. Hall (2001) examines the relationship between the stock market and intangibles he referred to as "e-capital" from tech-

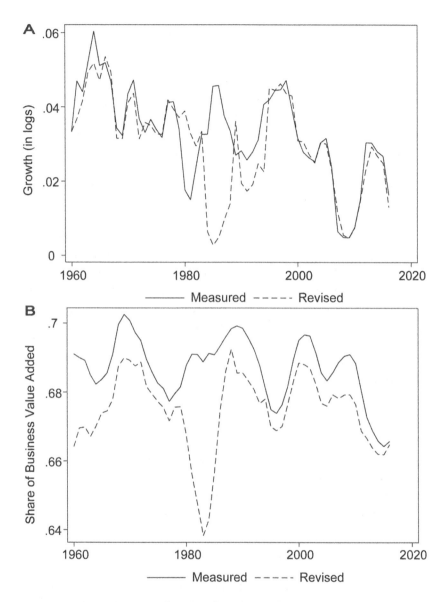

Fig. 8. Implications of mismeasured GDP, case *K*

nical resources and organizational know-how. He argues that e-capital accumulation from the 1990s resulted in an e-capital stock roughly 50% as large as measured GDP by 2000. McGrattan and Prescott (2005) attribute the gap between income and the sum of observed compensation to labor and imputed income to measured capital (what we call factorless income) to payments to intangibles. Their methodology restricts to balanced growth paths and implies a stock of missing capital equal to roughly two-thirds of output. Atkeson and Kehoe (2005) apply the same methodology for the US manufacturing sector and also arrive at the same estimate. Eisfeldt and Papanikolaou (2013) construct organizational capital from SG&A expenses and the perpetual inventory method. They find that the value of organizational capital typically exceeds that of physical capital.

Corrado et al. (2009) base their approach on more direct measurements. They show that, by 2000, investments in brand values and firm-specific resources account for up to 6% of measured output. But they assume these intangible capital stocks depreciate rapidly and set their values equal to zero in the decades preceding our data. Their implied estimates for the scale of these capital stocks are far smaller, therefore, than what we show in figure 7d. Barkai (2016) benchmarks in part to their work and argues that the size of missing capital would have to be implausibly large in order to account for factorless income. His calculations further assume that missing investment exceeds depreciation. By contrast, our estimated capital stock does not surge after 1980 in part because we allow the rate of investment to fall below the rate of depreciation.

C.   Case R

We now consider a third approach, which attributes factorless income entirely to the rental rate of capital faced by firms. For this analysis, we focus only on the business sector and ignore housing. Denoting by $\tilde{R}^j$ the revised rental rates (which may differ from the R^j used to calculate factorless income), we write

$$P^Q Q = WN + \tilde{R}^I K^I + \tilde{R}^N K^N + \Pi^Q, \tag{5}$$

where unlike case Π the level of business profits Π^Q is simply taken as given (i.e., chosen based on external information) and unlike case K there is no missing capital. There are multiple ways to calculate $\tilde{R}^j$ such that equation (5) holds given values for $P^Q Q$, WN, K^j, and Π^Q. To add more discipline to the exercise, we solve for the unique revised real interest rate $\tilde{r}$ such that the revised rental rates $\tilde{R}^j$ calculated according to equation (2) satisfy equation (5). The gap between $\tilde{r}$ and our measure r taken from Treasury yields and used in the other cases can be thought of as standing in for a time-varying risk premium or the impact of particular forms of adjustment costs or financial frictions. In our calculations, we set Π^Q to generate a constant $s_\Pi^Q = 0.06$, the value also used in case K.

Figure 9 compares 5-year moving averages of the resulting revised interest and rental rates (labeled "Revised" and plotted as dashed lines) with those calculated using the 10-year Treasury yields (labeled "Measured" and plotted as solid lines). Figure 9a offers the intuitive result that $\tilde{r}$ is generally higher than r because it absorbs factorless income. Additionally, $\tilde{r}$ does not decline in parallel with r after 1990s because higher levels of $\tilde{r}$ account for the increasing factorless income as a share of value added.

Given the lack of decline in $\tilde{r}$, the revised rental rates $\tilde{R}^j$ become flatter relative to the measured rental rates R^j calculated with r. The change in the real interest rate underlying the construction of the rental rates does not impact IT, non-IT, and housing capital income in the same way because these assets have different depreciation rates and investment price changes. The higher depreciation rate on IT capital means that the real interest rate is a less important driver of its rental rate compared with that of non-IT capital. The rental rate of IT capital declines rapidly due to the decline in the price of IT investment goods ξ^I, often attributed to productivity improvements in the development of communication, computers, and semiconductor technologies. Non-IT and housing rental rates, plotted in figures 9c and 9d, are more sensitive to the measure of the real interest rate. Relative to case II, these revised rental rates are all flatter after the 1980s.

Is there other evidence that risk premia or factors other than profits have caused an increasing wedge between Treasury rates and the opportunity cost of capital perceived by firms when making their investment decisions?[33] Our case R results relate closely to the conclusion in Caballero et al. (2017) that rising risk premia have generated a growing wedge between Treasury rates and corporate borrowing costs in recent decades. Their calibration exercises suggest that absent these rising risk premia since 1980, changes in the Treasury rates would have produced implausible factor share movements given the standard range of elasticities they consider. In a sample of 16 economies, the estimates of Jorda et al. (2017) suggest that the gap between the return on risky equity and housing and the return on safe assets has slightly increased between the 1990s and the 2010s. We acknowledge that the evidence for rising risk premia is mixed. Earlier research by Jagannathan, McGrattan, and Scherbina (2000) and Fama and French (2002) documents a decline in the US equity premium between 1980 and 2000. More recent work by Duarte and Rosa (2015), however, demonstrates that the first principle component of 20 model-based estimates

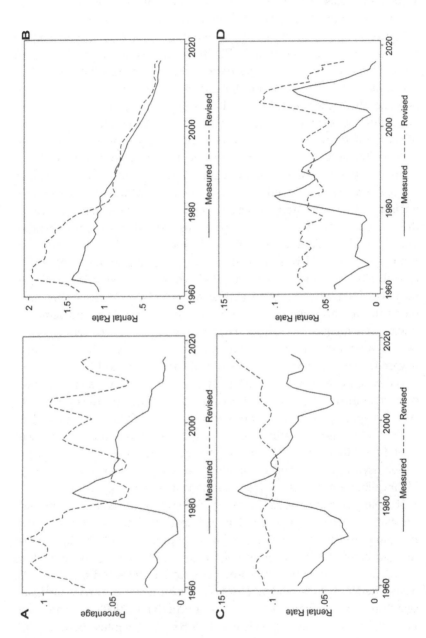

Fig. 9. Measured and revised real interest rate and rental rates, case R

of the equity risk premium has increased dramatically since the 2000s and reached again the historically high levels observed during the late 1970s.

D.   Implications for Total Factor Productivity

What are the implications of each of our three cases for productivity? Macroeconomists calculate Solow residuals to try to infer the rate of growth of technology or total factor productivity (TFP). Appealing to the assumption of perfect competition, the convention is to weight the growth of labor and capital input by the labor share and one minus the labor share. For the business sector, we write the growth of the standard or "Naive" measure of TFP as

$$d \ln \text{TFP}_{\text{Naive}} = d \ln Q - s_L^Q \times d \ln L - (1 - s_L^Q) \sum_{j \in \{I,N\}} \frac{s_{K^j}^Q}{s_K^Q} \times d \ln K^j, \quad (6)$$

where we also follow the convention in creating an index of business capital growth as a capital-j share weighted average of growth in IT and non-IT capital stocks.

As discussed in Hall (1990), Basu and Fernald (2002), and Fernald and Neiman (2011), when measured factor shares do not equal the true factor shares in costs, due to imperfect competition or measurement error, this standard Solow residual will fail to approximate technology. Rather, one must use revised factor shares of cost in what is called a "Modified" Solow residual:

$$d \ln \text{TFP}_{\text{Modified}} = d \ln Q - \frac{s_L^Q}{1 - s_\Pi^Q} \times d \ln L - \sum_{j \in \{I,N,U\}} \frac{s_{K^j}^Q}{1 - s_\Pi^Q} \times d \ln K^j. \quad (7)$$

All three of our interpretations of factorless income imply that modified TFP in equation (7) will differ from the naive TFP measure in equation (6). In case Π, the primary difference arises as the large and fluctuating profit share s_Π^Q drives a wedge between labor's share of costs and labor's share of revenues. Case K and case R also have nonzero profit shares, though they are typically smaller and are constant. Further, under case K, modified TFP will differ from the naive measure because of unmeasured value added and unmeasured capital. Finally, under case R, modified TFP will differ from the naive measure because the revised rental rates for IT and non-IT capital changes their relative shares in costs.

The solid black bars in figure 10 report the average growth rates of the naive TFP measure in equation (6) for 1960–65 and subsequent 10-year periods to 2015.[34] The evolution of these bars is consistent with the conven-

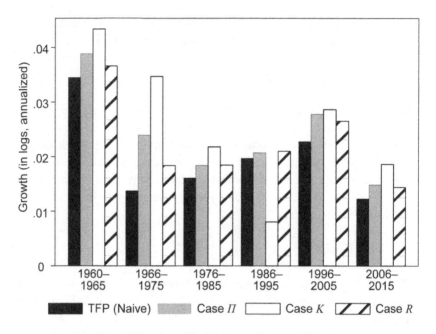

Fig. 10. Naive TFP and modified Solow residuals in US business sector

tional US productivity growth narrative, with high rates in the 1960s slowing down in the early 1970s, and a short-lived burst during the mid-1990s collapsing in the mid-2000s. The hollow red bars report the modified TFP measure in equation (7) under the case Π interpretation of factorless income. Capital input has generally grown faster than labor input, so the large markups in this case imply that the naive measure understates technology growth. The extent of this difference varies over time. Case Π suggests that in the most recent 10-year period, the naive measure implies growth rates 20% lower than what would be inferred from the modified Solow residual. It also suggests that during the 1966–75 period—a period often considered the start of the "Great Productivity Slowdown"—the modified TFP measure of technology growth was almost twice the rate implied by the naive measure.

For case K, the blue bars in figure 10 show that, in all periods aside from 1986–95, the growth of the naive measure of TFP is significantly lower than the growth implied by the modified measures. The basic logic for this difference is that GDP growth is not meaningfully affected by unmeasured investments but the stock of capital is. Given that the unmeasured capital stock is generally falling according to case K, the capital input growth used in equation (6) is too high.

For case R, the green bars show the smallest gap between the naive and the modified measures of TFP. Attributing a growing fraction of income to rental payments, as case R does, tends to decrease the growth of modified TFP relative to that of naive TFP. The small but nonzero profit share used in that case tends to increase the growth of modified TFP relative to naive TFP. These forces tend to offset each other, causing the naive measure of TFP to be closest to the modified measure of TFP in case R.

E. Taking Stock

To summarize our results, we have developed three strategies to allocate factorless income in an environment that, aside from a standard model-based formula for the rental rate of capital, relies on accounting identities to ensure an internally consistent allocation of the residual income. Case II requires a tight link between real interest rates and markups. While it implies rising profits from the early 1980s, it suggests that current profit levels remain below their levels in the 1960s and 1970s. Our implementation of case K leads to plausible results after the 1980s, but requires that unmeasured capital in the 1960s comprises more than half of total capital. Using a different selection criterion might allow for a smaller unmeasured capital stock in 1960 but at a cost or requiring more unmeasured flows later in the sample. Case R seems most promising as it stabilizes relative capital shares and preserves the traditional narrative of TFP's evolution. We recognize, however, that more evidence of rising risk premia or other wedges in firms' opportunity cost of capital is required before one more fully embraces this case. We next introduce a variant of the growth model with capital accumulation to make more progress at assessing the plausibility of these three interpretations of factorless income and to evaluate their implications for a richer set of macroeconomic outcomes.

III. A Multisector Model with Multiple Capital Types

We consider an economy with multiple sectors and multiple types of capital.[35] The business sector uses labor, IT capital, non-IT capital, and intangible or organizational capital—which is not measured in the fixed asset tables—to produce consumption and investment goods. The housing sector uses residential capital to produce housing services. The horizon is infinite and there is no aggregate uncertainty. The economy is populated by workers and capitalists who have perfect foresight about the evolution of all exogenous driving processes. The economy is small in the sense that it treats the path of the real interest rate as exogenous.[36]

A. Demographics and Growth

In each period t there is a measure L_t of identical workers. Labor-augmenting technology $\tilde{A}_t^L$ grows at an exogenous rate g_t, $\tilde{A}_t^L = (1 + g_t)\tilde{A}_{t-1}^L$. In the balanced growth path of the economy, the measure of workers and the growth rate of labor-augmenting technology are constant, $L_t = L$ and $g_t = g$. In what follows, we describe the model directly in terms of variables that are detrended by their respective growth rates in the balanced growth path. Thus, if $\tilde{x}_t$ is a variable growing at a rate $g_x = \{0, g\}$ along the balanced growth path, the detrended variable x_t is defined as $x_t = \tilde{x}_t/(1 + g_x)^t$.

B. Final Goods

The economy produces six final goods. The (nonhousing) consumption good is denoted by C and serves as the numeraire good. The consumption of housing services is denoted by H. There are four types of investment goods. We denote the jth investment good by X^j and, as before, denote the capital stocks by K^j for $j = \{I, N, U, H\}$, where I denotes IT capital, N denotes non-IT capital, U denotes unmeasured types of capital such as organizational and intangible capital, and H denotes residential capital. The first three types of capital are used in the production of consumption C and investments X^j. Residential capital is used in the production of housing services H.

Consumption C_t

Producers of final consumption are perfectly competitive. They operate a constant elasticity of substitution (CES) production function $C_t = (\int_0^1 c_t(z)^{(\varepsilon_t^Q-1)/\varepsilon_t^Q} dz)^{\varepsilon_t^Q/(\varepsilon_t^Q-1)}$, where $c_t(z)$ denotes the quantity of intermediate business variety z and $\varepsilon_t^Q > 1$ denotes the elasticity of substitution between business varieties. Denoting the price of consumption by P_t^C and the price of intermediate business variety by $p_t^Q(z)$, the profit-maximization problem yields the demand functions for varieties $c_t(z) = (p_t^Q(z)/P_t^C)^{-\varepsilon_t^Q} C_t$. Normalizing $P_t^C = 1$ and anticipating the symmetric equilibrium across all varieties z, we obtain $c_t(z) = C_t$.

Investments X_t^j

Producers of investment good $j = \{I, N, U, H\}$ are similar to the producers of consumption, with the difference being that they operate a CES production function $X_t^j = (1/\xi_t^j)\{\int_0^1 [x_t^j(z)]^{(\epsilon_t^Q-1)/\epsilon_t^Q} dz\}^{\epsilon_t^Q/(\epsilon_t^Q-1)}$, where ξ_t^j denotes the efficiency of producing investment good j. The price of investment good j relative to consumption is given by $P_t^j = \xi_t^j$. An improvement in the efficiency of producing investment (a lowering of ξ_t^j) is associated with a fall in the relative price of investment good j. Anticipating the symmetric equilibrium across all varieties z, we obtain $x_t^j(z) = \xi_t^j X_t^j$.

Housing Services H_t

Producers of housing services operate a CES production function $H_t = (\int_0^1 H_t^j(\zeta)^{(\epsilon_t^H-1)/\epsilon_t^H} d\zeta)^{\epsilon_t^H/(\epsilon_t^H-1)}$, where $H_t(\zeta)$ denotes the quantity of intermediate housing variety ζ and $\epsilon_t^H > 1$ denotes the elasticity of substitution between housing varieties. Differences in the elasticities of substitution across varieties in the business and the housing sector generate differences in markups across sectors. Denoting the price of housing services by P_t^H and the price of intermediate housing varieties by $p_t^H(\zeta)$, the profit-maximization problem yields the demand functions for varieties $H_t(\zeta) = (p_t^H(\zeta)/P_t^H)^{-\epsilon_t^H} H_t$. Anticipating the symmetric equilibrium across all varieties ζ, we obtain $H_t(\zeta) = H_t$ and $p_t^H(\zeta) = P_t^H$.

Market Clearing

The final consumption good C_t is consumed by workers C_t^L, by capitalists C_t^K, and by the rest of the world in the form of net exports NX_t. Each investment good X_t^j is used to augment the respective capital stock K_t^j. The market clearing condition in the business sector is given by $Q_t = C_t^L + C_t^K + NX_t + \Sigma_j \xi_t^j X_t^j$, where Q_t denotes business output in units of consumption. Housing services are consumed by workers and capitalists, $H_t = H_t^L + H_t^K$. Total output in units of consumption equals the sum of business and housing output, $Y_t = Q_t + P_t^H H_t$.

C.   *Intermediate Good Producers*

There are two types of intermediate good producers. The business sector produces varieties for consumption C_t and investments X_t^j. The housing sector produces varieties for final housing services H_t. The two sectors differ both in their production and in their demand functions.

Business Sector

There is a measure one of differentiated intermediate goods z. Business variety z produces output using a CES function of an aggregator of the three capital goods, $k_t^Q(k_t^I(z), k_t^N(z), k_t^{LI}(z))$, and labor $\ell_t(z)$:

$$q_t(z) = \left(\alpha(A_t^K k_t^Q(z))^{\frac{\sigma-1}{\sigma}} + (1-\alpha)(A_t^L \ell_t(z))^{\frac{\sigma-1}{\sigma}} \right)^{\frac{\sigma}{\sigma-1}}, \tag{8}$$

where σ denotes the elasticity of substitution between labor and capital, α is a distribution factor, A_t^K denotes capital-augmenting technology, and A_t^L denotes labor-augmenting technology. The bundle of capital inputs $k_t^Q(z)$ is rented at a rate R_t^Q and labor $\ell(z)$ is rented at a price W_t.

The producer of variety z sells $q_t(z) = c_t(z) + \Sigma_j \xi_t^j x_t^j(z)$ to final consumption and investment goods producers, internalizing the downward-sloping demand function for $q_t(z)$. The profit-maximization problem is

$$\max_{p_t^Q(z), q_t(z), \ell_t(z), k_t^Q(z)} \pi_t^Q(z) = p_t^Q(z)q_t(z) - R_t^Q k_t^Q(z) - W_t \ell_t(z), \tag{9}$$

subject to $q_t(z) = (p_t^Q(z))^{-\varepsilon_t^Q} Q_t$ and the production function in equation (8). In the symmetric equilibrium of the model, all varieties have the same production function and make identical choices of inputs and prices. Therefore, for all z we obtain $p_t^Q(z) = 1$, $q_t(z) = Q_t$, $\ell_t(z) = L_t$, $k_t^Q(z) = K_t^Q$, and $\pi_t^Q(z) = \Pi_t^Q$. Henceforth, we describe the model in terms of the aggregate variables denoted by capital letters.

The first-order conditions with respect to labor and capital are given by

$$(1-\alpha)(A_t^L)^{\frac{\sigma-1}{\sigma}} \left(\frac{Q_t}{L_t} \right)^{\frac{1}{\sigma}} = \mu_t^Q W_t, \tag{10}$$

$$\alpha(A_t^K)^{\frac{\sigma-1}{\sigma}} \left(\frac{Q_t}{K_t^Q} \right)^{\frac{1}{\sigma}} = \mu_t^Q R_t^Q, \tag{11}$$

where $\mu_t^Q = \varepsilon_t^Q / (\varepsilon_t^Q - 1)$ is the gross markup of price over marginal cost in the business sector. Variations in the elasticity of substitution ε_t^Q over time result in (exogenous) changes in μ_t^Q. Total business income is divided among labor payments, capital payments, and economic profits: $Q_t = W_t L_t + R_t^Q K_t^Q + \Pi_t^Q$.

Business Capital Aggregator

There is a perfectly competitive intermediary firm that transforms capital types K_t^I, K_t^N, and K_t^U into aggregate business capital K_t^Q with the CES production function

$$K_t^Q = \left(\sum_{j \neq H} (v_t^j)^{\frac{1}{\theta}} (K_t^j)^{\frac{\theta-1}{\theta}} \right)^{\frac{\theta}{\theta-1}}, \tag{12}$$

where θ denotes the elasticity of substitution between types of capital and v_t^j denotes j-specific capital-augmenting technology.

The intermediary firm rents the capital types from the capitalists at prices R_t^I, R_t^N, and R_t^U respectively and rents the capital aggregator to the business sector at a rate R_t^Q. From the cost-minimization problem we derive the first-order conditions for each type of capital,

$$K_t^j = v_t^j \left(\frac{R_t^j}{R_t^Q} \right)^{-\theta} K_t^Q, \tag{13}$$

where the rental rate of business capital is given by

$$R_t^Q = \left(\sum_{j \neq H} v_t^j (R_t^j)^{1-\theta} \right)^{\frac{1}{1-\theta}}. \tag{14}$$

Zero profits in the sector that intermediates capital implies $R_t^Q K_t^Q = \sum_{j \neq H} R_t^j K_t^j$.

Housing Sector

There is a measure one of differentiated intermediate goods ζ. Housing variety ζ uses only residential capital $k_t^H(\zeta)$ in the production process:

$$h_t(\zeta) = A_t^H k_t^H(\zeta), \tag{15}$$

where A_t^H is the technology in the housing sector. Residential capital is rented from the capitalists at a rental rate R_t^H.

The producer of variety ζ sells $h_t(\zeta)$ to final housing services producers, internalizing the downward-sloping demand function for $h_t(\zeta)$. The profit-maximization problem is

$$\max_{p_t^H(\zeta), h_t(\zeta), k_t^H(\zeta)} \pi_t^H(\zeta) = p_t^H(\zeta) h_t(\zeta) - R_t^H k_t^H(\zeta), \tag{16}$$

subject to $h_t(\zeta) = (p_t^H(\zeta))^{-\epsilon_t^H} (P_t^H)^{\epsilon_t^H} H_t$ and the production function in equation (15). In the symmetric equilibrium of the model, all varieties have the same production function and make identical choices of inputs and prices. Therefore, for all ζ we obtain $p_t^H(\zeta) = P_t^H$, $h_t(\zeta) = H_t$, $k_t^H(\zeta) = K_t^H$ and $\pi_t^H(\zeta) = \Pi_t^H$.

From the first-order condition for profit maximization, we obtain the price of housing services relative to consumption:

$$P_t^H = \mu_t^H \frac{R_t^H}{A_t^H}, \tag{17}$$

where $\mu_t^H = \varepsilon_t^H/(\varepsilon_t^H - 1)$ is the gross markup of price over marginal cost in the housing sector. Total income generated in the housing sector is divided between capital payments and economic profits, $P_t^H H_t = R_t^H K_t^H + \Pi_t^H$.

D. Households

The household sector consists of workers who simply consume their labor income and capitalists who choose how much of their capital income to consume, save, and invest.

Workers

There is a measure L_t of identical workers who provide labor inelastically and value nonresidential consumption C_t^L and housing services H_t^L according to a Cobb-Douglas utility function:

$$\max_{C_t^L, H_t^L} (C_t^L)^{1-\nu_t^H} (H_t^L)^{\nu_t^H}, \tag{18}$$

where ν_t^H denotes the time-varying preference for housing services. Workers do not have access to capital markets and consume their after-tax-and-transfers labor income. Their budget constraint is given by

$$(1 + \tau_t^c)C_t^L + P_t^H H_t^L = W_t L_t + T_t^L, \tag{19}$$

where τ_t^c denotes the tax rate on consumption expenditures and T_t^L denotes transfers from the government.

Workers maximize their utility function (18) subject to the budget constraint (19). Their optimal choice of housing to consumption is given by

$$\frac{H_t^L}{C_t^L} = \frac{\nu_t^H}{1 - \nu_t^H} \frac{1 + \tau_t^c}{P_t^H}. \tag{20}$$

The government rebates back to workers $T_t^L = \tau_t^c C_t^L$ and, therefore, in equilibrium the total expenditure of workers equals their labor income, $C_t^L + P_t^H H_t^L = W_t L_t$.[37]

Capitalists

There is a measure one of identical capitalists who own claims to all firms in the economy and the business and housing capital stocks. They value streams of utility according to

$$\max_{C_t^K, H_t^K, \{K_{t+1}^j\}, D_{t+1}} \sum_{t=0}^{\infty} \left(\prod_{k=0}^{t} \beta_k (1+g)^{\frac{1}{p}} \right) \left(\frac{1}{1 - \frac{1}{\rho}} \right) \left(\left((C_t^K)^{1-\nu_t^H} (H_t^K)^{\nu_t^H} \right)^{1-\frac{1}{\rho}} - 1 \right), \quad (21)$$

where ρ denotes the elasticity of intertemporal substitution and β_t denotes the time-varying transformed discount factor. Capitalists trade an international bond D_t at an exogenous interest rate r_t. Their budget constraint is given by

$$(1 + \tau_t^c)C_t^K + P_t^H H_t^K + (1 + \tau_t^x)\sum_j \xi_t^j X_t^j + \left(1 + \left(1 - \tau_t^k \right) r_t \right) D_t$$

$$(22)$$

$$= \left(1 - \tau_t^k \right) \left(\sum_j R_t^j K_t^j + \Pi_t^Q + \Pi_t^H \right) + (1+g)D_{t+1} + \tau_t^k \sum_j \delta_t^j \xi_t^j K_t^j + T_t^K.$$

In the budget constraint, τ_t^x denotes the tax rate on investment spending and τ_t^k denotes the tax rate on capital income (net of depreciation). The government rebates to capitalists a lump sum equal to $T_t^K = \tau_t^c C_t^K + \tau_t^x \sum_j \xi_t^j X_t^j + \tau_t^k(\sum_j R_t^j K_t^j + \Pi_t^Q + \Pi_t^H - r_t D_t - \sum_j \delta_t^j \xi_t^j K_t^j)$. Finally, the stocks of capital evolve according to the law of motion:

$$(1 + g)K_{t+1}^j = (1 - \delta_t^j)K_t^j + X_t^j, \quad (23)$$

where δ_t^j is the time-varying depreciation rate of the type j capital stock.

Capitalists maximize their value function (21) subject to the budget constraint (22) and the law of motion for capital (23). Capitalists' optimal choice of housing to nondurable consumption is

$$\frac{H_t^K}{C_t^K} = \frac{\nu_t^H}{1 - \nu_t^H} \frac{1 + \tau_t^c}{p_t^H}. \quad (24)$$

The first-order conditions with respect to bonds D_{t+1} yields a standard Euler equation,

$$U'(C_t^K) = \beta \left(\frac{1 + \tau_t^c}{1 + \tau_{t+1}^c} \right) (1 + (1 - \tau_{t+1}^k)r_{t+1})U'(C_{t+1}^K). \tag{25}$$

The first-order conditions with respect to the capital stocks K_{t+1}^j yield

$$(1 - \tau_{t+1}^k)R_{t+1}^j + \tau_{t+1}^k \delta_{t+1}^j \xi_{t+1}^j + (1 + \tau_{t+1}^x)\xi_{t+1}^j(1 - \delta_{t+1}^j)$$
$$= (1 + \tau_t^x)\xi_t^j(1 + (1 - \tau_{t+1}^k)r_{t+1}). \tag{26}$$

The left-hand side of equation (26) denotes the marginal benefit of purchasing capital in period t. This consists of the after-tax rental rate earned in period $t + 1$ plus the resale value of undepreciated capital in period $t + 1$. The right-hand side of equation (26) is the marginal cost of purchasing capital in period t. This equals the foregone gross return capital owners would have earned had they invested resources $(1 + \tau_t^x)\xi_t^j$ in the international bond with net return equal to $(1 - \tau_{t+1}^k)r_{t+1}$. Lagging by a period and rearranging this equation yields the formula we used in equation (2) to construct the capital shares.

E.   Driving Processes

We describe the exogenous processes in two groups. The first, grouped into the vector x_t^O, includes exogenous processes that we take directly from the data without solving for the equilibrium of the model. These include the real interest rate $\{r_t\}$, tax rates $\{\tau_t^c, \tau_t^x, \tau_t^k\}$, labor supply $\{L_t\}$, depreciation rates $\{\delta_t^I, \delta_t^N, \delta_t^U, \delta_t^H\}$, relative prices of investment $\{\xi_t^I, \xi_t^N, \xi_t^U, \xi_t^H\}$, markups in the business sector $\{\mu_t^Q\}$, and markups in the housing sector $\{\mu_t^H\}$.[38] The second, grouped into the vector x_t^I, includes exogenous processes that we infer so that model-generated variables match their counterparts in the data perfectly as we describe below. These include the discount factor $\{\beta_t\}$, labor-augmenting technology $\{A_t^L\}$, capital-augmenting technologies $\{A_t^K\}$ and $\{v_t^I, v_t^N, v_t^U\}$, housing preferences $\{v_t^H\}$, and housing technology $\{A_t^H\}$.

F.   Equilibrium

Households and firms have perfect foresight about the exogenous processes driving the economy. Given these exogenous processes, an equilibrium for this economy is defined as a sequence of prices,

$$\{W_t, R_t^Q, R_t^I, R_t^N, R_t^U, R_t^H, P_t^H\}, \tag{27}$$

and a sequence of quantities,

$$\{H_t^L, H_t^K, H_t, C_t^L, C_t^K, Q_t, K_t^Q, K_t^I, K_t^N, K_t^U, K_t^H, X_t^I, X_t^N, X_t^U, X_t^H, D_t\}, \tag{28}$$

such that the following conditions hold:

1. The business market clears, $Q_t = C_t^L + C_t^K + \Sigma_j \xi_t^j X_t^j + (1 + r_t) D_t - (1 + g)$ D_{t+1}, and the housing market clears, $H_t = H_t^L + H_t^K$.

2. Firms produce intermediate business varieties with the production function (8), their labor choice satisfies the first-order condition (10), and their capital choice satisfies the first-order condition (11).

3. The allocation of business capital satisfies the three first-order conditions (13) and the aggregate rental rate is given by equation (14).

4. Firms produce intermediate housing services with the production function (15) and their capital choice satisfies the first-order condition (17).

5. Workers' optimal choices satisfy their budget constraint (19) and their first-order condition for housing relative to consumption (20).

6. Capitalists' optimal choices satisfy their budget constraint (22), the four capital accumulation equations (23), their first-order condition for housing relative to consumption (24), their Euler equation (25), and the four equations for the rental rates (26).

The 23 endogenous variables of the model are pinned down from these 24 equations (one equation is redundant by Walras's law).

Recalling that we have transformed the model in terms of stationary variables, we define a steady state of the transformed model economy as an equilibrium in which all exogenous processes are constant and, as a result, all endogenous variables are constant.[39] In the balanced growth path, prices $\{R_t^Q, R_t^I, R_t^N, R_t^U, R_t^H, P_t^H\}$ are constant and the wage and all quantities in equation (28) grow at a constant exogenous growth rate g.

IV. Quantitative Results

In this section we present quantitative results from the model for case Π, case K, and case R. We begin by describing how we infer the exogenous stochastic processes and by reporting their values. We then present counterfactual experiments in which we shut down some of the exoge-

nous processes to assess their effects on macroeconomic outcomes. Differences across cases reflect both differences in the inferred exogenous
processes and differences in the responsiveness of the economy to the
dynamics induced by the exogenous processes.

A. Inference

We assume that the economy reaches a balanced growth path in 2017, the
year after our sample ends.[40] We drop time subscripts to denote variables
in the balanced growth path and assume that $r = .04$. We fix all other exogenous processes and endogenous variables in the balanced growth
path at their 2016 values. The only exceptions are the capital stocks. Consistency with the capital accumulation equations and the observed investment flows in 2016 requires setting their balanced growth values to
$K^j = X^j / (g + \delta^j)$.

We assume logarithmic preferences, $\rho = 1$, and set the growth rate in the
balanced growth path to its sample average of $g = 0.033$.[41] We consider
two values for the elasticity of substitution between capital and labor
in the production function (8), $\sigma = \{1.25, 0.75\}$, the first of which is close
to estimates in Karabarbounis and Neiman (2014) and the second of
which is close to the estimates in Oberfield and Raval (2014) and the
values discussed in Chirinko (2008). We normalize the level of labor-
augmenting technology in balanced growth to equal the wage, $A^L = W$,
and choose the distribution factor α in the production function (8) so that
the model generates a labor share that equals its data analog in the balanced growth path. We begin our analyses assuming a unitary elasticity
$\theta = 1$ across capital types in the production function (12).

Given parameter values and observed exogenous processes x^o_t taken
directly from the data, we infer the values of the exogenous processes
x^i_t such that the model-generated values of endogenous variables match
their analogs in the data. We note that our procedure guarantees that
the model perfectly replicates the time series on prices in equation (27)
and quantities in equation (28).

In figure 11 we plot time series of inferred exogenous processes for
each of the three cases. Inverting the production function for housing
services in equation (15), we calculate $A^H_t = (H_t / K^H_t)$. In figure 11a, we
see that A^H_t is growing until the 1990s and then remains relatively stable.
We calculate the parameter that determines the preference for housing

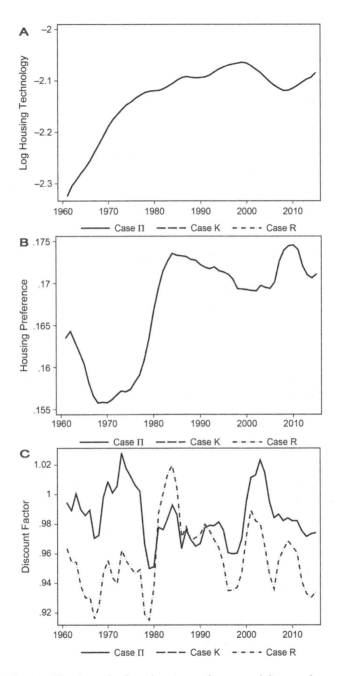

Fig. 11. Housing technology, housing preference, and discount factor

by solving the first-order conditions in equations (20) and (24) for the share $v_t^H = P_t^H H_t / [P_t^H H + (1 + \tau_t^c) C_t]$. Figure 11b shows that this share has remained relatively constant at roughly .17 over time.

We infer the path of the discount factor β_t in figure 11c by inverting the Euler equation for the capitalists (25) and substituting in the values of r_t, τ_t^c, P_t^H, v_t^H, and C_t^K. We calculate the analog of C_t^K in the data as the difference between nonhousing aggregate consumption C_t and the consumption of workers $C_t^L = [(1 - v_t^H) W_t L_t] / (1 + v_t^H \tau_t^c)$. Given the path of consumption growth for capitalists, we generally obtain a lower value of β_t under case R because the r_t under this case is generally higher. At annual frequencies, the inferred discount factors generally comove positively across the three cases.

Next, we use the first-order conditions for capital types in equation (13) to infer the capital-specific technologies v_t^j for $j = \{I, N, U\}$. In figure 12 we find that v_t^I has grown over time relative to v_t^N in all three cases. This trend reflects the increasing share of IT relative to non-IT capital income over time. To understand the differences across the three cases, recall that case R uses a revised real interest rate that is generally higher than the real interest rate in case II and case K. As equation (26) for the rental rate shows, the capital income accruing to IT is less sensitive to r_t than the capital income accruing to non-IT because the former has a higher depreciation rate. Therefore, a higher r_t increases the share of non-IT capital relative to IT capital and the dot-dashed line corresponding to case R lies below the solid black line corresponding to case II in figure 12a and the opposite in figure 12b. In case K, part of capital income is attributed to the unmeasured factor K_t^U. As a result, the share of capital income accruing to both IT and non-IT is smaller and both long-dashed lines shift down proportionally by the same factor relative to case II.

Figure 13 presents the inferred time series of (log) labor-augmenting technology A_t^L as a function of the elasticity of substitution between capital and labor σ. To understand how our results depend on which of the three interpretations of factorless income is used, together with the value of σ, we solve the first-order condition (10) for labor-augmenting technology:

$$A_t^L = (1 - \alpha)^{\frac{\sigma}{1-\sigma}} (s_{L,t}^Q)^{\frac{1}{\sigma-1}} (\mu_t^Q)^{\frac{\sigma}{\sigma-1}} W_t. \tag{29}$$

Labor-augmenting technology A_t^L in case R, a case featuring constant markups and no unmeasured capital, is plotted as the dot-dashed line and is declining over time. As equation (29) illustrates, with an elasticity of $\sigma > 1$, the decline in A_t^L reflects both the decline in $s_{L,t}^Q$ and the decline in W_t over time. With an elasticity of $\sigma < 1$, we still obtain a declining

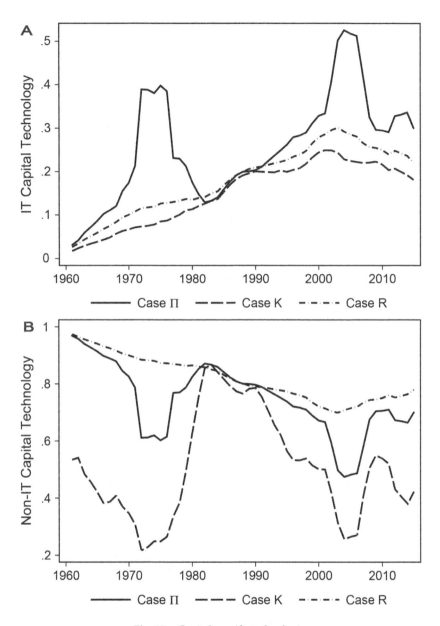

Fig. 12. Capital-specific technologies

A_t^L because quantitatively the decline in W_t is more important than the decline in $s_{L,t}^Q$.[42] Case K (long-dashed line) differs from case R only because $s_{L,t}^Q$ is the labor share of income, which now also includes capital income accruing to the unmeasured factor. While there are some differences in

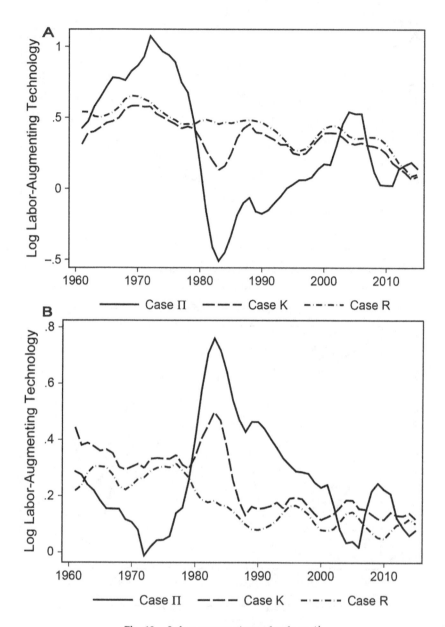

Fig. 13. Labor-augmenting technology A_t^L

the time series of A_t^L under the two cases (especially around 1980), all time series are declining over time for both values of σ.

The solid black line shows that A_t^L is significantly more variable under case Π, which allocates factorless income using time-varying markups.

Equation (29) shows that with $\sigma > 1$, the inferred A_t^l is positively associated with μ_t^Q. With $\sigma = 1.25$, the decline in markups between the 1970s and the early 1980s leads to a roughly 1.5-log-point decline in A_t^l. The increase in markups from the early 1980s is associated with an increase in A_t^l until roughly the Great Recession. These dynamics of A_t^l flip when $\sigma = 0.75$ because the inferred A_t^l is negatively associated with μ_t^Q. We view such large movements in A_t^l under case II as implausible.

Finally, figure 14 presents the inferred time series of (log) capital-augmenting technology relative to the rental rate of business capital, A_t^K/R_t^Q. To understand why our results differ across the three cases and two values for σ, consider the first-order condition (11) for capital-augmenting technology relative to the business rental rate,

$$\frac{A_t^K}{R_t^Q} = \alpha^{\frac{\sigma}{1-\sigma}}(s_{K,t}^Q \mu_t^Q)^{\frac{1}{\sigma-1}} \mu_t^Q, \qquad (30)$$

where the rental rate in the business sector R_t^Q is given by equation (14). We present the ratio A_t^K/R_t^Q because it is uniquely pinned down from equation (30), irrespective of how one normalizes the capital-specific technologies ν_t^i in equation (14) and A_t^K. By contrast, the individual components A_t^K and R_t^Q depend on how one normalizes the levels of ν_t^i and A_t^K.[43]

The dot-dashed line shows that for case R, A_t^K/R_t^Q is increasing over time when $\sigma = 1.25$, as shown in figure 14a, and is decreasing over time when $\sigma = 0.75$, as shown in figure 14b. As equation (30) shows, these dynamics reflect the increase in $s_{K,t}^Q$ over time under case R. Case K, plotted as the long-dashed line, differs from case R only because $s_{K,t}^Q$ is the capital share of income, which also includes capital income accruing to the unmeasured factor. While there are some differences in the time series of A_t^K/R_t^Q under the two cases (especially around 1980), the broad trends are similar across the two cases.

Similar to our inference of A_t^l, we find that the inferred A_t^K/R_t^Q becomes significantly more variable under case II with time-varying markups as seen in the solid black line.[44] This reflects the fact that the capital share $s_{K,t}^Q$ fluctuates significantly more under case II. By contrast, $s_{K,t}^Q$ is more stable either by imputing a revised real interest rate that makes factor shares sum to one in case R or by attributing the missing income to the unmeasured factor in case K. Equation (30) shows that with $\sigma > 1$, the inferred A_t^K/R_t^Q under case II is positively associated with the capital share of *costs*, $s_{K,t}^Q \mu_t^Q$ and the markup μ_t^Q. With $\sigma = 1.25$, we obtain a sharp increase in

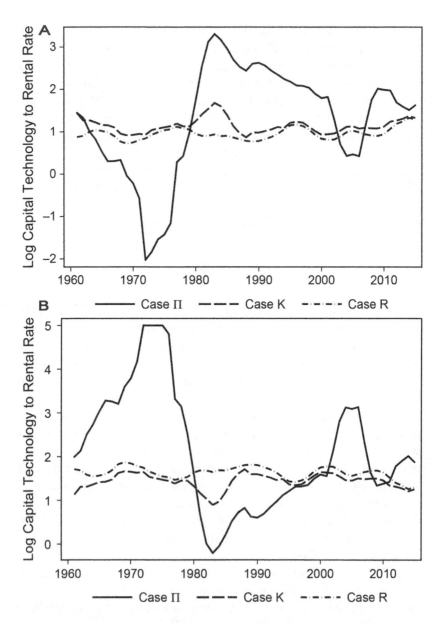

Fig. 14. Capital-augmenting technology to rental rate A_t^K/R_t^Q

A_t^K/R_t^Q between the 1970s and the early 1980s because the increase in the capital share of costs dominates the decline in the markup. With $\sigma = 0.75$ we obtain the opposite patterns. We again view such large movements in A_t^K relative to R_t^Q generated by case Π as implausible.

B. Counterfactuals

In this section we discuss several counterfactuals and show how our conclusions for the drivers of functional inequality, factor shares, and output depend critically on which case is used to account for factorless income. Our measure of inequality is the consumption of capitalists relative to workers C_t^K/C_t^L.[45] While admittedly stark, in our model C_t^K/C_t^L reflects the between income groups consumption inequality as workers earn all labor income and capitalists earn all capital income in the economy.

To understand the drivers of relative consumption C_t^K/C_t^L, we express it as a function of relative incomes net of depreciation across the two types of households, the investment behavior of capitalists, and the saving behavior of capitalists. We define the share of business depreciation in business output as $\psi_t^Q = (\Sigma_{j\neq H}\delta_t^j\xi_t^jK_t^j)/Q_t$ and the share of net business output in total net income as $\phi_t^Q = (Q_t - \Sigma_{j\neq H}\delta_t^j\xi_t^jK_t^j)/(Y_t - \Sigma_j\delta_t^j\xi_t^jK_t^j)$. Using the budget constraints of the capitalists and the workers, we arrive at the expression

$$\frac{C_t^K}{C_t^L} = \frac{1-\psi_t^Q}{s_{L,t}^Q\phi_t^Q}\left[1 - \frac{s_{L,t}^Q\phi_t^Q}{1-\psi_t^Q} - \frac{\Sigma_j\xi_t^j(X_t^j - \delta_t^jK_t^j)}{Y_t - \Sigma_j\delta_t^j\xi_t^jK_t^j} - \frac{(1+r_t)D_t - (1+g)D_{t+1}}{Y_t - \Sigma_j\delta_t^j\xi_t^jK_t^j}\right]. \quad (31)$$

A body of work since at least Weitzman (1976) has argued that the net concept of the labor share may be more closely associated with welfare and inequality than their gross counterparts because, unlike the rest of gross income, depreciation cannot be consumed by households. This logic appears in equation (31), which shows that relative consumption of capitalists is decreasing in the net labor share of total income $(s_{L,t}^Q\phi_t^Q)/(1 - \psi_t^Q)$. However, this equation shows there are additional factors that influence inequality. Investment motives affect relative consumption through the third term in the brackets, with relative consumption decreasing in the net investment rate of capitalists $[\Sigma_j\xi_t^j(X_t^j - \delta_t^jK_t^j)]/(Y_t - \Sigma_j\delta_t^j\xi_t^jK_t^j)$. Saving motives affect relative consumption through the last term in the brackets. Relative consumption decreases when capitalists decrease their stock of debt and the term $[(1 = r_t)D_t - (1 + g)D_{t+1}]/(Y_y - \Sigma_j\delta_t^j\xi_t^jK_t^j)$ is positive.[46]

We organize our discussion of the counterfactuals for relative consumption $\log(C^K / C^L)$ in table 2, for the business labor share s_L^Q in table 3, and for business output $\log Q$ in table 4. Each table is split into two panels. The top panel represents changes in these variables between the beginning of the sample (represented by the average value of each variable between 1961 and 1965) and the end of the sample (represented by the average value

Table 2
Counterfactuals: Relative Consumption Log(C^K/C^L)

	Elasticity $\sigma = 1.25$			Elasticity $\sigma = .75$		
	Case Π	Case K	Case R	Case Π	Case K	Case R
Changes between 1961–65 and 2011–15:						
Baseline	.427	.427	.427	.427	.427	.427
1. μ^Q	−.009	.002	.000	−.009	.002	.000
2. r	−.350	−.319	1.021	−.353	−.319	1.042
3. A^L	.415	.289	.370	.154	.259	.180
4. ξ^I	−.142	−.146	−.172	−.172	−.166	−.202
5. (A^K, v^I)	−.386	−.643	−.309	−.215	−1.005	−.206
6. ξ^N	.036	.035	.094	.032	.033	.083
7. (A^K, v^N)	−.093	−.752	−.110	.165	−.645	.078
8. L	−.183	−.183	−.183	−.183	−.183	−.183
9. τ^k	.103	.079	.156	.103	.081	.156
Changes between 1986–90 and 2011–15:						
Baseline	.335	.335	.335	.335	.335	.335
1. μ^Q	.151	.000	.000	.152	.000	.000
2. r	−.240	−.327	.527	−.242	−.320	.517
3. A^L	−.228	.340	.345	.342	.003	−.002
4. ξ^I	−.094	−.098	−.124	−.122	−.116	−.152
5. (A^K, v^I)	.216	−.313	−.276	−.402	−.214	.011
6. ξ^N	−.009	−.009	.057	−.009	−.008	.049
7. (A^K, v^N)	.433	.033	−.202	−.132	.615	.141
8. L	.019	.019	.019	.019	.019	.019
9. τ^k	.055	−.016	.115	.055	−.008	.115

Note: The table summarizes the counterfactual changes for relative consumption log(C^K/C^L). The rows labeled "Baseline" shows changes between 1961–65 and 2011–15 (upper panel) and 1986–90 and 2011–15 (lower panel) in the baseline model which, by construction, match the changes of log(C^K/C^L) in the data perfectly. Positive entries denote an increase in log(C^K/C^L). The entries for items 1–9 denote differences relative to the baseline. The differences are calculated as the change in the baseline minus the change in each counterfactual. A positive entry for items 1–9 means that the exogenous process causes log(C^K/C^L) to increase.

of each variable between 2011 and 2015). The bottom panel represents changes of these variables between the middle of the panel (averages between 1986 and 1990) and the end of the sample. The columns of the table present case Π, case K, and case R under the two different values of the elasticity of substitution between capital and labor σ.

The top row of each table, labeled "Baseline," shows changes which, by construction, match the changes of the corresponding variables in the data perfectly. For example, table 2 shows that from the beginning to the

Table 3
Counterfactuals: Business Labor Share s_L^Q

	Elasticity $\sigma = 1.25$			Elasticity $\sigma = .75$		
	Case II	Case K	Case R	Case II	Case K	Case R
Changes between 1961–65 and 2011–15:						
Baseline	−.016	−.003	−.016	−.016	−.003	−.016
1. μ^Q	.007	−.001	.000	.007	−.001	.000
2. r	−.005	.000	−.014	.005	.000	.011
3. A^L	.000	.000	.000	.000	.000	.000
4. ξ^I	−.024	−.025	−.029	.028	.027	.033
5. (A^K, ν^I)	−.064	−.114	−.055	.032	.154	.033
6. ξ^N	.006	.006	.015	−.005	−.006	−.014
7. $(A^K, \nu N)$	−.015	−.123	−.019	−.027	.109	−.013
8. L	.000	.000	.000	.000	.000	.000
9. τ^k	.001	−.003	.000	−.001	.003	.000
Changes between 1986–90 and 2011–15:						
Baseline	−.030	−.029	−.030	−.030	−.029	−.030
1. μ^Q	−.071	.000	.000	−.083	.000	.000
2. r	−.015	−.030	.012	.016	.029	−.011
3. A^L	.000	.000	.000	.000	.000	.000
4. ξ^I	−.016	−.016	−.021	.019	.018	.024
5. (A^K, ν^I)	.041	−.056	−.048	.063	.025	−.003
6. ξ^N	−.002	−.002	.009	.002	.002	−.008
7. (A^K, ν^N)	.075	.009	−.035	.023	−.094	−.024
8. L	.000	.000	.000	.000	.000	.000
9. τ^k	.000	−.012	.002	.000	.011	−.001

Note: The table summarizes the counterfactual changes for the business labor share s_L^Q. The rows labeled "Baseline" shows changes between 1961–65 and 2011–15 (upper panel) and 1986–90 and 2011–15 (lower panel) in the baseline model which, by construction, match the changes of s_L^Q in the data perfectly. Negative entries denote a decrease in s_L^Q. The entries for items 1–9 denote differences relative to the baseline. The differences are calculated as the change in the baseline minus the change in each counterfactual. A negative entry for items 1–9 means that the exogenous process causes s_L^Q to decrease.

end of the sample C^K/C^L increased by 0.427 log point. The other rows display counterfactuals in which we shut down particular exogenous processes that drive the transitional dynamics of the model. The entries in each counterfactual show the change in the baseline minus the change in each counterfactual. A positive entry means that the exogenous process causes a particular variable to increase. For example, row 1 in the upper panel of table 2 shows that under case II and $\sigma = 1.25$, markups led to a 0.009-log-point decrease in C^K/C^L.

Table 4
Counterfactuals: Output Log Q

	Elasticity $\sigma = 1.25$			Elasticity $\sigma = .75$		
	Case Π	Case K	Case R	Case Π	Case K	Case R
Changes between 1961–65 and 2011–15:						
Baseline	−.068	−.087	−.068	−.068	−.087	−.068
1. μ^Q	.000	−.001	.000	.000	.000	.000
2. r	.038	−.001	.103	.025	.000	.045
3. A^L	−.415	−.289	−.370	−.154	−.259	−.180
4. ξ^I	.177	.183	.215	.129	.125	.151
5. (A^K, v^I)	.482	.804	.386	.161	.754	.154
6. ξ^N	−.045	−.044	−.117	−.024	−.025	−.062
7. (A^K, v^N)	.116	.940	.138	−.124	.483	−.058
8. L	.183	.183	.183	.183	.183	.183
9. τ^k	−.005	.025	−.001	−.003	.014	−.001
Changes between 1986–90 and 2011–15:						
Baseline	−.147	−.148	−.147	−.147	−.148	−.147
1. μ^Q	−.046	.000	.000	−.028	.000	.000
2. r	.113	.221	−.094	.069	.128	−.048
3. A^L	.228	−.340	−.345	−.342	−.003	.002
4. ξ^I	.118	.123	.155	.091	.087	.114
5. (A^K, v^I)	−.270	.391	.345	.302	.160	−.008
6. ξ^N	.011	.012	−.071	.006	.006	−.037
7. (A^K, v^N)	−.541	−.041	.252	.099	−.461	−.106
8. L	−.019	−.019	−.019	−.019	−.019	−.019
9. τ^k	−.003	.086	−.013	−.001	.045	−.007

Note: The table summarizes the counterfactual changes for output log Q. The rows labeled "Baseline" shows changes between 1961–65 and 2011–15 (upper panel) and 1986–90 and 2011–15 (lower panel) in the baseline model which, by construction, match the changes of log Q in the data perfectly. Negative entries denote a decrease in log Q relative to a trend of $g = .033$. The entries for items 1–9 denote differences relative to the baseline. The differences are calculated as the change in the baseline minus the change in each counterfactual. A negative entry for items 1–9 means that the exogenous process causes log Q to decrease.

The first counterfactual we consider is setting the markup μ_t^Q to its average value in each of the three cases over the entire sample period. We illustrate the evolution of $\log(C_t^K/C_t^L)$ in figure 15 for $\sigma = 1.25$ and $\sigma = 0.75$. The solid black lines in figure 15 are labeled "Baseline" and correspond to the roughly 0.4-log-point increase in $\log(C_t^K/C_t^L)$ found in the data and perfectly reproduced by the model when all exogenous processes are active. Since markups are constant in case R and almost constant in case K, counterfactuals that eliminate markup variation in those

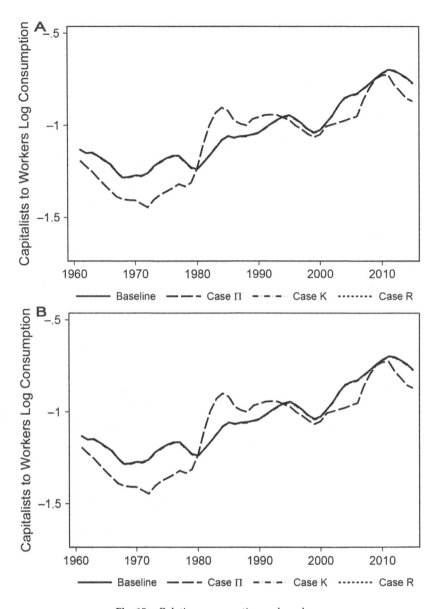

Fig. 15. Relative consumption and markups

cases do not affect endogenous variables. The lines corresponding to those cases, therefore, are visually indistinguishable from the baseline.[47]

The long-dashed lines in figure 15 show that eliminating the inferred markups from case Π over the full sample period makes little difference for the trend in inequality, because the long-dashed line starts and ends at a similar distance below the solid black line. We find that this conclusion is robust to the value of σ. Though markups have not significantly impacted the trajectory of relative consumption from 1960 to 2015, the long-dashed lines rise more steeply than the baseline during the first half of the sample and are flatter since the early 1980s. So, under case II, the interpretation is that the declining markups in the first half of our sample decreased the relative consumption of capitalists while the increasing markups in the second half restored it to near its initial value.

Eliminating the variation in markups results in movements in the business labor share in the opposite direction as the movements in inequality. This is expected from equation (31), which shows that, holding constant everything else, a lower s_L^Q increases C^K/C^L. Table 3 shows that markups are associated with a 0.7-percentage-point increase in the labor share since the beginning of the sample in 1960. Barkai (2016) and Eggertsson et al. (2018), by contrast, emphasize the increase of markups for the labor share decline. The difference in our conclusions stems from the different starting points of our samples, as shown in figure 2a. Similar to these authors who begin their analysis in the 1980s, we find that the increase in markups leads to a decline in the labor share of roughly 7 to 8 percentage points between 1986–90 and 2011–15 depending on the elasticity of substitution.[48] We also find declines in business output in these counterfactuals of roughly 0.03–0.05 log point during that period.

Next, we set the real interest rate equal to its value in the balanced growth path in all periods beginning in 1960, $r = .04$. Choosing the same level of r in all three cases guarantees that our results are not driven by differences in the long-run level of capitalists' consumption across the three cases. The short-dashed lines in figure 16 correspond to counterfactuals where $r = .04$ but where all other exogenous driving processes are preserved at their inferred values under case R. Unlike the baseline case, which features an increase in inequality, these short-dashed lines reveal a decline of inequality over time by nearly a log point. The high level of r in case R leads to an increase in C^K/C^L because capitalists save more to finance a growing consumption and this pushes down the last term of equation (31). Case II and case K feature lower and more declining values for r, so counterfactuals that remove that variation cause the lines corresponding to those cases to increase relative to the baseline case. We conclude, therefore, that the cost of capital is quantitatively significant for accounting for the increase in relative consumption under case R but not under case II and case K.

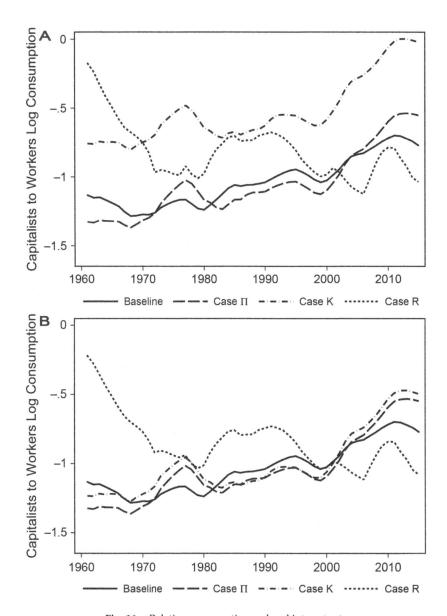

Fig. 16. Relative consumption and real interest rate

The impact of r on s_L^Q and Q is intermediated by changes in the business sector rental rate of capital R^Q. Given constant markups, equation (30) shows that a decline in r leads to a decline in s_L^Q when $\sigma > 1$ and R^Q declines, whereas it leads to an increase in s_L^Q if $\sigma < 1$ and R^Q increases or the reverse.[49] We also find that the lower r in the baseline compared with the counterfactual increases Q in most cases, as capitalists substitute from consumption toward capital accumulation. An important exception is the period between the end of 1980s and the 2010s under case R, in which the high baseline levels of r compared with the counterfactual lead to a decline in Q.

In figure 17 we plot the relative consumption path under the counterfactual that labor-augmenting technology A^L always equals its value in the first period of our sample. In all cases and for both elasticities, the lines exhibit either a decline or a more muted increase than the baseline case over the full sample. With $\sigma = 1.25$, A^L accounts for nearly all of the increase in C^K/C^L from the 1960s under case Π and for roughly 85% and 70% of the increase under case K and case R respectively. With $\sigma = 0.75$, A^L accounts for between roughly 35% and 60% of the increase in C^K/C^L.[50] We conclude that the decline in A^L since the 1960s can be robustly linked to an increase in C^K/C^L. The key force leading to the increased inequality is the decline in the investment rate of the capitalists as shown in the third term of equation (31). As shown in table 3, labor-augmenting technology A^L has no effect on the business labor share . Table 4 shows that the negative effects of A^L on output Q are larger in the higher substitution economy with $\sigma = 1.25$ than in the lower substitution economy with $\sigma = 0.75$.

Finally, figure 18 shows the relative consumption path when we remove the decline in the relative price of IT investment ξ^I and instead set it equal to its value in the first period of our sample. The decline in ξ^I increases capitalists' investment rate, which as the third term of equation (31) shows, leads to a decline in the relative consumption of capitalists. We conclude that IT-specific technological change lowered inequality and this conclusion is robust across different cases and values of the elasticity. On the other hand, the effects on s_L^Q depend on the elasticity of substitution. Given constant markups, equation (30) shows that a decline in ξ^I leads to a decline in s_L^Q when $\sigma > 1$ because R^Q declines and the opposite when $\sigma < 1$. Table 3 shows that, for $\sigma = 1.25$, the decline in ξ^I contributes to a decline in the labor share between 2.4 and 2.9 percentage points.[51] By contrast if $\sigma = 0.75$, the decline in ξ^I increases the labor share by roughly 2.7 to 3.3 percentage points. As shown in table 4, in all cases the decline in the relative price of IT causes business output to rise between 0.18 and 0.21 log point when $\sigma = 1.25$ and between 0.13 and 0.15 log point when $\sigma = 0.75$.

The other rows in tables 2, 3, and 4 present summary statistics for counterfactuals in which we keep constant at their 1960 values IT capital-augmenting technology (A^K and v^I), the relative price of non-IT invest-

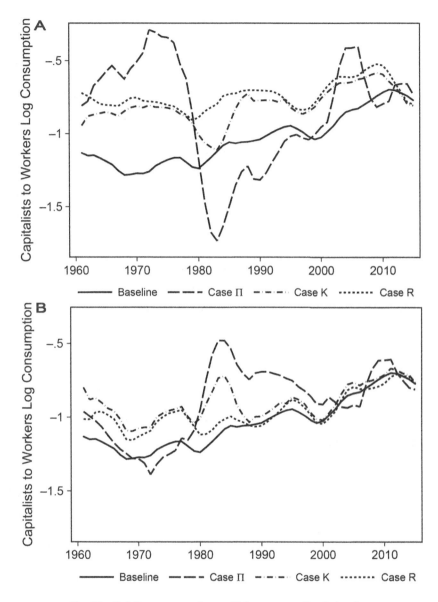

Fig. 17. Relative consumption and labor-augmenting technology

ment (ξ^N), non-IT capital-augmenting technology (A^K and v^N), labor supply (L), and capital taxes (τ^k). We find significant declines in C^K / C^L and increases in Q in response to IT capital-augmenting technology (A^K and v^I), with the effects being the largest in case K. Under an elasticity of $\sigma > 1$, IT capital-augmenting technology also accounts for large declines

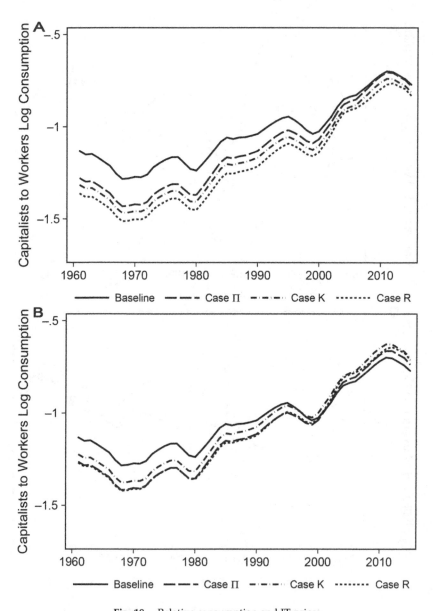

Fig. 18. Relative consumption and IT prices

in s_L^Q. The increase in labor supply L relative to the 1960s contributed to a decline in C^K/C^L and an increase in Q of roughly 0.18 log point in all three cases. Finally, the decline in capital taxes τ^k since the 1960s raised the after-tax return on saving and the consumption growth of capitalists and is associated with an increase in C^K/C^L between 0.08 and 0.16 log point across cases.

V. Conclusion

US GDP deviates significantly from the sum of measured payments to labor and imputed rental payments to capital. This deviation, or what we call factorless income, could reflect economic profits, missing capital, or a gap between the return on risk-free bonds and the cost of capital that firms perceive when making their investment decisions. In this paper we assess the plausibility of each of these strategies in allocating factorless income and demonstrate their implications for our understanding of macroeconomic outcomes such as functional inequality, factor shares, productivity, and growth.

We have laid out our skepticism of case II. Future work embracing this interpretation must articulate the mechanism by which a lower opportunity cost of capital is associated with higher markups and greater monopoly power. Further, if case II forms the basis for new calls for antitrust enforcement, it should be acknowledged that the logic for such calls was equally present in the 1960s and 1970s. We have similarly laid out our skepticism of case K and emphasize that future work embracing this interpretation must take a broad view of what constitutes unmeasured capital, potentially including forms of missing investment that far predate the IT revolution. However, we also recognize that more flexible analyses of missing capital may be able to cast this possibility in a more favorable light. We find case R the most promising and hope future work explores reasons why simple measures of the rental rate of capital might deviate from the rental rate that firms face when making their investment decisions. While we have considered the three methodologies in isolation to document with clarity their individual strengths and weaknesses, a direction for future research is to consider combinations of these methodologies.

Our interest in factorless income emerged from our prior work documenting a decline in the global labor share and associating it with capital-specific technological change. What do these three cases teach us about the labor share decline? Our skepticism about case II corroborates the view in Karabarbounis and Neiman (2014) that while rising markups likely contributed, much of the decline remains to be explained by technological change. Our skepticism about case K alleviates measurement concerns arising from missing output and reaffirms our measures of the labor share decline. Case R most closely approximates an environment with a stable opportunity cost of capital and in which IT-capital prices drive a significant amount of the variation in rental rates and factor shares, as in our earlier analyses.

Finally, though this study focuses on the United States, we note that the labor share decline has been a global phenomenon affecting developed countries in Continental Europe and Scandinavia and emerging economies such as China, India, and Mexico. We maintain our view that much can be learned from comparisons across this diverse set of experiences. In some countries, such as the United States, investment spending has been relatively low in recent decades. In others, such as China, investment has been increasing. We hope our methodology will be applied to many economies and that the study of factorless income around the world enhances our understanding of global changes in technology, product markets, and capital markets.

Endnotes

First draft: February 2018. We thank Anhua Chen for providing exceptional research assistance and Andy Atkeson, Emmanuel Farhi, Oleg Itskhoki, Greg Kaplan, Casey Mulligan, Richard Rogerson, Matt Rognlie, and Bob Topel for helpful comments. We gratefully acknowledge the support of the National Science Foundation. Karabarbounis thanks the Alfred P. Sloan Foundation and Neiman thanks the Becker Friedman Institute at the University of Chicago for generous financial support. The views expressed herein are those of the authors and not necessarily those of the Federal Reserve Bank of Minneapolis or the Federal Reserve System. For acknowledgments, sources of research support, and disclosure of the authors' material financial relationships, if any, please see http://www.nber.org/chapters/c14088.ack.

1. We acknowledge measurement difficulties that arise from a potential gap between the actual cost of employing labor and reported payments to labor. Measurement difficulties also arise from splitting sole proprietors' income between labor and capital. Gollin (2002) is a classic treatment on the topic, while Elsby, Hobijn, and Şahin (2013) examine this issue in the context of the recent decline in the labor share in the United States. Smith et al. (2017) offer evidence that labor income has increasingly been misreported as capital income in US S-corporations in order to minimize tax exposures, leading to an overstatement of the US labor share decline. Guvenen et al. (2017) find that US multinationals have increasingly shifted intellectual property capital income to foreign jurisdictions with lower taxes, leading to an understatement of the US labor share decline.

2. Piketty and Zucman (2014) and Dao et al. (2017) additionally offer detailed analyses of the labor share decline for various countries and periods.

3. Case Π follows a long tradition including Hall (1990), Rotemberg and Woodford (1995), and Basu and Fernald (1997). More recent analyses of longer-term factor share trends such as Karabarbounis and Neiman (2014), Rognlie (2015), and Barkai (2016) also used variants of this method. Recent work related to this approach focuses on the cyclicality of the inverse of the labor share to infer the cyclicality of markups. See, for instance, Gali, Gertler, and Lopez-Salido (2007), Nekarda and Ramey (2013), Karabarbounis (2014), and Bils, Klenow, and Malin (2018).

4. Examples in a large literature that follow this approach include Hall (2001), McGrattan and Prescott (2005), Atkeson and Kehoe (2005), Corrado et al. (2009), and Eisfeldt and Papanikolaou (2013).

5. Such an imputation of the rental rate underlies the internal rate of return in the prominent KLEMS data set. Similar approaches have been employed by Caselli and Feyrer (2007); Gomme, Ravikumar, and Rupert (2011); and Koh, Santaeulàlia-Llopis, and Zheng (2016).

6. The model we develop follows most of the related literature in assuming constant returns to scale production with no fixed costs, so the economic profit share is a fixed monotonic transformation of the markup of price over marginal cost. As such, unless otherwise noted, we use the terms profits and markups interchangeably.

7. Traina (2018) first showed the sensitivity of the markup estimate in De Loecker and Eeckhout (2017) to the split between COGS and SG&A. Further, Gutiérrez and Philippon (2017) estimate small changes in markups using the De Loecker and Eeckhout (2017) methodology but replace COGS with total expenses.

8. Similar to our case II, these authors back out implied markups for various parameterizations and demonstrate that the increase in risk premia is largely robust to the behavior of markups.

9. We also demonstrate that, among all three cases, case R generates the smallest gap between the growth of total factor productivity (TFP) as measured by the Solow residual and the growth of a modified measure of TFP that uses cost shares consistent with the allocation of factorless income.

10. As a baseline, we measure WL as compensation to employees. As we demonstrate below, this measure of the labor share produces fewer negative values for factorless income in the early 1980s than commonly used alternatives such as measures that allocate a fraction of taxes and proprietors' income to labor or labor's share of income in the corporate sector.

11. IT capital includes the subtypes of information processing equipment and software. Non-IT capital includes nonresidential structures, industrial equipment, transportation equipment, other equipment, research and development, and entertainment, literary, and artistic originals.

12. We construct the price of capital ξ^j for each j by dividing the total nominal value of type j capital by a chained Törnqvist price index constructed using the investment price indices for each capital subtype. Similarly, the depreciation rates δ^j are calculated by dividing the nominal value of depreciation for that capital type, itself the sum of depreciation across subtypes, by the nominal value of capital for that capital type, which itself equals the sum of the value of capital subtypes. The tax rates come from McDaniel (2007) and are effective average tax rates calculated from national accounts. Note that in a steady state and with zero taxes, eq. (2) reduces to the familiar $R = \xi\,(r + \delta)$.

13. To fill in Treasury rates for the small number of years early in the sample where they are missing, we grow later rates backward using growth in the AAA rate.

14. The online replication file is available at https://www.nber.org/data-appendix /c14088/KN_MacroAnnual_Replication.

15. Here and with all time series reported as moving averages, we use 3-year moving averages and then the 1-year change to fill in the series for the earliest and latest 2 years of the sample.

16. We wish to acknowledge that Matt Rognlie sent a figure in private correspondence documenting essentially this same pattern. Our methodology differs slightly from that used in Barkai (2016) due to our inclusion of taxes, different methods for smoothing, and focus on the entire business sector. The calculations, however, produce nearly identical results in terms of the time-series changes of our profit shares. When we apply his exact methodology to the business sector and lag by 1 year to account for different timing conventions, the resulting series has a correlation with that in fig. 2a of .90.

17. The timing of these changes accords well with the estimates of the real return on bonds presented by Jorda et al. (2017) for 16 countries.

18. The series in fig. 1b are much more volatile, and move more closely together, than the very similar plots of capital income shares by capital type offered in Rognlie (2015). The reason for this difference is exactly our point that case II implies a tight link of capital income and profit shares to the real interest rate. Rognlie uses a constant interest rate in constructing his plotted series, so they are less volatile and comove by less.

19. We note that the labor share in the housing sector is essentially zero because its value added in the national accounts is primarily composed of imputed rental income in owner-occupied housing and explicit rental payments.

20. We set $R^j = 0$ when we would otherwise impute a negative value and note that this is particularly commonly employed in the case of housing. To maintain consistency with the rest of our framework, we use the real interest rate based on 10-year Treasuries here. If we instead do this calculation using 30-year fixed rate mortgage rates, the level changes, but the time-series pattern for the most part does not.

21. Our measure of inflation is based on the price of nonhousing consumption. We considered inflation processes that belong in the ARMA(p, q) family. The Akaike information criterion selected $(p, q) = (3, 3)$ and the Bayesian information criterion selected $(p, q) = (1, 0)$.

22. We weight the ratios in this plot by firms' sales to mimic the weighting scheme used in the estimates of De Loecker and Eeckhout (2017) and multiply by a constant to normalize the series' levels in 1980.

23. Autor et al. (2017), Kehrig and Vincent (2017), and Hartman-Glaser, Lustig, and Zhang (2016) demonstrate that the reallocation of market share toward lower labor share firms underlies the trends of increasing concentration and declining labor share. This evidence is consistent with certain firms increasing their markups but also is consistent with technology-driven substitution toward firms operating more capital-intensive production methods in an environment with stable markups. Gutiérrez and Philippon (2017) confirm that concentration has risen in the US but do not find that to be the case in Europe.

24. The ratio of sales to operating costs (COGS+SG&A) fluctuated from 1.20 in 1953 to 1.14 in 1980 to 1.22 in 2014. Gutiérrez and Philippon (2017) have reported similar results when replacing COGS with total expenses.

25. While not all firms that report COGS also report SG&A, those that do represent a fairly stable share of total sales since 1980, ranging from about 72% to 82%. We further verified that the rise in sales to COGS looks similar in this subset of firms as in the whole set of firms, and in fact is even sharper.

26. These series use a quasi-Newton method in the second stage estimation of industry-specific output elasticity of variable cost. Using other methods such as Nelder-Mead only changes the level of the estimated markup and continues to result in a flat time-series.

27. We have tried using the perpetual inventory method, as well as directly using gross and net values for property, plant, and equipment. Our results presented here use the gross property, plant, and equipment measure for all North American firms, but little changes when using the other capital stock measures or restricting only to US firms.

28. We have experimented with removing expenditures associated with advertising (XAD), R&D (XRD), pension and retirement (XPR), and rent (XRENT), one at a time, from our measure of COGS+SG&A and do not find meaningful differences from the case when they are included. Many firms do not report these variables separately, however, so we cannot remove them all without excluding a large majority of firms in the data.

29. Chen, Karabarbounis, and Neiman (2017) document these patterns using firm-level data from many countries.

30. See Koh et al. (2016) for a helpful primer on these changes and their impact on the measured labor share decline.

31. See n. 14.

32. We note that the selection procedure in our algorithm plays a role in this. We focus on paths where nominal investment spending is small so GDP mismeasurement, discussed below, is also small. A consequence of this, however, is that there is little scope for the unmeasured capital stock to quickly grow prior to periods in which there is large or increasing factorless income. The initial stock of unmeasured capital therefore, according to this particular procedure, must be large. With less emphasis on minimizing the scale of unmeasured investment spending, we would likely be able to moderate the scale of initial unmeasured capital.

33. Following Barkai (2016), we have also calculated real interest rates using Moody's AAA borrowing rates. This change did not meaningfully alter any of our conclusions, but in that case the wedge calculated in case R should be interpreted as a risk premium over those AAA bond rates.

34. In performing the calculations, factor shares are calculated as the average values across adjacent periods corresponding to a Törnqvist index once chained together.

35. Greenwood, Hercowitz, and Krusell (1997) consider the macroeconomic effects of investment-specific technical change in a model that differentiates between equipment and structures. Related recent work with heterogeneous capital stocks includes Eden and Gaggl (2018), who consider a model with two types of capital, and Rognlie (2015), who considers multiple types of productive capital and housing.

36. We adopt the small open economy assumption with an exogenous real interest rate because it simplifies substantially our inference of the exogenous processes.

37. We abstract from labor income taxes because labor is provided inelastically and, to simplify the computation of the model, we rebate to each household the corresponding tax revenues. We model consumption taxes τ_t^c because their time-variation affects our inference of the time series of the discount factor β_t and the relative preference for housing ν_t^H. Similarly, we model capital τ_t^k and investment τ_t^x taxes because they affect the rental rate of capital R_t^j and our inferences of the exogenous processes driving the model.

38. The sequences of r_t, δ_t^j, ξ_t^U, μ_t^Q, and μ_t^H will in general differ across the three cases described above.

39. We assume that in the steady state the small open economy faces a real interest rate $r_t = \bar{r}_t + \psi(D_t - \bar{D})$, where $\bar{r}_t$ is an exogenous interest rate, $\bar{D}$ is a parameter, and ψ is a small but positive parameter that allows pinning down a unique steady state with $r = [1/(1 - \tau^k)][(1/\beta) - 1]$ and $D = \bar{D} + [(r - \bar{r})/\psi]$. We assume that r_t is exogenous during the transition, with the understanding that r_t approximates arbitrarily well $\bar{r}_t$ under a sufficiently small ψ.

40. Owing to the small open economy setup, the economy jumps to the balanced growth path once all exogenous variables settle down to a constant value.

41. As noted before, the growth rates of output are very similar between case K and the other cases.

42. Recall that we have detrended all variables that grow in the balanced growth path. So the decline in A_t^L is relative to a trend of $g = 0.033$ per year. We find that W declines by roughly 0.25 log point over the entire sample.

43. With J types of business capital, we have J equations (eq. [13] for the $J - 1$ relative shares and eq. [30] for the first-order condition for capital) to pin down $J + 1$ unknowns (the J capital-specific technologies ν_t^j and A_t^K). This means that we need one more condition that normalizes the ν_t^j relative to A_t^K. In our inference, we imposed the normalization $\Sigma_j \nu_t^j = 1$. To see how this normalization matters, denote the equilibrium of the model under our normalizing condition with the superscript 1 and the equilibrium of the model under some alternative normalizing condition with the superscript 2. Suppose that the aggregate rental rates in the two normalizing conditions are related by $(R_t^Q)^2 = x_t(R_t^Q)^1$, where x_t is a (potentially) time-varying factor. From eq. (30), we see that the ratio A^K/R^Q does not depend on the normalizing condition, so $(A_t^K/R_t^Q)^1 = (A_t^K/R_t^Q)^2$ and $(A_t^K)^2 = x_t(A_t^K)^1$. Since our inference of exogenous processes guarantees that we match perfectly business capital income $R_t^Q K_t^Q$ under any normalizing condition, we obtain that $(K_t^Q)^1 = x_t(K_t^Q)^2$. This implies that $A_t^K K_t^Q$ is identical under both normalizing conditions and so are output Q_t, consumptions C_t^K and C_t^L, and all other endogenous variables of the model. To summarize, the split of $R_t^Q K_t^Q$ and $A_t^K K_t^Q$ between K_t^Q and either R_t^Q or A_t^K depends on the particular normalizing condition that a researcher imposes, but all other variables do not.

44. Case II under an elasticity $\sigma = 0.75$ implies explosive values of $\log(A_t^K/R_t^Q)$ during the mid-1970s. To improve the visual presentation of the results, in fig. 14 we replace such explosive values with a value of 5.

45. With identical log preferences over a Cobb-Douglas bundle, the ratio of consumption completely characterizes welfare differences across the two types of households in a balanced growth path. We do not present welfare-based measures of inequality during the transition because these depend on ad hoc assumptions about when the economy reaches a balanced growth path. We also wish to acknowledge that our results for inequality depend crucially on the assumption that capitalists are infinitely lived and have perfect foresight. In this case C_t^K depends on the after-tax return on bonds (the substitution effect) and terminal consumption (the wealth effect) as seen from the Euler eq. (25).

46. In a balanced growth path with $g > 0$, the third term in the brackets becomes $(g\Sigma_j \xi^j K^j)/(Y - \Sigma_j \delta^j \xi^j K^j)$ and is positive because capitalists have to finance the growing cap-

ital of the economy. When $r > g$ and $D > 0$, the fourth term in the brackets becomes $[(r - g)D]/(Y - \Sigma_j \delta^j \xi^j K^j)$ and is positive because capitalists have to finance growing interest payments on their debt.

47. The small effects under case K are explained by the fact that in the baseline of case K we have set the profit share a constant fraction of measured business output $Q - \xi^U X^U$ rather than business output Q.

48. Barkai (2016) starts his sample in 1984. Eggertsson et al. (2018) show markup series starting in 1980 in all their analyses with the exception of fig. A.4 that starts in 1970. Consistent with our analysis, their fig. A.4 shows that the profit share has a similar level in 1970 and 2010.

49. Compositional changes across types of capital imply that the rental rate R^Q is differentially sensitive to changes in r across the three cases. In most cases, we find that r leads to a decline in s_L^Q when $\sigma > 1$, although the effects differ significantly across sample periods and cases.

50. We note that the effects of A^L on C^K/C^L change significantly when we begin our analysis in the mid-1980s. This is because the patterns of inferred A^L vary significantly both across cases and across values of σ when we begin our analysis in the mid-1980s, as shown in fig. 13.

51. In a model with a single investment good, Karabarbounis and Neiman (2014) argued that the decline in the aggregate price of investment goods led to a decline in the labor share of roughly 2.5 percentage points. Our results here with multiple types of capital are broadly consistent with Eden and Gaggl (2018), who estimate a production function with IT and non-IT capital and argue that the decline in the relative price of IT accounts for roughly half of the decline in the US labor share. Recent work by Autor and Salomons (2018) presents evidence across countries and industries that relates productivity-enhancing technological advances (potentially caused by the adoption of industrial robots and patenting flows) to declines in the labor share after the 1980s.

References

Atkeson, A., and P. Kehoe. 2005. "Modeling and Measuring Organization Capital." *Journal of Political Economy* 113 (5): 1026–53.

Autor, D., D. Dorn, L. F. Katz, C. Patterson, and J. Van Reenen. 2017. "Concentrating on the Fall of the Labor Share." Working Paper no. 23108, NBER, Cambridge, MA.

Autor, D., and A. Salomons. 2018. "Is Automation Labor-Displacing? Productivity Growth, Employment, and the Labor Share." *Brookings Papers on Economic Activity* 2018 (1): 1–87.

Barkai, S. 2016. "Declining Labor and Capital Shares." Working paper, University of Chicago.

Basu, S., and J. Fernald. 1997. "Returns to Scale in US Production: Estimates and Implications." *Journal of Political Economy* 105 (2): 249–83.

———. 2002. "Aggregate Productivity and Aggregate Technology." *European Economic Review* 46 (6): 963–91.

Bils, M., P. Klenow, and B. Malin. 2018. "Resurrecting the Role of the Product Market Wedge in Recessions." *American Economic Review* 108 (4–5): 1118–46.

Caballero, R., E. Farhi, and P.-O. Gourinchas. 2017. "Rents, Technical Change, and Risk Premia Accounting for Secular Trends in Interest Rates, Returns on Capital, Earning Yields, and Factor Shares." *American Economic Review* 107 (5): 614–20.

Caselli, F., and J. Feyrer. 2007. "The Marginal Product of Capital." *Quarterly Journal of Economics* 122 (2): 535–68.

Chen, P., L. Karabarbounis, and B. Neiman. 2017. "The Global Rise of Corporate Saving." *Journal of Monetary Economics* 89:1–19.

Chirinko, R. 2008. "σ: The Long and Short of It." *Journal of Macroeconomics* 30:671–86.

Corrado, C., C. Hulten, and D. Sichel. 2009. "Intangible Capital and US Economic Growth." *Review of Income and Wealth* 55 (3): 661–85.

Dao, M. C., M. Das, Z. Koczan, and W. Lian. 2017. "Why Is Labor Receiving a Smaller Share of Global Income? Theory and Empirical Evidence." Working paper, International Monetary Fund, Washington, DC.

De Loecker, J., and J. Eeckhout. 2017. "The Rise of Market Power and the Macroeconomic Implications." Working Paper no. 23687, NBER, Cambridge, MA.

De Loecker, J., and F. Warzynski. 2012. "Markups and Firm-Level Export Status." *American Economic Review* 102 (6): 2437–71.

Duarte, F., and C. Rosa. 2015. "The Equity Risk Premium: A Review of Models." Staff Report no. 714, Federal Reserve Bank of New York.

Eden, M., and P. Gaggl. 2018. "On the Welfare Implications of Automation." *Review of Economic Dynamics* 29:15–43.

Eggertsson, G., J. Robbins, and E. Wold. 2018. "Kaldor and Piketty's Facts: The Rise of Monopoly Power in the United States." Working Paper no. 24287, NBER, Cambridge, MA.

Eisfeldt, A., and D. Papanikolaou. 2013. "Organization Capital and the Cross-Section of Expected Returns." *Journal of Finance* 68 (4): 1365–406.

Elsby, M. W., B. Hobijn, and A. Şahin. 2013. "The Decline of the US Labor Share." *Brookings Papers on Economic Activity* 2013 (2): 1–63.

Fama, E., and K. French. 2002. "The Equity Premium." *Journal of Finance* 57 (2): 637–59.

Fernald, J., and B. Neiman. 2011. "Growth Accounting with Misallocation: Or, Doing Less with More in Singapore." *American Economic Journal: Macroeconomics* 3 (2): 29–74.

Gali, J., M. Gertler, and D. Lopez-Salido. 2007. "Markups, Gaps, and the Welfare Costs of Business Fluctuations." *Review of Economics and Statistics* 89 (1): 44–59.

Gollin, D. 2002. "Getting Income Shares Right." *Journal of Political Economy* 110 (2): 458–74.

Gomme, P., B. Ravikumar, and P. Rupert. 2011. "The Return to Capital and the Business Cycle." *Review of Economic Dynamics* 14:262–78.

Greenwood, J., S. Hercowitz, and P. Krusell. 1997. "Long-Run Implications of Investment-Specific Technological Change." *American Economic Review* 87 (3): 342–62.

Gutiérrez, G., and T. Philippon. 2017. "Declining Competition and Investment in the US." Working Paper no. 23583, NBER, Cambridge, MA.

Guvenen, F., R. Mataloni, D. Rassier, and K. Ruhl. 2017. "Offshore Profit Shifting and Domestic Productivity Measurement." Working Paper no. 23324, NBER, Cambridge, MA.

Hall, R. 1990. "Invariance Properties of Solow's Productivity Residual." In *Growth/Productivity/Unemployment: Essays to Celebrate Bob Solow's Birthday*, ed. P. Diamond, 71–112. Cambridge: Massachusetts Institute of Technology.

———. 2001. "The Stock Market and Capital Accumulation." *American Economic Review* 91 (5): 1185–202.

Hall, R., and D. Jorgenson. 1967. "Tax Policy and Investment Behavior." *American Economic Review* 57 (3): 391–414.

Hartman-Glaser, B., H. Lustig, and M. Zhang. 2016. "Capital Share Dynamics When Firms Insure Workers." Working Paper no. 22651, NBER, Cambridge, MA.

Jagannathan, R., E. McGrattan, and A. Scherbina. 2000. "The Declining US Equity Premium." *Federal Reserve Bank of Minneapolis Quarterly Review* (Fall):3–19.

Jorda, O., K. Knoll, D. Kuvshinov, M. Schularick, and A. Taylor. 2017. "The Rate of Return on Everything, 1870–2015." Working Paper no. 24112, NBER, Cambridge, MA.

Karabarbounis, L. 2014. "The Labor Wedge: MRS vs. MPN." *Review of Economic Dynamics* 17 (2): 206–23.

Karabarbounis, L., and B. Neiman. 2014. "The Global Decline of the Labor Share." *Quarterly Journal of Economics* 129 (1): 61–103.

Kehrig, M., and N. Vincent. 2017. "Growing Productivity without Growing Wages: The Micro-Level Anatomy of the Aggregate Labor Share Decline." Working Paper no. 244, ERID (Economic Research Intiatives @ Duke).

Koh, D., R. Santaeulàlia-Llopis, and Y. Zheng. 2016. "Labor Share Decline and Intellectual Property Products Capital." Working paper, University of Arkansas.

McDaniel, C. 2007. "Average Tax Rates on Consumption, Investment, Labor and Capital in the OECD 1950–2003." Working paper, Arizona State University.

McGrattan, E., and E. Prescott. 2005. "Taxes, Regulations, and the Value of US and UK Corporations." *Review of Economic Studies* 72 (3): 767–96.

Nekarda, C., and V. Ramey. 2013. "The Cyclical Behavior of the Price-Cost Markup." Working Paper no. 19099, NBER, Cambridge, MA.

Oberfield, E., and D. Raval. 2014. "Micro Data and Macro Technology." Working paper, Princeton University.

Piketty, T., and G. Zucman. 2014. "Capital Is Back: Wealth-Income Ratios in Rich Countries 1700–2010." *Quarterly Journal of Economics* 129 (3): 1255–310.

Rognlie, M. 2015. "Deciphering the Fall and Rise in the Net Capital Share: Accumulation or Scarcity?" *Brookings Papers on Economic Activity* 2015 (1): 1–69.

Rotemberg, J., and M. Woodford. 1995. "Dynamic General Equilibrium Models with Imperfectly Competitive Product Markets." In *Frontiers of Business Cycle Research*. Princeton, NJ: Princeton University Press.

Smith, M., D. Yagan, O. Zidar, and E. Zwick. 2017. "Capitalists in the 21st Century." Working paper, University of Chicago.

Traina, J. 2018. "Markup Estimation Using Financial Statements: Cost of Goods Sold vs. Operating Expense." Working paper, University of Chicago.

Vollrath, D. 2017. "An Update on the Profits from Housing." https://growthecon.com/blog/Ricardian-Housing.

Weitzman, M. 1976. "On the Welfare Significance of National Product in a Dynamic Economy." *Quarterly Journal of Economics* 90:156–62.

Comment

Richard Rogerson, Princeton University and NBER

The title of this paper tells us that the goal of this analysis is to account for something called "factorless income." Two immediate questions arise. What is factorless income? And why do we need to account for it? Although there are perhaps several motivations that might lead to this analysis, I think one prominent motivation stems from the interest in understanding the secular decline in the labor share that has been observed in the United States and other countries in the past several decades, a feature that the authors have documented in their previous work.

Figure 1 shows the decline in the labor share in the United States since 1960, with "labor share" here defined the same way that Karabarbounis and Neiman define it: total employee payroll as a fraction of gross domestic product. (This is what Elsby, Hobijn, and Sahin [2013] termed the "payroll share" to emphasize that it does not include all payments to labor. Importantly, much though not all of the secular trend in various measures of the labor share is accounted for by changes in the payroll share.)

I have also included a linear trend in the figure. It is important to emphasize up front that in my view, the feature of primary interest is the modest negative trend. The reason for this is that for many decades the labor share exhibited no trend, and it is this change, albeit somewhat modest, that is most striking. Although there are indeed some significant fluctuations around the linear trend, and one could seek to understand the source of the fluctuations, I think they are of second-order importance.

A question that many researchers have been asking is what lies behind the trend decline in the labor share, and the literature has suggested several possible answers. One dimension that usefully separates the explanations into two classes is the extent to which the decrease in

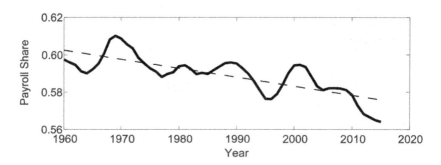

Fig. 1.   Trend change in the labor share

the labor share is accompanied by an increase in profits versus an increase in the share of income going to capital.

Unfortunately, separating the income that does not go to labor into these two components is challenging, and one of the contributions of this paper is to propose a new method for doing this. Before getting into the details of the authors' proposed method, it is useful to recognize the key challenge. In particular, whereas most of the payments to labor are recorded by payroll data, the fact that much of the capital stock is owned by the firms that use it implies that relatively few of the payments to capital are officially recorded and are therefore largely bundled with profits.

One could follow different approaches to decompose nonpayroll income into a piece representing payments to capital and a piece representing profit. One could try to measure profits directly and then impute the capital share as the residual. Indeed, several authors have sought to measure changes in markups over time as a way to implement this. The core strategy employed by Karabarbounis and Neiman is complementary to this: they use the Hall-Jorgenson formula for the user cost of capital to impute the rental price of capital and then combine this with data on the stock of capital to compute total payments to capital. The authors then also compute the residual income that goes to neither labor nor capital, a residual that they label "factorless income." As noted earlier, the behavior of this residual vis-a-vis the capital share is potentially relevant for distinguishing between different explanations for the trend decline in the labor share. Importantly, given the view that it is the trend decline in the labor share that interests us, it is the trend changes in the residual and capital share that are of interest.

Figures 2 and 3 display the time series behavior of the capital share and the residual that emerge from applying the authors' method.

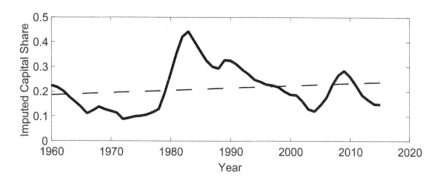

Fig. 2.   Trend change in the capital share

These figures indicate a small positive trend for the capital share and a small negative trend for the residual. Because the labor share was defined as the payroll share, the nonpayroll share of labor income is implicitly included in the residual. Elsby et al. (2013) argued that part of the decrease in the overall labor share is due to a decline in the share of nonpayroll payments to labor. They estimated this effect to be on the order of 2 percentage points. Taking this estimate as given, it would seem reasonable to conclude that the true profit component is close to trendless.

Taken at face value, the authors' method seemingly provides a sharp characterization: virtually all of the trend decline in the labor share is accounted for by a trend increase in the share of income going to capital, with effectively no trend in the share of income going to profits.

But a closer look at figures 2 and 3 gives one pause in taking the results at face value. In particular, it is of interest to take a closer look at the fluctuations about the linear trend in each of these figures. Without looking at the scale of the y-axis, one might think that each of these two series

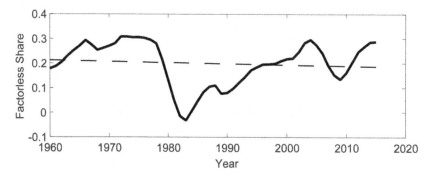

Fig. 3.   Trend change in the factorless income share

exhibits fluctuations similar to what we observed for the labor share. But a careful look at the scale of the y-axis reveals just how dramatic these fluctuations are: over a period of several years around 1980, the capital share increased by more than 30 percentage points, only to fall by roughly this same amount over the next 20 years. In contrast, the fluctuations in the labor share about trend are of the order of 1 or 2 percentage points.

At least to me, these fluctuations seem implausibly large. And this is problematic for the simple reason that we might be reluctant to take the estimated trend effects at face value given these large swings at high and medium frequency. Most of the paper is ultimately devoted to trying to rationalize these large swings. To this end, the authors consider three different possibilities. The first possibility is that these seemingly incredible swings reflect changes in markups and hence profits. The other two reflect the possibility that the large swings are an artifact of measurement, in particular mismeasurement of capital income. One of these measurement possibilities is that our measures of the capital stock are incorrect (due to the presence of unmeasured intangible capital) and the other is that the rental rate imputed from the Hall-Jorgenson cost of capital formula is incorrect.

The authors do an excellent job of assessing and contrasting the extent to which each of these three explanations can singularly account for the large swings in their imputed capital share, paying attention to what the associated implications are for a variety of driving forces, such as the extent and nature of technical change. Given that the reader was forced to choose one of the three explanations, I read the paper as basically preferring the third alternative, namely, that the issue lies with the user cost of capital implied by the Hall-Jorgenson formula when using a standard measure of the interest rate.

While I agree with this overall assessment, I would like to provide a somewhat different perspective. The Hall-Jorgenson formula is essentially an asset pricing equation: it expresses the seemingly sound economic intuition that the price of an asset today and tomorrow must be intimately connected to the flow value of the asset and the appropriate discount factor. Applied iteratively, this logic implies that the price of an asset is the appropriately discounted value of the stream of flow values.

While the logic of this seems reasonable, the asset pricing literature has taught us that this basic equality routinely fails miserably over both the short and medium run when applied using standard discount rates taken from the data, for example, either the rate on US Treasuries or some corporate bond rate. Put somewhat differently, we should not be surprised if the result of applying this formula with standard discount factors leads to large swings at high and medium frequency. And, in fact, this is exactly what the authors find.

Having obtained a series for the capital and factorless income shares that exhibit large swings, I think there are two main and intimately related questions of interest in the current context. First, can we trust the trend implications that result from applying the Hall-Jorgenson formula with a standard measure of the interest rate even if we do not trust the implications for the short and medium run? If so, then we possibly ignore the presence of the large swings from the perspective of understanding the trend changes in the labor share. But if the answer is no, the second question is whether there is any hope of finding the appropriate discount factor to use in the Hall-Jorgenson formula in order to uncover the true trend effect.

I do not know the answer to the first question, but if the answer is in the negative, I am somewhat pessimistic about being able to answer the second question in the affirmative. This being the case, I am at this point not yet convinced that the authors' method for computing the capital share and the factorless income share is able to provide powerful evidence to help us distinguish between alternative explanations for the trend decline in the labor share. But to be fair, it is important to recognize that other methods currently being used also have their limitations, and in view of this we should perhaps consider the method proposed in this paper as offering an additional perspective on an important and challenging issue.

As a final comment, I would like to raise a cautionary note about the interpretation of the results in the paper. For example, when the authors assess the ability of intangible capital to reconcile some of the seemingly implausible fluctuations in the capital share, I think the correct interpretation is that extending the analysis to allow a substantial role for intangible capital is not a very plausible way to eliminate the large movements in the capital share. This needs to be understood as quite distinct from assessing the extent to which incorporating intangible capital might be quantitatively important in affecting the implications for the trend behavior of the capital share. That is, the forces at work driving the large fluctuations in the factorless income share may be quite different from the forces at work driving the trend behavior of the factorless income share. While the current paper focused almost exclusively on accounting for the large swings, I think it would be of interest to adapt the methods of this paper to an analysis of trend changes.

Endnote

For acknowledgments, sources of research support, and disclosure of the authors' material financial relationships, if any, please see http://www.nber.org/chapters/c14089 .ack.

Reference

Elsby, M., B. Hobijn, and A. Sahin. 2013. "The Decline of the US Labor Share." *Brookings Papers on Economic Activity*. https://www.brookings.edu/bpea -articles/the-decline-of-the-u-s-labor-share/.

Comment

Matthew Rognlie, Northwestern University and NBER

I. Overview

This paper provides the most careful and clearheaded study to date of the factor distribution of income in the United States. Its most important contribution is the introduction of a new concept, "factorless income," which is the residual after assigning aggregate income to labor and capital. Unlike many other studies, which simply assume that factorless income corresponds to either economic profit, unmeasured capital, or a return premium, this paper is agnostic and entertains all three possibilities. It turns out that none of the three is a perfect match for the data, but economic profit is a particularly ill-fitting explanation. This calls into question some recent work on rising markups in the United States, and I suspect that Karabarbounis and Neiman's critique will quickly become central to the literature.

The following comment has two parts. First, I will provide my own brief tour of factor income trends in the United States, covering much of the same territory as Karabarbounis and Neiman but in a cursory and simplified way. Second, I will discuss the paper's key contributions, especially its rejection of "case II," the interpretation of factorless income as economic profit. I conclude that the paper is quite successful in making its case, and that future work should build upon it by combining the paper's three cases, with a special emphasis on "case R," the discrepancy between interest rates and the rate of return on capital.

II. Factor Income in the United States: A Whirlwind Tour

A. What Income Shares Should We Even Be Using?

In principle, the question is simple: What is labor's share of income? Sadly, this is a minefield for the casual observer. For the United States, the most commonly cited source is the Bureau of Labor Statistics' (BLS's) labor productivity and costs data, if only because this is the only official release of a "labor share" series. The BLS nonfarm business sector labor share series, however, suffers from several key weaknesses. The most severe is the imputation for the labor share of mixed income, which has bizarre features, documented by Elsby, Hobijn, and Şahin (2013), that exaggerate the decline in the labor share. Another limitation is that this is only a gross series, with no allowance for depreciation.

What are the other options? For casual discussion, another popular option is to look at corporate profits, normalized by either corporate value added or gross domestic product (GDP). This is intended to be the complement of the labor share, and at face value, it addresses the main weaknesses of the BLS series: it excludes proprietors' income altogether and is net of depreciation. But National Income and Product Accounts (NIPA) profits bring their own weaknesses. One is that the most common series includes profits from foreign investment, but we have no corresponding figures for labor compensation or value added.

Another much more serious—and almost entirely unknown—problem is the treatment of inflation. Profits are net of nominal interest payments and ignore the real capital gain from inflated-away debt. Traditionally, this downward bias in profits is offset by an upward bias from using nominal historical costs to measure depreciation, but this offset is not present in NIPA, which uses current costs instead. The consequence is a large downward bias in profits whenever there is substantial inflation—and in the US time series, this means an exaggerated decline centered around the 1970s and 1980s.[1]

B. *The Best Measure: Net Shares of Domestic Corporate Factor Income*

In short, the labor share should be a simple concept, but without an in-depth understanding of the national accounts, we can quickly be led astray. Amid the complexity, is there a standard measure of the labor share that we can use as our first pass at the question? Yes. The single best measure is the net labor share of domestic corporate factor income. This measure divides labor compensation by the sum of labor compensation and net operating surplus for the domestic corporate sector. This excludes proprietors' income, excludes depreciation, and is unaffected by the split between capital income accruing to debt versus equity. It also excludes income from foreign investments, which has no labor income counterpart and is conceptually not part of the domestic production function.

Two potentially serious biases remain, but we can take some consolation from the fact that they point in opposite directions. First, restricting to the corporate sector no longer means that we avoid all mixed income: as Smith and colleagues (2017) show, the remarkable rise of S corporations, which have a tax incentive to shift labor income to profits, has likely biased downward the trend in corporate labor share. On the other hand, in a world of tax havens and profit shifting, excluding all foreign profits is not really the right choice and will miss some capital income that actually corresponds to domestic production.[2] An important ongoing task for research is to quantify the magnitude of each bias.

When we look at this measure of the labor share, what do we see? Figure 1 shows its complement, the nonlabor share, which will be more natural once we begin to do accounting. Surprisingly, the postwar trend is ambiguous: nonlabor income is high now, but it was also high in the 1950s and 1960s. Moreover, its rise has been recent and sharp, having occurred entirely since 2000.

What accounts for this U-shaped pattern? If, as in many macroeconomic models, we interpret the nonlabor share of income as accruing to capital, it is natural to start our analysis by looking at the capital intensity of the corporate sector, as measured by the capital-income ratio. Indeed, conditional on a neoclassical production function, if there are no factor-augmenting technology shocks, the capital share should move one-for-one with the capital-income ratio—positively if the elasticity of substitution is greater than 1 and negatively if the elasticity is less than 1.

Figure 2 displays the ratio of capital to net income for the corporate sector.[3] This is a remarkably stable series: the ratio has been close to 200% for the entire postwar era. There is nothing to match the U-shape

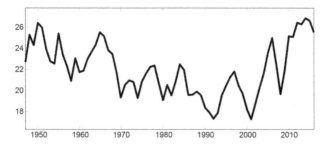

Fig. 1. Nonlabor share of net corporate factor income

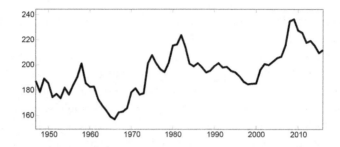

Fig. 2.   Ratio of fixed assets to net corporate factor income

in the nonlabor share, making it difficult to interpret figure 1 directly in terms of a neoclassical production function. Any proposed mechanism for the dynamics of the labor share that works through capital accumulation, as in Piketty (2014), is dead on arrival unless the stock of capital unmeasured by figure 2 is large and growing.

C.   Accounting for Capital's Share: An Enormous Residual

The puzzle worsens if we add information on prices. Abstracting from taxes, capital gains, and risk, the net return on capital should be the real interest rate. Since adequate historical data on inflation expectations are not available, this is difficult to obtain. But we can devise a rough measure, as in figure 3: the 10-year Treasury yield, subtracting the lagged 5-year rate of change of the GDP deflator as a proxy for inflation expectations.

This measure of the real interest rate shows an inverted U-shape, peaking in the 1980s.[4] This is exactly the wrong pattern for explaining figure 1: real interest rates are high when the nonlabor share is at its lowest!

We can make this mismatch even clearer. If r is the net return on capital and $K/(Y - \delta K)$ is the ratio of capital to net income, then their product

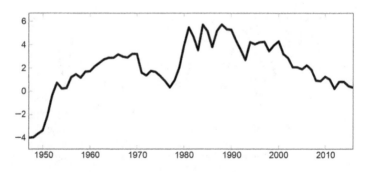

Fig. 3.   "Real" 10-year Treasury yield (lagged 5-year inflation proxy)

$rK/(Y - \delta K)$ should be capital's share of income. In figure 4, we compare $rK/(Y - \delta K)$—setting r equal to the rate in figure 3 plus 5% as an ad hoc equity premium—to the nonlabor share from figure 1. With so little movement in the capital-income ratio, movement in r dominates this series, and we obtain an inverted U for imputed capital income, which bears no resemblance to the actual time series for the nonlabor share. This result is robust across many formulations of the equity premium: although we can tweak the average levels, it is impossible to reconcile the dynamics.

It is difficult to overstate the puzzle that figure 4 poses for the usual macro analysis of the labor share. We are accustomed to writing models where capital is either the main or the only factor earning income other than labor. But when we try a simple accounting exercise to reconcile the observed nonlabor share with capital's share, we find that the two are completely disconnected. Rather than helping us distinguish between alternative neoclassical stories for the evolving labor share—say, savings versus technological change versus investment prices—figure 4 imperils the common assumptions on which all these stories rely. Indeed, the fall and rise of the actual nonlabor share, though a worthy puzzle in its own right, pales next to the discrepancy with the imputed capital share.

D.   Responding to an Empirical Dilemma

In the face of this seemingly intractable clash between model and data, the literature has moved in two directions.

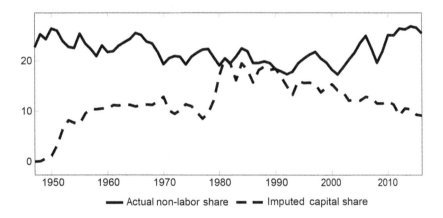

Fig. 4.   Actual nonlabor share vs. imputed ($r + 5\%$) capital income share

First, there has been an emphasis on other, less ambiguous trends in the factor income distribution. Figure 5 displays perhaps the two most striking: the rise in housing income and the rise in depreciation of intellectual property products. Both of these trends are omitted by construction in figure 1, since net figures exclude depreciation and the corporate sector excludes virtually all housing. But both come up in many other calculations of the labor share—for instance, as Rognlie (2015) documents, housing income is central to the postwar trends in Piketty (2014); and as Koh, Santaeulàlia-Llopis, and Zheng (2016) show, intellectual property has played a central role in the evolution of many gross labor share measurements.

These are important clarifications to our understanding. We want to know whether capital income is going to capitalists or to landlords and homeowners; we also want to know if it is merely echoing the capitalization of software in the national accounts.

But these clarifications may have, perversely, increased the general level of confusion among macroeconomists. The reason is that amid widespread discussion of a falling labor share, few observers are aware of the pattern in figure 1: that there is no postwar trend in the net corporate labor share. If we deviate from figure 1 along one dimension—say, by adding housing income or depreciation—then we will inevitably find that this deviation "explains" the entire trend in the labor share. Hence we have a proliferation of papers showing that some force or another accounts for a declining labor share: housing in Rognlie (2015), de-

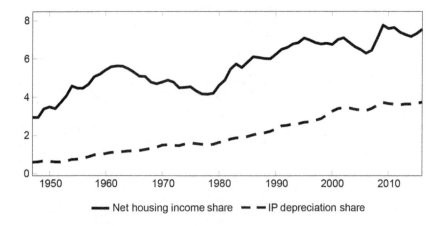

Fig. 5. Two unambiguous trends: housing and IP depreciation as shares of aggregate income.

preciation in Bridgman (2017), or intellectual property capitalization in Koh et al. (2016). There is no contradiction between these findings, all of which are accurate given their respective starting points. But to some extent they all bury the lede, which is that there have been two very sharp, but offsetting, postwar swings in the labor share.[5]

The other recent direction in the literature is to interpret the gap in figure 4 as a measure of economic profit, or markups. Most prominent in this vein is Barkai (2016), who starts in 1984 and takes the trends in figure 1 literally, arguing that the profit share has risen substantially while the capital share has actually fallen. Barkai attributes these trends to a decline in competition, joining a growing literature that ascribes changes in income distribution to market power in some form.

This interpretation, natural enough at first glance, becomes awkward if we look prior to 1984: in figure 4, the gap widens as we look back a few years into the 1970s, and grows vastly larger (even beyond current levels) as we extend the series to the 1950s and 1960s. If we interpret the entire series using markups, then these markups were enormous in the early postwar era, before contracting and then plummeting in the 1980s, then inflating back to their earlier levels in the 2000s and 2010s. This is not an inconceivable sequence, but it does defy the structural explanations (e.g., market concentration) usually put forward for thinking about markups, none of which should have induced such sharp reversals.

III. This Paper's Contribution

In the face of an increasingly jumbled literature, this new paper from Karabarbounis and Neiman is a beacon of clarity.

The basic idea of the paper is to document the part of aggregate income that we cannot assign to either labor or capital: "factorless income," to use the authors' very clever term. Factorless income is a residual, a much more sophisticated version of the gap in figure 4 between the nonlabor share and an imputed capital share. In studying factorless income, the authors must confront the central dilemma of the literature: Why is there such a gap between what we observe and what we can explain?

The brilliance of the term "factorless income" is that it is agnostic: it does not presuppose any particular source or explanation. To see why this is so important, one need only look at the existing literature, which interprets the same residual in several mutually exclusive ways: as economic profit, as rent on unmeasured capital, and as return premium. Rather than following the usual custom and writing a model in which only one of these three mechanisms is present, Karabarbounis and Neiman start with all three on equal footing, as cases Π (economic profit), K (unmeasured capital), and R (return premium). This is a practice that should be widely emulated.

A. A Much-Needed Critique of Case Π

The paper's single most important contribution is its critique of "case Π," the interpretation of factorless income as economic profit.

This critique is multipronged. First, Karabarbounis and Neiman show that factorless income has moved substantially in both directions, and that when the exercise of Barkai (2016) is extended backward, it implies very large markups in prior decades.[6] Furthermore, factorless income has moved very closely with the real interest rate. Although it is not strictly impossible that economic profits are responsible for all this, the authors point out that it is very difficult to think of a mechanism that would cause profits to replicate both the long-term fall and rise in factorless income and this tight connection with real interest rates.

Second, they highlight the difficulty by calculating a similar "profit" share for housing following Vollrath (2017) and obtaining a similar but even more volatile series. It is unclear what such large and volatile profits can even mean for the housing rental sector, which has little market power relative to the rest of the economy.[7]

Third, they document important caveats to other recent work showing rising markups. They find that it is difficult to replicate De Loecker and Eeckhout (2017), with deviations appearing in the step for handling measurement error. And as Traina (2018) has pointed out, De Loecker and Eeckhout's estimates of a rapid increase in markups are very sensitive to the assumption that cost of goods sold in Compustat represents variable cost, and the trend mostly disappears when we use an alternative measure of variable costs that includes sales, general, and administrative costs. Also important is Edmond, Midrigan, and Xu's (2018) observation that when sales weights are replaced by the more theoretically appropriate cost weights, there is a much smaller rise in markups.

A subtle but crucial point is that De Loecker and Eeckhout (2017) are not consistent with case Π in any case: their early markup estimates from the 1960s to the 1970s do not match the decline we see in factorless income, whereas their later markup estimates show a much larger rise than we see in factorless income.

Fourth, and perhaps most innovatively of all, Karabarbounis and Neiman calculate the implied series for labor and capital-augmenting technological change and show that case II leads to enormous fluctuations. In part, these numbers look extreme because the elasticity of substitution is close to 1.[8] But in any case, they are large and erratic enough that it seems very unlikely that technology could really be responsible for them.

The key economic insight here is that markups primarily drive a wedge between income and costs, and under reasonable parameters have relatively little effect on the split of costs between labor and capital. Although markups do reduce real wages relative to rental rates, this means that markups actually increase the capital share relative to total costs when the elasticity of substitution is less than 1. Even if the elasticity of substitution is greater than 1, the decrease in the capital share from higher markups is nowhere near what we see in the data, where there is a tight negative relationship between the capital share and factorless income.[9] Without much impact from markups, we are forced to infer very large technological fluctuations to match the data.

Altogether, this amounts to a timely and convincing argument against case II. It might seem natural to interpret the gap between income and imputed costs as a "markup," but this is not a story that stands up to scrutiny in other dimensions.

B. The Inevitability of Case R

In the end, Karabarbounis and Neiman conclude that their case R—a deviation of the rental rate of capital from the usual user cost formula based on bond returns—is the most promising. Their approach is careful and methodical, and the critique of case II is much needed, but to many of us (including, I suspect, the authors themselves) this is not a very surprising end point. The financial world is a lot more volatile than the macro world: bond yields and asset prices bounce around much more than the labor share or the capital stock. When we mix financial series with macro ones, we're bound to find big residuals, and these residuals will be too large and variable to admit any consistent macro interpretation.

Some form of case R, therefore, seems inevitable, and should really be the starting point for future work. This is not to dismiss the authors' contribution, which is a necessary step given how case R has been set aside in so much recent work in favor of case II. But it does make the analysis of case K somewhat less useful. It is clearly impossible to explain the factorless income series entirely using unmeasured capital—but at the same time, it's quite possible that unmeasured capital has made a large long-term contribution.

Indeed, as the authors acknowledge, it may well be that some combination of these three forces—fluctuations in markups, unmeasured capital, and the gap between user costs and bond returns—is needed to really understand factorless income.

C. Understanding the Reasons for Case R

Since case R is the most compelling, it is also an important object of study. Why exactly is the nonlabor share so disconnected from bond yields or other finance-based measures of the cost of capital, like equity valuations? While this disconnect is no surprise to anyone who has looked at the data, it is still not something that macroeconomists have fully modeled and understood. I suspect that capital adjustment costs, as usually calibrated, cannot come close to explaining it.

One possibility for this gap is an equity risk premium. As recent work by Farhi and Gourio (2018) shows, this improves our ability to account for capital income over the medium run, but I am skeptical that it is enough to explain case R entirely. Equity valuations are quite volatile and have less impact on high-frequency investment decisions than theory would suggest. Expected equity returns should have been quite high in the late 1970s and early 1980s, given low valuations, but this was precisely when the capital share was also low. Another challenge for this view, at least from a modeling perspective, is that when the price of investment goods is pinned down by technology, it is hard to explain why there should be a risk premium on investment at all, unless adjustment costs or other frictions allow for large temporary declines of capital prices below replacement cost.

An important test for this hypothesis is coming up. If equity valuations continue to rise while bond prices fall, the implied ex ante equity premium will shrink. It will be very interesting to see whether this coincides with a decline in factorless income.

My guess is that there is a deeper lack of transmission between financial market rates of return and the real rates used to make investment decisions. To some extent, this is already known: it is well established that corporate hurdle rates are usually far above stock or bond returns. Could this gap expand or contract over time, leading to variation in factorless income? Perhaps the rise of shareholder payouts and corporate "capital discipline" over the last few decades has propped up the required return on capital, even in the face of declining financial market returns. This hypothesis sounds similar to markups, but there is an important distinction: markups distort overall production, while high hurdle rates distort capital as an input to production.

D.   Alternative Measures of Capital-Labor Inequality

Finally, although the primary contribution of this paper is its study of factorless income, it also innovates in its measurement of capital-labor inequality. Usually, we talk about inequality in terms of income shares: some fraction goes to "labor" and some fraction goes to "capital." This is ambiguous on its face—for instance, it is not clear whether we should be measuring gross or net capital income.

If we care about consumption inequality or wealth accumulation, net income is a more natural measure, since capitalists can neither eat nor save depreciation. But this is still imperfect. Imagine two worlds, one in which "capitalists" earn net income at a rate of 6% on assets worth 200% of GDP and the trend growth rate is 0%, and another in which they earn the same amount but the growth rate is 3%. Capitalists can sustain consumption equal to 12% of GDP in the first world but only 6% of GDP in the second, where they are investing half their income so that the capital stock keeps up with economic growth.[10] Despite identical income shares, consumption inequality is much higher in the first case.

At a deeper level, the capital income share is a strange measure of inequality: capital is just an intermediate good that contributes to production with a time lag. Why should we give such special treatment to income from this part of the production process? In their counterfactual exercises in Section IV.B, Karabarbounis and Neiman try what I think is the best alternative: looking directly at the impact on consumption instead.

Unfortunately, though this is an important step, the authors are limited by the assumptions needed for the tractability of their overall analysis: perfect foresight, infinitely lived capitalists, and a small open economy. With these assumptions, the slope of capitalists' consumption is pinned down by the tax-adjusted exogenous real interest rate. This slope is unaffected by shocks to the income distribution at any date, which are anticipated under perfect foresight and smoothed across all periods. It is impossible, in this framework, to trace the connection between the time path of income shares and the time path of relative consumption.

To carry out this exercise, we probably need to modify the model on several dimensions: replace perfect foresight with some other model of expectations, replace capitalists with a household side that features richer heterogeneity and less-than-infinitely-elastic long-run savings, and drop the small open economy assumption in order to endogenize the real interest rate. This is likely to be messy and is far beyond the scope of the current paper, but it will build upon the excellent ideas here.

IV. Conclusion

Karabarbounis and Neiman have produced the state-of-the-art paper on factor income shares and should be applauded. Unlike many papers in this genre, they do not go all in arguing for one conclusive mechanism; the message is more subtle, steering us away from poorly fitting stories like case II and toward more promising avenues like case R. This might not be as viscerally satisfying as a paper that promises a decisive answer, but it has the great virtue of being correct, and it will prove an indispensable foundation for the coming literature.

Endnotes

For acknowledgments, sources of research support, and disclosure of the author's material financial relationships, if any, please see http://www.nber.org/chapters/c14090 .ack.
1. In their memorable work on inflation and equity valuation, Modigliani and Cohn (1979) discussed both of these accounting biases, although they were not the main focus.
2. See, e.g., Tørsløv, Wier, and Zucman (2018) for recent estimates of the growth in profit shifting.
3. For consistency with other figures, in fig. 2 we have the ratio with net income, as opposed to the more common ratio with gross income. Since figures 1 and 2 are net, we should interpret them in terms of net production function, which, as Rognlie (2015) emphasizes, always has a lower elasticity of substitution than the gross production function. In this case, however, the analysis is similar if fig. 2 is gross: the ratio is even more stable over time, meaning that accumulation of capital cannot explain factor income shifts in either direction.
4. The extremely low real interest rates in the beginning of the sample reflect the sharp postwar inflation—arguably a circumstance where lagged inflation was a poor measure of forward-looking inflation expectations. The same inverted U-shape, however, is present even if we throw out the first few years.
5. For instance, Rognlie (2015) starts with the accounting in Piketty (2014), which uses a measure of aggregate net income that includes housing; at this point, removing housing eliminates the postwar trend in the labor share, but only because the analysis already excluded depreciation and used a sensible imputation of mixed income. Housing is still an important issue, but not the only one; the author attempted to clarify this by putting the nonlabor share's "fall and rise" front and center in the paper's title!
6. To my knowledge, Karabarbounis and Neiman in this paper were the first to publicly make this observation. In a subsequent paper, Barkai and Benzell (2018) also extended Barkai's (2016) original series backward and obtained similar results.

7. On the other hand, long-lived assets like housing are especially sensitive to expectations of capital gains, which might be difficult to impute properly, so there is reason to expect that this series would be especially erratic.

8. In the limit, as we approach an elasticity of substitution of exactly 1, these blow up to infinity, since shares become independent of labor or capital-augmenting technology under Cobb-Douglas. Shocks to the production function could still produce changes in shares, but the shocks would have to affect the share parameters directly, which the authors do not consider.

9. Holding the rental rate of capital constant, one can show that the elasticity of the capital share of income with respect to markups μ is $-\sigma$, where σ is the local elasticity of substitution. The elasticity of the cost share of income with respect to μ is -1. If rising markups primarily cause a decline in the capital rather than the labor share, it must be that σ is close to $1/\alpha$, the inverse of the capital share α of costs. Since α is a small fraction, this requires it to be far above 1, contradicting almost all empirical evidence.

10. Or perhaps in the second world, saving is done less by a capitalist dynasty and more by wage earners who are constantly replenishing the stock of assets. In this case, we would probably also be less concerned about the capital-labor split.

References

Barkai, Simcha. 2016. "Declining Labor and Capital Shares." Working paper, University of Chicago.

Barkai, Simcha, and Seth Benzell. 2018. "70 Years of US Corporate Profits." New Working Paper Series no. 22, Stigler Center for the Study of the Economy and the State, University of Chicago.

Bridgman, Benjamin. 2017. "Is Labor's Loss Capital's Gain? Gross versus Net Labor Shares." *Macroeconomic Dynamics* 22 (8): 2070–87.

De Loecker, Jan, and Jan Eeckhout. 2017. "The Rise of Market Power and the Macroeconomic Implications." Working Paper no. 23687, NBER, Cambridge, MA.

Edmond, Chris, Virgiliu Midrigan, and Daniel Yi Xu. 2018. "How Costly Are Markups?" Working Paper no. 24800, NBER, Cambridge, MA.

Elsby, Michael W. L., Bart Hobijn, and Ayşegül Şahin. 2013. "The Decline of the US Labor Share." *Brookings Papers on Economic Activity* 2013 (2): 1–63.

Farhi, Emmanuel, and Francois Gourio. 2018. "Accounting for Medium-Run Macro-Finance Trends: A Rising Equity Premium?" Conference draft, *Brookings Papers on Economic Activity*. https://www.brookings.edu/wp-content/uploads/2018/09/BPEA_Fall2018_Accounting-for-Macro-Finance-Trends.pdf

Koh, Dongya, Raül Santaeulàlia-Llopis, and Yu Zheng. 2016. "Labor Share Decline and Intellectual Property Products Capital." Working paper, University of Arkansas.

Modigliani, Franco, and Richard A. Cohn. 1979. "Inflation, Rational Valuation and the Market." *Financial Analysts Journal* 35 (2): 24–44.

Piketty, Thomas. 2014. *Capital in the Twenty-First Century*. Cambridge, MA: Harvard University Press.

Rognlie, Matthew. 2015. "Deciphering the Fall and Rise in the Net Capital Share: Accumulation or Scarcity?" *Brookings Papers on Economic Activity* 2015 (1): 1–69.

Smith, Matthew, Danny Yagan, Owen Zidar, and Eric Zwick. 2017. "Capitalists in the Twenty-First Century." Working paper, University of Chicago.

Tørsløv, Thomas R., Ludvig S. Wier, and Gabriel Zucman. 2018. "The Missing Profits of Nations." Working paper, University of California, Berkeley.

Traina, James. 2018. "Is Aggregate Market Power Increasing? Production Trends Using Financial Statements." Working paper, University of Chicago.

Vollrath, Dietrich. 2017. "An Update on the Profits from Housing." https://growthecon.com/blog/Ricardian-Housing.

Discussion

The authors opened the discussion by thanking Richard Rogerson and Matthew Rognlie for their comments. They expressed their appreciation for Rognlie's effort to frame their paper in the context of the literature. The authors also shared his skepticism about the implications of case II.

Andrew Atkeson spoke next and pointed out that the ratio of after-tax net operating surplus to the capital stock for nonfinancial corporations has remained roughly constant since the 1960s, fluctuating between 6% and 8%. In support of this statement, Atkeson cited figures from the Bureau of Economic Analysis's annual report on the "Returns for Domestic Nonfinancial Business." Atkeson argued that the literature has mostly focused on decomposing this series into various components: the return on observed and unobserved physical capital, the return on intangible capital, and monopoly markups. In his view, the relevant source of variation in factorless income is government bond yields. Atkeson noted that a balanced growth model, where the return on capital is stochastic and has a mean of roughly 7%, would be consistent with the empirical evidence on the behavior of after-tax net operating surplus. In this model, the net operating surplus is entirely attributed to the return on physical capital.

The authors responded that case R in their paper focuses precisely on the role of bond yields. Although Atkeson's neoclassical benchmark implies zero profits, the authors mentioned that there is no consensus about the importance of profits and their evolution over time. In addition, there has been growing interest recently in the evolution of markups over the past few decades. The authors noted that when profits are not zero, the counterpart to Atkeson's measure of profits corresponds to the return on capital (R) plus firms' profits divided by the capital stock (Π/K).

Gita Gopinath followed up on a plot included in the authors' presentation, which depicted the business profit share under case II starting in 1960. She noted that case II predicts that markups were decreasing prior to the 1980s. She noted that the authors' approach to measuring markups requires data on payments to capital. She suggested that some alternative approaches don't rely on such data, and could address some of the issues with case II that the authors pointed out. In particular, Gopinath referred to the work of Jan De Loecker and Jan Eeckhout ("The Rise of Market Power and Macroeconomic Implications" [Working Paper no. 23687, NBER, Cambridge, MA, August 2017]). De Loecker and Eeckhout estimate production functions and identify markups using a first-order condition for a flexible input, such as intermediate goods. She reminded the audience that De Loecker and Eeckhout document a substantial rise in markups since the 1980s. Gopinath asked the authors how their own approach compares with De Loecker and Eeckhout's.

In response to Gopinath's question, the authors compared the markups obtained using the two approaches: case II in their own paper and the method of De Loecker and Eeckhout. Although the pattern is similar since the 1980s for both approaches, trending upward, the one before the 1980s differs substantially. Estimated markups declined up to the 1980s under case II but were roughly constant under De Loecker and Eeckhout's approach. The authors then elaborated on the differences between both approaches and what the associated markups capture.

To illustrate their comments, the authors displayed a plot on a backup slide, displaying three series starting in 1960. The first series corresponds to markups estimated using the De Loecker and Eeckhout method. The second corresponds to the ratio of total sales to total cost of goods sold (COGS). The third corresponds to the ratio of total sales to the sum of COGS and selling, general, and administration (SG&A) expenses. The authors noted that the second series closely tracks the first one, suggesting that the ratio of total sales to COGS is the first-order driver of the markups under De Loecker and Eeckhout. In contrast, the third series does not track to the first series and exhibits only a modest increase since the 1980s. The authors pointed out that this fact is consistent with the work of James Traina ("Markup Estimation Using Financial Statements: Cost of Goods Sold vs. Operating Expense" [Working paper, University of Chicago, 2018]), which documents that the ratio of COGS to the sum of COGS and SG&A fell over time.

The authors argued that this evidence suggests that both markups and fixed costs have increased over time. They cautioned, though, that

COGS and SG&A cannot be directly associated with variable and fixed costs, respectively. In particular, they pointed out that De Loecker and Eeckhout use Compustat, which does not classify a cost as COGS if the firm classifies it as SG&A and vice versa. In addition, the authors noted that changes in markups are no longer a sufficient statistic to understand changes in the labor share or capital share when fixed costs are changing. The authors argued that in this case, the relevant sufficient statistic is the average profit share, including fixed costs, which corresponds to their case II.

The authors mentioned that the increase in the ratio of SG&A to COGS is not specific to the United States, but occurred in many other countries. The authors replicated the exercise of De Loecker and Eeckhout for various countries, using the Compustat International data set. They found that the 10-year trend of sales divided by COGS is larger than the trend of sales divided by the sum of COGS and SG&A for many countries, including the United Kingdom.

To conclude, the authors acknowledged that case II only provides a partial picture of the rise in profits. They saw the work of De Loecker and Eeckhout as complementary to theirs.

Andrea Eisfeldt inquired about the allocation of profits, dividends, and rental rate on physical capital in the authors' model. In particular, she argued that understanding which agents own which types of assets is crucial to study income inequality. The authors responded that their model features two types of agents: capitalists, who receive the rental rate and profits, and workers, who earn labor income. As a consequence, the distinction between rental rates and profits does not affect income inequality. But this distinction matters along other dimensions in their model.

Alp Simsek was the last to comment. He pointed out that a difficulty in empirical asset pricing is that the expected return on assets is inherently difficult to observe. Simsek mentioned the work of Òscar Jordà and colleagues ("The Rate of Return on Everything, 1870–2015" [Working Paper no. 24112, NBER, Cambridge, MA, December 2017]), which studies real rates of return across developed economies, covering a very long horizon, and includes housing in addition to other assets. In Simsek's opinion, one of the most interesting results in their paper is that the series of aggregate ex post returns is rather flat. In contrast, the safe interest rate varies substantially over time. Simsek saw such variation in the risk premium as consistent with case R. The authors agreed with Simsek's point and confirmed that they cited Jordà et al. for this exact reason.

4

The Tail That Keeps the Riskless Rate Low

Julian Kozlowski, *Federal Reserve Board of St. Louis*
Laura Veldkamp, *Columbia University and NBER*
Venky Venkateswaran, *New York University and NBER*

I. Introduction

Interest rates on safe assets fell sharply during the 2008 financial crisis. This is not particularly surprising; there are many reasons, from an increased demand for safe assets to monetary policy responses, why riskless rates fall during periods of financial turmoil. However, even after the financial markets calmed down, this state of affairs persisted. In fact, by 2017, several years after the crisis, government bond yields still showed no sign of rebounding. In figure 1, we show the change in longer-term government yields in a number of countries since the financial crisis. Looking at longer-term rates allows us to abstract from transitory monetary policy and interpret the graph as evidence of a persistent decline in the level of riskless interest rates.

The decline in interest rates following the financial crisis took place in the context of a general downward trend in real rates since the early 1980s. Obviously, this longer-run trend cannot be attributed to the financial crisis. Instead, it may have come from a gradual change in expectations following the high inflation in the 1970s or a surge in savings from emerging markets seeking safe assets to stabilize their exchange rates. This longer-run trend taking place in the background is hugely important but distinct from our question. We seek to explain the fact that interest rates fell (relative to this long-run trend) during the financial crisis and failed to rebound.

We explore a simple explanation for this phenomenon: before 2008, no one believed that a major recession sparked by a financial crisis with market freezes, failure of major banks, and so forth could happen in the United States. The events in 2008 and 2009 taught us that this is more likely than we thought. Today, the question of whether the financial crisis might repeat itself arises frequently. Although we are no longer on the precipice, the knowledge we gained from observing 2008–9 stays with us and re-

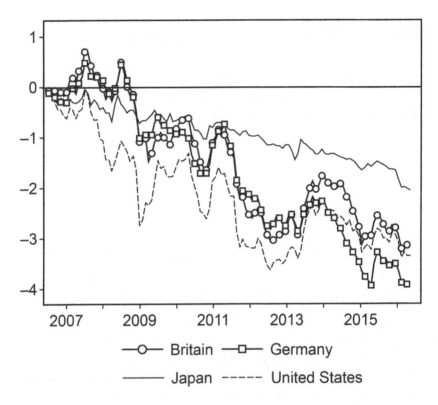

Fig. 1. Low interest rates are persistent. Change in percentage points of 10-year government bond yield since July 3, 2006 (Irwin 2016). A similar pattern emerges, even if we control for inflation.

shapes our beliefs about the probability of large adverse shocks. This persistent increase in perceived "tail risk" makes safe liquid assets more valuable, keeping their rates of return depressed for many years. The contribution of this paper is to measure how much tail risk rose, explain why it remains elevated, and quantitatively explore its consequences for riskless interest rates.

At its core is a simple theory about how agents form beliefs about the probability of rare tail events. Our agents do not know the distribution of shocks hitting the economy and use macro data and standard econometric tools to estimate the distribution in a flexible, nonparametric way. Transitory shocks have persistent effects on beliefs, because once observed, the shocks remain forever in the agents' data set. Then, we embed our belief formation mechanism into a standard production economy with liquidity constraints. When we feed a historical time series of macro data for the postwar United States into our model and let our agents reestimate the distribution from which the data are drawn each period, our belief revision mechanism goes a long way in explaining the persistent postcrisis decline in government bond yields since 2008–9.

The link between heightened tail risk and rates of return in the model comes from two intuitive mechanisms. First, the increase in consumption risk makes safe assets more valuable, lowering the required return on riskless government bonds. The second stems from the fact that government bonds also provide liquidity services that are particularly valuable in very bad states. Intuitively, in those states, the liquidity available from other sources falls. The main contribution of this paper is to combine these standard forces with the aforementioned theory of beliefs in a simple, tractable, and empirically disciplined framework and show that rare events like the 2008–9 recession generate large, persistent drops in riskless interest rates.

Apart from being quantitatively successful, our explanation is also consistent with other evidence of heightened tail risk. For example, in their value at risk (VAR) analysis, Del Negro et al. (2017) find that most of the decline in riskless rates is attributable to changes in the value of safety and liquidity. From 2007 to 2017, they estimate a 52-basis point change in the convenience yield of US Treasury securities (which is about 80% of the estimated drop in the natural riskless real rate over the same time period). A second piece of evidence comes from the SKEW index, an option-implied measure of tail risk in equity markets. Figure 2 shows a clear rise since the financial crisis, with no subsequent decline.[1] In our quantitative analysis, we show that the implied changes in tail probabilities are roughly in line with the predictions of our calibrated model. Finally, popular narratives about stagnation emphasize a change in "attitudes" or "confidence," which we capture with belief changes, and the reductions in debt financing that result: "Years after US investment bank Lehman Brothers collapsed, triggering a global financial crisis and shattering confidence worldwide . . . 'The attitude toward risk is permanently reset.' A flight to safety on such a global scale is unprecedented since the end of World War II" (Condon 2013).

In many macro models, including belief-driven ones, deviations of aggregate variables from trends inherit the exogenously specified persistence of the driving shocks (see, e.g., Maćkowiak and Wiederholt 2010; Angeletos and La'O 2013).[2] Therefore, these theories cannot explain why interest rates remain persistently low. In our setting, when agents repeatedly reestimate the distribution of shocks, persistence is endogenous and state dependent. Extreme events like the recent crisis are rare and thus lead

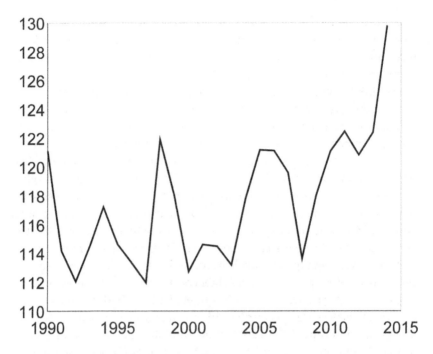

Fig. 2. The SKEW index. A measure of the market price of tail risk on the S&P 500, constructed using option prices (CBOE 2019).

to significant belief changes (and, through them, aggregate variables such as riskless rates) that outlast the events themselves. More "normal" events (e.g., milder downturns), in contrast, show up relatively more frequently in the agents' data set, and therefore additional realizations have relatively small effects on beliefs. In other words, although all changes to beliefs are, in a sense, long-lived, rarer events induce larger, more persistent belief changes and interest rate responses. Rare event beliefs are more persistent because rare event data are scarce. It takes many observations without a rare event to convince observers that the event is much more rare than they thought.

This mechanism for generating persistent responses to transitory shocks is simple to execute and can be easily combined with a variety of sophisticated, quantitative macro models to introduce persistent effects of rarely observed shocks. Although our focus in this paper is on interest rates, it could be applied to other phenomena, including labor force participation rates, corporate debt issuance and cash hoarding, house prices, export decisions, and trade credit. The crucial ingredients of the model are some nonlinearity (typically, a constraint that binds in bad states), some actions that compromise efficiency in the current state but that hedge the risk of this binding state, and then a large, negative shock. If those ingredients are present, then adding agents who learn like econometricians is likely to induce sizeable, persistent responses.

Because the novel part of the paper is using this belief formation mechanism to explore interest rates, Section II starts by examining the belief formation mechanism in a simple context. We construct a time series of "quality" shocks to US nonresidential capital and use it to show how our nonparametric estimation works. Agents estimate the underlying distribution of the shocks by fitting a kernel density function to the data in their information set. When they see extreme negative realizations from the financial crisis, it raises their estimation of large negative outcomes. More important, this effect is persistent. The theoretical underpinning of the persistence is the martingale property of beliefs. Intuitively, once observed, an event stays in the agents' data set and informs their probability assessment, even after the event itself has passed. Decades later, the probability distribution still reflects a level of tail risk that is higher than it was precrisis. Knowing that a crisis is possible influences risk assessment for many years to come.

We embed this mechanism into a standard production economy with a liquidity friction. Every period, in addition to their usual production, firms have access to an additional investment opportunity. However, to exploit this opportunity, they need liquidity in the form of pledgeable collateral. Both capital and government bonds act as collateral, but only a fraction of the former's value can be pledged. An adverse shock lowers the value of pledgeable capital and, therefore, liquidity.

Section V presents our quantitative results. We perform two sets of exercises. The first involves long-run predictions under the assumption that crises continue to occur. Specifically, we simulate long-run outcomes (i.e., stochastic steady states) drawing shocks from the updated beliefs. Our calibrated model predicts that the increase in tail risk is associated with a 1.45% drop in interest rates on government bonds in the long run. Most of this drop can be attributed to the liquidity mechanism. The modest degree of risk aversion in our calibration implies that the increase in consumption risk by itself induces only a very small change in interest rates. We also show that the implications of the model for changes in equity market variables (e.g., equity premium, tail risk implied by options) line up reasonably well with the data.

Next, we generate time paths for the economy under the assumption that the financial crisis we saw in 2008–9 was a one-off event and will never recur. Then, the economy eventually returns to its precrisis stochastic steady state, but we show that this occurs at a very slow rate. Even after several years, interest rates on safe assets remain depressed. Intuitively, learning about rare events is, in a sense, "local": probabilities in the tail respond sharply to extreme realizations but slowly to realizations from elsewhere in the support. As a result, it takes a very long period without extreme events to convince agents that such events can be safely ignored. Finally, to demonstrate that belief revisions are key to the model's ability to generate sustained drops in interest rates, we also generate counterfactual time paths with the belief mechanism turned off. In other words, we endow agents with knowledge of the true distribution from the very beginning. We find that the initial impact of the shock on interest rates is similar, but they start to rebound almost immediately and return to precrisis levels at a much faster rate. In other words, without changes to beliefs, the financial crisis would induce a fairly transitory fall in interest rates.

Comparison to the Literature

Our paper speaks to a large body of work that focuses on the macroeconomic consequences of beliefs.[3] Most of these papers focus on uncertainty (or second-moment changes) and, perhaps more important, rely on exogenous assumptions about the persistence of shocks for propagation. Essentially, beliefs about time-varying states are only persistent to the extent that the underlying states are assumed to be persistent.[4] Our mechanism, on the other hand, generates persistence endogenously and helps explain why some recessions have long-lasting effects while others do not. A second advantage of our contribution is that by tying beliefs to observable data, we are able to impose considerable empirical discipline on the role of belief revisions, a key challenge for this whole literature.

The nonparametric belief formation process specified in this paper is similar to other adaptive learning approaches. Kozlowski, Veldkamp, and Venkateswaran (2017) use a similar belief formation mechanism to explain persistence in real output fluctuations. That paper, however, abstracts from liquidity, an important amplification mechanism, and therefore cannot match the large decline in the riskless rate. In constant gain learning (Sargent, 1999), agents combine last period's forecast with a constant times the contemporaneous forecast error. Such a process gives recent observations more weight, similar to the behavior of agents in Malmendier and Nagel (2011) following the Great Depression. The reason why we use a nonparametric belief formation process is that we want to model time-varying changes in perceived tail risk, which requires a richer specification of the distribution of state variables.

Our belief formation process also has similarities to the parameter learning models by Johannes, Lochstoer, and Mou (2016) and Orlik and Veldkamp (2015) and is advocated by Hansen (2007). Similarly, in least-squares learning (Marcet and Sargent 1989), agents have bounded rationality and use past data to estimate the parameters of the law of motion for the state variables. However, these papers do not have meaningful changes in tail risk and do not analyze the potential for persistent effects on interest rates. Pintus and Suda (2015) embed parameter learning into a production economy but feed in persistent leverage shocks and explore the potential for amplification when agents hold erroneous initial beliefs about persistence. Sundaresan (2018) generates persistence by deterring information acquisition. Weitzman (2007) shows that the parameter uncertainty about the variance of a thin-tailed distribution can help resolve many of the asset pricing puzzles confronted by the rational expectations paradigm.

Finally, our paper contributes to a growing literature on low interest rates. Recent contributions include Bernanke et al. (2011), Barro et al. (2014), Bigio (2015), Caballero, Farhi, and Gourinchas (2016), Carvalho, Ferrero, and Nechio (2016), Del Negro et al. (2017), and Hall (2017). To this body of work, we add a novel mechanism, one that predicts persistent drops in riskless interest rates in response to rare transitory shocks, and demonstrate its quantitative and empirical relevance.

II. How Belief Updating Creates Persistence

The main contribution of this paper is to explain why tail risk fluctuates and to show how an extreme event like the Great Recession can induce a persistent drop in riskless rates. Before laying out the whole model, we begin by explaining the novel part of the paper: how agents form beliefs and the effect of tail events on beliefs. This will highlight the broader insight that unusual events induce larger and more persistent belief changes. Later, we layer the economic model on top to show how this mechanism affects interest rates.

The story that this model formalizes is that before the financial crisis hit, most people in the United States thought that such crises only happened elsewhere (e.g., in emerging markets) and that bank runs were a topic for historians. Observing the events of 2007–9 changed those views. Many journalists, academics, and policy makers now routinely ask whether the financial architecture is stable. But formalizing this story requires a departure from the standard rational expectations paradigm, where the distributions of all random events are assumed to be known. Then, observing an unusual event should not change one's probability assessment of that event in the future. Instead, we need a machinery that allows agents to not know the true distribution, so that upon seeing something they thought should not happen, they can revise their beliefs. There are many ways to depart from full knowledge of distributions. One that is realistic, quantifiable, and tractable is treating agents like classical econometricians. The agents in our model have a finite data set—the history of all realized shocks—and they estimate the distribution from which those shocks are drawn, using tools from a first-year econometrics class.

Learning models are not new to the macro literature. A common approach is to assume a normal distribution and to estimate its mean and variance. However, the normal distribution has thin tails, making it less useful to think about changes in the risk of extreme negative realizations. We could choose an alternative distribution with more flexibility in higher moments. However, this will raise obvious concerns about the sensitivity of results to the specific functional form used. To minimize such concerns, we take a nonparametric approach and let the data inform the shape of the distribution.

Instead, our agents take all the data they have observed and use a kernel density procedure to estimate the probability distribution from which these data were drawn. One of the most common approaches in nonparametric estimation, a kernel density essentially takes a histogram of all observed data and draws a smooth line over that histogram. There are a variety of ways to smooth the line. The most common is called the "normal kernel." It does not result in normal (Gaussian) distributions. We also studied a handful of other kernels and (sufficiently flexible) parametric specifications, which yielded similar results.[5] The kernel density approach allows for flexibility in the shape of the distribution while strictly tying the learning process to data that we, as economists, can observe. We do not need to guess or calibrate the precision of some signal. Instead, we take a macro data series, apply this econometric procedure to it, and read off the agents' beliefs.

Next, we describe the Gaussian kernel. Consider the shock ϕ_t whose true density g is unknown to agents in the economy. The agents do know that the shock ϕ_t is independent and identically distributed (i.i.d.). The information set at time t, denoted $\mathcal{I}_t$, includes the history of all shocks ϕ_t observed up to and including t. They use this available data to construct an estimate $\hat{g}_t$ of the true density g. Formally, at every date t, agents construct the following normal kernel density estimator of the probability density function g:

$$\hat{g}_t(\phi) = \frac{1}{n_t \kappa_t} \sum_{s=0}^{n_t-1} \Omega \left(\frac{\phi - \phi_{t-s}}{\kappa_t} \right),$$

where $\Omega(\cdot)$ is the standard normal density function, κ_t is the smoothing or bandwidth parameter, and n_t is the number of available observations at date t. As new data arrive, agents add the new observations to their data set and update their estimates, generating a sequence of beliefs $\{\hat{g}_t\}$.

Finally, back to the main point: Why does this estimated distribution change in such a persistent way in response to a tail event? We will explain this graphically and then mathematically. Figure 3 shows three panels. Figure 3a is the histogram of a data series. In this case, the data series happens to have some measures of capital quality, which we will describe in detail later. For right now, this is an arbitrary sequence of data generated from an unknown distribution. The smooth line over the histogram is the estimated normal kernel. Figure 3b shows what happens when two data points that are negative outliers are observed. The locations of the two new observations are highlighted (black rectangles) in the histogram. Notice that the new kernel estimator, and thus agents' beliefs, now places greater probability weight on the possibility of future negative outcomes. If in the next period the state returns to normal, those two rectangular data points are still in the histogram and still create the bump on the left. Although the tail event has passed, tail risk remains elevated. Figure 3c adds 30 years of additional observations, drawn to look just like the preceding years, except without any crisis events. The kernel on the right still shows a left bump. Smaller than it was before, but still present, elevated tail risk still persists 30 years after the tail event was observed.

The persistence in figure 3 has its origins in the so-called martingale property of beliefs—that is, conditional on time t information ($\mathcal{I}_t$), the estimated distribution is a martingale. Thus, on average, the agent expects her future beliefs to be the same as her current beliefs. This property holds exactly if the bandwidth parameter κ_t is set to zero.[6] In our empirical implementation, in line with the literature on nonparametric assumption, we use the optimal bandwidth (see Hansen 2015). This leads to smoother density but also means that the martingale property does not hold exactly. Numerically, the deviations are minuscule for our application. In other words, the kernel density estimator is, for all practical purposes, a martingale $\mathbb{E}_t[\hat{g}_{t+j}(\phi)|\mathcal{I}_t] \approx \hat{g}_t(\phi)$.

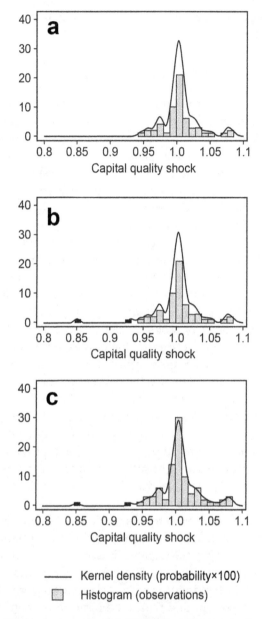

Fig. 3. The persistence of estimated probabilities. (*a*) Period 1950–2007. (*b*) Period 1950–2009. (*c*) Period 1950–2039. Data in the histograms are capital quality shocks, measured as described in Sec. IV. Kernel densities are constructed with the normal kernel in (3) and the optimal bandwidth.

Now, in the simulations underlying figure 3c, we drew future shock sequences from the precrisis distribution (i.e., $\hat{g}_{2007}$ instead of the revised belief $\hat{g}_{2009}$). This implies that beliefs will revert, namely, the bump in the left tail will eventually disappear. However, the rate at which this occurs is very slow. This has to do with the fact that under our nonparametric approach, outlier observations play a crucial role in learning about the frequency of tail events. Ordinary events are just not very informative about those tail probabilities. And since data on tail events are scarce, observing one makes the resulting belief revisions large and extremely persistent (even if they are ultimately transitory). It is worth pointing out that this slow convergence need not necessarily obtain with a parametric specification of the learning process. For example, suppose there is uncertainty about the standard deviation of a thin-tailed distribution, as in Weitzman (2007). Because all realizations are informative about standard deviations, the effect of observing a tail event is more muted (i.e., there is a lot more relevant data) and relatively less persistent (convergence to the true distribution occurs at a faster rate).

III. Model

Preferences and Technology

The economy is populated by a representative firm, which produces output with capital and labor, according to a standard Cobb-Douglas production function:

$$Y_t = AK_t^{\alpha}N_t^{1-\alpha}, \tag{1}$$

where A is total factor productivity, which is the same for all firms and constant over time. The firm is subjected to an aggregate shock to capital quality ϕ_t: formally, it enters the period with capital $\hat{K}_t$ and is hit by a shock ϕ_t, leaving it with "effective" capital K_t:

$$K_t = \phi_t\hat{K}_t. \tag{2}$$

These capital quality shocks are i.i.d. over time and are the only aggregate disturbances in our economy. The i.i.d. assumption is made to avoid an additional exogenous source of persistence.[7] They are drawn from a distribution $g(\cdot)$: this is the object agents are learning about.

As we see from equation (2), these shocks scale the effective capital stock up or down. This is not to be interpreted literally—it is hard to visualize shocks that regularly wipe out fractions of the capital or create it out of thin air. Instead, these shocks are a simple, if imperfect, way to model the extreme and unusual effects of the 2008–9 recession on the economic value and returns to nonresidential capital. It allows us to capture the idea that a hotel built in 2007 in Las Vegas may still be standing after the Great Recession but may deliver much less economic value. The use of such shocks in macroeconomics and finance goes back at least to Merton (1973), but they have become more popular recently (precisely to generate large fluctuations in the returns to capital), for example, in Gourio (2012) and in a number of recent papers on financial frictions, crises, and the Great Recession (e.g., Gertler and Kiyotaki 2010; Gertler and Karadi 2011; Brunnermeier and Sannikov 2014).

Finally, the firm is owned by a representative household, the preferences of which over consumption C_t and labor supply N_t are given by a flow utility function $U(C_t, N_t)$, along with a constant discount rate β.

Liquidity

We now introduce liquidity considerations, which will act as an amplification mechanism for tail risk changes. We model them in a stylized but tractable specification in the spirit of Lagos and Wright (2005): firms have access to a productive opportunity but require liquidity in the form of pledgeable collateral in order to exploit it. As in Venkateswaran and Wright (2014), both capital and riskless government bonds can be pledged, albeit to different degrees. Bonds are fully pledgeable, but only a fraction of the effective capital can be used as collateral. An increase in tail risk now has an additional effect—it reduces the liquidity value of capital, increasing the demand for an alternative source of liquidity, namely, riskless government bonds, amplifying the interest rate response.

Formally, at the beginning of each period, firms can invest in a project that costs X_t and yields a payoff $H(X_t)$ (both denominated in the single consumption/investment good). The function H is assumed to be strictly increasing and concave, which implies that the net surplus from the project, namely, $H(X) - X$, has a unique maximum at X^*. In the absence of other constraints, therefore, every firm presented with this opportunity will invest X^*. However, the firm faces a liquidity constraint:

$$X_t \leq B_t + \eta K_t$$

In other words, the investment in the project cannot exceed the sum of pledgeable collateral, which comprises a fraction η of its effective capital K_t and the value of its liquid assets (riskless government bonds) B_t.[8]

Therefore,

$$X_t = \min (X^*, B_t + \eta K_t).$$

After this stage, production takes place according to equation (1).

Timing and Value Functions

The timing of events in each period t is as follows: (i) the firm enters the period with capital stock $\hat{K}_t$ and liquid assets B_t, (ii) the aggregate capital quality shock ϕ_t is realized, (iii) the firm chooses X_t subject to the liquidity constraint, (iv) the firm chooses labor and production takes place, and (v) the firm chooses capital and liquid asset positions for $t + 1$.

Denoting the aggregate state S_t (described in detail later in this section), the economy-wide wage rate W_t, the price of the riskless bond P_t, and the stochastic discount factor M_{t+1}, we can write the problem of the firm in recursive form as follows:

$$V(K_t, B_t, S_t) = \max_{X_t, N_t, B_{t+1}, \hat{K}_{t+1}} H(X_t) - X_t + F(K_t, N_t) - W_t N_t + K_t(1 - \delta) + B_t$$

$$- P_t B_{t+1} - \hat{K}_{t+1} + \beta E_t M_{t+1} V(K_{t+1}, B_{t+1}, S_{t+1}) \tag{3}$$

$$\text{s.t.} \quad X_t \leq B_t + \eta K_t,$$

$$K_{t+1} = \phi_{t+1} \hat{K}_{t+1}.$$

The stochastic discount factor M_{t+1} and the wage W_t are determined by the marginal utility of the representative household:

$$W_t = -\frac{U_2(C_t, N_t)}{U_1(C_t, N_t)}, \tag{4}$$

$$M_{t+1} = \frac{U_1(C_{t+1}, N_{t+1})}{U_1(C_t, N_t)}. \tag{5}$$

The aggregate state S_t consists of $(\Pi_t, \mathcal{I}_t)$, where $\Pi_t \equiv H(X_t) - X_t + AK_t^\alpha L_t^{1-\alpha} + (1 - \delta)K_t$ is the aggregate resources available and $\mathcal{I}_t$ is the economy-wide information set. Standard market clearing conditions yield:

$$C_t = \Pi_t - \hat{K}_{t+1}, \tag{6}$$

$$B_t = \bar{B}. \tag{7}$$

where $\bar{B}$ is the exogenous supply of the riskless government bond. The interest expenses on these bonds is financed through lump-sum taxes.

Information, Beliefs, and Equilibrium

The set $\mathcal{I}_t$ includes the history of all shocks ϕ_t observed up to and including time t. For now, we specify a general function, denoted Ψ, which maps $\mathcal{I}_t$ onto an appropriate probability space. The expectation operator $\mathbb{E}_t$ is defined with respect to this space. In the following section, we make this more concrete using the kernel density estimation procedure to map the information set into beliefs.

For a given belief function Ψ, a recursive equilibrium is a set of functions for (i) aggregate consumption and labor supply that maximize household utility subject to a budget constraint; (ii) a bond price that clears the market for bonds; (iii) firm values and policies that solve equation (3), taking as given the stochastic discount factor and wages according to equations (4)–(5) and the bond price; and (iv) aggregate consumption and labor that are consistent with individual choices and thus the bond market clears.

Characterization and Solution

The equilibrium of the economic model is a solution to a set of nonlinear equations, namely, the optimality conditions of the firm and the household, along with resource constraints. The optimality conditions of the firm (3) are:

$$1 = \beta \mathbb{E}_t \{ M_{t+1} \phi_{t+1} [F_1(K_{t+1}, N_{t+1}) + 1 - \delta + \eta \mu_{t+1}] \}, \tag{8}$$

$$P_t = \beta \mathbb{E}_t \{ M_{t+1} (1 + \mu_{t+1}) \}, \tag{9}$$

$$\mu_t = H'(X_t) - 1, \tag{10}$$

$$W_t = F_2(K_t, N_t), \tag{11}$$

where μ_t is the Lagrange multiplier on the liquidity constraint. The first two equations are the Euler equations for capital and liquid assets, respectively. The value of liquidity services is reflected on the right-hand side (in the term involving μ_t). The third equation characterizes μ_t. In states of the world where liquidity is sufficiently abundant, $X_t = X^*$ and $\mu_t = 0$. Otherwise, $\mu_t > 0$. The expectation of μ_{t+1} (weighted by the SDF M_{t+1}) raises the price of the liquid bond P_t, or, equivalently, lowers the risk-free rate. An increase in tail risk—namely, the likelihood of large adverse realizations of ϕ_{t+1}—makes the constraint more likely to bind and thus raises the liquidity premium on the riskless bond.

Belief Formation

Next, we choose a particular estimation procedure for how agents form beliefs. Specifically, we employ the kernel density estimation procedure, which we described in Section II.

Consider the shock ϕ_t for which true density g is unknown to agents in the economy. The agents do know that the shock ϕ_t is i.i.d. The information set at time t, denoted $\mathcal{I}_t$, includes the history of all shocks ϕ_t observed up to and including t. They use these available data to construct an estimate $\hat{g}_t$ of the true density g. Formally, at every date t, agents construct the following normal kernel density estimator of the probability density function g:

$$\hat{g}_t(\phi) = \frac{1}{n_t \kappa_t} \sum_{s=0}^{n_t-1} \Omega \left(\frac{\phi - \phi_{t-s}}{\kappa_t} \right),$$

where $\Omega(\cdot)$ is the standard normal density function, κ_t is the smoothing or bandwidth parameter, and n_t is the number of available observations at date t. As new data arrive, agents add the new observations to their data set and update their estimates, generating a sequence of beliefs $\{\hat{g}_t\}$.

IV.   Measurement and Calibration

In this section, we describe how we use macro data to construct a time series for ϕ_t and pin down beliefs. A key strength of our belief-driven theory is that by assuming that agents form beliefs as an econometrician would, we can use observable data to discipline those beliefs. We also parameterize the model to match key features of the US economy and describe key aspects of our computational approach.

Measuring Capital Quality Shocks

To construct a time series of ϕ_t, we follow the approach in Kozlowski et al. (2017). They used data on nonfinancial assets in the US economy, reported in the "Flow of Funds" tables, both at historical cost, which we will denote NFA_t^{HC}, and at market value, NFA_t^{MV}. The latter series corresponds to the nominal value of effective capital, K_t in the model. Letting X_{t-1} denote investment in period $t-1$ and P_t^k denote the nominal price of capital goods in t, the two time series can be mapped onto their model counterparts as follows:

$$P_t^k K_t = \text{NFA}_t^{MV}$$

$$P_{t-1}^k \hat{K}_t = (1 - \delta)\text{NFA}_{t-1}^{MV} + P_{t-1}^k X_{t-1}$$

$$= (1 - \delta)\text{NFA}_{t-1}^{MV} + \text{NFA}_t^{HC} - (1 - \delta)\text{NFA}_{t-1}^{HC}.$$

To adjust for changes in nominal prices, we use the price index for nonresidential investment from the National Income and Product Accounts (denoted PINDX_t).[9] This allows us to recover the quality shock ϕ_t:

$$
\phi_t = \frac{K_t}{\hat{K}_t} = \left(\frac{P_t^k K_t}{P_{t-1}^k \hat{K}_t} \right) \left(\frac{P_{t-1}^k}{P_t^k} \right)
$$

$$
= \left(\frac{\text{NFA}_t^{MV}}{(1 - \delta)\text{NFA}_{t-1}^{MV} + \text{NFA}_t^{HC} - (1 - \delta)\text{NFA}_{t-1}^{HC}} \right) \left(\frac{\text{PINDX}_{t-1}^k}{\text{PINDX}_t^k} \right),
$$

(12)

where the second line replaces P_{t-1}^k / P_t^k with $\text{PINDX}_{t-1}^k / \text{PINDX}_t^k$.

Using the measurement equation (12) (and a value of $\delta = 0.03$), we construct an annual time series for capital quality shocks for the US economy since 1950, plotted in figure 4a. For most of the sample period, the shock realizations were in a relatively tight range around 1, but at the onset of the recent Great Recession, we saw two large adverse realizations: 0.93 in 2008 and 0.84 in 2009. To put these numbers in context, the mean and standard deviation of the series from 1950–2007 were 1 and 0.03, respectively.

We then apply our kernel density estimation procedure to this time series to construct a sequence of beliefs. In other words, for each t, we construct $\{\hat{g}_t\}$ using the available time series until that point. The resulting estimates for two dates, 2007 and 2009, are shown in figure 4b. They show that the Great Recession induced a significant increase in the perceived likelihood of extreme negative shocks. The estimated density for 2007 implies almost zero mass below 0.90, whereas the one for 2009 attaches a nontrivial (approximately 2.5%) probability to this region of the state space.

Calibration

We begin by specifying the functional form of preferences and technology. The period utility function of the household is $U(C, N) = \{C - [N^{1+\gamma} / (1 + \gamma)]\} / 1 - \sigma$. The risk aversion parameter σ is set to 0.5. The payoff

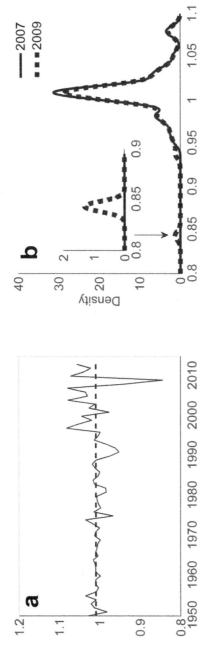

Fig. 4. Capital quality shocks and beliefs. (*a*) Capital quality shocks. (*b*) Beliefs. Panel (*a*) shows the capital quality shocks measured from US data using (12). Panel (*b*) shows the estimated kernel densities in 2007 (solid) and 2009 (dashed). The change in the left tail shows the effect of the Great Recession.

from the project is $H(X) = 2\zeta\sqrt{X} - \xi$. The labor supply parameter γ is set to 0.5, corresponding to a Frisch elasticity of 2 in line with Midrigan and Philippon (2011). The labor disutility parameter π is normalized to 1. The parameter ξ acts like a fixed cost and separates the liquidity premium (which is a function only of $H'[X]$) from the level of the net surplus, a flexibility that proves helpful in the calibration process.

A period is interpreted as 1 year. Accordingly, we choose the discount factor $\beta = 0.95$ and depreciation $\delta = 0.03$. The share of capital in the production is set to 0.40, while the total factor productivity parameter A is normalized to 1.

Next, we turn to the liquidity-related parameters. The parameter governing the pledgeability of capital η is set to match the ratio of short-term obligations of US nonfinancial corporations to the capital stock in the Flow of Funds. Short-term obligations comprise commercial paper (BGFRS 2017, table B.103, row 27), bank loans (row 31), and trade payables (row 34). Capital stock is the market value of nonfinancial assets (row 2). This ratio stood at 0.16 in 2007.[10]

There are three other parameters to be determined: the supply of liquid assets $\bar{B}$ and the technology parameters ζ and ξ. These are chosen to jointly target the following moments: (i) the ratio of liquid asset holdings of US nonfinancial corporations, which stood at 0.082 in 2007;[11] (ii) an interest rate of 2% on government bonds (which corresponds to the precrisis average for real interest rates in the United States); and (iii) a capital-output ratio of 3.5. In the model, the analogous objects are averages in the stochastic steady state under the precrisis belief distribution. Though this calibration is done jointly, a heuristic argument can be made for identification—the first moment is informative about $\bar{B}$, the second about ζ, and the third helps us pin down ξ. Table 1 summarizes the resulting parameter choices.

V.   Results

Our main goal in this section is to quantify the size and persistence of the response of risk-free rates to a large but transitory shock ϕ_t in an economy where agents are learning about the distribution. We begin by computing the stochastic steady state associated with $\hat{g}_{2007}$, the distribution estimated using precrisis data.[12] Then, starting from this steady state, we subject the model economy to the two adverse realizations observed in 2008 and 2009, namely, 0.93 and 0.84. As we saw in the previous section, this leads to a revised estimate for the distribution $\hat{g}_{2009}$, which shows an increase in perceived tail risk.

Table 1
Parameters

Parameter	Value	Description
Preferences:		
β	.95	Discount factor
γ	.50	1/Frisch elasticity
π	1	Labor disutility
σ	.5	Risk aversion
Technology:		
α	.40	Capital share
δ	.03	Depreciation rate
Liquidity:		
η	.16	Pledgeability of capital
$\bar{B}$	4.93	Supply of liquid assets
ζ	3.93	Investment technology (affects liquidity)
ξ	9.00	Investment fixed cost

We perform two exercises to demonstrate the quantitative bit of our belief revision mechanism. First, we compare the stochastic steady states implied by the two distributions $\hat{g}_{2007}$ and $\hat{g}_{2009}$ for both aggregate macroeconomic quantities (e.g., output, capital, and labor) and asset prices. This corresponds to the long-term behavior of the US economy under the assumption that crises continue to occur with the same likelihood as the updated beliefs (formally, if future shocks are drawn from the postcrisis distribution $\hat{g}_{2009}$). Second, we simulate time paths for the economy under the assumption that there are no future crises, namely, with future shocks drawn from the precrisis distribution $\hat{g}_{2007}$. In other words, we assume that the 2008–9 recession was a one-off adverse realization. As a result, beliefs will eventually revert to their precrisis levels. However, the effects of the tail events in 2008–9 on beliefs (and, therefore, aggregate outcomes) turn out to be quite persistent and remain significant over a relatively long horizon.

Long-Run Analysis

The results from the first exercise, where we compare long-run averages under $\hat{g}_{2007}$ and $\hat{g}_{2009}$, are reported in table 2. As the table shows, the rise in tail risk causes the economy to invest and produce less, leading to lower output and capital. This occurs because investing now has a lower mean return but is also significantly riskier. The change in beliefs leads to a sharp drop in the risk-free rate—in the new steady state, government bond yields are almost 1.3% lower. Two forces contribute to this

Table 2
Steady State Interest Rates and Macro Aggregates, Pre- and Postcrisis

	$\hat{g}_{2007}$	$\hat{g}_{2009}$	Change
ln $F(K, N)$	2.39	2.36	−.03
ln X	2.68	2.65	−.03
ln K	4.10	4.06	−.04
Riskless rate (R^f)	2.31	.86	−1.45
Return on capital (R^v)	5.30	5.29	−.01
Premium ($R^v - R^f$)	2.99	4.43	1.44

Note: R^f is the interest rate on government bonds, whereas R^v is the average expected returns on unlevered claims to the firm.

drop. First, future consumption is riskier, which has the usual effect of lowering the required return on risk-free claims. Second, the liquidity premium rises. This is partly because there is less liquidity in the economy (due to the lower levels of capital in the new steady state), but also due to the increase in liquidity risk. A tail event also implies states with very low levels of liquidity, which translates to a higher premium on liquid assets.

How do these predictions compare with the post-2008 data? The first row of table 3 compares the drop in interest rates predicted by the model to different measures of changes in risk-free rates since the Great Recession. The second row reports the change from 2007 to 2017 in short-term real rate. This is defined as the difference between 1-year nominal Treasury yield (taken from the H15 release [BGFRS 2019, table H15]) and 1-year expected inflation from the Federal Reserve Bank of Cleveland's inflation forecasting model. The next three rows contain estimates of changes in

Table 3
Interest Rates, Model and Data

	Change, %
Model:	
Riskless rate, R^f	−1.45
Data:	
1-year real rate	−2.48
5-year real rate, 5 years forward	−1.57
5-year real rate, 5 years forward (HP trend)	−1.78
Natural real rate*	−.66
Liquidity premium*	.52

Note: The changes in the data panel are differences between average levels in 2017 and 2007.
*From Del Negro et al. (2017).

longer-term real rates. The third row shows the change in the 5-year real rates 5 years forward. To estimate this, we use the nominal 5-year rate 5 years forward (computed from the constant maturity nominal Treasury yield curve) and the corresponding expected inflation (i.e., the expected 5-year inflation rate 5 years forward, which can be computed using the 5- and 10-year expected inflation series from the Federal Reserve Bank of Cleveland). The fourth row reports the change in the Hodrick–Prescott-trend component of the 5-year real rate 5 years forward (computed using annual data from 1982–2017 with a smoothing parameter of 6). The fifth row shows the change in the estimate of the long-run natural rate from Del Negro et al. (2017), who use a flexible VAR specification to extract the permanent component of the real interest rate from data on nominal bond returns, inflation, and their long-run survey expectations (from the Survey of Professional Forecasters).[13] Taken together, the data show that belief revisions can go long a way in explaining the drop in interest rates since the financial crisis.

For macroeconomic quantities, the predicted drops in table 2 generally underpredict the deviations from precrisis trends observed in the data. For example, at the end of 2017, output was about 14% below the 1952–2007 trend. This suggests a need for additional amplification mechanisms. In our related work in Kozlowski et al. (2017), we explore two such mechanisms—Epstein-Zin utility (which allows us to separate risk aversion and intertemporal elasticity of substitution) and defaultable debt (higher tail risk makes default debt less attractive, curtailing borrowing and investment)—and show that they help bring the model's predictions much closer to the data. Here, given our focus on interest rates, we abstract from these modifications. This allows us to highlight, in a more transparent fashion, the interaction of tail risk with liquidity considerations.

Role of Liquidity

To understand the role played by liquidity, we repeat the analysis above, setting the pledgeability of capital to 0. This implies that shocks to capital do not directly affect the available liquidity in the economy (because bonds are the only liquid asset in the economy). The remaining parameters are calibrated using the same strategy as before. The results are shown in table 4. The table shows that without liquidity effects, the increase in tail risk has a very small effect on the riskless rate. The interest rate on government bonds in the new steady state is only 2 basis

Table 4
Interest Rates and Macro Aggregates in the Long Run, without Liquidity Effects

	$\hat{g}_{2007}$	$\hat{g}_{2009}$	Change
ln $F(K, N)$	2.27	2.19	−.09
ln X	1.29	1.29	.00
ln K	3.93	3.80	−.13
Riskless rate (R^f)	2.31	2.29	−.02
Risky return (R^v)	5.28	5.27	−.01
Risk premium ($R^v - R^f$)	2.97	2.98	.01

Note: R^f is the interest rate on government bonds, whereas R^v is the average expected returns on unlevered claims to the firm.

points lower. In other words, almost all of the drop in our baseline analysis comes from the interaction of tail risk and liquidity.[14] This finding is consistent with that of Del Negro et al. (2017), who find that most of the change in the natural real rate comes from a rise in the convenience yield associated with US government bonds. Their VAR estimate is reported in the last row of table 3 (labeled "liquidity premium")—the change in convenience yield since 2007 constitutes almost 80% of the drop in real rates.[15]

Comparing the implications for macroeconomic aggregates in tables 2 and 4 shows that liquidity dampens the effect of increased tail risk on capital and output (the predicted drops in table 4 are smaller). Intuitively, when capital also provides liquidity, an increase in tail risk induces a precautionary response—firms hold more capital to buffer against the drop in liquidity due to an adverse shock. As a result, steady-state capital (and, therefore, output) does not fall by as much as it would have in the absence of liquidity considerations.

Evidence from Equity Markets

Our model stays relatively close to the standard neoclassical paradigm and inherits many of its limitations when it comes to matching asset pricing facts, particularly asset price volatility.[16] With that caveat in mind, we confront the model's predictions for equity markets with the data in table 5.

To do this, we interpret equity as a levered claim on the value of the firm in the model. The main role of leverage is to amplify the volatility of equity returns. We use a leverage (defined as the ratio of debt to total assets) of 0.8. This is higher than most estimates in the literature—for example, Kozlowski et al. (2017) use 0.7, an estimate that combines operating and financial leverage. We discuss the reasons behind the higher leverage assumption later.

Table 5
Implications for Equity Markets

	Changes	
	Model	Data
Return on equity, $\mathbb{E}(R^e)$ (%)	−.065	−.184
ln equity/capital	.010	.225
$\mathbb{E}(R^e - \bar{R}^e)^3$	−.002	−.002
$\Pr(R^e - \bar{R}^e \leq -0.30)$	.022	.015

Note: The model changes represent the difference between the average value under $\hat{g}_{2009}$ and that under $\hat{g}_{2007}$. The change in the data is the difference between the average value from 2013 through 2017 and the precrisis average (from 2005 to 2007).

The implications of the model for various equity market variables are shown in table 5. The increase in tail risk leads to a slight fall in the expected return on equity claims in the new steady state. Because rates on riskless assets drop significantly, this implies a big rise in the equity premium. In data, expected returns on the S&P 500, computed following the methodology of Cochrane (2011) and Hall (2015), also show a small drop relative to precrisis levels.[17] The small drop in expected returns also means that the model-implied value of equity claims (per unit capital) is actually higher in the new steady state. In the data, we observe a much larger run-up in equity prices over the past few years. We are not claiming that the model can rationalize such a large increase, but it is worth noting that increased tail risk does not necessarily imply a precipitous fall in valuations.

Evidence of returns and valuations is at best a very indirect measure of tail risk. We therefore turn to options prices, arguably a better source of evidence of changes in tail risk. The model, even with the relatively high leverage adjustment, does not generate sufficient variability in equity returns. The model-implied value for the Chicago Board Options Exchange (CBOE) Volatility Index (VIX) under the pre-2008 beliefs is 8.37 (the average from 1990–2007 in the data was 19). Furthermore, in the data, the VIX spiked in the immediate aftermath of the crisis, averaging 32 during 2008–9, but then fell sharply to historically low levels in 2017. The model, on the other hand, predicts a more modest but persistent increase (from 8.37 to 11.35). The SKEW index reported by the CBOE (2019) is a transformation of the standardized third moment:

$$\text{SKEW}_t = 100 - 10\,\frac{\mathbb{E}(R^e - \bar{R}^e)^3}{(\text{VIX}_t/100)^3}.$$

Because this is a function of the VIX, the model's difficulty in matching the time variation in the VIX also spills over to the SKEW index. For example, the SKEW spiked in part due to the sharp drop in VIX. Fixing these issues, that is, matching the levels and time variation in volatility measures, would require adding more shocks—almost certainly with heteroskedastic processes—and mechanisms to address the well-known excess volatility puzzles, an exercise beyond the scope of the current paper. Instead, we use the two reported indexes to construct two indicators of tail risk—namely, the nonstandardized third moment of the risk-neutral distribution (the numerator in the second term of the SKEW equation above) and the (risk-neutral) probability of an extreme negative return realization (defined as 30% below the mean).[18] As table 5 shows, the model predicts significant increases in both objects. These predictions line up reasonably well with the changes in their empirical counterparts relative to their precrisis levels. In other words, while the model cannot exactly match the time path of asset market variables, the evidence from asset markets appears to be broadly consistent with the idea that tail risk rose sharply since 2008.

What If There Are No More Crises?

Next, we compute time paths for riskless interest rates, starting from the average long-run values under $\hat{g}_{2007}$. These paths are generated using two different assumptions about future shocks. The first corresponds to the stochastic steady-state analysis from earlier and draws shocks from the updated belief distribution $\hat{g}_{2009}$. The second assumes that crises do not recur—that is, the shock sequences drawn from $\hat{g}_{2007}$. For each sequence of shocks, we compute beliefs, equilibrium prices, and quantities at each date. Finally, we average over all these paths and plot the mean change in interest rates (relative to the starting level) in figure 5a and 5b ("learning" line). It shows that under both assumptions, they remain depressed for a prolonged period. In the no-crisis version (fig. 5b), although the economy eventually returns to its precrisis stochastic steady state, learning about tail probabilities is sufficiently slow that interest rates are almost 1% lower 20 years after the crisis. This occurs because learning about tail events is "local" under our nonparametric approach: beliefs about the likelihood change a lot when such events are observed but are less responsive to realizations elsewhere in the support of the distribution. In contrast, if we imposed a parametric assumption (e.g., a normal distribution), then all realizations contain information about parameters (mean and variance) and so beliefs (and, therefore, interest rates) would converge back to their precrisis levels relatively quickly.

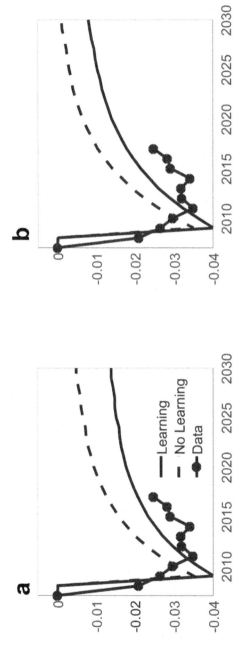

Fig. 5. Risk-free rate. (*a*) With crisis. (*b*) No more crisis. (*b*) shows an identical model in which future shocks are drawn from $\hat{g}_{2007}$. The "learning" line in both panels shows the solution when agents update their beliefs, and the "no learning" line shows the model with no learning. The circles show changes in 1-year real rates from US data for the period 2008–17.

Turning Off Belief Updating

To demonstrate the central role of learning, we also plot average simulated outcomes from an otherwise identical economy in which agents know the final distribution $\hat{g}_{2009}$ with certainty from the very beginning ("no learning" line in fig. 5). These agents do not revise their beliefs. This corresponds to a standard rational expectations econometrics approach, in which agents are assumed to know the true distribution of shocks hitting the economy and econometricians estimate this distribution using all available data. The post-2009 paths are simulated as follows: Each economy is assumed to be at its stochastic steady state in 2007 and is subjected to the same sequence of shocks—two large negative ones in 2008 and 2009. After 2009, the sequence of shocks is drawn from the estimated 2009 distribution.

In the absence of belief revisions, the negative shock causes the real rate to surge and then recover. The interest rate rises because as the economy recovers to the previous steady state, there is a lower demand for debt.[19] This shows that learning is what generates long-lived reductions in economic activity.

VI. Conclusion

No one knows the true distribution of shocks to the economy. Economists typically assume that agents, in their models, do know this distribution as a way to discipline beliefs. For many applications, assuming full knowledge has little effect on outcomes and offers tractability. But for outcomes that are sensitive to tail probabilities, the difference between knowing these probabilities and estimating them with real-time data can be large. In this paper, we present one such application: the effect of large, unusual events on riskless interest rates.

The central mechanism is that observing tail events like the Great Recession leads agents to assign a higher likelihood to such events going forward. Importantly, this change in beliefs is relatively persistent, even if crises never recur. As a result, assets that are safe and liquid, such as government bonds, become more valuable.

When we quantify this mechanism and use capital price and quantity data to directly estimate beliefs, the model predicts large, persistent drops in interest rates, similar to the observed decline in government yields in the years following the Great Recession. These results suggest that perhaps persistently low interest rates took hold because after seeing how fragile our financial sector is, market participants will never think about tail risk in the same way again.

Appendix

Role of Risk Aversion

In table A1, we show how higher risk aversion translates to a larger sensitivity of interest to tail risk, even in the absence of liquidity effects.

Computing Option-Implied Tail Probabilities

To compute tail probabilities, we follow Backus, Foresi, and Wu (2008) and use a Gram-Charlier expansion of the distribution function. The CBOE also follows this method in its white paper on the SKEW index to compute implied probabilities. This yields an approximate density function for the standardized random variable, $\omega = (x - \mu)/\sigma$:

$$f(\omega) = \varphi(\omega)\left[1 - \gamma\frac{(3\omega - \omega^3)}{6}\right] \quad \text{where} \quad \gamma = E\left[\frac{x - \mu}{\sigma}\right]^3,$$

where $\varphi(\omega)$ is the density function of a standard normal random variable and γ is the skewness. (The Gram-Charlier expansion also includes a term for the excess kurtosis, but it is omitted from the expansion because, as shown by Bakshi, Kapadia, and Madan [2003], it is empirically not significant.)

Table A1
Interest Rates in the Long Run, without Liquidity Effects

Risk Aversion	$\hat{g}_{2007}$	$\hat{g}_{2009}$	Change
$\sigma = 2$	2.31	2.23	−.08
$\sigma = 10$	2.31	1.67	−.64

Endnotes

Authors' email addresses: Kozlowski (kozjuli@gmail.com), Veldkamp (lveldkam@stern .nyu.edu), Venkateswaran (vvenkate@stern.nyu.edu). We thank Jonathan Parker, Marty Eichenbaum, and Mark Gertler for helpful comments and suggestions, and François Gourio and Robert E. Hall for their insightful discussions. For acknowledgments, sources of research support, and disclosure of the authors' material financial relationships, if any, please see http://www.nber.org/chapters/c14073.ack.

1. This index is constructed from market prices of out-of-the-money options on the S&P 500 (CBOE 2019). It is designed to mimic movements in the skewness of risk-adjusted skewness; a higher level indicates a more negatively skewed distribution. Note that this is different from the Chicago Board Options Exchange Volatility Index (VIX), which measures implied volatility (i.e., the second moment). The VIX rose dramatically in the immediate aftermath of the crisis but came down quite sharply afterward.

2. Backus, Ferriere, and Zin (2015) analyze propagation in business cycle models.

3. These include papers on news shocks (e.g., Beaudry and Portier 2004; Lorenzoni 2009; Veldkamp and Wolfers 2007), uncertainty shocks (e.g., Jaimovich and Rebelo 2006; Bloom et al. 2014; Nimark 2014; Berger, Dew-Becker, and Giglio 2017), and higher-order belief shocks (e.g., Angeletos and La'O 2013; Huo and Takayama 2015).

4. For example, in Moriera and Savov (2015), learning about a hidden two-state Markov process with exogenously known persistence changes the demand for shadow banking (debt) assets.

5. Other kernels we explored included other nonparametric kernels (e.g., Epinechnikov), kernels designed to better capture tail risk (e.g., Champernowne), and semiparametric kernels with Pareto tails and the g-and-h family, which covers several transformations of the normal distribution. Each alternative yielded similar economic predictions because new data increased the tail probabilities of each distribution in a similar way. For a detailed discussion of nonparametric estimation, see Hansen (2015).

6. As $\kappa_t \to 0$, the CDF of the kernel converges to $\hat{G}_t^0(\phi) = (1/n_t)\Sigma_{s=0}^{n_t-1}1\{\phi_{t-s} \le \phi\}$. Then, for any $\phi, j \ge 1$, $\mathbb{E}_t[\hat{G}_{t+j}^0(\phi)|\mathcal{I}_t] = \mathbb{E}_t\{[1/(n_t + j)]\Sigma_{s=0}^{n_t+j-1}1\{\phi_{t+j-s} \le \phi\}|\mathcal{I}_t\}$ and $\mathbb{E}_t[\hat{G}_{t+j}^0(\phi)|\mathcal{I}_t] = [n_t/(n_t + j)]\hat{G}_t^0(\phi) + [j/(n_t + j)]\mathbb{E}_t[1\{\phi_{t+1} \le \phi\}|\mathcal{I}_t]$. Thus, future beliefs are, in expectation, a weighted average of two terms: the current belief and the distribution from which the new draws of the data ϕ_t are made. When shocks are also drawn from the current belief distribution, the two terms are exactly equal, implying $\mathbb{E}_t[\hat{G}_{t+j}^0(\phi)|\mathcal{I}_t] = \hat{G}_t^0(\phi)$.

7. The i.i.d. assumption also has empirical support. In the next section (Liquidity), we use macro data to construct a time series for ϕt. We estimate an autocorrelation of .15, statistically insignificant.

8. It is straightforward to allow for some unsecured debt, and this has a negligible effect on our results.

9. Our results are robust to alternative measures of nominal price changes, e.g., computed from the price index for gross domestic product or personal consumption expenditure.

10. Calibrating to the average values during 1950–2007 yields almost identical results.

11. Liquid assets are defined as total financial assets (BGFRS 2017, table B.103, row 7) less long-term financial assets (rows 21–24).

12. The steady state is obtained by simulating the model for 1,000 periods using $\hat{g}_{2007}$ and the associated policy functions, discarding the first 500 observations and time-averaging across the remaining periods.

13. We thank Del Negro et al. (2017) for sharing their estimates with us.

14. This is in part due to the low level of risk aversion in our parameterization. In the appendix, we repeat this analysis with higher risk aversion (specifically, $\sigma = 2$ and $\sigma = 10$). Then, tail risk has a somewhat larger effect on interest rates, even in the absence of liquidity.

15. They add the spread between Baa corporate bonds and Treasuries to their VAR to identify the convenience yield component.

16. However, the model actually implies a sizable equity premium even in the pre-2008 steady state. This stems almost entirely from liquidity considerations, which drive down the required return on government bonds relative to all illiquid assets (e.g., equity). This is essentially the mechanism in Lagos (2010), who shows that a model with liquidity considerations can help rationalize many asset pricing anomalies, including the equity premium puzzle.

17. The 1-year-ahead forecast of returns is obtained using a regression where the left-hand variable is the 1-year real return on the S&P and the right-hand variables are a constant, the log of the ratio of the S&P at the beginning of the period to its dividends averaged over the prior year, and the log of the ratio of real consumption to disposable income in the month prior to the beginning of the period.

18. Details of the computation are in the appendix.

19. Since the no-learning economy is endowed with the same end-of-sample beliefs as the learning model, they both ultimately converge to the same level. But they start at different steady states (normalized to 0 for each series).

References

Angeletos, G.-M., and J. La'O. 2013. "Sentiments." *Econometrica* 81 (2): 739–79.

Backus, D., A. Ferriere, and S. Zin. 2015. "Risk and Ambiguity in Models of the Business Cycle." *Journal of Monetary Economics* 69:42–63.

Backus, D. K., S. Foresi, and L. Wu. 2008. "Accounting for Biases in Black-Scholes." SSRN Working Paper Series. https://papers.ssrn.com/sol3/papers.cfm?abstract_id=585623.

Bakshi, G., N. Kapadia, and D. Madan. 2003. "Stock Return Characteristics, Skew Laws, and the Differential Pricing of Individual Equity Options." *Review of Financial Studies* 16 (1): 101–43.

Barro, R. J., J. Fernández-Villaverde, O. Levintal, and A. Mollerus. 2014. "Safe Assets." Working Paper no. 20652, NBER, Cambridge, MA.

Beaudry, P., and F. Portier. 2004. "An Exploration into Pigou's Theory of Cycles." *Journal of Monetary Economics* 51:1183–216.

Berger, D., I. Dew-Becker, and S. Giglio. 2017. "Uncertainty Shocks as Second-Moment News Shocks." Working Paper no. 23796, NBER, Cambridge, MA.

Bernanke, B. S., C. C. Bertaut, L. Demarco, and S. B. Kamin. 2011. "International Capital Flows and the Return to Safe Assets in the United States, 2003–2007." International Finance Discussion Papers no. 1014, Board of Governors of the Federal Reserve System, Washington, DC.

BGFRS (Board of Governors of the Federal Reserve System). 2017. "Financial Accounts of the United States—Z.1: B.103 Balance Sheet of Nonfinancial Corporate Business." https://www.federalreserve.gov/releases/z1/current/html/b103.htm.

BGFRS (Board of Governors of the Federal Reserve System). 2019. "Selected Interest Rates (Daily)—H.15: H.15 Selected Interest Rates." https://www.federalreserve.gov/releases/h15/.

Bigio, S. 2015. "Endogenous Liquidity and the Business Cycle." *American Economic Review* 105 (6): 1883–927.

Bloom, N., M. Floetotto, N. Jaimovich, I. Sapora-Eksten, and S. Terry. 2014. "Really Uncertain Business Cycles." Working Paper no. 13385, NBER, Cambridge, MA.

Brunnermeier, M., and Y. Sannikov. 2014. "A Macroeconomic Model with a Financial Sector." *American Economic Review* 104 (2): 379–421.

Caballero, R. J., E. Farhi, and P.-O. Gourinchas. 2016. "Safe Asset Scarcity and Aggregate Demand." *American Economic Review* 106 (5): 513–18.

Carvalho, C., A. Ferrero, and F. Nechio. 2016. "Demographics and Real Interest Rates: Inspecting the Mechanism." *European Economic Review* 88: 208–26.

CBOE (Chicago Board Options Exchange). 2019. "Cboe SKEW Index (SKEW)." http://www.cboe.com/products/vix-index-volatility/volatility-indicators/skew.

Cochrane, J. H. 2011. "Presidential Address: Discount Rates." *Journal of Finance* 66 (4): 1047–108.

Condon, Bernard. 2013. "AP Impact: Families Hoard Cash 5 yrs after Crisis." *Associated Press*, October 6. https://apnews.com/10697d7ba73645eabe3e39adff0c190c.

Del Negro, M., D. Giannone, M. P. Giannoni, and A. Tambalotti. 2017. "Safety, Liquidity, and the Natural Rate of Interest." *Brookings Papers on Economic Activity* 2017 (1): 235–316.

Gertler, M., and P. Karadi. 2011. "A Model of Unconventional Monetary Policy." *Journal of Monetary Economics* 58:17–34.

Gertler, M., and N. Kiyotaki. 2010. "Financial Intermediation and Credit Policy in Business Cycle Analysis." In *Handbook of Monetary Economics*, vol. 3, ed. Benjamin Friedman and Michael Woodford, 547–99. Amsterdam: Elsevier.

Gourio, F. 2012. "Disaster Risk and Business Cycles." *American Economic Review* 102 (6): 2734–66.

Hall, R. E. 2015. "High Discounts and High Unemployment." Working paper, Hoover Institution, Stanford University.

———. 2017. "Low Interest Rates: Causes and Consequences." *International Journal of Central Banking* 13 (3): 103–17.

Hansen, B. E. 2015. "Econometrics." Working paper, University of Wisconsin. https://www.ssc.wisc.edu/~bhansen/econometrics/Econometrics2015.pdf.

Hansen, L. 2007. "Beliefs, Doubts and Learning: Valuing Macroeconomic Risk." *American Economic Review* 97 (2): 1–30.

Huo, Z., and N. Takayama. 2015. "Higher Order Beliefs, Confidence, and Business Cycles." Working paper, University of Minnesota.

Irwin, Neil. 2016. "'Brexit' Is Locking In the Forces That Already Haunt the Global Economy." *New York Times*, June 27. https://www.nytimes.com/2016/06/28/upshot/brexit-is-strengthening-the-forces-that-already-haunt-the-global-economy.html.

Jaimovich, N., and S. Rebelo. 2006. "Can News about the Future Drive the Business Cycle?" *American Economic Review* 99 (4): 1097–18.

Johannes, M., L. Lochstoer, and Y. Mou. 2016. "Learning about Consumption Dynamics." *Journal of Finance* 71 (2): 551–600.

Kozlowski, J., L. Veldkamp, and V. Venkateswaran. 2017. "The Tail That Wags the Economy: Belief-Driven Business Cycles and Persistent Stagnation." Working paper, New York University.

Lagos, R. 2010. "Asset Prices and Liquidity in an Exchange Economy." *Journal of Monetary Economics* 57 (8): 913–30.

Lagos, R., and R. Wright. 2005. "A Unified Framework for Monetary Theory and Policy Analysis." *Journal of Political Economy* 113 (3): 463–84.

Lorenzoni, G. 2009. "A Theory of Demand Shocks." *American Economic Review* 99 (5): 2050–84.

Maćkowiak, B., and M. Wiederholt. 2010. "Business Cycle Dynamics under Rational Inattention." *Review of Economic Studies* 82 (4): 1502–32.

Malmendier, U., and S. Nagel. 2011. "Depression Babies: Do Macroeconomic Experiences Affect Risk Taking?" *Quarterly Journal of Economics* 126 (1): 373–416.

Marcet, A., and T. J. Sargent. 1989. "Convergence of Least Squares Learning Mechanisms in Self-Referential Linear Stochastic Models." *Journal of Economic Theory* 48 (2): 337–68.

Merton, R. 1973. "An Intertemporal Capital Asset Pricing Model." *Econometrica* 41 (5): 867–87.

Midrigan, V., and T. Philippon. 2011. "Household Leverage and the Recession." Working Paper no. 16965, NBER, Cambridge, MA.

Moriera, A., and A. Savov. 2015. "The Macroeconomics of Shadow Banking." Working paper, New York University.

Nimark, K. 2014. "Man-Bites-Dog Business Cycles." *American Economic Review* 104 (8): 2320–67.

Orlik, A., and L. Veldkamp. 2015. "Understanding Uncertainty Shocks and the Role of the Black Swan." Working paper, New York University. https://www0.gsb.columbia.edu/faculty/lveldkamp/papers/uncertaintyOV.pdf.

Pintus, P., and J. Suda. 2015. "Learning Financial Shocks and the Great Recession." Working paper, Aix-Marseille School of Economics.

Sargent, T. J. 1999. *The Conquest of American Inflation.* Princeton, NJ: Princeton University Press.

Sundaresan, S. 2018. "Optimal Preparedness and Uncertainty Persistence." Working paper, Imperial College, London. https://docs.wixstatic.com/ugd/0da7cb _361e147bfbe24f27a92b7bf0b363ccd3.pdf.

Veldkamp, L., and J. Wolfers. 2007. "Aggregate Shocks or Aggregate Information? Costly Information and Business Cycle Comovement." *Journal of Monetary Economics* 54:37–55.

Venkateswaran, V., and R. Wright. 2014. "Pledgability and Liquidity: A New Monetarist Model of Financial and Macroeconomic Activity." *NBER Macroeconomics Annual* 28 (1): 227–70.

Weitzman, M. L. 2007. "Subjective Expectations and Asset-Return Puzzles." *American Economic Review* 97 (4): 1102–30.

Comment

François Gourio, *Federal Reserve Bank of Chicago*

I. Introduction

The paper by Kozlowski, Veldkamp, and Venkateswaran argues that economic agents rationally revised their estimates of tail risk following the Great Recession and that this revision explains, at least in part, the persistent decline of interest rates on safe and liquid assets such as US Treasury securities. In a previous paper (Kozlowski, Veldkamp, and Venkateswaran 2015), the authors argued that the same belief revision can explain the slow recovery of investment and output. One important contribution of this work is methodological: they propose a tractable approach to embedding learning dynamics in fairly standard quantitative models. Substantively, the overall argument is quite plausible, and I believe the remaining issues are really quantitative: How much did people's beliefs about tail risk change after the Great Recession? And how sensitive are interest rates (in this paper) or economic activity (in the previous paper) to perceived tail risk?

In this discussion, I will address the first question briefly, before turning to the second, and then dissect the mechanisms through which interest rates depend on tail risk in the paper. In Kozlowski and colleagues' model, the risk-free asset combines two qualities: it is safe, and it is excellent collateral. Conceptually, one can separate these two characteristics, even though they are joint in the model and, to some extent, in the data. This allows us to distinguish two mechanisms through which higher tail risk increases the value of the risk-free asset. First, agents' willingness to pay for safe assets increases with tail risk. I will call this the "safety channel." This is a standard precautionary savings effect, a well-known piece of canonical asset-pricing theory. Second, agents' willingness to pay for assets that are good collateral increases with tail risk, in large part because the tail risk reduces investment and thus the supply of collateral. I will call this the "liquidity channel." In the paper, the safety channel is largely irrelevant, which I will argue may not be the case in reality, thus strengthening the authors' case that interest rates are sensitive to tail risk. In contrast, the quantitative magnitude of the liquidity channel is fairly uncertain in my view, both because the quantitative credibility of the model is not fully established and because other changes since the Great Recession have affected the supply of and demand for collateral. Finally, I will present some preliminary results from a current project (Farhi and Gourio 2018) that broadly supports the overall conclusion of the authors: using a very different approach, we estimate that increased risk accounts for some of the decline of the risk-free interest rate.

II. How Much and When Did Beliefs about Tail Risk Change?

It may be useful to first contrast the mechanism of this paper with those of other papers that study the effect of tail risk on asset prices and macroeconomic dynamics (e.g., Gourio 2012, 2013). These papers argue that during some recessions, in particular the Great Recession, agents perceived a small but significant risk of a Great Depression (e.g., a 10% probability). This belief about tail risk, by itself, generates low investment and output as well as a low risk-free rate, a high credit spread, and a high-risk premium (i.e., expected excess return on risky assets). But in these studies, it is assumed that the belief normalized fairly quickly. Kozlowski and colleagues' key point is that the belief probably did not return to its precrisis value. They reach this conclusion by running their learning algorithm—which essentially calculates the historical distribution and updates it as more data become available—on a measure of "shock to capital." The shock to capital took extreme values in 2008 and 2009.[1]

The two approaches are complementary. In the first approach, the exogenous variable is the belief in a Great Depression scenario, and this belief acts as the input in a model that explains the patterns observed during the Great Recession as endogenous outcomes. In the approach of Kozlowski et al., the Great Recession is an exogenous large shock that endogenously generates changes in beliefs that lead to further changes in outcomes.

I do not think anyone will dispute that the severity of the financial panic in 2008 or the Great Recession constituted an extraordinary event that was perceived as unlikely ex ante. For instance, a few features that were stunning include the speed with which employment and production collapsed in fall 2008 in the United States, the degree of synchronization of this collapse throughout the world, the dysfunction in some asset markets, and the elevated default risk of many financial institutions. However, it is important to realize that Kozlowski and colleagues' conclusion would not have been nearly as striking had the authors run the same learning algorithm on more standard time series, such as gross domestic product (GDP) growth or stock returns. By these measures, 2008 and 2009 were not especially unusual events. Somehow, the authors managed to find a macroeconomic measure that captures the particular severity of the Great Recession.

Ideally, one would want to validate the change in beliefs that is imputed by Kozlowski and colleagues' learning algorithm using other sources of data, such as survey measures or asset prices that reflect people's beliefs. Unfortunately, commonly used surveys (e.g., the Survey of Professional Forecasters and the Michigan Survey) are not good proxies for tail risk. Asset prices embed expectations from economic agents, but these are expectations of payoffs under a risk-neutral distribution rather than the actual ("physical") distribution. Moreover, the mapping between asset prices and tail risk can be complicated because asset prices can depend on a variety of factors besides fundamental tail risk, such as expected long-term growth, idiosyncratic volatility, or leverage. With these caveats, it is comforting that the authors find evidence that the implied skewness of stock returns and implied tail risk became larger following the Great Recession.

Kozlowski and colleagues' model is, by necessity, fairly abstract. One could go one step deeper and ask which specific tail risk increased. Certainly people are more worried now about the possibility of a financial collapse and, in particular, a housing crash. Perhaps we are also less confident in the ability of monetary and fiscal policy to stabilize the economy. Possibly investors worry more about unusual political scenarios. Conversely, the risk of a massive deflation is probably lower now than before 2008, since we learned that inflation does not seem to engage in massive negative spirals today. In principle, these different tail risks could all have different effects on the economy or asset prices.

Another approach to validating the changes in beliefs would be to study intellectual history and, in particular, the beliefs of economists that may have evolved after the Great Recession. Lucas (2003) famously argued that "macroeconomics in this original sense has succeeded: Its central problem of depression prevention has been solved, for all practical purposes, and has in fact been solved for many decades" (1). After the

Great Recession, some people criticized this statement as too optimistic. However, Lucas was far from alone in thinking this. For instance, the most successful intermediate macro textbook cautiously said, "Because there is not yet agreement on the causes of the Great Depression, it is impossible to rule out with certainty another depression of this magnitude. . . . Yet most economists believe that the mistakes that led to the Great Depression are unlikely to be repeated" (Mankiw 2006, 323). But as a subsequent edition of the same intermediate macro textbook notes, "In 2008 the US economy experienced a financial crisis, followed by a deep recession. Several of the developments during this time were reminiscent of the events during the 1930s, causing many observers to fear that the economy might experience a second Great Depression" (Mankiw 2012, 348). In the end, indeed, Lucas and Mankiw were proven right: the Great Recession did not turn into a Great Depression. As Mankiw (2012) notes, "Policymakers could take some credit for having averted another Great Depression" (349).

III.   How Sensitive Is the Risk-Free Rate to Tail Risk?

As I explained in the introduction, I will first discuss how tail risk affects the willingness to pay for safety before discussing how tail risk affects the willingness to pay for liquidity.

A.   The Value of Safety

The willingness to pay for safety can be analyzed without loss of generality in a Lucas tree endowment economy. Given the focus of the paper on tail risk, I use the version of Rietz (1988) and Barro (2006). Assume a representative agent with expected utility preferences and constant relative risk aversion,

$$E\sum_{t=0}^{\infty}\beta^t \frac{c_t^{1-\gamma}}{1-\gamma},$$

and consumption follows the process

$$\Delta \log c_t = \mu + \sigma\varepsilon_t + x_t \log(1-b).$$

Here ε_t is independent and identically distributed (i.i.d.) $N(0,1)$ and corresponds to "standard business cycle shocks," whereas x_t is i.i.d. Bernoulli(p), that is, $x_t = 0$ with probability $1 - p$ and $x_t = 1$ with probability p. Probability p is the likelihood of a financial crisis or other economic disaster. When $x_t = 1$, the level of consumption falls by a factor b. For instance, $b = 0.1$ corresponds to a permanent 10% reduction in the level of consumption.

In this canonical framework, the sensitivity of the risk-free rate to the probability p of a crisis can be approximated for small p as

$$\frac{\partial r_f}{\partial p} \approx -(e^{\gamma b} - 1).$$

This formula reflects that the demand for insurance depends on the level of risk aversion γ and the size of the shock b. As a simple illustration, set $b = 0.1$ and $\gamma = 10$, then the sensitivity is approximately $-(e-1)$, or -1.72, so that an increase in the probability of a crisis by 1 percentage point (e.g., from 2% per year to 3% per year) would reduce the risk-free rate by about 172 basis points (bp), a very substantial effect.[2] This suggests that the safety channel can be an important mechanism through which tail risk lowers interest rates.

A possible reaction is that risk aversion of 10 is incredibly high. It is true that it is difficult to match this coefficient to microeconomic evidence. But this value is actually fairly small if one requires the model to account for other asset-pricing facts, such as the equity premium. Suppose, for instance, that one models stocks as an unlevered claim to consumption, and suppose that the probability of crisis is 2% per year and the size of a crisis is 10% per year, as above. With $\gamma = 10$, the equity premium is only 35 bp a year. To generate an equity premium of 2%, the risk aversion coefficient needs to be approximately 24.4, which would yield in turn much larger sensitivity (of -10.47). So in my view, from an aggregative perspective, it is somewhat compelling to use large risk aversion.

In the paper, this safety channel is largely irrelevant, however, mostly because the authors confine themselves to a low coefficient of risk aversion (and, to a smaller extent, because the shocks do not have perfectly permanent effects, as I assumed in the calculations above). Their motivation appears to be, in part, the desire for simplicity. First, raising risk aversion without changing intertemporal substitution would require using Epstein-Zin preferences (as they did in their previous paper), which some researchers still regard as less transparent. Second, and more important, the implications would then also depend on whether agents make decisions using anticipated utility or in a fully Bayesian rational manner. The authors, in both papers, assume anticipated utility, that is, agents make decisions taking their estimate of the distribution of shocks as certain; they do not take into account that future shocks will lead them to revise their estimates, as a fully rational Bayesian agent would. Solving the model with full rational choice is difficult. As Collin-Dufresne, Johannes, and Lochstoer (2016) nicely illustrate using some simple models, fully rational choice with Epstein-Zin preferences leads to a "revision risk," which may increase risk premiums (depending on the intertemporal elasticity of substitution [IES]). Intuitively, agents are even more fearful of future bad realizations because they also convey information that bad realizations are more likely. Overall, the safety channel would likely help the authors by strengthening the link between tail risk and the risk-free rate.

B. The Value of Liquidity

The other channel through which tail risk affects the risk-free rate is by affecting the willingness to pay for collateral. The mechanism is as follows. Assets can serve as collateral that produces some liquidity value each period, on top of the returns obtained from production (for private capital) or from principal and interest (for government debt). Government debt is excellent collateral, whereas private capital is poor collateral. The Great Recession led to a reduction in the supply of collateral because a significant amount of private capital "disappeared" overnight when the bad shock hit. Collateral became more scarce, which increased its marginal value, and thus increased the price of government debt, reducing its yield. The effect of the learning mechanism is somewhat more indirect here. If there were no learning, the economy would recover capital faster, so the supply of collateral would recover faster; however, the impact effect due to capital "disappearing" always occurs, regardless of the assumptions about learning. Therefore, the contribution of the mechanism is really the difference between the "learning" and "no learning" lines in Kozlowski and colleagues' figure 5.

The authors use what they view as a "standard" model of collateral. I first want to illustrate how the model works to better understand its mechanics and especially its quantitative implications. Besides wanting to generally "kick the tires" on the model, I believe this is an important question because Kozlowski et al. abstract from some other significant changes that have affected the demand for and supply of collateral since 2008. Two, at least, come to mind: (i) the supply of government debt increased due to the large federal budget deficits and (ii) the demand for collateral may have increased due to new financial regulations. A natural question is whether their model makes realistic predictions regarding the effect of these other changes. Moreover, one wonders if the model should be expected to account for the entirety of changes observed in the data (e.g., the "data" line is close to the "learning" line in figure 5), given that it abstracts from these changes. Finally, I want to close with a quick discussion of the kind of evidence that might be brought to bear on this liquidity channel.

Quantitative Implications

To study the effect of changes in collateral supply or demand simply, I solved the steady state of the model, which is characterized by the following five equations:

$$1 = \beta \times (F_1(K, N) + 1 - \delta + \eta L), \tag{1}$$

$$X = B + \eta K, \tag{2}$$

$$L = H'(X) - 1, \tag{3}$$

$$F_2(K, N) = \frac{U_2(C, N)}{U_1(C, N)}, \tag{4}$$

$$GDP = F(K, N) + H(X) - X = C + \delta K. \tag{5}$$

Here K is capital, N is labor, F is the production function, U is the utility function, B is government debt, X is the total amount of effective collateral, $H(X)$ is the amount of services produced by collateral, and L is the marginal value of collateral (i.e., the price for 1 unit of collateral services for one period). Equation (1) is simply a Euler equation where the return on capital is the sum of the usual marginal product and the collateral services rendered, ηL. Equation (2) states that total collateral is the sum of public debt and capital, but capital's efficiency as collateral is only η that of public debt. Equation (3) determines the marginal product of collateral according to the production function H. Equation (4) is a standard labor supply equals labor demand condition. Equation (5) is a resource constraint and definition of GDP as the sum of the value added of F and H (here X is treated as an intermediate input). As the authors do, I assume the functional forms $F(K, N) = K^{\alpha} N^{1-\alpha}$, $H(X) = 2\varsigma\sqrt{X} - \xi$, and $U(C, N) = u(C - N^{1+\gamma}/(1 + \gamma))$.

A key feature of the model is joint production: capital is an input that produces goods, through the usual production function F, and collateral services, through the function H. This is similar to the sheep-wool-meat example from Econ 101: if you raise sheep, you produce both wool and meat; as a result, shocks to the supply of or demand for wool affect the meat market, and vice versa.

The first natural question is how important collateral is in the model. There are at least two ways to look at this. First, if you assume that we did not need collateral services in this economy (i.e., if $H[X] = 0$), GDP would be about 50% lower, as shown in the first row of table 1. This occurs both because less value is created, since no collateral services are produced, and because the economy accumulates less capital, since collateral value is low. (In my sheep analogy, the demand for wool is zero, so we raise fewer sheep and get less meat.) This number may be reasonable, but it would be nice to have a discussion of how one could potentially compare it with data. The other measure of the importance of collateral is the liquidity premium. A perfect collateral asset generates a 5% flow return every year. Equities are 84% less perfect collateral than the risk-free asset ($\eta = 0.16$), so the wedge between capital and bonds is about 4% (84% $\times$ 5%). Here, essentially the entire equity premium is a liquidity premium.[3]

The second question regards the effect of an increase in the supply of government debt. Public debt crowds out private capital: by increasing the supply of collateral, the value of collateral, and thus the incentive to accumulate capital, is reduced. In my sheep analogy, you flood the market with wool, which reduces the number of sheep raised and the production of meat. Quantitatively, as shown in table 1, a 1% increase in the quantity of government debt reduces the capital stock by about 0.38%, GDP falls 0.15%, and the risk-free rate rises by 5 bp. This suggests that the risk-free rate should have been affected significantly by the very large increases in government debt observed after 2008.

The third question regards the effect of a change in the demand for collateral. Since 2008, more trades need to be collateralized, due to both

Table 1
Effect of Parameter Changes on Capital, Output, GDP, and the Risk-Free Rate in the Model

Experiment	ΔK %	$\Delta F(K, N)$ %	ΔGDP %	Δr_f bp
1. No demand for collateral ($\zeta = \xi = 0$)	−27.5	−19.3	−50.0	525
2. Higher supply of government debt ($\Delta B = 1\%$)	−.38	−.25	−.15	5
3. Lower pledgeability of capital ($\Delta \eta = -1\text{pp}$)	3.73	2.47	1.44	−89

government regulation and market demand. One can think of this as a reduction in the parameter η that governs the pledgeability of private capital (i.e., private capital is not as widely accepted as collateral, as previously). This change has two opposite effects in the model: On the one hand, it makes investing less attractive because the return from collateral services is reduced for capital. On the other hand, it decreases the effective supply of collateral, which stimulates capital accumulation. Intuitively, as usual when you change the efficiency in production of one good, the effect that dominates depends on the elasticity of demand. It turns out that for the parameters used in the paper, the second effect dominates, and a reduction in pledgeability leads to a large increase in capital accumulation. Going from 0.16 to 0.15 pledgeability increases the capital stock by 3.7% and GDP by 1.4% and decreases the risk-free rate by 89 bp. These effects are substantial; again, it would be interesting for the authors to discuss these implications further and whether the changes since 2008 in regulations may have had a similarly big effect on the risk-free rate.

Evidence

Another way to validate the model predictions, qualitatively and quantitatively, would be to study data on collateral quantity or prices. It is a little difficult to map collateral in the model to the data precisely, but at a broad level, the argument is that private capital fell significantly, leaving firms short of collateral and thus unable to borrow. As figure 1 shows, corporate borrowing (defined here as the sum of securities and loans issued and trade payables) indeed declined right after 2008, but only for a little while. However, one could argue that borrowing (e.g., GDP) did not catch up to the previous trend.

An alternative approach to gathering evidence is to look at prices rather than quantities, for instance, by studying the premium for assets that are good collateral over assets that are bad collateral. At the corporate level, researchers have compared spreads of bonds backed by assets that are easy to liquidate to those of bonds backed by assets that are harder to liquidate. At the micro level, one could study haircuts in repo markets on securities of different quality or liquidity.

IV. An Accounting Exercise

In this section, I present a preliminary result from a different quantitative exercise that, interestingly, reaches a conclusion similar to that of

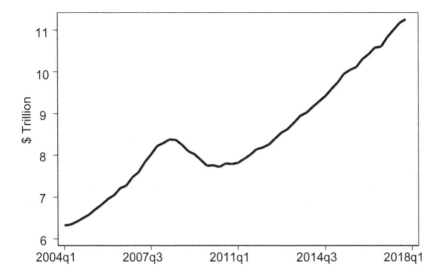

Fig. 1. Total liabilities of US nonfinancial corporation. Flow of funds = securities + loans + trade payables.

Kozlowski et al. The decline of the real interest rate over the past 2 decades has attracted a lot of attention. Various explanations have been offered; the current paper focuses on the role of higher perceived risk, but the role of savings supply (e.g., because of population aging and higher longevity) and lower expected growth have also attracted much attention. One approach to disentangling these potential explanations is to consider other data beyond the risk-free rate. The logic is that the different explanations for the risk-free rate have potentially different implications for other variables, for instance, investment and profitability of private capital. Low interest rates due to higher savings supply would stimulate capital accumulation, but low interest rates due to low expected growth or high perceived risk would likely deter capital accumulation. Similarly, low interest rates due to high savings would likely push the return on private capital down, whereas it could remain stable if higher risk is the culprit. As Gomme, Ravikumar, and Rupert (2011) show, the return on private capital has indeed remained stable or perhaps even risen. That said, it is also possible that the return on capital has been inflated recently by rising markups, as several studies have suggested.

Farhi and Gourio (2018) use a variant of the standard neoclassical growth model to formalize this intuition and examine the implications quantitatively. In the paper, we incorporate monopolistic competition and disaster risk in the neoclassical growth model. The key condition is the Euler condition for investment,

$$E_t\left[M_{t+1}R^K_{t+1}\right] = 1,$$

where M_{t+1} is the stochastic discount factor and R^K_{t+1} is the return on private capital:

$$R^K_{t+1} = \left(\frac{\alpha}{\mu}Z_{t+1}K^{\alpha-1}_{t+1}N^{1-\alpha}_{t+1} + (1-\delta)\frac{1}{q_{t+1}}\right)q_t e^{\chi_{t+1}},$$

where q_t is the relative price of consumption and investment goods, μ is the markup, Z_{t+1} is total factor productivity, and χ_{t+1} is a capital quality shock, assumed i.i.d. Along a balanced growth path, the capital-output ratio is given by

$$KY = \frac{\alpha}{\mu(r^* + g_q + \delta)},$$

where

$$r^* = \rho + \sigma g + \frac{1-\sigma}{1-\theta}\log E(e^{(1-\theta)\chi_{t+1}}),$$

and g_q is the growth rate of q_t, g is the growth rate of per capita GDP, ρ is the psychological discount rate, σ is the inverse of the IES, and θ is risk aversion. This formula illustrates how market power μ, technology (α, δ), technical progress (g, g_q), risk (θ, χ), and demographics (as proxied by ρ) all affect the capital-output ratio and thus the marginal product of capital. Similar to Kozlowski et al., we model χ as a rare shock, namely, a "disaster" or "crisis," which occurs with probability p.

In one preliminary exercise, we use eight data moments (labor share, profitability of capital, investment-capital ratio, population growth, investment prices, labor productivity growth, risk-free rate, and price-dividend ratio) to infer which of these underlying structural parameters (β, μ, α, δ, g_q, n, p, g_z) changed.[4] We estimate the model on 11-year centered rolling windows. One interesting preliminary finding is an increase in our estimate of the probability of a disaster shock, as shown in figure 2, in line with Kozlowski and colleagues' result, though the timing is somewhat different. Our result implies, as Kozlowski et al. also note, that the equity premium rose following a decline in the 1990s.

V.   Conclusion

Kozlowski et al. demonstrate how an appealing learning mechanism can be embedded in standard economic models. This methodological

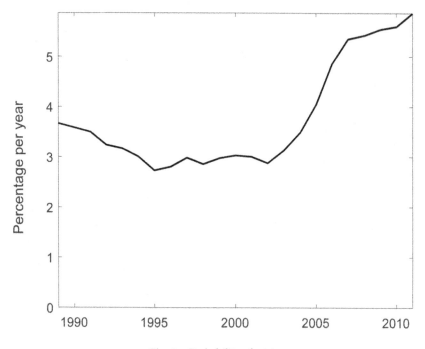

Fig. 2. Probability of crisis

contribution opens the path to many applications. The authors argue that belief revisions likely explain some of the decline in the risk-free interest rate post 2008, but exactly how much remains uncertain. Gathering more evidence on changes in beliefs and decomposing the role played by each of the safety and liquidity channels would be useful goals for future research.

Endnotes

Federal Reserve Bank of Chicago; email: francois.gourio@chi.frb.org. The views expressed here are those of the author and do not necessarily represent those of the Federal Reserve Bank of Chicago or the Federal Reserve System. I thank Gadi Barlevy and Francois Velde for comments. For acknowledgments, sources of research support, and disclosure of the author's material financial relationships, if any, please see http://www.nber.org/chapters/c14074.ack.

1. The authors discuss in detail the robustness of this conclusion to reasonable changes in the learning procedure, such as discounting past observations, including the Great Depression, in their learning sample, and so forth.

2. Note that because consumption is i.i.d., this reduction would apply to interest rates of all maturities equally, i.e., the yield curve, which is flat in this model, would simply shift in parallel fashion downward.

3. This raises some measurement issues because the returns measured in financial markets may include some of the collateral value provided. If I own a mutual fund of bonds,

and these bonds are used as collateral, my return may include the value of these services. Having the entire equity premium driven by liquidity also raises the question of why there are differences of returns within stocks of equal collateral value (e.g., the value premium).

4. In our model, only the safety channel is operative.

References

Barro, Robert. 2006. "Rare Disasters and Asset Markets in the Twentieth Century." *Quarterly Journal of Economics* 121 (3): 823–66.

Collin-Dufresne, Pierre, Michael Johannes, and Lars A. Lochstoer. 2016. "Parameter Learning in General Equilibrium: The Asset Pricing Implications." *American Economic Review* 106 (3): 664–98.

Farhi, Emmanuel, and François Gourio. 2018. "Accounting for Macro-Finance Trends." Working Paper no. 25282, NBER, Cambridge, MA.

Gomme, Paul, Ravi Ravikumar, and Peter Rupert. 2011. "The Return on Capital and the Business Cycle." *Review of Economic Dynamics* 14 (2): 262–78.

Gourio, François. 2012. "Disaster Risk and Business Cycles." *American Economic Review* 102 (6): 2734–66.

———. 2013: "Credit Risk and Disaster Risk." *American Economic Journal: Macroeconomics* 5 (3): 1–34.

Kozlowski, Julian, Laura Veldkamp, and Venky Venkateswaran. 2015. "The Tail That Wags the Economy." Working Paper no. 21719, NBER, Cambridge, MA.

Lucas, Robert E., Jr. 2003. "Macroeconomic Priorities." *American Economic Review* 93 (1): 1–14.

Mankiw, N. Gregory. 2006. *Macroeconomics*, 6th ed. New York: Worth.

———. 2012. *Macroeconomics*, 8th ed. New York: Worth.

Rietz, Thomas. 1988. "The Equity Risk Premium a Solution." *Journal of Monetary Economics* 22 (1): 117–31.

Comment

Robert E. Hall, *Stanford University and NBER*

This ingenious paper by Koslowski, Veldkamp, and Venkateswaran develops a model with two main components. The first is rooted in the financial economics of asset pricing. It describes a mechanism linking bad financial experiences to lengthy periods of low riskless interest rates. The second is rooted in corporate finance. It considers features of financial institutions and markets that explain why safe assets enjoy a larger increase in value in bad times than is captured in standard asset pricing models.

I will start by exploring the simple two-period, two-state Lucas (1978) model of asset pricing to develop a sense of the challenges in understanding the pricing of risky and riskless assets. Investor households receive 1 unit of endowment to consume now and a random endowment with two possible values to consume in the future, c_1 and c_2 in states 1 and 2. State 1 is normal and state 2 is a disaster with considerably lower consumption. The probabilities of the two consumption levels are $1 - \pi$ and π, respectively. These two values of possible consumption are constrained so that expected consumption growth is at a designated rate g:

$$(1 - \pi)c_1 + \pi c_2 = 1 + g.$$

Consumption in disaster state 2 is δ below consumption in normal state 1:

$$c_2 = c_1 - \delta.$$

Therefore,

$$c_1 = 1 + g - \pi\delta.$$

This setup defines a two-dimensional space of outcomes, indexed by the disaster probability π and disaster magnitude δ. The Arrow-Debreu equilibrium of the economy, as described by Lucas (1978), involves state prices: prices p_1 and p_2 of lottery tickets promising delivery of 1 unit of consumption in the respective states. With a utility discount rate β and a coefficient of relative risk aversion γ, the state prices are

$$p_s = \pi_s \beta c_s^{-\gamma}.$$

I take standard parameter values:

$$\beta = 0.987,$$

$$\gamma = 2.$$

The paper deals with the return to a safe claim:

$$\bar{r} = \frac{1}{p_1 + p_2} - 1.$$

Another interesting figure is the expected return to a claim to c_s. This is often taken as a proxy for the expected return in the stock market:

$$\bar{q} = \frac{\pi_1 c_1 + \pi_2 c_2}{p_1 c_1 + p_2 c_2} - 1.$$

The difference, $\bar{q} - \bar{r}$, is the equity premium.

Figure 1 shows the space defined by the pricing conditions over the possible values of the disaster parameters δ and π. At the upper right, no disasters occur—the disaster probability is zero and the magnitude is zero. This economy has no volatility. The riskless interest rate and the expected return in the stock market are the same, 3.4%, so the equity premium is zero. Down and to the left, each dot shows the riskless rate on the horizontal axis and the expected return to equity on the vertical axis. For example, one dot identified on the graph has a riskless rate of 0.017% and a stock return of 2.49%, with an equity premium of 2.47%. That point shows that the model can account for a riskless rate near zero and a somewhat positive expected return in the stock market.

Financial economists tend to regard normal current returns in the two markets as a real riskless rate around zero and an expected equity return around 6%. But this model cannot deliver that combination. The expected return to equity cannot be above 3.2%, and the safe rate is also 3.2% when the equity rate is at its highest. The introduction of a disaster possibility does explain the low value of the riskless rate but also depresses the expected return in the stock market.

For Koslowski et al., the disaster probability became 1.5% in 2009 and the disaster magnitude (measured by capital) was 0.15 (their fig. 4) This

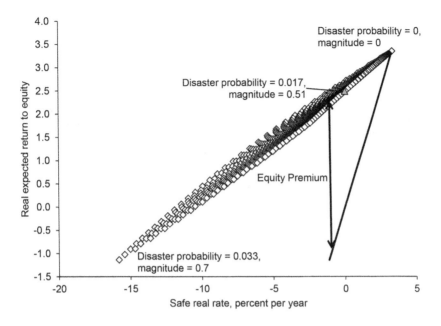

Fig. 1. Set of possible values of $\bar{r}$ and $\bar{q}$

produced a risk-free rate of 0.86% and an expected return on capital of 5.29% (their table 2), but that combination is way outside the feasible set within the model considered here (see fig. 2). So the first central idea of the paper—that beliefs about the probability of bad financial outcomes rose after the financial crisis in 2008 and 2009—cannot fully explain the decline in the risk-free rate while also recognizing the continuation of fairly high returns to equity. This finding sets the stage for the second major idea.

Koslowski et al. turn to ideas in corporate finance to amplify and alter the effects. The essential idea is to recognize that debt—a noncontingent promise to pay in all states of the world—has liquidity value beyond what is captured in the simple Lucas (1978) model considered here. The hypothesis that rising beliefs in rare disasters caused the decline in the real interest rate rests mainly on the strong financial amplification mechanism in the model

The Lucas (1978) model ties asset pricing to the marginal utility of the representative consumer—it is the simplest example of the consumption capital-asset pricing model. Another branch of modern financial economics drops the connection to marginal utility. It asks if there is a ran-

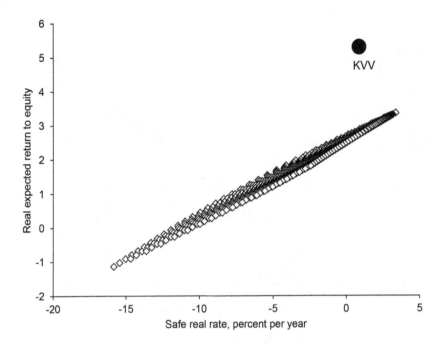

Fig. 2. The combination of returns found in the paper by Koslowski et al. lies far out of the feasible returns in Lucas's (1978) model.

dom variable playing the role of marginal utility that can account for debt and equity pricing. Continuing in the two-state setup from earlier with equity return q_s and debt return r_s, the state prices solve the pricing conditions:

$$1 = p_1(1 + q_1) + p_2(1 + q_2),$$
$$1 = p_1(1 + r_1) + p_2(1 + r_2).$$

From the data on Robert Shiller's website and using the definition of state 2 as a year when the stock market fell by 10% or more, I have solved for the state prices.[1] The idea is to interpret the prices in terms of a discount β, a disaster or tail probability π, and a factor $\mu < 1$ that expresses the high value of incremental consumption in the bad state of the world:

$$p_1 = \beta(1 - \pi),$$
$$p_2 = \beta\pi\mu.$$

Here, three parameters describe two data points. As Koslowski et al. stress, it is beliefs about π that control pricing, and we can think about those beliefs on their own. In particular, we can reverse-engineer beliefs from state prices.

Figure 3 describes ways of describing the two data points. It shows a curve in $\beta - \mu$ space corresponding to alternative beliefs π. Up and to the left on the curve is a point corresponding to the belief that the probability of state 2 is its frequency from 1971 to 2017, which is 13%. To make sense of that point, one has to believe that the time discount factor is $\beta = 0.75$, an absurdly large discount rate, and $\mu = 3.35$, severe pain while in that state. Down and to the right, with a disaster belief of 31%, absurdly high, are a reasonable $\beta = 0.95$ and a reasonably elevated value of consumption of 1.12. There is no point on the curve that makes good sense. Even without grounding the value of consumption in measured marginal utility, the standard principles of asset pricing cannot be made to deliver a plausible account of observed returns.

My take on Koslowski and colleagues' paper is that they are right that we should think seriously about relaxing the requirement that standard asset-pricing principles apply to risk-free investments.

One last remark: There must be more to the story of declining risk-free interest rates than the effects of the financial crisis. As figure 4 shows,

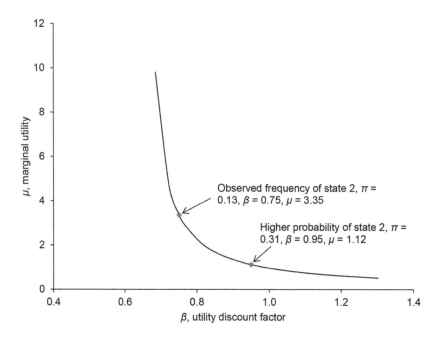

Fig. 3. Alternative parameter values consistent with observed state values. Color version available online.

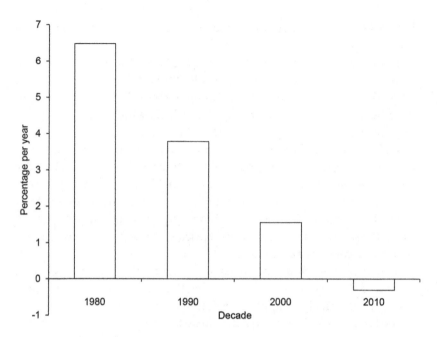

Fig. 4. Decline in the real rate began long before the disaster of 2009

realized real rates on 1-year Treasury bills have been declining since the 1980s, decade by decade.

Endnote

For acknowledgments, sources of research support, and disclosure of the author's material financial relationships, if any, please see http://www.nber.org/chapters/c14075 .ack.

1. Robert Schiller's website is available at http://www.econ.yale.edu/~shiller/data .htm.

Reference

Lucas, Robert E., Jr. 1978. "Asset Prices in an Exchange Economy." *Econometrica* 46 (6): 1429–45.

Discussion

The authors started by thanking both discussants. They agreed with Robert Hall's assessment that the paper contains two distinct parts but slightly disagreed on their characterization. They viewed the first part as proposing a mechanism for the propagation of a financial crisis and its effect on interest rates. The second part proposes a mechanism for the endogenous persistence of financial crises. The authors clarified that their paper focuses on persistence, whereas both discussants mostly focused on propagation. The authors argued that they opted for a simple yet quantitatively realistic propagation mechanism based on liquidity constraints. Their emphasis is on a novel persistence mechanism and its ability to explain a decrease in riskless interest rates over an extended period of time. Their persistence mechanism relies solely on agents not knowing the true distribution of shocks and estimating it over time.

Gregory Mankiw spoke next and asked the authors why they focused specifically on the recent financial crisis instead of taking a more general approach. He suggested that they could study other related episodes, including the Great Depression and the Great Moderation. Several participants proposed alternative approaches to validate the authors' mechanism. Gita Gopinath suggested looking at disasters in emerging markets. Valerie Ramey recommended investigating the response of land prices to earthquakes. Emmanuel Farhi proposed studying a broader class of assets and analyzing whether their behavior is consistent with the prediction of the authors' theory. He suggested looking into the cross-section of stocks and exchange rates during and following the Great Recession. The authors were sympathetic to these suggestions. They explained that they could not extend their analysis to the Great Depression due to data limitations.

Mankiw pointed out that real rates have decreased over time since the Great Depression, whereas the authors' persistence mechanism would predict a recovery following the initial decrease. The authors confirmed that their mechanism would indeed predict such a recovery but noted that real rates are affected by other factors outside the scope of their analysis. Robert Gordon followed up on the issue and questioned the existence of a secular decline in real interest rates. He argued that inspecting the series for real rates from the 1980s onward is misleading, referring to a plot displayed by Hall during his discussion. Gordon noted that the 1980s were times of tight monetary policy and easy fiscal policy, which led to high real interest rates. He added that real interest rates were actually low in the 1960s due to surprise inflation during the Vietnam War and in the 1970s due to an oil supply shock. Gordon suggested that notion of a secular decline in real interest rates may become obsolete over the next 5 years.

Andrea Eisfeldt followed up on the question of rare disasters and referred to the work of Tyler Muir ("Financial Crises and Risk Premia," *Quarterly Journal of Economics* 132, no. 2 [2017]: 765–809). Using a large cross-section of countries and a long time series, Muir documents that bond spreads respond to bank net worth shocks but not to wars or other events affecting consumption growth or the capital stock. Eisfeldt noted that this finding suggests that the response of bond spreads to leverage shocks may be muted. On the other hand, she raised the possibility that shocks to the collateral value of banks could have a sizable effect. The authors were very receptive to Eisfeldt's suggestion. They added that the response of spreads to an increase in perceived tail risk is quite modest in their model. The reason for this small response is that firms deleverage when credit risk increases. Eisfeldt noted that a friction to deleveraging would be required to obtain a larger effect.

The rest of the discussion focused on the nature of belief formation in the authors' model. Michael Woodford was very sympathetic to the idea that observing unusual events affects agents' beliefs about the probability of tail risk. He viewed the authors' evidence on options prices as compelling in this respect. Woodford was more skeptical, though, that the authors' simple model of learning could capture important features of the belief formation process. He emphasized that the size of the data set that agents use to form their expectations plays a critical role. Woodford noted that if this data set expands over time, agents will infer the true distribution of shocks asymptotically, so surprises about this distribution eventually disappear. He concluded that the window must be of finite length for the authors' mechanisms to be present in the long run. In Woodford's opinion, a window of fixed length wouldn't be particularly relevant either. As an example, he noted that prior to the Great Recession many economists assumed data prior to World War II was no longer relevant for assessing risks for the US economy, invoking policy and institutional changes. After the Great Recession, however, there was a renewed interest in the profession in the Great Depression and its policy lessons. Woodford argued that it is important to endogenize the window used for belief formation.

Pierre-Olivier Weill seconded Woodford's point and suggested that the natural next step would be a model of attention choice, where agents choose which episodes to consider when forming their beliefs. Wendy Edelberg noted that agents' beliefs may overshoot in response to a tail event. This response is not captured in the authors' model. She raised the possibility that this mechanism could decrease the degree of persistence in their model, as agents realize that their beliefs are incorrect. Martin Eichenbaum added that there is strong evidence of generational effects: old households put a lower weight on new observations when forming beliefs, relative to young households. Eichenbaum provided two examples: heterogeneity in inflation expectations by age and in risk taking in the financial industry between those who experienced the 2007–8 crisis and those who did not.

In response to Woodford, the authors said they saw a virtue in considering a modest deviation from rational expectation and showing that it yields a substantially different response to rare events. They added that they also performed an exercise in which they discounted the weights on observations by 1% a year, which may capture the generational effect mentioned by Eichenbaum.

Eichenbaum concluded the general discussion by inviting researchers to be less apologetic about deviating from rational expectations.

5

The Transformation of Manufacturing and the Decline in US Employment

Kerwin Kofi Charles, *University of Chicago and NBER*
Erik Hurst, *University of Chicago and NBER*
Mariel Schwartz, *University of Chicago*

I. Introduction

The period since 2000 has witnessed two profound changes in the US economy. One change has been the dramatic transformation of the manufacturing sector along several dimensions. Manufacturing employment fell by about 5.5 million jobs between 2000 and 2017, with much of these losses occurring even before the start of the Great Recession. Although manufacturing employment has been in decline since the 1970, this fall far surpasses the already substantial loss of 2 million jobs between 1980 and 2000. Despite employing less labor, however, the manufacturing sector has seen no persistent decline in its output. Instead, despite a decline during the recession, real manufacturing output is at least 5% higher today than it was in 2000. During this time, the manufacturing sector has become much more capital intensive. The capital-to-labor ratio of the manufacturing sector increased sharply and the labor share of manufacturing fell sharply during the 2000s relative to other sectors. Finally, workers employed in manufacturing are now less likely to be drawn from those with less education.

The other change, contemporaneous with these changes in the manufacturing sector, has been a large and sustained decline in employment and hours worked for prime-age workers. Between 2000 and 2017, employment rates for men aged 21–55 fell by 4.6 percentage points and hours worked fell by more than 180 hours per year. The declines in employment started prior to the Great Recession, accelerated during the Great Recession, and had only rebounded partially as of 2017. For comparison, the secular decline in annual hours worked for prime-age men from 2000 to 2017 is as large as the cyclical decline in their annual hours worked during the 1982 recession. The declines are even larger for prime-age workers with lower levels of accumulated schooling. Notably, less educated women also saw a pronounced decline in hours worked during the 2000s, reversing a century-long trend.

Although other sectors in the economy have undoubtedly changed in significant ways over the past few decades, the transformation of manufacturing is of particular interest to economists for several reasons.[1] The massive historical size of the manufacturing sector in the economy, accounting in 1980 for nearly a fifth of all jobs, is one reason to be especially interested in the effect of changes in manufacturing. Another reason is that manufacturing tends to be highly spatially concentrated compared with other sectors. Consequently, shocks to manufacturing may have larger labor market effects given both local spillovers and the fact that cross-region mobility is costly. In addition, compared with other sectors, manufacturing has traditionally occupied a disproportionate role in policy debates. This has been evident recently in the United States with discussions of how both trade and environment policies interact with the manufacturing sector. Finally, for many decades, the manufacturing sector has been one where relatively less educated Americans, and especially less educated men, have enjoyed labor market success. As of 1980, more than a third of employed men between the ages of 21 and 55 with a high school degree or less worked in the manufacturing sector.

In this paper, we examine how much, and by what mechanisms, changes in manufacturing since 2000 have affected the employment rates of prime-age men and women. We use a variety of data sources and empirical approaches to answer these questions. We document that the persistent, long-run decline in employment and hours for prime-age workers did not occur evenly across the United States. Furthermore, exploiting cross-region variation, we estimate a strong cross-commuting zone correlation between declining manufacturing employment and declining employment rates of prime-age workers. Using a shift-share instrument, we find that a 10-percentage-point decline in the local manufacturing share reduced local employment rates by 3.7 percentage points for prime-age men and 2.7 percentage points for prime-age women. To put the magnitude in perspective, naively extrapolating the local estimates suggests that between a third and a half of the decline in employment rates and annual hours for prime-age workers during the 2000s can be attributed to the decline in the manufacturing sector. This naive estimate ignores many important general equilibrium effects that will certainly alter the exact quantitative magnitude, but it suggests that the decline of the manufacturing sector is a first-order factor explaining the declining participation rate of prime-age workers in the United States during the past 2 decades. Our results are even larger for prime-age men with lower levels of accumulated schooling.

Because it is based, in part, on the national trend in manufacturing, the shift-share instrument captures the combined effect of all shocks that affected national manufacturing activity. One of these shocks, which has received considerable attention in the literature, is increased import competition because of rising trade with China. Yet, estimates in the literature suggest that import competition from China accounted for only about a quarter of the decline in manufacturing during the 2000s (see, e.g., Autor, Dorn, and Hanson 2013). The manufacturing sector has simultaneously experienced other dramatic changes over the past 2 decades, most notably in automation and the rise of robotics (see, e.g., Acemoglu and Restrepo 2017). We extend our shift-share instrumental variable (IV) analysis to examine how the effect of manufacturing decline from Chinese import competition compares to the effect of other shocks in manufacturing that are orthogonal to trade-related factors. We show that manufacturing employment declined substantially over the 2000s even in markets where there was essentially no manufacturing loss because of Chinese imports. Furthermore, we show that shocks to manufacturing that were unrelated to China or trade (including, presumably, things like rising automation) had very similar effects on local labor markets to the Chinese import shock. An implication of these results is that policy efforts to address the adverse labor market effects of trade will not reverse the broader trend in manufacturing employment that has significantly weakened labor market options, particularly for less educated workers.

We find that local employment losses from manufacturing decline were accompanied by reductions in wages. This suggests that the negative employment effects were not due to shifts in labor supply but were instead the result of falling labor demand, which likely adversely affected worker well-being. Consistent with this interpretation, we use data from a variety of sources to show that local manufacturing decline was associated with increased prescription opioid drug use and overdose deaths at the local level. We also show that manufacturing decline resulted in more failed drug tests among workers tested by their firms, confirming that much of this local increased drug use occurred among the affected workers themselves. Besides providing evidence about the adverse effect of negative manufacturing shocks on worker well-being, the drug results highlight how, by virtue of the effect on opioid use that they stimulate, negative local labor market shocks may have interacted with factors like changes in physician prescription behavior to drive the ongoing opioid epidemic in the United States. More generally, our findings contribute to an emerging consensus that labor market conditions may drive different dimensions of health (see, e.g., Charles and DeCicca 2008).

Why has the decline in the manufacturing sector led to such persistent declines in employment rates? The US economy has experienced sector declines throughout its history, and the manufacturing sector itself has, prior to the mid-2000s, shrunk as a share of total employment. Yet, rarely have the negative employment rate effects of these changes been as large or persistent, presumably because of various mediating mechanisms that have eased employment transitions. To highlight the differences with earlier periods, we use our shift-share methodology to show that local manufacturing employment declines during the 1980s had little effect on local employment rates during that time period. To help explain this difference, we present evidence on the role of three mediating mechanisms: transfer receipt from public and private sources, skill mismatch within the manufacturing sector, and regional migration.

We find some evidence that declining manufacturing labor demand is associated with increased disability take-up. However, the effects are quantitatively small and are not likely to explain why employment rates have remained so persistently low in the wake of declining manufacturing employment for most individuals. In addition, we find no evidence of altered cohabitation patterns—a measure of private transfers—in response to declining local manufacturing shares. We provide evidence of growing skill mismatch within the manufacturing sector. Manufacturing is becoming an increasingly skilled sector, particularly relative to other industries that have historically employed less educated workers, such as retail and construction. Consistent with this mismatch, we find that relative to other industries, the manufacturing sector has experienced the largest increase in the job opening rate during the 2000s. Finally, we show that the reduced propensity of workers to move across regions in response to a local manufacturing shock is a striking feature of the data during recent periods relative to prior periods.

Our work complements the growing literature exploring the declining employment-to-population ratio during the 2000s. Moffitt (2012) was one of the early contributors to this literature documenting that employment rates for younger and less educated men were declining sharply prior to the Great Recession. Krueger (2017) documented the change in labor force participation rates for different demographic groups based on age and sex. He found that both the aging of the population and an increase in school enrollment explained some of the declining labor force participation rate. Aguiar et al. (2017) documented declining employment rates and hours worked for individuals aged 21–30 and 31–55 by sex and education. They found that employment rates and hours worked fell most for young, less educated men. Abraham and Kearney (2018) surveyed the literature on declining employment rates during the 2000s.

Others have made the link between declining manufacturing employment and labor market outcomes during the 2000s. For example, Charles, Hurst, and Notowidigdo (2016, forthcoming) showed that manufacturing employment has declined sharply during the early 2000s and that local declines in the share of workers employed in manufacturing are strongly correlated with increased rates of nonemployment during the 2000–7 period. Acemoglu et al. (2016), Autor, Dorn, and Hanson (2013), and Pierce and Schott (2016) all highlighted the role of increased competition from China in declining manufacturing employment during the 2000s. Acemoglu et al. (2016) and Autor et al. (2013) used local labor market variation to show that increased Chinese import competition in the manufacturing sector led to declining local employment rates. In a separate line of work, Acemoglu and Restrepo (2017) showed that increased automation via the use of robots has led to a decline in manufacturing employment and a decline in employment. Our work complements both of these extensive studies by providing a broad overview of the link between declining manufacturing employment and labor market outcomes of prime-age wage workers during the 2000–17 period. We also discuss potential reasons why the decline in manufacturing demand may result in lower employment rates.

II.   Aggregate Trends in Labor Markets and Manufacturing during the 2000s

Two historically massive and significant changes in the economy occurred during the 2000s. One of these was a massive transformation in the manufacturing sector. The other was a sharp secular decline in work propensity among prime-age persons with few, if any, historical precedents. The bulk of our analysis in this paper examines whether and how much these two phenomena are causally related and evaluates alternative mechanisms that might account for the link between them. Before turning to this work, this section summarizes the magnitude and key features of national changes in manufacturing and employment rates over the 2000s.

A. Declining Work during the 2000s

We use two main data sources to study employment changes during the 2000s: several years of March supplements of the Current Population Survey (CPS; IPUMS 2019a) plus the 1980, 1990, and 2000 US Census, which we combine with the 2001–16 American Community Surveys (ACS; IPUMS 2019b).[2] The CPS allows us to study long time series, and the large samples in the Census/ACS facilitate cross-region analysis. For both data sets, we restrict the samples to persons aged 21–55 (inclusive) who are living outside of group quarters and who are not in the military. The data are weighted using survey weights provided by the CPS and Census/ACS.

Figure 1 plots the trends in annual hours worked for men aged 21–55 using the CPS sample. Annual hours worked are recorded by multiplying weeks worked during the prior calendar year by the number of hours per week the individual usually works. Year t measures of annual

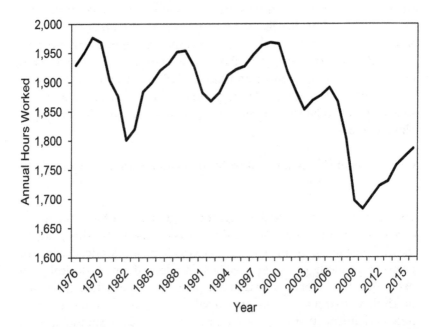

Fig. 1.   Annual hours worked, by year, for men aged 21–55 using the CPS sample

hours worked were reported by year $t + 1$ respondents. The figure shows that from 1976 through 2000, prime-age men worked slightly more than 1,950 hours per year on average at the peak of business cycles. Annual hours began falling before the Great Recession, declining throughout most of the period from 2000 to 2007. Hours plummeted during the Great Recession and rebounded only modestly after its end. By 2016, men aged 21–55 worked, on average, only 1,785 hours per year. These prime-aged men thus work, on average, 185 fewer hours per year than they did in 2000, which represents a massive decline in work activity by historical standards. Figure 1 shows that the secular decline in annual hours worked for prime-age men between 2000 and 2016 is larger than the drop in hours this group experienced during the severe 1982 recession.

A striking feature of the hours reduction between 2000 and 2016 is that almost all of the decline was the result of changes along the extensive margin of labor supply. Although unemployment rates have returned to prerecessionary levels, the employment rate for prime-age men as of 2016 was still 4.6 percentage points below its 2000 level. In 2016, only 82.2% of prime-age men were working, compared with 86.8% of men aged 21–55 worked in 2000. About half of this decline occurred prior to the Great Recession.

Figure 2 shows the annual decline in hours worked for men aged 21–55 relative to year 2000 for different education groups: persons with a bachelor's degree or more (accumulated education ≥16 years), persons with some college but no bachelor's degree (accumulated education = 13, 14, or 15 years), and persons with only a high school degree or less (accumulated educated ≤12 years). The declines in annual hours worked during the 2000s was largest for those with the least completed schooling. By 2016, prime-age men with a bachelor's degree experienced a decline in annual work hours of roughly 150 hours, or about 7%, whereas those with less than a bachelor's degree saw their annual hours of work fall by more than 200 hours relative to levels in 2000, a decrease of nearly 12%.[3]

Figure 3 plots the change over time in the share of men aged 21–55 who report not working during the year, separately by their level of education. In the mid-1980s, only about 9% of men aged 21–55 with education ≤12 years worked 0 weeks during the year. This number has increased with each successive recession and generally did not fall back to its original level when the recession was over. By 2016, a fifth of all men who had only a high school education or less worked 0 weeks during the year. Among men with some college training but no bachelor's

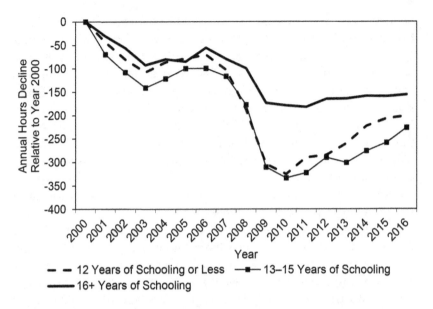

Fig. 2. Annual hours worked, by year, for men aged 21–55 by education using the CPS sample. Education groups include having a bachelor's degree or more (Ed ≥ 16), some college but no bachelor's degree (Ed = 13, 14, or 15), or no post-high school training (Ed ≤ 12).

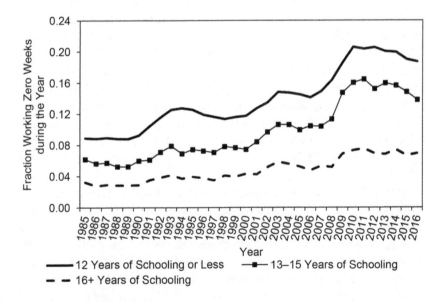

Fig. 3. Fraction of men aged 21–55 working 0 weeks during the year, by education, using the CPS sample.

degree, the fraction working 0 hours over the entire year rose from about 6% to about 15%. Long-term detachment from the labor market appears to be becoming a defining feature of the labor market experience of men who are not college graduates.[4]

Table 1 shows that the decline in annual work hours for men with less than a bachelor's degree spanned different races and locations. Columns 1 and 2 show results for native-born white and black men of prime age. Whereas white men worked more than black men in all years during the 2000s, the decline in annual hours worked was slightly larger for white men (233 vs. 201 hours per year). Columns 3–5 examine patterns for prime-age men with less than a bachelor's degree who live in city centers, those in the suburbs (within a metro area but outside the city center), and those living in rural areas (outside of a metro area). Although hours of work fell substantially for men everywhere, those living outside of city centers experienced the largest reductions.

We have thus far presented annual hours results only for prime-age men. Figure 4 presents trends in hours worked for prime-age women during the 2000s, separately by their level of education. We show results separately by gender chiefly because of the massive secular increase in women's hours worked over the past century. Showing results for the full population runs the risk of having this well-understood secular change for women be the dominant feature of the series, swamping the key features of men's annual hours patterns that we have shown. This point about how the overall working population has changed over the past several decades is relevant for how one thinks of post-2000 changes in manufacturing, which we discuss later.

Table 1

Annual Hours Worked for Men Aged 21–55 with Less Than a Bachelor's Degree, March CPS

	Native White	Native Black	City Center	Suburb	Rural
	(1)	(2)	(3)	(4)	(5)
2000	1,947	1,557	1,749	1,939	1,920
2016	1,716	1,357	1,572	1,715	1,698
Δ 2000–16	−231	−200	−177	−224	−222
% decline	−11.9	−12.9	−10.1	−11.6	−11.6

Note: Cols. 1 and 2 further restrict the sample to include whites and blacks born in the United States. Cols. 3–5 restrict the sample to those of all races living in center cities, suburbs, or rural areas.

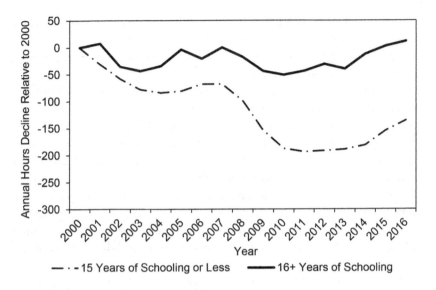

Fig. 4. Annual hours worked, by year, for women aged 21–55 by education using the CPS sample. Education groups include having a bachelor's degree or more (education ≥16 years) or less than a bachelor's degree (education <16 years).

Figure 4 shows that whereas annual hours worked for college-graduate women were relatively constant over the 2000s, women with less than a bachelor's degree experienced a decline of about 140 hours per year between 2000 and 2016. The pattern of changes in hours for these prime-age, less educated women was very similar to that of their male counterparts: declines predated the start of the Great Recession, accelerated over the course of the recession, and have only modestly recovered since. Also like less educated men, the decline in annual hours worked for less educated women was chiefly driven by falling employment propensities. Whereas 71% of women aged 21–55 with less than a bachelor's degree were employed in 2000, the shared was only 66% in 2017.

To summarize, during the 2000s, annual hours worked fell substantially for both prime-age men and women, with the declines concentrated among those with less than a bachelor's degree. Furthermore, nearly all of the reduction in hours was the result of falling employment rates. Although the US unemployment rate has returned to its prerecession level, employment rates for prime-age workers still lag behind where they were before the recession. What reconciles these two seemingly conflicting facts is the decision of many of those not working to cease searching for work.

B. The Transformation of the Manufacturing Sector during the 2000s

Although, as shown below, the manufacturing sector has been undergoing large evolution since at least the mid-1970s, the changes the sector has experienced since 2000 have been particularly profound. We highlight key features of these dramatic changes.

Perhaps the most stunning transformation in the sector has been the massive national decline in the number of manufacturing jobs. Figure 5 shows the trend in monthly employment in the US manufacturing industry from January 1977 through December 2017. These data come from the US Bureau of Labor Statistics (2019a) Current Employment Statistics establishment survey. The economy has been shedding manufacturing jobs for some time, but the changes since about 2000 have been particularly massive. Continuing a pattern that dates to the mid-1970s, the figure shows that the United States lost about 2 million manufacturing jobs between 1980 and 2000. After 2000, the trend decline in manufacturing employment accelerated dramatically. Six million manufacturing jobs disappeared between 2000 and 2010, with much of the job loss occurring prior to the start of the Great Recession. In the years after the Great Recession, US manufacturing employment has remained depressed, rebounding only slightly through 2017. On net, 5.5 million US manufactur-

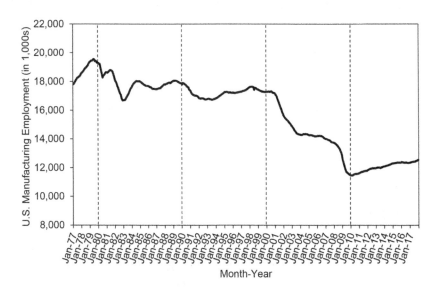

Fig. 5. Monthly US manufacturing employment, 1977–2014 (US Bureau of Labor Statistics 2018a). Vertical lines represent 1980, 1990, 2000, and 2010.

ing jobs were lost between 2000 and 2017. These large, recent declines dwarf those of the 1980s and 1990s.

Figure 6 presents another measure of work opportunities in manufacturing: the change in the number of manufacturing establishments. Corresponding to the reduction in the number of manufacturing jobs, which accelerated sharply after 2000, the figure shows that the number of manufacturing establishments also began to sharply decline at around the same time. Indeed, the number of manufacturing establishments rose between the late 1970s and late 1990s, before declining by more than 75,000 manufacturing establishments between 2000 and 2014. As with the reduction in manufacturing jobs, much of the decline in the establishments occurred before the Great Recession. Since the end of the Great Recession, the number of establishments in the manufacturing industry has not rebounded. As of 2014, the number of US manufacturing establishments was 50,000 lower than in 1977. The decline in the manufacturing employment during the 2000s is distinct in modern US history. Not only did manufacturing employment fall by a third since 2000, the declines were associated with a 20% reduction in the number of manufacturing establishments.

What has driven this decline in manufacturing employment and establishments? Figure 7 shows that manufacturers did not hire less labor because of falling demand for manufacturing output. The figure plots

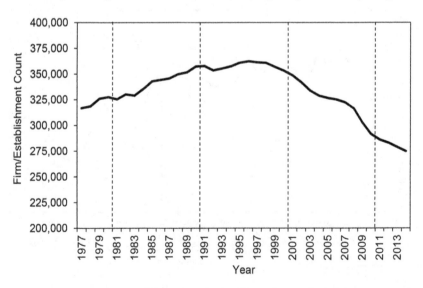

Fig. 6. Total manufacturing establishments in the United States, 1977–2014 (in thousands; US Census Bureau 2018). Vertical lines represent 1980, 1990, 2000, and 2010.

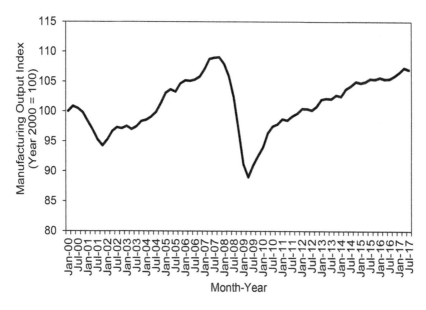

Fig. 7. US quarterly real output index for the manufacturing sector (2000Q1 = 100; US Bureau of Labor Statistics 2018b). All subsequent quarter-year pairs are percentage changes relative to 2000Q1.

the percentage deviations in real output for the US manufacturing sector relative to 2000Q1, which is anchored at 100 (US Bureau of Labor Statistics 2018b). The figure shows that, in spite of some reduction in manufacturing output during the Great Recession, a 27% decline in manufacturing employment, and a 21% decline in manufacturing establishments, US total manufacturing output is today 7% higher than its 2000 level. Thus, demand for manufacturing labor has not been accompanied by a commensurate decline in the demand for the goods made by manufacturers.[5]

The adoption of production techniques that use less labor in favor of technology and other inputs is a potential explanation for manufacturing's falling labor demand. Various pieces of evidence suggest that there has indeed been greater technology adoption and capital deepening in the sector over the past 2 decades.

Figure 8 plots the evolution of the labor share for the manufacturing sector and for the total nonfarm business sector from 1987 through 2015. Consistent with the findings of Karabarbounis and Neiman (2014), the labor share fell broadly in the US economy, with the declines concentrated in the post-2000 period. The labor share in the manufacturing sector fell by about 20% between 2000 and 2015. By comparison, the labor share in the broad nonfarm business sector (which includes the manufacturing

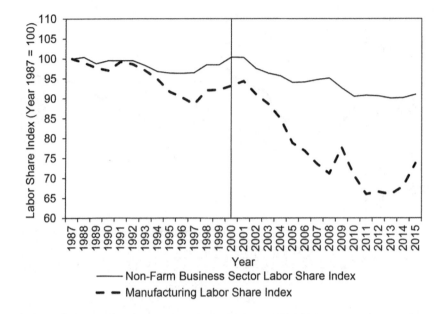

Fig. 8. Labor share annual index for US manufacturing (dashed line) and private non-farm business (solid line) sectors (US Bureau of Labor Statistics 2019c, 2019d). We index the labor share in both sectors to 100 in 1987; all subsequent years are percentage changes relative to 1987 (vertical line is 2000).

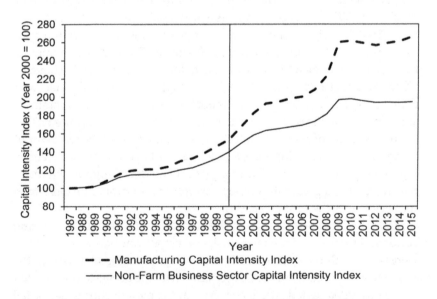

Fig. 9. Capital intensity annually for US manufacturing (dashed line) and private non-farm business (solid line) sectors (US Bureau of Labor Statistics 2019b, 2019e). We index the capital intensity measure to 100 in 1987; all subsequent years are percentage changes relative to 1987 (vertical line is 2000).

sector) fell by only about 10% over the same period. Figure 9 shows the capital intensity of the manufacturing sector and the nonfarm business sector during the 1987–2015 period. The figure shows clearly that manufacturing became substantially more capital intensive during the 2000s, both absolutely and relative to other nonfarm sectors in the economy. The manufacturing sector has not shrunk dramatically since 2000. Rather, the sector has grown and done so while sharply substituting capital for workers in production.

Another potential driver of decreased labor demand in manufacturing is the phenomenon of rising import competition from China during the 2000s. According to Autor et al. (2013), the real value of Chinese imports to the United States increased by 1,156% from the early 1990s through 2007, with much of the growth occurring after 2000. This surge in Chinese imports to the United States is relative to changes from other US trading partners both in terms of levels and growth rates (see table 1 of Autor et al. 2013).

Figure 10 shows the relationship between different four-digit manufacturing industries' exposure to Chinese import competition and the percentage decline in employment in the industry between 1999 and

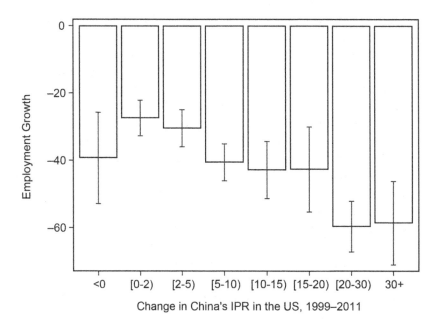

Fig. 10. Employment decline and import competition. The estimated percentage change in employment is shown by bins of the change in import penetration by China between 1999 and 2011 (Acemoglu et al. 2016; NBER 2016). Each bin also shows the 95% confidence interval around the employment decline.

2011 for the entire United States (the import competition measure is defined as the change in imports from China over the period 1999–2011, divided by initial absorption, measured as industry shipments plus industry imports minus industry exports).[6] As highlighted by Autor et al. (2013), the figure shows that employment losses were larger in manufacturing industries that experienced larger Chinese import competition shocks. For example, during 1999–2011, industries where Chinese import competition grew by at least 30% experienced a 60% reduction in employment, compared with the 40% employment decline in industries that saw import competition grow by between 5% and 10%. This variation in industry employment loss by the amount of import competition underlies the regional analysis in Autor et al. (2013) and Acemoglu et al. (2016). Consistent with our earlier results on capital deepening and capital substitution, the figure also shows that industries that experienced little or no growth in import competition from China, represented in the first two bins, also had substantial declines in employment, with reductions of about 30%–40% during the early 2000s. As Autor et al. (2013) noted, import competition from China explains only about a quarter of US manufacturing decline during the 1990–2007 period.

Although it is often analyzed in isolation, capital deepening of the manufacturing sector and import competition from China may be linked. Figure 11 shows the mean change in the ratio of real production worker wages to real capital stock for manufacturing industries between 1999 and 2011, according to the change in Chinese import competition. The large employment declines in manufacturing industries at all levels of Chinese import competition growth are matched by a marked change in the production technology, as indicated by a falling of the labor-to-capital ratio. The declines were largest in industries that faced the largest growth in Chinese import competition. We cannot disentangle whether the threat or reality of competition from imports induced manufacturers to automate their processes or whether imports happened to grow most in places where automation was rising for other reasons. In either case, this association between import shocks and automation suggests that policies that restrict trade with the aim of returning employment to its pre-China shock level confront the problem that the affected industries are now significantly more capital intensive than before. They are thus unlikely to raise labor demand to old levels even if they are protected from trade competition.

The reduction in the amount of labor used in the sector is only one of two major transformations in manufacturing. The other major change dur-

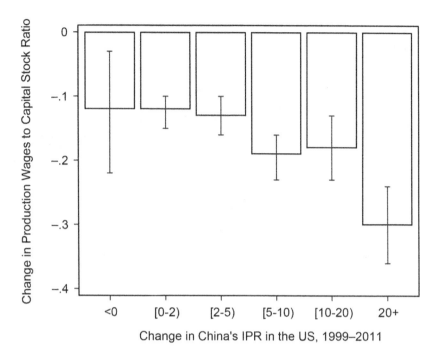

Fig. 11. Labor-to-capital ratio and import competition. The change in the ratio of real production worker wages to real capital stock is shown by bins of the change in import penetration by China between 1999 and 2011 (Acemoglu et al. 2016; NBER 2016). Each bin also shows the 95% confidence interval around the employment decline.

ing the past 2 decades has been a fundamental shift in the types of workers whom the sector employs, as measured by their completed schooling. Using data from several years of March Supplements to the CPS (IPUMS 2019a), we plot the time-series patterns in the share of men and women aged 21–55 of different education levels and regardless of employment status working in the manufacturing sector.

Figure 12 shows a large decline in the likelihood of working in manufacturing for men without any college training. Whereas 3 decades ago nearly one in three of such men worked in manufacturing, by 2017, the share had plummeted to only 12%. The manufacturing employment share among men with college training also fell between 1977 and 2017, but at only about 10 percentage points the decline was much smaller than that for less educated men and occurred from a much lower initial level of around 20% rather than 30%. Figure 13 shows results for women. Manufacturing has and continues to play a much smaller role in women's employment compared with men's, but the figure shows that the same

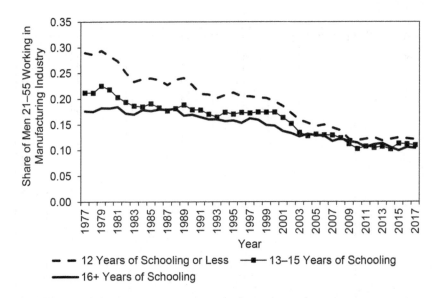

Fig. 12. Manufacturing share of population for prime-age men, 1977–2016, by educational attainment using the CPS sample (includes both men who are employed and not employed; see appendix for additional details).

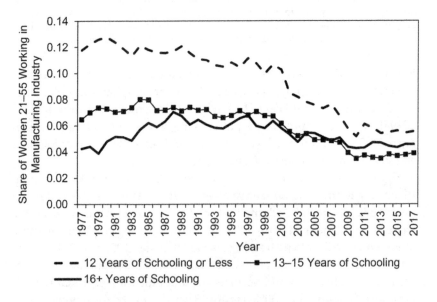

Fig. 13. Manufacturing share of population for prime-age women, 1977–2016, by educational attainment using the CPS sample (includes both women who are employed and not employed; see appendix for additional details).

qualitative patterns shown for men of different education levels occurred among women as well. Between 2000 and 2017, the share of prime-age women with no college training who worked in manufacturing fell by about 5 percentage points, from 11% to 6%. This reduction was larger than the retreat from manufacturing work experienced by more educated women, whose propensity to work in manufacturing fell by around 2 percentage points between 2000 and 2017.

A consequence of the differential changes in manufacturing employment shares by education level in figures 12 and 13 is that manufacturing has become a more highly skilled sector, as measured by workers' education. As of 2017, the manufacturing sector is no longer the disproportionately important source of employment for the less educated that it was in the late 1970s and early 1980s. At the same time, the share of manufacturing workers who are college educated and the fraction of college-educated workers employed in manufacturing have grown sharply.

Before concluding our discussion of the profound changes in the manufacturing sector, we note that another analysis might have sorted workers by occupation rather than industry. How much of what we summarize about manufacturing is really about particular occupations in the economy? More than three quarters of the prime-age men with less than a bachelor's degree working in manufacturing worked as production workers between 2000 and 2017, with little change in the share in that time.[7] By contrast, for prime-age men with at least a bachelor's degree working in the manufacturing industry, the share working in production occupations was only 15% during the same time period. Most college-educated men in manufacturing during the 2000s were managers, engineers, computer programmers, or software developers. Consistent with the shifts in education shares during the 2000s, the share of prime-age men in manufacturing working in production as opposed to other occupations fell from 61% in 2000 to 58% in 2017.[8]

C. Aggregate Relationship between Manufacturing Decline and Declining Employment

Taken together, the changes in the manufacturing sector summarized above point to a substantial decline in labor demand in the manufacturing sector over the past 2 decades. In the next section, we provide causal estimates of the effects of changes in manufacturing labor demand on employment and hours. Before turning to this causal evidence, we conclude this section by presenting some associational results from aggre-

gate time-series data that are consistent with the notion that the manufacturing decline may have played an important explanatory role in the
changes in employment and hours we have discussed.

To show these aggregate associations, figure 14*a* plots the manufacturing share of prime-age men (left axis) and the employment rate of

Fig. 14. Time-series relationship between manufacturing shares and employment rates
for prime-age men, using a CPS sample, 1977–2017. (*a*) Manufacturing share and employment rate. (*b*) Manufacturing plus construction share and employment rate.

prime-age men (right axis) using CPS data from 1977 through 2017 (IPUMS 2019a). Charles et al. (2016, forthcoming) highlighted how the construction boom during the late 1990s and early 2000s masked the adverse effects of the secular decline in manufacturing in aggregate statistics. With this in mind, figure 14*b* shows the association between the manufacturing plus construction share of prime-age men (left axis) and the employment rate of prime-age men (right axis).

A number of noteworthy results are evident in figure 14. First, the figure shows that the manufacturing share of employment for prime-age men fell sharply prior to the 2000s. Between 1977 and 2000, the manufacturing share of prime-age men across all education groups fell from 25% to about 18%. As shown previously in figure 5, total manufacturing employment only fell by 2 million jobs over the course of the 1980s and 1990s. The large decline in the manufacturing share of prime-age men during the period prior to the 2000s was therefore mostly driven by population growth as the baby boom generation entered the labor market. This stands in stark contrast to the decline in the manufacturing share since 2000, which has been primarily the result of massive losses in actual manufacturing jobs.

A second important result the figure shows is that the simple time-series correlation between the manufacturing share and the employment rate for prime-age men was weaker during the 1977–2000 period than it has been since 2000. Between 2000 and 2017, both the manufacturing share and the employment rate fell by roughly similar amounts (4.5 and 6.0 percentage points, respectively). However, during the 1977–2000 period, when the manufacturing share also fell by 6 percentage points, there was a decline of only 1.5 percentage points in the employment rate. Overall, the correlation between time-series movements and the employment rate for prime-age men was 0.44 between 1977 and 2000 and 0.85 between 2000 and 2017.

The tight time-series relationship between declining manufacturing employment shares and declining employment rates during the 2000s is the focus of our paper. In Section V, we explore some alternative potential explanations for the larger effect on employment of a given percentage decline in the manufacturing share during the 2000s than previously. In addition to the other factors we consider below, a key consideration to keep in mind is that, as we have shown, similar percentage reductions in manufacturing shares in the two periods were the result of fundamentally different underlying changes within manufacturing, which could have affected long-term employment quite differently. In particular, it is likely that a decline in the importance of manufacturing in overall employment arising mainly from the growth in the total number of workers in the economy was not associated with the same labor market challenges of adjustment and reallocation caused by the very large contraction in the absolute number of manufacturing jobs and establishments that occurred during the 2000s.

Another important result in figure 14 is motivated by results from Charles et al. (2016, forthcoming), who showed that accounting for cyclical movements in construction strengthens the relationship between changing manufacturing shares and changing employment rates. This is true during both the 2000s and the earlier period. Controlling for the cyclical movement in construction is important given the high degree of substitutability between these two sectors for prime-age men with lower levels of completed schooling. Figure 14*b* shows that there is a much tighter relationship between the manufacturing plus construction share and the employment rate of prime-age men than with the manufacturing alone. In 1980, more than a third of all men between the ages of 21 and 55 worked in manufacturing. The time-series correlation between the manufacturing plus construction share and the employment rate was 0.62 and 0.93 during the 1977–2000 and 2000–17 periods, respectively. Given that the construction share was similar between 2000 and 2017, the manufacturing plus construction share fell by 6 percentage points during this time period, and the employment rate fell by roughly 4.5 percentage points.

Finally, before leaving this section, we note that the associations documented in figure 14 line up across different education levels in a manner consistent with a causal link. The manufacturing share for men aged 21–55 with no more than a high school education fell by 7 percentage points between 2000 and 2017, as was previously shown in figure 12. This group's employment rate fell by 6 percentage points during that time period. Men in other education groups, whose manufacturing employment shares have historically been smaller, experienced much smaller changes in their employment rates as manufacturing has declined. To a first approximation, reductions in manufacturing shares for prime-age men were matched by roughly equal declines in employment rates during the 2000–2017 period, with particularly pronounced effects for less educated workers.

Collectively, these patterns in aggregate statistics suggest that declining manufacturing rates and declining employment rates were linked, especially during the 2000s.

III. The Effect of Local Labor Market Manufacturing Shocks on Employment since 2000

In this section, we move beyond suggestive aggregate evidence and apply IV methods to local labor market data to estimate the causal effect of declining local manufacturing labor demand in the 2000s on changes in local annual hours and employment rates for prime-age men and women.

We use data from the 2000 US Census and the pooled 2014–16 ACS (IPUMS 2019b). For ease of exposition, we will refer to the latter as 2016 data. Unlike the CPS, the large sample sizes in the Census/ACS allow us to explore labor market variables at detailed subregions of the United States.[9] As with the CPS analysis shown previously, we restrict the sample to nonmilitary individuals between ages 21 and 55 who live outside of group quarters. The local labor market we analyze is the commuting zone, which we classify using the commuting zone definitions outlines by Autor et al. (2013). There are 741 of these areas in our sample. These are relatively self-contained areas where the vast majority of residents also work. Unlike metropolitan areas, commuting zones span the entire United States. In the analysis, we weight commuting zones by the size of their population of prime-age workers in 2000 to mitigate the larger measurement error in sparsely populated commuting zones.

Figure 15 shows the commuting zones in the United States identified by the size of their manufacturing share of the population among 21- to 55-year-olds in 2000. Darker shading in a commuting indicates a higher manufacturing share. This regional variation will be a component of our identification strategy. The figure shows that community zones varied widely in terms of the importance of their manufacturing industries in 2000. For example, in most commuting zones in Nevada, less than 7% of the prime-age population worked in manufacturing in 2000. Conversely, in Indiana, most commuting zones had manufacturing shares of at least 15%. Another pattern the figure shows is that much of the manufacturing industry in the United States was concentrated in the Midwest and Southeast in 2000. For example, states like Georgia, Indiana, western Kentucky, Michigan, Minnesota, North Carolina, Ohio, Pennsylvania, South Carolina, Tennessee, West Virginia, and Wisconsin had commuting zones with very large fractions of the population working in the manufacturing sector as of 2000.

Figure 16 shows that commuting zones with the largest manufacturing share in 2000 experienced the largest decline in the manufacturing share between 2000 and 2016. This is not surprising. As aggregate

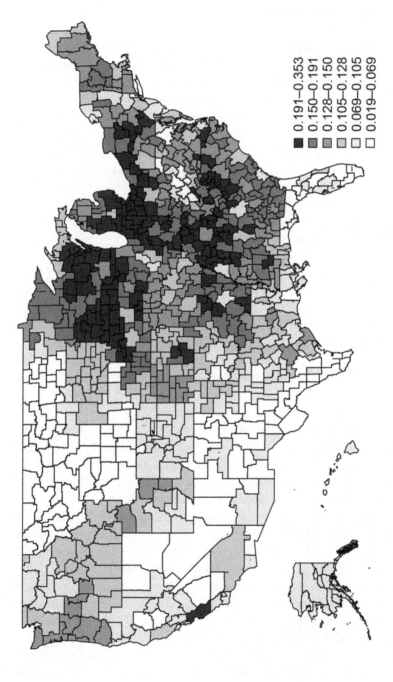

	0.191–0.353
	0.150–0.191
	0.128–0.150
	0.105–0.128
	0.069–0.105
	0.019–0.069

Fig. 15. Manufacturing share of prime-age population (aged 21–55 years) by commuting zone, 2000 Census. Shaded areas represent six quantiles of commuting zones based on 2000 manufacturing share; the darker the commuting zone, the higher the manufacturing share in 2000.

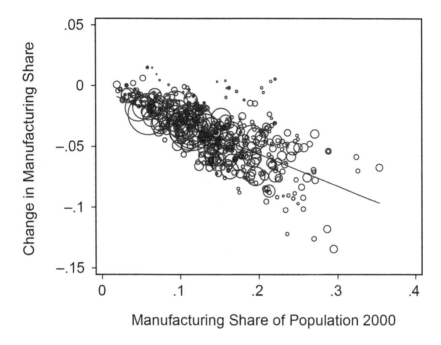

Fig. 16.   Change in manufacturing share for prime-age workers between 2000 and 2016 versus the initial manufacturing share in 2000. Each observation is a commuting zone. The size of the circle reflects the size of the 2000 prime-age population in each commuting zone. The slope of the weighted regression line of the scatter plot is −.26 with a robust standard error of −.02.

employment in the manufacturing industry declined, regions that specialized in manufacturing were most adversely effected. The weighted regression line through the scatter plot in figure 16 suggests that a 10-percentage-point higher manufacturing share in 2000 was associated with a 2.6-percentage-point decline in the manufacturing share between 2000 and 2016.

   Figure 17 provides some preliminary evidence linking declines in the manufacturing sector in a local area to changes in employment rates of prime-age men and women during the 2000s. The figure presents a scatter plot of the initial manufacturing share in the commuting zone in 2000 against the change in the employment rate of men (fig. 17*a*) and women (fig. 17*b*) in the commuting zone between 2000 and 2017. The manufacturing share, as above, is defined for all individuals aged 21–55 regardless of sex and education. The figure shows the strong negative relationship between a commuting zone's manufacturing share in 2000 and the subsequent change in employment rates there between 2000 and 2016.

(a)

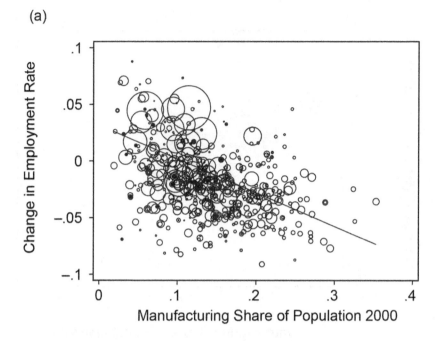

(b)

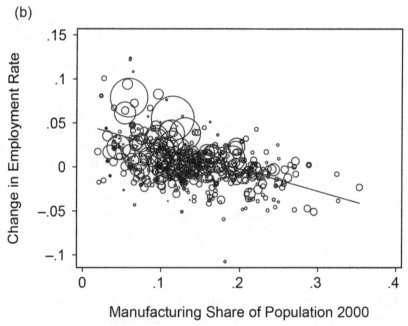

Fig. 17. Change in employment rate for prime-age individuals (21–55 years) between 2000 and 2016 versus the initial manufacturing share in 2000. (*a*) Men. The slope of the weighted regression line of the scatter plot is −.30 with a standard error of .04. (*b*) Women. The slope of the weighted regression line is −.25 with a standard error of .06.

For men, a 10-percentage-point increase in the manufacturing share in 2000 is associated with a 3-percentage-point decline in their employment rate (standard error = 0.4). The R^2 of the simple scatter plot for men was 0.24. For women, the results were similar, with a 10-percentage-point increase in the commuting zone's manufacturing share reducing their employment rate by 2.5 percentage points (standard error = 0.6). Thus, there is a strong cross-sectional relationship between initial manufacturing intensity and the subsequent long-run change in employment rates for both prime-age men and women.

We assume that the relationship between a commuting zone's decline in the manufacturing share and labor market outcomes is given by

$$\Delta L_{t+1}^{g,k} = \alpha^g + \beta^g \Delta Man_{t+1}^k + \Gamma^g X_t^k + \epsilon_{t+1}^{g,k}. \tag{1}$$

In the above specification, ΔMan_{t+1}^k denotes the change in the manufacturing share in commuting zone k between period t (2000) and $t + 1$ (2016) for all persons 21–55 years old. The variable $\Delta L_{t+1}^{g,k}$ measures the change in labor market outcomes between 2000 and 2016 in commuting zone k for demographic group g based on sex and education. The outcomes studied for each group g in k are the change in log average annual hours worked, the change in the employment rate, and the change in log hourly wages (described in the appendix). All regressions include a vector of year 2000 controls for k, denoted X_t^k, which includes the share of the prime-age population with a bachelor's degree, the prime-age female labor force participation rate, and the share of the population that is foreign born. These controls capture other potential determinants of labor market outcomes that might be correlated with initial manufacturing share. Our coefficient of interest is β^g, the responsiveness of local labor market conditions to changes in the local manufacturing share.

There are at least two potential threats to identification from estimating equation (3) via ordinary least squares (OLS). First, local labor supply shifts can simultaneously reduce local employment rates and draw individuals out of the manufacturing sector. For example, if individuals in a given area were to acquire a distaste for work, then observed employment might fall. As individuals stop working, some may be drawn out of the manufacturing sector. Thus, a positive correlation between changes in local employment rates and changes in local manufacturing shares need not imply that the decline in manufacturing labor demand caused a fall in local employment rates. Likewise, an increase in labor demand for a nonmanufacturing sector, such as the energy sector, could pull individuals out of the manufacturing sector and simultaneously increase local employment rates. This would cause a negative correlation between changes in local manufacturing shares and changes in local employment rates that is not due to the causal channel we wish to capture.

To overcome potential endogeneity concerns, we use a two-stage least squares (TSLS) approach, in which we use an IV for changes in the local manufacturing employment shares. Following Charles et al. (forthcoming), our IV, S_{t+1}^k, is given by

$$S_{t+1}^k = \sum_{n=1}^{J} \psi_{j,2000}^k (Man_{j,2016}^{-k} - Man_{j,2000}^{-k}), \qquad (2)$$

where $\psi_{j,2000}^k$ is the share of prime-age individuals in commuting zone k working in detailed manufacturing subindustry j in year 2000.[10] The shares are defined over all prime-age individuals regardless of sex and education. The term in the parentheses of equation (2) represents the change in aggregate employment shares in manufacturing industry j during the 2000s. When calculating the IV for region k, we calculate the aggregate change in employment in industry j excluding any changes in that industry within k. We define the change in aggregate employment shares within j for all 21- to 55-year-olds in the Census/ACS data.

The IV is an example of the well-known "shift-share" (or "Bartik") instrument, which has become a commonly used tool for identifying local labor demand shocks.[11] The instrument isolates two sources of variation that help with causal identification. First, as seen in figure 15, some commuting zones are more manufacturing intensive than others, so part of the identifying variation comes from a comparison across areas with high versus low initial manufacturing intensity. Second, because of differences in their specific industrial mix within the manufacturing sector, some commuting zones that were initially manufacturing intensive specialized in industries that declined more during the 2000s.

The validity of the shift-share instrument hinges on two assumptions. First, national changes in employment shares in manufacturing industry j need to be uncorrelated with local labor market conditions aside from their effect on local manufacturing labor demand. Second, initial local industry shares should be uncorrelated with changes in local labor market conditions aside from their effect on changes in local manufacturing labor demand. It is, as always, impossible to prove that the exclusion restriction holds. However, the literature has stressed that important components of national changes in manufacturing are the result of factors like import competition and trade policy at the national level (see Autor et al. 2013) and the exogenous secular changes at the national and international level in the development and adoption of automation and technology (Acemoglu and Restrepo 2017). These factors are arguably orthogonal to the factors other than manufacturing labor demand that determine local labor demand and labor supply.

Figure 18 relates the observed change in manufacturing in a commuting zone, $\Delta \ln Man_{t+1}^k$, to the change predicted by the shift-share IV, $\Delta \ln \widehat{Man}_{t+1}^k$. The figure shows that the IV strongly predicts actual changes in local manufacturing shares. Areas that had larger predicted declines in their manufacturing share had systematically larger actual declines in their manufacturing share. The slope coefficient from the simple weighted regression line of the scatter plot is 0.68 (standard error = 0.03) with R^2 = 0.68 and an $F(1, 739) = 511$.

Table 2 shows estimates of β^g from estimating equation (1) by TSLS and adapting for $\Delta \ln \widehat{Man}_{t+1}^k$ with S_{t+1}^k. We present separate estimates for different sex and education groups. Across the different regressions, the labor-market-dependent variables are specific to sex×education groups,

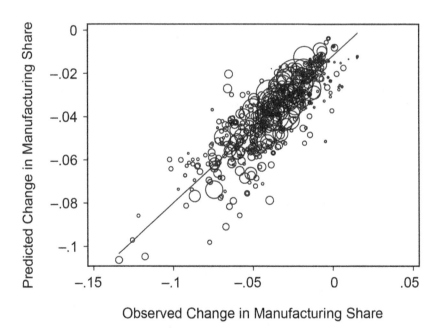

Fig. 18. Predicted change in manufacturing share between 2000 and 2016 and the observed change. The change is predicted using our shift-share instrument and local area baseline controls. Each observation is a commuting zone. The size of the circle reflects the size of the 2000 prime-age population in each commuting zone. The slope of the weighted regression line of the scatter plot is .68 with a robust standard error of .03.

Table 2
IV Regression of Changing Manufacturing Employment on Changing Labor Market
Conditions 2000–2016, by Sex and Education Groups

	Education			
	All	≤12	13–15	≥16
Change in employment rate:				
Men	.37	.46	.35	.13
	(.08)	(.13)	(.08)	(.06)
Women	.27	.56	.14	.09
	(.08)	(.08)	(.08)	(.08)
Change in log average annual hours worked:				
Men	.54	.79	.67	.04
	(.15)	(.24)	(.18)	(.11)
Women	.55	1.15	.43	.08
	(.15)	(.21)	(.16)	(.11)
Change in log average wage:				
Men	1.23	1.83	1.41	.68
	(.36)	(.34)	(.33)	(.35)
Women	1.00	1.34	1.28	.60
	(.30)	(.25)	(.36)	(.31)

Note: Table shows the two-stage least squares estimates of the effect of the change in the manufacturing share on changes in local labor market conditions. The change in the manufacturing share is instrumented using our shift-share instrument. In all specifications, we include the baseline share of the prime-age population with a bachelor's degree, the baseline prime-age female labor force participation rate, and the baseline share of the population that is foreign born as controls. Real wages are adjusted to account for the changing demographic composition between 2000 and 2016. Robust standard errors are shown in parentheses.

but both the change in manufacturing share and our instrument are defined at the commuting zone level. Having the same independent variable of interest facilitates comparisons of the coefficients across the various specifications.

We find that the decline in manufacturing shares between 2000 and 2016 led to large reductions in employment rates and annual hours worked for prime-age men and women. The 90–10 difference in the decline in manufacturing shares across commuting zones was roughly 5.7 percentage points.[12] Thus, commuting zones at the tenth percentile of the manufacturing change distribution experienced a decline in the employment rate for prime-age men between 2000 and 2016 (pooling across all education groups) that was 2.11 percentage points larger than commuting zones at the ninetieth percentile of the manufacturing change distribution $(0.057 \times 0.37 \times 100)$. The difference in the declines in annual hours worked for prime-age men between the tenth and ninetieth percentiles was 3.08% (0.057 × 0.54 × 100). The magnitudes were very similar for prime-age women.

Employment rates and annual hours worked of less educated men and women were affected particularly strongly by a declining local manufacturing sector. For example, comparing the tenth- and ninetieth-percentile commuting zones with respect to manufacturing decline, the decline in employment rates was 2.6 percentage points larger and the decline in annual hours worked was 4.5% larger for prime-age men with a high school degree or less. The comparable numbers for prime-age men with a bachelor's degree or more were much smaller, at 0.74 percentage point and 0.2%, respectively. Manufacturing decline had smaller effects on employment rates and hours worked the more educated the worker.

Table 2 also shows how changes in local manufacturing share affected average demographically adjusted real wages. As employment and hours fell, so did wages in the commuting zone. We take this as strong evidence that the reductions in employment and hours that we estimate do not primarily reflect reduced labor supply, but instead are primarily the product of decreased labor demand in commuting zones. Comparing the coefficients from the wage and hours regression provides a rough estimate of local labor supply elasticities.

As noted above, the TSLS results in table 2 based on the shift-share IV ultimately come from two types of comparisons. One of these is the contrast between commuting zones with large rather than small preexisting manufacturing shares—the importance of manufacturing in the area at the start of our study period. The other comparison is the contrast across areas based on whether the composition of their manufacturing industry in 2000 led there being bigger or smaller reductions when manufacturing declined nationally during the 2000s. One potential concern with the results in table 2 is that places with large manufacturing shares in 2000 might have been systematically different from places where manufacturing shares were smaller. To explore whether this concern is valid, we reestimated all the results in table 2, including the initial manufacturing share in 2000 as an additional regressor. Doing this generally increased both the coefficients and standard errors reported in table 2. However, the results are not statistically different from what we show in the table. For example, for all prime-age men, the coefficients on the change in the employment rate and the change in log annual hours worked become 0.64 (standard error = 0.21) and 0.82 (standard error =

0.45) when the 2000 manufacturing share is included as an additional control.

The estimates from the commuting-zone analysis shed light on how much the decline in manufacturing explains the aggregate decline in employment rates and hours worked for prime-age men and women. It should be stressed that cross-area estimates only provide an accurate assessment of the effects of aggregate manufacturing decline on aggregate changes in employment rates and labor market conditions under a stringent set of conditions. This point has been made in recent work by Beraja, Hurst, and Ospina (2016), Nakamura and Steinsson (2014), and Adão, Arkolakis, and Esposito (2019). The cross-region estimates ignore the mobility of labor, capital, and goods across space; changes in national monetary, fiscal, and regulatory policy that affect all regions; and the financial flows across regions through government transfer policies. All of these factors imply that the local employment elasticity to a local shock (e.g., the decline in manufacturing labor demand) differs from the aggregate employment elasticity to the same aggregate shock.

Given these concerns, we do not use estimates from our local labor market analysis to provide an exact counterfactual of how aggregate manufacturing declines affect aggregate employment rates. Instead, these estimates enable us to give a sense of the potential magnitudes of the role of declining aggregate manufacturing employment in explaining aggregate declines in employment and hours for prime-age workers, while holding these other general equilibrium forces and margins of adjustment constant.

Table 3 has two panels and shows four columns of results. Columns 1 and 3 show, respectively, the actual change in the employment rates (in percentage points) and the actual change in log annual hours (in percentages) for different demographic groups for the entire United States between 2000 and 2016. Columns 2 and 4 show the predicted change in these variables for the different demographic groups during the same period. To calculate the predicted change, we multiplied the demographic group specific coefficients in table 2 by the actual change in the manufacturing share for prime-age workers during the 2000–16 period.[13] Between 2000 and 2016, the decline in the prime-age manufacturing share using CPS data was 6.3 percentage points. The top panel of table 3 shows the results for men, and the bottom panel shows the results for women. Within each panel, we show results for the pooled education groups as well as for individuals with a high school degree or less, some college but no bachelor's degree, and a bachelor's degree or more.

Table 3
Predicted Employment Rate and Annual Hours Change Due to Declining
Manufacturing, by Sex and Education Groups

Education Group	Δ Employment Rate (Percentage Points)		Δ ln Annual Hours (PercentAges)	
	Actual Change (1)	Predicted Change (2)	Actual Change (3)	Predicted Change (4)
Men:				
All	−4.6	−2.3	−9.7	−3.4
≤12	−6.4	−2.9	−11.6	−5.0
13–15	−5.3	−2.2	−12.4	−4.2
≥16	−3.0	−.8	−7.4	−.3
Women:				
All	−2.8	−1.7	−4.2	−3.5
≤12	−7.5	−3.6	−14.1	−7.3
13–15	−4.9	−.9	−9.1	−2.7
≥16	−1.6	−.5	−.7	−.5

Note: Table shows the predicted and actual changes in the employment rate (in percentage points) and log annual hours (in percentages) for different demographic groups for the entire United States during the 2000–16 period. The predicted change is calculated by multiplying the demographic group specific coefficients in table 2 by the actual change in the manufacturing share for prime-age workers during the 2000–16 period. Between 2000 and 2016, the decline in the prime-age manufacturing share using CPS data was 6.3 percentage points.

One of the headline results from table 3 is that our regressions suggest that declining manufacturing employment was an important explanation of the aggregate decline in hours worked and employment rates for both men and women during the 2000s, holding potential general equilibrium forces constant. For example, our estimates suggest that 50% of the employment rate decline (−0.023/−0.046) and 35% of the annual hours decline (−0.034/−0.097) can be attributed to the decline in the manufacturing share of employment. For women, −1.7 percentage points of the −2.8-percentage-point decline in employment rates can be attributed to declining manufacturing. Collectively, these results suggest that the decline in the manufacturing sector was likely an important explanation for why employment rates and annual hours worked declined so sharply during the 2000s. As the literature evolves, understanding the general equilibrium forces associated with the decline in manufacturing will be an important contribution to the literature.[14]

Table 3 also reinforces the results in the aggregate time-series patterns. Our cross-region regressions imply that manufacturing declines have a greater impact on less educated workers. As the time-series patterns showed, these workers experienced the largest declines in employment rates and annual hours worked. Our estimates imply that manufacturing decline is responsible for a decline in annual hours worked of about 5% for prime-age men with a high school degree or less. By contrast, we find that manufacturing decline explains essentially none of the decline in annual hours for college graduates. Although hours and employment fell for these more highly educated persons at the aggregate level, our estimates imply that essentially none of that decline can be explained by a declining manufacturing sector, holding other general equilibrium forces constant.

The shift-share IV strategy discussed above captures the combined exogenous effect on local manufacturing of all national factors that change labor demand in the manufacturing sector: capital deepening and technology, Chinese import competition, new management techniques, etc. Yet, knowing something about these separate effects of the different factors might be important to policy makers contemplating alternative policies that affect specific mechanisms driving local manufacturing demand changes. Data limitations prevent us from providing evidence on the separate effects of the many different types of national shocks to manufacturing. However, because we have a direct measure of trade shocks in a commuting zone, we can say something about how the local effect of trade-related shocks compare with the local effect of all other shocks that are statistically orthogonal to trade.[15]

Our approach is straightforward. To isolate the part of the shift-share instrument that is purged of the effect of increased Chinese import competition, we estimate the following regression:[16]

$$S_{t+1}^k = \omega_0 + \omega_1 \text{Import}_{t+1}^k + \omega_2 X_t^k + v_{t+1}^k, \tag{3}$$

where S and X are defined as above and Import_{t+1}^k is the instrument for Chinese import competition measure as defined by Acemoglu et al. (2016). The residuals from this regression, which we denote $\tilde{S}_{t+1}^k$, are the portion of the shift-share measure that is orthogonal to the Chinese import competition measure ($S_{t+1}^k - \hat{\omega}_0 - \hat{\omega}_1 \text{Import}_{t+1}^k - \hat{\omega}_2 X_t^k$). We leave the instrument for Chinese import competition as is, so that any common component of the two instruments is loaded onto the import competition measure. We then predict the change in the local manufacturing share between 2000 and 2016 using the residualized shift-share measure and the Chinese import competition instrument:

$$\Delta Man_{t+1}^k = \gamma_0 + \gamma_1 \tilde{S}_{t+1}^k + \gamma_2 \text{Import}_{t+1}^k + \Gamma X_t^k + v_{t+1}^k. \tag{4}$$

Given the estimates from equation (4), we define the following two variables for each commuting zone:

$$\Delta \widehat{Man}_{t+1}^{\tilde{S},k} = \hat{\gamma}_1 \tilde{S}_{t+1}^k, \tag{5}$$

$$\Delta \widehat{Man}_{t+1}^{Import,k} = \hat{\gamma}_2 Import_{t+1}^k. \tag{6}$$

The variables $\Delta \widehat{Man}_{t+1}^{Import,k}$ and $\Delta \widehat{Man}_{t+1}^{\tilde{S},k}$ are the percentage-point change in a commuting zone's manufacturing share predicted by the Chinese import competition instrument and all other factors, respectively. We then estimate the regression below on the sample of prime-age men:

$$\Delta L_{t+1}^k = \alpha + \beta^S \Delta \widehat{Man}_{t+1}^{\tilde{S},k} + \beta^I \Delta \widehat{Man}_{t+1}^{I,k} + \Gamma X_t^k + \epsilon_{t+1}^k. \tag{7}$$

The results of the above regression are shown in table 4. The dependent variable in the regression is the change in the commuting zone's employment rate between 2000 and 2016. Column 1 includes the same X vector of controls as in table 2, and column 2 follows the work of Autor et al. (2013) and Acemoglu et al. (2016) and includes the initial manufacturing share out of total population in the year 2000 as an additional control. In column 2, the identification comes from variation in trends in

Table 4
Response of Changing Employment Rate 2000–16 to Variation in Manufacturing Decline, Prime-Age Men

	Δ Employment Rate	
	(1)	(2)
$\Delta \ln \widehat{Man}_{t+1}^{\tilde{S},k}$	.26	.66
	(.16)	(.24)
$\Delta \ln \widehat{Man}_{t+1}^{I,k}$	.42	.63
	(.08)	(.19)
p-Value of difference	.37	.92
Total R^2	.69	.69
Controls:		
Base controls from table 2	Yes	Yes
2000 manufacturing share	No	Yes

Note: Table shows the coefficients from a regression of changes commuting zone employment rate between 2000 and 2016 on $\Delta \ln \widehat{Man}_{t+1}^{\tilde{S},k}$ and $\Delta \ln \widehat{Man}_{t+1}^{I,k}$. Each observation is a commuting zone. The results in col. 1 include our base controls from table 2 as regressors. In col. 2, we also control for the manufacturing share in the commuting zone in year 2000 as an additional regressor. Bootstrapped standard errors are in parenthesis.

manufacturing employment among commuting zones with similar manufacturing shares in 2000.

The key takeaway from table 4 is that the local labor market effects
of local manufacturing employment due to Chinese import competition are very similar to the local labor market effects of manufacturing
declines due to other forces. For example, a 10-percentage-point reduction in the manufacturing share caused by the increased Chinese import competition leads to a decline in local male employment rates of
4.2 percentage points, whereas the male employment rate decline from
a 10-percentage-point decline in the manufacturing share from forces
orthogonal to increased Chinese import competition is 2.6 percentage
points. These estimates are not statistically different from each other.
If we control for initial manufacturing share, the small difference between these two estimated effects effectively disappears. These finding
suggest that, in terms of local employment effects, it is the fact of a local
manufacturing shock that matters and not its precise source.

At first blush, the findings above seem inconsistent with Autor, Dorn,
and Hanson (2015), whose results suggested that the labor market response to trade shocks were much larger than the labor market response
to technology shocks. This is not the case. When Autor et al. measured
the effect of a local area's exposure to routine occupations across all sectors, including services, they found automation had little effect on overall employment. This is due to the offsetting effect of increased demand
for abstract work, which typically dominates in areas with large service
sectors. When Autor et al. measured an area's exposure to routine occupations using only the manufacturing sector, however, they found that
automation does produce employment losses. This finding, which, like
our work, exploits variation from within the manufacturing sector, is
consistent with our findings that manufacturing areas subject to Chinese import competition experienced labor market outcomes that are
similar to manufacturing areas that experienced declining employment
for other reasons (including increased automation).

IV.   Effect of Manufacturing Decline on Well-Being:
Evidence from Opioid Use

The findings in the previous section show that the declines in the manufacturing sector lowered employment and wages of prime-age workers. These findings, which are consistent with reductions in the demand
for labor rather than voluntary labor supply shifts, suggest that manu-

facturing decline may have substantial adverse effects on agents' well-being in local markets. In this section, we provide some novel evidence about changes in well-being by examining the relationship between local manufacturing shocks and opioid drug use and addiction.[17]

According to the US Centers for Disease Control and Prevention (CDC), drug overdoses accounted for the deaths of nearly 64,000 people in the United States in 2016 and are now the leading cause of death for Americans under age 50 (Hedegaard et al. 2017). Opioid overuse accounts for much of the growth in drug-related deaths over the past 2 decades and for a growing addiction problem that has attracted the concerned attention of policy makers and analysts. Furthermore, according to the American Society of Addiction Medicine (2016), 2.6 million Americans in 2016 were addicted to prescription pain relievers or heroin. The opioid crisis facing the country was recently described by the *New York Times* as the "deadliest drug crisis in American history" (Salam 2017).

Although there is agreement among doctors and policy makers that the opioid epidemic started with a rapid increase in opioid prescriptions as pain relievers in the late 1990s and early 2000s, there is still some debate about the link between opioid use and labor market outcomes.[18] Although there is a correlation between high opioid use and low employment rates (Krueger 2017), there is little work interpreting causation. As labor market conditions worsen, and workers see their wages and employment prospects decline, the associated reduction in their well-being might induce an increased demand for opioids. On the other hand, local shocks to opioid demand, which presumably reduce worker productivity and reliability, might make firms unwilling to hire in a particular area.

Did local adverse shocks to manufacturing increase opioid use in the area? To address this question, we use data from the US CDC that tracks the amount of per capita opioids prescribed by doctors at both county and state levels. The data are provided at the level of morphine milligram equivalents (MME), which allows for a comparison of different opioid prescriptions in similar units of potency.[19] Figure 19 graphically represents the amount of opioids prescribed (in MME) per 1,000 individuals, separately by commuting zones. The darker areas show a higher per-capita prescription rate.[20] The figure shows that opioid prescriptions were much higher in the West, Midwest, and Southeast—the latter two being places that experienced particularly large reductions in manufacturing employment.

The simple scatter plot in figure 20 shows that there is a large, statistically significant relationship between the log of MME prescribed per

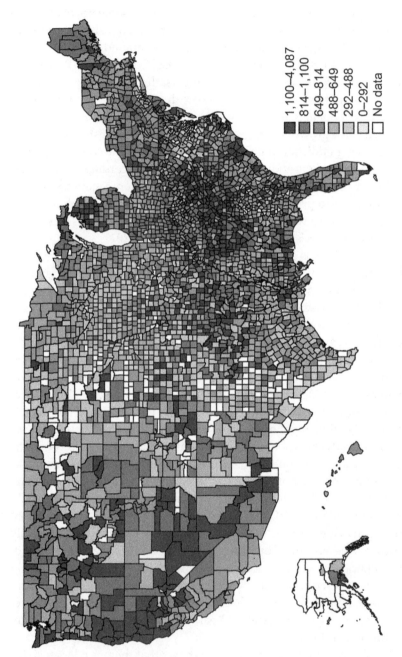

Fig. 19. MME prescribed per capita, 2015. Each observation is a US commuting zone

1,100–4,087
814–1,100
649–814
488–649
292–488
0–292
No data

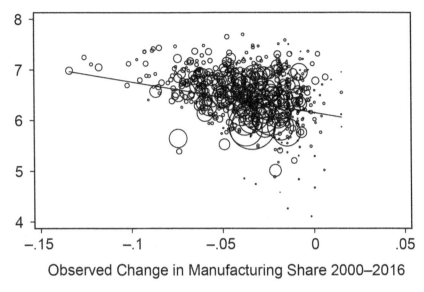

Observed Change in Manufacturing Share 2000–2016

○   Ln Morphine Milligram Equivalents Prescribed per Capita, 2015
──────   Fitted Line

Fig. 20.   Observed change in manufacturing share of population between 2000 and 2016 and log per capita MME prescriptions in 2015. Each circle represents a commuting zone, and the size of the circle represents the commuting zone population in 2000. The weighted regression line is shown. The estimated coefficient is –6.02 with a robust standard error of 1.67.

1,000 individuals in the commuting zone in 2015 and the change in the commuting zone's manufacturing share between 2000 and 2016. A 5.7-percentage-point decline in a commuting zone's manufacturing share (the 90–10 difference) is associated with a 34-log-point increase in MME prescribed per 1,000 individuals—an economically very large effect. Systematically, the commuting zones with the largest declines in the share of workers in the manufacturing sector are the commuting zones with the largest amounts of opioid prescriptions.

Column 1 of table 5 shows the response of log MME prescribed in commuting zone k in 2015 as a function of the change in the commuting zone's manufacturing share of prime-age workers between 2000 and 2016 (ΔMan_{t+1}^{k}), as well as controls for the commuting zone's age distribution.[21] We control for the age distribution in the commuting zone to account for the fact that older residents are more likely to be issued prescription medication. The top panel of the table presents OLS results. In the bottom panel, we present TSLS results, which instrument for ΔMan_{t+1}^{k} using the shift-share instrument discussed above. The TSLS results suggest

Table 5
OLS and IV Regressions of Opioid Use on Manufacturing Decline

	Opioid Prescriptions per Capita 2015	Opioid Prescriptions per Capita 2015	Δ Drug Deaths per 1,000	Δ Opioid Deaths per 1,000	Positive Drug Test Rate 2012–16
	(1)	(2)	(3)	(4)	(5)
OLS:					
Coefficient on ΔMan_{t+1}^k	−4.06	−8.69	−3.39	−2.31	−26.6
	(1.29)	(2.76)	(1.44)	(1.00)	(5.67)
R^2	.33	.42	.16	.14	.30
IV:					
Coefficient on ΔMan_{t+1}^k	−3.54	−8.67	−4.05	−2.20	−27.06
	(1.66)	(3.02)	(1.60)	(1.15)	(8.26)
R^2	.33	.42	.15	.14	.30
Unit of observation	Commuting zone	Zone	State	State	State
Sample size	724	51	47	45	51

Note: Table shows the response of various measures of opioid use to changes in the manufacturing share. Col. 1 examines cross-commuting zone variation in opioid prescriptions in 2015. Specifically, we use a measure of MME prescribed per capita as compiled by the US CDC. In col. 2, we aggregate the prescription data to the state level and perform a cross-state analysis. In cols. 3 and 4, we measure cross-state variation in the age-adjusted change in drug deaths and opioid deaths per 1,000 individuals between pooled 1999–2003 years and pooled 2012–16 years. In col. 5, we measure the fraction of drug tests that are failed at the state level pooled over the 2012–16 years. In cols. 1, 2, and 5, we include controls for the location's age distribution in 2000. In all specifications, we instrument the change in manufacturing share between 2000 and 2016 with our shift-share instrument. Robust standard errors are shown in parentheses.

that opioid prescription use in 2015 (as measured by MME) is about 20 log points higher in the commuting zone at tenth percentile of the manufacturing decline distribution relative to the commuting zone at the ninetieth percentile (0.057×-3.54).

Column 2 shows the cross-state relationship between opioid prescriptions and the decline in the manufacturing share.[22] Comparing the commuting-zone results in column 1 with the state-level results in column 2 shows that aggregating to the state level yields a stronger estimated relationship between 2015 opioid prescriptions and the change in local manufacturing shares. According to the state regressions, a 5.7-percentage-point decline in the state-level manufacturing share (the 90–10 difference) would increase local opioid prescriptions per 1,000 individuals by about 49 log points. These findings are consistent with deteriorating labor market conditions leading to higher opioid use. It appears that in places with declining demand for manufacturing workers, doctors prescribe more opioids, presumably to meet patient demand. Collectively, these results suggests that some of the opioid increase stems from weak labor market conditions resulting from the decline in labor demand.

A limitation of the results above is that the data on which they are based only allow us to estimate how the level of prescription opioid use varies with the change in manufacturing employment. Therefore, there may be a concern that the level of latent opioid demand was already higher in places where manufacturing declined the most. To further explore the relationship between deteriorating manufacturing employment and increased drug use, we use two additional measures from the CDC that track changes in per capita drug overdose deaths. The first measure tracks all drug overdose deaths, and the second measures only tracks deaths from opioid drug overdoses.[23]

Because the CDC suppresses drug overdose counts in counties with few overdose deaths, there are many counties with missing information. Given this, we explore the relationship between increased drug overdose deaths and manufacturing decline using state-level variation. To do so, we use age-adjusted drug and opioid overdose deaths per 1,000 individuals provided at the state level by the CDC.[24] Our dependent variable is the change in age-adjusted death rates for each state per 1000 individuals between 1999–2003 (averaged across years at state level) and 2012–16 (averaged across years at the state level). Figure 21 shows a simple scatter plot of the relationship between the percentage-point change in age-adjusted per capita drug overdoses during the 2000s and our measure of the decline in state level manufacturing share between 2000 and 2016. As seen from the figure, there is a strong statistically significant relationship between declining manufacturing employment and increasing death rates from drug overdose.

Columns 3 and 4 of table 5 show the OLS and IV estimates of the effect of declining manufacturing employment on both increased drug overdose deaths and increased opioid drug overdose deaths. For every 1-percentage-point decline in the manufacturing employment share of prime-age workers between 2000 and 2016, drug and opioid death rates per 1,000 individuals increased by 0.04 and 0.02, respectively, during the same time period. The mean drug overdose rate and opioid overdose rate per 1,000 in the pooled 1999–2003 years was 0.10 and 0.06, respectively, for the United States as a whole. For the pooled 2011–15 years, the national mean drug overdose rate and opioid overdose rate were 0.25 and 0.16, re-

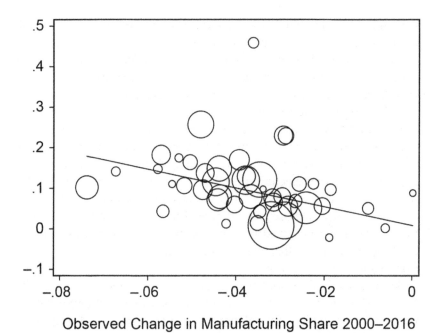

Observed Change in Manufacturing Share 2000–2016

Fig. 21. State-level variation in observed change in the manufacturing share of population between 2000 and 2016 and the change in per capita opioid overdose death rates between the early 2000s (1999–2003 pooled) and the late 2000s (2011–15 pooled). Each circle represents a US state, and the size of the circle represents the state population in 2000. The weighted regression line is shown. The estimated coefficient is –2.31 with a robust standard error of 1.00.

spectively. Our cross-region estimates are large relative to the time-series trends in aggregate death rates. Without more structure it is hard to extrapolate the cross-region estimates to the aggregate, yet the results in table 5 suggest that declining manufacturing demand—potentially through weakening employment conditions—had a role in increased opioid deaths at the aggregate level.

Our results complement recent analysis by Krueger (2017). Krueger documented that opioid prescriptions are higher in counties where employment rates have fallen the most. He interpreted access to opioids as being an important causal factor explaining why employment rates in the United States have fallen during the 2000s. His analysis controlled for initial manufacturing share when documenting the cross-county relationship between opioid prescriptions and declining employment rates. Our results suggest that declining manufacturing demand might partly explain why opioid use has increased during the 2000s. The shift-share instrument isolates arguably exogenous reductions in manufacturing labor demand in local areas. We find that opioid use rose the most in precisely those places that experienced the biggest exogenous adverse shocks to manufacturing, suggesting that weak labor demand could be a factor contributing to the rising opioid epidemic in the United States during the 2000s. This conclusion is consistent with findings from Pierce and Schott (2017) and from Autor et al. (2018), who showed that commuting zones that experienced greater manufacturing trade shocks had more deaths due to drugs and alcohol among 20- to 39-year-old men by 2015.[25]

The results thus far leave open the question of which persons in the community increase their drug use when jobs disappear. It might be persons who lose work or family members whose income falls when breadwinners are displaced. Similarly, the results shown thus far do not distinguish between increased use for persons who will be seeking jobs and those who will not. To the extent that current or future job-seekers are led to use drugs because of an adverse shock to well-being when their labor market opportunities worsen, even temporary well-being shocks might lead to future reductions in employment if job-seekers who become addicted to drugs find it difficult to find a new job or to acquire the skills necessary to fill open jobs. In other words, opioid use, manufacturing loss, and employment might be connected through employment hysteresis.

How does manufacturing decline affect drug use among people currently working or looking for work? To answer this question, we examine the incidence of positive results on drug tests given by employers to current and potential workers. We use novel data from Quest Diagnostics. Quest Diagnostics is a private company that performs and analyzes a number of health and wellness programs for employers. Among the services provided to employers is drug testing of existing and potential employees. Using their data, Quest Diagnostics (2017, 2018) puts out a Drug Testing Index that measures the fraction of their urine-based drug tests resulting in a positive result. Underlying the Drug Testing Index are millions of individual drug tests. In 2016 alone, Quest Diagnostics performed about 9 million urine-based drug tests on existing and potential employees. Although the sample is large, there are two potential selection issues with their data. First, the data are limited to only current and prospective employees of the firms that contract with Quest Diagnostics. To the extent that there is selection in these firms, this could make their Drug Testing Index not nationally representative. For example, Quest has a large sample of firms that are federally mandated to drug test their employees (e.g., pilots, truck drivers, workers in nuclear power plants, etc.). Second, within a given firm, not all drug tests are random. Although many firms test all potential employees prior to starting an employment relationship or randomly drug test existing employees, firms also drug test employees for cause. According to the Quest data, employees drug tested for cause have a probability of a positive drug test that is five times higher than a typical new employee. When compiling their Drug Testing Index, Quest pools together the results of potential new employees, randomly tested existing employees, and existing employees tested for cause.

Despite these caveats, we think it is interesting to use the data to explore both time-series and cross-region trends in their Drug Testing Index. In terms of units, the index measures the fraction of potential or existing employees with a positive drug test.[26] According to the Quest data, the propensity to fail a drug test has increased steadily since after the Great Recession. In 2010, 3.5% of their sample had a positive drug test. By 2016, the positive drug test rate increased to 4.2%. The increase was most pronounced in positive tests for marijuana, amphetamines, and opioids.

Since 2007, Quest has published state-level measures of the Drug Testing Index on their web page. Given that the data are only available from 2007 onwards, we cannot do a long difference to explore changes in the propensity for a positive drug test. Instead, we only explore the relationship between current propensity to have a positive drug test and the decline in the manufacturing share between 2000 and 2016. To average out potential noise in the index, we pool together the state-level Drug Testing Index over the 5-year period between 2012 and 2016. Figure 22 shows the relationship between the state-level Drug Testing Index (averaged between 2012 and 2016) and the change in the state-level manufacturing share for prime-age workers between 2000 and 2016 ($\Delta \ln Man_{i+1}^{k}$). The figure shows that states that experienced large declines in their manufacturing shares between 2000 and 2016 were much more likely to be home to a failed drug test in the 2012–16 period. According to the simple scatter plot, a 5.7-percentage-point decline in the manufacturing share (the 90–10 difference) is associated with a 1.5-percentage-point increase in the probability of failing an employer-provided drug test ($p < 0.01$). Given the base probability of testing positive for drugs is about 4%, the findings suggest an economically large relationship between manufacturing decline and the probability of testing positive for drugs.

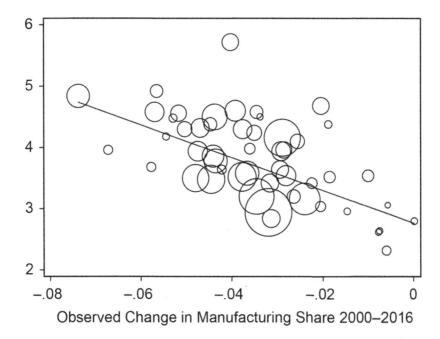

Fig. 22. Average drug test positivity rate by state between 2012 and 2016 and observed change in the manufacturing share of the population between 2000 and 2016. Circle size indicates state population in 2000. The slope on the linear fit is −26.7 (robust standard error = 6.2).

Column 5 of table 5 shows more causal estimates. The results in column 5 are analogous to column 2 of the table except that the dependent variable is the state-level Drug Testing Index (pooled over the years 2012–6). Like the results in column 2, we also control for the state's age distribution in 2000. Focusing on the TSLS results, a 5.7-percentage-point decline in the manufacturing share results in a 1.5-percentage-point increase in the propensity to have a positive drug test.

On the whole, our results strongly suggest that local well-being losses associated with job and wage reductions from local manufacturing decline led to greater opioid use and increased drug and opioid deaths at the local level. Although some of this increased use might have been among others in the community, it seems that workers and job-seekers accounted for some of the increased use, based on the results of drug test firms conduct on their workers. The latter finding raises the possibility that workers hurt by manufacturing decline, who salve the negative shock to their well-being by using drugs, may confront worse employment prospects in the future than they would have otherwise.

V.   Why Is There a Persistent Employment Effect?

The fact that the adverse employment effects from the decline in manu-facturing have lasted as long as they have is both striking and puzzling. Different sectors, including manufacturing before the 2000s, have rou-tinely grown and declined in the economy, yet various mediating mech-anisms ensure that affected workers generally do not have lowered em-ployment prospects many years after the initial dislocation. We have noted that the adverse employment effects might be different for a de-cline in the importance of manufacturing employment arising from the sector shedding jobs (as it has been since 2000) versus the sector becom-ing relatively smaller because employment rose in the economy overall (as was true in the 1980s and 1990s). Leaving aside this difference be-tween the 2000s and the prior period, it is clear that some traditional me-diating mechanisms have not worked, or else were not large enough, for post-2000 manufacturing change. For example, our local labor market shows that many workers of a given skill level who lost their jobs in man-ufacturing did not get jobs requiring the same skill in another industry in their same locality. Had this traditional mechanism of adjustment worked well, we would not have estimated negative within-location, within-skill employment effects from manufacturing decline. In this section, we pro-vide some evidence about the operation and importance of three other mediating mechanisms: public and private insurance, skill mismatch, and mobility.

A.   Disability and Private Transfers

One mediating mechanism that might be expected to affect the speed at which workers transition from job losses associated with sectoral de-cline is the availability of alternative sources of income to replace lost earnings because of nonwork. To the extent that workers are insured against earnings losses, from public or private sources, their transitions out of nonwork might be slowed. How important has public and private insurance been for affected workers since 2000?

Recent scholarship has argued that reduced labor demand for less educated workers has led to increased disability take-up.[27] Autor et al. (2013) use regional variation in the exposure to their Chinese import com-petition shock to show that declining manufacturing shares in a local area results in higher government transfers to that local area during the early 2000s. Using this previous work as motivation, we examine changes in government transfer take-up over the 2000s in response to our broader manufacturing changes. We measure the extent to which increased receipt of government transfers is associated with the dramatic decline in employment in response to declining manufacturing during the 2000s. We conclude that if the receipt of government transfers contributed to the low employment rates of prime-age workers during this period, its effect was most likely small.

We use our Census/ACS sample to conduct this analysis. From these data, we know whether individuals receive Supplemental Security Income (SSI) inclusive of Social Security Disability Insurance (SSDI) income. For persons in the age range we studied, essentially all of this income is SSDI associated with disability or blindness. Table 6 examines the fraction of individuals receiving SSI/SSDI income for various sex and age demographic groups. We split our sample into a younger group (aged 21–40) and an older group (aged 41–55). The age split allows us to compare labor market patterns between groups that are more likely to receive disability income (the older group) and less likely to receive disability income (the younger group).

The first two columns of table 6 show the fraction of each group receiving SSI/SSID income in 2000 and 2016. The third and fourth columns show similar statistics for nonworking members of each group. There are four key facts from table 6. First, only between 1% and 4% of all prime-age persons receive SSI/SSDI benefits in either 2000 or 2016.

Table 6

Share Receiving SSI/SSDI Income Received 2000 and 2016, by Demographic Group

	SSI/SSDI All		SSI/SSDI Nonworking	
	2000	2016	2000	2016
Age	(1)	(2)	(3)	(4)
Men:				
21–40	.01	.02	.06	.10
41–55	.02	.03	.10	.16
Women:				
21–40	.01	.02	.04	.06
41–55	.03	.04	.08	.11

Note: Table shows the share of individuals by age and sex that received SSI inclusive of SSDI income in 2000 and 2016. Cols. 1 and 2 do not restrict the sample based on employment status, whereas cols. 3 and 4 restrict the sample to nonworking individuals.

Second, the propensity to receive SSI/SSDI benefits is much lower for younger individuals relative to older individuals. Third, all four sex-age groups increased their propensity to receive SSI/SSDI benefits between 2000 and 2016. Fourth, and most importantly, most young and old non-working individuals did not receive SSI/SSDI benefits in either 2000 or 2016. For example, only 10% of younger, nonworking men and 16% of older, nonworking men received SSI benefits in 2016. Collectively, the table shows that the receipt of SSI/SSDI benefits is relatively rare among nonworking prime-age individuals.

Although rare, it is possible that SSI/SSDI benefits could explain a portion of the decline in employment rates in the 2000s. As seen from table 6, SSI/SSDI receipt has increased by 1 percentage point nationally for all prime-age sex groups between 2000 and 2016. Employment rates have fallen by about 4 percentage points for both younger and older men during this period. At most, increased access to disability could explain one quarter of declining employment rates for prime-age men during this period. There is an upper limit given that these aggregate relationships do not imply that access to disability caused declining employment.

Table 7 uses the cross-region variation exploited previously in the paper to more carefully assess how the change in the fraction of a group receiving SSI/SSDI/SSDI payments during the 2000s responds to changes in the manufacturing share. Specifically, we reestimate equation (1) with the dependent variable being the change in share of each demographic group within a commuting zone receiving SSI/SSDI benefits between 2000 and 2016 (col. 1) and reestimate the change in the share of the demographic group employed within a commuting zone between 2000 and 2016 (col. 2). Each entry in the table is the coefficient on the change in the manufacturing share in the commuting zone between 2000 and 2016 from different regression. The various regressions differ by dependent variable and demographic group. We only show the TSLS estimates where we instrument for ΔMan_{t+1}^k with S_{t+1}^k.

Column 1 of the table shows that manufacturing decline does raise SSI/SSDI receipt. For every 10-percentage-point decline in the manufacturing share, SSI/SSDI receipt by younger men, older men, and younger women increases by between 0.5 and 0.8 percentage point. There is no statistically significant effect on SSI/SSDI receipt for older women. These results are consistent with the findings reported by Autor et al. (2013), showing that manufacturing decline driven by increased import competition from China resulted in an increased take-up of public transfers during the early 2000s. However, table 7 also highlights why it is very unlikely

Table 7
IV Regression of Changing SSI/SSDI Receipt and
Changing Employment Rates to Changes in
Manufacturing Share 2000–2017, by Sex-Age Groups

Age	Δ Share Receiving SSI/SSDI, 2000–16	Δ Employment Rate, 2000–16
	(1)	(2)
Men:		
21–40	−.08	.40
	(.02)	(.10)
40–55	−.05	.35
	(.03)	(.07)
Women:		
21–40	−.06	.27
	(.02)	(.11)
40–55	.00	.30
	(.03)	(.08)
Sample size	741	741

Note: Table shows the coefficients from a regression of changes in the share of individuals receiving SSI/SSDI transfers (col. 1) or changes in employment rate between t and $t+1$ by age and sex on $\Delta \ln Man^k_{t+1}$ (col. 2) instrumented with S^k_{t+1}. Each observation is a commuting zone. All regressions include our base set of additional controls. Robust standard errors are in parenthesis.

that increased SSI/SSDI participation is a dominant driver of persistently low employment rates. Column 2 shows the change in the employment rate during the 2000s in response to the declining manufacturing share for the different demographic groups. The response of the change in the employment rate is roughly 5 to 7 times larger than the response of the change in SSI/SSDI take-up rate. This suggests SSI/SSDI participation could explain at most 15% –20% of the persistent decline in employment during the 2000s. We conclude that access to SSI/SSDI is at best only a small part of the story of why employment rates have remained low as manufacturing employment has declined during the 2000s.

Apart from any public source, workers displaced from manufacturing might also receive insurance against earnings losses from private sources, especially in the form of different types of assistance from friends and loved ones. Moving in with relatives might be one such form of assistance. Aguiar et al. (2017) documented that there has been a dramatic shift in the propensity for young individuals (those aged 21–30) to live with their parents or another close relative during the 2000s. For example, they found that roughly 30% of young men lived with a parent or close relative in 2000. By 2015, 45% of young men reported living with a parent or close relative. Given these time-series trends, we explored whether the propensity for young individuals to cohabitate with their parents or other close relatives increased more in places that experienced a larger declining in the manufacturing share during the 2000s. The results suggest that cohabitation patterns of 21- to 30-year-olds are not systematically related to declining manufacturing employment. The results of a regression of the change in the propensity to live with a parent between 2000 and 2015 by younger households on the decline in the manufacturing share in our base TSLS specification suggest that cohabitation patterns are not systematically related to declining manufacturing employment.[28] Based on this important measure of family support, we think that private insurance via cohabitation is not a first-order explanation for why declining manufacturing employment is leading to persistent declines in employment rates for young workers.

B.   Changes in Skill Composition of the Manufacturing Sector

A mechanism by which workers can adjust to sectoral transformation would be a switch to new jobs, either in their former sector or a new one. A factor that might act as a brake on the smooth operation of this adjustment mechanism, and lead to persistently lower employment, is if workers affected by sectoral transformation of the sort that occurred in manufacturing in the 2000s lack the requisite skills for work in either their transformed former sector or in another new sector. How important a role has this played in explaining the persistent employment losses we document?

The possible importance of "skill mismatch" has appeared frequently in the popular press in recent years (see, e.g., Davidson 2014; Elejalde-Ruiz 2016; Sussman 2016). Proponents of the view that rising skill mismatch is a primary driver of increasing labor market effects of manufacturing decline see evidence in support of their hypothesis in the sharp increase in the job opening rate for the manufacturing sector during the 2000s. The job opening rate is measured as the number of job openings in a given industry divided by the sum of employment in that industry and the number of job openings in that industry. We used data from the US Bureau of Labor Statistics (2019a) Job Opening and Labor Turnover Survey (JOLTS) to create table 8. This table documents the trend in the job opening rate for the total US economy and for various

Table 8
Job Opening Rate by Industry, 2001–2017

| | 2001 Rate | 2017 Rate | Change in Rate | Log Difference |
	(1)	(2)	(3)	(4)
All industries	3.32	4.16	.85	.23
Manufacturing	1.84	3.08	1.24	.52
Retail trade	2.66	3.80	1.14	.36
Professional services	3.98	4.97	.99	.22
FIRE	3.53	4.25	.72	.19
Leisure/hospitality	4.49	4.82	.33	.07
Construction	2.53	2.69	.17	.06
Education/health	4.63	4.74	.10	.02

Source: Data downloaded directly from the US Bureau of Labor Statistics (2019a) Job Opening and Labor Turnover Survey.
Note: To make yearly measures, we take the simple average of monthly observations over the year. For col. 3, the change in rate is defined as the simple difference between the 2017 and 2001 job opening rate. For col. 4, the log difference is defined as the difference in the log job opening rate in 2017 relative to the log job opening rate in 2000.

industries between 2001 and 2017.[29] As the table shows, the job opening rate has increased for the economy as a whole as well as for each broad industry. However, between the early 2000s and 2017, the largest increase in the job opening rate (in both absolute changes and percentage changes) was in the manufacturing sector. The job opening rate in manufacturing nearly doubled during the 2000s from an initial rate of 1.8% to the current rate of 3.1%.

The most obvious potential explanation for the increased job opening rate in the US economy is that it has become cheaper to post job openings. However, skill mismatch is an alternative explanation. In addition to firms posting more vacancies because it is now cheaper to do so, skill mismatch would cause the vacancies that firms post to stay unfilled longer because of the difficulty of finding qualified workers. The available information on job openings data does not allow us to distinguish between these two explanations. However, it is interesting to note that the job opening rate has grown the most (in both levels and percentage change) within the manufacturing industry. As there is no particular reason to suppose that it is somehow harder to post a job in manufacturing than in other sectors, this fact is consistent with job mismatch being more important for manufacturing than for other sectors in the economy. Construction is another sector that employs less educated men. Notice that the job finding rate in construction has not increased that much during the 2000s.

To further explore the potential for skill mismatch in the manufacturing industry during the 2000s, table 9 looks at the educational composition of the manufacturing sector over this time period. Our measure of educational composition is the share of workers who have at least a bachelor's degree within the industry. To illustrate the educational composition of the manufacturing sector over time, we use our CPS sample (IPUMS 2019a). To facilitate exposition, we focus on men between the ages of 25 and 29. The age restriction is imposed to look at workers post bachelor's degree but still young enough to be responsive to changing industry level skill demands. Given the narrow age range, we pool our CPS data over 4-year intervals between 1998–2001 (starting period) and 2013–17 (ending period). We show results for all men aged 25–29 (row 1) as well as men working in the manufacturing, retail trade, and construction industries. These three industries employ 45% of all working 25- to 29-year-olds and 57% of all working 25- to 29-year-olds with a high school degree or less in the 1998–2001 period. We pool data over the 1998–2001 samples (col. 1) and the 2014–17 samples (col. 2).

We would like to highlight three results from table 9. First, young men working in manufacturing, retail trade, and construction tend to be relatively less skilled compared with young men in the economy overall. In all periods, the share of men aged 25–29 with bachelor's degrees overall is higher than the proportion of 25- to 29-year-olds in these three industries who have college degrees. Second, young men in these sectors, as in the economy overall, became more skilled during 2000s, as least as measured by those with bachelor's degrees. Finally, the manufacturing sector has experienced the largest increase in the share of young men with a bachelor's degree or more over this time period compared with retail

Table 9
Percentage Bachelor's Degree or More by Industry Over Time, Men Aged 25–29

Men Aged 25–29	1998–2001 Share	2014–7 Share	Change in Share
All	26.5	31.9	5.4
Working in manufacturing	21.1	26.6	5.5
Working in retail trade	16.4	19.9	3.5
Working in construction	8.7	12.1	3.5

Source: Data from our CPS sample (IPUMS 2019a).
Note: We use the 1990 industry classification to define the manufacturing, retail trade, and construction industries. Table shows the share of men aged 25–29 with at least a bachelor's degree in the total population (row 1), working in the manufacturing industry (row 2), working in the retail trade industry (row 3), and working in the construction industry (row 4) in different years.

trade and construction. In the early 2000s, one in five younger workers in manufacturing had a bachelor's degree. By 2017, one in four workers in manufacturing had a bachelor's degree. The 5.5-percentage-point increase in the bachelor's degree share was larger than the increase in either retail trade or construction. In addition, it was on par with the increase in the bachelor's degree share for the population as a whole. Again, these results provide some additional evidence that the manufacturing sector is becoming more skilled relative to other industries historically populated by less educated workers such as construction and retail trade during the 2000s.

Collectively, the above results suggest a potential role for skill mismatch in explaining the sluggish response of employment to local manufacturing labor demand during the 2000s. Whereas many formerly lower-skilled sectors attracted more educated workers during the 2000s and job opening rates have increased in all sectors during the 2000s, the increases have been largest in the manufacturing sector. This is consistent with the substantial capital deepening that took place in the manufacturing sector during this time period. Overall, we conclude that skill mismatch can potentially explain some of the sluggish response of employment rates to declining employment needs in the manufacturing sector. Displaced manufacturing workers may not have the skills to fill the jobs currently available in their former sector. However, future work needs to be done to assess how quantitatively important this mechanism is relative to other mechanisms.[30] If the skill mismatch hypothesis is quantitatively important, it suggests that policies to promote the manufacturing sector may not substantively increase employment rates among less educated men.

C. Regional Mobility

A final mediating mechanism for adjustment to regional shocks of the sort that occurred in manufacturing during the 2000s is cross-region migration. If a region experiences a decline in labor demand relative to other areas, its residents may be more likely to out-migrate and people from other areas may be less likely to in-migrate. Both the increased out-migration and the reduced in-migration will lower the number of potential workers in the affected region to shrink. Because of cross-region migration, declining local labor demand shocks can lead to declining local labor supply. As local labor supply responds to declining local labor demand, equilibrium wage and employment responses are muted.

This is the mechanism at the heart of the seminal work of Blanchard and Katz (1992).

It is well documented that cross-region migration rates have fallen sharply in the United States over time. For example, Molloy, Smith, and Wozniak (2011) used data from the CPS, the Census/ACS, and the Internal Revenue Service to show that cross-region migration rates have consistently declined over the past 35 years. Although the magnitudes of the declines differed across the surveys, all three surveys showed declining interstate mobility in the US since 1980. Kaplan and Schulhofer-Wohl (2017) further explored the decline in cross-region mobility in the United States. Using data from the CPS, they found that for individuals between the ages of their early 20s and 55, annual interstate mobility rates had fallen from about 4% in 1990 to under 2% in 2011. Dao, Furceri, and Loungani (2017) found that interstate mobility in response to local labor demand shocks has been declining since the early 1990s, and Autor et al. (2014) found that workers in trade-exposed areas in 1994 do not increase employment or earnings in other commuting zones, suggesting that they do not shift labor supply across geographic areas. Not only are individuals moving across regions less over time, but they are also less likely to move across regions in response to relative changes in labor market conditions. Declining cross-area mobility and a reduced mobility response to local labor demand shocks might explain, in part, why local sectoral shocks in the 2000s are more likely to result in declining employment rates.

On the surface, the persistent employment effects we find for the manufacturing changes in the 2000s are strongly consistent with the greatly reduced role of the mediating mechanism of mobility. To explore this declining mobility hypothesis further, we examine how manufacturing declines in the 1980s affected employment rates during that time period and then compare cross-regional mobility in the earlier period to the 2000s. We proceed in two parts. First, we redo our cross-region analysis on the link between manufacturing decline and labor market outcomes for the 1980–90 period. As seen from figures 12 and 13, employment shares in manufacturing declined steadily during the 1980s. Figure 23 shows the shift-share instrument defined for the 1980s also has strong predictive power during the 1980–90 period.[31] Specifically, predicted manufacturing decline based on initial manufacturing shares and national trends between 1980 and 1990 are strongly predictive of actual manufacturing shares at the commuting zone level between 1980 and 1990. The scatter plot shows that the shift-share instrument predicts changes in the com-

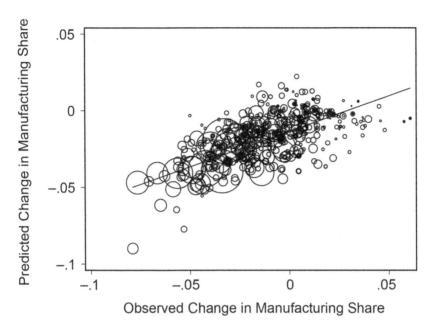

Fig. 23. Relationship between the predicted change in the manufacturing share between 1980 and 1990 and the observed change. The change is predicted using our shift-share instrument and local area baseline controls. Each observation is a commuting zone. The size of the circle reflects the size of the 1980 prime-age population in each commuting zone. The slope of the weighted regression line of the scatter plot is .46 with a robust standard error of .03.

muting zone's manufacturing share in the 1980s as well as the 2000s version does for the recent period ($R^2 = 0.46$, $F = 188.03$).

Row 1 of table 10 shows our IV estimates of manufacturing decline on employment rates of prime-age men and women during the 2000–16 period (col. 1) and during the 1980–2000 period (col. 2). The column 1 results in row 1 are analogous to those in table 2, except in this table we pool together men and women for ease of exposition. As before, during the 2000s, a 10-percentage-point decline in the manufacturing share reduced prime-age employment rates by 3.4 percentage points. The patterns during the 1980s are quite different. In column 2, we show that a decline in the local manufacturing share had no statistically significant effect on local employment rates. During the 1980s, there was essentially no persistent effect of manufacturing decline on local employment rates.[32]

To examine whether differential mobility patterns may have contributed to the differential findings between the 1980s and today, we esti-

Table 10
IV Response of Change in Log Population to Change Manufacturing Share
Over Time, Individuals Aged 21–55

	2000–16	1980–90
Dependent Variable	(1)	(2)
Δ employment rate	.34	−.14
	(.07)	(.10)
Δ ln Pop_{t+1}^{k}	.87	3.84
	(.45)	(1.04)
Standard controls	Yes	Yes
Sample size	741	741

Note: The first row of the table shows the coefficient on predicted manufacturing decline from a regression of changes in the employment rate between t and $t + 1$ to
$\Delta \ln Man_{t+1}^{k}$ instrumented with S_t^k and additional controls. The second row of the table
shows the coefficient on predicted manufacturing decline from a regression of changes
in log population between t and $t+1$ to $\Delta \ln Man_{t+1}^{k}$ instrumented with S_t^k and additional
controls. Each observation is a commuting zone. The results in col. 1 use $t = 2000$ and $t +
1 = 2016$, and the results in col. 2 use $t = 1980$ and $t + 1 = 1990$. All regressions include
our base set of additional controls, and the population change regressions additionally
include census division fixed effects. Robust standard errors are in parentheses.

mate the following regressions on both our 1980–2000 and 2000–16 samples:

$$\Delta \ln Pop_{t+1}^{k} = \alpha + \beta \Delta Man_{t+1}^{k} + \Gamma X_t^k + \epsilon_{t+1}^k, \tag{8}$$

where $\ln Pop_t^k$ is the log of all individuals between the ages of 21 and 55
living in k in period t and $\Delta \ln Pop_{t+1}^k$ is the change in $\ln Pop^k$ between periods t and $t+1$. As above, we instrument ΔMan_{t+1}^k using our time-period-
specific shift-share instrument. This regression is analogous to the regressions in table 2 except that the dependent variable is the change in
prime-age population rather than the change in labor market outcomes.
When estimating regression 8, we follow the lead of Autor et al. (2013)
and control for census division fixed effects, in additional to the same
X^k vector of controls in the models presented in table 2. Given the secular
shifts in population from the Northeast and Midwest to the southern and
western states during the last half century, one needs to include such
controls when assessing the causal relationship between manufacturing
decline and changes in population.

The second row of table 10 presents the estimation results for regression (8). The table shows that a 1-percentage-point change in the manufacturing share caused population to respond by only 0.87% over the
2000–16 period and by roughly 3.9% over the 1980–90 period. These re-

sults are consistent with the finding of Dao et al. (2017) showing that the population response to local labor market shocks is smaller in recent periods than it was in the 1980s. We also wish to note that the number of years over which the population is changing is not the same across the two regressions. Our 2000s regressions are over a 16-year period, whereas the 1980s regressions are over a 10-year period. If there is some sluggishness in the population response, a longer time period may allow for more population adjustments. However, if we annualized the coefficients, the differences between the 2000s and the 1980s became even more dramatic.[33] When we omit the census division controls, the same qualitative patterns emerge, in that manufacturing decline has a larger effect on population changes in the 1980s than it does in the 2000s.

These results suggest that declining cross-region mobility might, in fact, be an important reason for the large and persistent effects of manufacturing decline on employment rates during the 2000s compared with the 1980s. A question that arises immediately, however, is why mobility rates (and mobility in response to shocks) have fallen as much as they have. Although much more work needs to be one on this question, results from work by Molloy, Smith, and Wozniak (2014) indicate that reduced gains from job switching might be an especially key driver of these changes in mobility over time, compared with demographic factors like population aging or homeownership. Might these reduced gains workers receive from switching jobs, if true in manufacturing, be related to standardization of production processes through robotics or consolidation in firm ownership in the sector? If so, declining mobility would itself be a result of a change in the manufacturing sector rather than an explanation for why manufacturing reductions currently have larger employment effects than they once did. Questions of this sort remain to be answered before definitive conclusions can be drawn about the role of falling population mobility for the larger effect that manufacturing changes have on labor market outcomes today compared with the 1980s.

VI.   Discussion and Conclusion

Employment rates and annual hours worked have fallen substantially throughout the 2000–17 period. The declines have been most pronounced among those with lower levels of accumulated schooling. For example, prime-age men without a bachelor's degree are working more than 200 hours per year less than their counterparts in 2000. Much of this decline is due to individuals who have persistently left the labor market.

In this paper, we highlight the importance of the structural change in the manufacturing sector in explaining these patterns. Exploiting cross-region variation, we document that the persistent long-run decline in employment and hours for prime-age workers did not occur evenly across the United States. Furthermore, we document a strong cross-region correlation between declining manufacturing employment and declining employment rates of prime-age workers. Using a shift-share instrument, we find that a 10-percentage-point decline in the local manufacturing share reduced local employment rates by 3.7 percentage points for prime-age men and 2.7 percentage points for prime-age women. To put the magnitude in perspective, naively extrapolating the local estimates suggests that between one third and one half of the decline in employment rates and annual hours for prime-age workers can be attributed to the decline in the manufacturing sector. This naive estimate ignores many important general equilibrium effects that will certainly alter the exact quantitative magnitude. However, the naive results suggest that the decline of the manufacturing sector is a first-order factor in the depressed labor market outcomes for prime-age workers in the United States.

We present novel evidence showing how local manufacturing decline has adversely affected well-being. Using data from a variety of sources, we document that declining manufacturing employment is associated with increased prescription opioid use and increased death rates from drug overdoses. There is a growing literature suggesting that physician behavior is in part responsible for the opioid epidemic within the United States. Our results highlight how local economic conditions are interacting with these other potential causes of opioid behavior. These results suggest that a combination of both opioid supply and opioid demand are contributing to the rise in opioid use and opioid deaths during the 2000s.

One question is why the decline in the manufacturing sector is leading to persistent declines in employment rates. The US economy has experienced sector declines throughout its history, and the manufacturing sector itself has, at other periods, shed large numbers of jobs. Yet, rarely are the negative employment rate effects of these changes been as large or persistent—presumably because of various mediating mechanisms that, in general, might be expected to ease employment transitions. We present evidence relevant to the operation of three of these mediating mechanism during the 2000s: transfer receipt from public and private sources, skill mismatch and job finding, and regional migration. Our results suggest that whereas the other factors play some role in explaining long-term adverse employment outcomes from manufacturing loss, the reduced propensity of workers to move across regions is a striking feature of the data during recent periods relative to prior periods.

Our finding that opioid drug use has risen in areas hard-hit by manufacturing decline may have implications for future employment prospects in these areas. To the extent that these workers become addicted to drugs, which they might have taken in the first place because of the shock of a job loss, their likelihood of getting and retaining a job in the future will be lower. We know that employers are testing more for drug use and that the incidence of positive results on these tests is rising. Even if those individuals who are taking drugs want to find a job, employers may screen them out at the application phase.[34] Increased drug use in a local area arising from manufacturing job loss might itself lead to further reductions in employment. In other words, opioid use, manufacturing loss, and employment might be connected through employment hysteresis.

Finally, our results contribute to ongoing debates about policies concerning the manufacturing sector. There has been much recent discussion from policy makers about industrial, environmental, and trade policy—all with the aim of promoting employment in the manufacturing sector. This discussion appears to be based on the view that if policies like freer trade contributed to the decline in US manufacturing employment, restricting trade should cause lost manufacturing jobs to come back. As we have discussed, results from Pierce and Schott (2016), Autor et al. (2013), and Acemoglu et al. (2016) do indeed suggest that import competition has played an important role in the decline of US manufacturing employment during the 2000s.

However, our results also suggest that imposing trade barriers against the rest of the world is unlikely to substantially increase the employment prospects of workers with lower levels of accumulated schooling. For one thing, we have shown that the manufacturing sector is becoming increasingly highly skilled in terms of the education of the workers it hires. We have also shown that manufacturing has become much more capital intensive since 2000. Those manufacturing sectors that were most exposed to the trade shock from China actually experienced the largest declines in the labor share, suggesting that if they were to rebound they would do so with a much higher capital share relative to the early 2000s. Finally, the specific factories whose closings accounted for much of trade-related job loss during the 2000s were likely using "twentieth-century," more labor-intensive technology. Should trade barriers be erected, the new manufacturing plants created in the United States would almost surely use more capital-intensive, "twenty-first-century" technologies than the plants that were wiped out by trade shocks. Although certain policies to support the manufacturing sector (e.g., imposing tariffs on imports) may increase US manufacturing output, they will likely not have large effects on the employment rates of workers with lower levels of education.

Appendix

Capital intensity: The value of capital services relative to the value of hours worked in the production process.

Chinese import competition: The change in imports from China over the period 1999–2011, divided by initial absorption (measured as industry shipments plus industry imports minus industry exports; Acemoglu et al. 2016).

Manufacturing share: Also referred to as the "Manufacturing Share of the Population" and "Manufacturing to Population Ratio" and measured in the CPS, ACS, and Census. The manufacturing share is the ratio of the number of persons aged 21–55 in the relevant group working in manufacturing to the number of all such persons between 21 and 55, regardless of employment status. The data are weighted using survey weights provided in the relevant survey.

Demographically adjusted real wages at the commuting-zone level: We make wage measures by dividing annual labor earnings by annual hours worked for all individuals with positive labor earnings. We then compute average wages within each commuting zone. To adjust wages for demographic traits, we reweighted the 2016 sample to match the age, education, and gender distribution within each commuting zone in 2000, using 5-year age bins and three education groups. Finally, we compute the change in log demographically adjusted wages within each commuting zone.

Annual hours in the CPS: To create the annual hours measure, we multiply an individual's report of the number of weeks they worked during the prior calendar year by their report of usual hours worked per week. We then average the individual reports for annual hours worked over all prime-age males by year. Individuals who report not having worked at all during the prior year are assigned 0 hours. Given the CPS sample design, individuals from survey year t report their annual hours worked in survey year $t - 1$. Throughout the paper, we will refer to years in which hours were worked, not when they were reported. Thus, for CPS sample, hours worked in 1976 was reported by respondents in 1977.

Annual hours in the ACS: To create the annual hours measure in the ACS, we follow the same procedure as in the CPS, using intervalled weeks worked from 2000–16 because these are the only measure of weeks worked in the later years. Given the ACS sample design, individuals from survey year t report their annual hours worked in the previous 12 months. For this reason, we assign hours worked to the survey year, not the prior year as in the CPS.

Endnotes

We thank Mark Aguiar, David Autor, John Cochrane, Steve Davis, David Dorn, Bob Hall, Gordon Hanson, Matt Notowidigdo, Jonathan Parker, and seminar participants at the Hoover Policy Workshop for helpful comments. Authors' email addresses: Kerwin Kofi Charles (kerwin.charles@gmail.com), Erik Hurst (erik.hurst@chicagobooth.edu), and Mariel Schwartz (mes98@uchicago.edu). For acknowledgments, sources of research support, and disclosure of the authors' material financial relationships, if any, please see http://www.nber.org/chapters/c14081.ack.

1. Manufacturing decline has also attracted considerable attention recently. See, e.g., Quinones (2015) and Goldstein (2017).

2. We downloaded all CPS and the Census/ACS data directly from IPUMS (2019a, 2019b).

3. In 2000, prime-age men with at least a bachelor's degree worked 2,190 hours per year. The corresponding annual hours worked in 2000 for those with some college and those with a high school degree or less were 1,950 and 1,830 hours per year, respectively.

4. Excluding individuals enrolled full time in school has little effect on these time-series patterns.

5. There is a fair bit of heterogeneity across manufacturing subindustries with respect to output growth during the 2000s. Using data from the Bureau of Economic Analysis (2019), we measure annualized growth rates in real value added between 2000 and 2016 for each three-digit manufacturing subindustry. During this period, seven manufacturing subindustries had growth rates larger than 10%, another six had growth rates between –10% and 10%, and six had growth rates smaller than –10%. The largest positive growth rate was in "computer and electronic products" (more than 200% increase), whereas the largest contraction was in "apparel and leather and allied products" (more than 50% decline). Houseman, Bartik, and Sturgeon (2015) emphasize the importance of computer and electronic products in driving US manufacturing output growth during the 2000s.

6. For this analysis, we combine the Chinese import competition from Acemoglu et al. (2016) with data from the NBER-CES Manufacturing Industry Database (NBER 2016), which tracks employment by detailed manufacturing industry through 2011. See NBER (2016) for more details.

7. We define production workers as those with a 2010 occupation code over 6000.

8. During the 2000–17 period, roughly 60% of prime-age women working in manufacturing with less than a bachelor's degree worked in production occupations, compared with only 10% of prime-age women working in manufacturing with a bachelor's degree or more.

9. The time-series patterns in the Census/ACS and the CPS are nearly identical during this period.

10. We use the 2000 Census industry codes to define these 74 detailed manufacturing subindustries.

11. For examples of other papers that employ variants of this shift-share instrument, see Murphy and Topel (1987); Bartik (1991); Blanchard and Katz (1992); Bound and Holzer (2000); Charles et al. (2016, forthcoming); Autor et al. (2013); Acemoglu and Restrepo (2017); Goldsmith-Pinkham, Sorkin, and Swift (2017).

12. The tenth percentile of the actual decline in manufacturing shares across the 741 commuting zones was –0.065, whereas the ninetieth percentile was –0.008. Essentially all commuting zones experienced a decline in the manufacturing share of prime-age individuals during the 2000–16 period, with the mean decline of –0.034 and a standard deviation of 0.023.

13. As noted, for each demographic group, we defined the change in the manufacturing share in eq. (3) for all prime-age workers.

14. Some authors use detailed tables on input-output linkages to assess the spillover effects of declining local demand on other regions. Incorporating this general equilibrium force tends to amplify the aggregate effects relative to the naive calculation. For a discussion of these issues with respect to increased import competition from China, see, e.g., Acemoglu et al. (2016).

15. Recall, for example, our previous discussion showing that there was a correlation between technology adoption and capital deepening. Our approach would isolate the effect of trade and any the portion of technology correlated with trade.

16. We downloaded the import competition instrument directly from David Dorn's website (https://www.ddorn.net/data.htm).

17. Our examination of the link between opioid use and deteriorating local labor market conditions arising from broad manufacturing decline extends an emerging literature that studies the relationship between economic conditions and different measures of well-being. This literature includes the analysis of Case and Deaton (2017), documenting rising mortality rates for non-Hispanic whites, and recent work by Ruhm (2018), Currie, Jin, and Schnell (2018), Pierce and Schott (2017), and Autor, Dorn, and Hanson (2018), studying how local labor demand shocks affect drug use, suicide, or other social problems.

18. Laird and Nielsen (2016) exploit variation across doctors in Denmark to show that doctors with a higher propensity to prescribe opioids have patients with lower subsequent employment rates.

19. These data were also used by Krueger (2017).

20. Note that the CDC does not provide prescription data for all commuting zones. As a result, some parts of the map are blank.

21. Specifically, we include the three variables measuring the fraction of commuting zone residents between the ages of 21 and 40 in 2000, between 41 and 60 in 2000, and over 60 in 2000. We use the 2000 ACS to create these measures.

22. For this analysis, we recreate our measures of ΔMan_{t+1}^k and S_{t+1}^k at the state level using the Census/ACS data. As before, we exploit changes in the manufacturing share at the state level between 2000 and 2016.

23. The primary difference between the two measures are deaths associated from overdoses of cocaine and methamphetamines.

24. The CDC provides age-adjusted death rates given that different types of deaths (e.g., drug overdoses) occur with a higher frequency for some ages than others. Our results are nearly identical if we used the unadjusted drug overdose measures.

25. Currie et al. (2018) also examined the connection between labor market conditions and drug use, but found no evidence of a statistically significant relationship. Unlike our work and the findings from Pierce and Schott (2017) and Autor et al. (2018), which all examined changes in local drug use and local economic outcomes over longer time periods, Currie et al. (2018) exploited annual variation within a county. One reason for the difference between their results and the results in other recent papers could simply be that shocks to labor market conditions affect drug take-up with a lag that would be missed by exploiting high-frequency variation.

26. All data were manually collected from the information provided by Quest Diagnostics (2017).

27. For evidence, see, e.g., Autor and Duggan (2003) and Sloane (2017). The issue has also received attention in the popular press (Joffe-Walt 2013).

28. The full set of results is provided by the authors upon request.

29. The JOLTS data come monthly. For our yearly measures, we take the simple average of the monthly measures during the year.

30. Our results are broadly consistent with the recent findings of Weaver and Osterman (2017), who surveyed plant managers about their ability to hire qualified workers for their manufacturing facilities. Their survey evidence finds that while many manufacturers do not have trouble finding qualified workers, about one quarter of the manufacturers they surveyed may show signs of not being able to hire qualified workers.

31. We define our S_{t+1}^k variable for the 1980s analogously to the way we computed it for the 2000s.

32. These findings hold if we look at men and women separately or if we look at different skill groups by sex. In addition, our results are in line with the findings of Bound and Holzer (2000), who found demand shifts away from manufacturing had a small but significant effect on employment rates of men during during the 1970s and 1980s.

33. Our results contrast somewhat with the results of Autor et al. (2013), suggesting that the Chinese import shock did not have an effect on local population. In addition to using a broader source of variation, our sample period is over a much longer horizon. They examined patterns through 2007. We are looking at patterns through 2016. If migration is sluggish, the longer time period allows us to better uncover the sluggish population response to manufacturing decline.

34. In recent years, the popular press has reported that firms are struggling to hire workers who can pass a drug test (see, e.g., Calmes 2016).

References

Abraham, Katharine, and Melissa Kearney. 2018. "Explaining the Decline in the US Employment-to-Population Ratio: A Review of the Evidence." Working Paper no. 24333 (February), NBER, Cambridge, MA.

Acemoglu, Daron, David Autor, David Dorn, Gordon H. Hanson, and Brendan Price. 2016. "Import Competition and the Great US Employment Sag of the 2000s." *Journal of Labor Economics* 34 (S1): S141–S198.

Acemoglu, Daron, and Pascual Restrepo. 2017. "Robots and Jobs: Evidence from US Labor Markets." Working Paper no. 23285, NBER, Cambridge, MA.

Adão, Rodrigo, Costas Arkolakis, and Federico Esposito. 2019. "Spatial Linkages, Global Shocks, and Local Labor Markets: Theory and Evidence." Working Paper no. 25544, NBER, Cambridge, MA.

Aguiar, Mark, Mark Bils, Kerwin Kofi Charles, and Erik Hurst. 2017. "Leisure Luxuries and the Labor Supply of Young Men." Working Paper no. 23552, NBER, Cambridge, MA.

American Society of Addiction Medicine. 2016. "Opioid Addiction 2016 Facts and Figures." https://www.asam.org/docs/default-source/advocacy/opioid-addiction-disease-facts-figures.pdf.

Autor, David H., and Mark G. Duggan. 2003. "The Rise in the Disability Rolls and the Decline in Unemployment." *Quarterly Journal of Economics* 108 (1): 157–206.

Autor, David H., David Dorn, and Gordon H. Hanson. 2013. "The China Syndrome: Local Labor Market Effects of Import Competition in the United States." *American Economic Review* 103 (6): 2121–68.

———. 2015. "Untangling Trade and Technology: Evidence from Local Labour Markets." *Economic Journal* 125 (584): 621–46.

———. 2018. "When Work Disappears: Manufacturing Decline and the Falling Marriage Market Value of Young Men." Working Paper no. 23173, NBER, Cambridge, MA.

Autor, David H., David Dorn, Gordon H. Hanson, and Jae Song. 2014. "Trade Adjustment: Worker-Level Evidence." *Quarterly Journal of Economics* 129 (4): 1799–1860.

Bartik, Timothy. 1991. *Who Benefits from State and Local Development Policies?* Kalamazoo, MI: W. E. Upjohn Institute for Employment Research.

Beraja, Martin, Erik Hurst, and Juan Ospina. 2016. "The Aggregate Implications of Regional Business Cycles." Working Paper no. 21956, NBER, Cambridge, MA.

Blanchard, Olivier J., and Lawrence F. Katz. 1992. "Regional Evolutions." *Brookings Papers on Economic Activity* 1: 1–75.

Bound, John, and Harry J. Holzer. 2000. "Demand Shifts, Population Adjustments, and Labor Market Outcomes during the 1980s." *Journal of Labor Economics* 18 (1): 20–54.

Calmes, Jackie. 2016. "Hiring Hurdle: Finding Workers Who Can Pass a Drug Test." *New York Times*, May 17. https://www.nytimes.com/2016/05/18/business/hiring-hurdle-finding-workers-who-can-pass-a-drug-test.html.

Case, Anne, and Angus Deaton. 2017. "Mortality and Morbidity in the 21st Century." *Brookings Papers on Economic Activity*. https://www.brookings.edu/bpea-articles/mortality-and-morbidity-in-the-21st-century/.

Charles, Kerwin Kofi, and Philip DeCicca. 2008. "Local Labor Market Fluctuations and Health: Is There a Connection and for Whom?" *Journal of Health Economics* 27 (6): 1532–50.

Charles, Kerwin Kofi, Erik Hurst, and Matthew J. Notowidigdo. 2016. "The Masking of the Decline in Manufacturing Employment by the Housing Bubble." *Journal of Economic Perspectives* 30 (2): 179–200.

———. Forthcoming. "Housing Booms, Manufacturing Decline, and Labor Market Outcomes." *Economic Journal*.

Currie, Janet, Jonas Jin, and Molly Schnell. 2018. "US Employment and Opioids: Is There a Connection?" Working paper, Princeton University.

Dao, Mai, Davide Furceri, and Prakash Loungani. 2017. "Regional Labor Market Adjustment in the United States: Trend and Cycle." *Review of Economics and Statistics* 99 (2): 243–57.

Davidson, Adam. 2014. "The Future of US Manufacturing Jobs Will Require More Brain Than Brawn." *American Made*, November 7. https://www.npr.org/2014/11/07/362226235/future-u-s-manufacturing-jobs-will-require-more-brain-than-brawn.

Elejalde-Ruiz, Alexia. 2016. "Manufacturing's Big Challenge: Finding Skilled and Interested Workers." *Chicago Tribune*, December 17. https://www.chicagotribune.com/business/ct-manufacturing-talent-gap-1218-biz-20161217-story.html.

Goldsmith-Pinkham, Paul, Isaac Sorkin, and Henry Swift. 2017. "Bartik Instruments: What, When, Why, and How." Working Paper no. 24408. NBER, Cambridge, MA.

Goldstein, Amy. 2017. *Janesville: An American Story*. New York: Simon & Schuster.

Hedegaard, Holly, Margaret Warner, and Arialdi M. Miniño. 2017. "Drug Overdose Deaths in the United States, 1999–2016." NCHS Data Brief no. 294. National Center for Health Statistics, Hyattsville, MD.

Houseman, Susan, Timothy Bartik, and Timothy Sturgeon. 2015. "Measuring Manufacturing: How the Computer and Semiconductor Industries Affect the Numbers and Perceptions." In *Measuring Globalization: Better Trade Statistics for Better Policy, Volume 1, Biases to Price, Output, and Productivity Statistics from Trade*, ed. Susan Houseman and Michael Mandel, 151–93. Kalamazoo, MI: W. E. Upjohn Institute for Employment Research.

IPUMS (Integrated Public Use Microdata Series). 2019a. "Current Population Survey Data for Social, Economic and Health Research." http://cps.ipums.org/cps/.

IPUMS (Integrated Public Use Microdata Series). 2019b. "US Census Data for Social, Economic and Health Research." https://usa.ipums.org/usa/.

Joffe-Walt, Chana. 2013. "Trends with Benefits." Podcast, *This American Life*, March 22. https://www.thisamericanlife.org/490/trends-with-benefits.

Kaplan, Greg, and Sam Schulhofer-Wohl. 2017. "Understanding the Long-Run Decline in Interstate Migration." *International Economic Review* 58 (1): 57–94.

Karabarbounis, Loukas, and Brent Neiman. 2014. "The Global Decline of the Labor Share." *Quarterly Journal of Economics* 129 (1): 61–103.

Krueger, Alan B. 2017. "Where Have All the Workers Gone? An Inquiry into the Decline of the US Labor Force Participation Rate." *Brookings Papers on Economic Activity*. https://www.brookings.edu/bpea-articles/where-have-all-the-workers-gone-an-inquiry-into-the-decline-of-the-u-s-labor-force-participation-rate/.

Laird, Jessica, and Torben Nielsen. 2016. "The Effects of Physician Prescribing Behaviors on Prescription Drug Use and Labor Supply: Evidence from Movers in Denmark." Working paper, Harvard University.

Moffitt, Robert A. 2012. "The US Employment-Population Reversal in the 2000s: Facts and Explanations." Working Paper no. 18520, NBER, Cambridge, MA.

Molloy, Raven, Christopher L. Smith, and Abigail K. Wozniak. 2011. "Internal Migration in the United States." *Journal of Economic Perspectives* 25 (3): 173–96.

———. 2014. "Declining Migration within the US: The Role of the Labor Market." Working Paper no. 20065, NBER, Cambridge, MA.

Murphy, Kevin M., and Robert H. Topel. 1987. "The Evolution of Unemployment in the United States: 1968-1985." *NBER Macroeconomics Annual* 2: 11–58.

Nakamura, Emi, and Jon Steinsson. 2014. "Fiscal Stimulus in a Monetary Union: Evidence from US Regions." *American Economic Review* 104 (3): 753–92.

NBER. 2016. "NBER-CES Manufacturing Industry Database." http://www.nber.org/nberces/.

Pierce, Justin R., and Peter K. Schott. 2016. "The Surprisingly Swift Decline of US Manufacturing Employment." *American Economic Review* 106 (7): 1632–62.

———. 2017. "Trade Liberalization and Mortality: Evidence from US Counties." Working paper (October), Yale University.

Quest Diagnostics. 2017. "Drug Testing Index: Overall Positivity Rate in 2017." http://www.dtidrugmap.com/.

Quest Diagnostics. 2018. "Workforce Drug Positivity at Highest Rate in a Decade, Finds Analysis of More than 10 Million Drug Test Results." https://www.questdiagnostics.com/home/physicians/health-trends/drug-testing.

Quinones, Sam. 2015. *Dreamland: The True Tale of America's Opiate Epidemic*. New York: Bloomsbury.

Ruhm, Christopher. 2018. "Deaths of Despair or Drug Problems." Working Paper no. 24188 (January), NBER, Cambridge, MA.

Salam, Maya. 2017. "The Opioid Epidemic: A Crises Years in the Making." *New York Times*, October 26. https://www.nytimes.com/2017/10/26/us/opioid-crisis-public-health-emergency.html.

Sloane, Carolyn M. 2017. "Where Are the Workers? Technological Change, Rising Disability and the Employment Puzzle of the 2000s: A Regional Approach." Working paper (October).

Sussman, Anna Louie. 2016. "As Skill Requirements Increase, More Manufacturing Jobs Go Unfilled." *Wall Street Journal*, September 1. https://www.wsj.com/articles/as-skill-requirements-increase-more-manufacturing-jobs-go-unfilled-1472733676.

US Bureau of Economic Analysis. 2019. "Interactive Access to Industry Economic Accounts Data: GDP by Industry: Value Added by Industry." https://apps.bea.gov/iTable/iTable.cfm?ReqID=51&step=1.

US Bureau of Labor Statistics. 2018a. "CES National Databases: Employment, Hours, and Earnings—National (Current Employment Statistics—CES)." https://www.bls.gov/ces/data.htm.

US Bureau of Labor Statistics. 2018b. "Major Sector Productivity and Costs—Sector." https://data.bls.gov/cgi-bin/dsrv?pr.

US Bureau of Labor Statistics. 2019a. "Databases, Tables, and Calculators by Subject: Employment." https://www.bls.gov/data/#employment.

US Bureau of Labor Statistics. 2019b. "Manufacturing Sector: Capital Intensity (MPU9900082)." https://fred.stlouisfed.org/series/MPU9900082.

US Bureau of Labor Statistics. 2019c. "Manufacturing Sector: Labor Share (PRS30006173)." https://fred.stlouisfed.org/series/PRS30006173.

US Bureau of Labor Statistics. 2019d. "Nonfarm Business Sector: Labor Share (PRS85006173)." https://fred.stlouisfed.org/series/PRS85006173.

US Bureau of Labor Statistics. 2019e. "Private Non-Farm Business Sector: Capital Intensity (MPU4910082)." https://fred.stlouisfed.org/series/MPU4910082.

US Census Bureau. 2018. "Business Dynamics Statistics: Establishment Characteristics Data Tables." https://www.census.gov/ces/dataproducts/bds/data_estab.html.

Weaver, Andrew, and Paul Osterman. 2017. "Skill Demands and Mismatch in US Manufacturing." *Industrial and Labor Relations Review* 70 (2): 275–307.

Comment

Lawrence F. Katz, Harvard University and NBER

Kerwin Kofi Charles, Erik Hurst, and Mariel Schwartz provide an insightful and comprehensive empirical examination of the link between the transformation of the US manufacturing sector and the substantial decline in the employment rates and average annual hours worked of prime-age adults (those aged 21–55), especially men and less educated women, since 2000. Charles et al. document that US manufacturing experienced a massive decline in employment of 5 million jobs, a large increase in capital intensity, and substantial skill upgrading from 2000 to 2017. They exploit geographic variation in manufacturing employment decline across commuting zones (CZs) in the 2000s using a Bartik (shift-share) instrument to assess the "causal" impact of local manufacturing employment demand shocks on employment outcomes. Charles et al. find that CZs with larger manufacturing employment declines have larger declines in employment rates, hours worked, and wages for prime-age workers from 2000 to 2016, regardless of whether the adverse manufacturing shocks were related to China trade shocks or other sources. Charles et al. conclude that manufacturing decline can account for about half of the prime-age male employment rate decline since 2000. Geographic areas with bigger manufacturing employment losses in the 2000s also experience greater social problems as seen in more severe drug and opioid addiction problems. Finally, Charles et al. show that adverse manufacturing employment shocks have generated less geographic mobility (less of a regional migration response) and more persistent impacts on employment rates in the 2000s than in the 1980s.

I find the analysis of Charles et al. to be well crafted and quite convincing. Their findings of adverse labor demand shocks against less educated workers being a driving force in declining employment rates in the 2000s complement other work using cross-area variation in China trade exposure (Autor, Dorn, and Hanson 2013) and automation shocks from industrial robots (Acemoglu and Restrepo 2017). Charles and colleagues' results also echo Krueger's (2017) findings of a clear link across US geographic regions between the opioid epidemic and labor force participation declines, and the patterns parallel to the findings of Autor, Dorn, and Hanson (forthcoming) that areas with larger declines in manufacturing jobs from China trade shocks experience an increase in a wide range of social problems. Gould (2018a, 2018b), in related work examining US cross-city variation in manufacturing employment declines similarly using an industry shift-share instrument, finds that areas with larger manufacturing employment losses also experience greater declines in employment rates and relative wages for less educated workers, larger increases in inequality, and increases in racial economic disparities. And Gould (2018b) parallels the results in Charles et al. in finding larger persistent negative local labor market impacts of manufacturing employment declines in recent decades than in the 1960s to the 1980s.

I do have one minor quibble with the Charles et al. presentation of the decline in work of prime-age men during the 2000s. Charles et al. emphasize, using retrospective data from the March Current Population Survey (CPS) in their figure 3, that the decline in prime-age male employment is dominated by a rise in long-term detachment from the labor market as seen in a rapidly increasing share of full-year dropouts (those working 0 weeks during an entire year). Recent research by Coglianese (2018) using longitudinal matched CPS data and other longitudinal data sets shows there has been a substantial rise of "in-and-outs" (those who take temporary labor force breaks and move in and out of the labor force within a year) that can account for about a third of the decline in the employment rate of prime-age men in recent decades. Coglianese further shows that the rise of full-year dropouts is substantially overstated and the rise of "in-and-outs" is missed in the retrospective March CPS data used by Charles et al. Coglianese documents a sharp increase in the rate of recall bias in the March CPS in which a larger share of individuals who reported themselves to be employed for at least one month in the monthly CPS during a year then report zero weeks worked for that same year in the retrospective survey in the March CPS of the following year. The rise in recall bias leads to an overstatement of the increase in permanent dropouts versus in-and-outs of 1.5 percentage points in the 2000s in the March CPS. Coglianese's findings raise the question of the extent to which the persistent declines in employment rates in areas with larger adverse manufacturing employment shocks reflect a rise in those permanently disconnected from the labor force versus more in-and-outs who churn through periods of unstable work and periods of nonemployment. Tighter labor markets as the United States has experienced over the past few years might be more successful in moving in-and-outs back into more stable employment than reaching the truly long-term jobless.

A key point of Charles et al. is that the labor market outcomes of prime-age men and less educated workers are strongly connected to the state of employment opportunities in manufacturing. Charles et al. argue that the adverse manufacturing employment shock of the 2000s is larger than in the late twentieth century and the distinctive transformation of manufacturing since 2000 helps explain the large decline in prime-age male employment rates from 2000 to 2017 as compared with almost no change in the prime-age male employment rate from 1980 to 2000. Charles et al. emphasize the large absolute decline in manufacturing employment of the early twenty-first century in contrast to little change in the total number of manufacturing jobs in the late twentieth century. And, as can be seen in my figure 1, the massive decline of 6 million manufacturing jobs from 2000 to 2010 is historically unprecedented over the last 80 years and is of similar magnitude to the number of manufacturing jobs added in the massive mobilization of World War II from 1939 to 1944. In contrast, if one views the size of the shock to manufacturing employment as the share of workforce that needs to be reallocated from manufacturing, then the post-2000s period does not appear to be a pe-

Fig. 1. US manufacturing employment, 1939–2017, thousands (BLS 2019, Current Employment Statistics, Establishment Survey, payroll employment, series CES3000000001).

riod of a particularly large manufacturing employment decline, as illustrated in my figure 2. Manufacturing employment as a share of total (nonfarm) employment has been secularly declining at a steady rate since the 1950s. And, if anything, the rate of decline of the manufacturing share of total employment is slower in the 2000s than in previous decades.

A third metric of manufacturing employment opportunities that adheres more closely to the cross-area empirical specifications used by Charles et al. is the number of manufacturing jobs per prime-age adult (here defined as those aged 25–54). My figure 3 plots the ratio of manufacturing employment to prime-age adults from 1948 to 2017, showing stability in the mid-twentieth century and substantial decline starting in the 1970s, as does the prime-age male employment to population ratio. Manufacturing jobs per prime-age adult has a correlation with the prime-age male employment rate of 0.91 over the full period and remains strongly positively related even after including a linear time trend. But puzzles remain for the Charles et al. hypothesis, with a much larger decline in manufacturing jobs per prime-age adult from 1980 to 2000 than from 2000 to 2017 in contrast to stability in the prime-age male employment rate in the earlier period and steep decline in the latter period.

Thus, as Charles et al. point out, it must be either (a) declines in the absolute number of manufacturing jobs rather than declines in manu-

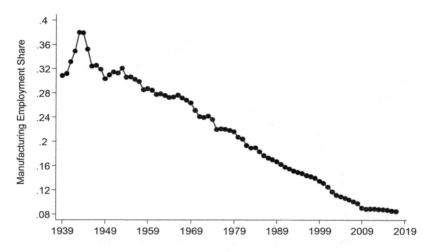

Fig. 2. Manufacturing share of total nonfarm employment, 1939–2017 (BLS 2019, Current Employment Statistics, manufacturing employment over total nonfarm employment).

Fig. 3. Manufacturing jobs per prime-age adult, 1948–2017 (BLS 2019, Current Employment Statistics, manufacturing employment and CPS series on civilian noninstitutional population of prime-age adults [25–54 years old], series LNU00000060).

facturing jobs scaled by employment or population that matter for declines in the employment rate of prime-age workers or (*b*) something is different about the transformation of manufacturing in the 2000s so that similar shocks to manufacturing jobs per prime-age adult now lead to more adverse and persistent labor market impacts. Charles et al. argue that rapid skill upgrading in manufacturing in the 2000s with a shift toward employing college-educated workers may partially explain larger impacts of negative manufacturing employment shocks in the 2000s than earlier periods such as the 1980s. Yet, rapid educational upgrading in manufacturing relative to other less educated sectors such as construction and retail trade was already present in the 1980s and 1990s in CPS tabulations analogous to table 9 of Charles et al.

What does seem most distinctive about the 2000s is declining geographic mobility in response to local area (CZ) manufacturing employment shocks as seen in table 10 of Charles et al. where the migration (population) response to such shocks is more than four times larger in the 1980s than in the 2000s. The large migration responses to local labor market shocks meant essentially no permanent impacts on employment rates of local labor demand shocks through the 1980s as found in Blanchard and Katz (1992) and corroborated by Charles et al. Blanchard and

Katz (1992) showed that adjustments to US local economic shocks from 1947 to 1990 largely took place through migration from declining to expanding areas, with the adverse local shocks having only transitory negative impacts on the local labor force participation, unemployment, and employment rates. Dao, Furceri, and Loungani (2017) find a decline in the interstate migration response to state economic shocks in the past couple decades. And Ganong and Shoag (2017) document declining directed interstate migration rates since the 1990s being related to the rising restrictiveness of land-use and housing regulations in high-productivity areas (e.g., the San Francisco Bay Area) reducing housing supply elasticity in potential receiving destinations. The presence of more-affordable housing along with the greater drug and health problems of job losers and other potential migrants from CZs that experienced larger manufacturing employment declines may be leading to more individuals remaining out of the labor force in such areas despite poor employment prospects rather than moving to thriving areas with much more expensive housing.

Some extensions worth exploring to further assess the Charles et al. manufacturing decline hypothesis include examining whether the loss of manufacturing jobs per se are important or whether what matters is the loss of jobs offering high wage premia (high wages conditional on observed worker characteristics such as education and age) especially for non-college-educated workers. One could divide the shift-share measures of manufacturing employment shocks into high-wage and low-wage premia manufacturing sectors and see if the impacts on local labor market outcomes are larger and more persistent for high-wage employment losses. And the shift-share analysis could look at shocks to high-wage jobs outside manufacturing as well. Furthermore, the role of decline in union jobs and the loss of unions as a key provider of local social capital might also be a distinctive feature of the large concentrated loss of manufacturing jobs. A final heterogeneity analysis to pursue would be to examine whether areas with higher overall education levels (greater local human capital) or the presence of colleges and research universities may be more resilient to adverse manufacturing employment shocks.

Endnote

For acknowledgments, sources of research support, and disclosure of the author's material financial relationships, if any, please see http://www.nber.org/chapters/c14082 .ack.

References

Acemoglu, Daron, and Pascual Restrepo. 2017. "Robots and Jobs: Evidence from US Labor Markets." Working Paper no. 23285 (March), NBER, Cambridge, MA.

Autor, David H., David Dorn, and Gordon H. Hanson. 2013. "The China Syndrome: Local Labor Market Effects of Import Competition in the United States." *American Economic Review* 103 (6): 212–68.

———. Forthcoming. "When Work Disappears: Manufacturing Decline and the Falling Marriage Market Value of Young Men." *American Economic Review: Insights*.

Blanchard, Olivier J., and Lawrence F. Katz. 1992. "Regional Evolutions." *Brookings Papers on Economic Activity* Spring: 1–75.

BLS (US Bureau of Labor Statistics). 2019. "Databases, Tables and Calculators by Subject: Employment." https://www.bls.gov/data/#employment.

Coglianese, John. 2018. "The Rise of In-and-Outs: Declining Labor Force Participation of Prime Age Men." Working paper (February), Harvard University.

Dao, Mai, Davide Furceri, and Prakash Loungani. 2017. "Regional Labor Market Adjustment in the United States: Trend and Cycle." *Review of Economics and Statistics* 99 (May): 243–57.

Ganong, Peter, and Daniel Shoag. 2017. "Why Has Regional Income Convergence in the US Declined?" *Journal of Urban Economics* 102: 76–90.

Gould, Eric D. 2018a. "Explaining the Unexplained: Residual Wage Inequality, Manufacturing Decline and Low-Skilled Immigration." *Economic Journal*. Advance online publication. https://doi.org/10.1111/ecoj.12611.

———. 2018b. "Torn Apart? The Impact of Manufacturing Employment Decline on Black and White Americans." CEPR Discussion Paper no. 12992, Center for Economic and Policy Research, Washington, DC.

Krueger, Alan B. 2017. "Where Have All the Workers Gone? An Inquiry into the Decline of the US Labor Force Participation Rate." *Brookings Papers on Economic Activity* Fall: 1–86.

Comment

Valerie A. Ramey, *University of California, San Diego, and NBER*

Introduction

This fine paper by Charles, Hurst, and Schwartz investigates the link between the post-2000 decline in manufacturing employment and the decline of the employment rate, and also analyzes the supporting roles played by transfer payments, geographic mobility, and opioid use. The paper is a particularly useful synthesis because it brings together threads from a number of other papers, including the authors' own work, and it explores some competing explanations in a standardized empirical framework. The paper is a wonderful read because it tells a clear story based on an impressive marshalling of evidence.

The paper contains numerous findings that shed light on a variety of changes that occurred around the same time. The span of the analysis from aggregate to commuting zone level is particularly enlightening. Here are highlights of a just a few of the many interesting results:

• A 10-percentage-point decline in the local manufacturing employment share of population reduced the local employment rate by 3.7 percentage points for prime-age men and 2.7 for prime-age women.

• Manufacturing decline in local markets had similar effects on the prime-age employment rate whether the decline was due to the China shock or other shocks.

• The correlation between manufacturing share changes and employment rate changes holds only in the post-2000 period, not the 1980–90 period. Decreased geographical mobility appears to play a key role in this changing relationship.

In my discussion, I will begin by putting the changes post-2000 in historical context. I will then consider the validity of the shift-share instrument in light of the long-term effects of initial conditions in manufacturing as well as in light of some new work on the econometrics of Bartik instruments. I will conclude by questioning whether one can draw aggregate inferences from cross-sectional data.

How New Are These Trends?

The authors focus on what they call "two profound changes in the US economy" since 2000: the secular declines in manufacturing employment and in the employment rates of prime-age individuals. In this section I will suggest that the movements post-2000 are largely a continuation of past trends, though I will highlight one key exception.

Consider figure 1, which shows the labor force participation rates for prime-age individuals.[1] I use labor force participation rates instead of employment-population rates to remove the cyclicity of unemployment so that I can focus on the secular trends.

The "All Prime Age" graph in figure 1a shows that the rise in the labor force participation rate slowed during the 1990s and then declined somewhat since 2000. It is this decline since 2000 that is the focus of Charles and colleagues' investigation. The graphs separated by sex (fig. 1b and 1c) show that, contrary to the emphasis on men and manufacturing in much of the paper's discussion, the aggregate trend appears to be driven by the behavior of prime-age female labor force trends. This feature is particularly striking once one takes account of the different scale of the graphs: the changes in female labor force participation rates swamp those of the men. Female labor force participation rates rose 43 percentage points from 1948 to the peak in 2000, and then declined 2 percentage points from 2000 to 2018. Prime-age male labor force participation rates declined gradually, with the average annual rate of decline after 2000 similar to the rate from the late 1960s to 2000. Thus, what changed after 2000 was not the behavior of the prime-age male labor force participation rate but rather the cessation of the decades-long rise in female labor force participation rates. This fact calls into question the role of manufacturing in explaining the aggregate participation rate because the authors' own evidence suggests that manufacturing plays a much smaller role for female employment.

The second change the authors highlight is the decline in the share of manufacturing employment. I would argue that the decline in the share is part of a long-term trend, but the decline in the level is indeed unprecedented. Figure 2a shows manufacturing employment as a percentage

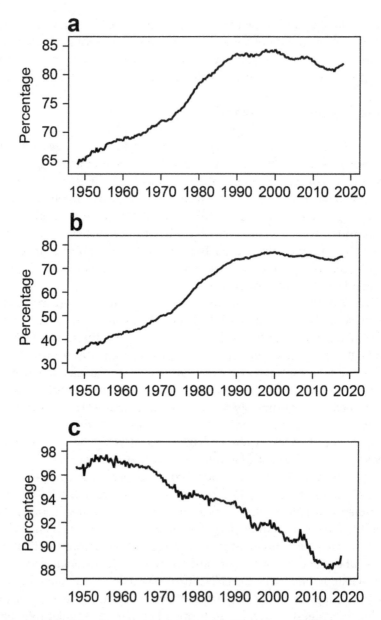

Fig. 1. Trends in labor force participation rates. (*a*) All prime age. (*b*) Prime-age female. (*c*) Prime-age male.

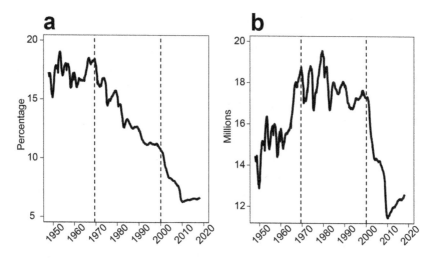

Fig. 2. US manufacturing employment percentage of population ages 20–64. (*a*) Employment share of population. (*b*) Employment level.

of the working-age population, ages 20–64. The average annual loss rate in the share was 0.25 percentage points per year from 1970 to 2000 and 0.22 percentage points per year from 2000 to 2018. Thus, the employment share in manufacturing is following a long-standing trend. On the other hand, as the graph in figure 2*b* shows, the decline in the level of employment in manufacturing since 2000 is unprecedented for the post-WWII period. Thus, to make the link to recent declines in the employment rate, it seems that explanations should focus on absolute levels of manufacturing employment rather than on shares. However, all of Charles and colleagues' key evidence, such as figure 14 at the aggregate level and the estimates from commuting zone regressions in table 2, is in terms of the manufacturing employment share relative to population, not changes in the levels. Thus, the estimates cannot inform us about the role of the actual variable that changed post-2000—the level of manufacturing employment. Such an investigation might shed further light on the role of manufacturing.

The Long Decline in Manufacturing and Why Less Educated Workers Were Adversely Affected

As my graphs in the previous section showed, the decline in manufacturing employment relative to the working-age population began just before 1970. A question that the current paper's focus on manufacturing brings up is, What makes manufacturing special? The US economy has experienced other dramatic sectoral shifts in its history, such as the movement of workers out of agriculture. Why is the decline in manufacturing seen as such a negative shock to workers, particularly to the less educated?

George Borjas and I offered one possible answer to this question in a series of papers written in the 1990s (Borjas and Ramey 1994a, 1994b, 1995). In that work, which explored the role of the decline in durable goods manufacturing employment in the rise in wage inequality, we presented time series evidence and evidence from a panel of cities, as well as a theoretical model that told the following story. At the end of World War II, US manufacturing was dominant in the world, particularly in the durable goods industries such as automobiles and steel. US companies enjoyed market power at home and abroad and earned significant rents as a result. American unions, which were strengthened by the New Deal legislation during the 1930s, compelled the companies to share their rents with their workers in the form of higher wages. Because the manufacturing workers who benefited from these high wage premia were less educated, the education wage premium was lower in the 1950s and 1960s.

But circumstances began to change in the 1970s. Europe and Japan completed their recovery from World War II and their companies began to compete with US firms. For example, Japan's success in the automobile industry beginning in the 1970s competed away many of the rents previously earned by US automobile companies. Later, in the 1990s and 2000s, China became a significant competitive force faced by US companies and workers. The net effect was fewer rents earned by US companies to share with the workers, and increased direct worker competition against less educated US workers. The result, we argued, was a rise in the education premium because fewer less educated workers could find work in the high-wage manufacturing industries.

In Borjas and Ramey (2000), we went on to investigate the long-term consequences for employment and wages in manufacturing industries. We found very high correlations of industry wage premia over decades, suggesting institutional barriers to lowering long-standing wage premia in the face of competition. However, we found that firms responded in other ways to the rise in competition. In particular, we found that industries that paid higher wage premia in 1960 experienced significantly slower employment growth over the subsequent decades relative to industries with lower wage premia. Further investigations found that the high initial wage industries responded by replacing workers with capital and ended up experiencing faster growth in capital-labor ratios and faster labor productivity growth. In follow-up work, Shim and Yang (2018) showed that this process has continued up to the present, with the high initial wage premia industries investing much more in ICT (information and communication technology) and replacing their routine workers. Thus, it appears that the decline in manufacturing employment share is tied to its initial high rent/high wage status after World War II.

In sum, our story suggests that researchers and policy makers are correctly focused on the negative consequences of the decline in manufacturing for less educated workers. However, that decline was driven by forces that one should not expect to reverse. It also highlights the very long-term effects of the initial conditions. These effects might affect the exogeneity of Charles and colleagues' instrument, as I will argue in the next section.

Comments on the Cross-Sectional Commuting Zone Estimates

An important part of the Charles et al. paper is the extension of the previous research using variation at the level of the commuting zone to estimate causal effects of the decline in the manufacturing share. They use a Bartik-type shift-share instrument to estimate the differential decline in the employment rate of prime-age individuals across commuting zones caused by differential declines in manufacturing employment shares. Their estimates (shown in table 2 of their paper) indicate that a commuting zone that experienced a demand-driven 1 percentage point larger decline in manufacturing than another commuting zone suffered a 0.37-percentage-point larger decline in the employment rate of prime-age men. The estimated effect for prime-age women was 0.27. In both cases, the effects were larger for less educated individuals.

The commuting zone estimates are quite interesting and suggest important effects on individual worker outcomes. As Charles et al. discuss, manufacturing tends to be highly spatially concentrated relative to other sectors. This implies that the decline in manufacturing might have larger effects on local labor markets than on aggregate ones. Decades ago, Blanchard and Katz (1992) showed that the departure of industries from local areas leads to a rise in the unemployment rate that falls only slowly afterward, and does so not because other firms move in but because the population eventually moves out. Their results raise a puzzle: Why don't other firms move into the local area to take advantage of the weak labor market? This question deserves far more attention from the literature. The Blanchard and Katz finding, along with the evidence that geographic mobility has declined, can perhaps explain why the long-run declines in manufacturing are now having more serious consequences for individuals. If firms do not move in to take the place of those that left, and if workers will no longer move out, then the result is local areas with large shares of prime-age individuals who are no longer economically productive. As the Charles et al. paper suggests, these areas may be more prone to ills such as opioid abuse.

My final comments consist of two observations about the cross-sectional estimates, one about the instrument and the other about the link between cross-sectional estimates and aggregate implications.

Charles et al. use a shift-share Bartik instrument as a demand instrument for the local manufacturing share. This type of instrument has been used in a number of recent papers. They construct their instrument as the sum over all of the local industries of the product of two terms: (i) the share of prime-age individuals in commuting zone k working in manufacturing industry j in the year 2000, and (ii) the change in aggregate employment (less commuting zone k) in manufacturing industry j from 2000 to 2016. Essentially, the first term measures the exposure of the commuting zone to the aggregate shock measured in the second term.

A recent paper by Goldsmith-Pinkham, Sorkin, and Swift (2018) analyzes the econometrics of Bartik instruments and reveals a number of previously unknown or underappreciated aspects. They summarize one of their key findings as: "Bartik is formally equivalent to a GMM [generalized method of moments] estimator with the industry shares as instruments. Hence, we argue that the identifying assumption is best stated in terms of the industry shares—the national growth rates are simply a weight matrix" (25). This insight implies that Charles and colleagues' identifying assumption requires that the initial distribution of manufacturing industries across commuting zones in 2000 has no effect on the change in the employment-population ratio from 2000 to 2016 except through the demand-channel effect on the change in the manufacturing share in the commuting zone. It is at this point we can link back to my discussion in the previous section of the unique history of the manufacturing sector in the United States and the long-term effects of the initial high rent/high wage premia in US manufacturing in the couple of decades after World War II. It is very possible that those long-term features also affect the employment-population ratio in other ways, and perhaps might be able to explain the reluctance of other industries to move into local areas.

Goldsmith-Pinkham et al. (2018) also analyze the Autor, Dorn, and Hanson (2013) commuting zone estimates of the effect of China, and one of the findings might be relevant to the Charles et al. paper because the instruments share similarities. Goldsmith-Pinkham et al. show that despite the fact that Autor et al. have more than 700 Bartik instruments, only a few instruments are actually driving their estimates. In particular, it turns out that the highest-weight instrument in their sample is electronic computers in the 2000s, which implies that their estimator is "comparing outcomes in locations with high and low shares of the electronic computers industry" (Goldsmith-Pinkham et al. 2018, 3). If this feature is also true for the closely related Charles et al. shift-share instrument, then the interpretation of their estimates would change dramatically. In particular, because they are estimating only relative effects across regions, their results might be reinterpreted as an explanation for why the employment rate of prime-age individuals rose in Silicon Valley.

This last point brings me to my second comment regarding the link between cross-sectional estimates and aggregate implications. In several places in the paper, Charles et al. use their commuting zone estimates to make inferences about aggregates. Cognizant of the leap required, they always preface these extrapolations with the adjective "naive." As they recognize, one cannot identify aggregate effects from cross-sectional estimates (because the constant term nets out aggregate effects). The additional identifying assumptions required to translate cross-sectional estimates to the aggregate are very strong, a crucial point overlooked by some of the recent literature. Muendler's (2017) recent World Trade Organization report discusses the pitfalls and potentially faulty inference that can result when naively extrapolating cross-sectional estimates. These issues should be kept in mind when assessing how much the fascinating cross-commuting zone estimates of Charles and colleagues' paper can tell us about the aggregate trends.

Endnotes

For acknowledgments, sources of research support, and disclosure of the author's material financial relationships, if any, please see http://www.nber.org/chapters/c14083 .ack.
1. Charles et al. define prime age as ages 21–55. I define prime age as 25–54 because it corresponds to the age category aggregate published by the Bureau of Labor Statistics.

References

Autor, David, David Dorn, and Gordon Hanson. 2013. "The China Syndrome: Local Labor Market Effects of Import Competition in the United States." *American Economic Review* 103:2121–68.

Blanchard, Olivier Jean, and Lawrence Katz. 1992. "Regional Evolutions." *Brookings Papers on Economic Activity* (1):1–75.

Borjas, George J., and Valerie A. Ramey. 1994a. "The Relationship between Wage Inequality and Trade." In *The Changing Distribution of Income in an Open US Economy*, ed. J. H. Bergstrand, T. F. Cosimano, J. W. Houck, and R. G. Sheehan. Amsterdam: Elsevier.

———. 1994b. "Time Series Evidence on the Sources of Trends in Wage Inequality." *American Economic Review* 84 (May): 10–16.

———. 1995. "Foreign Competition, Market Power and Wage Inequality." *Quarterly Journal of Economics* 110 (November): 1075–110.

———. 2000. "Market Responses to Interindustry Wage Differentials." Working Paper no. 7799, NBER, Cambridge, MA.

Goldsmith-Pinkham, Paul, Isaac Sorkin, and Henry Swift. 2018. "Bartik Instruments: What, When, Why, and How." Working Paper no. 24408, NBER, Cambridge, MA.

Muendler, Marc-Andreas. 2017. "Trade, Technology and Prosperity: An Account of Evidence from a Labor Market Perspective." Staff Working Paper ERSD-2017-15 (November), World Trade Organization, Geneva.

Shim, Myungkyu, and Hee-Seung Yang. 2018. "Interindustry Wage Differentials, Technology Adoption, and Job Polarization." *Journal of Economic Behavior and Organization* 146:141–60.

Discussion

Andrew Atkeson pointed out that rural-to-urban transitions are typically associated with a selection effect. Those who leave early are more skilled and adaptable. As time goes by, those who haven't migrated are less likely to transition to a different job and remain in place. Atkeson asked whether the same phenomenon is at play in the United States. The authors mentioned that mobility among the young is usually an important margin of adjustment. They noted that a striking feature of the data is that the young aren't moving out with the same propensity as in the past.

Several participants offered comments and formulated conjectures regarding the possible causes for the lack of mobility. Richard Rogerson shared Atkeson's view that selection might play an important role. Rogerson suggested that migration of skilled workers out of manufacturing towns leads to a collapse of the tax base and a deterioration in the provision of services. Guido Lorenzoni noted that relocating is an investment activity. As such, the return on this investment is crucial for geographic mobility. Lorenzoni inquired about the evidence on the returns to moving out of manufacturing towns. Robert Gordon argued workers may not be able to pay the costs of moving simply because their wages are too low. Gordon pushed back on the idea that land-use regulation is an impediment for mobility, an idea that was raised by both discussants. He reminded the audience that most population growth in the United States is in large flat areas, which do not have exorbitant real estate prices. Valerie Ramey joined the discussion and referred to Michael W. L. Elsby and Matthew D. Shapiro ("Why Does Trend Growth Affect Equilibrium Employment? A New Explanation of an Old Puzzle," *American Economic Review* 102, no. 4: 1378–1413). Their work emphasizes the role of labor productivity growth for the decline in labor mobility. When labor productivity growth is low, as it currently is, workers are not willing to move away for low-wage jobs.

The authors responded that the lack of mobility could indeed be a cause or a symptom. They were sympathetic to the view that low mobility reflects poor prospects of moving out. The authors also suggested that the decline in manufacturing cannot account entirely for the decline in labor force participation.

The authors then followed up on a point raised by Ramey in her discussion. She noted the difference between the authors' results on drug use compared with those found in other recent studies. The authors confirmed that other studies find a weaker effect of economic conditions on opioid drug use. The authors pointed out that these papers use relatively short time spans and allow for commuting zone fixed effects. They argued that the inclusion of such fixed effects does not leave enough variation in the data to identify the effect of interest. Their paper, instead, exploits cross-section variation.

Andrea Eisfeldt commented on another point raised by Ramey in her discussion. Ramey had noted that firms don't move into declining manufacturing towns, despite low wages. Eisfeldt pointed out that complementarity between capital and high-skilled labor might be an important factor in explaining this fact. High-skilled labor is scarce in these towns, so firms do not find it profitable to move there. The authors agreed with Eisfeldt's comment. They also emphasized the potential role of agglomeration forces. A firm relocating unilaterally to a declining manufacturing town wouldn't benefit from positive spillovers.

Martin Eichenbaum wondered how people living in declining manufacturing towns survive, despite poor economic outcomes. In particular, he inquired about the role of intrahousehold transfers, with women potentially supporting men. The authors agreed that the question is particularly interesting, and said they don't have an answer to it. They noted that most people do not receive any direct government transfer. The young do not cohabitate more. And the decline in employment in those locations affects both men and women. The authors confirmed the presence of some forms of intrafamily transfers. Lawrence Katz joined the discussion and pointed out that informal or short-term work might be important in this context. He noted that this type of employment is poorly measured. He cited the work of John Coglianese ("The Rise of In-and-Outs: Declining Labor Force Participation of Prime Age Men" [Mimeo, Harvard University, February 2018]), which documents that the same people who report no work at all in the March Current Population Survey (CPS) supplement for the past year often report some work in one or two other CPS monthly surveys. Katz suggested that this extensive margin of adjustment, with frequent and informal in-and-outs of the labor market, could help explain how people make ends meet.

Richard Rogerson followed up on a point raised separately by Katz and Ramey. Both discussants had pointed out that the manufacturing employment share has been steadily decreasing since the 1950s. This fact suggests that the decline in manufacturing employment in the 2000s simply reflects a secular trend. Rogerson noted that a stable decline in manufacturing employment jobs could have very different implications for employment, depending on the growth rate of the labor force. When the labor force is not growing rapidly, such a decline can happen without any existing worker being forced to switch occupation. On the contrary, when the labor force is growing rapidly, the adjustment must come from workers in the manufacturing sector losing their job.

Jonathan Parker seconded Rogerson's point by providing an example from the economics job market. He compared two situations where the ratio of job openings to population size increases, but with very different implications for employment: one where job openings increase whereas the population is steady, and one where job openings are steady whereas the population decreases. To address Rogerson's concern, Ramey suggested controlling for whether there was an absolute decline in manufacturing employment.

Gordon offered some comments regarding the secular decline in manufacturing employment, and its origins. He noted that the period ranging from the 1970s to the beginning of the Great Recession was characterized by a dramatic increase in the capital-to-labor ratio and a decline in the share of manufacturing employment. In contrast, the capital-to-labor ratio and the share of manufacturing employment stabilized after the Great Recession. Gordon noted that this revival of employment took place despite low growth in labor productivity and total factor productivity (TFP). He argued that the decline and subsequent recovery of the share of manufacturing employment could be partly attributed to a satiation of investment. Gordon noted that evolution of the manufacturing capacity, that is, the ratio of the Industrial Production Index to the capacity utilization rate, is consistent with this explanation. He pointed out that the annual growth in manufacturing capacity was 2%–3% in the 1970s and 1980s, and even reached 8% over a 5-year period in the late 1990s. In contrast, manufacturing capacity increased by only 1%–2% a year since the mid-2000s. In Gordon's opinion, this evidence suggests that substitution from labor to capital was an important determinant of the evolution of manufacturing employment. He dismissed the view that competition from Chinese imports could account entirely for the decline in the share of manufacturing employment.

Gita Gopinath inquired about the authors' conclusion that recent policy proposals by the Trump administration, such as tariffs and trade wars, would be ineffective in bringing back manufacturing jobs. Gopinath pointed out that increased automation in the manufacturing industry could indeed mitigate the effect of such policies when it comes to manufacturing employment. She wondered whether the authors' conclusion relates to their evidence on the decline in workers' geographic mobility. The authors responded that their conclusion does not rely on their evidence regarding the decline in mobility. In their view, the nature of the manufacturing industry has changed substantially over time. This change could mitigate the response of manufacturing employment to tarriff and trade policies. Katz joined the discussion and argued that the types of tariffs being proposed could have adverse labor market consequences. Although trade is generally viewed as a major contributor to the decline in labor share in the manufacturing sector, Katz noted that the relation between trade shocks and declining labor share within the manufacturing sector is weak.

Katz offered some comments about what he calls "mediocre technological change." He provided an example in the context of autonomous vehicles. He compared two scenarios. In the first, autonomous vehicles work effectively, increase TFP substantially, decrease transportation costs, stimulate trade between locations, and ultimately lead to an increase in employment. In the second scenario, the technology only leads to a modest decrease in costs, leaves five million vehicle operators unemployed, and doesn't lead to substantial productivity gains. Katz viewed this second scenario as a fair description of what happened in the manufacturing sector over the past decade. In Katz's opinion, disruptive technological changes led the manufacturing sector to substitute away from labor, without sustained productivity growth or positive spillover effects.

Katz also offered some thoughts on location-based economic development policies. He pointed out that areas with a more educated workforce and those hosting a university are more resilient to negative shocks, referring to the work of Edward Glaeser. Katz noted that there could be significant returns to multiplying higher education institutions, including state universities, across modest-sized cities in the Midwest. He suggested that the United States had cut back on such effort several decades ago, investing instead in higher education through Pell Grants, student loan programs, and for-profit fly-by-night institutions. In Katz's opinion, investing in higher education infrastructures is the only location-based economic development policy that could attract high-skilled labor and have a significant impact on local economies.

Emmanuel Farhi asked how the authors' results for the United States compared with that for other countries. The authors responded that the decline in employment rates for prime-age workers is not specific to the United States, but has been observed in other Anglo-Saxon countries. Canada, Australia, and the United Kingdom experienced such declines, though the magnitude was lower than in the United States. Germany, on the other hand, did not. In the Anglo-Saxon countries, employment rates of people in their 20s have also declined. The authors noted that these observations are based on aggregate statistics, and that they haven't replicated their analysis using micro data sets for other countries. Eichenbaum followed up on the question and mentioned that the decline in prime-age employment rates in Canada was not nearly as severe as in the United States. Eichenbaum noted that Canada hasn't had a substantial growth in populism during this period, and wondered whether these two patterns are connected. The authors argued that Canada's abundant natural resources might have played a role in limiting the decline in manufacturing employment, compared with the United States.

6

The Macroeconomics of Border Taxes

Omar Barbiero, *Harvard University*
Emmanuel Farhi, *Harvard University and NBER*
Gita Gopinath, *Harvard University and NBER*
Oleg Itskhoki, *Princeton University and NBER*

I. Introduction

Border adjustment is a feature of certain tax policies, in particular of the value-added tax (VAT) and in certain cases of the corporate profit tax (C-BAT), which makes export sales tax deductible, while levying the tax on imported inputs.[1] The economic consequences of these adjustments are poorly understood and highly politicized in the public debate. Superficially, a border adjustment tax (BAT) can indeed appear mercantilistic because it taxes imports but not exports.

Economists have long recognized that, ironically, it is precisely the border adjustment feature that guarantees the absence of protectionist effects. For example, without the rebate of VAT on exports, a VAT would act like an export tax, which by Lerner (1936) symmetry is equivalent to an import tariff (see Feldstein and Krugman 1990). Similarly, it also follows from Lerner symmetry that a C-BAT is neutral, with no real effects on the economy (see Grossman 1980).

It is fair to say that these arguments have held limited sway outside the ivory tower. In part, it is because they rely on long-run general equilibrium effects mediated by multiple price changes, which, on top of being difficult to understand, might take time to materialize if prices and wages do not adjust immediately. In this paper, we focus squarely on the dynamic effects of C-BAT and VAT tax reforms, from the short run to the long run. These effects are complex and poorly understood, even among economists. We address this hole in the literature.[2]

Our analysis arrives at the following main conclusions. First, C-BAT is unlikely to be neutral at the macroeconomic level, as the conditions required for neutrality are unrealistic. The basis for neutrality of VAT is even weaker.[3] Second, in response to the introduction of an unanticipated permanent C-BAT of 20% in the United States, the dollar appreciates strongly, by almost the size of the tax adjustment, and US exports and imports decline significantly, while the overall effect on output is small. Third, an equivalent change in VAT, by contrast, generates only a weak appreciation of the dollar and a small decline in imports and exports, but has a large negative effect on output. Last, border taxes increase government revenues in periods of trade deficit; however, given the net foreign asset (NFA) position of the United States, they result in a long-run loss of government revenues and an immediate net transfer to the ROW.

The vehicle for our investigation is an open-economy New Keynesian dynamic stochastic general equilibrium model with trade in intermediate goods, sticky prices and wages, and monetary policy following a Taylor rule. With nominal rigidities, the short-run pass-through of taxes and exchange rates into different prices becomes crucial. Our model can be specialized to capture different international pricing assumptions, namely producer currency pricing (PCP), local currency pricing (LCP), and dominant currency pricing (DCP). It can also be studied under various tax pass-through assumptions. Finally, the model also features pricing to market with variable markups and incomplete desired pass-through of costs into prices. With the United States in mind, we take our benchmark specification to be DCP, so that both imports and exports are denominated in the domestic currency (the dollar). We also assume that the immediate pass-through of VAT taxes into sticky prices is full (akin to the sales taxes in the United States), but that the immediate pass-through of the border adjustment associated with the corporate profit tax is zero. We analyze the dynamic effects of a one-time unanticipated introduction of a VAT and of a border adjustment for the corporate profit tax.

We start with the C-BAT, a tax proposal that was hotly debated as a part of the corporate tax reform in the United States (Auerbach et al. 2017). The C-BAT disallows deductions of imported input costs from corporate revenue when computing taxable corporate profits, and excludes export revenue from taxation. Loosely, this policy can be thought as the combination of an import tariff and an export subsidy. In this paper we focus on the macroeconomics of border adjustment; that is, the dynamic effects from border taxes that arise due to nominal rigidities in wages and prices and from nominal contracts in asset markets. We therefore deliberately leave aside some important long-run benefits of border adjustment in terms of transfer pricing, profit shifting, and business location (see, e.g., Auerbach et al. 2017; Auerbach and Devereux 2018).

We specify conditions under which the C-BAT would be completely neutral, not just in the long run, as predicted by Lerner symmetry, but also in the short run. By neutrality we mean an outcome in which the equilibrium path of the macro variables remains unchanged independently of whether the border adjustment is implemented or not as a part of a tax policy reform. The conventional static analysis of the border adjustment relies on the trade balance logic, and concludes that C-BAT neutrality is an immediate implication of the country's budget constraint (see Auerbach and Holtz-Eakin 2016; Feldstein 2017). We show here, however, that BAT neutrality in a dynamic monetary macro model is a much taller order.

First, when prices are sticky, C-BAT neutrality requires that the nominal exchange rate appreciates on impact by the magnitude of the BAT to offset its effect on import and export prices. The equilibrium extent of this nominal appreciation depends both on the intertemporal budget constraint of the country and on the monetary policy regime. We show that conventional Taylor rules that respond to output gap and effective consumer price inflation are consistent with C-BAT neutrality. Yet, neutrality fails if monetary authorities react, directly or indirectly, to the nominal appreciation associated with the border adjustment.[4]

Second, beyond a specific type of monetary regime, C-BAT neutrality imposes restrictions on the timing and implementation of the C-BAT reform. In particular, exact neutrality requires that the border adjustment is an unexpected permanent policy shift that applies uniformly to all import and export flows.[5] If the border adjustment is expected ahead of time, is expected to be reversed in the future, or creates expectations of retaliation by trade partners, these expectation effects translate into additional exchange-rate movements, which, given price stickiness, result in distortions to the relative import and export prices. In addition, these expectation effects may alter the dynamic savings and portfolio choice decisions made by the private sector.

Third, the specific nature of import and export price stickiness also matters for the neutrality result. In particular, C-BAT neutrality requires symmetry in the short-run pass-through of exchange-rate and tax changes into import and export prices. While the theoretical PCP and LCP benchmarks satisfy this symmetry requirement, the more empirically motivated case of DCP may fail this requirement, and hence result in deviations from BAT neutrality, which we study in Section IV. Interestingly, we find that the extent of nominal appreciation is not particularly sensitive to the nature of price stickiness and to the extent of exchange-rate pass-through. Instead, it depends more on the trade openness and the relative duration of wage and price stickiness in the economy adopting BAT.

In particular, in our quantitative model calibrated to the United States, a complete and immediate appreciation of the dollar by the extent of the border adjustment remains a good approximation even when exact neutrality fails.[6]

Last, C-BAT neutrality depends on the currency composition of the NFA position of the country. Border adjustment is, in general, associated with important distributional consequences, both within and across countries. In our analysis, we focus on two types of such distributional effects—namely, between the private sector and the government, and across international borders. The international transfer results from the currency appreciation, provided there exists a nonzero NFA position denominated in home currency. Indeed, currency appreciation triggered by C-BAT leads to a capital loss on home-currency net debt. Under these circumstances, C-BAT is, of course, not neutral. Interestingly, if the NFA position is entirely in foreign currency, C-BAT is neutral and there is no associated valuation effect, as under these circumstances the purchasing power of the ROW does not change with the currency appreciation. This is because the valuation loss on foreign-currency assets is exactly compensated by the BAT, which subsidizes exports, leaving the foreign-currency trade prices unchanged.

Independent of the currency of NFA and C-BAT neutrality, border adjustment results in a transfer between the private sector and the government in the home country. In particular, in each period the C-BAT applies, the transfer from the private sector to the government is proportional to that period's trade deficit of the country. If border adjustment is permanent, the country's intertemporal budget constraint implies that the net present value of these transfers equals the NFA position of the country at the time of the policy implementation. The nature of this transfer is akin to a capital levy on the existing NFA position, which is transferred in proportion to the future flow trade deficits.[7] In our model, we make the conventional assumption that macro aggregates do not depend on the distribution of wealth within the home economy, and in particular the Ricardian equivalence holds. As a result, C-BAT neutrality is not violated by this transfer between the home private sector and the government. More generally, currency appreciation associated with C-BAT has distributional consequences between borrowers and lenders, which may trigger departures from C-BAT neutrality in richer models.

Finally, we study quantitatively the trade effects emerging from border adjustment in the plausible cases when C-BAT neutrality is violated. As trade prices and wages adjust, there are no long-run consequences of

C-BAT for trade flows, and therefore all effects are confined to the short run. Under DCP, we find that border adjustment and the associated appreciation, even if incomplete, are likely to depress both imports and exports, with only second-order effects on the overall trade balance. This happens despite the increased profit margins of the home exporters, as they pocket the border adjustment without reducing their dollar export prices in the short run.

Our quantitative model is calibrated to the specific case of the United States and the policy proposal under consideration. The US economy is distinct in a number of ways. First, the United States holds large gross foreign asset positions, with the majority of liabilities denominated in dollars. This results in net foreign dollar liabilities of the order of one US annual gross domestic product (GDP), and hence the dollar appreciation triggered by a 15% BAT results in a transfer from the United States to the ROW of the order of magnitude of 20% of the US GDP. Second, the US dollar enjoys the status of the dominant currency for world trade flows, and thus both imports and exports of the United States are priced in dollars, violating another requirement for C-BAT neutrality.

We find that, despite these departures from neutrality, the US dollar still appreciates on impact of the policy reform by almost the exact amount of the BAT. This is because, while the capital loss on the NFA position is large, it is still dwarfed by the present value of all future US gross trade flows. Also, because the US economy is fairly closed, with a trade-to-GDP ratio of 30%, the nonneutrality arising from the dollar pricing assumption has only a small effect on the exchange rate. At the same time, dollar price stickiness results in depressed short-run trade flows, both imports and exports, which gradually recover as trade prices become flexible. Therefore, we find that C-BAT policy cannot be used to stimulate US exports, with at best a very mild effect on the US trade balance. Instead, it is likely to reduce all international gross trade flows, including those between third countries (see Boz, Gopinath, and Plagborg-Møller 2017).[8]

Another distinct feature of the US economy is its current trade deficit, despite the fact that it is a net debtor country. As discussed above, this implies that the BAT results in a transfer from the private sector to the government budget in the short run, but away from the government budget in the long run. Therefore, in the case of the United States, C-BAT cannot be considered a robust long-run source of government revenues. We also discuss possible caveats to this argument associated with transfer pricing of US imports and the differential rate of return on US gross assets and liabilities.

We also consider the case when the ROW retaliates by announcing their own implementation of the border adjustment at a future date. Such a retaliation stimulates US exports in the time period prior to the ROW implementing C-BAT. This is because the dollar remains mostly unchanged given the expected retaliation in the future, while US exporters gradually pass through the tax cut to foreign buyers and therefore sell more. At the same time, US imports decline immediately and consumer prices rise because of the US border tax. The combined effect is to generate a short-term improvement in the US trade balance, which also stimulates US output and employment.

After having analyzed the C-BAT, we turn to the VAT. While the C-BAT tax reform can be loosely thought of as the combination of two offsetting taxes from the point of view of Lerner symmetry, the VAT tax reform would have to be coupled with a reduction in domestic payroll taxes in order to satisfy this equivalence and be generally neutral under flexible prices. We have studied such coupled policies in Farhi, Gopinath, and Itskhoki (2014). Here, we are interested instead in a tax reform that introduces a VAT without a corresponding reduction in payroll taxes, and hence creates a long-run distortion to the equilibrium labor supply.

We also establish a neutrality result for the VAT, but it is much more restrictive than for the C-BAT. In particular, it holds when labor supply is perfectly inelastic or when nominal wages are completely rigid—the two cases in which the VAT-induced labor wedge does not affect equilibrium employment. Under the circumstances of VAT neutrality, there is no effect on the exchange rate, a stark contrast with the appreciation of the exchange rate that was necessary to deliver neutrality for C-BAT tax reforms. The reason for this lack of exchange-rate adjustment is the symmetric VAT treatment of both domestically and internationally produced goods, so that their relative prices remain unaffected.

When equilibrium employment is not fully inelastic, the VAT tax reform leads to a reduction in domestic labor and a partial appreciation of the exchange rate, reflecting the negative productivity effects of distortionary taxation. For our baseline calibration, the appreciation remains modest (2%) in comparison to the tax change (20%). In addition, exports and imports decline much more modestly than under the C-BAT tax reform. This prediction that with VAT the real exchange-rate appreciation occurs mainly through prices and not the exchange rate is consistent with empirical evidence in Freund and Gagnon (2017).

The rest of the paper is organized as follows. We lay out the general model environment in Section II. We establish the exact conditions for neutrality of the border tax adjustment and of the VAT in Section III.

We proceed in Section IV to study the quantitative implications of various departures from the exact neutrality of the two tax reforms respectively, and conclude in Section V.

II. Model

The model economy features two countries, home H and foreign F. There are three types of agents in each economy—consumers, producers, and the government—and we describe each in turn below. Several ingredients follow from Farhi et al. (2014) and Casas et al. (2016). We focus on two types of tax reforms: a corporate tax reform with a BAT (C-BAT) and a VAT reform.

A. Consumers

The home country is populated with a continuum of symmetric households. Households are indexed by $h \in [0, 1]$, but we often omit the index h to simplify exposition. In each period, each household h chooses consumption C_t, holdings of H and F bonds, and trades a complete set of Arrow-Debreu securities domestically. Each household also sets a wage rate $W_t(h)$ and supplies labor $N_t(h)$ in order to satisfy demand at this wage rate.

The household h maximizes expected lifetime utility, $\mathbb{E}_0 \Sigma_{t=0}^{\infty} \beta^t U(C_t, N_t)$, subject to the flow budget constraint:

$$P_t C_t + B_{t+1} + B_{t+1}^* \mathcal{E}_t + \int_{s \in \mathcal{S}_{t+1}} Q_t(s) \mathcal{B}_{t+1}(s) ds$$

$$\leq (1 + i_t) B_t + (1 + i_t^*) B_t^* \mathcal{E}_t + \mathcal{B}_t + W_t(h) N_t(h) + \Pi_t + T_t, \tag{1}$$

where $\mathcal{E}_t$ is the home-currency price of the foreign currency (i.e., an increase in $\mathcal{E}_t$ is a depreciation of the home currency) and P_t is the price of the domestic final consumption good C_t. Π_t represents domestic post-tax profits that are transferred to households that own the domestic firms. Households also trade risk-free international bonds denominated in H and F currency that pay nominal interest rates i_t^* and i_t respectively. B_{t+1} and B_{t+1}^* are the holdings of the H and F bonds respectively. $\mathcal{B}_t$ is the payout on the Arrow-Debreu security that is only traded domestically with $Q_t(s)$ the period-t price of the security that pays one unit of H currency in period $t + 1$, and state $s \in \mathcal{S}_{t+1}$, and $\mathcal{B}_{t+1}(s)$ are the corresponding holdings. Finally, T_t captures domestic lump-sum transfers from the government.

The per-period utility function is separable in consumption and labor and given by

$$U(C_t, N_t) = \frac{1}{1 - \sigma_c} C_t^{1-\sigma_c} - \frac{\kappa}{1 + \varphi} N_t^{1+\varphi}, \tag{2}$$

where $\sigma_c > 0$ is the household's coefficient of relative risk aversion, $\varphi > 0$ is the inverse of the Frisch elasticity of labor supply, and κ scales the disutility of labor. Intertemporal optimality conditions (Euler equations) for H bonds and F bonds are standard.

Households are subject to a Calvo friction when setting wages: in any given period, they may adjust their wage with probability $1 - \delta_w$, and maintain the previous-period nominal wage otherwise. They face a downward-sloping demand for the specific variety of labor they supply, given by $N_t(h) = \{[W_t(h)]/W_t\}^{-\vartheta} N_t$, where $\vartheta > 1$ is the constant elasticity of labor demand and W_t is the aggregate wage rate. The standard optimality condition for wage setting is given by

$$\mathbb{E}_t \sum_{s=t}^{\infty} \delta_w^{s-t} \Theta_{t,s} N_s W_s^{\vartheta(1+\varphi)} \left[\frac{\vartheta}{\vartheta - 1} \kappa P_s C_s^{\sigma} N_s^{\varphi} - \frac{\bar{W}_t(h)^{1+\vartheta\varphi}}{W_s^{\vartheta\varphi}} \right] = 0, \tag{3}$$

where $\Theta_{t,s} \equiv \beta^{s-t}(C_s^{-\sigma_c}/C_t^{-\sigma_c})(P_t/P_s)$ is the stochastic discount factor between periods t and $s \geq t$, and $\bar{W}_t(h)$ is the optimal reset wage in period t. This implies that $\bar{W}_t(h)$ is preset as a constant markup over the expected weighted average between future marginal rates of substitution between labor and consumption and aggregate wage rates, during the duration of the wage.[9] This is a standard result in the New Keynesian literature, as derived, for example, in Galí (2008).

The foreign households are symmetric.

B.   Producers

Production

In each country there is a continuum $\omega \in [0, 1]$ of firms producing different varieties of goods using a technology with labor and intermediate inputs. Specifically, a representative home firm produces according to

$$Y_t(\omega) = e^{a_t} L_t(\omega)^{1-\alpha} X_t(\omega)^{\alpha}, \qquad 0 < \alpha < 1, \tag{4}$$

where a_t is the (log) aggregate countrywide level of productivity, $L_t(\omega)$ is the firm's labor input, and $X_t(\omega)$ is its purchase of intermediate inputs. The labor input L_t is a constant elasticity of substitution (CES) aggregator of the individual varieties supplied by each household, $L_t = [\int_0^1 L_t(h)^{(\vartheta-1)/\vartheta} dh]^{\vartheta/(\vartheta-1)}$ with $\vartheta > 1$, at a variety-specific wage $W_t(h)$. This implies that the cost of the basket of labor inputs is $W_t = [\int W_t(h)^{1-\vartheta} dh]^{1/(1-\vartheta)}$ and the demand for individual type of labor is $L_t(h) = \{[W_t(h)]/W_t\}^{-\vartheta} L_t$.

Furthermore, we adopt the Basu (1995) roundabout production structure, where the intermediate input X_t is the same as the local final good. The price of the final good is P_t, the domestic price index, but the effective price for firms is $(1 - \tau_t^V)P_t$, because they are reimbursed the VAT τ_t^V on intermediate good purchases. With this, the marginal cost of a domestic firm is given by

$$MC_t = \kappa e^{-a_t} W_t^{1-\alpha}[(1 - \tau_t^V)P_t]^\alpha, \tag{5}$$

where $\kappa \equiv 1/(\alpha^\alpha(1-\alpha)^{1-\alpha})$, and the optimal intermediate good and labor expenditures, respectively, are

$$(1 - \tau_t^V)P_t X_t = \alpha MC_t Y_t \quad \text{and} \quad W_t L_t = (1 - \alpha)MC_t Y_t. \tag{6}$$

The firm sells its product to both the home and foreign market, and we denote the respective quantities demanded by $Q_{HH,t}(\omega)$ and $Q_{HF,t}^*(\omega)$. Therefore, goods market clearing requires $Y_t(\omega) = Q_{HH,t}(\omega) + Q_{HF,t}^*(\omega)$. The profits of a home firm ω are given by

$$\Pi_t(\omega) = (1 - \tau_t^\Pi)\left[(1 - \tau_t^V)(P_{HH,t}(\omega)Q_{HH,t}(\omega) - P_t X_t(\omega)) + \frac{P_{HF,t}(\omega)Q_{HF,t}^*(\omega)}{1 - \iota_t \tau_t^\Pi} - W_t L_t(\omega)\right], \tag{7}$$

where τ_t^Π is the profit tax and $\iota_t \in \{0, 1\}$ is an indicator for whether the profit tax features border adjustment; that is, that exports are deductible from the base of the profit tax. We assume that the VAT τ_t^V is not assessed on the export sales of the firm, as is the case in practice.

Competitive Bundlers

We assume that the final good is not tradable internationally and is used for final consumption, government consumption, and as an intermediate input in production of the domestic firms:

$$Q_t = C_t + G_t + X_t. \tag{8}$$

The final good in each country is assembled in a sector of competitive bundlers that combine all domestic and imported varieties using a

Kimball (1995) aggregator, which defines implicitly the resulting output of the final good Q_t:

$$\int_0^1 \left[\gamma_H \Upsilon \left(\frac{Q_{HH,t}(\omega)}{\gamma_H Q_t} \right) + \gamma_F \Upsilon \left(\frac{Q_{FH,t}(\omega)}{\gamma_F Q_t} \right) \right] d\omega = 1, \tag{9}$$

where $Q_{iH,t}(\omega)$ is the input of variety ω produced in country $i \in \{H, F\}$ and γ_i is the preference parameter, and which in particular captures home bias when $\gamma_H > \gamma_F$. The function Υ is increasing and concave, with $\Upsilon(1) = 1$, $\Upsilon'(\cdot) > 0$, and $\Upsilon''(\cdot) < 0$. This demand aggregation structure gives rise to strategic complementarities in price setting resulting in variable markups and pricing to market (Dornbusch 1987, Krugman 1987). The Kimball (1995) structure also nests the CES case with Υ as a power function.

The profits of the bundlers are given by

$$\Pi_{Ht}^B = (1 - \tau_t^Y)(1 - \tau_t^\Pi) \left[P_t Q_t - \int_0^1 P_{HH,t}(\omega) Q_{HH,t}(\omega) d\omega - \frac{1}{1 - \iota_t \tau_t^\Pi} \int_0^1 P_{FH,t}(\omega) Q_{FH,t}(\omega) d\omega \right]. \tag{10}$$

Since bundlers only use intermediate goods, the VAT applies to their profits, akin to a profit tax. At the same time, profit tax with a border adjustment ($\iota_t = 1$) prevents the deduction of imported products from the base of the profit tax. The competitive bundlers are flexible-price zero-profit firms and price the final output according to the marginal cost of assembly; that is, they immediately pass through their input price changes into the final good price P_t, which is the consumer price index at home. The final good price satisfies

$$P_t = \int_0^1 \left[P_{HH,t}(\omega) \frac{Q_{HH,t}(\omega)}{Q_t} + \frac{P_{FH,t}(\omega)}{1 - \iota_t \tau_t^\Pi} \frac{Q_{FH,t}(\omega)}{Q_t} \right] d\omega, \tag{11}$$

where the quantities demanded satisfy

$$\frac{Q_{HH,t}(\omega)}{Q_t} = \gamma_H \psi \left(\frac{P_{HH,t}(\omega)}{P_t/D_t} \right) \quad \text{and} \quad \frac{Q_{FH,t}(\omega)}{Q_t} = \gamma_F \psi \left(\frac{P_{FH,t}(\omega) D_t}{1 - \iota_t \tau_t^\Pi P_t} \right), \tag{12}$$

where $\psi(\cdot) \equiv \Upsilon'^{-1}(\cdot)$ is the demand curve with $\psi'(\cdot) < 0$ and D_t is an auxiliary variable.[10] Note that the definition of the price index in (11) ensures zero profits for bundlers.

We adopt this formulation with bundlers to reflect that in reality virtually all imports are made by firms, subject to the profit tax, rather than directly by consumers. We return to this assumption and evaluate the robustness of our results in Section IV.

Foreign Firms

Foreign firms are symmetric, producing output according to a counterpart to (4) and facing marginal costs $\mathcal{MC}_t^*$ in parallel with (5). The produced output is split between home and foreign markets: $Y_t^*(\omega) = Q_{FF,t}^*(\omega) + Q_{FH,t}(\omega)$. The profits of the foreign firms (in foreign currency) are given by

$$\Pi_t^*(\omega) = P_{FF,t}^*(\omega)Q_{FF,t}^*(\omega) + \frac{1 - \tau_t^V}{\mathcal{E}_t} P_{FH,t}(\omega)Q_{FH,t}(\omega) - W_t^*L_t^*(\omega) - P_t^*X_t^*(\omega),$$

(13)

where we quote $P_{FF,t}^*(\omega)$ in foreign currency and $P_{FH,t}(\omega)$ in home currency, hence the nominal exchange rate $\mathcal{E}_t$ in the expression. The VAT τ_t^V is levied at the border on all imports, creating a wedge between the consumer price $P_{FH,t}(\omega)$ paid by the home bundlers and the producer price $(1 - \tau_t^V)P_{FH,t}(\omega)$ received by the foreign firms. For simplicity, we assume that the foreign country does not levy profit or VAT, which should be viewed as a normalization without loss of generality for our dynamic analysis.

The foreign bundlers assemble the foreign final good Q_t^* according to an aggregator as in (9), with preference parameters $\gamma_F^* > \gamma_H^*$, reflecting home bias. The foreign bundlers are also competitive flexible-price firms with profits

$$\Pi_{Ft}^{B*} = P_t^*Q_t^* - \int_0^1 P_{FF,t}^*(\omega)Q_{FF,t}^*(\omega)d\omega - \int_0^1 \frac{P_{HF,t}(\omega)}{\mathcal{E}_t} Q_{HF,t}^*(\omega)d\omega = 0.$$

The price index P_t^* and demand schedules for $Q_{FF,t}^*(\omega)$ and $Q_{HF,t}^*(\omega)$ are given by equations similar to (11) and (12).

C.   Price Setting

Markets are assumed to be segmented so firms can set different prices by destination market and invoicing currency, with prices reset infrequently. We consider a Calvo pricing environment where firms are randomly chosen to reset prices with probability $1 - \delta_p$ in any given period. In setting prices, the firms maximize the discounted present value of expected profits conditional on the price staying in effect. Furthermore, we consider three pricing paradigms—PCP, LCP, and DCP, respectively, with home currency (dollar) being the dominant currency. In an extension in Section IV, we additionally discuss alternative assumptions about short-run pass-through of taxes, as well as about the incidence of the C-BAT, to study the robustness of our results.

To fix ideas, it is useful to define three types of prices: (i) producer prices (net prices received by producers in producer currency); (ii) consumer prices (net prices paid by consumers in local currency); and (iii) border prices (net prices paid/received by foreigners at the border in dollars). Depending on the pricing paradigm (PCP, LCP, or DCP), either type of price can be sticky, while others move in the short run together with the exchange rate and taxes. We summarize the three types of prices in table 1 (omitting indicators ω for brevity).

Desired Prices

Before we characterize equilibrium price setting, we first define desired prices of the firms; that is, prices they would set if they could flexibly adjust them. The desired producer prices for home and foreign firms, respectively, are given by

$$\tilde{P}^p_{Hj,t} = \frac{\sigma_{Hj,t}(\omega)}{\sigma_{Hj,t}(\omega) - 1} \mathcal{MC}_t \quad \text{and} \quad \tilde{P}^{p*}_{Fj,t} = \frac{\sigma_{Fj,t}(\omega)}{\sigma_{Fj,t}(\omega) - 1} \mathcal{MC}^*_t, \quad j \in \{H, F\},$$

where $\sigma_{ij,t}(\omega)$ is effective elasticity of demand by

$$\sigma_{iH,t}(\omega) \equiv -\frac{\partial \log Q_{iH,t}(\omega)}{\partial \log \tilde{P}^c_{iH,t}(\omega)} \quad \text{and} \quad \sigma_{iF,t}(\omega) \equiv -\frac{\partial \log Q^*_{iF,t}(\omega)}{\partial \log \tilde{P}^{c*}_{iF,t}(\omega)}, \quad i \in \{H, F\},$$

where $\{\tilde{P}^c_{iH,t}, \tilde{P}^{c*}_{iF,t}\}_i$ are the local-currency consumer prices associated with the desired producer prices $\{\tilde{P}^p_{Hj,t}, \tilde{P}^{p*}_{Fj,t}\}_j$ in producer currency, according to the transformation summarized in table 1. Because of strategic com-

Table 1
Types of Prices

Transaction Price	Producer Price (in Producer Currency)	Consumer Price (in Local Currency)	Border Price (in Dollars)
$P_{HH,t}$	$P^p_{HH,t} = (1 - \tau^V_t)P_{HH,t}$	$P^c_{HH,t} = P_{HH,t}$	...
$P_{HF,t}$	$P^p_{HF,t} = \frac{1}{1-\tau^I_t}P_{HF,t}$	$P^{c*}_{HF,t} = \frac{1}{\mathcal{E}_t}P_{HF,t}$	$P^b_{HF,t} = P_{HF,t}$
$P_{FH,t}$	$P^{p*}_{FH,t} = \frac{1-\tau^V_t}{\mathcal{E}_t}P_{FH,t}$	$P^c_{FH,t} = \frac{1}{1-\tau^I_t}P_{FH,t}$	$P^b_{FH,t} = (1 - \tau^V_t)P_{FH,t}$

Note: Transaction prices are conventionally used in the formulas above and in fig. 1. The border prices refer to the net prices paid/received by foreigners but evaluated in dollars. We omit $P^*_{FF,t}$ for brevity, since it involves no taxes.

plementarities, the desired markup is not constant, in general, and depends on the relative price of the firm.

Local Market

We assume that all domestic prices are sticky in the local currency and exhibit a full pass-through of the VAT in the short run. Therefore, in all pricing regimes, the optimal reset price for domestic sales of home firms satisfies (see appendix, "Price Setting," for details):

$$\mathbb{E}_t \sum_{s=t}^{\infty} \delta_p^{s-t} \Theta_{t,s} (1 - \tau_s^{\Pi}) Q_{HH,s} (\sigma_{HH,s} - 1) \left(\bar{P}_{HH,t}^{p} - \frac{\sigma_{HH,s}}{\sigma_{HH,s} - 1} \mathcal{MC}_s \right) = 0, \quad (14)$$

where $\Theta_{t,s}$ is the stochastic discount factor of home households, as defined in (3), and we omit firm indicator ω for brevity. This expression implies that $\bar{P}_{HH,t}^{p}$ is preset as a markup over expected future marginal costs during the duration of the price. All firms adjusting prices at t set their producer price at $\bar{P}_{HH,t}^{p}$, because we assume no idiosyncratic productivity shocks. In periods of price duration $s \geq t$, the associated consumer price is $P_{HH,s}^{c} = \bar{P}_{HH,t}^{p}/(1 - \tau_s^{V})$, and it fluctuates in proportion with the VAT. The price setting by foreign firms for the foreign market is characterized by a symmetric equation.

Border Prices

We consider three types of border pricing—PCP, LCP, and DCP. We view PCP and LCP as the pure theoretical benchmarks (Obstfeld and Rogoff 2000, Engel 2003) in which either net producer prices (in producer currency) or net consumer prices (in consumer local currency) remain fixed during the period of price nonadjustment. Therefore, under PCP there is full pass-through of both exchange rates and border taxes into the consumer prices, while under LCP both pass-through elasticities are zero. We consider dollar pricing as the third alternative, in which both import and export prices are sticky in dollars (home currency), so that currency fluctuations are absorbed in the short run into the profit margins of foreign firms. At the same time, we assume that BATs are absorbed into the margins of the US (home) firms during the period of price nonadjustment. While there are many other possible departures from the limiting theoretical benchmarks of PCP and LCP, we view our formulation of DCP as the empirically relevant case, at least given our focus on the US economy, but arguably even more generally (see

Gopinath, Itskhoki, and Rigobon 2010; Casas et al. 2016; Boz et al. 2017). These three types of price setting correspond to the three notions of prices in table 1.

Producer Currency Pricing

In this case prices are sticky in H currency for H firms and in F currency for F firms. Furthermore, we assume that the firm presets the pretax price, and BATs operate on top of the preset price. This way, the firm targets an optimal level of markup over its producer-currency marginal cost, and both exchange rate and taxes are added on top of this factory-gate price. This means that under PCP, $P^p_{HF,t}(\omega)$ and $P^{p*}_{FH,t}(\omega)$ are kept unchanged during the period of price nonadjustment, while consumer and border prices move with the exchange rate and border taxes.

Therefore, the optimal reset price of home firms for foreign sales satisfies (again omitting indicator ω for brevity)

$$\mathbb{E}_t \sum_{s=t}^{\infty} \delta_p^{s-t} \Theta_{t,s}(1 - \tau_s^{II}) Q^*_{HF,s}(\sigma_{HF,s} - 1)\left(\bar{P}^p_{HF,t} - \frac{\sigma_{HF,s}}{\sigma_{HF,s} - 1} \mathcal{MC}_s \right) = 0,$$

which exactly parallels the price-setting equation for the home market, allowing however for a different desired markup due to pricing to market. Note that the exchange rate and BAT do not enter this expression directly, as the firm only wants to maintain a certain desired level of markup over its home-currency marginal cost. The exchange rate and BAT affect price setting indirectly, as the foreign-currency consumer price $P^{c*}_{HF,s} = (1 - \iota_s \tau_s^{II})\bar{P}_{HF,t}/\mathcal{E}_s$ affects both the quantity sold abroad $Q^*_{HF,s}$ and the elasticity of demand $\sigma_{HF,s}$. Finally, note the asymmetry between the effects of the VAT and BAT (associated with the profit tax): τ_s^V affects directly the consumer price to home consumers, but not to foreign consumers, while in contrast $\iota_s \tau_s^{II}$ affects the foreign consumer price, but not the home.

A symmetric equation characterizes optimal price setting by foreign PCP firms for the home market:

$$\mathbb{E}_t \sum_{s=t}^{\infty} \delta_p^{s-t} \Theta^*_{t,s} Q_{FH,s}(\sigma_{FH,s} - 1)\left(\bar{P}^{p*}_{FH,t} - \frac{\sigma_{FH,s}}{\sigma_{FH,s} - 1} \mathcal{MC}^*_s \right) = 0,$$

and the associated consumer price at home is $P^c_{FH,s} = (\mathcal{E}_t \bar{P}^{p*}_{FH,t})/[(1 - \iota_s \tau_s^{II})(1 - \tau_s^V)]$, that is, the VAT and the BAT affect it symmetrically.

Local Currency Pricing

In this case, prices are sticky in the destination currency and inclusive of the border adjustment, so that consumers face a constant effective price during the period of price nonadjustment. This means that for prices set at t, effective consumer prices at $s \geq t$ are $\bar{P}^{c*}_{HF,t}$ and $\bar{P}^{c}_{FH,t}$. At the same time, prices received by exporting firms change with both the exchange rate and the BAT according to $P^{p}_{HF,s} = \bar{P}^{c*}_{HF,t}\mathcal{E}_s/(1 - \iota_s\tau^{II}_s)$ and $P^{p*}_{FH,s} = (1 - \tau^{V}_s)(1 - \iota_s\tau^{II}_s)\bar{P}^{c}_{FH,t}/\mathcal{E}_s$. Therefore, the optimal price-setting equations are given by

$$\mathbb{E}_t\sum_{s=t}^{\infty}\delta^{s-t}_p\Theta_{t,s}(1 - \tau^{II}_s)Q^{*}_{HF,s}(\sigma_{HF,s} - 1)\left(\frac{\mathcal{E}_s\bar{P}^{c*}_{HF,t}}{1 - \iota_s\tau^{II}_s} - \frac{\sigma_{HF,s}}{\sigma_{HF,s} - 1}\mathcal{MC}_s\right) = 0,$$

$$\mathbb{E}_t\sum_{s=t}^{\infty}\delta^{s-t}_p\Theta^{*}_{t,s}Q_{FH,s}(\sigma_{FH,s} - 1)\left(\frac{(1 - \tau^{V}_s)(1 - \iota_s\tau^{II}_s)\bar{P}^{c}_{FH,t}}{\mathcal{E}_s} - \frac{\sigma_{FH,s}}{\sigma_{FH,s} - 1}\mathcal{MC}^{*}_s\right) = 0.$$

Dominant Currency Pricing

In this case, we assume that both import and export prices are sticky in dollars (the home currency); however, domestic firms face the BAT on top of the preset prices. In particular, the home exporters preset the border price $\bar{P}^{b}_{HF,t}$ for $s \geq t$, so that the foreign consumers pay $P^{c*}_{HF,s} = \bar{P}^{b}_{HF,t}/\mathcal{E}_s$, while the home producers receive on net $P^{p}_{HF,s} = \bar{P}^{b}_{HF,t}/(1 - \iota_s\tau^{II}_s)$. In this case, the producer price responds immediately to C-BAT, while the consumer price responds immediately to the exchange rate, resulting in an asymmetry in pass-through of exchange rate and border taxes. Similarly, foreign firms also preset the border price $\bar{P}^{b}_{FH,t}$, and therefore the price that they receive changes with the exchange rate, $P^{p*}_{FH,s} = \bar{P}^{b}_{FH,t}/\mathcal{E}_s$, while the net price paid by home importers responds immediately to C-BAT and VAT: $P^{c}_{FH,s} = \bar{P}^{b}_{FH,t}/[(1 - \tau^{V}_s)(1 - \iota_s\tau^{II}_s)]$.

Note the two types of asymmetries relative to the PCP and LCP pricing regimes. The first obvious one is the asymmetry in currency use, as home exports are priced in producer currency, while foreign exports are priced in the consumer (local) currency. Second, there is also an asymmetry in the pass-through of the exchange-rate movements and the border taxes—while foreigners absorb all of the exchange-rate movements, domestic firms absorb the border taxes into their profit margins in the short run. We view this as a realistic description of dominant currency price-setting strategies for US import and export flows.

Given this price-setting assumption, optimal preset prices under DCP satisfy

$$\mathbb{E}_t \sum_{s=t}^{\infty} \delta_p^{s-t} \Theta_{t,s} (1 - \tau_s^{\Pi}) Q_{HF,s}^* (\sigma_{HF,s} - 1) \left(\frac{\bar{P}_{HF,t}^b}{1 - \iota_s \tau_s^{\Pi}} - \frac{\sigma_{HF,s}}{\sigma_{HF,s} - 1} \mathcal{MC}_s \right) = 0,$$

$$\mathbb{E}_t \sum_{s=t}^{\infty} \delta_p^{s-t} \Theta_{t,s}^* Q_{FH,s} (\sigma_{FH,s} - 1) \left(\frac{\bar{P}_{FH,t}^b}{\mathcal{E}_s} - \frac{\sigma_{FH,s}}{\sigma_{FH,s} - 1} \mathcal{MC}_s^* \right) = 0.$$

D. Government and Country Budget Constraints

We assume that the government must balance its budget each period, returning all tax revenues from the VAT and the profit tax in the form of lump-sum transfers T_t to households after financing exogenous government expenditure G_t. This is without loss of generality since Ricardian equivalence holds in this model. Hence, the period t government budget constraint is

$$T_t + P_t G_t = TR_t^{\Pi} + TR_t^V, \tag{15}$$

where (see derivation in the appendix, "Country Budget Constraint")

$$TR_t^{\Pi} = \frac{\tau_t^{\Pi}}{1 - \tau_t^{\Pi}} \Pi_t + \frac{\iota_t \tau_t^{\Pi}}{1 - \tau_t^{\Pi}} (P_{FH,t} Q_{FH,t} - P_{HF,t} Q_{HF,t}^*), \tag{16}$$

$$TR_t^V = \tau_t^V [P_{HH,t} Q_{HH,t} + P_{FH,t} Q_{FH,t} - P_t X_t], \tag{17}$$

where we used the convention that $P_{HH,t} Q_{HH,t} = \int_0^1 P_{HH,t}(\omega) Q_{HH,t}(\omega) d\omega$, and similarly for other variables (including aggregate profits Π_t).

The VAT simply applies to the total value added at home. Similarly, in the absence of border adjustment ($\iota_t = 0$), tax revenues from the profit tax are proportional to aggregate profits Π_t. However with BAT ($\iota_t = 1$), profit tax revenues are instead proportional to aggregate profits minus the trade balance (the difference between the value of aggregate exports and imports).

Combining the above expressions with the household budget constraint (1) and aggregate profits (7), we arrive at the aggregate country budget constraint (see appendix, "Country Budget Constraint"):

$$B_{t+1} + \mathcal{E}_t B_{t+1}^* - (1 + i_t) B_t - (1 + i_t^*) \mathcal{E}_t B_t^* = NX_t, \tag{18}$$

where net exports NX_t are defined as the value of exports minus the value of imports, evaluated at the effective border prices paid/received by foreigners (see table 1):[11]

$$NX_t \equiv P_{HF,t}Q^*_{HF,t} - (1 - \tau^V_t)P_{FH,t}Q_{FH,t}. \tag{19}$$

E. Monetary Policy

The domestic risk-free interest rate is set by H's monetary authority and follows a Taylor rule:

$$i_t - i^* = \rho_m(i_{t-1} - i^*) + (1 - \rho_m)(\phi_M\pi_t + \phi_Y\tilde{y}_t) + \varepsilon_{i,t}. \tag{20}$$

In equation (20), ϕ_M captures the sensitivity of policy rates to domestic price inflation $\pi_t = \Delta\ln P_t$; ϕ_Y captures the sensitivity to the domestic output gap $\tilde{y}_t$, measured as the distance between equilibrium output and flexible price output; ρ_m is the interest rate smoothing parameter; and $\varepsilon_{i,t}$ is the monetary policy shock.

III.   Border Adjustment Neutrality

We start this section by considering the case of the corporate profit tax with and without the border adjustment (C-BAT), assuming there is no VAT. We lay out the conditions for C-BAT neutrality, as well as discuss what happens when they are not satisfied. We also explore the implications for the government budget. We finish the section with an analysis of the VAT.

A.   C-BAT Neutrality

In this section we study the dynamic effects of a corporate profit tax τ^{Π}_t reform at some date t_0, in the absence of any changes in the VAT, so for simplicity we normalize $\tau^V_t = 0$ for all t. More specifically, we are interested in analyzing the circumstances under which the border adjustment associated with the corporate profit tax is consequential for macroeconomic allocations. Therefore, we compare the dynamic paths of the economy under the two scenarios: a corporate tax reform with ($\iota_t = 1$) and without ($\iota_t = 1$) the border adjustment, and we refer to the former case as the C-BAT. In fact, for the neutrality analysis it is inessential whether the profit tax rate τ^{Π}_t changes itself at t_0 or that there is simply a switch from a no C-BAT to a C-BAT profit tax system.

We introduce the following notion of C-BAT neutrality.

Definition 1 (C-BAT neutrality).   Border adjustment associated with the corporate profit tax is neutral if the equilibrium path of all real macroeconomic variables does not depend on whether the border adjustment is implemented or not; that is, whether $\iota_t = 0$ or $\iota_t = 1$.

The neutrality concerns only real macro variables, and does not concern prices, exchange rates, and distributional outcomes across agents or between the private and public sectors, a topic to which we return in Section III.B. The C-BAT neutrality property means that the choice of whether to implement the profit tax with or without the border adjustment is immaterial for the equilibrium path of the economy.

We introduce two additional definitions that prove useful below. First, as we will see, the border adjustment is often associated with an exchange-rate appreciation. In particular, we call this appreciation "complete" if it meets our definition 2.

Definition 2 (complete appreciation).   The dollar appreciation caused by the C-BAT is said to be complete if $[\mathcal{E}_t^1/(1 - \tau_t^{\Pi})] = \mathcal{E}_t^0$ for all t, where $\mathcal{E}_t^1$ and $\mathcal{E}_t^0$ denote the equilibrium values of the exchange rate in otherwise identical economies with ($\iota_t = 1$) and without ($\iota_t = 0$) the C-BAT.

Recall that a fall in $\mathcal{E}_t$ corresponds to an appreciation of the home currency, as fewer units of the home currency are needed to buy one unit of the foreign currency. Therefore, definition 2 implies an appreciation in the home currency proportional to the size of the profit tax τ_t^{Π} when the profit tax is implemented together with the border adjustment. Alternatively, for a given value of the profit tax $\tau_t^{\Pi} = \tau^{\Pi}$ for all t, a reform can involve a switch from no border adjustment $\iota_t = 0$ for $t < t_0$ to a C-BAT $\iota_t = 1$ for $t \geq t_0$ at some date t_0, which triggers an exchange-rate appreciation at t_0 proportional to the existing level of the profit tax τ^{Π}.

The final definition concerns the short-run response of border prices, both to the border tax and to the exchange rate. It turns out to be convenient to use foreign-currency border prices for this definition, namely $P_{ij,t}^{b*}(\omega) = P_{ij,t}^b(\omega)/\mathcal{E}_t$ for $i, j \in \{H, F\}$ and $i \neq j$, where $P_{ij,t}^b(\omega)$ are the home-currency border prices defined in table 1. Therefore, $P_{ij,t}^{b*}(\omega)$ corresponds to the net foreign-currency price paid/received by foreigners for cross-border transactions. The corresponding effective home prices (producer price for exports and consumer price for imports, respectively) in the home currency are

$$P_{HF,t}^p(\omega) = \frac{\mathcal{E}_t}{1 - \iota_t \tau_t^{\Pi}} P_{HF,t}^{b*}(\omega) \quad \text{and} \quad P_{FH,t}^c(\omega) = \frac{\mathcal{E}_t}{1 - \iota_t \tau_t^{\Pi}} P_{FH,t}^{b*}(\omega).$$

The reason for this focus on $P^{b*}_{ij,t}(\omega)$ is that C-BAT neutrality requires, among other things, that foreign relative prices remain unchanged. Hence, we define a symmetric short-run pass-through.

Definition 3 (symmetric short-run pass-through).   During the period of price stickiness, the response of border prices is symmetric for the C-BAT $\iota_t \tau_t^\Pi$ and the exchange rate $\mathcal{E}_t$:

$$\frac{\partial \log P^{b*}_{ij,t}(\omega)}{\partial \log \mathcal{E}_t} = -\frac{\partial \log P^{b*}_{ij,t}(\omega)}{\partial \log(1 - \iota_t \tau_t^\Pi)}, \qquad i,j \in \{H, F\}, \quad i \neq j. \tag{21}$$

Note that this is not an assumption about the strategic price-setting behavior of the firms. Instead, it is an assumption on the mechanical behavior of prices during the period of price stickiness. There are two notable cases in which short-run pass-through is symmetric. The first case is that of PCP pricing, in which the firm fixes the net of tax home-currency price (i.e., $P^p_{HF,t}$ and $P^{p*}_{FH,t} = P^{b*}_{FH,t}$). In this case, any changes in taxes and exchange rates have an immediate complete pass-through into the foreign-market consumer price, and the symmetric short-run pass-through assumption holds. The second case is that of LCP, where the firm fixes the export market consumer price in foreign currency (i.e., $P^{c*}_{HF,t} = P^{b*}_{HF,t}$ and $P^c_{FH,t}$). In this case, changes in taxes or exchange rates have a zero short-run pass-through into the consumer price, and again the symmetry assumption holds. The alternative scenarios, in which the firm absorbs in the short run the tax changes but adjusts in response to the exchange-rate movements, or vice versa, would violate the symmetric short-run pass-through assumption. This, in particular, is the case under our definition of the DCP pricing regime, in which the home-currency border prices $P^b_{ij,t}$ are inflexible, and hence $P^{b*}_{ij,t}$ are fully responsive to the exchange rate but have a zero pass-through to the C-BAT in the short run.

With these definitions in hand, we now introduce the following set of assumptions and prove our main neutrality result below.

Assumptions

1. Border prices are either flexible or exhibit a symmetric short-run pass-through (according to definition 3).
2. The monetary policy rule depends only on the output gap and the effective consumer price index (CPI) inflation (or its expectation), as in (20), and does not depend on the exchange rate or trade price inflation.

3. The foreign assets and liabilities of the countries are exclusively in terms of foreign-currency bonds; $B_t \equiv 0$ for the home-currency bonds.
4. The BAT is a one-time permanent and unanticipated policy shift, with no retaliation (or its expectation) by foreign country.
5. The BAT is uniform and applies to all imports and exports of the home country.

Proposition 1.   When assumptions 1–5 are satisfied, the C-BAT is neutral and the associated currency appreciation is complete, as defined above.

This proposition can be viewed as a complementary result to proposition 3 in Farhi et al. (2014) for the polar opposite case of a fixed exchange-rate regime. Farhi et al. demonstrate that, under a fixed exchange-rate regime, an equivalent fiscal policy to the BAT has the same effect as a nominal devaluation. In contrast, when the exchange rate is flexible and monetary policy follows a conventional Taylor rule, the BAT results in an instantaneous and complete nominal appreciation, and the policy has no real consequences for the macroeconomy; that is, it is neutral.

We now describe the logic behind the proof, which is presented in the appendix ("Proof of C-BAT Neutrality Proposition 1"). Consider an equilibrium allocation in an economy without border adjustment ($\iota_t \equiv 0$ for all t). We check that the same path of macroeconomic variables remains an equilibrium allocation in an economy with the border adjustment ($\iota_t \equiv 1$) and a complete exchange-rate appreciation, $\mathcal{E}_t^1 = (1 - \tau_t^\Pi)\mathcal{E}_t^0$ for all t. The combinations of assumptions 1 and 5, together with the complete exchange-rate appreciation result, ensure that all relative prices in the economy remain unchanged, both in the short and the long run. Indeed, the pass-through is symmetric in the short run, and firms have no incentives to change prices later when they have the opportunity to do so. This can be seen by investigating the optimal price-setting equations from Section II.C; because the costs of the firms remain unchanged, they have no incentive to adjust their producer prices. Assumption 2 then ensures that the monetary policy stance is also unchanged, despite the appreciation, and hence so is aggregate demand in the economy. Assumption 4 ensures that there are no expectation effects that would alter the savings and portfolio choice decisions of the agents. Finally, assumption 3 is needed to guarantee that there are no international wealth transfers triggered by the border adjustment and the associated nominal appreciation. Indeed, this can be observed from the country budget constraint (18), which in this case can be rewritten as

$$B^*_{t+1} - (1 + i^*_t)B^*_t = P^{b*}_{HF,t}Q^*_{HF,t} - P^{b*}_{FH,t}Q_{FH,t}.,$$

with the foreign-currency border prices $P^{b*}_{ij,t}$ following the same equilibrium path regardless of the border adjustment, due to assumption 1. Therefore, we conclude that the same macroeconomic allocation (consumption, output, trade flows, effective price levels, and interest rates) still characterizes the equilibrium path of the economy in the border adjustment regime, coupled with a nominal appreciation of the home currency.

The neutrality result relies on strong assumptions 1–5. In Section III.C, we discuss these assumptions in detail and what goes wrong for the neutrality result when some of them fail. Then, in Section IV, we explore quantitatively the various departures from the neutrality result. Before turning to the violations of the border adjustment neutrality, we look into the government budget consequences of this policy when neutrality holds.

B. Government Budget Revenues

We consider here the case when assumptions 1–5 and this proposition 1 hold, and therefore the C-BAT is neutral for macroeconomic outcomes. Nonetheless, this does not exclude the possibility of the distributional effects, for example between borrowers and lenders, which in our model have no macroeconomic consequences. We focus here on another distributional effect, namely the transfer between the government and the private sector. Indeed, while the overall country budget constraint does not change—there is no transfer from foreign to home—the BAT is associated with a lump-sum transfer between the private sector (households) and the government budget constraints. In particular, this transfer is given by $\Delta^{II}_t = -[\iota_t \tau^{II}_t / (1 - \tau^{II}_t)]NX_t$, as follows from the expression for the profit tax revenues TR^{II}_t in (16) and the definition of net exports NX_t in (19). That is, if a country runs a trade deficit, the border adjustment is associated with a lump-sum transfer from the private sector to the government proportional to the size of the trade deficit and the magnitude of the border adjustment. In contrast, when the trade balance is in surplus, the border adjustment policy is associated with an equivalent transfer, but now from the government toward the households.

Over the long run, the net present value of these transfers depends on the initial NFA position of the country, which from the intertemporal budget constraint is equal to the present value of future trade surpluses and deficits:

$$B_t^* = -\sum_{s \geq t} \frac{\mathcal{E}_s NX_s}{\prod_{j=0}^{s-t}(1 + i_{t+j}^*)}.\tag{22}$$

Therefore, the present value of the government budget surplus from a C-BAT reform at t_0 is $\Sigma_{t_0}^{\Pi} = [\tau^{\Pi}/(1 - \tau^{\Pi})]B_{t_0}^* \mathcal{E}_{t_0}^1$, or equivalently $\Sigma_{t_0}^{\Pi} = \tau^{\Pi} B_{t_0}^* \mathcal{E}_{t_0}^0$ if evaluated under at the pre-reform value of the exchange rate.[12] Note that for the home households, which face an unchanged price level P_t under C-BAT neutrality, this nominal transfer also corresponds to the real loss/gain in household wealth, which is transferred over time to/from the government as the country runs trade deficits/surpluses along the future equilibrium path.

We summarize these results in proposition 2.

Proposition 2. Under assumptions 1–5 ensuring C-BAT neutrality, the border adjustment is associated with a lump-sum transfer Δ_t^{Π} from the private sector to the government in periods of trade deficit, and vice versa. The net present value of these transfers $\Sigma_{t_0}^{\Pi}$ toward the government is proportional to the initial NFA position of the country. In particular,

$$\Delta_t^{\Pi} = -\frac{\tau^{\Pi}}{1 - \tau^{\Pi}} NX_t \quad \text{for} \quad t \geq t_0 \quad \text{and} \quad \Sigma_{t_0}^{\Pi} = \frac{\tau^{\Pi}}{1 - \tau^{\Pi}} B_{t_0}^* \mathcal{E}_{t_0}^1,\tag{23}$$

where τ^{Π} is the profit tax rate after the C-BAT reform at t_0.[13]

What is the nature of this transfer? Consider a representative household holding $B_t^* > 0$ of foreign-currency assets at $t = t_0$. An appreciation ($\mathcal{E}_t\downarrow$) reduces its home-currency purchasing power, $B_t^* \mathcal{E}_t/P_t$, since the home consumer price index P_t is not affected, while the home-currency value of the assets $B_t^* \mathcal{E}_t$ declines. Similarly, it reduces the purchasing power of B_t^* in terms of foreign goods in the home market, $B_t^*(1 - \tau_t^{\Pi})/P_{FH,t}^{b*}$, but not in terms of the pre-border-tax prices, $B_t^*/P_{FH,t}^{b*}$. (Recall that the foreign-currency price paid to foreigners, $P_{FH,t}^{p*} = P_{FH,t}^{b*}$, stays unchanged). As a result, this generates a gap between the price paid by the US private sector and the border price received by the foreigners.[14] The net present value of this gap is exactly $\tau^{\Pi} B_{t_0}^*$, in terms of foreign-currency purchasing power. This capital loss on the asset position of households is realized gradually as households unwind it by purchasing foreign goods and running trade deficits. Trade deficits result in the transfer of funds to the government that pockets the difference in the trade prices that emerged at the border.

The opposite happens in the case of a negative foreign asset position, $B_t^* < 0$, and the government loses revenues to the households.[15]

Why is this transfer nondistortionary? Indeed, we refer to it as a lump-sum transfer because it is associated with no change in relative prices and macroeconomic allocations, as follows from proposition 1. The reason is that the combination of the border adjustment on both import and export flows with the complete offsetting exchange-rate movement ensures that no relevant relative price is affected. Perhaps surprisingly, while home households now pay more for imports than foreign exporters receive due to the border adjustment wedge, this wedge does not alter the relative price of the home- and foreign-produced goods for domestic households due to the home-currency appreciation. Furthermore, due to the Ricardian equivalence, this distributional consequence of the C-BAT does not alter the equilibrium allocations determined by the combined wealth of home households and the home government. This combined wealth remains unchanged when the assumptions underlying C-BAT neutrality (in particular assumption 3) are satisfied, ensuring no wealth transfers across the border.

What are the implications of proposition 2 for the proposed C-BAT reform in the United States? The United States currently holds a large accumulated NFA deficit against the ROW, and simultaneously runs persistent trade deficits. Under these circumstances, the intertemporal budget constraint (22) requires that the US trade deficits eventually convert into trade surpluses in the long run. Therefore, proposition 2 suggests that a C-BAT reform in the United States would generate government surplus in the short run and government deficits in the long run when the trade balance reverses. Over the long run, a C-BAT reform would create a net transfer away from the government budget in proportion with the current US net foreign liabilities.

There are two caveats to this conclusion. First, our analysis here assumes a single international bond, which in particular implies a common rate of return on both the US foreign assets and foreign liabilities. The analysis, however, can be immediately extended to a richer asset market structure (as we do in Farhi et al. [2014]), which allows for the case where the United States holds a riskier foreign asset portfolio commanding a higher expected rate of return relative to the ROW (consistent with the empirical patterns documented by Gourinchas and Rey [2007] and Curcuru, Thomas, and Warnock [2013]). In this case, proposition 2 still applies, and in particular expression (23) for $\Sigma_{t_0}^{\Pi}$ still holds, but now in terms of the risk-adjusted net present value using the stochastic discount factor. In other words, the higher returns on the US foreign assets reflect their higher risk, and hence have to be discounted more heavily, while without adjusting for risk, the United States would indeed run an average trade deficit over time.[16]

Second, there is an issue of mismeasurement of the US NFA position, both due to imprecise valuation of the US assets abroad (e.g., the understated capital gains on foreign direct investment [FDI] and portfolio investment abroad) and the transfer pricing by US importers, which inflated the value of the past trade deficits by overstating the value of the imported goods (Guvenen et al. 2017). In this case, again, proposition 2 applies, but the value of B_t^* used in the calculation of the transfer in (23) needs to be corrected. If transfer pricing is indeed the concern, the C-BAT has an added benefit of reducing incentives for transfer pricing and hence increasing the base of the corporate profit tax at home (as discussed in, e.g., Auerbach et al. 2017).

C.   Departures from BAT Neutrality

We now consider in turn what happens when certain assumptions fail and the neutrality result of proposition 1 does not hold. Consider first the case when the pass-through assumption 1 does not hold. In particular, assume that instead of PCP or LCP, the DCP regime applies. In this case export prices are fixed in the home currency (complete short-run exchange-rate pass-through), but are set inclusive of the BAT (zero short-run C-BAT pass-through). Import prices are set in home currency (zero pass-through), but the BAT is paid by home importers (complete pass-through). We view this as a likely scenario for the United States. In this case, even if the exchange rate appreciates fully, the relative price of imported and domestic goods will be distorted in the short run, before prices adjust, and therefore neutrality fails. We explore this case quantitatively in the next section.

When neutrality does not hold, the appreciation of the exchange rate does not necessarily have to be complete. However, there are two limiting cases, which result in a complete appreciation even when assumption 1 fails. The first is the limit of a closed economy ($\gamma_H^* = \gamma_F \to 0$); as imported goods become a trivial part of the consumption basket, the behavior of their prices is irrelevant for equilibrium outcomes, and the exchange rate appreciates fully. By continuity, the economies that trade little are likely to experience a full appreciation in response to a border adjustment, independently of the nature of price stickiness. The second is the limit in which wages are increasingly more sticky relative to prices, $[(1 - \delta_w)/(1 - \delta_p)] \to 0$, because once prices adjust, this case is akin to PCP. In our quantitative analysis below, we establish that indeed for an economy calibrated to a low degree of trade openness as is the case for the United States and relative price and wage stickiness, a complete exchange-rate appreciation on impact of C-BAT provides a reasonable approximation even when C-BAT neutrality does not hold. Under DCP and with a nearly complete appreciation, border prices increase on impact of the reform— due to the dollar appreciation for exports and due to the border adjustment for imports—and are only gradually adjusted back down. As a result, both exports and imports are depressed in the short run, as we further explore in the next section.

Next consider the case when assumption 2 fails, and the foreign country targets a particular value of the exchange rate $\bar{\mathcal{E}}_t$ so as to prevent its own currency depreciating excessively relative to the dollar. This could arise, for instance, if the banking system in the foreign country has net liabilities in dollars, and the central bank has an incentive to avoid a negative shock to banks' balance sheets. This would lead the foreign central bank to raise its interest rates, resulting in a reduction in foreign demand for both foreign- and home-produced goods, possibly triggering a recession.

Assumption 3 is violated when home holds NFA in home currency; that is, $B_t > 0$. Due to the home-currency appreciation, there is a capital gain on the home-currency NFA position. In particular, if the appreciation is complete (recall definition 2), home receives a capital gain equal to $B_t[(\mathcal{E}_t^0/\mathcal{E}_t^1) - 1] = [\tau^{II}/(1 - \tau^{II})]B_t$, which would be a net transfer from the foreign and would improve the budget constraint of home as a country. As a result, this cannot be an equilibrium, and the appreciation needs to be more than complete for $B_t > 0$ and less than complete for $B_t < 0$. In the case of the United States, $B_t < 0$ (large home-currency foreign liabilities), and hence the BAT with the resulting appreciation generates a large net transfer from the United States to the ROW, as we discuss quantitatively in the next section.[17]

If border adjustment is anticipated (assumption 4 fails), then the movement of the currency takes place prior to the policy implementation, at least in part, resulting in extra short-run dynamics prior to the reform, which would be absent under a reform featuring no C-BAT. If the policy is expected to be reversed, then appreciation is likely to be incomplete on impact, affecting the relative price of traded goods and therefore trade flows. Whether this stimulates or hinders net exports becomes then a quantitative matter, which we address in the next section.

Last, if the border adjustment policy is not uniform across all goods (assumption 5 fails), then it acts effectively as a trade policy of a differential tariff on certain products. For example, assumption 5 is violated if some businesses can avoid BAT on imports as they are not subject to the corporate tax, but instead pay the personal income tax (e.g., as the S corporations do in the United States). It is also violated for services sold domestically to foreigners, such as tourism, education, and health services.

This discussion suggests that the border adjustment neutrality is a tall order, as the assumptions 1–5 are strong and clearly violated in the case of the United States. Once exact neutrality fails, analytical results in a dynamic environment become largely infeasible. This is why, in Section IV, we turn to a quantitative exploration of a calibrated model to assess the likely consequences of a BAT in practice.

D. The Value-Added Tax

We close this section with a brief analysis of an alternative tax reform, which also features the border adjustment, namely the VAT reform. In the long run, with flexible prices and wages, the VAT is a distortionary tax, which unlike the profit tax creates a "labor wedge" in the economy, depressing equilibrium employment. When combined with the labor subsidy, the VAT has the same effects as the border adjustment associated with the corporate profit tax (the C-BAT). Therefore, our above results for C-BAT also apply to a tax reform that jointly increases VAT and reduces the payroll tax, as we study in Farhi et al. (2014). Here instead we consider an alternative reform that only increases the VAT rate τ_t^V at some date t_0, without an associated reduction in the payroll tax.

Due to the induced labor wedge, such VAT policy reform cannot be neutral in general. Nonetheless, in the special case where the equilibrium employment allocation is not sensitive to the VAT labor wedge, the VAT is neutral. For example, in one such special case wages are infinitely sticky and employment is demand-determined given the constant nominal wage $\bar{W}$. The other special case features fully inelastic labor supply $\bar{N}$ and wages of an arbitrary degree of flexibility. Furthermore, the neutrality in this case requires no exchange-rate adjustment, provided the VAT pass-through into prices is complete and instantaneous for all products subject to the VAT—an assumption we adopt here and relax quantitatively later in

Section IV.D. We summarize these results in proposition 3 (see the appendix, "Proof of VAT Neutrality Proposition 3," for a formal proof).

Proposition 3.   Assume (i) wages are infinitely sticky at some $\bar{W}$ or labor supply is inelastic at some $\bar{N}$; (ii) the pass-through of VAT into prices is complete in the short run; and (iii) the monetary policy rule does not respond to a one time-time jump in the price level. Then a one-time unanticipated VAT reform is neutral for the real macroeconomic allocation (consumption, output, trade flows), triggers a one-time instantaneous increase in the consumer price level and an associated reduction in the real wage, and no adjustment in the nominal exchange rate.

How can a VAT reform remain neutral for consumption, output, and international trade, even when it results in a large jump in the price level and a reduction in the home real wage? Consider for concreteness the case with infinitely sticky wages (the case with infinitely inelastic labor supply is similar). With unchanged wages, home producers have no incentive to change producer prices, while consumer prices instantaneously increase by the magnitude of the VAT (see table 1). Similarly, if foreigners do not adjust their producer prices, the price of imported goods at home also increase by the size of the VAT. As a result, the consumer price P_t instantaneously jumps by the same amount.[18] However, because the VAT is reimbursed on intermediate input purchases, the marginal cost of the home producers are not affected (see eq. [5]). Export prices are also unaffected, because export sales are not subject to the VAT and therefore there is no reallocation of purchasing power across the international border. There is, however, a distributional effect within home—the government collects VAT and the households become poorer in real terms due to the jump in the price level. Yet this does not affect aggregate wealth and consumption in the home economy, due to Ricardian equivalence. However, if wages are not fully sticky and labor supply not fully inelastic, the reduction in the real wage associated with the VAT triggers an adjustment akin to that to a negative productivity shock, and the VAT reform is no longer neutral.

The stark difference of this result from the C-BAT neutrality in proposition 1 is the lack of the exchange-rate appreciation following a VAT reform. This is the case because the VAT by itself introduces no asymmetry in the treatment of domestically and internationally produced goods—both home and foreign goods are subject to the VAT when they are purchased for domestic final consumption, but not for intermediate use, and home goods are not subject to the VAT when they are exported. Therefore, VAT introduces no wedge in the relative price of home and foreign goods in the absence of any exchange-rate movements. This is not the case for C-BAT, which treats home- and foreign-produced goods differentially, and hence requires an exchange-rate adjustment to maintain constant the relative prices of foreign goods. While proposition 3 applies to a much narrower set of circumstances then the earlier BAT neutrality result, we find nonetheless that the prediction for the lack of the exchange-rate adjustment is a rather robust feature of VAT reforms, as we show in the following quantitative section.

IV. Quantitative Analysis of Border Adjustment Taxes

In this section we numerically evaluate the impact of BAT, for the case of corporate tax reform (C-BAT) and for the case of VAT. In Section III, we described conditions under which neutrality is obtained. Here we explore the short-term and long-term implications when we depart from neutrality by presenting impulse response functions within the model environment described in Section II. We calibrate to the United States economy and consequently refer to the home country as the United States and the home currency as the dollar.

A. Benchmark Specification

Our benchmark specification is one of a small open economy in that we keep all foreign variables unchanged except for the prices at which they sell to the home market. We allow for both sticky wages and sticky prices. For the pricing environment we choose DCP as the benchmark given the extensive evidence of the dominant role of the US dollar in trade invoicing for US imports and exports (see Goldberg and Tille 2008; Gopinath and Rigobon 2008; Gopinath et al. 2010). Under DCP all border prices are assumed to be sticky in dollars.

In the benchmark case, international asset markets are assumed to be incomplete with only bonds denominated in foreign currency traded, an assumption we later relax. The world interest rate faced by domestic households depends on the amount borrowed by the country as a whole. Specifically

$$i^*_{t+1} = i^* + \psi \left(e^{-(B^*_{t+1} - \bar{B}^*)} - 1 \right),$$

where $\bar{B}^*$ is the exogenously specified steady-state level of foreign-currency assets held by households and $i^* = 1 / \beta - 1$. This assumption ensures that the model is stationary in a log-linearized environment.

For Kimball demand, which gives rise to strategic complementarities in pricing, we adopt the functional form in Klenow and Willis (2016). This gives rise to the following demand for individual varieties:

$$Q_{FH,t}(\omega) = \gamma_F(1 - \epsilon \ln Z_{FH,t}(\omega))^{\sigma/\epsilon} Q_t,$$

where $Z_{FH,t}(\omega) \equiv \{[P_{FH,t}(\omega)]/P_t\}[\sigma D_t/(\sigma - 1)]$, with P_t and D_t as previously defined, and σ and ϵ are two parameters that determine the elasticity of demand and its variability. The elasticity of demand and the elasticity of the desired markup, respectively, are given by

$$\sigma_{FH,t}(\omega) = \frac{\sigma}{1 - \epsilon \ln Z_{FH,t}(\omega)} \quad \text{and}$$

$$\Gamma_{FH,t}(\omega) \equiv -\frac{\partial \log \frac{\sigma_{FH,t}(\omega)}{\sigma_{FH,t}(\omega)-1}}{\partial \log Z_{FH,t}(\omega)} = \frac{\epsilon}{\sigma - 1 + \epsilon \ln Z_{FH,t}(\omega)}.$$

In a symmetric steady state $Z_{ij,t}(\omega) = 1$ for all i, j, and ω, the elasticity of demand is σ, and the elasticity of markup $\Gamma \equiv \mathcal{E}/(\sigma - 1)$. When $\epsilon = 0$, the demand collapses to the CES case with elasticity σ.

B.   Calibration

The parameter values used in the simulation are listed in table 2. The time period is a quarter. Several parameters take standard values as in Galí (2008). We follow Christiano, Eichenbaum, and Rebelo (2011) and set the wage stickiness parameter $\delta_w = 0.85$, which corresponds to roughly a 1.5-year wage duration on average. The average price duration is 1 year, and hence $\delta_p = 0.75$. The steady state elasticity of substitution between home and foreign varieties and between varieties within the home region is assumed to be the same and set to $\sigma = 2$ following Casas et al. (2016). We set $\epsilon = 1$ so as to generate a steady state markup elasticity of $\Gamma = 1$ consistent with the estimate by Amiti, Itskhoki, and Konings (2019). The foreign bond holdings are set to $\bar{B}^* = -7$, to obtain a NFA position of –60% of GDP in steady state. The home bias share is set to $\gamma_H = 0.9$ to obtain a 15% steady state value of imports over GDP.

C.   C-BAT Reform

At time $t = 0$, the economy is in its nonstochastic steady state with a corporate tax of 20%. In the first quarter ($t_0 = 1$) BAT is implemented. Consequently, export sales become fully deductible for home good produc-

Table 2
Parameter Values

	Parameter	Value
Household preferences:		
Discount factor	β	.99
Risk aversion	σ_c	2.00
Labor Frisch elasticity	$1/\varphi$	.50
Disutility of labor	κ	1.00
Production:		
Labor share	$1-\alpha$	.33
SS log-productivity	$\bar{a}$	1.90
Rigidities:		
Wage	δ_w	.85
Price	δ_p	.75
Monetary rule:		
Inertia	ρ_m	.50
Inflation sensitivity	ϕ_m	1.50

Note: Other parameter values are reported in the text.

ers, while home bundlers face a 20% tax increase on imported goods, which they pass on as a cost to consumers and home good producers. Unless otherwise specified, the shock is assumed to be unanticipated and permanent.

The Impact of Pricing Regimes

Figure 2 plots the impulse responses to the permanent introduction of a C-BAT under PCP, LCP, and DCP. In the long run, when prices and wages are flexible, the tax is neutral in our benchmark specification; therefore, we focus on the short-run effects.

First, consider the response under the PCP and LCP regimes. Consistent with proposition 1, the dollar instantaneously appreciates by the full amount of the border tax reform and there is no effect on real variables or on inflation.[19] The symmetry in pass-through of border taxes and exchange rates into buyers' prices neutralizes the impact of the tax reform. In the absence of an output gap or inflation, policy rates are unchanged, which under uncovered interest parity (UIP) is consistent with a one-time permanent exchange rate appreciation.

In the more realistic case of DCP, prices are sticky in dollars for both US exporters and foreign exporters to the United States. In this case the sharp dollar appreciation is associated with a decline in imports and in

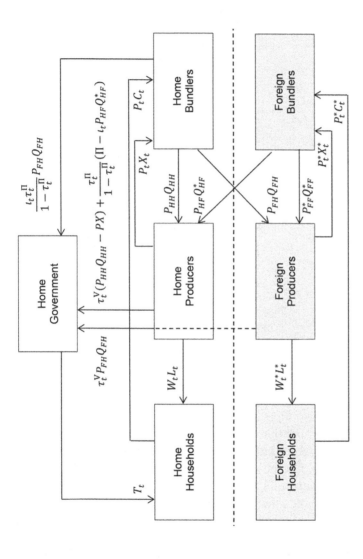

Fig. 1. Value flows. Transaction value flows between agents in the economy. All flows with "Home" are in home currency. Flows within "Foreign" are in foreign currency. For brevity, we suppress government consumption flow $P_t G_t$, as well as time subscript t on certain flows. The direction of arrows indicates the direction of payments; the goods/factors flow in the reverse direction. VAT is represented as τ_t^V, and τ_t^Π is the profit tax with $\iota_t = 1$ if it includes the BAT.

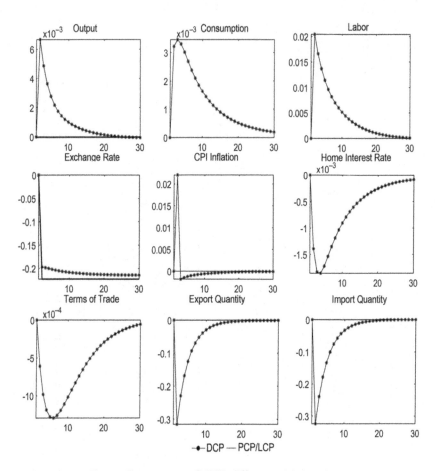

Fig. 2. Response to a C-BAT: different pricing regimes

exports. This is because under DCP, import prices at-the-dock are sticky in dollars and respond minimally to the exchange-rate appreciation in the very short run. On the other hand, the bundlers pass through the C-BAT to their buyers fully. Consequently, from the perspective of producers and households there is an increase in the relative price of imports to home goods, resulting in a 30% drop in demand for imports. On the export side, the sticky export price in dollars does not respond to the C-BAT and consequently the nearly complete (18%) dollar appreciation raises the price of US exports in foreign currency, leading to a drop in exports of almost 30% as foreign buyers switch away from home goods. The DCP case effectively implies a significant decrease in trade compared with PCP and LCP. The terms of trade remain stable as border prices in dollars adjust sluggishly, and the trade balance remains stable due to the counterbalancing effects on imports and exports.

The increase in the consumer price of imported goods generates a transitory spike in CPI inflation in the first quarter that turns slightly negative due to the gradual negative adjustment of import prices in response to the dollar appreciation.[20] Given that the monetary policy rule reacts to the persistent components of inflation as opposed to the highly transitory short-term inflation, the central bank cuts interest rates (negligibly) to mitigate the expected deflation triggered by import price adjustment. Output increases by 0.4% due to both the effect of import substitution on the production of home goods and the effect of the negative real rate in stimulating consumption. Overall, the impact on output and consumption is small owing to the low level of openness of the US economy. This is also consistent with a close to one-time appreciation of the dollar as interest rates remain broadly unchanged.

Valuation Effects

We now discuss the case where the home country holds debt in both foreign currency and home currency. In the benchmark case, when debt is fully denominated in foreign currency, the exchange-rate appreciation is not associated with wealth transfers across countries, despite the possible redistribution effects within countries (see proposition 2). In contrast, when debt is partially owed in home currency, the home-currency appreciation triggers a capital loss and generates a net transfer from the debtor to the lender country. If the home country is a debtor, like the United States, it experiences a negative valuation effect.[21]

We calibrate the valuation effect to the features of the US NFA position. US external liabilities are 180% of GDP, of which 82% are in dollars. US external assets are 120% of GDP, of which 32% is in dollars. Therefore, the NFA position in dollars is $B_0/GDP_0 = 0.82 \cdot 1.8 - 0.32 \cdot 1.2 = 1.09$, and we simulate an economy with a negative valuation effect of $B_0 \cdot (1 - \mathcal{E}_1/\mathcal{E}_0)$, or 15% of GDP.

Figure 3 plots simulation results when the debt is partially held in dollars, under the benchmark simulation along with the baseline DCP pricing. In this case neutrality is violated both in the short run and in the long run. As depicted in figure A3, the exchange rate also appreciates instantaneously to (almost) its long-run value; however, compared with the case without valuation effects, the size of this appreciation is smaller for reasons discussed in Section III.C. The negative wealth effect that re-

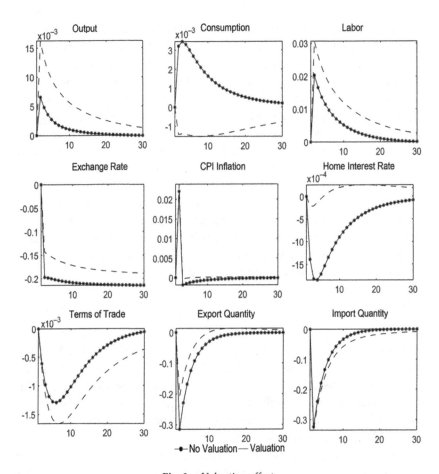

Fig. 3. Valuation effects

sults in a transfer from the United States to the ROW along with the dollar appreciation then results in a decline in imports as US consumption demand declines and imports become relatively more expensive. Despite the smaller appreciation of the dollar, the negative impact on imports is as large as the case without valuation effects because in the short run, exchange rate pass-through is low and the entire effect is driven by the tax, which has not changed. On the other hand, the smaller appreciation of the dollar mutes the negative impact of the C-BAT on exports and on net the trade balance, and output increases. The quantitative difference from the no-valuation-effect case is, however, not very large, as the transfer to the ROW, while large as a fraction of annual GDP, is still small relative to home wealth.

Retaliation/Shocks to UIP

We now consider the impact of retaliation from the ROW, modeled in an admittedly stylized way. In particular, we model this as a shock to the UIP condition that occurs alongside the imposition of C-BAT and prevents the dollar from appreciating by the extent of the tax. This can occur when countries try to prevent a large depreciation of their currency relative to the dollar.[22] The UIP shock is calibrated to have a half-life of 2 years and to reduce the impact effect of the C-BAT on the exchange rate by half. Figure 4 depicts the results in this case.

The calibration imposes the benchmark values along with DCP. In this case long-run neutrality and a long-run appreciation of the dollar that offsets the tax completely continue to hold. However, short-run

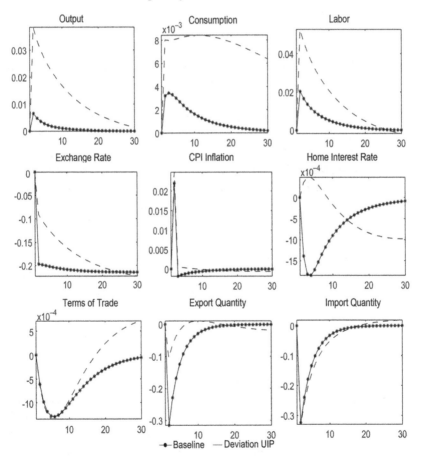

Fig. 4. Deviation from UIP

dynamics are significantly different as the dollar appreciates by half of its long-run value in the short run and then gradually appreciates over time to its long-run value, consistent with the UIP shock fed in. The smaller appreciation of the dollar leads to a significantly smaller drop in exports as export prices in destination currency rise by less. On the other hand, imports decline by almost as much as in the case without the UIP shock in the short run. This is because under DCP, short-run exchange-rate pass-through is low and consequently the weaker dollar appreciation makes little difference to the level of import demand. The combined effect of a weaker drop in exports and a similar decline in imports (as compared with the case without the UIP shock) results in a larger improvement in the trade balance through the expenditure-switching effect on output.

Border Adjustment Retaliation

Instead of targeting the exchange rate, other countries can react by border-adjusting their existing corporate taxes. To simulate this scenario we extend the model to include two large countries: the United States representing 25% of the world economy and the ROW. In figure 5, we consider the case when the ROW makes an announcement to retaliate in the future (1 year, or 4 quarters, later), once the United States has introduced the C-BAT. The US policy change with the ROW retaliation announcement creates the long-term expectation of a counteracting border adjustment, which results in nearly no exchange rate adjustment—neither on impact, nor in the future. This implies that US exports do not decline in the year in which the retaliation is announced, but not implemented. In fact, as more US producers are able to update prices and pass through the export deduction, exports increase, with positive effects on domestic production, consumption, employment, and trade balance. There is also a temporary spike in consumer price inflation from the tax on imports. As the ROW retaliates, these effects subside.

Nonuniform Implementation of C-BAT

We now model the possibility that a fraction of importers are not subject to the border adjustment. The C-BAT may not be universal whenever exemptions apply to certain industries, such as tourism, or when some companies engage in tax avoidance. We call such companies "X-Corps."

Figure 6 compares the simulation results when the import tax applies to all imports and when X-Corps make up 50% of imports; that is, half of

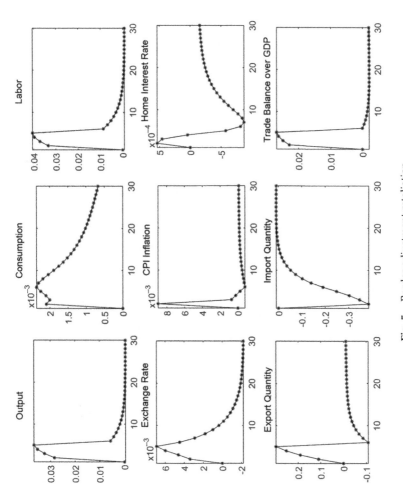

Fig. 5. Border adjustment retaliation

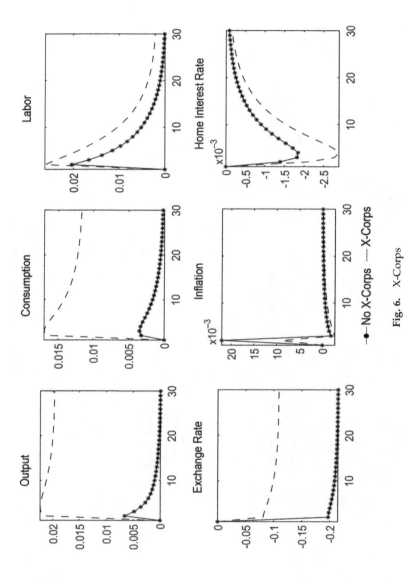

Fig. 6. X-Corps

432

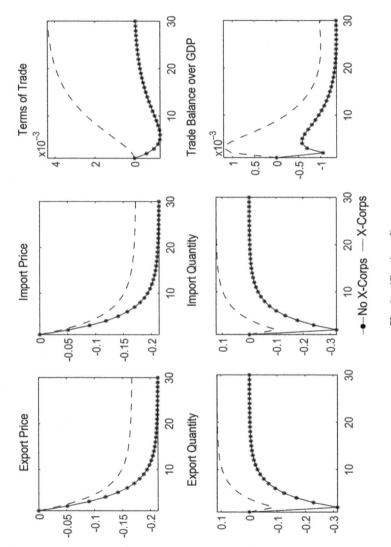

Fig. 6. (Continued)

bundlers are exempted from C-BAT. When X-Corps are present, long-run neutrality does not hold anymore. The border adjustment effectively works as a net export subsidy because the tax discount on export sales is not matched by an equivalent import tax. As a result, the equilibrium dollar appreciation is smaller by about a half. As in the benchmark, the instantaneous appreciation of the dollar, paired with the short-term dollar price stickiness, makes imports and exports fall in the short run but by a smaller amount because of the weaker appreciation of the dollar in the case of exports and the exemption of half of importers from the C-BAT in the case of imports.

D.   *VAT Reform*

In this section we numerically evaluate the implementation of a 20% VAT in the US economy. The model is specified and calibrated in the same way as before. In Section III, we demonstrated that under the assumption of a full pass-through of the tax and inelastic labor supply, the VAT is neutral and the value of the dollar remains unchanged. In this section we explore the importance of assumptions on pricing, labor supply elasticity, and tax pass-through on the neutrality of VAT both in the short run and in the long run.

At time 0, the economy is in its nonstochastic steady state, with zero VAT or BAT. Figure 7 depicts the response to an unexpected and permanent onset of a 20% VAT tax in the first quarter. The VAT is levied on all goods sold in the domestic market and rebated back for the purchase of intermediaries. The VAT is not levied on exports to the ROW. When introduced, the tax is assumed to be fully passed through to domestic and import prices. In other words, firms do not absorb the VAT into their short-run profit margins. Figure 7 presents the case with DCP and PCP producers facing elastic labor supply, and we contrast that to the case with inelastic labor supply.

When labor is inelastically supplied, VAT has no impact on employment and output by construction and the tax is neutral both in the short run and in the long run. The introduction of the VAT results in an instantaneous increase in the price of domestic goods and of imports by 20% given our assumption of full pass-through, and dollar export prices remain unchanged because they are exempt from the VAT. Consequently, there are no expenditure-switching effects either at home or in the ROW. Aggregate demand is also unaffected as all revenues are returned lump-sum to households. The decline in real wages takes place entirely through

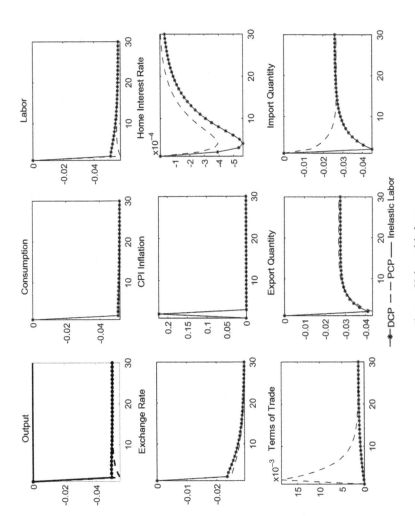

Fig. 7. Value-added tax

the increase in prices, and nominal wages remain unchanged. Though the price of intermediate inputs faced by domestic producers increases by 20%, it is fully offset by the VAT deduction. Because nominal marginal costs of domestic producers stay fixed, domestic firms do not desire to update their prices. Even though the VAT includes a border adjustment feature, unlike the case of the C-BAT, neutrality is associated with no exchange-rate appreciation. This is because all relative prices (inclusive of taxes) remain unchanged even without a dollar adjustment, which is not the case under C-BAT. With nominal marginal costs unchanged for domestic producers and no change in the dollar's value, neither domestic producers nor foreign exporters have a desire to change their pretax price; consequently the choice of currency of invoicing is irrelevant in the case with perfectly inelastic labor supply.

Next, we consider the realistic case of elastic labor supply with a benchmark Frisch elasticity of 0.5. In this case we no longer have long-run neutrality and this holds for either PCP or DCP. In either case the decrease in real wages is associated with a decline in labor supply. The general equilibrium effect is around a 5% decrease in output, consumption, and labor. The instantaneous full pass-through of the VAT makes nominal marginal costs relatively stable at their initial level. As a consequence, inflation is negligible in the quarters after the VAT introduction. The decline in output generates a cut in interest rates that is associated with an expected appreciation of the dollar. On impact the exchange rate appreciates, but not nearly as much as the magnitude of the VAT tax or the response documented in Section IV for a C-BAT of the same size.

The effects under DCP and PCP are similar because of the low dollar appreciation, and because both cases assume the same tax pass-through. One exception is with regard to import quantities that take a larger hit under DCP because import prices do not instantaneously pass through the effect of the dollar appreciation.

Sensitivity to Elasticity of Labor Supply

We demonstrate here that the low response of the exchange rate remains even as we increase the elasticity of labor supply, the size of the demand elasticity parameter, or the measure of relative risk aversion. Figure 8 plots the impulse responses to a 20% VAT rise, under four different parameterizations. The first case corresponds to the calibration in table 2: Frisch elasticity $\varphi^{-1} = 0.5$, risk aversion $\sigma_c = 2$, and elasticity of substitution between varieties σ = 2. The other three cases test the effect of changing these parameters to stimulate a larger appreciation.

Changing the Frisch elasticity from 0.5 to 2 almost doubles the effect on output and labor, but the dollar appreciates by only 3% because relative import and export prices move again closely to the benchmark case. Decreasing the risk aversion parameter from 2 to 1 implies a change to the Walrasian labor elasticity, and the effects are similar to the high Frisch elasticity case. Finally, making demand more inelastic by setting σ = 1.5 can cause a somewhat larger dollar appreciation but the general equilibrium effect is again similar to the benchmark case.

Sensitivity to VAT Pass-Through

We now discuss the case where we relax the assumption of instantaneous pass-through of the VAT into consumer prices. Under partial pass-through, both the short-term output drop and the appreciation of the dollar are amplified. Moreover, the slow dynamics of inflation imply that the assumptions on monetary policy response start to matter.

We present the results only under DCP. Using the notation in table 1, partial pass-through can be introduced by assuming that only a fraction $\lambda \in [0, 1]$ is passed through instantaneously into the consumer prices:

$$P^b_{FH,t} = (1 - \tau^V_t)^\lambda P_{FH,t}$$
$$P^p_{HH,t} = (1 - \tau^V_t)^\lambda P_{HH,t}.$$

As a consequence, a fraction $1 - \lambda$ of the VAT will be absorbed into the short-term profit margins of importers and domestic producers.

Figure 9 depicts the effect of a 20% VAT introduction when $\lambda = 1$ (the benchmark case in figs. 7 and 8) and $\lambda = 0.5$. When the VAT is passed through 50%, the import and aggregate price levels only rise by 10% in the first quarter. The rest of the tax is absorbed by foreign exporters and domestic producers with sticky prices. Firms start updating their prices in the following quarters to offset the 10% tax incidence on their margins. This generates expected positive inflation that the central bank responds to. In this case, we assume that the Taylor rule fights expected inflation but not the output gap. And the implied boost in interest rate leads to a larger dollar appreciation and a more intense recession. The large dollar appreciation causes export sales to drop by 20% in the short term. Import quantities are less responsive because prices are sticky in dollars and the tax pass-through between domestic goods and imported goods is symmetric.

In conclusion, with a partial VAT pass-through, assumptions on price stickiness and monetary policy response count. Under a BAT,

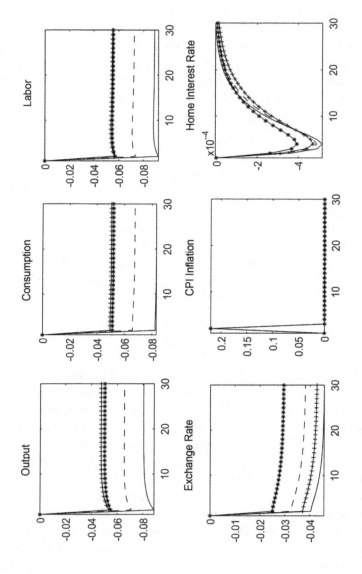

Fig. 8. VAT: alternative parameterizations

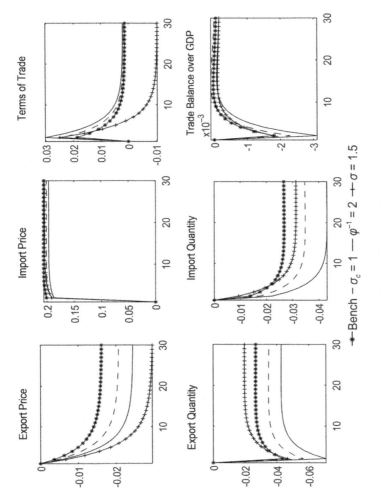

Fig. 8. (Continued)

439

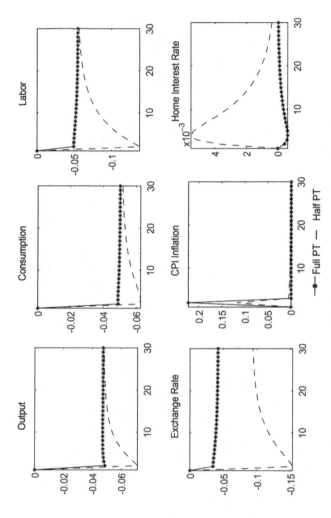

Fig. 9. VAT: alternative pass-through assumptions

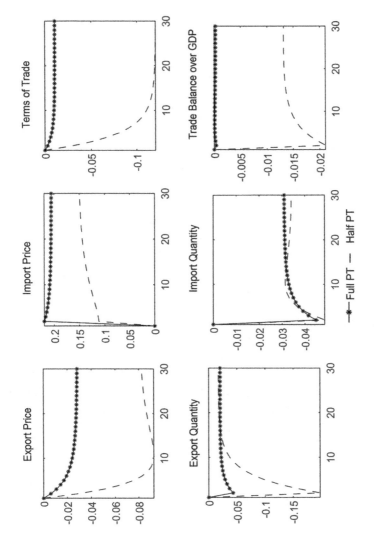

Fig. 9. (Continued)

441

the calibration of the Taylor rule is of second-order importance because the inflation and the output responses are small, as the BAT only affects international prices. Instead, a VAT with partial pass-through affects inflation dynamics of both imports and domestically produced goods, which entails a sharp response of monetary policy that can generate a large short-term appreciation as in figure 9.

V. Conclusion

Our analysis of BAT demonstrates that the Lerner (1936) symmetry result holds only under very special circumstances that are unlikely to hold up in reality. As discussed, the C-BAT is unlikely to be neutral either in the short run or in the long run once we recognize that there is a differential pass-through of taxes and exchange rates into the prices buyers face, the accompanying exchange appreciation can lead to large valuation effects and net transfers to the ROW, and the policy can trigger retaliation from the ROW. In the case of the VAT, neutrality breaks down under weaker conditions. There are other important differences between a VAT and C-BAT. For the United States, a VAT generates only a weak exchange-rate response, while a C-BAT generates a strong exchange-rate response and consequently strong valuation effects.[23] On the other hand, a VAT is far more distortionary to output as compared with a C-BAT. While there is some empirical evidence that confirms the theoretical predictions of a VAT for the exchange rate, much less is known empirically about the impact of a C-BAT or its equivalent of a VAT-payroll tax swap, and so this remains an avenue for future research. Finally, our analysis evaluates the impact of various tax policies, assuming that monetary policy follows a Taylor rule. There is of course the important question of what the outcomes would look like under optimal monetary policy and how that monetary policy differs from a Taylor rule—an exploration that we leave for future research.

Appendix

Price Setting

Consider the profit maximization by the home firms:

$$\max \; \mathbb{E}_t \sum_{s=t}^{\infty} \delta_p^{s-t} \Theta_{t,s} \Pi_s(\omega),$$

where $\Pi_s(\omega)$ is defined in (7), and subject to production

$$Y_s(\omega) = e^{a_s}L_s(\omega)^{1-\alpha}X_s^\alpha = Q_{HH,s}(\omega) + Q_{HF,s}^*(\omega)$$

and demand constraints

$$Q_{HH,s}(\omega) = \gamma_H\psi\left(\frac{P_{HH,s}(\omega)}{P_s/D_s}\right)Q_s \quad \text{and} \quad Q_{HF,s}^*(\omega) = \gamma_H^*\psi\left(\frac{P_{HF,s}(\omega)/\mathcal{E}_s}{P_s^*/D_s^*}\right)Q_s^*.$$

Under PCP, maximization is with respect to preset producer prices $\bar{P}_{HH,t}^p(\omega)$ and $\bar{P}_{HF,t}^p(\omega)$, such that

$$P_{HH,s}(\omega) = \frac{\bar{P}_{HH,t}^p(\omega)}{1-\tau_s^V} \quad \text{and} \quad P_{HF,s}(\omega) = (1 - \iota_s\tau_s^{\Pi})\bar{P}_{HF,t}^p(\omega).$$

Under LCP, maximization is with respect to preset consumer prices $\bar{P}_{HH,t}^c(\omega)$ and $\bar{P}_{HF,t}^{c*}(\omega)$, such that

$$P_{HH,s}(\omega) = \bar{P}_{HH,t}^c(\omega) \quad \text{and} \quad P_{HF,s}(\omega) = \mathcal{E}_s\bar{P}_{HF,t}^{c*}(\omega).$$

Under DCP, maximization is with respect to preset export border price in dollars $\bar{P}_{HH,t}^b(\omega)$, such that

$$P_{HF,s}(\omega) = \bar{P}_{HF,t}^b(\omega).$$

Formal differentiation results in price-setting equations in the text upon simplification, in particular using the definition of demand elasticity $\sigma_{Hj,s}(\omega)$ and marginal cost $\mathcal{MC}_s$. Similar formulation applies to the price setting by foreign firms, and making use of the definitions of prices in table 1.

Country Budget Constraint

Define $\Delta^{NFA} = B_{t+1} + \mathcal{E}_tB_{t+1}^* - (1 + i_t)B_t - (1 + i_t^*)\mathcal{E}_tB_t^*$. Then we reproduce (1), (7), (10), and (15) as the following system:

$$\Delta^{NFA} = W_tL_t + \Pi_t + T_t - P_tC_t,$$

$$\Pi_t = (1 - \tau_t^{\Pi})\left[(1 - \tau_t^V)(P_{HH,t}Q_{HH,t} - P_tX_t) + \frac{P_{HF,t}Q_{HF,t}^*}{1 - \iota_t\tau_t^{\Pi}} - W_tL_t\right],$$

$$0 = \Pi_{Ht}^B = (1 - \tau_t^V)(1 - \tau_t^{\Pi})\left[P_tQ_t - P_{HH,t}Q_{HH,t} - \frac{1}{1 - \iota_t\tau_t^{\Pi}}P_{FH,t}Q_{FH,t}\right],$$

$$T_t + P_tG_t = TR_t^V + TR_t^{\Pi} = TR_t,$$

where

$$TR_t = \tau_t^V [P_{HH,t}Q_{HH,t} + P_{FH,t}Q_{FH,t} - P_tX_t]$$
$$+ \tau_t^{\Pi}\left[(1 - \tau_t^V)(P_{HH,t}Q_{HH,t} - P_tX_t) - W_tL_t\right] + (1 - \iota_t)\tau_t^{\Pi}P_{HF,t}Q_{HF,t}^*$$
$$+ \tau_t^{\Pi}(P_tQ_t - P_{HH,t}Q_{HH,t}) - (1 - \iota_t)\tau_t^{\Pi}P_{FH,t}Q_{FH,t}.$$

Using the definitions of profits, we simplify the expression for tax revenues:

$$TR_t = \tau_t^V [P_{HH,t}Q_{HH,t} + P_{FH,t}Q_{FH,t} - P_tX_t] + \frac{\tau_t^{\Pi}}{1 - \tau_t^{\Pi}}\Pi_t$$
$$- \frac{\iota_t\tau_t^{\Pi}}{1 - \tau_t^{\Pi}}\left[P_{HF,t}Q_{HF,t}^* - P_{FH,t}Q_{FH,t}\right],$$

which corresponds to (16) and (17) in the text.

Finally, we combine the government and the household budget constraints (using $Q_t = C_t + G_t + X_t$) to arrive at the country budget constraint
(18) in the text:

$$\Delta^{NFA} = W_tL_t + \Pi_t + TR_t - P_t(C_t + G_t)$$
$$= P_{HH,t}Q_{HH,t} + \frac{P_{HF,t}Q_{HF,t}^*}{1 - \iota_t\tau_t^{\Pi}} - P_tQ_t + \tau_t^V P_{FH,t}Q_{FH,t} - \frac{\iota_t\tau_t^{\Pi}}{1 - \tau_t^{\Pi}}\left[P_{HF,t}Q_{HF,t}^* - P_{FH,t}Q_{FH,t}\right]$$
$$= P_{HF,t}Q_{HF,t}^* - (1 - \tau_t^V)P_{FH,t}Q_{FH,t} = NX_t,$$

where net exports

$$NX_t = P_{HF,t}Q_{HF,t}^* - (1 - \tau_t^V)P_{FH,t}Q_{FH,t},$$

as defined in (19) in the text.

Proof of C-BAT Neutrality Proposition 1

Consider an equilibrium path of macro variables at home $\mathbf{Z} \equiv \{P_t, W_t, C_t,$
$L_t, Q_t\}_{t\geq 0}$ in an economy without border adjustment, $\iota_t = 0$ for all t, and
also an associated equilibrium path of the nominal exchange rate $\{\mathcal{E}_t^0\}$.
We prove that the same path of variables at home and abroad $(\mathbf{Z}^*)$ remains an equilibrium in an economy with a one-time unanticipated
C-BAT reform at $t_0 > 0$ at home, that is $\iota_t = 1_{\{t\geq t_0\}}$ with $\tau_t^{\Pi} = \tau^{\Pi}$ for all
$t \geq t_0$, with a new equilibrium path of the exchange rate given by

$$\mathcal{E}_t^1 = (1 - \iota_t\tau_t^{\Pi})\mathcal{E}_t^0.$$

Assuming this is the case, we check in turn:

1. That the relative consumer prices in every period are unaffected. C-BAT and exchange rate do not directly affect $P_{HH,t}$ and $P^*_{FF,t}$, so we only need to check the international prices. Under assumption 1, the path of consumer prices $P^c_{FH,t} = (P^{b*}_{FH,t}\mathcal{E}^1_t)/(1 - \iota_t\tau^{II}_t)$ and $P^{c*}_{HF,t} = P^{b*}_{HF,t}$ is unchanged on impact, as $\mathcal{E}^1_t/(1 - \iota_t\tau^{II}_t) = \mathcal{E}^0_t$, and pass-through into $P^{b*}_{FH,t}$ and $P^{b*}_{HF,t}$ is symmetric (see definition 2). With this (and with assumption 5), P_t, P^*_t, and consumer demand $Q_{iH,t}$ and $Q^*_{iF,t}$ remain unaffected on impact of the reform.

2. That firms do not want to change the path of their price changes at all dates. This follows directly from the price-setting equations in Section II.C for the PCP and LCP cases since either $\mathcal{E}_t$ and ι_t do not enter at all or enter jointly as $\mathcal{E}^1_t/(1 - \iota_t\tau^{II}_t)$, and hence there is no change to the price-setting outcome relative to the economy without border adjustment. This confirms that the path of all prices and product demand remains the same for all t.

3. Given demand for goods, the demand for labor and intermediate goods remains unchanged. Therefore, the wage setting remains unchanged. These equations do not feature either $\mathcal{E}_t$ or ι_t. This means that W_t, L_t and Q_t follow the same path with and without border adjustment.

4. Next we confirm that Euler equations continue to hold for the same path of C_t. This is indeed the case since consumer price level P_t follows the same path, and so does the interest rate set by monetary policy in the absence of changes to the path of inflation and output gap (assumptions 2 and 4).

5. Last, we check that the country budget constraint (18) continues to hold under the same allocation. This is indeed the case under assumption 3 ($B_t \equiv 0$), as we can rewrite (18) as

$$B^*_{t+1} - (1 + i^*_t)B^*_t = \frac{P_{HF,t}}{\mathcal{E}_t}Q^*_{HF,t} - \frac{P_{FH,t}}{\mathcal{E}_t}Q_{FH,t} = P^{b*}_{HF,t}Q^*_{HF,t} - P^{b*}_{FH,t}Q_{FH,t},$$

with the path of border prices unaffected (see point 1 above).

This confirms that $\mathbf{Z}$ remains an equilibrium path of macro variables in an economy with border adjustment. QED.

Proof of VAT Neutrality Proposition 3

The proof of VAT neutrality follows the same steps as that of the C-BAT neutrality above, with the difference that now $\mathbf{Z}^V \equiv \{\mathcal{E}_t, W_t, C_t, L_t, Q_t, Q_{iH,t}\}_{t\geq0}$ is the path of macro variables (including nominal exchange rate), which remains unchanged after the introduction of a VAT, while the consumer price level jumps on impact of the VAT reform by the magnitude of the tax:

$$P_t^1 = \frac{P_t^0}{1 - \tau_t^V} \quad \text{for} \quad t \geq t_0.$$

As a result, the real wage W_t/P_t falls on impact by the same magnitude. Assuming this is the case, we verify:

1. The relative prices do not change on impact, since $P_{HH,t}^1 = P_{HH,t}^0/(1 - \tau_t^V)$ and $P_{FH,t}^1 = P_{FH,t}^0/(1 - \tau_t^V)$, that is, both increase by value of the VAT due to the complete pass-through assumption, resulting in a jump in P_t as described above. The prices in the foreign are unaffected by VAT and there is no exchange-rate movement, so the relative prices there are also unchanged. As a result, the quantities of the products demanded are unchanged on impact.

2. The marginal costs (due to VAT reimbursement on intermediate inputs), producer prices, sales, and profits of the firms remain unchanged, and therefore they do not change their price-setting behavior when they adjust prices.

3. Since there is a one-time jump in the price level and no change to the following path of inflation, there is no change in the monetary policy, and consumption-saving decisions remain unchanged.

4. There is no change to the border prices paid/received by the foreigners, and therefore the country budget constraint remains unchanged.

5. It only remains to verify that the old path of $\{W_t, L_t\}$ is consistent with equilibrium. If wages are infinitely sticky, $W_t \equiv \bar{W}$ in both cases, the path of L_t is demand determined, and product demand did not change, therefore equilibrium L_t is unchanged. If labor is in perfectly inelastic supply at some $L_t \equiv \bar{N}$, then we need to verify that the equilibrium path of wages W_t remains unchanged. This is the case because the firm would demand the same amount of labor $\bar{N}$ only if wages do indeed remain unchanged.

This completes the proof of the proposition. QED.

Extensions

Strategic Complementarities and Incomplete Pass-Through

Figure A1 plots the impulse response for the DCP case with different values of markup elasticity, $\Gamma \in \{0, 1, 6\}$, with the $\Gamma = 1$ case corresponding to the baseline and $\Gamma = 0$ corresponding to the CES (constant markups). A larger value of Γ corresponds to a lower pass-through of marginal costs into prices, or equivalently stronger strategic complementarities in the price setting (see Amiti et al. 2019). The figure indicates only very mild differences between our baseline and the constant markup case. Raising $\Gamma = 6$, an implausibly high value empirically, still results in about the same exchange-rate movement, but leads to more protracted future deflation, triggering a larger monetary policy response and hence a bigger swing in consumption and output.

Alternative LCP Formulation

Figure A2 shows the impulse response to the introduction of a BAT in the case of LCP when import taxes are levied on top of the initially pre-set import prices (LCP, BA post-border). The figure additionally reproduces the PCP and DCP impulse responses from figure 2 for comparison. Import prices are sticky in US dollars while export prices are sticky in foreign currency. The dollar instantaneously appreciates by 19% and later reaches 20% appreciation in around 5 years. Foreign exporters to the United States cannot update their dollar prices right away and once the tax is levied on their products, US import demand drops by 30%. US exporters, in contrast, barely change their foreign-currency export prices because the border adjustment they receive is almost fully offset by the dollar appreciation. In large part, export quantities do not react. Border price movements imply a 15% deterioration in the terms of trade and a 1.5-percentage-point increase in the trade balance over GDP.

Robustness to Parameters

Figure A3 quantifies the importance of trade openness and wage stickiness for the extent of dollar appreciation under DCP, when BAT neutrality fails. Specifically, figure A3 compares the benchmark DCP case with (i) a case with greater trade openness ($\gamma_H = 0.6 \ll 0.9$) and (ii) a case where wages are more flexible than prices ($\theta_p = 0.85$ and $\theta_w = 0.75$). Indeed, as we explain in Section III.C, in both of these cases the dollar appreciates by less than in the benchmark. Quantitatively, home bias plays a more important role: in a more open economy, the dollar appreciation on impact is far from complete.

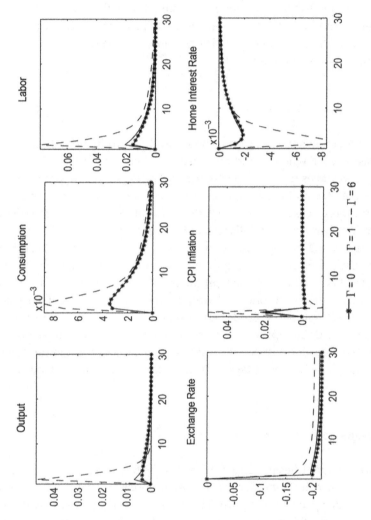

Fig. A1. Dominant currency pricing with strategic complementarities

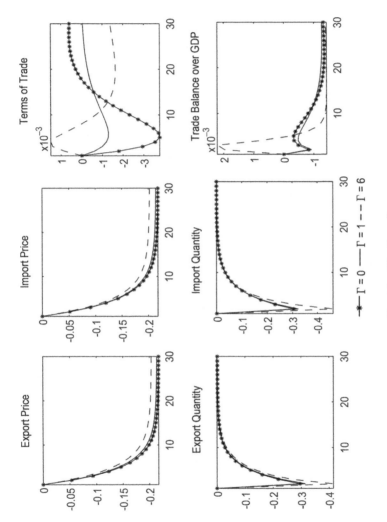

Fig. A1. (Continued)

449

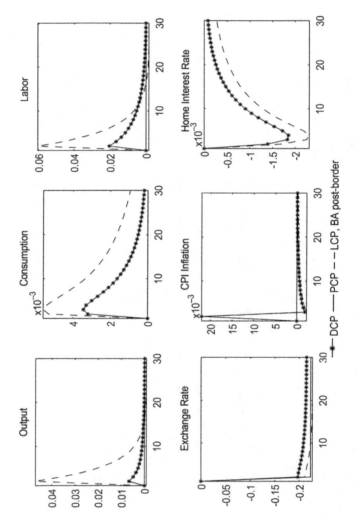

Fig. A2. Response to a BAT across pricing regimes

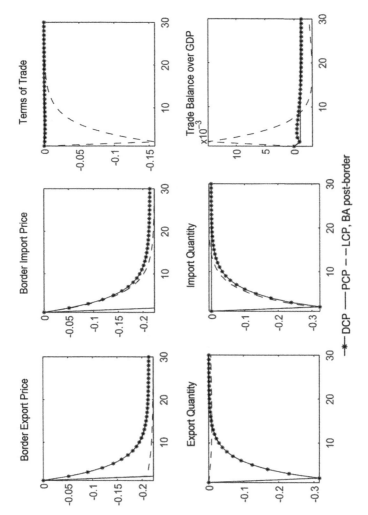

Fig. A2. (Continued)

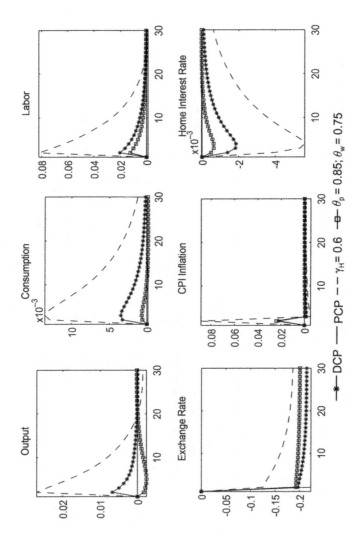

Fig. A3. Dynamics under different openness and stickiness assumptions

452

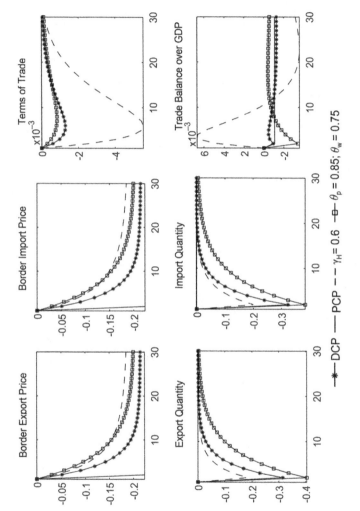

Fig. A3. (Continued)

Endnotes

We thank Alan Auerbach and Greg Mankiw for helpful comments. Gopinath acknowledges that this material is based upon work supported by the National Science Foundation (NSF) under grant no. 1628874. Any opinions, findings, and conclusions or recommendations expressed in this material are those of the authors and do not necessarily reflect the views of the NSF. All remaining errors are our own. Author email addresses: Barbiero (obarbiero@g.harvard.edu), Farhi (efarhi@harvard.edu), Gopinath (gopinath@harvard.edu), Itskhoki (itskhoki@princeton.edu). For acknowledgments, sources of research support, and disclosure of the authors' material financial relationships, if any, please see http://www.nber.org/chapters/c14069.ack.

1. The C-BAT often goes by the acronym DBCFT, which stands for "destination-based cash flow tax."

2. Other recent papers that contribute to our understanding of BAT include Erceg, Prestipino, and Raffo (2018) and Lindé and Pescatori (2017).

3. The two policy experiments we consider are different in an important way. In the case of C-BAT, we study the incremental effect emerging from the border adjustment for a given corporate tax reform. In the case of VAT, we examine the full effects of a VAT introduction, which by definition features the border adjustment. As we explain below, if a VAT were combined with a payroll subsidy (or a payroll tax reduction), the resulting effect mimics the net effect of the border adjustment, because such policy does not introduce a permanent tax wedge.

4. Note that neutrality requires that both: (a) the monetary authority of the country implementing C-BAT does not change its policy stance in response to the currency appreciation; and (b) the monetary authorities of its trade partners let their respective currencies depreciate. Each of these assumptions may be problematic in practice.

5. It is difficult to apply C-BAT to exports of some services, such as education, health care and recreation. In the particular case of the United States with C-BAT proposed to be part of the corporate tax, an arguably bigger concern are the S corporations, which are not subject to corporate taxes and pay instead individual income taxes with no border adjustment.

6. This approximation appears to be robust more generally, and fails only if there are strong expectation effects either about the policy reversal or foreign retaliation, which are, however, difficult to discipline quantitatively.

7. The nominal appreciation triggers a capital loss on the foreign-currency debt held by the private sector, but not by the government, due to the wedge in the border prices faced by the home private sector and by the foreigners. The home government pockets this wedge in proportion to the trade deficits, which over time cumulates to the amount proportional to the size of the initial NFA position.

8. One might argue that if the tax on US imports had to be paid by foreign exporters then this would leave unchanged the dollar price that US consumers face and consequently leave import demand unchanged, on the assumption that exporters keep their dollar prices unchanged despite the tax. However, this is an unrealistic assumption. Such a policy we expect even under DCP will lead to full tax pass-through into US (higher) dollar prices. The issue remains that foreign exporters do not pass through the dollar appreciation, consistent with evidence on low exchange rate pass-through into the US despite large movements in the dollar. This asymmetry in pass-through rates between the tax and exchange rates is potentially consistent with some of the evidence on asymmetric pass-through rates between trade tariffs and exchange rates. There is of course the separate concern of how exactly to implement a US corporate tax reform that has the foreign exporters paying the tax.

9. Note that in the limiting case with flexible wages ($\delta \to 0$) and perfectly substitutable labor inputs ($\vartheta \to \infty$), the wage-setting condition (3) simplifies to the conventional labor supply condition $\kappa C_t^\sigma N_t^\varphi = W_t/P_t$.

10. The auxiliary variable satisfies $D_t = \int_0^1 (\Upsilon'\{[Q_{HH,t}(\omega)]/\gamma_H Q_t\}\{[Q_{HH,t}(\omega)]/Q_t\} + \Upsilon'\{[Q_{FH,t}(\omega)]/\gamma_F Q_t\}\{[Q_{FH,t}(\omega)]/Q_t\})d\omega$. In the special case of CES, $\Upsilon(z) = z^{(\sigma-1)/\sigma}$, so that $\psi(x) = \{[\sigma/(\sigma-1)]x\}^{-\sigma}$, $D_t = [(\sigma-1)/\sigma] = const$, and $P_t = \int_0^1 (\gamma_H\{[P_{HH,t}(\omega)]/P_t\}^{1-\sigma} + \gamma_F\{[P_{FH,t}(\omega)/P_t]/[1 - \iota_t \pi_t^\Pi]\}^{1-\sigma})d\omega$.

11. Note the difference between this definition of NX_t and the C-BAT term in (16), which we can rewrite as $TR_t^{\Pi} = \{[\pi_t^{\Pi}/(1 - \pi_t^{\Pi})]\Pi_t\} - \{\iota_t[\pi_t^{\Pi}/(1 - \pi_t^{\Pi})]NX_t\} + \{\iota_t[\pi_t^{\Pi}/(1 - \pi_t^{\Pi})][\pi_t^V/(1 - \pi_t^V)]P_{FH,t}Q_{FH,t}\}$. The last term reflects the compounding effect of the border adjustment associated with VAT and C-BAT.

12. Two clarifications are in order. First, by assumption 4, the C-BAT is one-time permanent change, so that $\iota_t\tau_t^{\Pi} = 0$ for all $t < t_0$ and $\iota_t\tau_t^{\Pi} = \tau^{\Pi}$ for all $t \geq t_0$. Second, by assumption 3, $B_{t_0} = 0$, and therefore the nonzero NFA are entirely in foreign currency, $B_{t_0}^* \neq 0$.

13. The profit tax reform may or may not involve a change in the profit tax rate itself. What is essential for proposition 2 is that ι_t switches from 0 to 1 at t_0. This analysis can also be extended in a straightforward way to the changes in the profit tax rate while the border adjustment is in effect throughout.

14. A symmetric gap emerges for US exports, where the US private sector receives more than what is paid by foreigners.

15. Note that the discussion above assumes that NFA are held privately. In the alternative case, where all NFA are held by the government (e.g., the central bank), there is no distributional gain or loss for the government.

16. The matter is different, however, if the higher rate of return on the US portfolio reflects financial market imperfections rather than the equilibrium price of risk. This could be the case if, for example, the United States has a monopoly power in supplying international safe assets. In this case, the United States indeed can run a permanent trade deficit even in the risk-adjusted terms, and hence it is possible to have $\Sigma_t^{\Pi} > 0$ even with a negative initial NFA position.

17. The same applies to the cross-border portfolio and FDI investment into the US stock market and companies.

18. Note that the monetary policy stance is not affected as long as this is a one-time jump in the price level resulting in no inflation thereafter.

19. The exchange rate impulse response function shows a 22% rather than a 20% appreciation as $\log(\mathcal{E}^1) - \log(\mathcal{E}^0) = \log(1 - \tau) = \log(0.8) = -0.22$.

20. The results are qualitatively the same for various degrees of strategic complementarity in price setting, as captured by ϵ and Γ, as we explore in the appendix ("Extensions") and fig. A1. In particular, the CES case ($\Gamma = 0$) is almost indistinguishable from our baseline case with $\Gamma = 1$.

21. We have assumed that all home firms are owned locally. If instead the firms are owned partly by foreign nationals then again the dollar appreciation leads to a negative valuation effect.

22. This can also capture a risk-premium or an expectation shock to the UIP (see Itskhoki and Mukhin 2017).

23. One of the sources of nonneutrality arises from sticky dollar prices in the case of DCP. One could argue that, given the large size of the tax adjustment (20%), the appropriate assumption is that foreign exporters will cut the foreign currency price at which they sell to the United States following the large appreciation of the dollar. This argument fails to recognize that most exporters to the United States are also importers and therefore have a significant fraction of costs that are stable in dollars. As the value added share of trade is much smaller than trade flows and with most trade invoiced and sticky in dollars even for trade with non-US partners, the scope to cut dollar prices is limited. Factors such as these explain why, despite a substantial and rapid appreciation of the dollar by 15% between the third quarter of 2014 and third quarter of 2015, the pass-through into border prices remained low at around 35% (as opposed to a full pass-through of 100%).

References

Amiti, M., O. Itskhoki, and J. Konings. 2019. "International Shocks, Variable Markups, and Domestic Prices." http://www.princeton.edu/~itskhoki/papers/DomesticPrices.pdf.

Auerbach, A. J., and M. P. Devereux. 2018. "Cash-Flow Taxes in an International Setting." *American Economic Journal: Economic Policy* 10 (3): 69–94.

Auerbach, A. J., M. P. Devereux, M. Keen, and J. Vella. 2017. "Destination-Based Cash Flow Taxation." Working Paper 17/01, Oxford University Center for Business Taxation. https://papers.ssrn.com/sol3/papers.cfm?abstract_id=2908158.

Auerbach, A. J., and D. Holtz-Eakin. 2016. "The Role of Border Adjustments in International Taxation." American Action Forum. https://www.americanaction forum.org/research/14344/.

Basu, S. 1995. "Intermediate Goods and Business Cycles: Implications for Productivity and Welfare." *American Economic Review* 85 (3): 512–31.

Boz, E., G. Gopinath, and M. Plagborg-Møller. 2017. "Global Trade and the Dollar." Working Paper no. 23988, NBER, Cambridge, MA.

Casas, C., F. Diez, G. Gopinath, and P.-O. Gourinchas. 2016. "Dominant Currency Paradigm." Working Paper no. 22943, NBER, Cambridge, MA.

Christiano, L., M. Eichenbaum, and S. Rebelo. 2011. "When Is the Government Spending Multiplier Large?" *Journal of Political Economy* 119 (1): 78–121.

Curcuru, S. E., C. P. Thomas, and F. E. Warnock. 2013. "On Returns Differentials." *Journal of International Money and Finance* 36 (C): 1–25.

Dornbusch, R. 1987. "Exchange Rate and Prices." *American Economic Review* 77 (1): 93–106.

Engel, C. 2003. "Expenditure Switching and Exchange Rate Policy." *NBER Macroeconomics Annual* 17:231–72.

Erceg, C., A. Prestipino, and A. Raffo. 2018. "The Macroeconomic Effect of Trade Policy." Presented at the Society for Economic Dynamics annual meeting, Mexico City, June 29.

Farhi, E., G. Gopinath, and O. Itskhoki. 2014. "Fiscal Devaluations." *Review of Economics Studies* 81 (2): 725–60.

Feldstein, M. 2017. "The House GOP's Good Tax Trade-Off." *Wall Street Journal*, January 5. https://www.wsj.com/articles/the-house-gops-good-tax-trade-off-1483660843.

Feldstein, M. S., and P. R. Krugman. 1990. "International Trade Effects of Value-Added Taxation." In *Taxation in the Global Economy*, ed. Assaf Razin and Joel Slemrod, 263–82. Cambridge, MA: NBER.

Freund, C., and J. E. Gagnon. 2017. "Effects of Consumption Taxes on Real Exchange Rates and Trade Balances." Working Paper Series WP17-5, Peterson Institute for International Economics, Washington, DC.

Galí, J. 2008. *Monetary Policy, Inflation and the Business Cycle: An Introduction to the New Keynesian Framework*. Princeton, NJ: Princeton University Press.

Goldberg, L. S., and C. Tille. 2008. "Vehicle Currency Use in International Trade." *Journal of International Economics* 76 (2): 177–92.

Gopinath, G., O. Itskhoki, and R. Rigobon. 2010. "Currency Choice and Exchange Rate Pass-Through." *American Economic Review* 100 (1): 306–36.

Gopinath, G., and R. Rigobon. 2008. "Sticky Borders." *Quarterly Journal of Economics* 123 (2): 531–75.

Gourinchas, P.-O., and H. Rey. 2007. "From World Banker to World Venture Capitalist: US External Adjustment and the Exorbitant Privilege." In *G7 Current Account Imbalances: Sustainability and Adjustment*, ed. Richard H. Clarida, 11–66. Cambridge, MA: NBER.

Grossman, G. M. 1980. "Border Tax Adjustments: Do They Distort Trade?" *Journal of International Economics* 10 (1): 117–28.

Guvenen, F., R. J. Mataloni Jr., D. G. Rassier, and K. J. Ruhl. 2017. "Offshore Profit Shifting and Domestic Productivity Measurement." Working Paper no. 23324, NBER, Cambridge, MA.

Itskhoki, O., and D. Mukhin. 2017. "Exchange Rate Disconnect in General Equilibrium." Working paper, Princeton University. http://www.princeton.edu /~itskhoki/papers/disconnect.pdf.

Kimball, M. 1995. "The Quantitative Analytics of the Basic Neomonetarist Model." *Journal of Money, Credit and Banking* 27:1241–77.

Klenow, P. J., and J. L. Willis. 2016. "Real Rigidities and Nominal Price Changes." *Economica* 83:443–72.

Krugman, P. 1987. "Pricing to Market When the Exchange Rate Changes." In *Real Financial Linkages among Open Economies*, ed. S. Arndt and J. Richardson, 49–70. Cambridge, MA: MIT Press.

Lerner, A. P. 1936. "The Symmetry between Import and Export Taxes." *Economica* 3:306–13.

Lindé, J., and A. Pescatori. 2017. "The Macroeconomic Effects of Trade Tariffs: Revisiting the Lerner Symmetry Result." Discussion Paper no. DP12534, Center for Economic and Policy Research, Washington, DC. https://papers.ssrn .com/sol3/papers.cfm?abstract_id=3095584.

Obstfeld, M., and K. Rogoff. 2000. "New Directions for Stochastic Open Economy Models." *Journal of International Economics* 50 (1): 117–53.

Comment

Alan J. Auerbach, *University of California, Berkeley and NBER*

Introduction

The tax reform process that culminated in the December 2017 enactment of the Tax Cuts and Jobs Act followed an unusual pattern regarding business tax reform. In particular, the original proposal, the "Blueprint" put forward by Republicans in the House of Representatives in June 2016 (Tax Reform Task Force 2016) called for the adoption of an approach that, at the time, was unfamiliar to many in the economics profession, a destination-based cash-flow tax (DBCFT). The DBCFT would have represented a sharp break from current policy, and the general lack of familiarity with it led many business leaders, policy makers, and economists to misinterpret its aims, characteristics, and properties. The paper by Omar Barbiero, Emmanuel Farhi, Gita Gopinath, and Oleg Itskhoki represents part of a small and growing literature seeking to analyze the DBCFT, or at least one of its key components: a border tax adjustment on imports and exports. In reading the paper, one is reminded of the advantages of following the more standard tax reform approach of analyzing new proposals before voting on them. This is not to say that I agree with all the paper's modeling assumptions or conclusions, because I do not. But without such concrete analysis, it is difficult to identify key points of professional disagreement and, more importantly, to try to resolve them.

The paper analyzes the short-run macroeconomic effects of adopting border tax adjustments on their own, although this is not what was being proposed. However, this is equivalent in the model to analyzing adoption of a full DBCFT, that is, a "source-based" cash-flow tax—a tax on domestic producers' cash flows—plus border adjustment that removes tax on exports and imposes tax on imports. This equivalence follows because in the model, a cash-flow tax without border adjustment is a nondistortionary tax on pure profits—a lump-sum tax that would then be rebated via an equal-size lump-sum transfer. In particular, the channels through which companies might respond to a source-based cash-flow tax by shifting profitable operations or simply reported profits to lower-tax countries (as discussed by Auerbach and Devereux [2018]) are absent. Thus, only the border-adjustment component of the DBCFT has real effects in the model. The paper contrasts the effects of the border adjustment/DBCFT to those of a traditional value-added tax (VAT), which is equivalent to a DBCFT plus a payroll tax at the same rate, both in the model and in the real world.

Why Consider the DBCFT?

One thing the paper does not do is explain the motivation for proposing the DBCFT in the first place. Here, it is useful to distinguish the effects of the DBCFT from those of a more traditional cash-flow tax without border adjustment, which we might label simply a cash-flow tax. While the DBCFT is a relatively unfamiliar proposal, arguments in favor of the cash-flow tax are more common and of longer standing. A cash-flow tax even without border adjustment would represent a major change from the traditional approach to business taxation by eliminating the distinction between debt and equity finance, removing the tax wedge facing marginal investment decisions, and making tax administration and compliance simpler by not requiring the calculation of income. For reasons such as these, many economists have long argued in favor of business cash-flow taxation (see, e.g., Institute for Fiscal Studies 1978; Hall and Rabushka 1983).

Arguments for imposing the cash-flow tax on a destination basis—for the DBCFT—are newer and less familiar.[1] First, by eliminating any tax on the foreign-source income of US corporations, it would remove incentives for companies to use corporate inversions to relinquish US residence. Second, by making US tax liability independent of the prices charged for imports and exports, the DBCFT would eliminate the possibility of using internal transfer pricing to reduce US tax liability. The loss of interest deductibility would make it impossible to use the location of borrowing in the United States to shift profits elsewhere. Third, as a tax based on the location of sales, the DBCFT would impose no additional tax on the inframarginal profits from US production, encouraging companies to locate profitable activities in the United States. Fourth, as a tax only on the nonlabor component of value added, the DBCFT would be progressive, particularly because companies would have no incentive to move capital out of the United States to escape taxation. Finally, unlike other attempts to reform the treatment of multinational businesses, the DBCFT would be self-reinforcing among countries; the incentive for US adoption would not require cooperation with other countries, and other countries would have a stronger incentive to follow suit after US adoption. As to why the case for the DBCFT might be more compelling now than in the past, one need look no further than the changing nature of business activity. The increased importance of multinational companies and the stronger reliance on the use of intellectual property in the production process have made it easier for companies to shift production and profits around the globe and more difficult for tax authorities to pin the location of profits and production.

The paper acknowledges that such potential advantages exist and sets them to the side, based on the idea that one can separate such advantages as being of a longer-run nature not relevant to the short-run macroeconomic effects that are its major focus. I will return to this issue below.

In addition to these economic arguments for the DBCFT, at least two additional characteristics helped generate political appeal during the US debate. First, to many noneconomists for whom the Lerner symmetry theorem is not self-evident or even plausible, border adjustments appeared to be protectionist. Of course, only some saw this apparent proexport bias as an advantage. Second, during the 10-year budget window, the border adjustment—effectively a tax applied to the US trade deficit—was estimated to raise a substantial amount of money, well in excess of $1 trillion at the 20% tax rate initially proposed (Nunns et al. 2016). While this attribute would have made it much easier for legislators to "pay for" tax cuts, it was also the focus of sharp criticism from those who argued that one could not view such a revenue gain as permanent. The basic argument, as laid out in this paper, follows the standard long-run condition that the present value of a country's trade deficits equals the initial value of its international investment position. With a negative international position, this predicts that the United States would lose money, at its present value, by imposing border adjustments. However, as the paper also notes, this calculation requires adjustment if some of the US trade deficit arises from mismeasurement of trade. Put simply, if some of the reported trade deficit arises from the understatement of net exports to related parties in foreign tax havens, that trade deficit generates offsetting foreign source income and does not occasion any accumulation of net US liabilities that must be serviced through future trade surpluses.[2] Given estimates of the large magnitude of such mismeasurement, border adjustments could have generated substantial tax revenue well beyond the official 10-year estimation period.

Of course, there were also arguments against the DBCFT. The concerns of importing industries may have been the most important politically, and these are closely related to this paper's analysis. Additional concern arose about potential conflicts with respect to international tax agreements, notably the World Trade Organization. The key issue here was the extent to which border adjustments, explicitly permitted in the context of the VAT and trade neutral from an economist's perspective, would somehow violate international trade norms if applied outside the VAT. I return to this issue below when discussing the paper's modeling approach. Finally, there was concern about the possible wealth transfers associated with exchange rate appreciation, which this paper explicitly discusses and for which it provides an estimate. Although this wealth effect is relevant in evaluating the DBCFT, it requires more context than the paper provides.

As discussed by Auerbach (1997), adding border adjustments to a source-based cash-flow tax amounts to imposing a cash-flow tax on net foreign investment positions or, equivalently, imposing a cash-flow tax on outbound foreign investment positions and a cash-flow subsidy on inbound foreign investment positions. While a cash-flow tax generates no revenue in present value on new marginal investments, it does collect revenue on the positive cash flows from past investments and new inframarginal investments. Thus, the cash-flow tax on outbound investment generates tax revenue in present value, representing a net flow from domestic individuals to the government, whereas the cash-flow subsidy on inbound investment represents a transfer to foreign investors. This is, essentially, the wealth transfer to foreigners that the current paper discusses, although there are further complications associated with the nominal currency denomination of assets and liabilities that affect the distributions of gains and losses.

However, there are two things to keep in mind about this wealth transfer. First, applied in the context of imposing a DBCFT rather than on its own, the border adjustment is just undoing the imposition of a cash-flow tax on foreign investment. That is, a source-based cash-flow tax applies to domestic cash flows. The border adjustment adds in foreign cash flows of domestic residents and takes out domestic cash flows of foreign residents. Thus, the cash-flow subsidy for inbound investment offsets a tax that otherwise would be imposed on foreign investors by the domestic cash-flow tax. Second, the extent to which one is transferring wealth to foreigners by adopting a border adjustment depends on how much of a burden the tax system without border adjustment would impose on them in the first place, that is, the extent to which the incidence of source-based business taxes falls on foreign owners. There is a general view that, through capital flight as well as tax avoidance, much of the burden of traditional business income taxes falls on domestic fixed factors, notably labor.

In summary, one should measure the wealth transfer to foreign investors in net terms, which is not something that can be done using this paper's modeling approach. All this being said, adopting a DBCFT does mean giving up on attempts at "tax exporting," and this should be weighed against the associated economic gains, a trade-off modeled by Auerbach and Devereux (2018). For example, if a country's primary source of domestic business income were from the development of natural resources, fixed in location and relatively easy to measure in value, a border adjustment would provide a windfall to foreign investors with little offsetting economic benefit. As such, it would make sense, if imposing a DBCFT, to maintain some source-based taxation on industries where the distortionary behavior of modern multinationals is not so important a problem (Auerbach et al. 2017).

Interpreting the Paper's Simulation Results

One additional argument made in 2017 against adopting the DBCFT was that it represented a major change not only from past US policy but also with respect to what other countries had done, leaving considerable uncertainty about its economic impact, particularly in the short run. Would the large nominal appreciation predicted by basic theory occur? Would there be disruptions to the level and pattern of trade? The heart of this paper is directed to address such questions. After highlighting the conditions needed to guarantee the simple outcome of full dollar appreciation and a neutralization of trade disruptions, the authors develop an elaborate model aimed at incorporating various real-world frictions to assess what might actually happen.

Perhaps most important among these frictions is the dominant currency (i.e., dollar) pricing of imports and exports, which makes such prices sticky in dollars in the short run, even if substantial dollar appreciation occurs. This means that US exporters fail to pass along the benefits of border adjustment of exports to their foreigner buyers, and US importers do not see much of a change in the dollar price they pay for imports, making such imports more expensive once the border adjustment is taken into account. Consequently, both exports and imports fall substantially in the short run. These offsetting trade effects still result in strong dollar appreciation but without the trade neutrality that exists in simpler models in the short run or in this model in the longer run. The net impact is a small short-run increase in gross domestic product (GDP; Barbiero and colleagues' fig. 2), which becomes larger when considering wealth effects (their fig. 3) because of the resulting moderation in import demand. Perhaps most striking is the impact of retaliation by other countries, which is modeled initially by assuming that other countries defend their currencies against the dollar. Why other countries would seek to do this is unclear, given that the result is a stronger short-run improvement in the US trade balance and a much larger positive jolt to the US GDP. Of course, international trade policy is an area where decisions are not always easily explained, so it is hard to predict how other countries might react. However, an alternative response in other countries to US adoption of a DBCFT might have been to follow the US lead, either by adopting a DBCFT as well or by simulating a move in that direction by increasing existing VATs and reducing employment taxes. If countries were to adopt this alternative approach, then one would expect muted effects in the United States with respect to exchange rates, trade, and output. Indeed, this is what the paper finds in modeling a response by the rest of the world to announce adoption of the DBCFT once the United States does. In a parallel universe, important economies might take such a coordinated approach to smooth the path for adopting DBCFT-based reform.

The paper's findings for a VAT are quite different. Whereas adopting the border adjustment alone, which, again, is equivalent to adopting a DBCFT, is mildly stimulative in the short run, adopting a VAT has a sharply negative impact on output. To understand why, note again how these two tax systems differ. The VAT is equivalent to a DBCFT plus a tax at the same rate on domestic labor income, imposed at the employer level. Thus, whereas the DBCFT is a nondistortionary tax (at least when prices are flexible), the VAT imposes a tax wedge on the labor market, whose impact on labor supply is exacerbated in the paper's model, because with all taxes refunded, the impact on labor supply is through a pure substitution effect. There is no negative income effect to dampen the demand for leisure. However, before concluding that the authors finally arrived at an explanation for why the United States chose not to adopt a VAT, one should keep in mind that, unlike in the paper, VATs have not simply been added to existing tax systems. Rather, VATs have arisen around the world either to replace more distortionary taxes, such as turnover taxes or sales taxes that (like those at the US-state level) miss much of consumption and tax many intermediate products, or to cover funding imbalances, which without the VAT would have eventually required the introduction of other taxes.

One other key difference between the effects of the VAT and those of the DBCFT that does make sense, and that I think would be present more generally, is that a price adjustment to the VAT would occur largely domestically, through an increase in the price level rather than an appreciation of the nominal exchange rate. The paper explains this difference in terms of the DBCFT treating foreign and domestic goods differently, but I find much simpler intuition in the fact that for a VAT not to result in a price-level increase would require a fall in the sticky nominal wage rate. Put another way, adjustment to the VAT could occur through dollar appreciation plus a fall in nominal wages, whereas for the DBCFT dollar appreciation alone would suffice.

Returning to the results for the DBCFT, a central question is what to assume about the pricing behavior of importers and exporters. The authors argue in favor of dominant currency pricing over, for example, producer currency pricing, which would lead to an immediate adjustment rather than a short-run trade contraction. Their argument is based on empirical evidence of such behavior. I do not dispute the evidence, but I question whether one can treat it as reflecting a structural model of behavior, invariant to the cause of exchange rate fluctuations. Put simply, while it might be quite rational for an optimizing producer to maintain a fixed dollar price in the short run in the face of a fluctuating exchange rate, a large, onetime, permanent change in relative costs induced by a border adjustment would call for a different response. If such changes do not feature prominently in the data used to estimate pricing behavior, then one may need to apply the resulting empirical evidence with considerable caution.

As an illustration of the potential pitfalls, consider an alternative method of implementing border adjustment. While the approach proposed in the United States, and the one modeled in the paper, is to implement border adjustment through the US firms involved in cross-border transactions—denying a deduction for imports and exempting export revenues from taxation—one could also impose border adjustments on the foreign parties to these transactions. That is, one could tax companies exporting to the United States and provide tax rebates to purchasers of US exports. Indeed, this alternative approach to the border adjustment of imports is not just a conceptual experiment, it has been suggested as a way of ensuring the compatibility of the tax with WTO rules (Grinberg 2017), and so represents more than just an intellectual exercise. This transfer of tax liability from importers to foreign exporters would be very large—a 20% tax rate would mean a transfer of 20% of the purchase price from seller to buyer. Yet under the paper's modeling assumptions, it might appear that this shift would have no immediate impact on the dollar price of imports. The authors argue (in n. 9) that an assumption of no pass-through of a 20% tax rate on producers is unrealistic, and I wholeheartedly agree. But I disagree just as strongly with their contention that a permanent 20% tax rate would be passed through fully while a concurrent permanent 20% exchange rate depreciation would have very limited immediate pass-through. Unlike the authors, I don't see evidence of asymmetric past responses to exchange rate fluctuations and tariffs as being potentially very informative here, given the much closer underlying economic symmetry of the exchange-rate and tax-rate changes in this case, in terms of their effects on relative prices, their size, and their permanence. I cannot cite clear empirical evidence in favor of my argument, because the experiment would represent a sharp break from historical practice, but my own sense is that adoption of a DBCFT with a standard approach to implementing border adjustment would lead to a much faster adjustment of dollar prices than is assumed in the paper's calibration.

Finally, in a more realistic modeling of the macroeconomic effects of the DBCFT (and not simply a border adjustment), one would expect there to be a short-run impetus to invest coming from the removal of source-based taxation on the profits from domestic production. This would likely lead to capital inflows and higher short-run dollar appreciation.

Looking Ahead

The paper concludes with a call for more research. Papers often end this way, but in this instance the call is clearly warranted. The US proposal for a DBCFT might have fared better or might have been modified to make it more attractive if the proposal and its effects were better understood by policy makers, but especially by economists. In addition to giving further consideration to the modeling issues just discussed (as well as the assumption regarding monetary policy, which the authors highlight in the conclusion), one useful thing to consider would be how a DBCFT might appeal to different countries, acting either unilaterally or together. As the paper notes, the effects would be quite different within a currency union where the implicit fiscal devaluation could not be offset by a nominal exchange rate adjustment. However, there are also differences in exposure to trade, domestic market flexibility, and, of course, the currencies in which prices are set.

In light of the failure of the United States to adopt the DBCFT in 2017, a potential researcher might ask whether time would be better spent exploring other research questions. As to this, one can observe that, even though the DBCFT as originally proposed was not part of the Tax Cuts and Job Act, the DBCFT proposal had an impact on the law. The new tax system contains provisions that reflect some of the same motivations as those behind the DBCFT: to make the system less distortionary, to encourage production in the United States, and to limit the ability of multinational companies to shift profits to lower-tax jurisdictions. On the domestic side, the law has introduced (if only temporarily, and applying only to some assets) expensing of investment and a limit on (although not elimination of) interest deductibility by businesses, moving in the direction of cash-flow taxation. Regarding cross-border transactions, the law did not adopt full border adjustment but did introduce two new provisions not found in other countries' tax systems that effectively implement partial, limited border adjustment. These are a minimum tax on domestic income (the base erosion and antiabuse tax, or BEAT), which allows no deduction for certain imports from related foreign businesses, and a reduced tax rate on income (over a threshold rate of return on tangible assets) attributable to exports (i.e., on foreign-derived intangible income, or FDII). These provisions represent a more modest and therefore potentially less controversial move in the direction of the DBCFT, but at the cost of much greater complexity and a variety of new distortions.[3] Given the new law's built-in instability (because of its many expiring provisions), new opportunities to consider tax reform are clearly in our future. With the same economic factors that drove US consideration of the DBCFT at work in other countries as well, the value of additional research should be high.

Endnotes

For acknowledgments, sources of research support, and disclosure of the author's material financial relationships, if any, please see http://www.nber.org/chapters/c14070.ack.

1. See Auerbach (2017) for details regarding these arguments.
2. Auerbach (2017) discusses the adjusted calculation in more detail.
3. For example, the base erosion and antiabuse tax may lead companies to spin off related foreign parties in order to avoid losing a deduction for imports.

References

Auerbach, Alan J. 1997. "The Future of Fundamental Tax Reform." *American Economic Review* 87 (2): 143–46.
———. 2017. "Demystifying the Destination-Based Cash-Flow Tax." *Brookings Papers on Economic Activity* 2017 (2): 409–32.
Auerbach, Alan J., and Michael P. Devereux. 2018. "Cash-Flow Taxes in an International Setting." *American Economic Journal: Economic Policy* 10 (3): 69–94.
Auerbach, Alan J., Michael P. Devereux, Michael Keen, and John Vella. 2017. "Destination-Based Cash-Flow Taxation." Working Paper 17/01, Oxford Centre for Business Taxation.

Grinberg, Itai. 2017. "A Destination-Based Cash Flow Tax Can Be Structured to Comply with World Trade Organization Rules." *National Tax Journal* 70 (4): 803–18.

Hall, Robert E., and Alvin Rabushka. 1983. *Low Tax, Simple Tax, Flat Tax.* New York: McGraw-Hill.

Institute for Fiscal Studies. 1978. *The Structure and Reform of Direct Taxation.* London: George Allen & Unwin.

Nunns, Jim, Len Burman, Ben Page, Jeff Rohaly, and Joe Rosenberg. 2016. *An Analysis of the House GOP Tax Plan.* Washington, DC: Urban–Brookings Tax Policy Center. http://www.taxpolicycenter.org/publications/analysis-house-gop-tax-plan/full.

Tax Reform Task Force. 2016. *A Better Way: Our Vision for a Confident America.* Washington, DC: US House of Representatives. https://www.novoco.com/sites/default/files/atoms/files/ryan_a_better_way_policy_paper_062416.pdf.

Comment

N. Gregory Mankiw, *Harvard University and NBER*

Let me start with a Rorschach test, which I am borrowing from Charles L. Schultze, the late Brookings economist and once-Council of Economic Advisers chair under President Jimmy Carter. In the following sentence, fill in the blanks with the words "long" and "short":

Take care of the _____ run and the _____ run will take care of itself.

Any well-trained economist is tempted to say that this question is not well posed, or that neither statement is really true, or something like that. But this is meant to be a psychological gauge of one's predispositions, not an analytic exercise. So humor me and write down your answer. I will get back to it in a minute.

Now, back to border taxes.

There is no doubt in my mind that the broad issue addressed in this paper is an important one. In Washington policy circles, a common argument is that Europe's value-added taxes (VATs) are adverse to American trade interests. After all, the European VAT taxes imports and exempts exports. From the mercantilist perspective that (unfortunately) dominates public discussion of trade, what could be worse that a policy that encourages American imports and hurts American exports?

Needless to say, Washington policy circles are not dominated by PhD economists steeped in general equilibrium theory and the Lerner symmetry theorem. I recall one conversation I had about this issue with a colleague when I worked in the Bush administration. He was not an economist, but rather an Ivy League-educated lawyer. He was a smart guy with a lot of experience in the policy and politics of international trade negotiations.

I told him that economists don't view value added taxes that way, that equilibrium exchange rates adjust to ensure that these border taxes do not impede trade. I recall his response: "Yeah, I have had a lot of economists tell me that, but to tell you the truth, I have never really understood it." And, of course, because he didn't understand the argument, he wasn't persuaded by it.

The bottom line I took from this experience is that economists need to do a better job of explaining the economics of border adjustment to the broader policy community. If someone could write an article that explains the relevant issues to an intelligent layman, that would be a great service.

That article, however, would not look anything like this one. For one thing, the machinery in the paper is pretty complicated. When putting together a slide deck to brief your favorite presidential candidate, you really shouldn't include a diagram anything like this paper's figure 1.

More important, the purpose of the paper is not so much to explain Lerner symmetry as it is to suggest that Lerner symmetry might not apply in the real world. It does not go so far as to justify the naïve view, popular in some policy circles, that European VATs are adverse to American trade interests. But it does mean that there are enough deviations in the world from the frictionless model that we should not be confident in the neutrality implied by Lerner symmetry.

As such, this is an impressive paper. Keeping track of all the interactions depicted in figure 1 within the context of a dynamic general equilibrium model with sticky wages and prices is no mean feat. For me, reading this paper is a bit like watching a grandmaster play 20 simultaneous games of blindfolded chess. I can follow what the grandmaster is doing, but I would never even begin to try to do it myself.

At the end of the paper, however, I was left wondering how seriously I should take the results. The results are predicated on a Calvo model of price adjustment, for both wages and prices. Many of the important deviations from neutrality follow from these rigidities, together with assumptions about which currencies are used as units of account to set particular prices.

It is worth pointing out that there are good reasons to doubt the Calvo model. As I and others have written in the past, it has dynamic properties that are hard to square with the data. That is why empirical implementations of dynamic stochastic general equilibrium models often include some kind of ad hoc fix, such as indexing prices to past inflation. The sticky-information model I proposed some years ago with Ricardo Reis was an attempt to remedy the problems we saw with the Calvo model. I am not confident that our answer was the right one, but I am confident that the Calvo model is the wrong one.

My guess is that the authors chose the Calvo model not out of a strong conviction that it is the right model for wage and price dynamics, but because it is a conventional one, with a desirable balance between Keynesian plausibility and theoretical elegance. And it might well be true that other models of sticky wages and prices would yield results that are qualitatively similar to those presented here, even if the precise dynamic paths would no doubt be different.

But there is also a harder and more important question: Should we be confident that the Calvo model, or any alternative model of sticky prices, is structural in response to a major change in tax policy? The assumption here is that prices change when the Calvo fairy taps the price-setter's shoulder and that these shoulder taps come randomly. And the Calvo fairy is assumed not to notice when the government makes a major change in tax policy that influences equilibrium prices. She just keeps doing her job, ignoring the change in tax policy and tapping shoulders randomly.

Now, I am as big a believer in short-run sticky prices as anyone, but I still find this assumption hard to swallow. As a result, I am inclined to view the results in this paper as an illustration of how Lerner symmetry and border-tax neutrality could fail, not as an iron-clad demonstration of how it likely would fail.

A similar issue arises regarding monetary policy. The assumption made in this paper is that the central bank consistently follows a Taylor rule. I am not sure, but I am guessing that this behavior is not optimal in the face of changes in tax policy. It might be worth exploring what optimal monetary policy is in this environment, and what the dynamic response to tax policy looks like under an optimal monetary policy.

In light of these concerns, I left the paper wondering how much they should inform actual policy. In other words, how much weight should one give to these results when deciding to border-adjust the corporate tax?

This brings me back to the Schultze Rorschach test. I responded to the test by saying, "Take care of the long run, and the short run will take care of itself." According to Charlie Schultze, this is the answer most often given by conservative economists, while liberal economists say the opposite.

I think that my answer is definitely the right one when thinking about the details of the tax code. The long-run benefits of border adjustment are significant and are, by the way, excluded in the model in this paper. In particular, with multinational corporations and global supply chains, it is hard to know where goods are produced. As a result, the current tax regime invites all kinds of games with transfer pricing as companies try to move the tax base to low-tax jurisdictions. It is much easier to know where goods are consumed. This means that destination-based taxes are harder to evade. This is the main argument for the kind of border adjustment that was proposed in the original Republican tax bill.

These benefits of border adjustment are ongoing, not just transitory, and their size likely grows with the economy. It is hard to know for sure, but my guess is that the present value of these benefits exceeds any short-run costs that arise from sticky wages and prices. And if, as seems plausible, price-setters and central bankers respond sensibly to major changes in tax policy, rather than mechanically following the rules proposed by Calvo and Taylor, the short-run dislocations from a border tax are likely to be smaller than this paper suggests.

Endnote

For acknowledgments, sources of research support, and disclosure of the author's material financial relationships, if any, please see http://www.nber.org/chapters/c14071 .ack.

Discussion

The authors opened the discussion by addressing two points raised by Gregory Mankiw in his discussion. First, they argued that their model allows for sizeable long-run effects. They explained that an adjustment of border taxes leads to an appreciation of the US dollar in their model. Because the United States is a net debtor in its own currency, this appreciation leads to a negative valuation effect, corresponding to a transfer from the United States to the rest of the world of roughly 16% of US gross domestic product. This valuation effect possibly outweighs the short-term benefits of border adjustment. Second, the authors challenged the idea put forth by Mankiw that there is a clear dichotomy between short-run and long-run effects when it comes to trade policy. The authors insisted on the importance of political economy considerations in the short run, which may prevent the adoption of desired tax changes and the realization of long-run benefits.

The authors next replied to questions from both discussants regarding the role of dollar pricing and the importance of Calvo pricing in the context of a large tax policy change. They pointed out that dollar pricing plays a key role in the failure of the Lerner symmetry in their model. The adoption of a border tax on imports has two effects on US consumer prices. The direct effect raises these prices, while the indirect effect reduces them by leading to an appreciation of the US dollar. In the presence of dollar pricing, the direct pass-through of a tax is full, whereas the short-run pass-through of the exchange rate to consumer prices in the United States is low. This asymmetry is responsible for the failure of the Lerner symmetry. The authors noted that dollar pricing is consistent with recent evidence: the dollar appreciated and then depreciated by 10%–12% while border prices remained roughly unchanged. They provide a rationale for dollar pricing as an equilibrium phenomenon. International firms decide to set prices in US dollars because US inputs account for a significant fraction of their marginal cost. The authors acknowledged that Calvo pricing is a simplifying assumption but view it as a modeling tool. They noted that the predictions of their model about the pass-through of a tax and the exchange rate are consistent with the data.

Andrew Atkeson asked one of the discussants, Alan Auerbach, about the desirability of adjusting border taxes at the US-state level. Auerbach mentioned that some US states, including California, have adopted similar taxes in the form of apportioned corporate taxes. The profits of a company are taxed in each state in proportion to the sales realized there. Auerbach noted that this tool differs from adjusting border taxes in various respects and has been proposed as an alternative to it. In particular, both taxes would not necessarily have the same implications for exchange rates in an international context.

The rest of the discussion mostly focused on two topics: valuation effects and profit repatriation.

On the first topic, Atkeson pointed out that valuation effects such as those in the paper would result from any other policy change, leading to an unanticipated appreciation of the US dollar. The authors acknowledged that these effects aren't specific to an adjustment of border taxes but insisted that these effects should be taken into account when designing trade policy.

Robert Hall offered a comment on the same topic. He first highlighted that the US economy borrows at low interest rates from abroad and invests domestically with high equity returns. Hall advocated that macroeconomic models should take these spreads seriously. The authors suggested that these spreads may reflect differences in risk and the special role of the US dollar in the international monetary system. They also acknowledged that the exact source of these spreads hasn't been fully understood, either theoretically or empirically.

Guido Lorenzoni noted that profit margins of importers and exporters may be affected differently when adjusting border taxes if prices are sticky. He inquired about the value of stocks of importers and exporters in the model, and about the presence of associated valuation effects. The authors mentioned that an earlier version of the paper explicitly modeled equity holdings. They pointed out that valuation effects are still present in their model, through bond holdings. The authors confirmed that the adjustment of border taxes leads to large losses for US importers in their model. They noted that such losses are in line with some of the public concerns voiced about this policy.

Turning to the topic of profit repatriation, Atkeson referred the authors to a recent paper by Robert J. Barro and Jason Furman ("The Macroeconomic Effects of the 2017 Tax Reform," Conference drafts, Brookings Papers on Economic Activity [2018]), which studies the macroeconomic effects of the 2017 tax reform through the lens of a closed-economy neoclassical growth model with capital taxation. Atkeson inquired about the quantitative importance of capital flows to and from the United States for the effect of adjusting border taxes. The authors noted that their model abstracts from physical capital, but they acknowledged that the question was interesting for two reasons. First, an adjustment of border taxes could affect capital accumulation and output in the long run. Second, the associated capital flows may lead to profit repatriation, which would increase government revenues. The authors contrasted the financial gains from profit repatriation with the more uncertain benefits resulting from a reallocation of businesses with high inframarginal profits in the United States.

Mankiw offered some comments on the subject, based on his experience as chairman of the Council of Economic Advisors. He mentioned that the council analyzed and eventually was opposed to a repatriation holiday that was being proposed. In their view, such a repatriation would have important effects beyond revenue implications only if it affected the ultimate allocation of firms' savings. The affected firms typically hold liquid deposits in international financial institutions investing worldwide, so the council's assessment was that repatriation was unlikely to trigger an investment boom. The authors seconded this point and noted that profit repatriation by itself was unlikely to cause an appreciation of the US dollar, contrary to popular arguments, as the ultimate allocation of firms' savings would be mostly unchanged. Auerbach noted that the effects of a repatriation holiday and of profit repatriation due to an adjustment of border taxes would be different, as the latter may affect long-run incentives to produce in the United States.

Following up on his earlier question, Atkeson suggested that the analysis of Barro and Furman does not account for entry decisions by domestic or foreign firms. He argued that these decisions could be distorted by the level of corporate taxes, which itself would be affected by the levy of import and export taxes. The authors responded that their model abstracts from entry and exit dynamics. They noted that an adjustment of border taxes does not per se affect the level of the corporate taxes, it only affects the composition of fiscal revenues.

To conclude, Jonathan Parker pointed out that the paper focuses on valuation effects across countries associated with the adjustment of border taxes but remains silent on efficiency considerations and restricts its attention to the case of a unilateral adjustment of border taxes. Valuation effects correspond to transfers between countries, he argued, and do not affect global welfare (absent inequality concerns), whereas efficiency gains do, especially if they are coordinated. The authors were very sympathetic to this point and noted that coordinated adjustment of border taxes would be less contentious than a unilateral one. They mentioned that the focus of the paper on unilateral adjustment reflects the recent policy discussion in the United States.